The Cambridge Economic History of Modern Britain
Volume I: Industrialisation, 1700–1860

The Cambridge Economic History of Modern Britain provides a readable and comprehensive survey of the economic history of Britain since industrialisation, based on the most up-to-date research into the subject. Roderick Floud and Paul Johnson have assembled a team of fifty leading scholars from around the world to produce a set of volumes which are both a lucid textbook for undergraduate and postgraduate students and an authoritative guide to the subject. The text pays particular attention to the explanation of quantitative and theory-based enquiry, but all forms of historical research are used to provide a comprehensive account of the development of the British economy. Volume I covers the period 1700–1860 when Britain led the world in the process of industrialisation. Volume II examines the period 1860–1939 when British economic power was at its height. The focus of volume III is 1939–2000, when Britain adjusted to a decline in manufacturing, an expansion of the service economy, and a repositioning of external economic activity towards Europe. The books provide an invaluable guide for undergraduate and postgraduate students in history, economics and other social sciences.

RODERICK FLOUD is Vice-Chancellor of London Metropolitan University, a Fellow of the British Academy, an Academician of the Social Sciences and a Fellow of the City and Guilds of London Institute. His publications include *An Introduction to Quantitative Methods for Historians* and (with D. McCloskey) *The Economic History of Britain since 1700*.

PAUL JOHNSON is Professor of Economic History at the London School of Economics and an Academician of the Social Sciences. He has authored or edited seven books and over fifty articles and chapters on various aspects of the economic, social and legal history of modern Britain, and on the economics of ageing and pensions. Publications include *Saving and Spending: The Working-Class Economy in Britain* 1870–1939; *Ageing and Economic Welfare*; and *Old Age: From Antiquity to Post-Modernity*.

The Cambridge Economic History of Modern Britain

Volume I: Industrialisation, 1700–1860

Edited by Roderick Floud
London Metropolitan University

and Paul Johnson
London School of Economics

CAMBRIDGE
UNIVERSITY PRESS

CAMBRIDGE UNIVERSITY PRESS
Cambridge, New York, Melbourne, Madrid, Cape Town, Singapore, São Paulo, Delhi

Cambridge University Press
The Edinburgh Building, Cambridge CB2 8RU, UK

Published in the United States of America by Cambridge University Press, New York

www.cambridge.org
Information on this title: www.cambridge.org/9780521527361

First published 2004
Fourth printing 2008

Printed in the United Kingdom at the University Press, Cambridge

A catalogue record for this publication is available from the British Library

Library of Congress Cataloguing in Publication data
The Cambridge economic history of modern Britain / edited by Roderick Floud
and Paul Johnson.
    p.   cm.
Includes bibliographical references and index.
Contents: v. 1. Industrialisation, 1700–1860 – v. 2. Economic maturity, 1860–1939 – v. 3.
Structural change and growth, 1939–2000.
ISBN 0 521 82036 7 (v.1) – ISBN 0 521 52736 8 (pb.) – ISBN 0 521 82037 5 (v.2) –
ISBN 0 521 52737 6 (pb.) – ISBN 0 521 82038 3 (v.3) – ISBN 0 521 52738 4 (pb.)
1. Great Britain – Economic conditions.   2. Great Britain – Economic
conditions – 18th century.   3. Great Britain – Economic conditions – 19th century.
4. Great Britain – Economic conditions – 20th century.   I. Title: Economic history of
modern Britain.   II. Floud, Roderick.   III. Johnson, Paul (Paul A.)
HC253.C36   2003
330.941′08 – dc21   2003046169

ISBN 978-0-521-82036-3 hardback
ISBN 978-0-521-52736-1 paperback

To Louisa and Oriana

Contents

List of figures   ix
List of tables   xi
List of contributors   xiv
Preface   xvii

Chapter 1   Accounting for the Industrial Revolution   *1*
JOEL MOKYR

Chapter 2   Industrial organisation and structure   *28*
PAT HUDSON

Chapter 3   British population during the 'long' eighteenth century, 1680–1840   *57*
E. A. WRIGLEY

Chapter 4   Agriculture during the industrial revolution, 1700–1850   *96*
ROBERT C. ALLEN

Chapter 5   Industrialisation and technological change   *117*
KRISTINE BRULAND

Chapter 6   Money, finance and capital markets   *147*
STEPHEN QUINN

Chapter 7   Trade: discovery, mercantilism and technology   *175*
C. KNICK HARLEY

Chapter 8   Government and the economy, 1688–1850   *204*
RON HARRIS

Chapter 9   Household economy   *238*
JANE HUMPHRIES

Chapter 10   Living standards and the urban environment   *268*
HANS-JOACHIM VOTH

Chapter 11   Transport   *295*
SIMON VILLE

Chapter 12   Education and skill of the British labour force   *332*
DAVID MITCH

Chapter 13   Consumption in eighteenth- and early
nineteenth-century Britain   *357*
MAXINE BERG

Chapter 14   Scotland   *388*
T. M. DEVINE

Chapter 15   The extractive industries   *417*
ROGER BURT

Chapter 16   The industrial revolution in global perspective   *451*
STANLEY L. ENGERMAN AND
PATRICK K. O'BRIEN

Bibliography   465
Index   505

Figures

3.1 English population totals, 1681–1841   *page* 61
3.2 Changes in English demographic rates, 1681–1841   66
3.3 The combined effect of fertility and mortality in
     determining intrinsic growth rates, 1666–1841   68
3.4 Long-term trends in birth intervals   72
3.5 Mean age at marriage: bachelor/spinster marriages   74
3.6 Marriage age combinations: bachelor/spinster marriages   75
3.7 Crude first marriage rates and real wage trends   78
3.8 Urban growth in England, France and the Netherlands   89
4.1 Output per worker in agriculture, 1300–1800   98
6.1 Sectoral shares of London stock market in 1873   149
6.2 Deposits, bills, coins and banknotes in 1873   150
6.3 Innovation of the payment system, 1688–1870   152
6.4 Supply and demand for industrial finance *c.* 1790   161
6.5 Price of gold in London, 1790–1830   163
7.1 British exports, 1660s, 1700s and 1770s   178
7.2 Terms of trade, 1796–1913   194
7.3 Exports as proportion of national income,
     1700–1913   199
7.4 Tariff revenues as percentage of value of retained imports   201
8.1 Total tax revenue, 1665–1805   215
8.2 Employees in fiscal bureaucracy, 1690–1782/3   216
8.3 Growth of national debt, 1690–1780s   217
8.4 Allocation of government expenditure, 1665–1805   218
9.1 Contributions to household income   259
10.1 Real earnings in Great Britain, 1781–1855   272
10.2 Working hours in Britain in the long run   278
10.3 Composition of working-class expenditures, 1788/92   282
10.4 Life expectancy at birth (in years) in selected cities and
     areas, 1841   285
10.5 Pseudo-HDI for Britain, the USA, Sweden and Germany   290
11.1 Transport's share of gross domestic fixed capital formation
     in Great Britain, 1761–1860   321
12.1 Estimated illiteracy of men and women in England,
     1500–1900   344

12.2 Estimated annual percentage of males and females unable
to sign at marriage, 1754–1840   345
14.1 Scotland   390
14.2 The Central Lowlands of Scotland   405
15.1 Volume and value of mine output, 1720s and 1857   421

Tables

1.1 Estimated annual rates of growth of real output,
1700–1871   *page* 4

1.2 Total factor productivity, computed from product
accounts   8

1.3 Total factor productivity, computed from income
accounts   9

1.4 The world according to Clark, all in average percentage
change per year   10

3.1 Quinquennial demographic data: population totals,
fertility and mortality data, intrinsic growth rates and
dependency ratio   64

3.2 Age-specific marital fertility rates per 1,000 woman-years
lived; and total marital fertility rates   70

3.3 Long-term trends in birth intervals (months): thirty-year
overlapping periods   71

3.4 Mean age at marriage in bachelor/spinster marriages   73

3.5 Adult mortality, sexes combined ($1,000\ q_x$)   80

3.6 Mortality within the first year of life in England,
1650–1837 ($1,000\ q_x$)   81

3.7 Childhood mortality in England and the Princeton model
North life tables   82

3.8 Maternal mortality rates (per 1,000 birth events)   83

3.9 Male and female adult mortality ($1,000\ q_x$)   85

3.10 Male and female infant and child mortality ($1,000\ q_x$)   86

3.11 Percentage of total population living in towns with
5,000 or more inhabitants   88

4.1 Agricultural output, 1700–1850   102

4.2 Utilisation of English and Welsh land, 1700–1850   104

4.3 Employment in English and Welsh agriculture, 1700–1850   105

4.4 Capital in English and Welsh agriculture, 1700–1850   107

5.1 Patents for capital goods, 1750–99   124

5.2 Selected product and ornamenting patents,
1720–1800   125

6.1 British banks in 1873   148

6.2 Changes in the number of railways listed by stock
exchange   173

7.1 Official values of British trade, 1663–1774   177
7.2 Circulation of precious metals, 1550–1800   180
7.3 The terms of trade, 1820–1910   193
7.4 Cotton textile production and consumption yielded, 1815–41: effects of terms of trade   200
8.1 Size of navies, 1689–1815 (ships of the Line)   217
8.2 The number of patent law cases, 1750–1849   234
9.1 Number of persons per household (percentage in various communities)   242
9.2 Percentage of households with kin, lodgers and servants for various communities   242
9.3 Structure of the families of household heads   245
9.4 Expenditure on necessities as a proportion of men's earnings   265
10.1 Selected indicators of the standard of living, 1760–1850   271
10.2 Consumption of luxury goods and standard-of-living indicator   281
10.3 Alternative indices of living standards in Britain, 1760–1850   289
10.4 Estimates of productivity growth in England, 1770–1860   292
11.1 Growth of the London carrying trade, 1681–1840   298
11.2 Growth in passenger services to selected provincial centres, 1715–1840   298
11.3 Growth of inland waterways, 1760–1830   300
11.4 Shipping registered in the United Kingdom, 1790–1900   303
11.5 Construction of the rail network, 1830–1900   305
11.6 Growth of railway services, 1842–1900   307
11.7 Productivity growth in transport by mode   322
11.8 Sectoral contributions to productivity: annual percentage growth, 1780–1860   323
12.1 Exact-title occupational inheritance at marriage, 1839–43   337
12.2 Literacy for selected areas in Europe and North America *c.* 1700   344
12.3 Proportion of population under 20 in England and Wales who were scholars, 1818–71   346
12.4 Distribution of men in the manual labour classes across wage categories following Baxter's 1867 classification   349
12.5 Illiteracy and school enrolments in Europe and North America, *c.* 1860   351
12.6 Illiteracy by social structure and occupation group, 1580s to 1780s   355
13.1 The composition of British imports, 1699–1800   365
13.2 The source of English imports, 1700–98   365
13.3 Consumption per head of groceries   367

13.4 English East India Company imports of chinaware and
porcelain　369
13.5 Estimated East India Company textile imports compared
with other commodities　369
13.6 Estimated average cost of country houses by estate size,
1770–1800　372
13.7 Ownership of goods, 1675–1725　374
13.8 Expenditure in working-class budgets　376
14.1 Occupational structure in Scottish cities, 1841　415
14.2 Occupational structure in Scottish cities, 1841, by sector　415
15.1 Estimated value of some construction and industrial
materials, 1858　422
15.2 Men and women employed in coal and metal mining in 1854　422
15.3 Causes of death among 10,000 males over 15 years old,
1860–2　424
15.4 Mineral exports as a percentage of domestic annual
production　429
15.5 The geographical distribution of mineral exports,
1790　430
15.6 Index of coal and metal prices, 1700–1830　431
15.7 Employment structure of Manchester cotton firms, 1841,
and Cornish metal mines, 1837　437
16.1 World population, 1500–1900　453
16.2 Population of selected western European nations, 1500–1870　454
16.3 GDP per capita by region, 1500, 1820 and 1913　455
16.4 Income per capita in Netherlands relative to Britain,
1500–1913　456
16.5 Number of years nations were at war, 1450–1900　461
16.6 GDP per capita, selected countries, 1820–1913　463

Contributors

ROBERT C. ALLEN is Professor of Economic History at Oxford University

MAXINE BERG is Professor of History at the University of Warwick

KRISTINE BRULAND is Professor of Economic History at the University of Oslo

ROGER BURT is Professor of Mining History at Exeter University

T. M. DEVINE is Research Professor of Scottish History at Aberdeen University

STANLEY L. ENGERMAN is Professor of Economics and of History at the University of Rochester

RODERICK FLOUD is Vice-Chancellor of London Metropolitan University

C. KNICK HARLEY is Professor of Economics at the University of Western Ontario, and University Lecturer in Economic History at Oxford University

RON HARRIS is Senior lecturer in Law and Legal History at Tel Aviv University

PAT HUDSON is Professor of Economic History at Cardiff University

JANE HUMPSRIES is Reader in Economic History at Oxford University

PAUL JOHNSON is Professor of Economic History at the London School of Economics

DAVID MITCH is Associate Professor of Economics at the University of Maryland Baltimore County

JOEL MOKYR is Robert H. Strotz Professor of Arts and Sciences and Professor of Economics and History at Northwestern University

PATRICK K. O'BRIEN is Centennial Professor of Economic History at the London School of Economics

STEPHEN QUINN is Associate Professor of Economics at Texas Christian University

SIMON VILLE is Professor of Economics at the University of Wollongong, New South Wales

HANS-JOACHIM VOTH is Associate Professor of Economics at the Universitat Pompeu Fabra, Barcelona

SIR TONY (E. A.) WRIGLEY was formerly Professor of Economic History and Master of Corpus Christi College, Cambridge

Preface

In their gloomier moments, academics are prone to predict the demise of their subject. As the tastes of students change, as the economy waxes and wanes, as the number of academic jobs fluctuates and the average age of academics increases, so it is easy to discern a long-term decline in the attractiveness of any subject.

Economic historians, above all, ought to be wary of such speculation. After all, if there is one single thing which is taught by study of the subject of economic history, it is that change is continuous and usually slow. As economists put it, 'change is at the margin'; it proceeds by tiny increments or decrements and the end, or even the direction, is rarely to be seen by those who are living through the changes. But change is always with us, a lesson which needs to be learned by each generation. It should be learned particularly by those eminent economic commentators who, at each stage of the business cycle, confidently predict that that stage, whether of boom or bust, will go on forever. But it must be learnt also by those who predict that an academic subject is in terminal decline.

On the evidence of the three volumes of *The Cambridge Economic History of Modern Britain*, reports of the death of economic history are clearly premature and probably mistaken. The volumes demonstrate a vibrant subject, reaching out into new areas of research and using new techniques to explore new and old problems. Economic history, as revealed in these pages, is a true interdisciplinary subject, a point emphasised also by the contributors to *Living Economic and Social History* (Hudson 2001) which was published to celebrate the 75th anniversary of the Economic History Society, the guardian of the subject in the United Kingdom.

As Pat Hudson emphasises, the subject has certainly changed. The rotund phrases of Ephraim Lipson, the beautifully crafted analyses of John Clapham, have given way to equations, to the quantitative analysis of bizarre sources such as human skeletal remains and to the increasing emphasis on the study of national economic histories within their global environment. Yet the essence of the subject remains: in the words which used each Sunday to advertise the *News of the World*, 'all human life is here'. Economic history is about the behaviour of human beings in an uncertain world, as they struggle to earn a living, as they decide when to have a child, as they band together in a common cause or, all too often, fall out and resort to conflict or war.

The economic history of modern Britain, the subject of these volumes, has seen all these and billions more human acts, collective and individual. In most cases, economic history is about collective behaviour. There are few 'great men' (and even fewer 'great women') in British economic history, mainly because economic change can very rarely be attributed to a single person. Even if, on occasion, economic historians identify one person as an inventor who has changed the world, other historians will usually jump in to claim the credit for another, or at the extreme will claim that, counter-factually, the invention really did not make much difference. This alone is enough to keep the subject changing. But also, because we cannot directly observe collective behaviour or describe myriad individual acts, the subject has to theorise as well as describe. Only through theory can we hope to make sense of the economic past.

Some academic subjects, in such circumstances, turn in on themselves and allow theory to predominate. Often, they become the preserve of the favoured few, writing and publishing for each other, theorising in increasingly arcane language. New technologies of academe, the email and the working paper, abet these tendencies as the results of research are circulated within an inner circle and only emerge, months or years later, to inform a wider audience.

The Cambridge Economic History of Modern Britain, by contrast, belongs to a tradition which believes that research has no purpose if it is not used, if it is not disseminated as soon as possible to as wide an audience as possible. In other words, its editors and authors have a mission to explain. This certainly does not obviate the use of the most ingenious and complex techniques to tease out the mysteries of the past; it does demand, however, that the techniques and the results that stem from them are explained clearly, concisely and in language which anyone interested in the topic can understand. This was the aspiration which lay, for example, behind *The Economic History of Britain since 1700* (Floud and McCloskey 1981, 1994) and it still animates these volumes. They belong to an academic tradition exemplified by Lord Rutherford, the great Cambridge scientist, who believed (in somewhat antiquated parlance) that 'The good scientist should be able to explain his results to the charlady in his lab.'

These volumes, therefore, are textbooks, in the best sense of books which explain their subject. They are written by leading researchers, drawn from many countries around the world, who have themselves recently contributed to our understanding of British economic history; usually with pleasure, they accept the obligation to tell students and others with an interest in their subjects about the results of academic enquiry by themselves and others in the field. It is not always possible, of course, to be sure of the background knowledge which each reader will possess; most of the techniques and technical terms have been explained as they are used in the chapters which follow, but some readers – if they are puzzled – may need to consult a dictionary or a dictionary of economics.

All authors need critics. A phrase which seems limpidly clear to one person may baffle another and only an informed critic can help the author to express complex notions in a comprehensible way. For this reason, all the drafts of the chapters which follow were discussed, not only by the editors, but by all the other authors within each volume and by a number of invited commentators who gathered together at a conference held in London Guildhall University. The editors are grateful to those commentators: Martin Daunton, Tim Leunig, Richard Smith, Emmett Sullivan, Barry Supple, Rick Trainor and Peter Wardley. Our grateful thanks go also to the Economic and Social Research Council, the British Academy, the Gatsby Foundation, and Cambridge University Press for their support for the conference and the production of these volumes. Richard Fisher, Elizabeth Howard and Helen Barton at Cambridge University Press have encouraged us throughout the process of publication and we have also had the invaluable support of an exemplary research assistant, Claudia Edwards.

Roderick Floud and Paul Johnson

1

Accounting for the Industrial Revolution

JOEL MOKYR

Contents

Introduction   1
Accounting and 'accounting' for the Industrial Revolution   4
Explaining the Industrial Revolution   14
The intellectual origins of economic growth   17
Conclusions   27

INTRODUCTION

How do we account for the Industrial Revolution?[1] In recent years, economic historians have had to redefine what they mean by the industrial revolution and to reassess its significance. On the one hand, the findings published in the 1990s by Crafts, Harley (Crafts and Harley 1992; Harley 1998) and others have reduced estimates of the rate of economic growth during the classic years of the industrial revolution, 1760 to 1830. These findings have been reinforced by recent work by scholars such as Antràs and Voth (2003) and Clark (2001b), who have shown that the sharp revisions downward to Deane and Cole's (1967) estimates of the rates of growth and productivity change during the industrial revolution made by Crafts and Harley were, if anything, too optimistic and that little if any real per capita growth can be discerned in Britain before 1830. These conclusions are consistent with Feinstein's (1998) recalculations of the growth in real wages, which showed very little secular increase before the mid-1840s. As a macroeconomic phenomenon, then, the Industrial Revolution in its 'classical years', 1760–1830, stands today diminished and

---

[1] I am grateful to Gregory Clark and Joachim Voth for making unpublished papers easily accessible and to E. A. Wrigley, Knick Harley and Maxine Berg for insightful comments. Some of the materials in this chapter are adapted from my editor's Introduction, 'The new economic history and the industrial revolution', in Mokyr (1999); from my chapter 'Knowledge, technology, and economic growth during the industrial revolution', in Van Ark *et al.* (2000); and from Mokyr (2002).

weakened. It is now also widely realised that the Industrial Revolution was not 'industrialisation'. On the eve of the Industrial Revolution Britain was a highly developed, commercialised, sophisticated economy in which a large proportion of the labour force was engaged in non-agricultural activities, and in which the quality of life as measured by the consumption of non-essentials and life expectancy was as high as could be expected anywhere on this planet. In many ways, life did not improve all that much between 1750 and 1850. So perhaps the concept of an industrial revolution is indeed the product of an obsolete historiography.

It is possible to exaggerate this view. We need to recall first that the Industrial Revolution took place in a period of almost incessant war, and that wars in these years – as Ricardo pointed out in an almost forgotten chapter in his *Principles* (1951 [1817]) – meant serious disruptions in the patterns of trade and hence income loss through foregone gains from trade. The peace of Paris (1763) was soon followed by the American Independence Wars, the Revolutionary Wars, Napoleon, Jefferson's embargo and the war of 1812–14. These were compounded by harvest failures, the worst of which (1816) occurred right after the wars ended. Finally, between 1760 and 1830 the population of England rose from 6.1 million to 13.1 million, an increase that had no precedent in the country's history or equal in the European experience outside the British Isles in this period. One does not have to be a committed Malthusian to accept that for most 'pre-industrial' economies such a sudden demographic increase would have created serious stresses and resource scarcities. The very fact that despite these pressures Britain was able not only to maintain living standards and prevent truly damaging scarcity, but also to finance a set of expensive wars on the continent, demonstrated that by 1780 or 1790 her economy had reached a resilience and strength that exceeded by a large factor that found by William III upon arrival in Britain in 1688. Indeed, had the years of the Industrial Revolution coincided with peace and more abundant harvests, or had population growth been less fast, real wages and income per capita would have in all likelihood increased faster.

Moreover, the striking historiographical phenomenon is that the importance of the Industrial Revolution as a historical dividing line has recently been underlined by scholars writing in the traditions of 'world history' because of the growing realisation that until late in the eighteenth century the economic gap between Europe and the Orient was less than earlier work had suggested. As early as 1988, Eric Jones suggested in his *Growth Recurring* that episodes of growth took place in Asia as much as in Europe, and that before the industrial revolution it would have been hard to predict that the one episode that would 'break through' and create *sustained* growth would happen in Europe and specifically in Britain. This work has suggested that the differences in the early modern age between Europe and parts of the Orient have been overdrawn and that as late as 1750 the gap between West and East was comparatively minor: a number of scholars have argued that economic performance and living standards in western Europe did not really diverge from those in the Orient (specifically the Yangzi delta in China and Japan) until the nineteenth century (Hanley 1997; Pomeranz 2000; Vries 2001a, 2001b; Goldstone 2002). Given the huge gap between the West and the rest in 1900, the realisation that the gap may not have been all that large in 1750 places an additional onus of responsibility for historical change on the period after the mid-eighteenth century.

It is ahistorical to think about industrial revolutions as events that abruptly raise the rate of sustained economic growth by a considerable amount. Most of the effects of invention and diffusion on income per capita or economic welfare are slow in coming and spread out over long periods. All the same, we should recognise that even though the dynamic relation between technological progress and per capita growth is hard to pin down and measure, it is the central feature of modern economic history. We do not know for sure how to identify the technology-driven component of growth, but we can be reasonably sure that the unprecedented (and to a large extent undermeasured) growth in income in the twentieth century would not have taken place without prior technological changes. It seems therefore more useful to measure 'industrial revolutions' in terms of the technological *capabilities* of a society based on the knowledge it possesses and the institutional rules by which its economy operates. These technological capabilities include the potential to produce more goods and services which enter GDP and productivity calculations, but they could equally affect aspects that are poorly measured by our standard measures of economic performance, such as the ability to prevent disease, to educate the young, to preserve and repair the environment, to move and process information, to co-ordinate production in large units, and so on.

These historiographical developments underlie what we may call the paradox of the Industrial Revolution, which I will attempt to account for in this chapter. With the lowering of the estimates of economic growth, some scholars have attempted to suppress the entire notion of the British industrial revolution (J. Clark 1986; Wallerstein 1989; Cameron 1990, 1994; G. Clark 2001b). This attempt has failed, because the notion that contemporaneous economic growth – as traditionally measured using standard national income accounting procedures – was the essence of the 'classical' Industrial Revolution was never established as an axiom. Changes in the British economy and in the larger social and intellectual environment in which production technology operated occurring before and during the classical years of the Industrial Revolution were critical. In the end, this is what accounted for the period of indisputable economic expansion that we observe in Britain after 1830 and the rest of Europe after 1850 and that created the vast gap between Europe and the rest of the world that had emerged by 1914 and still seems to dominate the literature on 'divergence'.

Period	National income per cap. (Deane and Cole)	National income per cap. (Crafts)	Indust. product (Hoffmann)	Indust. product (Deane and Cole)	Indust. product (Harley)	Indust. product (Crafts)	Indust. product (Cuenca)
1700–60	0.44	0.3	0.67	0.74	n.a.	0.62	–
1760–1800	0.52	0.17	2.45	1.24	1.6[a]	1.96	2.61[c]
1800–30	1.61	0.52	2.70	4.4	3.2[b]	3.0	3.18
1830–70	1.98	1.98	3.1	2.9	n.a.	n.a.	–

Table 1.1   Estimated annual rates of growth of real output, 1700–1871 (in percentages)

[a] 1770–1815
[b] 1815–41
[c] 1770–1801

Sources: Computed from Harley 1998; Hoffmann 1965; Cuenca 1994.

ACCOUNTING AND 'ACCOUNTING' FOR THE INDUSTRIAL REVOLUTION

The national income accounting concept of GDP or GNP growth has become associated with economic change for good reason. In principle, it measures what happens to the economy as a whole, not to selected industries or sectors that seem to be unusually dynamic and that may bias the picture. It is the very embodiment of the admonition made by Sir John Clapham, one of the great figures of British economic history of the twentieth century, that any proof by example should face the quantifier's challenge: How large? How long? How often? How representative? It seems all too easy to focus on the dramatic and well-documented inventions in cotton, steam, iron and engineering, and forget the handicraft, construction, food processing, farming and services sectors, which employed the majority of Britons in 1760 in which changes were far slower or non-existent.

Any kind of macroeconomic analysis of the British economy in this period is, as already noted, severely limited by the unavailability of data. Most of what economic historians know about the British economy at the aggregative level has been pieced together from little fragments of data usually collected for a totally different purpose, and held together by a healthy dose of economic analysis. Although the issue still remains a matter of some dispute, it seems that today's consensus is that, at a high level of aggregation, the British economy experienced little growth during the years typically associated with the Industrial Revolution. Most of the computations come from the output side of the national income accounts, and are summarised in Table 1.1.

Compared to Deane and Cole's national income statistics, Crafts' figures reveal an aggregate growth that was much slower during the Industrial Revolution. Industrial production is more ambiguous: Hoffmann's data, computed in the 1930s, clearly show a rapid acceleration during the period of the Industrial Revolution, but Deane and Cole's series is much more erratic and, like the revisionist data of Harley and Crafts, shows that most of the quantitative expansion occurred after 1800.[2] The point to be stressed is that in an economy that is undergoing rapid change in one sector but not in another, aggregate change depends on the relative size of each sector at the *initial moment* and on the interaction between the two sectors. Part of the economic logic of the Crafts–Harley view of slow growth was that productivity growth and technological progress were confined to a few relatively small sectors such as cotton, wool, iron and machinery whereas much of the rest of manufacturing remained more or less stagnant till after 1830. Two-sector growth models imply that abrupt changes in the economy *as a whole* are a mathematical impossibility when the more dynamic sector is initially small, because the aggregate rate of growth of any composite is a weighted average of the growth rates of its components, the weights being the respective shares in output.[3] The British economy as a whole was changing much more slowly than its most dynamic parts such as cotton and machine tools, because growth was 'diluted' by slow-growing sectors (Pollard 1981: 39). It is hardly surprising that it took until 1830 or 1840 for the economy-wide effects of the industrial revolution to be felt.

Berg and Hudson (1992) have argued that sharp dividing lines between the traditional sector and the modern sector are inappropriate; that even within cotton, the most dynamic industry, there were large islands of traditional domestic production which actually grew as a result of mechanisation elsewhere. On the other hand, some service industries such as land transportation before 1830 were experiencing productivity growth without much dramatic technological progress. Such refinements do not weaken the arithmetic power of the argument unless the relative sizes of the two sectors are radically revised. More serious is the critique that this exercise assumes that the rates of growth are independent. Much as is true today for today's high-tech sector, this independence seems unlikely because of input–output relations between the different sectors. If the 'modern sector' during the Industrial Revolution helped produce, for

---

[2] All the same, Crafts and Harley explicitly deny adhering to a school that would negate the profound changes that occurred in Britain during the Industrial Revolution and restate that 'industrial innovations . . . did create a genuine industrial revolution reflected in changes in Britain's economic and social structure', even if their impact on economic growth was more modest than previously believed (1992: 3).

[3] Even if changes in the modern sector itself were discontinuous and its growth rate very high, its small initial size would limit its impact on the economy-wide growth rate, and its share in the economy would increase gradually. In the long run, the force of compound growth rates was such that the modern sector swallowed the entire economy. How long was the long run? A numerical example is illuminating here. Suppose there are two sectors, a modern one growing at 4 per cent per year and a traditional one growing at 1 per cent per year, and suppose that initially the modern sector produces only 10 per cent of GNP. It will therefore grow relative to the economy as a whole, but it will take seventy-four years for the two sectors to be of equal size and a full century after the starting point the traditional sector will have shrunk to about 31 per cent of the economy. These hypothetical numbers fit the actual record rather well.

instance, cheaper and better iron, that would have affected the tools used by farmers and artisans who otherwise would belong to the slow-growth part of the economy. Devices, materials and ideas from the modern sector slowly penetrated into the traditional industries, and some of them, such as steam power, seem in many ways similar to the modern notion of General Purpose Technology (Helpman 1998).

The exact limits of the 'modern sector' remain in dispute, since industry-specific output and productivity statistics do not exist. Temin (1997) has maintained that the Crafts–Harley 'minimalist' argument is inconsistent with the patterns of British foreign trade, which clearly show that Britain maintained a comparative advantage not just in the few rapidly expanding 'new industries' but in a host of small, older industries such as linen, glass, brewing, pottery, buttons, soap, candles, paper, and so on. Temin relies on export figures to make a point about comparative advantage and to infer from it indirectly that technological progress occurred on a variety of fronts or at least that the input–output effects from the technologically dynamic sectors to the laggards were significant. Anecdotal evidence and examples of progress in industries other than the paradigmatic high-flying industries can be culled from specialised sources.[4] On the other hand, as critics have pointed out, maintaining comparative advantage is not the same as attaining rapid productivity growth. Moreover, the growing reliance on imported food would have implied higher manufacturing exports even in the absence of technological progress in the industrial sector (Crafts and Harley 2000). Even with the sectors that Temin believes to be progressive, the modern sector would still include only a relatively small proportion of GNP and employment in 1760 or even 1800.

The sense in which technological progress is supposed to have led to economic growth is through efficiency-increasing innovation. By that it is understood that a given quantity of output or GNP can be produced with fewer inputs and thus the economy becomes more productive. A growth in efficiency is not a necessary condition for *economic* growth. Income per capita could increase through a rise in the capital/labour ratio, or through a rise in diligence through longer work-years and higher participation rates. In a pair of pathbreaking papers Jan de Vries (1993, 1994) has argued for an 'industrious revolution' in which more household members participated in market activities (which get counted as part of GDP) and replaced goods produced in the household by goods purchased in the market. Voth (2001) has confirmed this increase in diligence, although it is complicated by changes in the age structure of the

---

[4] On the hardware industry, see Berg (1994: ch. 12). On many of the other industries, classic industry studies carried out decades ago have not yet been supplanted such as Coleman (1958) on the paper industry, Mathias (1953, repr. 1979a) on brewing, Clow and Clow (1952) and Haber (1958) on the chemical industries, Church (1970) on the shoe and boot industry, McKendrick (1961, 1982b) on potteries, and Barker (1960) on glass.

population (Britain was, on average, getting younger during the years of the Industrial Revolution). On the other hand, an economy that experiences persistent total factor productivity growth is likely to experience per capita income growth.

Economists have remained loyal to total factor productivity (TFP) analysis, perhaps more than the concept deserves. The idea is to look at the productivity of all inputs, because a growth in that of one factor, say labour, could occur simply as the result of a growth in the level of complementary factors that make it work more efficiently. The literature on the calculation of the residual is enormous, and this is not the place to sing its praises or to criticise it. The actual logic is to subtract a weighted sum of input growth from output growth, and to define the 'residual' as productivity growth. An equivalent procedure is to use the 'dual' approach, estimating the growth of weighted real returns to factors (McCloskey 1981; Antràs and Voth, 2003). In order to identify these numbers as a correct approximation of total factor productivity, we need to assume perfect competition, constant returns to scale, the correct identification of the production function, and Hicks-neutral technological change.[5] Without that, the use of factor shares as proxies for the elasticities of output with respect to inputs would no longer hold.[6] Any errors, omissions, mismeasurements and aggregation biases that occur on either the output or the input sides would, by construction, be contained in the residual. For instance, we simply do not know much about the flow of capital services and their relationship to the stock of capital. If horses or machines worked longer hours or factory buildings were occupied for more than one shift, it is unlikely to be registered in our estimates as an increase in capital inputs. Even if properly measured, the identification of total factor productivity growth with technological progress requires the suspension of disbelief on a number of fronts, above all as far as the quality of the data is concerned.

The best-known attempts to compute total factor productivity for Britain during the Industrial Revolution were made by Crafts and Harley. Between 1760 and 1800, Crafts and Harley estimate, total factor productivity 'explained' about 10 per cent of total output growth; in the period 1801–31 this went up to about 18 per cent. This seems rather unimpressive, but it should be kept in mind that growth is concerned with output per worker (or per capita). If we look at output per worker, we observe that for the period 1760–1830 practically the entire growth of per capita income – such as it was – is explained by technological change.

---

[5] Hicks-neutral technical change leaves the marginal rate of substitution between any two inputs unaffected by the technological change, and thus the relative contribution of each input to the production process is unaltered.

[6] As Antràs and Voth (2003), in the most recent contribution to this literature, point out, whatever weaknesses are embodied in the primal approach will be entirely reflected in the dual as well.

Table 1.2   Total factor productivity, computed from product accounts

	Per capita growth	Contrib. of capital/ labour ratio	Contrib. of resources per capita ratio	Total contrib. of non-labour inputs	Total factor productivity growth	Productivity as % of total per capita growth
1760–1800	0.2	0.2*0.35 = 0.07	−0.065*0.15 = −0.01	0.06	0.14	70
1800–30	0.5	0.3*0.35 = 0.105	−0.1*0.15 = −0.015	0.09	0.41	82

Source: Computed from Crafts 1985a: 81 and Crafts and Harley 1992: table 5.

The contribution of total productivity towards per capita output are presented in Table 1.2, where the standard ('primal') procedure is used, and Table 1.3 where the dual procedure is used. Both procedures require making assumptions about the shares of labour, capital and land in national income. The shares used are labour 50 per cent, capital 35 per cent, land 15 per cent. These figures were originally proposed by Crafts based on computation made by Deane and Cole who estimated the share of labour in national income to be 44 per cent in 1801 and 49 per cent in 1860. Crafts notes that the 44 per cent figure seems low, and his proposed adjustment seems uncontroversial. While the computation of the primal is not sensitive to misspecifying the shares of labour and capital (which grow at similar rates between 1760 and 1830), the share of land matters since resources were growing at a much slower rate than labour or capital (and hence if the share of land used is too low, the estimate of total input growth would be biased upward and that of total productivity would be biased downward).

To judge from Tables 1.2 and 1.3, British economic growth was slow in this period, but what little there was seems to be explained by the residual. The assessment of the importance of TFP in the critical period 1770–1800 is difficult because it relies on the division of one small growth rate by another, and because a lot depends on the inclusion of the government (which extracted a large amount of income in terms of higher taxes). Until 1830, however, the increase in TFP is about equal to the growth in product per capita: for the entire period 1770–1860, product per capita increased at an average rate of 0.6 per cent per year, of which 0.41 (or almost exactly two thirds) is explained by Antràs and Voth's estimates of total productivity growth. Because all numbers are small, however, this result is rather sensitive: a ratio of two numbers very close to zero rarely produces a robust result. Even a minor revision in computation means a major difference in the conclusions. By varying their sources for capital and resource income growth, Antràs and Voth show that productivity growth either could be made negative or could over-explain income per capita growth. Furthermore, just by varying the assumptions on factor shares (the most assumption-driven part of the calculation) total factor productivity growth could be made to vary from 0.18 per cent to 0.38 per cent in 1770–1800, and between 0.24 per cent and 0.46 per cent in 1830–60 (the difference in 1800–30 is smaller).

Table 1.3 Total factor productivity, computed from income accounts

'Preferred estimates':

	Per capita output growth	Total factor productivity growth					
		capital income	labour income	land income	Total private sector	Government	TFP growth
1770–1801	0.2	−0.40*0.33 = −0.132	0.35*.45 = 0.157	0.26*0.14 = 0.036	0.061	2.60*.08 = .208	0.27
1801–31	0.5	0.71*0.33 = 0.234	0.25*0.45 = 0.112	0.76*0.14 = 0.106	0.452	1.11*.08 = .088	0.54
1831–60	1.1	−0.21*0.33 = −0.069	0.68*0.45 = 0.306	0.48*0.14 = 0.067	0.304	0.31*.08 = .025	0.33

Sensitivity analysis:

1770–1801 <lower bound, upper bound>[a]							<−0.09, 0.64>
1801–31 <lower bound, upper bound>[b]							<0.48, 1.26>
1831–60 <lower bound, upper bound>[c]							<0.31, 1.26>

Source: computed from Antràs and Voth 2003.

Notes:
[a] minimum: using Clark 'charity returns'; maximum: using Lindert–Williamson price index.
[b] minimum: using Clark 'charity returns'; maximum: using wholesale price index.
[c] minimum: using Clark 'real rents'; maximum: using Lindert–Williamson price index.

Table 1.4 The world according to Clark, all in average percentage change per year				
	Real per capita GDP growth	Total factor productivity growth	TFP growth attributable to cotton and wool alone	TFP attributable to other sectors
1760–1800	−0.05	0.04	0.21	−0.17
1800–30	0.58	0.68	0.30	0.38
1830–60	0.13	0.20	0.27	−0.07

Source: Clark 2001b.

The most robust conclusion that the recent literature offers is that, as far as it can be measured, there was little total factor productivity growth at the aggregate level during the classical Industrial Revolution. This conclusion seems unsurprising, since a very slow per capita growth is irreconcilable with rapid TFP growth unless there is dramatic decumulation of capital or a reduction in natural resources.[7] Precisely because growth per capita was so slow and there is little to explain, small differences in procedures and estimation will produce radically different residuals.[8]

A different approach to the same issues is proposed by Gregory Clark (2001b). Clark has employed the data he has collected from the charities commission to revise the growth of real per capita GDP between 1760 and 1800 and finds it to be essentially zero. After 1800 there was some recovery, but then his data show a sudden and unexpected slow-down after 1830. Clark's conclusions are still tentative, but because he uses new sources they should be noticed. In this line of work, an ounce of new evidence is worth a pound of theory, but the representativeness of samples and the calculation of proper price indices remain difficult questions, especially when they fly in the face of other evidence.

On the basis of the data summarised in Table 1.4, Clark dismisses the entire Industrial Revolution as a historical phenomenon, and takes exception to the Berg–Hudson–Temin view of a broad-based set of technological advances. The very slow growth he observes for the decades after 1830 (much slower than for the 1800–30 period) seems to fly in the face of much other historical evidence and must be regarded as preliminary. It is also somewhat odd that in these calculations TFP growth consistently *over*explains per capita income growth. This difference is not quite impossible (for instance, capital/labour ratios could be declining or the

[7] In an open economy, there could also be a dramatic decline in the terms of trade that would be consistent with a possible situation of widespread technological progress without growth (so that the economy has to produce more for the export sector to pay for ever more expensive imports). Such a decline would also bias the estimated TFP growth in the dual procedure downward, and a correction for this after 1800 does increase the estimated value of TFP growth from 0.49 per cent per year to 0.61 per cent.

[8] For instance, Voth (1998, 2001) has radically revised labour inputs and claimed that because labour input per capita increased in the fifty years before 1800, the residual is extremely small and possibly negative.

labour-year might have become shorter), but for this period these explanations seem inapplicable: capital grew slightly faster than labour and, as we have seen, the labour year grew, if anything, longer. All the same, Clark's data confirm the overall picture of slow pace of growth during the Industrial Revolution, and that what growth occurred is attributable to total factor productivity.

Moreover, recent attempts to improve our estimates of the inputs that went into the production function seem to indicate that those estimates are still too conservative. For instance, if Voth is correct about people working longer hours and the quantitative importance of the decline of St Monday (see p. 277), labour inputs estimated from population data *under*estimate labour inputs and thus overestimate productivity growth. Clark (2001b) has re-examined the housing and real estate market, always one of the weakest links in the computation of the income accounts, and discovered that the property income estimates based on the property tax of 1803 seriously underassessed the value of land and houses, and as a result the rise of this component of income in the following decades is seriously overstated. Real rental income per capita by this account actually fell from the late eighteenth century to the middle of the nineteenth. Given that population almost tripled in this period, that is not an implausible finding, especially in view of the growing dependence on the importation of land intensive products. If correct, the computations of income per capita growth are *over*estimated and so are productivity computations derived from them.

It is not only that income per capita and productivity grew slowly, but what little growth there was, argues Clark, was due to a set of adventitious circumstances.[9] The advances in textile technology, in his view, happened to occur in a large sector with an elastic demand, and much of the rest of the economy was not really affected until the closing third of the nineteenth century. This ultra-narrow view of the Industrial Revolution resonates strangely with the 'energy-interpretation' that regards the invention of steam engines and the emergence of the capability to convert stored-up (fossil) energy into work as the macroinvention that changed all (Cipolla 1965; Wrigley 2000; Goldstone 2002). Yet the energy interpretation is too narrow itself. What the aggregative accounting approach conceals is what went on inside people's minds, which prepared the ground and planted the seeds of what was to come. The years 1760–1815 witnessed more than just some lucky breaks in a handful of industries: it was also the period in which people defied gravity through hot-air balloons, began the conquest of smallpox, and learned to can food, to use binary codes for manufacturing purposes, to infer geological strata from fossil

---

[9] The idea that the Industrial Revolution was in some sense a fortunate 'accident' or at least highly contingent was first proposed by Crafts (1977). For a recent argument along those lines see Goldstone (2003).

evidence and to burn gas for lighting. They advanced and improved old and tried techniques as much as they introduced radical new ones. Not just steam but water power, too, was greatly improved.[10] The invention of stearic candles kept an old technology thriving despite the threats from new sources of light. In pottery, one of the oldest techniques known to mankind, Josiah Wedgwood and others introduced new materials, new moulding techniques and improved oven-firing. It may well have been inevitable that the time it took for these improvements to filter through enough barriers to affect national income is longer than was thought in the past. Indeed, it seems surprising that it could have been thought otherwise. But that does not reduce the achievement. As McCloskey (1981: p. 118) put it, the Industrial Revolution was not the Age of Cotton, nor the Age of Steam; it was an age of improvement.

Yet, as noted, improvement was not ubiquitous. Large sectors of the economy, employing the majority of the labour force and accounting for at least half of gross national product in 1830 were, for all practical purposes, only little affected by innovation before the middle of the nineteenth century. Even in textiles, the finishing industries such as tailoring, haberdashery and millinery remained largely manual until the advent of the sewing machine in the 1860s. Domestic servants, construction workers, retailers, teachers, sailors and dockworkers, to pick a few examples, were but little affected. Some industries changed and others did not, for reasons that in part reflected the demand side of the economy or the supply of raw materials and energy, but above all had to do with technological capabilities. Yet we should also recognise that some of the inventions, especially in energy, engineering and materials, found applications in many industries, and that general purpose technologies spread throughout the economy.

What makes the use of national accounts particularly difficult as a measure of economic progress is that further refinements of the total factor productivity computation are yielding ambiguous results and require data that are not available on an aggregate level. On the one hand, economists have increasingly realised that rapid technological progress implies both product and process innovation. The appearance of new products and their growing availability, and improvements in the quality of existing ones, would not show up in the output statistics. In that regard, perhaps, the first Industrial Revolution was less problematic than the second, since most of the major breakthroughs were process innovations. The improvements in cotton quality and variety introduced perhaps the most significant large-scale bias of this sort (Cuenca 1994: 78), but the

---

[10] In Britain, the greatest names in the improvements in water power were John Smeaton and John Rennie. They designed the so-called breast wheel that combined the advantages of the more efficient overshot waterwheels with the flexibility and adaptability of the undershot waterwheel. The increased use of iron parts and the correct setting of the angle of the blades also increased efficiency. The great French engineer Poncelet designed the so-called Poncelet waterwheel using curved blades, and theoretical hydraulics gradually merged with the practical design of waterwheels.

possible impact of the mismeasurement implied on changes in economic performance has not been addressed. In so far as technological advances increase consumer surplus or some other indicator of utility, all measures of economic growth during the 1760–1830 years miss the invention of the smallpox vaccination process. Vaccines became available right at the midpoint of the 'classical' Industrial Revolution period (1796). What economist would deem that invention 'insignificant'? In other words, the computed residual *under*states the economic significance of technological change simply because the procedures used miss the introduction of new products and improvements in quality.[11] Economists interested in a true welfare measure of technological change should try to estimate growth in social surplus. This counterfactual mental experiment asks how much of GNP would consumers who enjoyed a certain invention have been demanding to be paid to do 'without'. Applied to steam power, as Von Tunzelmann showed in 1978, this may not have been all that much because water power provided an alternative. Of course, as we have seen, water power itself was improving dramatically during the same period, and hence the social savings calculations understate the gains from steam power compared to 1750 (as opposed to a hypothetical world of 1830 without steam). Yet even beyond that, the calculation must leave some pessimists uncomfortable. How much, for example, would someone who did not have access to anaesthesia (introduced in surgery in the 1850s) be willing to pay to have it? All the same, using the standard definitions of national income accounting, it seems unlikely that new product and quality improvements would radically change the computations reported above simply because there were few new products by comparison with the late nineteenth century.

The apparent dominance of invention over abstention suggested by total factor productivity analysis, once one of the most striking findings of the New Economic History, seems somehow less secure now than it did in the 1990s. Most of the payoff to technological creativity occurs in a more remote future and is spread over a longer period than was previously believed. Despite the fragile nature of many of the estimates, the conclusion that seems to emerge is that in the closing decades of the eighteenth century, the classical period of the Industrial Revolution, the changes in technology and organisation, however pregnant of future change, were insufficient to affect broad measures of the overall economy. After 1800, and especially after 1820, these effects became more noticeable, but their impact on aggregate variables was inevitably gradual and slow.

---

[11] There are other examples indicating qualitative improvements in this period. One of those was recently emphasised by Nordhaus (1997) in a paper arguing that the history of lighting suggests that product innovation may be the cause of a radical understatement of the advantages of technological progress. Among the important innovations introduced in this time was the Argand oil lamp, invented in the 1780s, and of course the introduction of gas lighting in the first decades of the nineteenth century.

EXPLAINING THE INDUSTRIAL REVOLUTION

None of the above reduces the significance of the Industrial Revolution. What has come under attack is the view, suggested originally by Deane and Cole in 1967, that the Industrial Revolution *itself* was a period of rapid economic growth. Instead it may be better regarded as a period of incubation in which the groundwork to future growth was being laid. Such preparation is historically important because without it we cannot possibly understand how Europe managed to break out of the negative feedback cycle of recurring episodic growth followed by retrenchment that had characterised economies before 1750 both in Europe and elsewhere.

Explaining the sudden change from a world of slow growth to one in which expansion became the norm has remained a central issue in modern scholarship. Before we can 'account' for the Industrial Revolution, some underbrush needs to be cleared.

The first point is that the industrial revolution in its wider sense was not really a British affair but a European (or perhaps north Atlantic) event. One interpretation has suggested that without Britain's leadership it might not have happened at all (Wrigley 2000; Goldstone 2003). Eric Jones (1987) has called this 'the little Englander' view of economic history. It is true, of course, that the first signs that something dramatic was brewing emerged in Britain, and that by 1820 much of the rest of Europe in some way felt 'left behind'. But Britain's primacy is a different-order problem and has a different historical explanation than the dramatic advance of Europe over the rest of the world. Confounding these two issues could lead to misleading conclusions. For instance, Pomeranz insists that the reason that the Industrial Revolution occurred in Europe but not in China was the access to coal and the 'ghost acreage' that Europe derived from its colonies. But coal was as localised in the north Atlantic as it was in China, and some regions such as Switzerland and New England were able to substitute around it by choosing low-energy-intensive industries and using alternative sources such as water power or peat. An industrial revolution led by continental economies would have been delayed by decades and differed in some important details. It might have relied less on 'British' steam and more on 'French' water power technology and 'Dutch' wind power, less on cotton and possibly more on wool and linen. But given the capabilities of French engineers and German chemists and the removal of many institutions that hampered their effective deployment before 1789, it would have happened. Even without Britain, by the twentieth century the gap between Europe and the rest of the world would have been there (Mokyr 2000).

Technological change is not just a 'residual' or a shift in an isoquant. It is something that takes places inside a human mind and from there is mapped successfully onto an object, a substance or an action. The 'mind' part is especially crucial. The intellectual foundations of the technology which made the Industrial Revolution came out of the Enlightenment, the scientific advances of the seventeenth and eighteenth centuries, the Renaissance, the Reformation and the printing press. These were all pan-European phenomena, and while Britain was an active participant and then became a leader, the reasons for its position were in a different class from those that explain the deeper historical roots of the phenomenon altogether.

Second, what made the Industrial Revolution such a watershed phenomenon was not just the dramatic inventions of Watt, Smeaton, Harrison, Cort and Crompton during the years of *Sturm und Drang* (approximately 1760–1800). Dramatic inventions before the Industrial Revolution were not unknown in Europe or elsewhere. Some of these breakthroughs undeniably had an effect on growth, such as the invention of the spinning wheel and the horizontal loom in the twelfth century, or that of the blast furnace and navigational and shipbuilding technology in the fifteenth. The increased industrial use of coal as a source of heat for industry and improvements in agricultural productivity (in part owing to investment in land improvements and livestock rather than technological change) did lead to higher income per capita and the ability to sustain a larger population on a given resource base (Wrigley 2000). But none of these 'episodes' resulted in sustainable per capita growth, even if each time they ratcheted living standards up to a higher level. Each of these episodes created a negative feedback effect that eventually eliminated growth. Identifying such feedback effects in earlier periods, and then checking whether they may have weakened or even turned positive may provide a better understanding of what happened.

The critical period in which West and East diverged may thus have been not the classical years of the Industrial Revolution but the decades that followed. Attention may have been diverted away from post-1815 developments by the spectacular inventions of the *annus mirabilis* as Donald Cardwell (1972) has termed the year 1769. In other words, what made the Industrial Revolution into the 'great divergence' was the *persistence* of technological change after the first wave. To see this, we might well imagine a counterfactual steady state of throstles, wrought iron and stationary steam engines, in which there would have been a one-off shift from wool to cotton and from animate power to stationary engines. But this is not what happened: the true miracle is not that the classical Industrial Revolution happened, but that it did not peter out like so many earlier waves of innovation. It was followed after 1820 by a secondary ripple of inventions that may have been less spectacular, but these were the ones that provided the muscle to the downward trend in production costs, spread the application to new and more industries and sectors, and eventually showed up in the productivity statistics.

Among those we may list the perfection of mechanical weaving; the invention of Roberts's self-acting mule in spinning (1825); the extension and adaptation of the techniques first used in cotton to carded wool and linen; the continuing improvement in the iron industry through Neilson's hot blast (1829) and other inventions; the continuing improvement in steam power that kept raising the efficiency and capabilities of the low-pressure stationary engines, while introducing the high-pressure engines of Trevithick, Woolf and Stephenson; the breakthroughs in engineering and high-precision tools by Maudslay, Whitworth, Nasmyth, Rennie, Brunel and the other great engineers of the 'second generation'; the growing interest in electrical technology leading to electroplating and later to the telegraph; the continuous improvement in crucible steelmaking through co-ordinated crucibles (as practised for example by Krupp), the work of Scottish steelmakers such as David Mushet (father of Robert Mushet, celebrated in one of Samuel Smiles's *Industrial Biographies*), and the addition of manganese to crucible steel known as Heath's process (1839). These advances – always excepting the telegraph – were in the nature of microinventions, but they did not run into diminishing returns nearly as fast and as early as they had before.

How, then, do we account for the Industrial Revolution? The literature has identified a number of themes around which the transition can be explained. But, as noted, it is important to separate out the 'little' question of why Britain was first from the 'big' question of why there was an Industrial Revolution in the West. The former is no mean question either, but from the point of view of the global economy it is the lesser one. I have dealt with the question of 'why Britain first' elsewhere (Mokyr 1994, 1998) and for a detailed discussion the interested reader is referred there. Little has been done in recent years to weaken the view that Britain's advantages were real, but it seems now agreed upon that they were to some extent temporary if not adventitious. Its ability to stay out of military conflicts on its own soil, a political system that was capable of reinventing itself and introducing reforms without violence, a capitalist, productive and progressive agricultural sector, an institutional agility that allowed it to adapt to a changing environment, all must be at the top of any such list. Britain was spared the upheavals of the French Revolution and its subsequent disruptions, even if it had to bear substantial financial costs of the Wars. Its closest continental rivals, the Low Countries, France and the western parts of Germany, were by contrast severely affected.

Furthermore, Britain could rely on a class of trained artisans and mechanics who were capable of carrying out clever designs and actually making things that worked and were still affordable. What Britain had in relative abundance is what Stevens (1995) has called 'technical literacy', which required, in addition to literacy, a familiarity with the properties of materials, a sense of mechanics, and the understanding of notation and spatial-graphic representation. Technical competence was a major factor in the leadership role that Britain played in the Industrial Revolution. Explaining this ability harks back in part to economics and in part to natural endowments: Britain already had a relatively large proportion of people in non-agricultural activities, both full-time artisans and part-time in cottage industries. It had a shipbuilding industry, a mining sector and a developed clock- and instrument-making sector. Smeaton, Watt, Ramsden, Harrison, Murdoch, Trevithick and so many other successful inventors of the time possessed the complementary skills needed for successful invention, including that ultimate umbrella term for tacit knowledge we call 'dexterity'. In the little workshop he used as a teenager, John Smeaton taught himself to work in metals, wood and ivory and could handle tools with the expertise of a regular blacksmith or joiner (Smiles 1891). What made the difference between a James Watt and a Leonardo was that Watt had Wilkinson and Leonardo did not. Britain by no means monopolised these skills: the millwrights of the Zaan area in the Netherlands and French engineers and craftsmen such as Jacques de Vaucanson and Honoré Blanc were obviously as competent as anyone Britain had to offer, and Smeaton himself travelled extensively to the continent to study these techniques. Yet Britain had more of them, and British society channelled their creative energies to those activities that were most useful to future technological development in the eyes of that most discerning of all masters: the market.

In Britain, these skills were transmitted through an apprenticeship system, in which instruction and emulation were intertwined, and thus codifiable and tacit knowledge were packaged together. Engineers worked for the private sector, not for the state, and thought mostly in terms of profit and economic efficiency. As long as the application of the technology did not require a great deal of formal knowledge, this system worked well for Britain. Britain also benefited from a social elite with an unusual interest in technical improvement, its ability and willingness to absorb and apply useful ideas generated elsewhere (without the 'not invented here' kind of arrogance), a well-functioning transport system favoured by nature and improved by investment, and the propitious location of some resources, especially coal. None of those factors was necessary or wholly unique to Britain, and while their fortunate conjuncture in Britain helped Britain secure its leadership, they do not explain the Great Divergence.

THE INTELLECTUAL ORIGINS OF ECONOMIC GROWTH

What made modern and sustained growth possible was the weakening of the negative feedback effects that had restrained economic expansion before 1750. Some of these feedbacks may even have switched sign and become positive. To make such an interpretation more than a tautology, we need to specify their nature in more detail. Many scholars following the work of Douglass North and Mancur Olson have insisted that modern growth became possible because of institutional changes that reduced the opportunities for rent-seeking behaviour. The decline of arbitrary taxation and state enforced monopolies (excepting patents), the gradual emergence of freer trade, the weakening and eventual abolition of guilds, the streamlining of the legal environment in which economic activity took place, and the growth of personal safety and contract enforcement through courts must have had an effect on the dynamic behaviour of the economy. From 1688 to 1848, institutional change in the western world was trending in these directions, haltingly and hesitantly perhaps, but the move was unmistakable. In this way the political enlightenment and the institutional changes it inspired brought about a more liberal environment, in which the kind of parasitic and predatory behaviour that had hamstrung growth before gradually weakened. This movement over time reached deeper and deeper into the darker institutional corners of eastern and southern Europe, but it started in Britain and the Low Countries.

The negative feedback from classical demographic response also changed. E. A. Wrigley (1988, 2000) has pointed out that the transition from a land-based or 'organic' to an 'inorganic' (mineral) economy is key to the understanding of the dissolution of the Malthusian dynamic. There is no doubt that economic performance at all times depends on the way the economy deploys energy and materials. The growing role of fossil fuels and iron was the defining characteristic of the first Industrial Revolution just as the use of steel and electric power characterised the second industrial revolution. In both cases this rising consumption of energy and materials clearly implied that the classical relation of diminishing returns to the fixed factor no longer held in its old form. It also seems plausible, as some economists have argued (Galor and Weil 2000; Galor and Moav 2002; Lucas 2002) that profound changes in demographic behaviour were driven by changes in the desired number of children. The logic here is based on a growth in the return to human capital, which makes it more attractive to have fewer children but invest more in their education. The eventual result was a sharp decline in fertility rates, driving up per capita income. Moreover, classical models inspired by Malthusian thinking implicitly assumed closed economies. Land was fixed in these models and they were driven by diminishing returns to the fixed factor. The growing access of the industrialising world to 'ghost acreage' (land and mineral resources located at a considerable distance from the final consumer, whether in the same political unit or not) obviated the old models. Countries with rapidly growing population did not starve – they imported food.

All the same, many of these changes were in their turn driven by changes in knowledge. We cannot possibly understand the transition to a mineral economy without realising the extent to which resources and knowledge were complementary. The coal that Britain dug out of its land had been there all along, but only in the seventeenth century was it applied to a wide variety of industrial uses, and only in the eighteenth century could it convert its natural form of energy (heat) to kinetic energy and thus do 'work'. Locating coal seams, digging it out of the ground and transporting it to its markets are complex activities. The demographic changes were similarly driven in part by variables that depended on useful knowledge. The rise in the rate of return to human capital and the rising effectiveness of contraceptive technology both belong to that category. If we are to search for a clue as to what really made the difference, we should look at what people knew, who knew what was known, how others had access to it, and how knowledge expanded both in terms of more being known and in terms of making what was known more accessible.

The Industrial Revolution, then, was driven by an expansion of technology or 'useful knowledge', in the classic sense formulated by Nobel prize winner, economist Simon Kuznets. Technology, after all, is the manipulation of natural regularities and phenomena in the service of our material well-being. To observe and register such regularities does not require that they be wholly 'understood'. But *something* has to be known. The most obvious example is the steam engine. Much of the physics that explained why and how steam power worked the way it did was not established until the middle of the nineteenth century and was certainly not available to Newcomen or Watt. But the idea of an atmospheric device that converts heat into work did require the notion of an atmosphere and atmospheric pressure, and the realisation that a vacuum creates the opportunity of moving a piston with force.[12] This is not a plea for technological determinism. On the contrary, the argument is that technology itself depended on the existence of a minimum amount of knowledge. Moreover, how much and what kind of knowledge was generated and what was done with it was a function of institutions. Technology could open a door, but it could not force a society to walk through it.

The continuation of technological progress at an accelerating pace in the nineteenth century depended on a phenomenon that pervaded much of the western world in the seventeenth and eighteenth centuries and which, failing a better term, I have termed the *Industrial Enlightenment* (Mokyr 2002). What I mean by that is a number of related phenomena, all of them quite novel (in extent, if not entirely in their essence).

First, the scientific developments of the seventeenth century mark an important foundation of the Industrial Enlightenment, despite the

---

[12] Similarly, the invention of chlorine bleaching required, at the very least, the knowledge of the existence of chlorine – discovered in 1774 by a Swedish chemist named Scheele. Of course, there was still a lot to be learned: Scheele and Berthollet still believed chlorine to be a compound, and its true nature as an element was shown by Humphry Davy in 1812.

often-repeated truism that before the 1780s there was little in the actual knowledge of natural philosophers that was of much direct use to people in production. This takes too narrow a view of the achievements of the great minds from Copernicus to Newton. Beyond their specific discoveries, they basically persuaded themselves and growing portions of the world around them that nature was 'rational' and followed knowable laws and regularities. Such knowledge should be open and made widely available (as opposed to more narrow technical knowledge which often remained private). A penchant for secrecy and privacy had characterised medieval alchemists, astrologers, botanists, geographers, and so on. This secrecy made room for a knowledge culture in which publicity and fame were rewarded and priority conveyed prestige (Eamon 1994).

The Industrial Enlightenment sought to understand why techniques worked by generalising them, trying to connect them to the formal propositional knowledge of the time. These would lead to extensions, refinements and improvements, as well as speed up and streamline the process of invention. This idea eventually penetrated the 'useful arts'. Important technical books in fields from mining techniques to botany were increasingly written in the vernacular or translated. The arrangement of topics either alphabetically (in technical dictionaries and encyclopaedias) or by topic (in technical manuals and descriptions of arts and crafts) created 'search engines' that made knowledge more accessible. A great effort was made to survey and catalogue artisanal practices out of the dusty confines of workshops, to determine which techniques were superior and to propagate them. The best-known example is Diderot's justly famous *Encyclopédie*, the epitome of Enlightenment literature, with its thousands of very detailed technical essays and plates (Headrick 2000).[13] Encyclopaedias were supplemented by a variety of textbooks, manuals and compilations of techniques and devices that were (or could be) in use somewhere. In machinery and in dyeing technology, to pick two examples, comprehensive treatises tried to catalogue and fully describe every technique known at the time.[14] Graphical representation and a standardisation of notation and units of measurement made the transfer of knowledge more efficient. Moreover, access to technical knowledge became in part a market

---

[13] In the *Encyclopédie*, in his article on 'arts', Diderot himself made a strong case for the 'open-ness' of technological knowledge, condemning secrecy and confusing terminology, and pleading for easier access to useful knowledge as a key to sustained progress. He called for a 'language of [mechanical] arts' to facilitate communication and to fix the meaning of such vague terms as 'light', 'large' and 'middling' to enhance the accuracy of information in technological descriptions. The *Encyclopédie*, inevitably perhaps, only fulfilled these lofty goals very partially and the articles on technology varied immensely in detail and emphasis. For a recent summary of the work as a set of technological representations, see Pannabecker (1998).

[14] The redoubtable Andrew Ure published his *Dictionary of Arts, Manufactures and Mines* in 1839 (an earlier edition, dedicated mostly to chemistry, had appeared in 1821), a dense book full of technical details of crafts and engineering covering over 1,300 pages of fine prints and illustrations, which by the fourth edition (1853) had expanded to 2,000 pages.

phenomenon: over-the-counter knowledge became available from experts such as civil engineers, coal viewers and other consultants.

Moreover, the ideology and rhetoric of natural philosophy changed. Aristotelian science had set as its main purpose to 'understand' nature. During the scientific revolution and the eighteenth century the idea that the purpose and the justification of the search for natural regularities was to harness and exploit them, as Bacon had argued, kept gaining ground. In the days of Bacon, the notion that useful knowledge was to be exploited for material improvement was more hopeful than realistic, and even for the founders of the Royal Society the idea was in large part a self-serving device for lobbying rather than a sincere objective. Yet, the Industrial Revolution eventually proved them right: after 1800, useful knowledge became the dynamic force that Bacon had hoped for.[15]

The Industrial Enlightenment was characterised by an attempt to expand what was known and therefore what would work. For decades, the role of useful knowledge in the Industrial Revolution has been dominated by long debates about the 'role of science' in which minimalists such as David Landes (1969) and Rupert Hall (1974) debated Musson and Robinson (1969). It is hard to disagree with Shapin (1996: 140–1) that 'it appears unlikely that the "high theory" of the Scientific Revolution had any substantial direct effect on economically useful technology either in the seventeenth century or in the eighteenth . . . historians have had great difficulty in establishing that any of these spheres of technologically or economically inspired science bore substantial fruits'. Yet the methods of scientific endeavour spilled over into the technological sphere: concepts of measurement, quantification and accuracy, which had never been an important part of the study of nature, gradually increased in importance.[16] The precision skills of the clockmaker blended with the scientific and mathematical rigour of the post-Galileo natural philosopher were personified in key figures such as Christiaan Huygens, who perfected the pendulum clock and also sketched the first internal combustion engine. His assistant, Denis Papin, built the first model of an atmospheric engine. The 'ideology of precision' influenced later key figures such as James Watt, John Smeaton and John Harrison, whose contributions to economically significant inventions are not in doubt. Quantification, measurement and a sense for the orderly arrangement of information into what we today would call 'data' constituted one of the most precious gifts that science gave to technology (Heilbron 1990; Headrick 2000).

---

[15] The relation between pre-Lavoisier chemistry and the Industrial Revolution is particularly enlightening, since it was widely believed that 'chemical philosophy' would help to advance agriculture, manufacturing and medicine. Yet in the eighteenth century, this remained, in the words of the leading scholar on the topic, 'more of a promissory note than a cashed-in achievement' (Golinski 1992).

[16] The noted historian of science Alexandre Koyré (1968) argued that the scientific revolution implied a move from a world of 'more or less' to one of measurement and precision.

The intellectual background of the Industrial Revolution is thus more complex than the ability of natural philosophy to provide *direct* insights into the natural regularities and phenomena that could be applied in a straightforward manner. The unintended spillover of the flourishing of natural philosophy in the seventeenth century was the creation of a 'scientific culture', as Margaret Jacob (1997, 1998) has called it. The widespread interest in physics, chemistry, mechanics, botany, geology and so on created a technical literacy she feels was at the root of the innovations that made the Industrial Revolution. The Industrial Enlightenment spawned figures for whom the economic promise of bridging between natural philosophy and the practical and mechanical arts was axiomatic. One thinks of Dr John Roebuck, a physician and iron-monger, early supporter of James Watt's improvements to the steam engine, and inventor of the lead process in the manufacture of sulphuric acid, or of Joseph Black, the Scottish chemist and friend of James Watt. For progressive industrialists such as pottery maker Josiah Wedgwood, reliance on scientists (such as his close friends Erasmus Darwin and Joseph Priestley) was essential (McKendrick 1973). Others, such as Leeds woollen manufacturer Benjamin Gott, read French chemistry books applicable to his dyeing business.

The formal institutional manifestations of this culture are well known. The many scientific and philosophical societies created contact and interaction between the people who knew things and those who were hoping to apply that knowledge. The Society of Arts, a classic example of an access-cost reducing institution, was founded in 1754, 'to embolden enterprise, to enlarge science, to refine art, to improve manufacture and to extend our commerce'. Its activities included an active programme of awards and prizes for successful inventors: over 6,200 prizes were granted between 1754 and 1784. Perhaps the epitome of this culture of access and encouragement was the founding of the Royal Institution in London in 1799, which was meant to disseminate useful knowledge to the public at large. It was associated with three of the greatest names of the period: Count Rumford was one of its founders, and Humphry Davy and Michael Faraday were among its earliest public lecturers. All three shared the ability to look for laws in nature and think of useful technical applications of what they knew. Davy's most famous invention was the 'miner's friend' (a lamp that reduced the danger of fires in coal mines) but he also wrote a textbook on agricultural chemistry and discovered that a tropical plant named *catechu* was a useful additive to tanning. Rumford, besides his famous refutation of heat being a 'substance', invented a better stove, improved the oil lamp, and made the first drip percolator coffee maker.

Scientific (formal, consensual) knowledge was, however, a small part of what counted. Most of the knowledge on which continued technological expansion rested was far more mundane in nature than the body of knowledge which we think of today when we talk of 'science'. The popular distinction between 'science-based' techniques and 'empirical' techniques refers to the degree of formalisation and generality of the knowledge on which they rest, but this dichotomy seems less than helpful for the economic historian examining the early nineteenth century. Natural regularities may be as 'unscientific' as the cataloguing of trade winds and the apprehension of the rhythmic movements of the tides, which were harnessed for the techniques of transportation and shipping, or the relation between crop rotations and agricultural productivity. The line between 'science' and 'informal useful knowledge' is arbitrary. Our modern notions of 'science' may look as primitive to some future person as pre-Copernican astronomy and pre-Lavoisier chemistry do to us. In the eighteenth century the useful knowledge underlying the new techniques consisted in large part of practical and artisanal knowledge, based on experiments and experience, trial and error, the collection and cataloguing of facts and the search for patterns and regularities in them.[17]

The systematisation and perfection of these methods delivered far more to the industrial revolution than formal science. In this respect, the unsung heroes of the period were the engineers such as John Smeaton, John Rennie and Richard Trevithick. Smeaton's approach was pragmatic and empirical, although he was well versed in theoretical work. He limited himself to ask questions about 'how much' and 'under which conditions' without bothering too much about the 'why'. Yet his approach presupposed an orderliness and regularity in nature exemplifying the scientific mentality. Vincenti (1990: 138–40) and Cardwell (1994: 195) attribute to him the development of the method of parameter variation through experimentation, which is a systematic way of cataloguing what works and how well. By establishing regularities in the relationships between relevant variables, even without knowing why these relationships are true, it can extrapolate outside them to establish optimal performance. It may well be, as Cardwell notes, that this type of progress did not lead to new macroinventions, but the essence of progress is the interplay between 'door-opening' and 'gap-filling' inventions. This work, even

---

[17] An example of how such incomplete knowledge could lead to a new technique was the much hailed Cort puddling and rolling technique. The technique depended a great deal on prior knowledge about natural phenomena, even if science properly speaking had very little to do with it. Cort realised full-well the importance of turning pig iron into wrought or bar iron by removing what contemporaries thought of as 'plumbago' (a term taken from phlogiston theory and equivalent to a substance we would today call carbon). The problem was to generate enough heat to keep the molten iron liquid and to prevent it from crystallising before all the carbon had been removed. Cort knew that reverberating furnaces using coke generated higher temperatures. He also realised that by rolling the hot metal between grooved rollers, its composition would become more homogeneous. How and why he mapped this prior knowledge into his famous invention is not exactly known, but the fact that so many other ironmasters were following similar tracks indicates that they were all drawing from a common pool. Cort surely was no scientist: Joseph Black famously referred to him as 'a plain Englishman, without Science'.

more than his inventions, stamps Smeaton without question as one of the 'Vital Few' of the industrial revolution.

Pragmatic and experimental knowledge was at the base of many of the key inventions of the classical Industrial Revolution. The great inventions in cotton spinning in the early years of the Industrial Revolution were significant mechanical advances, but it is hard to argue that they depended on any deep scientific insights or even methodology. If they had been all there was to the Industrial Revolution, the scepticism about the role of intellectual factors in economic growth would be well placed. But what needs to be explained is not so much Arkwright's and Crompton's famous 'gadgets' but their continuous improvement beyond their original breakthrough.

To sum up: accounting for the Industrial Revolution involves an understanding of the changes in the culture and technology of useful knowledge that had been in the making since at least the era of Bacon and Galileo. These changes explain the difference between sustained growth and 'just another' episode that would have tapered off to the stationary state that most political economists of the period still expected.

Two further examples will illustrate this argument. One is the career of the engineer Richard Roberts (Hills 2002). Roberts was far from a scientist and never had a scientific education. His invention of the self-actor in 1825 is a famous episode in the history of technology since it was triggered by a strike of mule-operatives. Roberts, however, was a universal mechanical genius with an uncanny ability to access what knowledge was available and turn it into new techniques that worked. His application of the concept of binary coding of information embodied in the Jacquard loom was more immediately useful than the analytical engine of Charles Babbage (which was based on the same principle): he perfected a multiple spindle machine, which used a Jacquard-type control mechanism for the drilling of rivet holes in the wrought iron plates used in the Britannia tubular bridge (Rosenberg and Vincenti 1978). Despite his lack of formal education, he was well networked, elected to the famous Manchester Literary and Philosophical Society in 1823, where he rubbed shoulders with leading natural philosophers such as John Dalton and William Henry. In 1845 he built an electromagnet which won a prize for the most powerful of its kind and was placed in the Peel Park museum in Manchester. When first approached, he responded, characteristically, that he knew nothing of the theory or practice of electromagnetism, but that he would try and find out. By this time, if someone wanted to 'find out' something, one could do so readily by talking to an expert, consulting a host of scientific treatises and periodicals, encyclopaedias and engineering textbooks, as Roberts no doubt did.

The other example is the early applications of chemistry to industry. Most of what chemistry could do for the economy had to await the development of organic chemistry in the 1830s by von Liebig and Wöhler, and the breakthroughs in the fertiliser and dye industries in the second half of the nineteenth century. There were a few famous breakthroughs, of course, such as Leblanc's soda-making process (1787), yet before Lavoisier these all rested on slender or confused chemistry, and without further breakthroughs would have run into diminishing returns.

The insights provided by the new chemistry, coupled to the economic importance of mordants, dyes and soap for the growing textile industry, were such that new work on the topic kept appearing. Among those, the *Art de la teinture* by Claude Berthollet (Lavoisier's most illustrious student) appeared in 1791, not many years after he had shown how chlorine could be turned into an industrial bleaching agent (an idea promptly appropriated by enterprising Britons, among them James Watt, whose father-in-law was a bleacher). Berthollet's book explained dyeing in terms of chemical affinity and summarised the state of the art for a generation. He served as director of dyeing at the *Manufacture des Gobelins*, and his *Statique chimique* (1803) 'was not only the summation of the chemical thought of the entire eighteenth century . . . but also laid out the problems that the nineteenth century was to solve' (Keyser 1990: 237). The knowledge gathered by chemists and manufacturers formed the basis for William Partridge's *A Practical Treatise on the Dyeing of Woollen, Cotton and Silk* that appeared in New York in 1823 and for thirty years remained the standard text 'in which all the most popular dyes were disclosed . . . like cookery recipes' (Garfield 2001: 41). Berthollet's successor at the *Gobelins*, Michel Eugène Chevreul, was interested in lipids, discovered the nature of fatty acids and isolated such substances as cholesterol, glycerol and stearic acid. He discovered that fats are combinations of glycerol and fatty acids, easily separated by saponification (hydrolysis) which immediately improved the manufacture of soap.[18] For some reason, the European continent seemed better at producing advances in chemistry than Britain; this seems to have bothered the British not one iota. They simply sent their chemistry students to study across the channel, or imported the best chemists to teach in Britain. Here as elsewhere during the Industrial Revolution, the advances were pan-European.

In chemicals, much as was the case in mechanical devices, the bulk of the inventions between Berthollet's pathbreaking bleaching process (1785) and the discovery of Aniline Mauve by Perkin in 1856 (which set into motion the synthetic dye industry based on organic chemistry) were relatively small microinventions. However, they rested on ever more chemical knowledge and thus continued to pour forth, instead of slowly petering out. Much of this knowledge was gathered by empirical experimentation

---

[18] Clow and Clow in their classic account (1952: 126) assess that his work 'placed soap-making on a sure quantitative basis and technics was placed under one of its greatest debts to chemistry'. His better understanding of fatty substances led to the development of stearic candles, which he patented in 1825 together with another French chemist, Gay-Lussac. His work on dyes and the optical nature of colours was also of substantial importance.

rather than based on coherent theory, and thus to some extent a matter of good luck, but clearly the growth of chemical knowledge prepared the fortunate minds of the chemical revolution and thus streamlined the pragmatic and somewhat randomised 'search'.

Thus, for instance, the adoption of early gas lighting was hampered by the ghastly smell caused by sulphur compounds. The pioneers of gas lighting, William Murdoch and Samuel Clegg discovered that the introduction of lime in industrial gas removes the sources of bad odour. Access to the requisite chemical knowledge proved easier than before: Antoine Fourcroy's magisterial *Système des connaissances chimiques* (1800) which codified the new Lavoisier chemistry around the concepts of elements, bases, acids and salts was widely available in Britain. Similarly, the early post-Lavoisier chemistry of Gay-Lussac informed the Scottish ironmaster James Neilson in his invention of the famous hot blast technology which is one of the most pronounced productivity-enhancing invention of the post 1815 era, reducing fuel requirements in blast furnaces by a factor of three. It is hard to see those advances happening in a world without accurate measurement and systematic and informed experimentation. It is perhaps too strong to argue with Clow and Clow (1952: 355) that 'Neilson the scientist succeeded where the practical ironmasters failed' – Neilson had taken some courses in applied chemistry in his twenties, and was a member of the Glasgow Philosophical Society, but he was hardly a 'trained scientist'.

The knowledge revolution meant not only that technological progress could proceed without hitting a conceptual ceiling. The interaction between the two was bi-directional, creating positive feedback. Indeed, some scholars, most notably Derek Price (1984), have argued that the 'loop' going from technology to science was possibly more important than the traditional mechanism in which science informs technology. New instruments and laboratory techniques undoubtedly helped science immensely. Moreover, new techniques whose mode of operation was poorly understood created a 'focusing device' for scientific work by raising the curiosity and possibly financial hopes of scientifically trained people. The most celebrated example of such a loop is the connection between steam power and thermodynamics, exemplified in the well-known tale of Sadi Carnot's early formulation, in 1824, of the Second Law of Thermodynamics by watching the difference in fuel economy between a high pressure (Woolf) steam engine and a low pressure one of the Watt type.[19] Power technology and classical energy physics developed hand-in-hand, culminating in the career of the Scottish physicist and engineer William

---

[19] It is interesting to note that Carnot's now famous *Reflexions sur la puissance motrice du feu* (1824) was initially ignored in France and eventually found its way second hand and through translation into Britain, where there was considerably more interest in his work because of the growing demand by builders of gigantic steam engines such as William Fairbairn in Manchester and Robert Napier in Glasgow for theoretical insights that would help in making better engines.

Rankine, whose *Manual of the Steam Engine* (1859) made thermodynamics accessible to engineers and led to a host of improvements. In steam power, then, the positive feedback can be clearly traced: the first engines had emerged in the practical world of skilled blacksmiths, mechanics and instrument makers with only a minimum of theoretical understanding. These machines then inspired theorists to come to grips with the natural regularities at work. These insights were in turn fed back to engineers to construct more efficient engines. This kind of mutually reinforcing process can be identified, in a growing number of activities, throughout the nineteenth century.

CONCLUSIONS

Drawing attention to the intellectual sources of the Industrial Revolution does not invalidate any of the traditional economic arguments about the causes of the Industrial Revolution. Relative factor prices and demand played an important role in directing technological progress in particular directions. Incentives to inventors such as the hope of securing a pension or patent royalties motivated ingenious and creative individuals. Secure property rights were essential for continuing investment in the capital goods that embodied the new technology. British institutions did what institutions are supposed to do: they reduced uncertainty. Britain's markets were well developed; its infrastructure was rapidly improving. It provided a healthy environment for would-be entrepreneurs who were willing to take risks and work hard. By 1688 it was already a wealthy and sophisticated country by many standards. Yet in 1700 there still was no way to tell that its wealth and sophistication had the capacity to unleash a force that would change human life on this planet more than anything since the emergence of Christianity. The Industrial Enlightenment increased useful knowledge not only at a rate that was faster than ever before, but at a rate that has been accelerating since.

Britain played a crucial role as spearhead in this movement, and the effects of Britain's leadership on its economy and polity dominated the country until at least 1914. But the *global* significance of the Industrial Revolution is much deeper, since it had the capacity to raise living standards in a wide range of societies. This process had barely taken off by the time the Industrial Revolution was over, but by 1914 it was unmistakable. The full implications of this event are still as mind-boggling today as they were in 1776.

2

Industrial organisation and structure

PAT HUDSON

Contents

Introduction   28
Proto-industrialisation   29
  The environment of proto-industry   30
  Households, families, demographic change and
    occupational cultures   34
The rise of the factory   36
  Why the large integrated factory did not triumph   37
  The factory debate   40
  The variety of factory forms of enterprise   42
  Labour, skills and collective innovation   45
Evolution, adaptation, risk and trust   47
  The business environment and family firms   48
  Business networks and industrial agglomeration   49
  Capital and credit   53
Conclusion   55

INTRODUCTION

Most accounts of industrialisation stress the rapid rise of the factory, of powered technologies, and of large-scale plants and firms.[1] Indeed the factory more than anything else has come to symbolise the industrial revolution and dominates popular imagery of the period. However, factories were slow to spread and uneven in their hold over sectors of manufacturing. Their development was a notable feature of the industrialising economy, and requires explanation, but their rise was limited and accompanied by a proliferation of small-scale enterprises, workshops, and domestic and dispersed forms of manufacturing employing a handful of workers and using hand tools as much as advanced machinery. Most

---

[1] I am grateful to Joel Mokyr and Maxine Berg for detailed comments on an earlier draft and to the other contributors to the volume for their help and advice.

concerns remained small and family firms predominated. These were not just lingering pre-industrial forms but an integral part of the modern industrial economy.

This chapter analyses the causes and consequences of variation in business organisation and structure. Consideration is given to the nature of products, markets and factor supplies and the interplay between technological change and organisational adaptation. Particular emphasis is placed upon the economic, social and cultural contexts in which enterprises operated, and which shaped their form and success. Communities, institutions and business networks, embodying knowledge, skills, experience and reciprocities, were crucially important in the high-risk, information-poor environment of the later eighteenth and early nineteenth centuries. These social and organisational structures did much to support varied rather than monolithic forms of enterprise.

The chapter is divided into three main sections. The first covers the spread of household production for distant markets, paying particular attention to regional and local contexts. The second addresses the development of the factory. Both of these sections demonstrate that overarching theories cannot accommodate the great diversity of forms of manufacturing: there was certainly no single or linear path of development in the emergence of modern industry. The third section provides an explanation of diversity in organisation and structure by emphasising the way in which adaptation to local circumstances produced different outcomes whilst imperfect competition and various reactions to high transaction costs prevented a competitive drift towards a unique industrial form. Late eighteenth- and early nineteenth-century conditions encouraged different, often very localised and sector-specific development pathways based upon various mechanisms for minimising risk.

PROTO-INDUSTRIALISATION

Industrialisation in Europe was preceded by a century or more of marked expansion of regionally concentrated rural domestic industries, serving distant markets: cotton, woollen and linen textiles, hosiery, lace, a range of metalwares and many other goods came to be mass-produced in this way. Frequently artisans ran small businesses, alongside agriculture, using family labour, buying their own raw materials and completing a finished or semi-finished product for sale. More commonly, merchants distributed raw materials to domestic workers who often worked on just one process such as spinning or weaving. In this, the putting-out system, the merchant controlled access to raw materials and to markets and benefited from low overhead costs.

Since the 1970s the growth of household industries in this period has come under considerable scrutiny: it has been argued that this process

of 'proto-industrialisation' was sufficiently pervasive and dynamic, economically, socially and culturally, to have impelled regions, if not whole
economies, forward into the urban machine age (Mendels 1972, 1975,
1980; Kriedte, Medick and Schlumbohm 1981; Cerman and Ogilvie 1996;
for notable earlier work on rural industries in England see Heaton
1920; Wadsworth and Mann 1931; Thirsk 1961; Jones 1968; Mann 1971;
Chambers 1972). The build up of capital and manufacturing skills, labour
supply, marketing knowledge and local infrastructures and institutions
during proto-industrialisation is argued to have paved the way for the
specialised manufacturing regions of the later industrialised economy.

The environment of proto-industry

Early studies stressed the association between rural industries and pastoral farming. In the Midlands a major shift from arable to grass occurred
in the eighteenth century, accompanied by enclosure. This generated high
levels of unemployment which were partly soaked up by rural industries
including lace making, hosiery and metalwares (Jones 1968; Rowlands
1989; Carpenter 1994). The Pennine upland areas of both Lancashire and
Yorkshire became the home of linen/cotton and wool cloth making respectively in the seventeenth and eighteenth centuries (Heaton 1920;
Wadsworth and Mann 1931; Sigsworth 1959; Hudson 1986; Walton 1989;
Timmins 1993). But proto-industries were also found in areas which were
not primarily pastoral or upland: woollen manufacture in East Anglia;
linen on the Norfolk/Suffolk border; the silk industry of Essex; knitting
in arable parts of Leicestershire; pillow lace and straw plait industries
of Buckinghamshire, Bedfordshire, Hertfordshire and Huntingdonshire;
cloth making in lowland Lancashire and Yorkshire. The importance of
particular rural settings has been attributed to seasonal complementarity in labour demands between agriculture and industry, particularly in
arable contexts (Mendels 1975). But the seasonality of farming often coincided with the seasonality of manufacture and the division of labour between agriculture and industry was as likely to be determined by gender-
specific demands for labour as by seasonal factors (Snell 1985; Marshall
1989; Whyte 1989; Sharpe 1994). Much domestic manufacture of consumer goods utilised the underemployed labour and indigenous skills of
females and juveniles (Berg 1987, 1994; Hudson 1995)

Cheap labour was not the only determinant of the location of dispersed forms of mass manufacture. Institutional factors were also important. Rural industries often flourished where there was little co-operative
agriculture, where freeholders and customary tenants had firm property rights, and where partible inheritance (division of land between
surviving male children) led to the fragmentation of holdings (Thirsk
1961: 70–2, 86–8; Zell 1994). Unigeniture (inheritance by one child only)
could also support rural industry by encouraging proletarianisation as

in north-east Lancashire (Swain 1986). Areas of weak manorialism which allowed in-migration and the division of land among small cultivators were favoured sites for putting-out industries as in the Vale of Trent (Chambers 1963: 428–9) whilst access to common rights, which enabled squatters to settle, was important in attracting rural metal working to the north-west Midlands (Hey 1972). Similarly in Derbyshire, lead mining by small independent producers (free miners) continued only on those manors where they were able to preserve their common law rights (Wood 1999). In west Yorkshire the putting-out system of worsted manufacture expanded in the eighteenth century where the ownership of land was dispersed, where freehold predominated over copyhold land and where the process of proletarianisation was advanced. The rural artisan structure of woollen manufacture, by contrast, endured in more fertile areas where manorialism had been more entrenched, where there was more control over landholding and where the predominantly copyhold land was rented out in plots suitable for the dual occupation of clothier/farmer (Hudson 1986: 57–96; 1991). Framework knitting was earliest developed by independent yeomen farmers in Midland villages of middling wealth and relatively egalitarian social structures but the breakdown of landholding patterns in Nottinghamshire during the eighteenth century resulted in the rise of larger landholders and growing numbers of landless squatters. This, coupled with changes in the market for stockings and the introduction of silk and cotton mixes, led to the growth of large putting-out concerns and impoverished outworkers. Thus prior histories and established institutions could influence not only the presence of proto-industry but also its organisational form and, with this, its potential for growth and change.

As important as the agrarian and institutional context in determining the location, form and success of manufacturing was the sort of communities they supported and which enabled them to respond to new developments whether as a reaction to unemployment or to additional opportunities for profit. In Staffordshire and parts of south and west Yorkshire the agrarian environment supported smallholders with some capital who became rural artisans and whose activities created an atmosphere of common purpose and (to an important degree) mutual support (Hey 1969, 1972; Frost 1981; Hudson 1983). Elsewhere the context favoured putting-out systems as in the worsted region of west Yorkshire but here again the success of merchants depended in large part upon their integration into local middle-class society and its networks of power, wealth and influence. It was upon this that they relied for trade contacts, information flow and credit and capital supply (Hudson 1986; Smail 1994).

Different trades adapted to, or were encouraged by, a variety of types of agricultural context, institutional history and cultural milieu. Thus specialisation of production was often highly localised. In the West Midlands many of the varied products and processes of the metalwares trades were in concentrated enclaves in both towns and the countryside (Rowlands 1975, 1989; Berg 1990). In south Yorkshire, cutlery, saw, scythe and nail making clustered in very different contexts (Hey 1972). In Lancashire the cotton, woollen, linen and silk industries were all important in different parts of the county, each having a different set of relationships with agriculture and landholding and each spawning a distinctive set of networks, relationships, cultures and practices which contributed to their viability and growth (Wadsworth and Mann 1931; Walton 1989; Timmins 1993; Rose 2000). The success of proto-industries in the Birmingham area has been related to lack of institutional regulation, religious toleration, skill traditions, artisan mutuality and the socio-economic advantages of agglomeration (Sabel and Zeitlin 1985; Rowlands 1989; Berg 1990, 1994). By contrast, the relative inflexibility and decline of much of the West Country woollen industry from the later eighteenth century arose from the staid culture of large putting-out employers, aggravated by craft-conscious communities of workers who resisted the introduction of new techniques and machinery (Wilson 1973; Randall 1989).

Local adaptation to national taxation and welfare policies, in line with the distinctive social structures and patterns of culture and influence in different regions, may also have had a significant impact upon early industrialisation. The harsher nature of poor relief in some of the heartlands of industrial expansion by the later eighteenth century may indicate that there were strong cultures of self-reliance and family support networks in many manufacturing parishes (as well as more work available) (Smith 1998; King 2000; compare Solar 1995). Light local taxation was in the interests of the rate-paying manufacturing classes and parsimonious relief payments would tend to keep the cost of labour low. The relatively light burden of land tax in the north of England and systems of excise collection which encouraged the short-term local investment of such funds in areas of capital shortage may also have had a significant effect in promoting economic growth by creating further differentials in factor endowments and costs (Pressnell 1956; Pollard 1981; Turner and Mills 1986). Central and local government policies regarding industry and trade directly influenced the location of manufacturing and even the markets served. Local magistrates in Nottingham were able to prevent the London Company of Framework Knitters from limiting entry to the trade in 1728 and this encouraged the migration of the craft from London to the East Midlands (Daniels 1920: xxviii–xxix, 3–6; Chapman 1967: 18). A decisive factor in the growth of fustian manufacture in Lancashire in the sixteenth and seventeenth centuries was that local employers were able to take advantage of exemption from the Weavers' Acts of the 1550s which restricted the number of apprentices to be employed by master weavers. The county's later exemption from the Calico Acts, as applied to fustians, and the stimulus which these same Acts gave to the export of printed cotton cloths from Lancashire are further examples of the regionally differentiated incidence of national policies.

The sorts of products made and the markets served also affected the organisation of production and its growth. When worsted manufacture expanded in Yorkshire it had to compete with established manufacturing in East Anglia and to find its way in difficult, predominantly export, markets. The long turnover time of capital was a further factor necessitating the presence of substantial putting-out merchants as catalysts of the trade. The same was the case in the Lancashire cotton industry (Farnie 1979; Hudson 1986; Rose 2000). In the West Country woollen industry the mass production of high-quality woollen cloths necessitated a putting-out system there in contrast to the artisan structure in Yorkshire which mainly produced lower-grade products (Mann 1971; Wilson 1973). Elsewhere small masters flourished where products included a high degree of batch or individual variation and served niche markets, both domestic and foreign. Their success was often aided by the development of co-operative forms of production for certain processes best done in bulk such as in the scribbling, carding and fulling mills of West Yorkshire, the public grinding wheels of Sheffield and the co-operative ventures in centralised processing in the Birmingham hardware trades which supplied brass and copper inputs (Pollard 1959: 54–7; Sabel and Zeitlin 1985; Hudson 1986: 76–81; Berg 1994: 128).

Rural manufacturing took a great variety of forms which adapted themselves to local cultures and circumstances. It is impossible to match these to a crude proto-industrialisation model of linear progression from artisans to putting-out systems to the factory. Different agrarian histories and institutional legacies within regions and localities were important in creating the setting for expanding industrial enterprise. They conditioned the availability of capital and labour, receptiveness or resistance to change, the nature of individualism or co-operation, bonds of family, kinship and neighbourhood and the impact of central and local government. All of these influenced the form and the success of manufacturing: history mattered.

Only four out of the ten most prominent proto-industrial areas thrived in the long term to become the foundations of success in the coal-based, more mechanised and urbanised economy of nineteenth-century England: west Yorkshire, south Lancashire, south Yorkshire and the West Midlands (Coleman 1983). The fate of many former proto-industrial regions such as East Anglia and the Weald of Kent was deindustrialisation (Coleman 1983; Houston and Snell 1984; Short 1989; Zell 1994; Sharpe 1994; Hudson 1996). Coalfield locations clearly became more vital in the new age of steam power and mass-production technologies but other factors were involved to do with the varied potential for growth and adaptation of different forms of proto-industrial organisation, with path dependency and with the broader cultural and institutional infrastructure of regions which could either promote or retard development beyond proto-industry (Ogilvie 1993; Cerman and Ogilvie 1996; Leboutte 1996; Hudson 1999). Some proto-industrial areas disappeared but some whole regions and many pockets of dispersed manufacturing survived and flourished whilst small-scale units arose in new areas, proving themselves to be viable, successful and necessary, alongside factories, throughout and beyond the nineteenth century (Samuel 1977; Sabel and Zeitlin 1986; Rowlands 1989; Berg 1991a, 1993a; Behagg 1998).

The industrial revolution did not displace proto-industry but rather 'encompassed, integrated and further developed it' (Deyon 1996). The institutional environment of proto-industries not only underpinned the fortunes of proto-industrial areas in the eighteenth century but also conditioned the nature and extent of factory and mixed forms in the nineteenth. Although it has not stood up to empirical testing the proto-industrialisation thesis has stimulated research which highlights organisational variety and the roots of this in different institutional, social and cultural as well as economic contexts (Eley 1984; Cerman and Ogilvie 1996). This has had the effect of making historians acutely aware of the difficulty of separating industrial history from the social and cultural circumstances in which it is embedded. It has encouraged integrated studies of manufacturing, agriculture, the socio-cultural and institutional environment, demography and family life. (This literature is much more developed on the continent but for English examples see Wrightson and Levine 1979; Rollison 1992; Hudson 1986; King 1993; Zell 1994; Sharpe 2002).

Households, families, demographic change and occupational cultures

The proto-industrial literature has highlighted not only the influence of culture and institutions upon industrial forms but also the impact of different occupational cultures upon many aspects of personal and social life. Heaton argued that as it took six people to make a piece of broadcloth in the eighteenth century, many west Yorkshire households were of this size, additional adults being taken on as journeymen or apprentices within a household where men, women and children worked together as a production unit, buying raw wool from staplers and selling unfinished cloths at weekly cloth markets in Leeds and elsewhere (Heaton 1920). In the Yorkshire worsted sector whole families were sometimes involved in textile manufacture but individuals were often employed for separate processes (females mainly on spinning and men, predominantly, on weaving or combing) by different employers. It was also very common for proto-industrial workers in Yorkshire, especially women, to live in households in which other individuals were engaged in entirely different sectors such as agriculture or mining. Similarly in the lace making areas of the Midlands and south-west and in areas which became centres of straw plaiting in the late eighteenth and early nineteenth centuries, women were engaged in low-wage, labour-intensive domestic industries in households in which men were often underemployed or seasonally employed in agriculture (Sharpe 1994). In the making of nails, chains, nuts, bolts, files and stirrups in the Black Country, expansion depended upon the use of female workers and children from the age of 5 or 6 upwards (Berg 1987). Sometimes, here as in other parts of the country, female and child workers were subcontracted via the male head of household and were paid only through him. In other cases women received their wages independently. These very different structures of household employment have important implications when one comes to consider the impact of commercial manufacturing upon such crucial social and demographic variables as the age of leaving home, the ability to set up new households, family and household size, living standards, and the status and independence of women and children.

Analysis of the marked acceleration of population growth in the eighteenth century has recently focused upon regional and local variations in demographic experience, and their relationship to dominant occupational cultures. Family reconstitution results broadly confirm the expectation that marriage ages fell, and marriage rates and illegitimacy rose most noticeably in manufacturing areas (Wrigley *et al.* 1997, and chapter 3 below). Proto-industrialisation theory emphasises that areas of rural industry were likely to become the fastest growing in terms of population because earnings of young people allowed them to leave home and marry earlier and thus to have larger families (Mendels 1972; Levine 1977). It is argued that industrial earnings gave young people more social and sexual freedom which may be one cause of the notable rise in illegitimacy and prenuptial pregnancy in the eighteenth century (Levine 1977, 1987; Seccombe 1992). The existence of expanding rural industry in a region might also encourage in-migration which would further boost population increase, whilst institutional obstacles to early marriage such as formal apprenticeships and live-in farm service were not characteristic of proto-industrial regions. Not all studies have found an association between proto-industry and high rates of demographic growth, not least because the earnings of young women could delay marriage by keeping them in the parental home and by taking away the economic necessity of marriage. Shifts in nuptiality may also have been less characteristic of artisan than putting-out communities (Hudson and King 2000).

Research on the demographic transition from the later nineteenth century (the shift to slower rates of population growth, largely through family limitation) has done even more to underpin our understanding of distinctive and localised occupational cultures, and their socio-demographic implications. Szreter has shown that the general trend towards smaller families was very varied in both timing and speed from one locality to another and that these variations bore a strong relationship to economic specialisation and to the family life and customary behaviour associated with distinctive occupations and with their gender- and age-specific labour demands (Szreter 1996; Garrett *et al.* 2001). Death rates also varied markedly in relation to regional and local industrial concentrations, further adding to distinctive industrial/demographic patterns (Woods 2000: 203–381).

The social and agrarian character of regions where commercial industry grew shaped the structure and nature of emergent manufacturing, as we have seen. But industrial intensification, and the development of factories and coalfield sites, related urbanisation and migration flows, and the great geographical concentrations of shipbuilding and iron and steel, made industrial localities even more distinctive as the nineteenth century progressed (Pollard 1981; Langton 1984; Langton and Morris 1986; Hudson 1989). The regional and local concentration of particular sectors of industry was accompanied by distinctive patterns of gender- and age-specific employment, of work culture, and of home and family life which influenced household structure, demographic experience, living standards and a host of other social, cultural and political networks and institutions. Such regional differences, which extended from skill transmission to social and political identity, voting behaviour and trade union membership, were important in influencing regional industry and commerce, and they lasted long after the material foundations of such regional patterns began to disappear in the twentieth century (Savage 1987; Southall 1988; Hudson 1989; Massey 1995).

THE RISE OF THE FACTORY

If we define a factory as a place where workers and equipment are concentrated, where work is supervised and monitored and where there is usually some application of powered machinery, we can agree that a growing proportion of output in many sectors, and especially in textiles, came to be factory-produced in Britain during the nineteenth century. In addition, the numbers of workers employed in shipbuilding, blast furnaces and major building works, none of which was suited to small-scale or domestic operations, multiplied. Thus a growing proportion of industrial workers (approaching the majority by the second half of the nineteenth century) worked alongside masses of their fellows in a hierarchically organised, closely supervised environment.

By 1835 there were 1,330 woollen mills, 1,245 cotton factories, 345 flax mills and 238 silk mills at work in the UK (Jenkins 1973: 26–46). Some of the major textile establishments employed several hundred workers in the 1840s and 1850s but these were exceptions. In 1851 the average number of workers in woollen mills was fifty-nine, in worsted mills 170 and in cotton mills 167 (Clapham 1926: 196; Fong 1930; Gattrell 1977; Rose 2000). But in each case the median firm was much smaller – nearer to half these numbers of employees – suggesting that the majority of firms were small and that a large range of firm sizes co-existed. Only a tenth of cotton firms employed more than 100 workers in 1841 and very few employed more than 150. Many used second-hand plant, shared power and premises and relied on water rather than steam power (Gattrell 1977: 97; Lloyd Jones and Le Roux 1980: 75) A similar variety of sizes characterised iron working. The Scottish Carron works employed 200 as early as 1814 but at this time the average Scottish foundry had twenty workers and the average English foundry few more. Overcapacity following the Napoleonic Wars led to major restructuring and the concentration of almost half of the national output in South Wales. Here the giant Cyfarthfa and Dowlais ironworks both employed around 5,000 men by 1830 (John 1950) but there were also many firms with under fifty workers. In 1851 there were 677 engineering firms but two thirds had under ten employees and only fourteen had more than 350. However the largest textile engineering firm, Platts of Oldham, employed 7,000 by 1875, again indicating the coexistence of a huge range of very different concerns (Crouzet 1985: 35, 249–50). As late as 1871 the average manufacturing establishment had fewer than twenty employees and many industrial workers remained self-employed, working in twos and threes (Mokyr 2002).

Why the large integrated factory did not triumph

The growth of factories in all industrialising countries was accompanied by an upsurge in the number and variety of smaller-scale units, and a notable continuation of self-employment. Home working and putting out (predominantly employing women and juveniles) remained prominent in manufacturing in the second half of the nineteenth century and beyond, especially in the urban sweated trades of tailoring, stationery and small (particularly seasonal) fancy goods manufacture (Samuel 1977; Schmiechen 1984; Schwarz 1992; August 1994). There was certainly a drift towards placing production under one roof, promoted in many industries by the adoption of water and steam powered technologies which sometimes required a minimum size of building and/or a particular location. But the shift to factory production was slow and uneven, and remained partial. The inexorable benefits of scale and scope, identified by Chandler as the key to explaining the development of large business plant and firm size in industrialised economies, were only a small part of the story, more applicable to the American than to European economies (Chandler 1990; Casson and Rose 1997: 1). In many contexts there were in fact few advantages of scale and scope, and most sectors, as we have seen, had a vast range of firm and plant sizes, the majority very small. Factory labour was often more expensive and more difficult to recruit than underemployed outworkers. Thus many manufacturers continued to engage in domestic alongside factory production: labour and overhead costs were cheaper and domestic workers could easily be laid off in depressions or multiplied quickly if conditions improved. In an era of market volatility and uncertainty the benefits of scale were not always present and the dangers of size were great. Circumstances were ever changing and a balance of investment between different technologies, equipment and labour supply was often the wisest policy (Gattrell 1977: 107–8; Hudson 1986). Gattrell has shown that there was no optimal factor composition (labour to capital ratio) even in the cotton industry (in 1841), a fact which was probably true of many other sectors (Gattrell 1977: 107). Size-related labour-saving opportunities in cotton were probably negligible before the innovation of Roberts's self-acting mule in the 1830s, whilst in the 1840s and 1850s weaving technologies improved and many small separate powered weaving factories were established. This kept the average size of plant low in cotton in the period and the first generations of factory owners continued to be of very modest means (Gattrell 1977; Honeyman 1982; Crouzet 1985; Rose 2000: 65). The steep rise in yarn exports in the 1830s and 1840s in both cotton and worsteds also served to check further vertical integration between spinning and weaving establishments and the growing average size of plant which might have resulted.

Early factory entrepreneurs faced the relatively new challenge of sinking large amounts of capital, including fixed capital, into business and of making effective accounting calculations about costs and prices which would allow for depreciation and the phasing of investments. Entrepreneurs lacked the computational skills and accountancy tools needed to measure such variables with accuracy and it is therefore unlikely that large firms took best advantage of scale economies even where they could be found (Gattrell 1977; Hudson 1986). The challenge proved too much for many and often ended in bankruptcy. The threat of bankruptcy was magnified by the large amount of circulating capital required by bigger concerns, especially if they were involved in vertical integration which involved marketing or controlling raw material supplies (Sigsworth 1959; Hoppit 1986; Hudson 1986; Chapman 1979a). For these reasons most sectors and businesses comprised mixes of large and smaller concerns, factories and various forms of outwork. This spread risks for entrepreneurs and also made them less vulnerable to threats from organised labour.

Small-scale workshop forms also proliferated because of the widespread practice of external subcontracting, frequently associated with factories. In west Yorkshire labour-intensive cloth mending was almost always subcontracted in the nineteenth century, as were many sorts of specialised finishing, whilst gun manufacture in the Birmingham area remained the province of small masters who relied extensively upon outwork (Timmins 1967: 387–93; Behagg 1998). The subcontracting of work to smaller firms also characterised much of the brass, copper and iron trades (Hamilton 1926: chs. 3, 10, 12; Allen 1929: ch. 5). Subcontracting lowered the fixed capital requirements and the risks for entrepreneurs. A further factor encouraging small-scale units was technology. Early steam engines were expensive and unreliable whilst domestic and workshop industries often proved remarkably receptive to small but productive technological innovations and adaptations. The spinning jenny was first introduced in the 1760s as a hand powered machine that fitted into workers' homes and remained in use there for decades. Many forms of intermediate technology, such as the stamp and press, used in the Birmingham button and pin industries, were equally at home in domestic and workshop premises as in factory environments. Silk weavers worked at home in the 1840s and 1850s with a steam engine at the end of the street (Jones 1987: 77). Furthermore, organised labour sometimes blocked or delayed those forms of technical change which threatened older ways of working and living associated with smaller-scale concerns. In the late 1770s, riots in Lancashire slowed the adoption of jennies of more than twenty-four spindles (which could be accommodated in the home) and machine wrecking in Yorkshire significantly slowed innovation of the gig mill and shear frame in cloth finishing which was feared to signal the death knell of the skilled workshop trade. The threat to established, more flexible and more independent working, and the association of factories with the workhouse, were major reasons why factory employers often found it difficult to recruit workers (Wadsworth and Mann 1931: 496–502; Thompson 1963; Pollard 1965).

Finally, the factory did not replace other forms of production either rapidly or completely because factory production just did not suit many trades, particularly those dependent upon short-batch production, volatility in fashion, and/or requiring a great deal of specialist workmanship, individual tailoring or ornamentation (Allen 1929; Sabel and Zeitlin 1985). This was also true in certain coarse trades where the products were of low quality and required little supervision. And where there was no obvious technological or organisational advantage of factories over workshops, large numbers of small producers could tip the balance in their own favour by co-operating to create an innovative and dynamic environment. The small masters of the Sheffield and Birmingham metal trades, for example, flourished because they were flexible in the face of market changes and because collectively they encouraged new work methods and new designs. Regionally based institutions encouraged firms to compete through product and process innovation rather than through price and wage cuts (Sabel and Zeitlin 1985; Berg 1991a).

The existence of specialist traders and intermediaries is also important in understanding variation in industrial structure, particularly over time. The industrial revolution was marked by the emergence of significant numbers of merchant-manufacturers in the industrial regions. Manufacturers extended into merchanting and merchants extended their finance and entrepreneurial involvement backwards into manufacturing (Chapman 1979b; Price 1980; Hudson 1986; Rose 2000). Some of the biggest concerns, like the Drinkwaters, Dales, Gregs, Fosters, Salts and Gotts in textiles, for example, established integrated concerns with capital in a combination of factories, transport, banking, mining and estate development as well as directly importing raw materials and exporting cloth. But after the commercial crisis of 1826 this began to change as specialist firms came to control trade and the manufacturers themselves withdrew. The big acceptance houses of London and Liverpool dominated overseas trade by the 1830s and 1840s and most of the manufacturers and merchants of the major industrial centres, Manchester, Birmingham, Sheffield and west Yorkshire, came to depend upon them and upon the credit which they advanced (see chapter 6 below). This left most industrialists free to concentrate on production and militated against the growth of giant vertically integrated firms.

The factory debate

There has been much debate about the rise of the factory (well summarised in Jones (1994) and developed much further by Geraghty (2002)). Traditionally, historians stressed that the ability to employ powered machinery gave factories superiority over dispersed manufacture and accounted for their proliferation (Ashton 1996; Mantoux 1961; Heaton 1965; Mathias 1983; Landes 1986; Clark 1994; Langlois 1999). New machine technologies are argued to have placed a minimum on the efficient scale of plant, and adoption of the factory became essential in order to benefit from economies of scale and from indivisible new technologies such as the steam engine (Landes 1986: 615; von Tunzelmann 1995). Others (especially Marglin 1974) have argued that factories were introduced primarily to ensure control over the labour process and thus to secure greater output and profit for capitalists from their workers. In this view the existence of factories stimulated the adoption of powered machinery not the other way round.

As dispersed industries spread over wider geographical areas and as competition intensified in many trades, the costs and penalties of trying to supervise domestic workers rose. It was difficult for entrepreneurs to ensure uniform quality of output and hard to work to deadlines without controlling workers' time. Embezzlement of raw materials also became a more important problem in putting-out systems as competition intensified and profit margins were squeezed. Many establishments of the late eighteenth century did not employ technologies vastly superior to domestic industry but simply gathered workers under one roof in order to operate more efficiently. Often this appears to have been associated with control over the time input and the quality of labour. For example, following a strike by Macclesfield silk workers in 1815 over a reduction in piece rates, manufacturers established hand factories and paid significantly lower rates of pay (Jones 1987: 78–80). Benjamin Gott's factory in Leeds housed only handworkers for twenty-five years in order to bring the labour under stricter control and Peter Stubs of Warrington gathered file makers under one roof initially with no change in technology (Crump 1931: 24–5, 31; Ashton 1939). Hand factories had a long history before as well as during the industrial revolution. Jenny factories and large handloom shops were as common in the late eighteenth century as powered premises (Crouzet 1985: 32; Clapham 1926: 53–5, 59; Jones 1994: 43). The large cotton mills of the Peels, the Oldknows and the Gregs all started out as hand factories. Such establishments have parallels in the information age. An apocryphal example is the call centre, which has no technological justification but which enables employers to enforce a highly disciplined labour regime (Westall 1997).

Recently the idea that factories multiplied because they were organisationally superior has been examined with greater analytical rigour. Incorporating different processes and smooth product flow in a hierarchically organised plant lowered the transaction costs associated with dispersal and allowed manufacturers to respond more effectively to changes in demand (O. Williamson 1980, 1985, 1989, following Coase 1937). In a variant of this, Szostak argued that increases in the efficiency of transport and reductions in transport costs in the late eighteenth century favoured factories. Transport improvements stimulated shifts in consumer demand and marketing policies which made quality and output control in the workplace more vital (Szostak 1989). But if the costs of transport had unequivocally favoured factories by the late eighteenth century, it becomes difficult to explain why so much scattered workshop and domestic production expanded alongside the factory long after that date, proving flexible and receptive to shifts in consumer demand (Jones 1994: 55–6). This was particularly so with the production of goods with a low value to weight ratio as these were much less affected by transport costs, for example ribbons, lace, hosiery, hats and gloves. Williamson's broader argument can also be criticised for exaggerating the transaction cost and efficiency gains of factory organisation over putting-out systems. The eleven efficiency criteria which he explores concerning product flow, incentive structures, the better use of skills, co-ordination and leadership are very difficult to quantify (Jones 1994), and such efficiencies were also possible in linked but dispersed forms of enterprise. Furthermore, embezzlement and shirking continued to be a problem in factories, and capital tied up in stock was often high because factory owners had to produce whatever the state of the market or see their capital lying idle.

Mokyr has argued that what determines the optimal scale and location of production units is the relative costs of moving people, goods and information (Mokyr 2002). These are in turn influenced by technological change, product mix and the sort of knowledge needed for production to take place most efficiently. During the century or so after the industrial revolution it became much cheaper and easier to move people and goods, whilst many production technologies favoured large units of production. Where raw materials or equipment were expensive or complex, factory discipline and continuous adaptation of knowledge and skills became more important to ensure consistent effort and quality of output, to minimise pilfering and to ensure that workers took good care of the equipment (Lazear 1986; Mokyr 2002). Only close supervision and time rates rather than piece rates provided an appropriate incentive structure for labour in these circumstances, particularly where it was difficult to disentangle individual contributions to output because workers were part of a team. In many nineteenth-century factories such as the large cotton spinning mills (especially those using water frames), and in some flax spinning, iron manufacturing and glass making establishments, close supervision was essential because production could be slowed by any individual worker who was not pulling her weight (Alchian and Demsetz 1972; North 1981). Thus in Mokyr's view the rise of the factory was linked to changing technology, but only indirectly: 'organisational and technological forces created interaction effects that increased the total advantage of the factory by more than just the sum of the individual components' (Mokyr 2002: 134). This may explain why the early centralisation of hand weaving by the Gregs of Styal in 1784 was phased out after a short time, not to be reintroduced until mechanisation in the 1830s which probably raised the gains to supervision. Geraghty has further developed this 'complementarity thesis' by stressing that the introduction of machinery typically increased transaction costs and agency problems associated with ensuring output quality and volume as well as good asset maintenance. This increased the need for more intensive supervision and new incentive structures based largely upon the time rates, fines and bonuses which we associate with factory regimes (Geraghty 2002).

The variety of factory forms of enterprise

Deterministic accounts of the way in which the transition to time rates and close supervision within factories was associated with the introduction of new technologies during the industrial revolution can be overplayed. In practice many variations occurred in hiring arrangements, payment systems, supervision in the workplace and incentive structures within and between factories, and these make general arguments difficult to sustain. One important variant in the transition to factories, which highlights the weakness of relying solely upon transaction costs reasoning, was the provision of shelter, space, light and power to small concerns in return for a rental income. In these environments, common in wool textile weaving, machinery was leased to artisans who worked on their own account (on just one process) and at hours chosen by them. In west

Yorkshire it remained common for individual weavers and small weaving concerns to rent room and power in a mill until well into the nineteenth century whilst Kidderminster carpet weavers worked in this way, on hand-looms, as late as the 1860s. Similar arrangements often occurred with internal subcontracting whereby different divisions within a factory were worked by independent agents who employed and disciplined their own labour. In the giant Winlaton works of Abraham Crowley, for example, there was a complex of forges, mills, furnaces, workshops and warehouses each of which operated as a separate business. The engineering works of Boulton and Watt in the 1770s was organised in a series of shops each carrying out one process and separately employing workers on piece rates. Teams of steam engine fitters were later contracted internally in a similar way (Roll 1930; Tann 1977). The idiosyncratic power of cotton mule spinners in England has also been viewed as resulting from internal subcontracting: a head spinner, on piece rates, in turn employed and supervised his own assistants, paying time rates. The strength of organised labour in mule spinning exacted this arrangement (Lazonick 1991: 77–100, 124–8; Huberman 1996: 53–6). Thus, whilst internal subcontracting was rife and the integrated benefits of scale were equivocal, Marshall's view that 'a large factory is only several smaller factories under one roof' (Marshall 1921: 281) rings substantially true. Such could be argued for many branches of the textile industry, including cotton, at least before the 1870s (Gattrell 1977: 108).

Biernacki has recently emphasised that the nature of factory regimes varied considerably between countries. Woollen weavers in Germany were paid time rates in a classical way, but in many British textile areas weavers continued to be paid by the piece on a sliding scale to take account of the quality and density of the cloth. Workers arriving late were simply locked out and denied access to 'their' looms. German owners and workers had long viewed employment as involving close command over the person and capacities of the labourer. British owners and workers in the textile sector, on the other hand, saw employment rather as the appropriation of the products of labour: the buying and selling of labour embodied in commodities. These divergent definitions were reflected in language (the German *Arbeitskrafte* compared with English labour) and led to differences in the definition of wages, the rights of employment, factory discipline and even the design of factory buildings. Such international contrasts arose from deep-rooted differences in cultural understandings of labour (Biernacki 1995). There were also significant differences in conceptions of work, payment structures, factory discipline and factory architecture from one industrial sector and region to another within each national context. The architecture of spinning factories for example, which operated time rates almost exclusively, involved serried rows of machinery with observational platforms for overlookers, whilst weaving establishments generally did not. Pottery and glass making factories are easily distinguished architecturally from textile plant, not just as a result of technological determinants but because of the nature of factory labour, payment systems and product flow. It thus seems wise to incorporate vernacular understandings of labour and labour discipline in analysing the transition to a variety of factory regimes.

Contemporaries appear to have distinguished between manufactories which merely brought labour under one roof and mills which contained power driven machinery (Berg 1994: 144). But in practice hand working in factories could be accompanied by little supervision or by much hierarchical ordering, time and work discipline and division of labour. Likewise powered plants were not always dominated by standard hierarchical or sophisticated systems of labour discipline. They often included internal subcontracting to independent groups or might contain a multitude of independent small concerns or artisans renting room, power and/or machinery whilst retaining a large degree of work autonomy. It is also the case that size could involve managerial diseconomies: a fact which concerned contemporaries. Marshall stressed the importance of small proprietorships with little bureaucracy: 'The master's eye is everywhere; there is no shirking by his foremen or workmen, no divided responsibility, no sending half understood messages backwards and forwards from one department to another' (Marshall 1890: 237). Furthermore, the master and servant legislation could effectively be used by small employers and putting-out merchants to bolster long contracts and bonds of service. It was possible to manipulate credit and wage payments to secure subordination and hard work without bringing labour into a factory (Berg 1985: 280–2; 1994: 147).

These facts caution against a monocausal explanation for the rise of the factory. The lure of increasing returns to scale, the solution to asymmetric information difficulties, agency problems and high transaction costs and, finally, the benefit of the division of knowledge and labour all probably played a significant part, their relative weights differing between sectors and over time. Technological imperatives were clearly important but they were not the sole cause. Once technology is regarded as only a partial determinant of plant or firm size it becomes easier to explain the coexistence of a variety of manufacturing structures in terms of relative organisational demands and efficiencies and of different economic, social and cultural contexts and legacies. That the latter were important is illustrated by differences in the character of firms and plant in the Lancashire cotton industry. Small masters using water frames and later throstles predominated in Rochdale, a result of the earlier tradition of woollen manufacture in the town, whilst the persistence of handloom weaving in north-east Lancashire has been associated with the long tradition of craft-organised handwork in the area (Swain 1986; Timmins 1993). The concentrated persistence of small-scale jenny workshops in Wigan arose partly because there were better opportunities for men in mining but there was also a machine making tradition focused on the jenny and local demand for sail cloths and sacking for which jenny-spun yarns were suitable (Rose 2000: 36–7). Oldham and Bolton both concentrated upon spinning in 1811, using the mule, but their products and firm sizes varied. Oldham had generally small firms set up by men who had previously been involved in hatting or fustian weaving, and produced coarse yarns. Bolton produced finer yarns in much larger establishments financed by men who had made some wealth in the town's pre-factory concentration on muslin manufacture (Honeyman 1982: 87–114). Similar variations occurred between towns in most industrial regions even though they were only a few miles apart.

Labour, skills and collective innovation

The factory debate has been accompanied by discussion of the conditions which favour the most efficient utilisation of skills and knowledge, as well as labour power, and which support the most innovation in products and processes. Developing arguments first emphasised by Adam Smith (1776) and, later, by Charles Babbage (1835), Mokyr has stressed the greater specialisation and division of labour which the factory allowed compared with smaller units of production, particularly the household. In a period of substantial technological change, more and more knowledge was necessary to operate best-practice techniques and state of the art technologies: efficient production came to require more experience than a single household could possess. The knowledge transmitted from parent to child and from master to apprentice worked efficiently when technologies were relatively straightforward and where they did not alter much between the generations. In the later eighteenth century this changed so that large firms and factories became the primary locus of such skill transmission: factories were thus a substitute for incomplete markets in technical knowledge (Becker and Murphy 1992; Saviotti 1996; Nooteboom 2000; Mokyr 2002). But this argument ignores the complementary role of occupational cultures and industrial communities in sustaining and transmitting knowledge between as well as within manufacturing units of various sizes. Reciprocities and networks based on artisan communities could provide a similar function to the factory in terms of knowledge, innovation and the transmission of skills. There are many examples of artisans and small firms working in close collaboration, exchanging knowledge through informal co-operation and collectively forming institutions for mutual aid and technical education. Such communities often had the edge over larger firms and/or factories, particularly where flexible specialisation was required (Piore and Sabel 1984; Sabel and Zeitlin 1985). It may have been the case that free riders and defectors were more prevalent in such communities of small firms than with factory organisation. It was virtually impossible to keep technological secrets in an artisan or putting-out context. But this could be a strength as much as a weakness. Rapid innovation often occurred through collective and co-operative forms of invention in environments where knowledge was freely available.

Innovations were vital, from the introduction of new production technologies and ways of organising, employing and paying labour to innovations in design, products, salesmanship and marketing. Continuous adaptation was very important in both technological and organisation innovation and this was stimulated by on-the-job responses to problems and opportunities rather than by managerial training, formal science, patents or secrecy. Large firms and plants had no necessary advantage in this process. Such incremental innovations were usually not novel in the legal sense and therefore not patentable: they were a by-product of day-to-day operations where the processes of invention and innovation were fused (see chapter 5 below). Even in sectors like textiles, steam turbines and civil engineering, characterised by significant and patented macro-inventions, smaller innovations which turned the major inventions into workable and efficient machines for use in a variety of regional and local contexts played a key role. These were often promoted by collective effort and a culture of sharing between communities of entrepreneurs or artisans, rather than by secrecy. Technical experts in many fields often released data to consolidate their reputations and this frequently developed into a professional ethos of disclosure and the sharing of experiences (MacLeod 1988).

It would have been costly to keep incremental technical changes secret, and in fact there was often a relatively free exchange of information between firms during the industrial revolution about everything from markets and fashion to new techniques and plant design. The frequently close geographical proximity of firms and of specialised suppliers of tools, machinery and equipment was conducive to the transfer of knowledge about mechanical improvements. In west Yorkshire, for example, there was a continuous circulation of textile manufacturers and engineering workers: in each others' premises, at markets, trading, chasing debts, socialising, all of which provided opportunities to learn and to borrow ideas (Cookson 1997). Firms could often gain from releasing information because they would share in the success of the entire sector, community or region. Larger blast furnaces in Cleveland in the 1870s, for example, increased the value of local ore deposits, which were owned by the manufacturers, as well as giving considerable advantage to iron firms located in the region. The increasing height of blast furnaces in the mid-nineteenth century was a response to freely available technical information about the fuel consumption and performance of different sizes of furnace and with different sorts of ores. The technology of capping the blast furnace so that waste gases could be used for fuel was also collectively invented (Allen 1983). Spreading the costs and risks amongst firms yielded high rates of incremental improvements in many industries. The thermodynamic efficiency of the Cornish pumping engine, for example, occurred after the expiry of Watt's patent in 1800 because an environment of competitive firms favoured publication of detailed information of all new installations suited to local needs. The 'cost book system' whereby mining rights were leased to overlapping groups of shareholders meant that the mine adventurers had most interest in the aggregate profitability of the district rather than of individual firms. By pooling accumulated experience and experimenting with a variety of different approaches, technical change proceeded apace, doubling the efficiency of pumping engines between 1821 and 1844, without being trapped in just one optimum configuration (Nuvolari 2001). Collective inventions and innovations tended to be biased in responding to factor prices in the region or locality over which the collective information and effort was spread. Indeed interregional competitiveness between firms in the same industry was one of the sparks to collective invention. Significant rates of technological advance occurred in this way particularly where there was a multitude of small firms involved (who could not afford independent research and development facilities) and as long as there was a high rate of capital formation (which reduced the costs of experimenting) (Allen 1983).

Alfred Marshall emphasised the importance to innovation of such environments and industrial clustering in the later nineteenth century:

> so great are the advantages which people following the same skilled trade get from near neighbourhood to one another. The mysteries of the trade become no mysteries; but are as it were in the air, and children learn many of them unconsciously. Good work is rightly appreciated, inventions and improvements in machinery, in processes and the general organisation of the business have their merits promptly discussed: if one man starts a new idea, it is taken up by others and combined with suggestions of their own; and thus it becomes a source of further new ideas.   (Marshall 1890: 225)

EVOLUTION, ADAPTATION, RISK AND TRUST

It is a truism that firms and businesses which are most suited to their environment generally proliferate compared with those that lack certain elements, but there is nothing deterministic about the process and no unique solution emerges. This is partly because there are localised social and cultural elements in the environment which complicate and vary the responses to market conditions. But pluralism also exists because of poor market information and undeveloped skills of management and accounting, and also because of lock-in (path dependency) and conservatism in the face of environmental change. Furthermore, in an environment which is constantly changing, there are no unique criteria for success: survival and success do not depend upon optimal design or optimal management because the goal posts are constantly moving. This was particularly the case in our period; thus the optimising characteristics of particular structures were almost always local and myopic (Penrose 1959; Hodgson 1993; Nelson 1995).

The rival strengths of small firms and plants *vis-à-vis* large are also determined by the life-cycles of firms and products and by the nature of innovation. Product innovation and process innovation were both a marked feature of the eighteenth and nineteenth centuries (Berg 2002). Process innovation is closely related to firm size; product innovation is not. The presence of many firms can result in rapid product innovation, but as profitable firms grow and invest more in process innovation, entry barriers rise. Shake-out arises from bankruptcies which occur because of rivalry between firms who increasingly compete on the basis of cost. At this point, new smaller firms enter to extend and to sophisticate the product range, keeping the business structure varied. Evolutionary theory, with its stress upon adaptation to varied and changing environments, helps to explain the creation and maintenance of plurality in business organisation, especially in a highly volatile business climate. It suggests that a plural rather than a monolithic structure is one best placed to accommodate growth and change (Penrose 1959; Hodgson 1993).

The business environment and family firms

To explore the varied paths and patterns of industrial development it is necessary to consider further the character of the business environment of the time: it was rapidly changing, unstable, high risk and information poor. Trust was at a premium and institutions as well as social and cultural relationships and practices which promoted trust, reliability and predictability were vital. This often gave a premium to evolutionary and incremental rather than revolutionary and radical changes in technologies and business forms.

The nature and efficiency of information flows and transport meant that markets were highly imperfect, especially at interregional and international levels. In an age which was only starting to appreciate the information revolution of print culture, an expanding national and provincial press and improved transport and postal services, tapping into the sorts of networks and contacts through which reliable business knowledge was acquired, filtered and processed was of vital importance. Business operators were always dependent upon their networks and contacts in order to use as well as to acquire commercially important knowledge. The boundaries of the firm were necessarily fluid, and transaction costs and informational asymmetries could be reduced by activity as much outside the firm as within it (Casson 1991: 169–70; 1993: 30–54).

Given the problems of information flow, delays caused by transport difficulties, bankruptcies of trading partners and the constant threat of uninsurable losses, almost all business activity was uncertain and few risks were measurable. Uncertainty abounded in business dealings between investors and industrialists, between trading partners, and between principals and agents in various management and subcontracting arrangements. Public controls against fraud were weak and it was difficult to use the law to enforce accountability in business dealings. In a climate of unlimited liability and ubiquitous credit, confidence and trust were pivotal: the vital ingredients in business success. In large measure these were secured by a predominance of face-to-face and personalised transactions through networks of families and friends, and by trade and information centred upon clearly defined, often localised, and self-conscious business communities. Such networks were also important in long-distance trade. Use of a trusted partner or family connection in the metropolis or in an overseas port was frequently vital in securing commercial intelligence and in reducing risks and costs (Heaton 1920; Hudson 1986; Chapman 1992; Farnie 1997; Smail 1999; Rose 2000).

In the eighteenth century, with some notable exceptions in foreign trade, mining and ship owning (all of which needed large investments), the typical concern was small and individual entrepreneurs or small common law partnerships predominated. Family firms proliferated because manufacturers and traders preferred the lower risks of family, kinship and community connections to those with outsiders. Amongst other things, this allowed a great deal of scope for female entrepreneurship. After several decades in which historians have assumed that business women generally withdrew to the household and domesticity in the Victorian age (if not earlier) the key role of women in a large number of capacities and trades and in the networks which surrounded them is starting to be recognised (Berg 1993c; Barker 1997; compare Pinchbeck 1969 [1930]; Davidoff and Hall 1987). Family networks reduced the costs of commercial transactions, helped to minimise the risk of free riding and cheating and provided access to finance, and commercial and technological knowledge (Casson 1997). Thus family firms, once argued to have been symptomatic of Britain's incomplete industrialisation and relative failure in the later nineteenth century, can be seen to have been a dynamic, flexible and rational response to the needs of Britain, the pioneer industrialiser, in the economic circumstances of the time (compare Chandler 1990; Lazonick 1991 with Jones and Rose 1993: 1–16; Church 1993: 17–43).

Business networks and industrial agglomeration

The family was a major foundation of business networks during the industrial revolution and beyond, but other networks operated alongside the family to cement the trust and personal loyalty essential to commercial success. Religion was often very important, and is one reason why nonconformists, Quakers in particular, were very prominent amongst successful business families. They had a common moral outlook and set of beliefs, cemented by friendships and intermarriage, centred around the social life of the chapel or meeting house (Briggs 1963: 204; Seed 1982, 1986; Prior and Kirby 1993; Ashton 1996: 14–15). This provided the foundation for business dealings and the extension of credit and loans within the group. Such networks made it easier to raise capital and to reduce internal borrowing costs. Commercial news and technological information were, in the same way, often shared across a web of friends and acquaintances. Other networks which transcended religion and family can be seen operating in the growing industrial towns of the period. From the 1830s and 1840s the new entrepreneurial classes came to dominate the municipal administrations, charities, and social and cultural lives of most industrial cities (Briggs 1963; Hennock 1973; Morris 1990). Participation in local government or charities and civic duties raised the profile and respectability of businessmen whilst creating opportunities for regular meetings and ceremonies which enhanced the integration and legitimacy of local commercial elites (Trainor 1993: 246–7). Good character, reliability and personal integrity were demonstrated through cultural patronage and membership of clubs and societies. These eroded internal differences and created a radius of trust cemented by appropriate displays of hospitality, sober personal behaviour, dress sense, self-presentation and language, and by fitting combinations of restraint and innovation in domestic consumption (Hudson 1986; Seed 1986; Morris 1993; Trainor 1993; Fukuyama 1995: 154).

Shared values and attitudes, and shared knowledge as well as skills, were reinforced by an array of institutions and informal arrangements. Churches and chapels were joined by literary and philosophical societies, chambers of commerce, employers' associations, friendly societies, charities, the governing bodies of schools and hospitals. Whether the main function of an institution was religious, economic or social, it fulfilled similar functions in relation to business networks and information flows amongst established business families. The Lunar Society in Birmingham provided a vital meeting point for men of business and science (Uglow 2002a), whilst the Manchester Royal Exchange acted as 'a coffee house, a news room and a trading floor' (Seed 1982: 4, 85–6) centralising the supply of information both private and public and providing a congenial place for the conduct of business (Farnie 1979: 97–8). Here, and in the Manchester Literary and Philosophical Society, the dominant circle of Unitarian businessmen, the Phillipses, Potters and Gregs, conducted their social and commercial lives as one (Gattrell 1982: 25; Seed 1986: 25–46). The leading business families throughout the Lancashire cotton area came primarily from nonconformist groups, their families bonded through intermarriage. The regular social interaction which family relationships and a common religion spawned increased the levels of trust in business dealings and formed the basis for an array of interlocking family partnerships, reduced transaction costs and improved information flows without the need for formal integration. The Lees and the Armitages of Salford and the Boltons and Kershaws of Stockport and Manchester were linked by marriage in the second half of the nineteenth century. Similar family ties can be traced in Bolton and in Blackburn and Darwen, where family networks spread across cotton, engineering and iron-making over several generations (Joyce 1980: 12–19; Howe 1984: 6–15, 77; Rose 2000: 74–5). In west Yorkshire, family connections in the textile manufacturing districts were similarly active and underpinned the personal knowledge of creditworthiness, respectability and reputation which were the key to acceptability and to gaining the most from the local business environment (Hudson 1986; Morris 1990; Caunce 1997a). The Birmingham business elites also operated in cliques in which religious affiliation, intermarriage and involvement in municipal enterprise were key elements (Briggs 1963) endorsed by rivalries with their counterparts in family networks of the nearby Black Country (Trainor 1993).

The role of such networks in stimulating collective diversification and hence local and regional economic development across a broad front was also important. Close links between businessmen across a range of interlocking partnerships have been identified in Leeds, Liverpool, Manchester and the West of England between 1776 and 1824 (Pearson and Richardson 2001). These relationships bridged political and religious divisions, being cemented by residential stability over generations, and by intermarriage. On the basis of relationships initiated in the fire insurance sector, businessmen collectively shifted into joint-stock canal investment and banks, dock, water, gas, retail and property companies. They created institutions and conventions to increase mutual trust and co-operation. These were embodied in deeds of partnership and in the constitutions of joint-stock companies, which received no formal recognition at law and needed such conventions and mutual trust to operate. In Liverpool groups of businessmen drew bills on each other, sold shares in ships, bought each others' property and invested together in cloth mills, sugar refineries, theatres and turnpikes. They invested money in ventures only where fellow investors were known personally, where they were deemed respectable and reliable and where there was additional security provided by the formal and informal codes of their associations (Pearson 1991: 413; 1993; Pearson and Richardson 2001: 669). The source of such knowledge, institutions and mutual trust lay in the clearly defined regional business community.

Industrialisation was accompanied by increasing regional specialisation and the concentration of whole sectors of manufacturing into one or a small number of key locations (Langton 1984; Hudson 1989). In considering the variety of forms of business enterprise, technological change and the role of business networks in the eighteenth and early nineteenth centuries, recognition of the regional context is vital. Industrialisation endorsed existing spatial differences in economy and society by making regions more functionally distinct. Dominant specialised sectors spawned regional transport, finance and service infrastructures, concentrations of specialist suppliers, traders, bankers, insurers and other services as well as institutional forms and overlapping familial, social, religious political and economic networks which did much to create the character and energy of the industrialisation process. The critical mass of interacting families and firms created significant external economies, and local reserves of knowledge, skills and commercial intelligence from which individual entrepreneurs could benefit (Pollard 1981; Hudson 1986, 1989; Rose 2000: 58–98). Specialised, regionally concentrated mercantile institutions could significantly reduce transaction costs in the purchase of raw materials and the sale of finished or semi-finished goods, facilitating the finance and operation of a range of types and sizes of business (Hudson 1986).

The advantage of geographical concentration of industry has traditionally been associated with the way in which certain locations generated physical and economic benefits via product specialisation, and vertical or horizontal integration, but the processes of institution building amongst employers, workers and families are now seen as the key element in understanding the vitality of industrial agglomerations. Employers, for example, depended upon regional co-operation to control such matters as unreasonable credit practices and embezzlement by workers and to curtail the role of labour activists. Collective activities and collusive arrangements of all kinds were widespread. There were regional and trans-regional trade associations and pricing agreements in a broad range of industries including tobacco, insurance, brewing, pins and paper. Interfirm co-operation and collective action aimed at reducing risks and cutting information and labour costs made industry more workable and more profitable without the need for formal business integration. Meanwhile, workers developed strong occupational cultures from regional organisations, trade unions, friendly societies and social networks, whilst family links at all levels could generate the reciprocities and mutual aid vital to stability in an uncertain and volatile business climate. One must not exaggerate the degree of harmony in industrial districts. Co-operation often existed alongside cut-throat competition, industrial espionage and bitter law suits. There was friction, jealousy and secrecy. Wedgwood, for example, did not co-operate with the community of Staffordshire potters and jealously guarded his designs against ubiquitous copiers (McKendrick 1961). However, industrial regions in the eighteenth and early nineteenth centuries, as today, did provide extensive institutional support which could encourage innovation and risk taking, stability and efficient management; social consensus, common purpose and high levels of interfirm collaboration; local skill transmission, the circulation of ideas, trust, reciprocities and the presence of a common discourse (Grabher 1993; Granovetter 1985; Hirst and Zeitlin 1991; Storper 1993).

Capital and credit

The 'market' for capital and credit in the period illustrates the practical operation and importance of institutions and networks, particularly in regional settings. This was a social market based largely upon face-to-face relationships, personal knowledge, reputation, esteem and trust, all of which were aided by conventions and common understandings and by accepted, often ritualised, modes of self-presentation, hospitality and communication. Manufacturing and commerce were expanding amongst individuals who were often distanced (geographically and socially) from the old concentrations of landed, rentier and mercantile wealth. Firms thus had to rely upon the formal and informal networks which arose in the expanding industrial regions. Attorneys were key figures in the eighteenth century, able to put borrowers in touch with lenders through the personal contacts and information that they acquired in their regional legal work (Anderson 1969a). Private banks in industrial areas in the later eighteenth century were developed as an adjunct to manufacturing or commerce, and their activities in bill discounting and lending were underpinned by the social and business networks from which they had grown. The levels of trust which these networks encouraged significantly reduced the transaction costs of bill discounting but the close ties between local industry, commerce and banking also increased financial interdependency and the danger of local collapse (Hudson 1986; Hoppit 1987).

Joint stock banks which developed in the industrial regions after 1826 similarly reflected and served the business groups from which they arose. There was some 'blind' investment, but more typically access to both attorneys and bankers throughout the period depended upon being known and respected in the social and business circles in which industrialists moved. The formal and informal elements of the capital market overlapped. The lending activity of both private and early joint-stock banks was highly dependent upon personal recommendation. Indeed, the partners and shareholders themselves, their families and their immediate business clients were frequently the most favoured borrowers (Collins and Hudson 1979; Hudson 1986; Collins 1991; Newton 1996). Banks in principle avoided long-term commitments to industrialists but many short-term loans became longer term by default and banks often held title deeds to industrial premises as collateral for such investments (Hudson 1986). Start-up and longer-term investment funds generally came from taking on extra partners in family firms, from loans from close friends or kin and from the mortgage of land. In west Yorkshire dense, often reciprocal, patterns of land mortgage were common, suggesting that these were determined by social as well as by economic considerations (Hudson 1986: 96–104).

Credit was vital and ubiquitous. Manufacturers were caught in a web of credit in which their personal contacts and reputation played a key role. They could fall victim to its pressures or they could manipulate it to their advantage. Sometimes they were able to buy raw materials, and pay labour, on long credits whilst selling final products for immediate returns. This could mean that much of the turnover time of the production process was effectively financed by merchants, banks and discount houses. West Yorkshire clothiers bought wool on long credits and sold for cash or short bills in the cloth halls. This made it easier for small firms to operate alongside the giants who were involved with direct trade. There was always a trade-off between credit and costs or prices, so a juggling act was necessary, but in general the long open credits which characterised the period to the 1830s and 1840s worked to keep entry thresholds for manufacturers low and created a credit matrix generally favourable to small concerns who were well integrated in the local business community (Hudson 1986; Rose 2000).

Most buying and selling was done on trust involving credit, without legally binding instruments or money changing hands. Debts arising from commerce were handled as book debts and were unsecured either by mortgage or by a bond with a third party. If debts were bad enough, suing for bankruptcy was possible, but it was difficult, expensive and rarely yielded enough to justify the risks (Hoppit 1986; Marriner 1986). Similarly the system of credit using bills of exchange (in which several parties endorsed a paper instrument) depended upon regional and national networks of trust and commercial knowledge because there was no legally enforceable way of guaranteeing payment. In eighteenth-century Lancashire this network underpinned the growth of the fustian and cotton trades (Ashton 1954; Hoppit 1986: 91–2) and it was just as vital in west Yorkshire. Such structures could not have worked without widespread recognition that the firms and institutions of the regional financial and business community were highly interdependent. A chain of bankruptcies could occur from just one weak link, and banks and businesses often bailed each other out in the short term to avoid greater region-wide calamities (Hudson 1986; Hunt 1996). Credit systems were volatile and it only took a few to be demanding repayment or drawing in their credit for the whole structure to come under immense strain (Hoppit 1986b; Johnson 1993; Muldrew 1998).

There long remained a tension between economic rationality in credit dealings and the use of credit as an instrument of friendship or mutual support within communities (Fontaine 2001). Credit created bonds of mutual dependence vertically and horizontally and acted as a force binding localities and regions together (Hudson and King 1996; Muldrew 1998). People were involved in tangled webs of economic dependency based only on each other's word, or the word of third parties. The high degree of trust required by such a system was both acquired and maintained through neighbourly relations. These took many forms, including participation in church or chapel, and being active within local government, charities and civic good works. It also meant observing certain habits and rituals of manner and conversation, keeping a well-ordered domestic environment, being able to entertain clients in appropriate ways (Hudson 1986; Hunt 1996). The first to be hit in a crisis were often those latest established in the business community, even though they were not in deepest debt. Being able to tap into the bonds of credit and mutuality involved not just familial and social contacts but also local knowledge of how things were done in business and in social life. This came from familiarity, habit and routine, and assimilation for new entrants could be slow and difficult. Old hands were protected by their creditors because they were more deeply embedded in the mutuality of their business environment (Hudson 1986; Muldrew 1998). Merchants often waited a year or more for payment for goods and services. This was the price of retaining the goodwill of clients and maintaining good working relationships with other local traders (Mackelworth 1999).

The growing anonymity of longer-distance trade created institutional responses to the additional uncertainties generated where face-to-face trading was impracticable and where principal agent problems could be costly. Trust between anonymous trading partners was aided by symbolic and ritualistic forms of communication. The phraseology and polite conventions of commercial correspondence and the increasing use of the ideal of honour and personal reputation in business correspondence illustrate the importance of a common language of reputation and morality in bolstering trading confidence (Smail 2001). Creditworthiness gradually came to depend more upon formal commercial intelligence, estimates of future profitability, the capital of an enterprise or the collateral involved. But such a shift did not occur overnight, and personal contacts, habit, trust, reputation and reciprocity remained the keys to success in the later nineteenth century and beyond.

CONCLUSION

Social and familial networks were engaged to underpin economic exchange in the uncertain, high-risk, information-poor business environment of the industrial revolution. Institutions evolved to promote trust, to reduce risks and to minimise transactions costs and agency problems. The rise of larger centralised concerns had technological and organisational imperatives but these were varied and seldom overriding. Factories were only one way of reducing transaction costs and agency problems and of ensuring the efficient production of goods for a variety of market needs. Technologies and institutions encouraging small-scale undertakings also proliferated. A pluralistic business structure, the prevalence of private family firms of generally very modest size and a complex variety of plant size, created considerable flexibility and adaptiveness in the face of changes in the market and business climate. It was the workshop as much as the factory, and families and communities as much as heroic entrepreneurs and inventors, that created the dynamism of industrialisation in Britain.

3

British population during the 'long' eighteenth century, 1680–1840

E. A. WRIGLEY

Contents

The setting	57
The components of population growth	60
Fertility and nuptiality	69
Mortality	79
Lopsided growth	87
Conclusion	93

THE SETTING

Although large for an island, Britain does not rank among the bigger countries of western Europe. The land surface of the island is 230,000 square kilometres: that of France, the largest west European country, is 552,000 square kilometres; Spain is almost as large as France (505,000 square kilometres), while Germany (357,000 square kilometres) and Italy (301,000 square kilometres) are also substantially larger than Britain. If, for purposes of comparison, western Europe is taken to consist of the area now comprising the Scandinavian countries, Poland, Slovakia, Hungary, the Czech Republic, Austria, Switzerland, Italy, Germany, the Netherlands, Belgium, France, Britain, Ireland and the Iberian peninsula, then Britain occupies only 5.7 per cent of the land surface of western Europe. In the early modern period the British population did not greatly exceed the total to be expected from its proportionate share of the land surface of western Europe. For example, in 1680 the population of Britain was about 6.5 million, or 7.6 per cent of the west European total of about 86 million.[1]

[1] There are comparatively good data on the size of the English population from 1541 onwards. In 1681 the total was 5.1 million (Wrigley *et al.* 1997: tab. A9.1, 614–15). The Welsh population, was assumed to bear the same relationship to that of England as was the case when the 1801 census was taken: Wales, including Monmouth, was then 6.6 per cent of

Yet in 1840 the British share had risen to 10.5 per cent (18.5 million out of a total of 177 million). By 1860 the comparable totals were 23.1 and 197 million and the British percentage had reached 11.7, an increase of almost 60 per cent compared with the situation 180 years earlier. Since 1860 there has been a further rise in the British share of the west European total, but it has been much slower and more modest. In 1990 the population of Britain was 56 million, 13.1 per cent of the west European total of 429 million.[2] The 'long' eighteenth century, therefore, was a period of striking change in the relative demographic size of Britain within Europe.

In the later seventeenth century the population of Britain was static in number; fertility and mortality were in balance. In the early decades of the nineteenth century the population was increasing more rapidly than at any earlier or later period. Before considering the changes which brought about this dramatic acceleration in the growth rate, however, it is of interest to take note of a possibility which would place the long eighteenth century in a different perspective.

Although the impact of the Black Death was both massive and widespread, it appears to have been universally the case that by the later sixteenth century populations had more than recovered their medieval peaks to judge from the estimates presented by McEvedy and Jones (1978). This remained true a century later, even in countries, like Germany, which suffered huge losses in the middle decades of the seventeenth century. According to McEvedy and Jones, Britain conformed to the same pattern: they suggest a pre-Black Death maximum of between 3.75 and 4.00 million for England and Wales and 0.5 million for Scotland, totals which in both cases were matched by 1550 and exceeded by 1600 (McEvedy and Jones 1978: 43, 47). But more recent work suggests a different picture, at least as far as England is concerned. After a critical survey both of the available empirical data and of the views of leading scholars, Smith concluded 'that the English population total prior to 1310 is very unlikely to have been less than 5.0 million and most probably exceeded 6.0 million' (R. M. Smith 1991: 49; but see also Campbell 2000: 399–410 for the view that 4.25 million was the probable maximum).

the total for England and Wales. The Scottish population total was taken as 1.1 million (Flinn 1977: 241–2). Houston suggests a figure of 1.23 million in 1691 (Houston 1996: 119). The west European total was arrived at by combining the estimates for each of the constituent countries given by McEvedy and Jones (1978: 53, 57, 63, 65, 69, 75, 85, 87, 89, 93, 101, 103, 107).

[2] For the data relating to 1840 and 1860 see Mitchell 1981: tab. B1, 29–37. In order to estimate totals for Hungary, Austria and Czechoslovakia (i.e. the Czech Republic and Slovakia combined) in 1840 and 1860, it was assumed that the rate of growth in each of these countries was the same as the overall rate of growth in Cisleithenia and Transleithenia. The totals for each of the three countries in 1910 were reduced in the ratio of the 1840 and 1860 combined totals for Cis- and Transleithenia to their combined total in 1910. For Poland it was assumed that the country as a whole grew at the same rate as Russian Poland, for which an estimate can be derived by a similar exercise (Mitchell 1981: 36, nn. 46 and 47). For the 1990 calculation see Maddison 2001: tab. A1a, 183; the population of Northern Ireland was taken as 1.6 m. at that date.

As Smith pointed out, a figure as high as 6 million for England would imply that the medieval peak was not exceeded until the middle of the eighteenth century. It is therefore possible that England was unusual, even unique, in having failed to recover the population level of the early fourteenth century before the long eighteenth century. If this was the case, at least a part of the exceptional spurt which followed might be regarded as the restoring of an earlier position rather than a novel phenomenon, and the key *explicandum* would be the failure of the British population to recover the losses experienced during the Black Death and its aftermath for more than a quarter of a millennium (R. M. Smith 2002). If, for argument's sake, the population of Britain is taken to have been 6 million in the early fourteenth century, and the estimates for other west European countries made by McEvedy and Jones are taken as broadly accurate, then the British share of the west European total in *c.* 1310 was 9.0 per cent, a much higher figure than in 1680 and only modestly smaller than in 1840.[3] Of course, it may be that further reassessment of medieval peak populations in other countries will produce upward revisions elsewhere and so restore the pattern to be found in the estimates of McEvedy and Jones.

Two other preliminary remarks are needed. First, the system of Anglican registration of baptisms, burials and marriages instituted in England in 1538 has made it possible to reconstruct English demographic history from the mid-sixteenth century in fair detail. Neither Wales nor Scotland possesses sources which permit their demographic history to be reconstructed with comparable precision. The discussion which follows, therefore, will be based almost exclusively on English history. It is possible, though not demonstrable, that events in Wales and Scotland followed a broadly similar course to that in England. Scottish population, for example, probably grew at much the same pace as the English in the later eighteenth century, but when good data are first available regional differences were pronounced in Scotland and it may well be true that in earlier periods also regional contrasts were more pronounced north of the border than south of it.[4] Second, a number of topics of much interest and importance will be touched on only briefly or obliquely, notably migration, both internal and external. Such topics are neglected solely because constraints of space impose selection; they are no less worthy of attention than the topics which are treated at length.

During the second half of the seventeenth century the intrinsic growth rate (IGR) in England was very close to zero (−0.023 per cent per annum: Wrigley *et al.* 1997: tab. A9.1, 614–15). It reached a peak of 1.75 per cent per annum in the quinquennium 1821–6, and during the first quarter

---

[3] The west European total in the early fourteenth century calculated in this fashion is 67 million (McEvedy and Jones 1978: 53, 57, 63, 65, 69, 75, 85, 87, 89, 93, 101, 103, 107).

[4] The county data on nuptiality and marital fertility in the nineteenth century illustrate this point (Teitelbaum 1984: tab. 5A.2, 113 and tab. 6.4b, 129); or for regional contrasts in illegitimacy (Leneman and Mitchison 1987).

of the nineteenth century averaged 1.62. The IGR measures the rate at which a population will rise or fall, given the persistence of current fertility and mortality rates long enough to ensure that any transient features related to initial age structure have disappeared. The IGR may therefore be regarded as a truer measure of the rate of increase than a rate expressed, say, as the difference between the crude birth and death rates, or derived from successive census counts. The extent of the contrast between the demography of the English population in the late seventeenth century and in the early nineteenth century is striking. A stable population[5] experiencing the IGR of the period 1651–1700 would fall by about 2 per cent in the course of a century: a stable population experiencing the IGR of the period 1801–25 would grow fivefold in a century. Far higher IGRs became common in Third World countries in the second half of the twentieth century, but the level attained in England towards the end of the long eighteenth century was most exceptional in the pre-industrial world, except in countries of new settlement with abundant supplies of fertile land, such as the settlers in colonial North America enjoyed. Such a rapid rate of growth would normally soon have produced widespread misery, given the constraints upon productive capacity experienced by all organic economies. It is a vivid testimony to the remarkable gains in productive capacity taking place in parallel with the population increase in England that, rather than falling, living standards rose substantially.

THE COMPONENTS OF POPULATION GROWTH

In conducting the 1801 census Rickman made the enterprising decision to require each parish minister to make returns of the totals of baptisms, burials and marriages in his parish for selected years throughout the whole period of Anglican parochial registration. This provided for the first time a basis for estimating population totals over the preceding quarter millennium, though for a long time it proved impossible to avoid circularity of reasoning in attempting to convert these data into authoritative estimates of population size or measures of fertility and mortality. Hence Flinn's dismissal of work based on parish register material (Flinn 1970: 20). Nevertheless, from Rickman's own first estimates until the present day there has been unanimity that there was rapid growth in the eighteenth century. Nor have estimates of the absolute size of the population in this period changed greatly. Rickman himself, Finlaison,

---

[5] A stable population is one which is closed to migration and in which the prevailing levels of fertility and mortality have been maintained sufficiently long for any transient features to have disappeared. As a result, although the population may be increasing or decreasing in size, its age structure will be unchanging and the age patterns of fertility and mortality will be constant (the special case in which fertility and mortality are equal is termed a stationary population). A stable population is never encountered in reality, of course, but is a most helpful analytical concept.

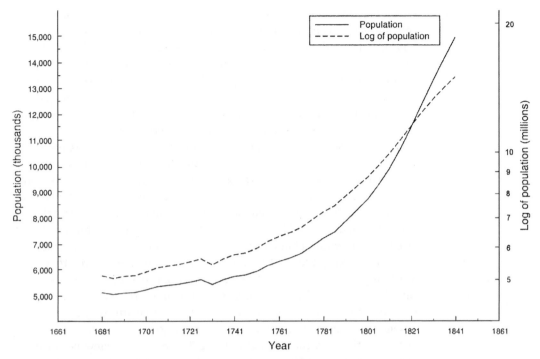

Figure 3.1 English population totals, 1681–1841

Source: Wrigley *et al.* 1997: tab. A9.1, 614–15.

Farr, Brownlee, Griffith and Ohlin, writing at intervals over a period of 150 years from 1801 to 1955, differed only modestly in their estimates (Wrigley and Schofield 1989: app. 5, 563–87).

Recent decades have seen both the development of new techniques of analysis and the construction of new data series. Figure 3.1 shows the estimates of total population for the period 1681to 1841 produced by the application of the technique of generalised inverse projection to national totals of births and deaths derived until 1837 from aggregated baptism and burial totals taken from the registers of 404 Anglican parishes, and thereafter from the Registrar-General's returns of births and deaths. The raw totals drawn from Anglican registers were extensively modified to take account of deficiencies in the original data; of the problems associated with the unrepresentative character of the sample of parishes; and of the presence of rising numbers of nonconformists. Further modifications were made to take advantage of the information contained in the early censuses and of the findings of family reconstitution studies, before the resulting totals were inflated by a multiple intended to produce national estimates from the sample data (Wrigley and Schofield 1989: chs. 3–5).[6] The figure plots the data both naturally and logarithmically: the latter enables changes in the rate of growth to be appreciated more easily.

---

[6] These totals were in turn modified slightly after the analysis of data from a total of twenty-six family reconstitution exercises had suggested that some of the assumptions made earlier could be improved (Wrigley *et al.* 1997: 520–31).

Agreement among those working on English population history in the eighteenth century did not extend beyond population totals and the phasing of population growth. There was no lasting consensus over the related question of the relative importance of changes in mortality and fertility in bringing about the growth which occurred. The dominant view until the later decades of the twentieth century was that falling mortality accounted for the bulk of the change. Griffith, for example, wrote in 1926: 'As the primary cause of the increase in the population in this period, therefore, we are confronted by a remarkable decrease in the death rate, which must be the main cause, backed up by a birth rate at a level distinctly above the death rate and rising steadily, except for 1760, from 1710 to 1790' (Griffith 1926: 42). A belief that mortality change was the key variable was sustained also by the example of Sweden. Sundbärg's work had made available detailed and authoritative information about Swedish population characteristics from the mid-eighteenth century onwards (Sundbärg 1907). The acceleration in the rate of growth of the Swedish population in the nineteenth century was almost exclusively a function of reduced mortality: fertility remained relatively high and invariant for many decades after death rates had begun to decline. In the absence of equally secure data for other countries, it was natural to suppose that this was the normal pattern. The prevailing view began to be questioned in the 1950s, initially by Habakkuk, but then in quick succession also by Ohlin and Krause, but the issue was impossible to resolve with certainty for lack of an appropriate technique for deriving detailed and dependable estimates of fertility and mortality from parish register data (Habakkuk 1953; Ohlin 1955; Krause 1958).

The basic difficulty is easily described but proved hard to overcome. Most standard measures of fertility and mortality require knowledge of the size of the population at risk and of the incidence of a particular type of event. To gain insight into marital fertility by constructing age-specific marital fertility rates, for example, it is necessary to obtain information about, say, the number of married women aged 25–9 and the number of children born to women in this age group in a defined period of time, and to secure similar data for all the other child-bearing age groups. The census normally provides information of the first type, vital registration information of the second. In England parish registers, since they record baptisms, marriages and burials, are capable of providing the close equivalent of vital registration from their inception in 1538, but the first census was not taken until 1801. Although the church, because of its interest in establishing the number of Anglican communicants and the scale of dissent, and the state, in order to raise taxes more efficiently or to assess the number of men capable of bearing arms, sometimes collected information which can be exploited to provide approximate estimates of population totals, there is no data source before the nineteenth-century censuses which routinely yields tolerably accurate estimates of numbers at risk to complement the information which the parish registers can provide about totals of events. This is true of estimates of overall population totals, and true *a fortiori* of subdivisions of the population, such as totals by five-year age groups. This appeared to represent an impasse which was beyond resolution. It seemed impossible to determine such questions as the relative importance of fertility and mortality in causing the surge in population growth in the long eighteenth century, except by making assumptions which, in effect, preordained the answers.

The situation was transformed by two advances in technique, each of which makes it possible to secure detailed demographic measures from vital registration alone. These were family reconstitution and generalised inverse projection (GIP). The first was deployed to great effect by French scholars in the 1950s and 1960s, though it had been foreshadowed earlier in Scandinavia, and has subsequently been widely employed wherever suitable parish registers exist (Edin 1915; Hyrenius 1942; Henry 1956; Gautier and Henry 1958; see also Terrisse 1975). The second stemmed from the pioneering work of Lee in 1974 but was greatly extended, refined and generalised by Oeppen (Lee 1974; Oeppen 1993a, 1993b). Family reconstitution, as the name suggests, is genealogical in nature but focuses on a whole community rather than on a lineage. It produces reliable results only when the nominal record linkage procedures employed are rigorous, and when the periods of time during which a family can be taken to be 'in observation' for a given type of demographic measurement are defined in such a way as to eliminate bias from the result. It was Henry's achievement in providing appropriate rules for defining periods of observation which transformed family reconstitution into a major research tool (Fleury and Henry 1956).

Whereas family reconstitution is based on linking records, GIP depends on counting them. The heavy labour still involved in the former, even though many of the operations involved have been computerised, has meant that only small populations can be tackled, characteristically consisting of a single parish or small group of parishes. GIP, in contrast, needs only annual totals of births and deaths preceding an accurate census, and it is no more onerous to process annual totals numbering hundreds of thousands than totals numbering hundreds only. Space does not permit a detailed description of either technique, nor of the tests needed to establish the suitability of a given data source. Both techniques may, in certain circumstances, give rise to bias or distortion in the hands of the unwary, but since the issues involved are complex and have been discussed extensively elsewhere, it is otiose to rehearse them in this chapter.[7]

Table 3.1 and Figure 3.2 provide an overview of population change during the long eighteenth century. They display the results produced by the application of GIP to annual totals of births and deaths. Table 3.1 provides population totals at five-year intervals and estimates of crude

---

[7] In relation to aggregative methods see Wrigley and Schofield 1989: xiii–xxx; Goldstone 1986; Henry and Blanchet 1983; Lee 1985; Mokyr 1983. In relation to family reconstitution see Razzell 1993 and 1994; Ruggles 1992; Wrigley 1994 and 1997; Rogers 1988; Desjardins 1995.

Table 3.1 Quinquennial demographic data: population totals, fertility and mortality data, intrinsic growth rates and dependency ratio

Year	Pop. (000s)	CBR	CDR	CMR	GRR	e_0	IGR	DR
1681	5109	30.32	32.14	7.91	2.03	31.27	−0.26	642
1686	5036	31.87	28.56	7.17	2.23	35.93	0.47	644
1691	5094	30.05	28.06	6.61	2.16	36.35	0.42	678
1696	5118	31.25	26.67	7.70	2.27	38.06	0.71	711
1701	5211	32.06	26.39	7.72	2.34	38.47	0.83	740
1706	5334	28.48	25.67	7.05	2.07	38.50	0.45	754
1711	5382	29.47	26.77	8.03	2.09	36.89	0.34	741
1716	5428	31.65	27.91	8.21	2.19	35.75	0.38	716
1721	5503	32.80	28.21	9.01	2.22	35.49	0.39	676
1726	5602	31.16	36.99	9.00	2.05	25.34	−0.95	689
1731	5414	35.13	27.46	9.16	2.30	36.34	0.58	647
1736	5599	33.79	28.47	7.99	2.28	35.26	0.46	671
1741	5723	31.71	28.78	8.15	2.18	34.27	0.24	689
1746	5782	32.68	27.02	8.11	2.30	36.47	0.62	723
1751	5922	32.97	24.61	8.05	2.37	39.77	0.99	714
1756	6149	31.87	25.82	8.50	2.27	38.12	0.75	727
1761	6310	33.48	28.29	8.88	2.34	35.37	0.61	749
1766	6449	33.88	27.69	8.79	2.33	36.19	0.68	754
1771	6623	34.90	25.47	8.48	2.38	39.09	1.01	736
1776	6913	35.76	26.57	8.67	2.44	37.74	0.99	756
1781	7206	34.86	27.81	8.57	2.40	35.81	0.76	776
1786	7434	36.89	25.23	8.56	2.56	38.97	1.25	767
1791	7846	37.17	26.07	8.38	2.60	37.92	1.22	762
1796	8256	35.51	24.82	8.19	2.49	38.93	1.15	782
1801	8671	37.60	24.08	8.90	2.64	40.02	1.43	798
1806	9232	37.90	23.68	8.08	2.67	40.58	1.52	800
1811	9864	39.18	23.25	8.42	2.77	41.25	1.69	810
1816	10,628	39.48	23.54	7.91	2.81	40.84	1.70	844
1821	11,457	40.22	23.73	8.35	2.88	40.47	1.75	850
1826	12,374	37.30	22.40	7.70	2.66	41.43	1.56	857
1831	13,254	36.03	22.43	8.12	2.53	40.89	1.36	836
1836	14,100	35.27	22.47	7.96	2.43	40.56	1.19	808
1841	14,937							

Notes: The population totals refer to the year shown in col. 1. All other data refer to a five-year period beginning at the date shown: thus the CMR for 1681–5 is 7.91 per 1,000. Key to table headings: CBR, CDR, CMR, crude birth, death and marriage rates per 1,000; GRR, gross reproduction rate; e_0, expectation of life at birth in years; IGR, intrinsic growth rate (per cent per annum); DR, dependency ratio (1,000 × ((0 − 14 + 60 and over)/15–59)).

Source: Wrigley et al. 1997: tab. A9.1, 614–15.

birth, marriage and death rates, the gross reproduction rate,[8] expectation of life at birth, the intrinsic growth rate, and the dependency ratio for

[8] This rate measures the average number of children who would be born to a woman during her lifetime if she survived to the end of the childbearing period and experienced the average age-specific rates prevailing in a given period of time (or in the case of the equivalent cohort measure, the average age-specific rates experienced by a given cohort).

five-year periods between 1681 and 1841. Figure 3.2 plots the same data in graphical form, except for the population totals (see Figure 3.1).

During the 160 years from 1681 to 1841 the English population almost trebled in size from 5.1 to 14.9 million. Overall, this represents a moderate rate of growth of 0.67 per cent a year, but over the last 100 years of the period, from 1741 to 1841, the pace was much brisker, at 1.01 per cent (in the first 60 years, 1681 to 1741, the rate of growth was almost glacial, at only 0.2 per cent a year). It increased to a crescendo between 1791 and 1831, when the annual rate stood at 1.32 per cent.

That fertility increased and mortality declined is evident both from the crude birth and death rates and from changes in the gross re-production rate (GRR) and in expectation of life at birth (e_0), mea-sures which are more reliable and informative because free from the potentially distorting effects of changing age structure which can af-fect crude rates.[9] Expectation of life at birth was exceptionally low in the first five-year period, 1681–5, lower indeed than in any compara-ble five-year period in the entire parish register period, other than in the late 1550s and the late 1720s, both periods when widespread epi-demic mortality produced individual years in which the crude death rate rose above 40 per 1,000 (Wrigley and Schofield 1989: tab. A3.3, 531–5). There was no individual year in the early 1680s in which such a high level was reached but all five years 1681–5 were very sickly. Thereafter the sec-ular trend in mortality was generally favourable, in spite of occasional relapses, of which that in the late 1720s was the most pronounced. This was the last peacetime quinquennium in which there were more deaths than births. Over the period as a whole the IGR rose dramatically from zero to a peak of 1.75 in 1821–6. In round figures the GRR increased from 2.0 to 2.9 from trough to peak, while e_0 increased by nine years from 31 to 40 years between the first quinquennium and the early 1820s.

It is clear from Table 3.1 that both fertility and mortality were chang-ing in a manner to increase the growth rate but their relative importance in engendering accelerated growth is not immediately clear. Figure 3.3 serves to elucidate this issue. The grid of diagonal lines represent intrin-sic growth rates. Any one line represents the locus of all combinations of fertility and mortality which result in a particular growth rate; 0.0 per cent per annum, 0.5 per cent, and so on. Any vertical movement on the graph represents a change in fertility (GRR); any horizontal movement a

---

[9] Symbols are widely used in the representation and analysis of mortality for the sake of economy and precision. The symbol e which refers to expectation of life and the symbol q which refers to the life table death rate are used in this chapter. Other such symbols are common in relation to the construction of life tables. Examples will illustrate the meaning and use of the symbols. Thus e_0 refers to expectation of life at birth; e_{25} refers to expectation of life at age 25; $_{20}e_{25}$ refers to the expectation of life in the twenty years between age 25 and 45 (that is the average number of years lived between these two ages). Similarly, $_1q_0$ refers to mortality between age 0 and age 1; $_5q_{15}$ refers to mortality between the ages of 15 and 20; and so on. If $_1q_0 = 236$ per 1,000, this means that of every 1,000 children born, 236 will die before reaching their first birthday.

(a)

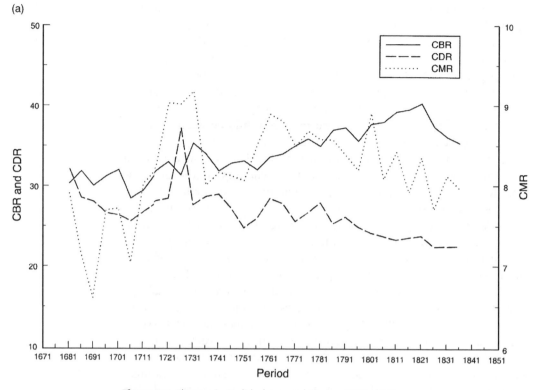

Figure 3.2 Changes in English demographic rates, 1681–1841

Notes: CBR, CDR, CMR: crude birth, death and marriage rates per 1,000 population. GRR: gross reproduction rate. e_0: expectation of life at birth (years). IGR: intrinsic growth rate (per cent per annum). DR: dependency ratio (1,000 × ((0 − 14 + 60 and over) /15–59)).

Source: Wrigley *et al.* 1997: tab. A9.1, 614–15.

change in mortality (e_0). Since the two axes are isometric with respect to the IGR, the relative scale of movement in the two directions will show the relative importance of the contributions made by changes in fertility and mortality to any change in the IGR taking place over time. Fuller details of the mode of construction and characteristics of graphs of this type may be found elsewhere (Wrigley and Schofield 1989: 236–48). It should be noted that the key mortality variable which is captured indirectly by plotting e_0 is the proportion of women surviving to the mean age at maternity.

In general, vertical movement is more pronounced than horizontal in Figure 3.3, though the savagery of the mortality setback in the late 1720s shows through vividly. This may best be appreciated from the heavy black line which begins in a black square on the zero growth diagonal, rises vertically, and then makes a rectangular turn to the right to join the second black square just beyond the diagonal representing an IGR of

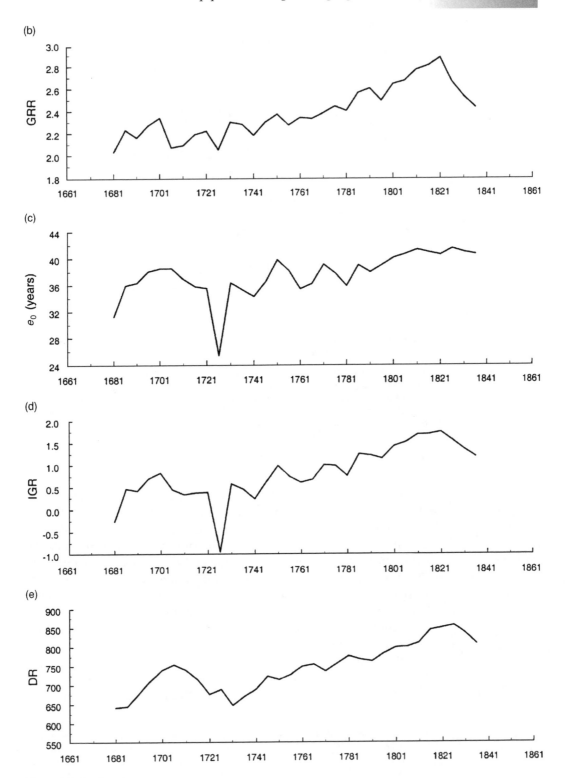

Figure 3.2 *Continued*

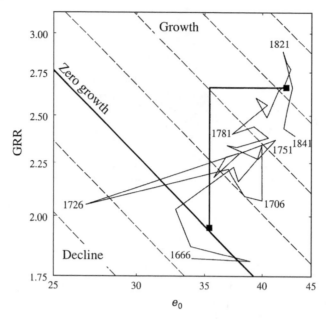

Figure 3.3 The combined effect of fertility and mortality in determining intrinsic growth rates, 1666–1841 (quinquennial data: growth contours at 0.5 per cent intervals)

Notes: The heavy diagonal line represents the locus of all combinations of fertility and mortality resulting in an intrinsic growth rate of zero. Each successive diagonal line to the 'north-east' of the zero line represents positive growth rates of 0.5 per cent per annum, 1.0 per cent per annum, and so on, while each successive line to the 'south-west' represents similar but negative growth rates. See text for an explanation of the heavy black line joining the two black squares.

Source: Wrigley *et al.* 1997: tab. A9.1, 614–15.

1.5 per cent per annum. The vertical section of the line captures the change in fertility: the horizontal section the change in mortality between the two black squares. The two squares plot the combinations of fertility and mortality prevailing in the two quarter centuries 1666–90 and 1816–40, at the beginning and the end of the great acceleration. In the former period e_0 averaged 33.9 years while the GRR averaged 1.95: in the latter period the comparable figures were 40.8 years and 2.66.[10] The ratio of the vertical section of the heavy black line to the horizontal section is 1.8:1.0. By this measure, therefore, fertility accounted for about 64 per cent of the increase in the IGR between the two periods. Griffith's conviction, it seems, was not well founded. The course of population change in England had a principally 'vertical' character in marked contrast to that of Sweden where it was strongly 'horizontal', and both

[10] It may be noticed that the first black square is plotted at an e_0 of slightly more than 35 years rather than at the 33.9 years quoted in the text. This is because a measure of female mortality rather than overall mortality is appropriate since it is the mean age at maternity which is relevant, and female expectation of life exceeded male expectation.

countries were at odds with the French experience, which, in terms of Figure 3.3, slid slowly down the zero growth diagonal in the later eighteenth and early nineteenth centuries (Wrigley and Schofield 1989: fig. 7.13, 246).

The age structure of a population is largely determined by its fertility. It comes as no surprise, therefore, to see the marked change in the dependency ratio which occurred over the long eighteenth century. In the last twenty years of the seventeenth century the ratio averaged 669; in 1821–40 it averaged 838. In the same two periods the population aged 0–14 rose from an average of 303 per 1,000 total population to 387 per 1,000; the large rise in this component of the dependent population being somewhat offset by a decline in the proportion of the population over 60 from 97 to 69 per 1,000. *Ceteris paribus* the living standards both of the working population and of its dependants must tend to be significantly reduced by such a big rise in the dependency ratio.

FERTILITY AND NUPTIALITY

The results presented in the last section were chiefly based on aggregative data and were derived from generalised inverse projection. Those to be presented in this section and the next were chiefly based on nominal data, structured by record linkage using the technique of family reconstitution. It is natural to wonder whether the results obtained by these two different methods, which are logically independent of each other and based on data sets with little overlap, reinforce one another or are at odds. This question has been considered elsewhere (Wrigley *et al.* 1997: ch. 8; Oeppen 2000). The results are reassuring. There is close agreement in all the main demographic series derived by the two methods.

Aggregative methods may establish the outlines of population change and the relative importance of fertility and mortality in bringing about the striking acceleration in the rate of population growth, but reconstitution produces in addition a wealth of more detailed information, turning the sketch into a portrait, and at the same time suggesting questions which can only be resolved by entering the areas in which social, economic and demographic terrains overlap.

That fertility increased considerably during the long eighteenth century is sufficiently evident from the rise in the GRR which took place. But fertility may rise for many different reasons, either singly or in combination: because the fertility rates of married women increase; because women marry earlier in life; because the proportion of women who remain single throughout life falls; even because there is a marked rise in the fertility rates of unmarried women. An increase in the GRR as great as that which occurred is, of course, most unlikely to be due exclusively to one of these four factors, especially as they are closely interlinked. It is rather the relative importance of changes in the four factors which

Table 3.2 Age-specific marital fertility rates per 1,000 woman-years lived; and total marital fertility rates

	15–19	20–4	25–9	30–4	35–9	40–4	45–9	TMFR 20–49	TMFR 15–49
1680–1729	315	410	366	315	240	111	22	7.32	8.90
1730–79	430	418	364	314	254	134	22	7.53	9.68
1780–1829	532	429	390	312	255	148	23	7.79	10.45

Source: Wrigley *et al.* 1997: tab. 7.37, 450.

needs to be established. All four changed in England in the long eighteenth century.

Table 3.2 summarises English age-specific marital fertility rates in three fifty-year periods. Both the dramatic rise in the rate in the 15–19 age group and the more modest rise in the next age group, 20–4, are attributable to the marked rise in the proportion of women who were pregnant on marriage. In the early nineteenth century about a quarter of all first births were prenuptially conceived and a further quarter were illegitimate, whereas in the later seventeenth century the comparable proportions were about 7 per cent in each case (Wrigley 1981: 162 and more generally 155–63). Since the early months of marriage represent a far higher proportion of the total of woman-years lived in marriage among teenagers than among older women, this change in behaviour has a much greater impact on the fertility rate in the age group 15–19 than in older age groups. Fertility also rose in the age groups 25–9, 35–9 and 40–4 but was stable in the remaining age groups. The total marital fertility rate summarises the individual rates, showing the number of children who would be born to an average woman living in marriage either between the ages of 15 and 49 or 20 and 49. Both rates rose steadily during the period as a whole, but the former much more than the latter because of the massive rise in the rate for the age group 15–19.

The marked increase in illegitimacy and in prenuptial conceptions in the course of the eighteenth century is a notable phenomenon in itself. At first sight it might be thought strange that in a period when marriage age fell substantially, and when therefore the proportion of sexually mature women who were single was greatly reduced, illegitimacy should have risen sharply. Viewed in a different light, however, it is less surprising. If entry into marriage is restricted, the average age at marriage advanced, and overall fertility consequently held to a modest level, normative forces may also restrain fertility before marriage and outside marriage; whereas in an era when marriage is early and universal both intercourse before marriage and illegitimacy may be more readily countenanced. One of the more intriguing features of this aspect of English fertility history is the contrast it affords with contemporary France. In France in this period both age at marriage and the proportion never marrying were rising but illegitimacy rose significantly, rather than declining, conforming to what might be thought 'natural' expectation. The contrasts between the two countries extend further, since prenuptial pregnancy became commoner in England among young brides than in older ones in the course of the long eighteenth century, though in earlier periods the reverse was true, but in France prenuptial pregnancy was always more widespread among older brides, though brides at all ages in France were less likely to be pregnant on marriage than in England. Space prevents further discussion of this aspect of fertility behaviour, which is both intriguing and potentially illuminating (data and some further analysis may be found in Wrigley 1981: 174–82).

Table 3.3 Long-term trends in birth intervals (months): thirty-year overlapping periods			
1670–99	32.11	1740–69	31.33
1680–1709	31.84	1750–79	30.85
1690–1719	31.61	1760–89	30.72
1700–29	31.69	1770–99	30.62
1710–39	31.65	1780–1809	30.85
1720–49	31.93	1790–1819	30.54
1730–59	31.44	1800–37	30.57

Notes: The number of birth intervals on which the averages shown in the table were based was usually between 10,000 and 13,000. Intervals to first birth and intervals following the death of the previous child when less than 1 year old were excluded. Extensive tests showed that using all other classes of birth interval produced no detectable bias in the results.

Source: Wrigley *et al.* 1997: tab. 7.36, 447.

The age-specific rates shown in Table 3.2 suggest rising marital fertility. However, a firmer indication of marital fertility trends can be gained from the birth interval data set out in Table 3.3 and Figure 3.4. Birth intervals provide a more reliable indication of fertility trends because they are based on a far larger number of events than age-specific rates. Family reconstitution forms which lack the date of birth of the wife and/or the date of marriage can still yield useful data on birth intervals, whereas both types of information are essential if marital fertility rates are to be derived from them. Between 1670–99 and 1800–37 the mean birth interval fell by 5 per cent, enough to have accounted for about a seventh of the rise in the GRR over the period.

There is good reason to suppose that the reduction in the mean birth interval is attributable to a major decline in the stillbirth rate. By the mid-nineteenth century the stillbirth rate in England was probably in the range 40–50 per 1,000 total births whereas in the later seventeenth century it was probably between 100 and 125 per 1,000 (Wrigley 1998: 447–52). Stillbirths were very rarely recorded in a systematic fashion in English parish registers so that evidence of their prevalence is inevitably largely indirect. However, deaths in the later stages of pregnancy and deaths soon after birth are largely determined by the same factors, and trends in the two mortality rates are usually closely similar. Indeed, the widespread use of the perinatal mortality rate[11] as a measure of mortality close to birth reflects this fact (the perinatal mortality rate measures the combined impact of stillbirths and neonatal mortality). The

---

[11] Perinatal mortality is a measure of the combined impact of foetal mortality in the later stages of pregnancy, or stillbirths, and of neonatal mortality. Stillbirths are commonly defined as mortality after twenty-eight weeks of pregnancy. Neonatal mortality is defined as the mortality of live-born children during the first four weeks of life.

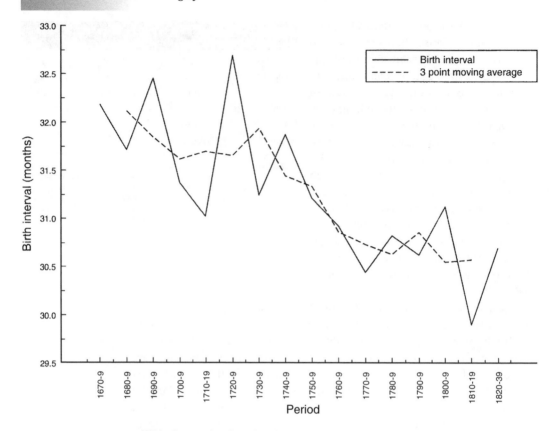

Figure 3.4 Long-term trends in birth intervals (all parities except parity 0: earlier child of pair survives infancy)

Source: Wrigley *et al.* 1997: tab. 7.36, 447.

stillbirth rate is also closely correlated with the endogenous infant mortality rate.[12] Since both neonatal mortality and endogenous infant mortality can be measured using family reconstitution data, indirect estimates of the level and the trend of stillbirth mortality are possible for the early modern period. If the stillbirth rate fell from 100 to 50 per 1,000 total births between the late seventeenth century and the early nineteenth century, the live birth rate would have risen by 5.6 per cent. The change in the mean birth interval corresponds closely with this figure. There are also other indications that a fall in the stillbirth rate underlies the rise in marital fertility, notably the disproportionate rise in age-specific rates among older women. Since the incidence of stillbirth rises markedly with age, a major fall in the incidence of stillbirths, other things being equal, will cause fertility rates in the older age groups to

---

[12] All infant mortality can in principle be divided under two heads, endogenous and exogenous. The latter refers to deaths caused by the invasion of the body by external agents, for example infections such as smallpox or scarlet fever. The former refers to the effects of prematurity, the birth trauma itself, and inherited genetic defects. Almost all endogenous deaths occur within the first month of life. The distinction is valuable in historical studies because estimates of the level of endogenous and exogenous mortality can be made from any data source which enables the age distribution of deaths within the first year of life to be determined, even in the absence of any information about cause of death. The technique for making this estimation was devised by Bourgeois-Pichat (1951).

rise more than those among younger women. A more refined analysis of the changes in age-specific rates shows this pattern clearly (Wrigley 1998: tab. 7, 455).

Analyses of the proximate determinants of stillbirth rates consistently show that by far the most important single factor is birth weight. Low birth weight babies, especially at full term, are subject to very much higher perinatal mortality rates than those close to the optimum weight, usually taken to be in the range

Table 3.4 Mean age at marriage in bachelor/spinster marriages					
	Male	Female		Male	Female
1680–9	27.7	25.8	1760–9	25.9	24.5
1690–9	27.1	25.9	1770–9	26.1	24.3
1700–9	27.4	26.0	1780–9	25.9	24.0
1710–19	27.3	26.3	1790–9	25.3	24.0
1720–9	27.0	25.9	1800–9	25.3	24.0
1730–9	26.9	25.5	1810–19	25.1	23.6
1740–9	26.5	24.8	1820–9	25.2	23.8
1750–9	26.1	25.0	1830–7	24.9	23.1

Source: Wrigley *et al.* 1997: tab. 5.3, 134.

3,500–3,900 grams. The stillbirth rate at an average birth weight of 2,500 grams (the conventional point for defining low birth weight) is between ten and thirty times higher than the rate at an average of 3,500 grams (Wrigley 1998: 442). Since low birth weight in turn is strongly conditioned by maternal nutrition, the marked fall in the stillbirth rate during the long eighteenth century is strong evidence against the supposition that levels of nutrition deteriorated during this period. It is noteworthy that endogenous infant mortality, which is subject to similar influences, fell roughly in parallel with the fall in stillbirths, from almost 90 per 1,000 live births in the late seventeenth century to less than 40 per 1,000 in the early nineteenth century (Wrigley 1998: tab. 6).

Changes in nuptiality can exercise a powerful influence in raising or lowering total fertility rates. In most societies in the past the scope for such changes was limited because convention required women to be married at or soon after reaching sexual maturity, but marriage in early modern England was strongly influenced by economic circumstance as well as physiological maturation. Marriage was not mandatory for either sex and a significant proportion of both sexes in each rising generation remained single. Self-evidently if, say, the percentage never marrying were to rise from 10 to 20 per cent, overall fertility, other things being equal, would fall proportionately. But changes in the mean age at marriage could be equally influential in altering fertility levels. For example, at the age-specific fertility rates prevailing in 1730–79, a mean age at marriage of 26 would result in the average woman who survived in marriage to age 50 giving birth to a total of 5.08 children (Table 3.2). If the mean age of marriage were to fall by one year to 25 the comparable figure would rise to 5.44 children, an increase of 7 per cent, a substantial change. But this calculation understates the full impact of such a change, since there would also be a slight fall in the mean age at childbirth, and, with unchanged mortality, a higher proportion of each cohort of women would reach the mean age at maternity, thereby ensuring a small further increase in effective fertility.

Table 3.4 and Figures 3.5 and 3.6 show the trend in the mean age at marriage in bachelor/spinster marriages between the 1680s and the 1830s.

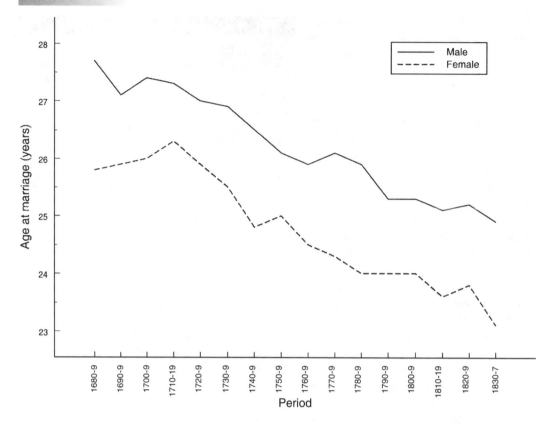

Figure 3.5 Mean age at marriage: bachelor/spinster marriages

Source: Wrigley *et al.* 1997: tab. 5.3, 134.

This category of marriage comprised about 75 per cent of all marriages at the beginning of the period, rising to about 82 per cent towards its end, but bachelor/spinster marriages accounted for a far higher proportion of all births, so that the trend in average age of such marriages is a telling statistic in relation to marital fertility (Wrigley *et al.* 1997: 164–5). Between the first and last decades of the period, male marriage age dropped by 2.8 years from 27.7 to 24.9, while female marriage age fell by an almost identical amount, by 2.7 years from 25.8 to 23.1. Since the totals of marriages from which the average ages for each decade were derived are relatively modest (in the range 400–1,100 for women, increasing over time, and about 80 per cent of these totals for men), it is perhaps safer to measure change from thirty-year rather than ten-year periods. Between 1670–99 and 1810–37 the male average fell from 27.6 to 25.1, and the female average from 26.0 to 23.5, in both cases a fall of 2.5 years. Using the method of estimation just described, the fall in marriage age for women would produce a rise of 20 per cent in completed marital fertility. This is a minimum figure since the associated fall in mean age at maternity would increase the pure fertility effect slightly. The three-dimensional representation of the change in marriage age shown in Figure 3.6 emphasises the increasing degree to which marriage was becoming the preserve of the

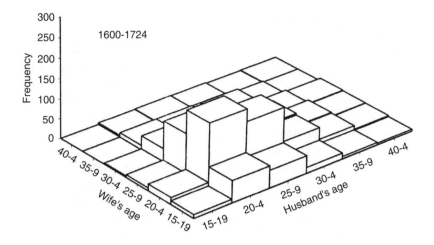

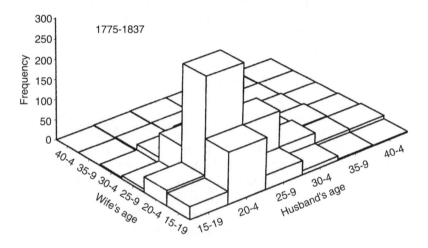

young. Marriages in which the groom was aged 20–4 and the bride was either in the same age group or in her teens constituted 41 per cent of all marriages in the period 1775–1837, whereas in 1600–1724 the corresponding figure was only 22 per cent.

The combined effect of changes in stillbirth rates and of the fall in the mean age of marriage for women would have served to raise fertility by 27 or 28 per cent. Since the GRR rose by 36 per cent in the course of the long eighteenth century, these two changes alone account for at least three-quarters of the rise in the GRR.

A further change which boosted fertility lay not in fertility within marriage but in extra-marital fertility. In the last quarter of the seventeenth century 1.8 per cent of all births were illegitimate; in the first quarter of the nineteenth century the comparable figure had risen to 6.2 per cent. Since the proportion of young women who were unmarried fell sharply over this period as marriage age declined, the rise in

Figure 3.6 Marriage age combinations: bachelor/spinster marriages (frequency per 1,000 marriages)

Source: Wrigley *et al.* 1997: tab. 5.5, 142.

the age-specific illegitimate fertility rate was, of course, far greater than might appear from the rise in the illegitimacy ratio (Wrigley 1981: 155–63; Wrigley and Schofield 1989: tab. 6.2, 219). The increase in illegitimate fertility would have increased overall fertility by about 4.7 per cent ((100 × (100/93.8)/(100/98.2)) = 104.7). Adding this rise to the rises attributable to changes in marriage age and the stillbirth rate would have raised the GRR by 33 or 34 per cent, thus accounting for the great bulk of its rise.

There remains the question of the proportion of each generation of young men and women who never married. Before 1851, when the census first provides reliable information about this topic, only indirect estimation of this variable is possible. It is essentially a residual derived from other variables which can be estimated directly. The work of Weir and Schofield has suggested that there were major changes in the proportion never marrying in the sixteenth and seventeenth centuries, but that, beginning with the birth cohort which married chiefly in the 1690s, there was little subsequent change in this variable in the course of the long eighteenth century. Throughout this period the proportion of each cohort never marrying probably lay in the range between 10 and 15 per cent (Weir 1984; Schofield 1985; Schofield 1989: fig. 8.8, 297). It has not proved possible to estimate the percentage separately for men and women, though it is unlikely that they diverged widely. At the time of the 1851 census the proportion of men above the age to marry who had never married was 11.4 per cent, and of women 12.3 per cent.[13] That there was little change in the proportion never marrying is, of course, also an implication of the combined effect of changing marriage age, a decreasing stillbirth rate and the sharp increase in illegitimate fertility in accounting in full for the rise which took place in the GRR. The level and trend of abstention from marriage, however, remains subject to greater uncertainty than other aspects of marriage behaviour.

That economic circumstances exercised a powerful influence on marriage decisions became clear when *The Population History of England* was first published in 1981. It was difficult to resist the view that secular economic and nuptiality trends were closely related, though the parallel movement in the two series also appeared to pose a difficulty, since there was a time lag between the turning points in the two series (Wrigley and Schofield 1989: fig. 10.9, 425). The question proved controversial (Wrigley and Schofield 1989: xx–xxx and fig. 3.1, xxii). The accuracy of the real wage series was questionable. Even if it were demonstrably accurate, because of its nature, changes in the proportion of family income provided by women and children, or in the number of days worked during the year, could play no part in influencing its level or trend (de Vries 1994; Voth 2000). And there were other problems with both data series. But

---

[13] The proportion never marrying was taken as the average of those single in the age groups 45–9 and 50–4. For the relevant statistics see Mitchell 1988: tab. I.5, 20–2.

the big issue proved to be the apparent time lag. In principle, at one extreme, it might be argued that there should be no time lag: at the other extreme, that, for example, random fluctuations in the real wage tied to the fortunes of the annual harvest were so substantial that turning points in the secular trend of the real wage could not be detected with confidence until some time after they had occurred; that, in other words, the 'signal' was difficult to interpret since there was so much 'noise' in the system.

Figure 3.7 puts a different complexion on this question. There are a number of differences between this and previous graphs of the variables. The assumptions made in deriving the series totals are enumerated in the notes to the figure. They produce significant changes in some data points in both series compared with earlier graphs. A further change, however, also makes a substantial difference to the appearance of the graph. The data are plotted as decennial averages rather than as twenty-five-year moving averages as in earlier exercises. As a result it is clear that mid-seventeenth-century lag in the turning points of the two series, apparent when moving averages are employed, is absent if the 1660s and 1670s are ignored. Whether they *should* be ignored is debatable. The registration of marriages during the Civil War and the Commonwealth period suffered very severely and remained poor following the Restoration until the Marriage Duty Act of 1695. It is inherently easier to identify a period when there is an abrupt or wide departure from a preceding pattern than to do the same if the change is less marked or is gradual. Thus, paradoxically, the radical disruptions of the 1640s and 1650s posed fewer problems to the programme used to detect underregistration and introduce replacement values than those associated with the prevalence of clandestine marriage in the period following the Restoration. In this period the replacement estimates suggested that 10.9 per cent of marriages were not recorded, a figure which dropped to 3.3 per cent following the passage of the Marriage Duty Act, but the true figure for the Restoration period was probably higher, especially in the 1660s and 1670s (Wrigley and Schofield 1989: tab. 1.5, 32 and app. 12, 687–704). It is possible, therefore, that the agreement between the trends in the real wage index and the crude first marriage rate would be still closer if this problem did not exist. In that case the two series might be said to follow very similar paths during the first two and a half centuries of the period. Only in the early decades of the nineteenth century was the relationship less close.

It has long been known that in organic economies there was normally a strong relationship between the fortunes of harvest, which had a major impact on the economic well-being of a community, and fluctuations in the marriage rate. The relationship was positive: years of bad harvest severely reduced the number of marriages; good harvests brought many more couples to the church porch. This was true of England in common

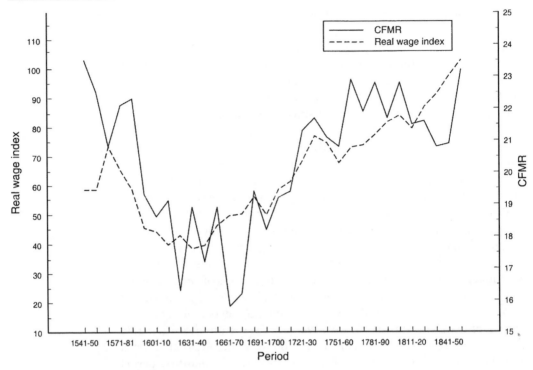

Figure 3.7 Crude first marriage rates and real wage trends

Notes: The crude first marriage rate was calculated by relating the decennial totals of first marriages to the population aged 15–34 at the midpoint of the ten-year period. The population totals for the four five-year age groups 15–19 to 30–4 were weighted 1:5:3:1 to reflect approximately the distribution of marriages between the four age groups (previously the simple total of population aged 15–34 had been used). First marriages were calculated from the totals of all marriages using the assumptions set out in Wrigley and Schofield (1989: 426–7). The real wage index was calculated using the decadal real wage estimates of Goldstone (1986) for the period down to 1691–1700; the Phelps Brown and Hopkins index modified to include a 'northern' component as described in *ibid*.: 432–3 for the period 1701–10 to 1771–80; and Feinstein's (1998a) estimates thereafter. The Goldstone and PBH series were joined by treating the decadal value for 1691–1700 as 50 in both cases. The PBH and Feinstein series were joined by indexing the Feinstein series to the value of the PBH series for 1771–80.

Sources: Wrigley and Schofield 1989: tab. A9.2, 642–4; Wrigley *et al*. 1997: tab. A9.1, 614–15, and the related and more detailed Cambridge Group tabulations of the age structure of the population at quinquennial intervals: Goldstone 1986: tab. A1, 32; Feinstein 1998a: app. tab. 1, 652–3.

with other European countries (Galloway 1988; Wrigley and Schofield 1989: 348–53, 368–77). The foregoing shows that there was also a strong link between economic circumstances and marriage trends in the longer term. In the absence of any major change in age-specific marital fertility rates, wide variations in nuptiality are certain to produce parallel movements in overall fertility. The existence of a link between economic circumstances and marriage decisions, and the absence of any comparable link with mortality, sustain the presumption that what Malthus termed the preventive check was much more influential than the positive check in early modern England (Wrigley and Schofield 1989: ch. 10). The issue was much more doubtful in Scotland. The 1690s showed vividly how vulnerable large tracts of the country remained to harvest failure. Aberdeenshire was as cruelly affected as, say, the Beauvaisis in that decade. In England, in contrast, even in the sixteenth century, *crises de subsistances* had a greater impact on nuptiality and fertility than on mortality (Goubert 1960; Tyson 1986; Wrigley and Schofield 1989: 320–42; Schofield 1994: 81–4; Houston 1996).

MORTALITY

Figure 3.3 showed that the fall in mortality was less influential than the rise in fertility in increasing the intrinsic growth rate during the long eighteenth century, but the mortality history of the period is none the less remarkably interesting. Perhaps the point of widest significance which is brought to light is that the assumption that age-specific mortality rates tend to move roughly in parallel with each other, which is fundamental to the construction of model life tables, should not be accepted uncritically when considering populations in the past. Model life tables are widely employed to extrapolate from the known to the unknown, as, for example, when there is information about mortality in the childhood age groups but none for the higher age groups. It may be true in general that a major improvement or deterioration in childhood mortality is likely to be paralleled by similar changes in adult mortality, and vice versa, but this rule is not universally valid. It did not hold true for England in the long eighteenth century, when adult mortality improved sharply while child mortality changed little. The mortality history of early modern England, therefore, suggests that it is unsafe to make use of a knowledge of mortality rates in a particular age range to infer rates in other age groups using model life tables. For example, it is possible to calculate male e_{20} for the monks living in Canterbury in the fifteenth century when it was about 27.6 years. Using the model North Princeton life tables this implies an e_0 of only about 18 years, yet if the relationship between adult and child rates in the fifteenth century were the same as in the seventeenth century e_0 would be much higher, probably more than 30 years (Wrigley *et al.* 1997: 349; the Canterbury data are from Hatcher 1986: tab. 2, 28). Family reconstitution data show that in Stuart England adult mortality rates were radically higher relative to those earlier in life than would be expected from the Princeton life tables, yet that in the course of the eighteenth century age-specific rates came to conform quite closely to the model North pattern across their whole range, a feature which remained apparent when William Farr produced the influential third English life table, reflecting the mortality recorded under the new civil registration system during the first seventeen years

Table 3.5 Adult mortality, sexes combined (1,000 q_x)			
	1640–89	1750–1809	Third English life table modified
25–9	75.9	53.6	47.8
30–4	82.0	54.1	52.6
35–9	97.4	62.3	58.4
40–4	92.8	68.1	66.2
45–9	115.0	89.0	76.8
50–4	142.5	101.1	94.3
55–9	204.9	124.1	123.3
60–4	226.1	172.1	170.7
65–9	295.5	237.7	242.8
70–4	431.4	375.8	350.7
75–9	514.5	439.0	480.9
80–4	627.4	607.5	618.9
e_{25}	30.4	35.4	36.3
$_{20}e_{25}$	17.0	17.8	18.0
$_{20}e_{45}$	14.9	16.2	16.5
$_{20}e_{65}$	9.1	10.2	10.2

Note: The original rates in the third English life table above the age of 50 understated the prevailing mortality rates because there was a marked overstatement of age by the elderly in the censuses of 1841 and 1851. The rates shown in the table have been corrected to offset this source of inaccuracy. Wrigley and Schofield 1989: 709–12, esp. tab. A14.3, 711.

Source: Wrigley et al. 1997: tab. 6.20, 291.

of its existence, 1838–54. For this reason model North would appear to be a natural choice for use in making inferences from partial data for an earlier period, but doing so can demonstrably lead to dubious results.

Table 3.5 shows adult mortality rates at the beginning and the end of the long eighteenth century. The periods are relatively long to minimise the random variability to be found in decennial estimates based on limited numbers of events. Rates from the third English life table are also shown to illustrate the similarity between mortality towards the end of the parish register era and that revealed by national statistics for the middle years of the nineteenth century. In contrast, mortality rates in the late seventeenth century were at a far higher level. In the period 1640–89 e_{25} was 30.4 years, roughly equivalent to level 5 of model North. At this level, expectation of life at birth for the two sexes combined is only 28.5 years. When mortality was at its worst in the 1680s e_{25} was less than 28 years, which in model North terms is equivalent to an e_0 of less than 20 years. In contrast by the period 1750–1809 e_{25} was 35.4 years, equivalent to level 9 in model North (Wrigley et al. 1997: tab. 6.19, 290; the technicalities of deriving accurate estimates of adult mortality preclude the estimation of rates based on parish register data later than the decade 1800–9: ibid., app. 6, 581–600). Level 9 has a combined sex e_0 of 38.4 years. If, therefore, adult mortality data were the sole guide to mortality change during the long eighteenth century, there would appear to have been a pronounced rise in e_0 of at least ten years, and possibly approaching twenty years, depending on whether the estimate were based on lengthy periods, or from the trough in the 1680s to the plateau in the late eighteenth century. If this line of argument had been valid, the increase in life expectancy between the two periods would have been as great, measured in years of life gained, as over the equivalent period of time separating the mid-nineteenth and early twentieth centuries. Measured as a percentage rise in life expectancy, the earlier period would have the more impressive record.

Matters appear very different, however, when infant and child mortality is also taken into account. Here the picture is turned on its head, for if estimates of e_0 were to based on mortality rates in the first fifteen years of life, the conclusion would be virtual stasis rather than rapid change.

Table 3.6	Mortality within the first year of life in England, 1650–1837 (1,000 q_x)								
	Days within the first year of life								
	0–29	30–59	60–89	90–179	180–273	274–365	$_1q_0$	Endogenous	Exogenous
1650–99	107	17	11	22	15	15	176	88	88
1700–49	104	20	14	26	22	19	191	82	109
1750–99	75	17	11	26	23	18	160	57	103
1800–37	54	15	11	25	23	19	139	38	100

Notes: The rates shown are averages of two quarter-century periods (e.g. 1650–99 is the average of 1650–74 and 1675–99; the final period 1800–37 is the weighted average of 1800–24 and 1825–37, where the later period is given half the weight of the earlier period). Rounding may give rise to apparent error, as in the endogenous/exogenous split of $_1q_0$ in 1800–37.

Source: Wrigley *et al.* 1997: tab. 6.4, 226.

Overall childhood mortality ($_{15}q_0$) was 323 per 1,000 in 1650–99 and had declined only modestly to 303 per 1,000 in 1750–99 (Wrigley *et al.* 1997: tab. 6.12, 256). In terms of model North the two are closely equivalent to level 10 and level 11 with combined sex e_0's of 40.9 and 43.4 years respectively. If childhood mortality were representative of mortality as a whole, therefore, and were used to estimate overall life expectancy, there would appear to have been only very limited improvement between the later seventeenth and later eighteenth centuries, a very different conclusion from that suggested by adult mortality. This comparison may be thought misleading in that the phasing of change in childhood and adult mortality was different. Childhood mortality was at its height in the quarter century 1725–49 and declined further between the later eighteenth century and the final parish register period 1800–37, but even between these two periods the implied decline in overall mortality would only be that from level 9 to level 12, or about seven years, perhaps half the peak to trough fall implied by adult mortality.

Differential movement was not confined to the contrast between adult and childhood mortality, for the pattern in childhood itself was far from uniform. Table 3.6 shows how vivid was the contrast between the trend in mortality during the first month of life and that in the remainder of the first year. The former halved in the course of the long eighteenth century; the latter rose somewhat at first but stabilised thereafter. Since the distinction between endogenous and exogenous mortality is capturing a similar phenomenon, the same pattern is visible in the trends in these two measures (Wrigley *et al.* 1997: 223–7).

Childhood mortality rates, shown in Table 3.7, display similar characteristics to those within the first year of life, other than the first month. Mortality in each of the three age groups either rose slightly or was unchanged between the first and second periods but then declined between the first and second halves of the eighteenth century, quite sharply in the case of the age group 5–9. This age group also experienced a further decline between the penultimate and last periods, but in early and late childhood any further change was slight, a small fall in $_4q_1$, a modest rise

Table 3.7   Childhood mortality in England and the Princeton model North life tables

	$_4q_1$	$_5q_5$	$_5q_{10}$	Equivalent levels in model North			
				$_1q_0$	$_4q_1$	$_5q_5$	$_5q_{10}$
1650–99	109	48	27	8.5	11.3	11.0	10.6
1700–49	114	48	28	7.5	10.9	11.0	10.3
1750–99	108	38	24	9.2	11.5	13.0	11.6
1800–37	98	29	25	10.5	12.2	14.9	11.4

Notes: The rates shown are averages of two quarter-century periods (e.g. 1650–99 is the average of 1650–74 and 1675–99; the final period 1800–37 is the weighted average of 1800–24 and 1825–37, where the later period is given half the weight of the earlier period). The rates for $_1q_0$ are set out in Table 3.6.

Source: Wrigley et al. 1997: tab. 6.14, 262.

in $_5q_{10}$. The table also shows the equivalent model North mortality levels for each age group and period. For the childhood age groups the model North levels show a substantial internal consistency, except that $_5q_5$ drifts apart somewhat during the two final periods. Space does not permit a fuller discussion of this apparently aberrant development here, nor the consideration of a comparison with the childhood rates in the third English life table but both issues are discussed at some length elsewhere (Wrigley et al. 1997: 255–61). In contrast, infant mortality was substantially more severe than childhood mortality in model North terms but the gap closed rapidly towards the end of the period as infant rates fell more markedly than childhood rates.

Another way of characterising the changes shown in this section of Table 3.7 would be to describe the move towards conformity with the model North pattern as the result of the drastic fall in mortality in the first month of life. As evidence of the fundamentally different fortunes of children and adults, consider the following. At the mortality rates prevailing in 1650–99, of 1,000 infants surviving the first month of life 761 would still be living on their fifteenth birthday, a figure which had improved only marginally, to 778, in 1800–37. In contrast, at the mortality rates which obtained in 1640–89, of 1,000 adults living on their 25th birthday, only 419 would still be living at age 60, whereas in 1750–1809 the comparable figure had jumped to 561, a rise of more than one third. During the long eighteenth century the striking fall in adult mortality, combined with a significant decline in infant mortality, over a period in which childhood rates changed very little, was gradually producing a 'modern' pattern in age-specific mortality which had been conspicuously absent at the start of the period. Overall expectation of life at birth was improving but the increase was modest because of the contrasting fortunes of adults and children.

There are many other aspects of the mortality history of early modern England which are of great interest. The seasonality of death in relation to age, for example, can be explored effectively with family reconstitution data and is most instructive (Wrigley et al. 1997: 322–43). Again, there was a notable improvement in mortality in London during the later eighteenth century (Landers 1993; Laxton and Williams 1989). Nor was London alone in this regard. Many other English cities, like London, had ceased to be demographic 'sinks' by the end of the century; birth surpluses replaced the previous excess of deaths. The improvement was not continuous, however, since the second quarter of the nineteenth century saw widespread deterioration in urban mortality as urban authorities failed to cope with the public health problems associated with urban life (Szreter and Mooney 1998). The failure of national expectation of life to improve significantly over the first three-quarters of the nineteenth century, however, is easily misinterpreted: it was due in part to migratory movements which

Table 3.8	Maternal mortality rates (per 1,000 birth events)
1650–99	16.3
1700–49	12.9
1750–99	9.3
1800–37	5.8

Note: The rates shown are averages of two quarter-century periods (e.g. 1650–99 is the average of 1650–74 and 1675–99; the final period 1800–37 is the weighted average of 1800–24 and 1825–37, where the later period is given half the weight of the earlier period).

Source: Wrigley *et al.* 1997: tab. 6.29, 313.

resulted in a steadily rising fraction of the population living in the least salubrious environments. Villages and small towns housed a steadily declining share of the population, while the rapidly growing industrial and commercial centres bulked larger and larger within the national whole. It was therefore quite possible for expectation of life to improve in each category of settlement and yet for there to be little change nationally (Woods 1985, 2000: ch. 9).

Though space prevents a fuller consideration of these and many other aspects of mortality in the long eighteenth century, one other set of related topics demands consideration, sex differential mortality.

Perhaps the most dramatic development in any aspect of mortality during the long eighteenth century was the fall in maternal mortality. Table 3.8 shows that maternal mortality fell by two thirds between 1650–99 and 1800–37, from 16.3 to 5.8 per 1,000 birth events. The remarkable nature of the change is underlined by the fact that maternal mortality thereafter stabilised throughout the balance of the nineteenth century, and indeed had declined only very slightly by the outbreak of the Second World War. In the five decades 1850–9 to 1890–9 the rate averaged 4.8 per 1,000; in 1910–19 it was 4.0, and as late as 1930–9 still 3.7 (Loudon 1992: app. 6, tab. 1, 542–4). The proportionate fall in maternal mortality in the long eighteenth century was similar to that in endogenous infant mortality (from 88 to 38 per 1,000 birth events), and parallels the presumptive decline in the stillbirth rate described above, a set of linked changes which accord with expectation. The period immediately before birth, birth itself and the period immediately after birth became radically less dangerous to both mother and child during the long eighteenth century.

A satisfactory explanation for the remarkable fall in maternal mortality is still to seek, but it is clear that it was not a phenomenon peculiar to England. There is a striking similarity in both the level and trend of maternal mortality in England and Sweden from the middle of the eighteenth century onwards (Swedish data are available only from 1751 onwards). The same is true of rural France. In London maternal mortality was substantially higher than in the country as a whole, but the trend was almost identical (Schofield 1986: tab. 9.1, 238; Wrigley *et al.* 1997: fig. 6.22, 314).

The close interrelationship between maternal mortality, the stillbirth rate and endogenous infant mortality illustrates another point worthy of emphasis. Fertility, mortality and nuptiality are often treated as separate topics, but they are always necessarily closely interlinked. It is entirely arbitrary to treat life as beginning with parturition, for example. If conception were regarded as the start of life, what appears as an increase in fertility in the course of the eighteenth century would be treated as a fall in mortality, with fertility rates in all probability unchanged. Or again, a rise in infant mortality, by causing the average length of birth intervals to fall, will provoke a rise in marital fertility as conventionally measured, yet the 'true' level of fertility may not have altered.[14] Such examples could be multiplied almost indefinitely.

Maternal mortality was a major element in female mortality generally during the peak years of childbearing in early modern England. With an average birth interval of thirty months, for example, maternal mortality as high as in the second half of the seventeenth century is equivalent to annual death rate of 6–7 per 1,000, or over a five-year period to a life table death rate of 30–5 per 1,000 (that is, of 1,000 married women entering the period 30–5 would die from childbirth and its associated hazards before its end). This was equivalent to roughly a third of all deaths among married women in the age groups 25–39 in 1640–89, and largely explains the excess of female deaths in these age groups visible in Table 3.9. Although adult mortality in general declined substantially during the long eighteenth century, the much sharper proportionate fall in maternal mortality meant that it was a smaller element in female mortality towards the end of the period than at its beginning.

The third English life table mortality rates in Table 3.9 show a far smaller female disadvantage in the childbearing age groups than in the reconstitution data for 1750–1809, but any direct comparison is misleading. The reconstitution data refer to married women only, given the nature of the rules of observation which govern the derivation of such data, whereas the third English life table refers to the whole female population. The younger the age group, the higher the proportion of single women, and single women experienced lower mortality since their exposure to the risks of childbirth was far less than for married women. Appropriately adjusted to take this point into account, the reconstitution death rates in the age groups 25–39 and those in the third English life table are closely similar. In the age groups above the age of 40, when childbirth was a rapidly diminishing hazard, there is a good agreement between the

---

[14] An infant death caused the cessation of breast feeding and brought about an early return of ovulatory cycles. The average birth interval following an infant death was about eight months shorter than the average following a child who survived. Where the mean interval in the latter case was, say, thirty-two months and in the latter only twenty-four months, therefore, a rise in infant mortality from 150 per 1,000 to 200 per 1,000 would reduce the overall average birth interval from 30.8 to 30.4 months, *ceteris paribus* (Wrigley *et al.* 1997: tab. 7.35, 438–9).

Table 3.9	Male and female adult mortality (1,000 q_x)									
	1640–1809		1640–89		1750–1809		Third English life table			
	(1) M	(2) F	(3) M	(4) F	(5) M	(6) F	(7) M	(8) F	(9) (1)/(2)	(10) (7)/(8)
25–9	39.1	74.8	50.9	99.1	25.8	73.4	46.7	49.0		
30–4	55.3	79.0	60.3	92.6	37.2	70.5	51.5	53.6		
35–9	71.6	89.0	85.5	111.3	57.8	67.1	58.1	58.7		
40–4	84.1	83.8	90.9	95.6	68.5	68.0	67.5	64.9		
45–9	106.1	95.7	114.8	114.8	99.0	77.5	80.8	72.8	111	111
50–4	127.5	110.6	154.4	126.6	116.3	83.3	101.0	87.1	115	116
55–9	182.6	139.7	216.3	189.0	133.1	113.0	130.1	116.6	131	112
60–4	203.3	189.3	221.8	232.6	182.8	160.0	176.9	165.7	107	107
65–9	259.0	267.7	286.3	310.3	222.1	254.5	246.8	240.9	97	102
70–4	387.1	374.4	454.9	406.5	372.7	380.0	355.7	348.7	103	102
75–9	469.3	476.0	492.7	555.3	423.9	451.8	489.3	477.3	99	103
80–4	609.7	596.4	537.2	766.0	643.5	556.2	626.2	615.9	102	102

Note: The original rates in the third English life table above the age of 50 understated the prevailing mortality rates because there was a marked overstatement of age by the elderly in the censuses of 1841 and 1851. The rates shown in the table have been corrected to offset this source of inaccuracy. Wrigley and Schofield 1989: 709–12, esp. tab. A14.3, 711.

Source: Wrigley et al. 1997: tab. 6.26, 303.

reconstitution data for 1750–1809 and the third English life table. Outside the years of childbearing the normal tendency for male mortality rates to exceed female rates is clearly evident in the reconstitution data, as may be seen in the ratios in columns 9 and 10 of Table 3.9. The pattern is more regular in the third English life table since it was based on millions of deaths in the period 1838–54, whereas the comparatively small number of events in the parishes which provided data for the reconstitution exercise was insufficient to suppress random variation. Nevertheless the general similarity between the relative levels of male and female adult mortality in the early modern period and in the mid-nineteenth century is clear.

Finally, it is instructive to consider sex differences in infant and child as well as adult mortality. Table 3.10 shows that the ratio of male to female rates for infants was stable over time and very close to the ratios to be found in the model North and model West tables of Coale and Demeny (which are extrapolated respectively from the mortality experience of Scandinavian countries principally in the nineteenth century on the one hand and advanced countries chiefly in the twentieth century on the other: Coale and Demeny 1966: 12–14). There were many infant deaths in the reconstitution parishes and these ratios are stable partly because they are subject to little random variation. The same was not so true of mortality later in childhood, when the absolute number of deaths on which the rates were based was substantially smaller. Nevertheless a tendency for female mortality to worsen relative to male mortality seems probable in the age group 1–4 and clear-cut for the age group 5–14, though it should be noted that the average pattern over the whole

Table 3.10 Male and female infant and child mortality (1,000 q_x)						
	$_1q_0$		$_4q_1$		$_{10}q_5$	
	M	F	M	F	M	F
1650–99	178.0	151.3	111.1	107.0	71.6	76.1
1700–49	201.2	177.5	115.8	113.1	76.2	73.0
1750–99	169.4	148.9	103.3	111.4	60.3	63.5
1800–37	148.0	128.4	97.5	99.8	48.5	57.2
Male/female ratios						
1650–99	1.177		1.038		0.941	
1700–49	1.134		1.024		1.044	
1750–99	1.138		0.927		0.950	
1800–37	1.153		0.977		0.848	
Level 8 North	1.168		1.045		1.003	
Level 8 West	1.163		1.001		0.916	

Notes: The rates shown refer to legitimate births only. The rates shown for each half century are averages of the two quarter centuries which comprise it (e.g. 1650–99 is the average of 1650–74 and 1675–99), except that the rates shown for 1800–37 are derived by averaging 1800–24 and 1825–37 after giving double weight to 1800–24 relative to 1825–37.

Source: Wrigley *et al.* 1997: tab. 6.22, 296 and tab. 6.23, 299.

period 1650–1837 is not dissimilar from the ratios to be found in the model life tables. What might have caused the relative deterioration in female childhood mortality?

Cause of death is very rarely mentioned in parish registers but was a main concern of William Farr during the long period during which he was Statistical Superintendant at the General Register Office. In 1861 respiratory tuberculosis claimed a steadily rising proportion of all deaths in each successive age group from birth to adolescence in England and Wales. The absolute rate for girls was higher than that for boys throughout, and the disproportion rose with age so that in the age group 10–14 the rate was almost twice as high for girls as for boys. In that age group respiratory tuberculosis caused 30 per cent of all female deaths, a proportion which rose still higher to more than 50 per cent in the age group 15–19. Excluding deaths from respiratory tuberculosis, male rates in each age group from 1 to 15 years of age were higher than female rates in 1861 (Preston *et al.* 1972: 224–7). Since the incidence of tuberculosis was already declining sharply in 1861, it is likely that rates were even higher early in the nineteenth century. Assuming that the rates were rising during the eighteenth century, it may well be that the proximate cause of the increasing sex differential in childhood mortality visible in Table 3.10 was the differentially severe impact of respiratory tuberculosis upon the health of young girls. As with most such issues, of course, establishing the proximate cause of a particular feature may be only a first step towards providing a fuller explanation. Further work on this issue might prove illuminating.

LOPSIDED GROWTH

Although fertility, mortality and nuptiality necessarily form the core of a description of the population history of Britain in the long eighteenth century, to regard the story as consisting solely of the development of these three variables and their interrelationships would be to overlook some of the most interesting and thought-provoking aspects of the population history of the period. The rapid increase of population which occurred was not the result of proportionate growth in all types of economic activity or categories of settlement.

Proportionate growth may take either an extensive or an intensive form. When, as may happen in lands of new settlement, population growth is rapid because new areas are taken into cultivation, the resulting expansion consists essentially of replicating an existing pattern over a larger and larger area; in short, extensive growth. In a long-settled territory proportionate growth may also be possible for a time, perhaps following the pattern which Geertz described as agricultural involution, a more and more intensive use of an unchanging area of farming land without significant structural change, though growth of this kind is apt to be accompanied by increasing immiseration (Geertz 1963a: 33). Geertz had in mind wet rice cultivation but his model is also applicable, for example, to the cultivation of the potato in Ireland in the century preceding the famine. Ricardo identified the implications of this type of intensive growth when developing the concept of decreasing marginal returns to land and labour (Ricardo 1951 [1817]: 120–7, esp. 125–6). This type of intensive growth might also be termed balanced. Much the same percentage of the labour force is engaged in each major type of economic activity at the end of a period of intensive growth of this kind as was involved at its beginning. But intensive growth can also be unbalanced, or lopsided, as in early modern England: and such growth may long escape the drawbacks of balanced growth, even within the constraints imposed by an organic economy. (Wrigley (1988) develops the concept of an organic economy.)

The long eighteenth century saw, towards its end, the early stages of a fundamental change in the economic constitution of society, a change which has come to be termed the industrial revolution; but the bulk of the growth and change during the long eighteenth century is better characterised as 'Smithian' growth than as a foretaste of the industrial revolution; growth, that is, arising from the interrelated benefits associated with growing market size, improved transport, better commercial facilities, increasing working capital and the division of labour. Such growth caused profound change in many aspects of economic life in England, as it had done previously in the Netherlands, and the change is readily visible in the secondary population characteristics of the period.

Table 3.11   Percentage of total population living in towns with 5,000 or more inhabitants

	England	France	The Netherlands
1600	8	9	29
1700	17	11	39
1750	21	10	35
1800	28	11	33
1850	45	19	39

Sources: Wrigley 1987c: tab. 7.2, 162; tab. 7.8, 182; tab. 7.9, 184–5: Bairoch 1988: tab. 13.4, 221.

Two such changes in particular deserve attention: those in occupational structure and in the urban share of total population.

It is a major handicap to tracing the course of development in the long eighteenth century that information about the changing occupational structure of the country is as yet so sparse. It is therefore hazardous to provide a sketch of such change, yet impossible to resist the temptation to attempt it. We are better served with information about urban development. These two aspects of population structure are necessarily closely connected and may conveniently be treated together.

In Elizabethan times it is clear that England was less urbanised than continental Europe as a whole, and substantially less urbanised than those parts of Europe which were economically the most advanced: northern Italy, the Rhine corridor and the Low Countries. It is highly likely that agriculture dominated the occupational structure of the country at least as completely as was the case beyond the Channel, though this assertion is less easy to substantiate with reliable data than the comparable point about urbanisation. It is probable that at least three-quarters of the labour force was engaged in agriculture. Early in the nineteenth century England became the most urbanised country in western Europe. A far smaller proportion of its labour force worked on the land than on the continent, even though the country remained largely self-sufficient in food (Jones 1981; Thomas 1985: tab. 2, 743). Much of this profound transformation took place in the long eighteenth century.

Before considering the implications of urban growth and a changing occupational structure, an attempt to quantify the scale of the changes in question is appropriate. Table 3.11 and Figure 3.8 show the percentage of the population which was urban in England, France and the Netherlands from 1600 to 1850.[15] The Netherlands was the most advanced economy in Europe from the mid-sixteenth century until the early eighteenth century. The pattern of urban growth in France was typical of that of continental Europe as a whole throughout this period (Wrigley 1987c: tabs. 7.5 and 7.9, 176, 184–5). These two countries, therefore, form suitable comparitors for England during the long eighteenth century. The contrasts between the three countries are striking. The Netherlands was far

---

[15] Urban populations are defined as those living in towns with 5,000 or more inhabitants. Any division between urban and rural is bound to be arbitrary and will prove unsatisfactory for some purposes. In many contexts setting the dividing line at 5,000 inhabitants would appear inconveniently high. Its advantage in this context is that there were few towns of this size in which agricultural employment was other than trivially small as a fraction of the labour force.

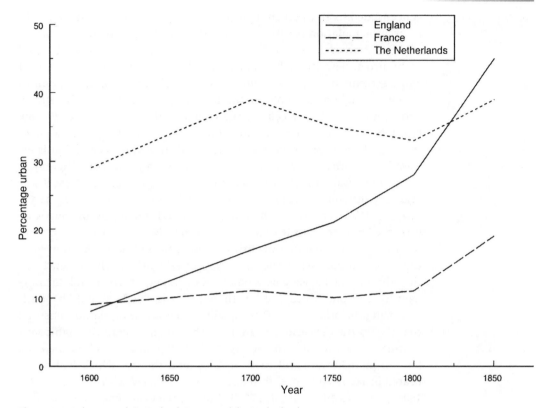

Figure 3.8 Urban growth in England, France and the Netherlands

Notes: The urban proportion was taken as the percentage of the total population living in towns with 5,000 or more inhabitants.

Sources: Wrigley 1987c: tab. 7.2, 162; tab. 7.8, 182; tab. 7.9, 184–5: Bairoch 1988: tab. 13.4, 221.

more urbanised than England or France in 1600, the two latter being roughly on a par with each other at that date. Urbanisation continued in the Netherlands during the seventeenth century and was gathering momentum in England, but in the following century declined in the former while continuing strongly in the latter. By 1850 the position in the Netherlands was little different from that in 1700, whereas growth had continued unabated in England. Meanwhile in France there was no significant change from the initial level of urbanisation until after 1800, and in 1850 France was still much less urbanised than the Netherlands had been in 1600, having reached a level similar to that reached in England a century earlier.

The truly exceptional character of the surge of urbanisation in England in the eighteenth century is only partially apparent from Figure 3.8. Urban growth became widespread throughout western Europe in the first half of the nineteenth century, but in the preceding century it was concentrated to an astonishing degree in England alone. If the 'net' gain in urban population between any two dates is defined as the number by which the urban population exceeded that which would have obtained if the urban percentage had not changed in the interim, then England alone accounted for 57 per cent of the net gain in urban population in western Europe as a whole in the first half of the eighteenth century and as much as 70 per cent in the second half (Wrigley 1987c: 177–80, esp. tab. 7.7, 179). Since even in 1800 England contained such a small fraction of the population of Europe, this degree of concentration is extraordinary. Urban growth in England was not only radically different in scale from urban growth elsewhere in the long eighteenth century, it was also very different in character. In England only four of the ten largest towns in 1670 were still in the top ten in 1801. London was, of course, always the largest city. In 1670 it was followed by Norwich, Bristol, York and Newcastle. Of these four, only Bristol, Newcastle and Norwich survived in the top ten in 1801, when they were respectively fifth, ninth and tenth. All the others in the list were newcomers. Manchester, Liverpool and Birmingham were second, third and fourth, with Leeds, Sheffield and Plymouth occupying the other places. The equally meteoric rise of Glasgow ensured that the Scottish experience paralleled that of England in the eighteenth century. In France, in contrast, eight of the ten cities which formed the top ten in 1650 were still there in 1800, and the two which had disappeared in 1800 had been eighth and tenth in 1650 (Wrigley 1987c: tab. 7.1, 160–1; de Vries 1984: app. 1, 273–5). The French experience was common throughout the continent. The urban hierarchy was radically revised in England far earlier than in other European countries. It is also noteworthy that, although London was always by far the biggest city in England, during the long eighteenth century it grew little faster than the population of the country as a whole. London held about 9.5 per cent of the national total in 1670 and 11 per cent in 1801, whereas other urban centres expanded spectacularly from 4.0 to 16.5 per cent of the national total over the same period (Wrigley 1987c: tab. 7.2, 162).

Given the scale of urban growth, it is hardly surprising that there were also major changes in occupational structure in early modern England. Until the nineteenth century the available information about this aspect of economic life is limited and frequently either difficult to interpret with confidence or subject to wide margins of error. Some things, however, are clear. In 1800 a much lower percentage of the labour force was working on the land in England than anywhere else in Europe, with the exception of the Low Countries. It is probable that the absolute size of the agricultural labour force changed very little between 1600 and 1800. Since population was rising fast, this implies a major fall in the proportion of the workforce on the land, from perhaps 70 per cent in 1600 to about 55 per cent in 1700 and close to 40 per cent in 1800. By 1851 agriculture employed less than 25 per cent of the male labour force (Wrigley 1987c: tab. 7.4, 170;

1986: tab. 11.12, 332: the figures for 1800 and 1851 refer to the male labour force; those for 1600 and 1700 relate to the proportion of the population dependent on agriculture for a living). The change appears to have been progressive throughout the period 1600–1800. King and Massie, who each made estimates of the social and economic composition of the national population, divided the population into categories which do not readily equate with the divisions which are now conventional. As a result, assumptions must be made about the allocation to occupational groupings of categories which represented status rather than occupation: the allocation, for example, of cottars between agriculture and other employments. In my view, however, their estimates support the figures just quoted. My interpretation of their data yields a figure of about 60 per cent of families working in agriculture for King (1688) and 50 per cent for Massie (1760). If the assumptions made in arriving at this interpretation of their work are justified, they support the picture just outlined (Wrigley 1987c: 171–2; see also Mathias 1979b).

Urban growth accounts for only part of the rapid rise in the proportion of the population finding a living from non-agricultural occupations. By 1800 about half of the population of rural England was no longer dependent on agriculture for employment. Indeed, between 1600 and 1800 rural non-agricultural employment may well have accounted for a slightly larger share of the overall growth in employment outside agriculture than is attributable to the growth of urban employment (Wrigley 1987c: tab. 7.4, 170). This was the fruit of Smithian growth, of the successful exploitation of the opportunities for growth afforded by an organic economy. Its momentum dominated the growth process throughout the long eighteenth century. It remained powerful until well into the nineteenth century. When Rickman made provision for more extensive occupational returns in the 1831 census than he had in the three earlier censuses, the distinction which he drew between manufacturing on the one hand, and retail trade and handicraft on the other, though not very clearly defined in the instructions sent to the overseers of the poor, proved in practice to correspond closely to the distinction between the production of goods for large, dispersed, national or international markets and the production of goods and services for a local market. The former, in other words, embraced both factory-based production and forms of employment, such as framework knitting, where production was still domestic but the market was large and remote. Both such forms of employment were heavily concentrated in limited areas. The retail trades and handicrafts, in contrast, were widely spread throughout the country, forming a stable fraction of local employment and serving the immediate locality almost exclusively (Wrigley 2002).

Manufacturing employment in England in 1831 was dwarfed by employment in retail trade and handicraft. The former employed 314,000 males aged 20 and over compared with a total of 964,000 engaged in the latter, 10.4 per cent and 32.0 per cent respectively of the total of males aged 20 and over; and while 55 per cent of all manufacturing employment was to be found in Lancashire and the West Riding of Yorkshire alone, retail trade and handicraft employment was distributed in a notably even fashion throughout the kingdom (Wrigley 1986: 297 n. 8 and tab. 11.2, 300–1). The largest individual occupations in the latter in declining order of size in 1831 were: shoemaker, carpenter, tailor, publican, shopkeeper, blacksmith, mason, butcher, bricklayer and baker. The first four of these occupations alone between them employed almost as many men as the whole of manufacturing. Furthermore, employment in the ten trades collectively grew by 39.3 per cent between 1831 and 1851, a period during which the national population increased by only 26.2 per cent (Wrigley 1986: tab. 11.2, 300–1; Wrigley et al. 1997: tab. A9.1, 614–15). Any account of the early nineteenth century which focuses exclusively on those industries which were ultimately to dominate the national economy will overlook some of the most substantial growth areas of the time.

The dominant feature of the English economy in the long eighteenth century was the transformation in agricultural productivity which took place between the end of Elizabeth's reign and the beginning of Victoria's. The striking increase in output per acre has long been remarked; that in output per head less so, but the latter underwrote success elsewhere in the economy. Although the scale of the change may be difficult to pinpoint accurately, and both the timing and the causes of the change remain controversial, it was certainly substantial. Overton offers two calculations of its size, based on 'population' and on 'output'. The two methods produce a contrasting picture of the phasing of the increase between 1700 and 1850, but are in agreement that productivity per head roughly doubled over the period as a whole (Overton 1996a: tabs 3.8(b) and 3.8(c), 82). Nor should it be overlooked that, since agricultural labourers earned less than workers in most other employments, the parallel rise in non-agricultural employment implies a rise in average incomes through compositional change independent of any additional benefits gained from rising wages in particular employments.

The great majority of those no longer working on the land were employed, as we have seen, in local service and handicraft industries. To many of these industries the parable of the pinmakers, which Adam Smith told to illustrate the vast possibilities for rising output per head where the scale of the market allowed division of function, hardly applied. Shoemakers, carpenters, tailors, publicans, butchers and the like, if they continued to serve only a local market, possessed neither the means nor the opportunity to achieve large gains in productivity, yet such occupations remained the source of livelihood for a very substantial fraction of all non-agricultural employment until well into the nineteenth century. The significance of the increase in production per head in agriculture is underlined by this consideration.

CONCLUSION

The long eighteenth century was a period in which the demographic history of Britain presented a great contrast with that of the continent. Population growth was far faster than across the Channel, though not swifter than in much of Scandinavia. Demographic growth, however, though notable, was outstripped by economic growth. The British economy in the long eighteenth century achieved a degree of aggregate growth unrivalled elsewhere in Europe. In 1820 it appears from Maddison's estimates that gross domestic product per head in Britain was about 36 per cent higher than in the Netherlands and 44 per cent higher than in France (Maddison 1982: tab. 1.4, 8 and 167). For England alone the gap would be still wider (Wrigley 2000: 118–19). The British advantage compared with Germany, Italy or Spain must have been substantially greater. If, for argument's sake, it is assumed conservatively that GDP per head was 50 per cent higher than in France, the Netherlands, Germany, Spain and Italy combined in 1820, and noting that whereas population in these five countries combined rose by about 50 per cent between 1680 and 1820, the British population rose by 140 per cent, the scale of the contrast in overall growth is evident (Wrigley 1987c: tab. 9.1, 216; the Scottish population was assumed to have been 1.0 million in 1680, 2.1 million in 1820). How large the gap between British and continental levels of GDP per head had been at the start of the long eighteenth century is uncertain, indeed essentially guesswork. Suppose, however, that the difference in 1680 was 25 per cent rather than 50 per cent, and suppose further that GDP per head on the continent rose on average by 20 per cent during the period. On these assumptions, the GDP of the continental countries would have increased by 80 per cent ($100 \times 1.5 \times 1.2$): over the same period the British GDP would have risen by 246 per cent ($100 \times 2.4 \times (180/125)$), a massive relative gain.

During the period 1680–1820, the great bulk of the expansion taking place was attributable to the 'old' rather than the 'new' economy, to the remarkably successful exploitation of the possibilities of an advanced organic economy rather than to the prospects opened up by the new mineral-based energy economy. Contemporaries were doubtful about the future and their forebodings were not without foundation (Wrigley 1987b). Adam Smith feared that no country would prove able to avoid the fate which was overtaking the Dutch Republic (A. Smith 1961 [1776]: I, 101–10). The work of de Vries and van der Woude in describing and analysing the dynamic rise and subsequent stagnation of the Dutch economy shows that 'modernity', the advent of a capitalist economy, is not a guarantee of indefinite growth (de Vries and van der Woude 1997: 711; Wrigley 2000: 133–7).

All pre-industrial economies experience a tension between production and reproduction, the tension which Malthus, as a young man, attempted to capture by contrasting arithmetical and geometric growth rates (Malthus 1986a [1798]: 8–10). Ultimately, Britain might well have found it impossible to avoid crippling difficulties if it had not succeeded in gradually ceasing to be an organic economy. In areas of ancient settlement the mass of the population in organic economies usually paid a bitter price for rapid population growth. As the eighteenth century drew towards its close there were signs that the familiar pattern was about to be repeated in Britain. That the signs faded over the next half century, to be replaced by harbingers of a new age, was made possible *inter alia* by the transformation of the energy base of the economy and the concomitant escape from the constraints imposed on the output of secondary industry as long as its raw materials were almost exclusively derived from plants and animals, and therefore limited by the productivity of the land (Wrigley 1988: chs. 2 and 3). Yet the advent of the new should not obscure what was achieved within the older, organic economy. Britain experienced its greatest growth relative to its neighbours during the long eighteenth century while still dominantly an organic economy, managing to cope successfully, if not without strain, with a prolonged period of population growth which, at its peak, was faster than at any other time in British history.

Despite the rapidity of the population growth which took place, there was nothing remarkable about the strictly demographic attributes of the English population in the long eighteenth century. Marital fertility was not exceptionally high. In much of France and Germany it was higher. Nor was mortality notably low. Throughout the period there was a close similarity in both level and trend between mortality in England and in Scandinavia, especially so in the case of Denmark. Moderate levels of marital fertility and unremarkable levels of mortality, however, proved sufficient to produce a surge in population unmatched elsewhere in Europe.

More unusual perhaps were the constraints and feedback mechanisms, the economic structures and cultural conventions which influenced the attitudes and behaviour of individual men and women. The tendency for nuptiality trends to mirror secular changes in the real wage, for example, was potentially of major importance in preserving or enhancing living standards and so creating an aggregate demand structure favourable to innovation and investment. Though the nature of the link between the two trends and its explication remain controversial, it is none the less clear that its possibility turned on the existence of a particular set of conventions and a distinctive social milieu. A combination of the general rule that there should be no more than one married couple per household with the fact that a majority of young people of both sexes spent a part of their adolescence and early adulthood in service away from the parental household meant that on marriage a young couple needed to command the resources to establish a new household and further that their ability to do so was often dependent principally on their prior earnings rather than a decision made by the older generation (Hajnal 1965, 1983; Laslett 1972a, 1977; Anderson 1980, 1990; Kussmaul 1981; R. M. Smith 1981).

But there were many other features of early modern English society which may have played an important role in helping to maintain an easy balance between production and reproduction. It seems probable, for example, that the nature of the poor law was important in enabling the victims of life-cycle difficulties – the elderly, the crippled, the sick, the widowed, the orphaned – to survive with a degree of dignity. The poor law must have tended to lessen the importance of kinship ties and obligations, and it may also have encouraged freer movement between parishes. Or again, as Malthus in his maturity pointed out, the nature of an increasingly capitalist agriculture may have had highly important implications both for living standards and for mobility. He sketched a distinction widely employed at times by development economists when analysing the weaknesses of traditional, 'peasant' society. If, as he re-marked, a capitalist farmer has no reason to retain in his employment any man whose product does not at least equal the value of the wage paid to him, the failure of the *marginal* producer to be a net contributor to income will provoke movement off the land.[16] In contrast the peasant family's system of values may be such that no one leaves the family hold-ing until the *average* product has fallen to the level of subsistence. The two contrasting cases are extreme and artificially simple, but a structural difference in this regard may help to explain why in the nineteenth cen-tury the percentage of total income contributed by the agricultural sector in England was roughly equal to its share of the labour force, whereas in many continental countries the former was far smaller than the latter (Crafts 1985: tab. 3.4, 57).

A very long list of comparable topics might be compiled. The inter-weaving of production and reproduction is fundamental to the life of any society in any age. Elucidating the relationship presents a host of op-portunities, balanced by as many challenging difficulties. In one respect, however, matters have advanced substantially in recent decades. The mar-gin of uncertainty relating to changes in the main demographic variables determining reproduction, which in this sense, of course, includes mor-tality and nuptiality no less than fertility, has narrowed to the point where it seems reasonable to assert that it is little if any greater for the long eighteenth century than for the century which succeeded it.

---

[16] 'Upon the principle of private property . . . it could never happen [a situation in which population growth was pushed to a limiting extreme]. With a view to the individual interest, either of a landlord or farmer, no labourer can ever be employed on the soil, who does not produce more than the value of his wages; and if these wages be not on an average sufficient to maintain a wife, and rear two children to the age of marriage, it is evident that both the population and produce must come to a stand' (Malthus 1986b [1826]: 405).

4

Agriculture during the industrial revolution, 1700–1850

ROBERT C. ALLEN

Contents

Introduction   96
The rise of the great estate   98
Outputs   101
Inputs   103
   Land   103
   Labour   104
   Capital   106
Productivity growth   107
   Farm methods and productivity growth   108
   Farm size and productivity growth   110
   Enclosure and productivity growth   110
Agrarian change and economic growth   114
A longer-term perspective   116

INTRODUCTION

British agriculture developed in a distinctive manner that made important contributions to economic growth. By the early nineteenth century, agricultural labour productivity was one third higher in England than in France, and each British farm worker produced over twice as much as his Russian counterpart (Bairoch 1965; O'Brien and Keyder 1978; Wrigley 1985; Allen 1988, 2000). Although the yield per acre of grains was no higher in Britain than in other parts of north-western Europe, the region as a whole reaped yields twice those in most other parts of the world (Allen and O'Gráda 1988; Allen 1992.)

Most accounts of British farming link the high level of efficiency to Britain's peculiar agrarian institutions. In many parts of the continent, farms were small, operated by families without hired labour and often owned by their cultivators. Farms often consisted of strips scattered in open fields, and animals were often grazed on commons. Peasant farming of this sort was consolidated by the French Revolution. In contrast, in Britain, the open fields were enclosed, farm size increased and tenancy became general. While this transformation had been underway since the middle ages, it reached its culmination during the industrial revolution. Furthermore, it is often claimed that the agrarian transformation made important contributions to industrialisation by increasing output and supplying the industrial economy with labour and capital.

One of the most basic questions is the timing and nature of the agricultural revolution. Toynbee (1969 [1884]), Mantoux (1905), Ernle (1961) and mostly recently Overton (1996a, 1996b) located the agricultural revolution in the eighteenth century, and their revolution comprised both institutional change and the modernisation of farm methods. In contrast, most twentieth-century historians have emphasised that much productivity growth occurred before 1700 and have tended to decouple improvements in farming from enclosure and farm size increases. Certainly by 1700 crop yields were higher than in the middle ages, labour productivity had increased, and output per worker in English farming was already 55 per cent higher than in France. The first half of the nineteenth century was also a time of sustained improvement, but a question mark hangs over the eighteenth century: some scholars see it as a period of stasis; others as a century of steady progress. The importance of enclosure and large-scale farming as bases for productivity growth is not independent of this issue since enclosure and farm amalgamation progressed so substantially during the eighteenth century. The relationships between productivity growth, rural social structure and agriculture's role in economic development remain fundamental questions of historical research.

A broad chronological and geographical perspective is needed for an assessment of British agriculture during the industrial revolution. Historians of farming concentrate on biological indicators like the yield of an acre or the weight of a fleece, but from an economic perspective the productivity of labour is a more critical variable since a larger fraction of the population can be employed off the farm if each cultivator produces more food. Figure 4.1 shows output per worker in six European countries from 1300 to 1800, and this helps put the achievements of British farming into perspective. In Italy, France and Germany agricultural labour productivity declined slowly after 1400, although France shows slight improvement in the eighteenth century. The renowned husbandry of medieval Flanders meant that productivity was exceptionally high in present-day Belgium. Population pressure in later centuries meant that output per worker slumped, but it still remained above the level on most of the continent. The well-known agricultural revolutions of the early modern period – those of the Dutch and the English – stand out in the figure. Output per worker in English farming leapt from the continental norm in 1600 to a

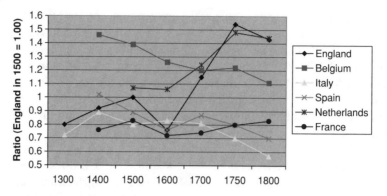

Figure 4.1 Output per worker in agriculture, 1300–1800

Source: Allen 2000: 21.

leading position in 1750. It is important that this advance occurred before the industrial revolution, and, indeed, that there was no further advance between 1750 and 1800. It is also important that England's advances did not push her efficiency above that of the Low Countries.

The modernisation of agriculture took place in the context of fluctuating farm prices. They fell during the second quarter of the eighteenth century – the so called agricultural depression – and then increased erratically until the 1790s. Corn prices doubled and tripled during the harvest years of 1795, 1799 and 1800, and the price level remained high and volatile until the end of the Napoleonic Wars. Then began a slide of prices that lasted until the middle of the nineteenth century. The pace of improvement of farm methods may have been a determinant of the price history through its impact on agricultural supply, but tariff policy and increased market integration also played a role. The fluctuations in the price level certainly affected the evolution of farming and rural society in general. Rising prices after 1750 and especially during the Napoleonic Wars accelerated enclosure; the high prices of the 1790s threatened the standard of living of the rural poor, gave rise to radicalism, and brought on changes in poor relief like the Speenhamland system; landowners who had gained from the high prices of 1795–1815 sought to preserve their rent rolls in the succeeding deflation through the corn laws, which imposed substantial duties on imported grain (Hueckel 1981).

THE RISE OF THE GREAT ESTATE

Eighty per cent of Britain's farm land lay in England and Wales, which produced 89 per cent of Britain's farm output in the mid-nineteenth century (Feinstein 1978: 635, n. 55; cf. Solar 1983 and Table 4.1). While the agriculture of the Scottish Highlands was revolutionised by the clearances, the changes that affected the largest share of British agriculture occurred mainly in England and comprised the enclosure of the open fields, the growth in farm size and the consolidation of the great estate. Hence, discussion will focus on the English story. Many of the changes in farm methods and management affected Scottish agriculture as well.

Over half of the farm land in medieval England was organised in open fields and commons. Under this system, the land of the village was divided rigidly between arable and pasture. Holdings of arable consisted of strips scattered around the village. The strips were grouped into several large fields, which were also often units in a crop rotation. Three fields were common, in which case one was planted with wheat or rye, the second with barley, oats, beans or peas, and the third was fallow. Each year the fields shifted to the next phase in the sequence. Every farmer had to follow this communally agreed plan. The grass of the village included the meadow on which hay was cut, and the common where the sheep and cattle were pastured in a village herd. In densely settled regions, the commons were small, but in many parts of the kingdom there were great tracts of waste used as common pasture for sheep. The herd was also turned onto the fallow field, as well as the other fields after they were harvested, in order to eat weeds and manure the land.

Enclosed farming was the antithesis of the open field system. When land was enclosed, the owners usually exchanged strips and divided commons, so that each proprietor had large, consolidated blocks of property. Communal rotations and grazing were abolished. Each owner acquired exclusive control over his property, so every farmer could cultivate as he pleased without reference to the rest of the community. In 1500, about 45 per cent of the farm land in England was already enclosed, and most of that had probably never been open. The open fields in 1500 included much of the grain growing land in the country. In 1700, 29 per cent of England remained open or common, and the proportion shrank to 5 per cent in 1914, where it remains today (Wordie 1983: 502). This phase of the enclosure movement was particularly intense in the Midlands, where over half of the farmland was enclosed in the eighteenth and nineteenth centuries (Wordie 1983: 500). Most of the remaining open land was common pasture.

In the eighteenth century, much of the enclosing was accomplished by parliamentary act. In such an enclosure the principal landowners of the village petitioned parliament for a bill to enclose their village. Unanimity of the owners was not required: in general the owners of 75 per cent to 80 per cent of the land had to be in favour in order for the bill to proceed. Since landownership was highly concentrated, an enclosure could – and often did – proceed with a majority of small proprietors opposed. In the memorable phrase of the Hammonds (1924: 25), 'the suffrages were not counted but weighed'. The bill named commissioners, who carried out the enclosure, and endorsed their award in advance. The commissioners held hearings in the village, identified the proprietors, appointed a surveyor who mapped the village and valued each holding, and finally reallocated the land so that each proprietor (including those who opposed the enclosure) received a grant of land in proportion to the value of his or her holdings in the open fields. A total of 3,093 acts enclosed 4,487,079 acres of open field and common pasture in this manner. A further 2,172 acts were concerned exclusively with the enclosure of an additional 2,307,350 acres of common pasture and waste (Turner 1980: 26, 178).

A second major change was an increase in farm size. In the middle ages demesnes were already several hundred acres, but the farms of serfs were usually 30 acres or less (Kosminski 1956; Allen 1992). During the population decline in the fourteenth and fifteenth centuries, farm size increased. Estate surveys show that the average farm – including demesnes, copyholds and leased land – in northern England and in open field villages in southern England was 65 acres in *c.* 1700. Enclosed farms in the south were already larger, however. In the eighteenth century, small farms were amalgamated into large ones in open field villages in the south, and throughout the north. By 1800, 150 acres was the average across all types of farms in the south, and 100 acres was the average in the north (Wordie 1974; Allen 1988).

The growth in farm size was accompanied by a revolution in land tenure. Many small farms in 1700 either were owned outright by their occupiers or were held on very long term agreements like copyholds for lives or beneficial leases. During the eighteenth century, small freeholds were bought up by great estates and manorial lords stopped renewing copyholds for lives and beneficial leases. The formerly yeomen lands passed into the hands of the gentry and aristocracy. The small farms were amalgamated into large and were then leased to large-scale farmers. The result was the consolidation of the great estate and the emergence of the three-tiered social structure of rich landlord, substantial tenant farmer and poor landless labourer.

Eighteenth-century agricultural improvers regarded enclosure and the creation of large farms as prerequisites for the modernisation of agriculture, and this view has become widespread among historians. Since enclosing began on a large scale in the late fifteenth century, the defenders have argued that it led to the adoption of modern methods. Quesnay, the French physiocrat, advanced the view that higher farm output required more investment, and that only large-scale farmers had access to the requisite capital. Arthur Young adopted this view and merged it with the claim that enclosure also led to modernisation. For Young (1774: 287–8), the large 'farmer, with a greater proportional wealth than the small occupier, is able to work great improvements in his business . . . He also employs better cattle and uses better implements; he purchases more manures, and adopts more improvements.' Open fields inhibited this style of farming since they gave the small, backward farmers the power to check the initiative of the large-scale entrepreneur. Enclosure was essential to set free the process of investment and modernisation.

In the eighteenth century, there was a consensus that enclosure and large-scale farming raised output. There was, however, a deep difference of opinion about the impact of these changes on employment. One group, whose origins ran back to the earliest critics of enclosure, argued that enclosures and large farms reduced employment in agriculture. By the seventeenth century, in an ironic twist, some advocates of this view were defending enclosures on the grounds that the expulsion of people from farming created a manufacturing workforce (Fortrey 1663). This, of course, became Marx's view on the subject. The other group argued that enclosures and large farms increased agricultural employment since they led to more intensive cultivation. Young endorsed this position, and argued that, none the less, large farms and enclosures stimulated manufacturing since they increased food production, which led to a larger population, most of whom were employed off the farm. The claims that enclosure raised employment and that the industrial workforce was the result of population growth (rather than the release of labour from agriculture) have become standard views since their restatement by Chambers (1953).

The role of enclosure and large farms in raising output, the impact of these changes on employment, the contribution that agricultural change made to manufacturing development – these issues remain central questions of English history. A first step in analysing them is to consider broad trends in agricultural outputs and inputs.

OUTPUTS

Despite its importance, the rate of output growth remains a controversial issue. In the absence of agricultural censuses, estimates must be constructed from diverse data using indirect methods and strong assumptions. Alternative approaches point to different periods as those of fastest growth. Moreover, agriculture has recapitulated the experience of industry as more recent estimates of the growth rate are lower than earlier ones. There are four important approaches.

Direct aggregation is the most straightforward. In this approach, output is measured by valuing the production of the various farm products with a set of constant prices. Chartres (1985) and Holderness (1989) estimated the output of the main farm products in 1700, 1800 and 1850. Valuing them with 1815 prices implies that output grew at 0.8 per cent from 1700 to 1800 and at 0.9 per cent per year in the next half century. The similarity of the growth rate in the two periods is unique.

Income deflation is the second approach. It relies on the accounting identity that the value of agricultural output equals value added (on the assumption of no purchased inputs), which, in turn, equals the sum of agricultural incomes (wages plus rents plus profits). For 1800–50, Deane

Table 4.1 Agricultural output, 1700–1850		
	1700–1800	1800–50
Deane and Cole	0.4%	1.5%
Crafts	0.5%	1.2%
Aggregation of farm products	0.8%	0.9%
Population	0.5%	1.1%
Demand curve I	0.3%	–
Demand curve II	0.2%	1.1%

Notes and sources: Deane and Cole (1969: 78, 170) used a population-based extrapolation for 1700–1800 and deflated income for 1800–50. The figure shown here for 1800–50 is their estimate for 1811/21–1841/51.
Crafts (1985: 42) used a demand curve for 1700–1800 and deflated income for the nineteenth century. The estimate for 1800–50 shown here applies to 1801–31.
Aggregation of farm products – Allen 1994: 102.
Population – Overton 1996a: 86
Demand curve I – Jackson 1985.
Demand curve II – Allen 1999.

and Cole (1969: 72–5, 164–73) deflated estimates of the latter with an index of agricultural prices to compute real agricultural production. Crafts followed the same procedure for this period. The output index, of course, is no better than the quantity and price series of labour, land and capital that go into the calculation. All of these are uncertain. Deflation is particularly difficult in the early nineteenth century when the price level was so volatile.

Population is the basis of the third approach. It assumes that per capita consumption of agricultural goods was constant, and then uses population as an index of agricultural output, making an allowance for imports and exports. Deane and Cole used this procedure for the eighteenth century, and Overton applied it to the whole period 1500–1850. These calculations show little output growth in the first half of the eighteenth century but rapid growth thereafter in line with the increase in the population.

A demand curve is posited in the fourth approach. Crafts (1976, 1985a: 38–44) effectively debunked the population method by pointing out that constant per capita consumption was inconsistent with the high income and price elasticities of demand found for developing countries as well as for eighteenth-century England. Clark, Huberman and Lindert (1995) forcefully pressed the point for the first half of the nineteenth century. Crafts specified a demand curve for farm goods in which quantity demanded depended on population, per capita income, and the price of agricultural and manufactured goods. Jackson (1985), Clark (1993), Clark *et al.* (1995) and Allen (1999) have proposed variants of this approach. All indicate slow growth in the second half of the eighteenth century: the rise in farm prices from 1750 to 1800 implies that output was growing less rapidly than population and demand.

Table 4.1 summarises the output growth rates implied by the various methods. For the eighteenth century, the aggregation of the Chartres–Holderness production figures gives distinctly the fastest growth. In all likelihood, however, farm output is underestimated in 1700. Wheat has been studied intensively by other scholars. Holderness put the yield at 16 bushels per acre *c*. 1700, and Overton (1996a: 77) concurred, although his own work on probate inventories for Norfolk, Suffolk and Lincolnshire implied an average yield of about 18.5 for the early eighteenth century (Overton 1991: 302–3). More recent scholarship points to higher values. Turner, Beckett and Afton (2001: 129), who have compiled information from farmers' account books, put the yield of wheat in excess of 20 bushels early in the eighteenth century. Brunt (1999) arrived at a similar figure using econometric models of weather and farming methods. Turner *et al.*'s (2001: 163–4) yields for barley and beans are also considerably in excess of the yields assumed by Holderness–Chartres. The upward revisions in the yield estimates for the early eighteenth century cast considerable doubt on the production aggregation approach especially *c.* 1700.

The population-based estimates of Deane and Cole and Overton imply slower growth, but their maintained assumption of constant per capita consumption is hard to credit. Crafts's estimate based on a demand curve is superior methodologically. It implies faster output growth than the calculations of Jackson and Allen, which are also based on demand curves. The difference arises since Crafts used GDP to measure income, whereas Jackson and Allen used wages, which grew less rapidly. The latter is probably more pertinent to the food market than GDP, which also includes profits and rents. These considerations suggest that agricultural output grew at 0.2–0.3 per cent per year in the eighteenth century.

In the first half of the nineteenth century, Deane and Cole's deflation of agricultural income gives distinctly the highest estimate of output growth. There is remarkable agreement among the other procedures. The consensus is that agricultural production grew at about 1.1 per cent per year in the first half of the nineteenth century. This was markedly faster than in the eighteenth century.

INPUTS

Farm output went up for two reasons: the land, labour and capital used by agriculture increased, and those inputs generated more output owing to improvements in farm methods and organisation. As with output, there is considerable uncertainty as to the exact magnitudes of the inputs. The figures discussed here relate to England and Wales rather than Great Britain.

Land

The main sources that describe land use are contemporary estimates. As part of his social accounts for 1688, Gregory King estimated the acreage of arable, pasture, etc. W. T. Comber did the same in 1808, and his estimates agree in broad outline with B. P. Capper's figures for 1801. The noted agricultural writer James Caird produced further estimates for 1850–1. Table 4.2 applies King's, Comber's and Caird's figures to 1700, 1800 and 1850, respectively. The most remarkable development was the growth in arable, pasture and meadow, which increased from 21 million acres *c.* 1700 to 29.1 million *c.* 1800 to 30.6 million *c.* 1850. In the eighteenth

Table 4.2 Utilisation of English and Welsh Land, 1700–1850			
	c. 1700	*c.* 1800	*c.* 1850
Arable	11	11.6	14.6
Pasture and meadow	10	17.5	16.0
Woods and coppices	3	1.6	1.5
Forest, parks, commons	3		
Waste	10	6.5	3.0
Buildings, water, roads	1	1.3	2.2
Total	38	38.5	37.3
Total agricultural	34	35.6	33.6
Index of land input	1.00	1.35	1.37

Source: Allen 1994: 104.

century, the growth was mainly in pasture and meadow; in the nineteenth century, it was the arable that expanded. These increases were accomplished by corresponding reductions in wood, common and waste. Some of this change was spurious: 'waste' has always been used to graze sheep, and thus has always been agricultural land. However, there was probably also a real improvement in the quality of the land – pastures were drained, fertilised and reseeded. Great tracts of land in northern and western England were developed into improved grazing in this way. In eastern England, arable was often the result. Young's (1813a: 2, 99, 100) account of Lincolnshire gives a flavour of the changes. He described the improvement of the heath near Lincoln 'which formerly was covered with heath, gorse, &c. and yielding, in fact, little or no produce, converted by enclosure, to profitable arable farms'. Much land had been improved, 'for these heaths extend near seventy miles'. On the coast, 'there spreads a great extent of lowland, much of which was once marsh and fen; but now become, by the gradual exertions of above 150 years, one of the richest tracts in the kingdom'.

Labour

The agricultural workforce is much more difficult to count than the acreage of farm land or even the volume of production. The subject is bedevilled by the problems of part-time work, unpaid family work, and people dividing their time between farming and proto-industry. Perhaps for these reasons, King tallied much of the population as 'labourers' and 'cottagers' without assigning them to agriculture, commerce or manufacturing. Massie did the same with his social table for 1759 (Lindert and Williamson 1982). Estimates of the agricultural workforce must be erected on a basis other than contemporary estimates.

The oldest view about the size of the agricultural workforce – and one that appeals to common sense – is that it declined during the industrial revolution. This view is supported by the long-standing notion that enclosures were driving people off the land into the factories. Both of these positions have been called into question by historians. In particular, Deane and Cole (1969: 142–3) have used the occupational information in the nineteenth-century censuses to argue that farm employment in Great Britain increased from 1.7 million in 1801 to 2.1 million in 1851. Although they describe their 1801 employment estimates as 'little more than guesses', the idea that agricultural employment expanded during the industrial revolution (albeit at a slower rate than manufacturing employment) has become the standard view.

While the 1851 census does provide an acceptable basis for calculating the agricultural workforce at the end of the industrial revolution, the early censuses are not nearly so reliable, and, in any event, cannot be used to push the esti- mates back before 1800. Indirect meth-

Table 4.3   Employment in English and Welsh agriculture, 1700–1850 (thousands)

	1700	1800	1850
Men	612	643	985
Women	488	411	395
Boys	453	351	144
Total	1553	1405	1524
Index of labour input	1.00	0.95	1.16

Source: Allen 1994: 107.

ods are necessary. One procedure is to combine information from estate surveys with the returns collected by Arthur Young on his English tours (Allen 1988). Young was a noted agricultural improver and prolific writer. He travelled through most English counties in the 1760s and reported the details of several hundred farms. Since the information includes the size and land use pattern of the farm as well as the number of regu- larly employed men, women and boys, equations can be estimated that correlate employment with variables like farm size. Applying those rela- tionships to the distribution of farm sizes shown by estate surveys allows estimates of the agricultural labour force. The estimates encompass only those steadily employed: additional labour was hired during peak periods like the harvest. While important, the total number of hours worked by the additional labourers was small compared to the contribution of the regularly employed.

Table 4.3 shows that there was little long-run change in the English agricultural workforce. The total number employed fell between 1700 and 1800, then rebounded to 1851 when the total was still less than it had been in 1700. Weighting the employment of men, women and boys by the wage rates recorded by Young produces an index of the quantity of labour. It increased marginally over the period. Since the acreage of improved farm land was also rising, employment per acre (as measured by the ratio of the index of labour to the index of land) fell from a value of 1.00 in 1700 to 0.70 in 1800 and then returned to 0.85 in 1850. Even though farm employment was roughly constant, employment per acre declined, especially in the eighteenth century.

The composition of the agricultural workforce also changed signifi- cantly from 1700 to 1850. First, the share of adult males increased from 39 per cent of the workforce to 64 per cent. Second, more of these men were employees rather than farmers since the number of farms was prob- ably falling. Third, most of the hired men in 1851 were day labourers while most had been servants hired by the year in 1700 (Kussmaul 1981). Fourth, while the servants in 1700 had been continuously employed over the year, about one third of the male labourers in 1851 were only em- ployed in peak periods like the harvest. The contrast between 1700 and 1851 is far reaching: in 1700, the agricultural workforce had been built around family labour supplemented by young adults in their late teens and early twenties hired on annual contracts as servants. These categories were still present in 1851, but the workforce had become much older, more male and more erratically employed.

Wrigley (1985, 1986) has also analysed the agricultural labour force over the eighteenth and nineteenth centuries. He estimated that the 'agricultural population' was about 3 million people over the eighteenth century. This figure includes non-working children and retired people. Assuming that the average household had 4.5 members, 3 million people corresponds to 667,000 households – a figure close to the 612,000 and 643,000 adult men shown in Table 4.3. An exact match is not expected, since male servants did not head households and since some women did. Nevertheless, the correspondence confirms the order of magnitude of both calculations. Wrigley's procedure does not permit a separate examination of the employment histories of men, women and children, and so does not pick up the falls in the employment of women and boys.

Wrigley (1986) has also estimated the growth of the adult male agricultural labour force in the first half of the nineteenth century. He found it grew about 10 per cent from 1811 to 1851 when it equalled 1 million, a figure that includes men who only worked in peak periods as well as those steadily employed. Wrigley's estimate of the rate of growth is the right order of magnitude for the growth rate of the total, regularly employed agricultural labour force over the period. However, the number of steadily employed men grew more rapidly than Wrigley's estimate, as men displaced women and boys in farm labour.

Capital

The provision of capital was divided between landlords and tenants. Landlords financed most of the permanent improvements to the property – structures, roads, fences and enclosures. Tenants financed implements and livestock. Tenants also financed a few improvements to the soil such as marling or draining. Their benefits lasted a decade or two and were worthwhile from the tenant's point of view only if the tenant had adequate security. The tenants also had to pay wages, rent, taxes, etc. in advance of the sale of the crops. These expenses did not result in capital formation, strictly speaking, since they did not create assets that lasted longer than one year.

Landowners could finance their investments by mortgaging their property. Tenants obtained their capital in more diverse ways. At the outset, most farmers took over their parents' farms and secured their livestock and implements in that way. Thereafter, they bred their animals. Cash to pay wages and rents was saved from the sale of the previous year's output. Sometimes landlords provided their tenants with capital, for instance when drains were installed. 'At Marston, much draining has been performed on a farm of Mr. Foster's, who pays all of the bushes [to line the drains], except what could be obtained from the farm, and the tenant is to allow interest for the money thus sunk by the landlord' (Batchelor 1808: 476). Money could be borrowed from relatives and other villagers (Holderness 1976). Corn merchants often bought the crop while it was still standing in the fields. According to Defoe (1727: II, part II, 36), 'These Corn-Factors in the Country ride about among the Farmers, and buy the Corn, even in the Barn before it is thresh'd, nay, sometimes they buy it in the Field standing, not only before it is reap'd but before it is ripe.' Whether or not the factors were 'cunningly taking advantage of the farmers by letting them have Money before-hand, which they, poor Men, often want', credit was being extended.

Table 4.4 Capital in English and Welsh agriculture, 1700–1850				
	1700	1750	1800	1850
Landlords				
structures, etc.	112	114	143	232
tenants				
implements	10	8	10	14
farm horses	20	20	18	22
other livestock	41	53	71	85
Total	183	195	242	353

Source: Allen 1994: 109.

Feinstein (1978, 1988) and Holderness (1988) have estimated the growth of capital supplied by farmers and landlords. Their results are shown in Table 4.4. Between 1700 and 1850, both components of capital approximately doubled. During the eighteenth century, capital grew at the same rate as improved farm land, so capital per acre remained constant. From 1800 to 1850, capital per acre rose 40 per cent. Capital was the fastest-growing input.

PRODUCTIVITY GROWTH

The history of outputs and inputs implies that productivity grew from 1700 to 1850. Over that period, land grew 37 per cent, labour 16 per cent and capital 93 per cent. Giving equal weight to each input implies that inputs *in toto* grew by a factor of 1.45 from 1700 to 1850. Output grew by a factor of 2.2 according to the demand curve approach. Total factor productivity increased by 50 per cent (1.52 = 2.2/1.45) or about 0.3 per cent per year over the whole period. In the eighteenth century, inputs grew at 0.2 per cent per year. According to Allen's and Jackson's demand curve estimates, output grew at 0.2–0.3 per cent per year, implying negligible productivity growth (0.0–0.1 per cent per year). From 1800–50, input growth increased to 0.4 per cent per year, but output grew much faster by all measures. Accepting output growth of 1.1 per cent per annum implies TFP growth of 0.7 per cent per year – a much better performance.

Other estimates of output growth, of course, imply other estimates of productivity growth. One can side-step the difficulties in measuring the *quantities* of inputs and outputs by inferring productivity from their *prices*. If efficiency rises, then a farmer can cut his price and still cover his costs.

Hence, a fall in product prices with respect to input prices indicates productivity growth. McCloskey (1981: 114, 126) used this reasoning to compute productivity growth of 0.5 per cent per year for the first half of the nineteenth century. In contrast, Turner, Beckett and Afton's (1997) rents imply higher productivity growth, while Clark (1993: 247; 1998b: 208) has calculated rates ranging from nil to about 0.5 per cent per annum from 1700 to 1850.

The lack of consensus indicates that the price approach is not a quick fix to the productivity measurement problems. Not only does this method require good information on product and factor prices, but it presumes that they equalled marginal costs and the values of marginal products. This condition was probably not satisfied for many inputs, in particular land. Rents, for instance, were not adjusted annually and so could fall behind changes in land values (Allen 1982). In such cases price calculations can give spurious measures of productivity change. The measurement of both prices and quantities needs to be refined to pin down the chronology of the agricultural revolution.

Farm methods and productivity growth

Agricultural productivity rose because output increased and employment per acre declined. No single innovation or institutional change explains these increases. Many reinforcing changes were involved.

Corn output increased because of changes in yields and acreage. In the case of wheat, the yield rose from perhaps 10 bushels per acre – certainly more in Norfolk (Campbell 1983) – at the end of the middle ages to 20 bushels or more in the early eighteenth century (Rogers 1866: I, 38–45; Salzman 1938: II, 60–1; Titow 1972: 121–35; Clark 1991b; Overton 1991; Allen 1992, 1999; Brunt 1997, 1999; Turner *et al.* 2001: 129). Between 1700 and 1850, yields rose little, and output increased because more land was planted as fallow was reduced. The yields of barley, oats and beans also increased in the early modern period; they continued to rise after 1700 so the increase in the production of these crops was not simply due to greater acreage.

The causes of the rise in corn yields are diffuse. First, there were improvements in seed. Farmers collected the seeds from the best plants and grew them separately to isolate high-yielding and disease resistant strains. This practice, which began in the seventeenth century and was responsible for some of the pre-1700 advance of yields over medieval levels, was carried on by enterprising farmers through the eighteenth and probably into the nineteenth centuries (Plot 1677: 151; Marshall 1788: II, 4). Second, heavier manuring may have raised fertility, although Brunt (2000) has called this into question. Third, the cultivation of legumes (beans, peas, clover) increased during the eighteenth century. These crops fixed atmospheric nitrogen and thereby raised soil fertility (Chorley

1981). Fourth, soils were improved by marling and draining. During the Napoleonic Wars, the high price of corn relative to labour made it profitable to install bush drains on heavy clays. By the 1840s, the price of drain tiles fell enough to precipitate another round of drainage investment. Other investments that improved the quality of the soil included paring and burning and the application of lime. Fifth, the diffusion of seed drills and other improved farm machinery resulted in a better seed bed. Historians have not yet been able to pin down the relative importance of these factors, but together they were responsible for the rise in corn output (Brunt 1997). Sixth, regional specialisation increased, so that crops were grown where the natural conditions were most favourable.

Livestock output increased because the herds and flocks became more productive rather than because there were more animals. The number of cattle probably fell from about 4.5 million at the end of the seventeenth century to 3.9 million in the middle of the nineteenth, but the share of productive animals (i.e. dairy cows and those slaughtered) increased. Moreover, the weight of a carcass and the product of a cow rose. Likewise, the number of swine scarcely increased, so the main reason for the rise in pork output was a much greater rate of slaughtering and a very sharp rise in meat per carcass. In the case of sheep, the stock doubled between 1700 and 1850, but the weight of a fleece and the meat per carcass both increased (King 1696: 430; Holderness 1988: 32; 1989: 147–159, 169–70).

Meat per carcass increased for several reasons; improvements in the breed and increases in feed consumption were the main factors. A shift in tastes away from veal and young lamb towards the meat of older animals may have played a minor role as well (Holderness 1989: 155). Stockbreeders created new varieties of sheep, pigs and cattle in an effort to increase the rate of weight again. The earliest and most famous breakthrough was the development of the New Leicester sheep by Robert Bakewell in the mid-eighteenth century. It reached a large size at a younger age than other breeds and it had a higher proportion of flesh to bone. Ellman's subsequent creation of the Southdown had a similar objective. Cattle breeds were also improved. Bakewell and Robert Fowler improved the Longhorn in the mid-eighteenth century, and it had a vogue for fifty years. After 1800 the Shorthorn gained popularity in the north and east as it was improved by Robert and Charles Colling, and by Thomas, John and Richard Booth. In the first half of the nineteenth century, the Hereford emerged as an important fattening breed. Likewise, pigs were improved through the introduction of foreign, particularly Chinese, breeds. Rapid weight gain was the objective of most of these improvements.

The quantity of feed consumed by British livestock was increased by upgrading commons and waste into improved pasture and by cultivating animal feed in the arable rotations. Feed had always been grown by farmers. Much of the oat crop, for instance, was consumed by the farm horses, and peas and beans were often eaten by livestock. In the seventeenth century, the production of feed was increased with the cultivation of turnips and clover on a large scale. By the mid-eighteenth century, the classic Norfolk rotation (turnips–barley–clover–wheat) had emerged. The fallow was eliminated, and the clover and turnips provided winter fodder for animals. Other fodder crops like sainfoin and roots like swedes and mangolds were also introduced into British rotations and fed to livestock. A big reason that sheep and cattle weighed more when they were slaughtered in 1850 than they had in 1750 was because they were eating better.

Farm size and productivity growth

The second reason that agricultural productivity increased during the industrial revolution was because labour per acre declined. The employment of women and boys fell. The employment of men grew slightly but much less than the growth of improved land. The drop in labour per acre resulted from the growth in farm size.

Higher rent was the motive behind the creation of large farms. Big farms could afford to pay a higher rent since their costs were less – in particular, their labour costs. Large farms employed fewer boys per acre than small farms since boys were hard to supervise. The employment of women was also curtailed since their work was often tied to dairying and large mixed farms kept fewer cows per acre. There were also economies in the employment of men. Specialists replaced the ordinary labourer in tasks like tending hedges and caring for sheep. Activities like transporting grain and manure were carried out more efficiently when they were performed by groups of workers than when they were done by individuals. 'In harvest; two drivers, two loaders, two pitchers, two rakers, and the rest at the rick, or in the barn, will dispatch double the work that the same number of hands would do if divided into different gangs on different farms' (Arbuthnot 1773: 8). The growth in the average size of farms was the reason that the total employment of women and boys declined in the eighteenth century, and the employment of men remained constant even as the improved acreage expanded.

Enclosure and productivity growth

The most long-standing explanation for the rise in efficiency is enclosure. Eighteenth-century commentators regarded it as a prerequisite for improvement since the open field system was supposed to have blocked advance. The rigid division of lands into arable and pasture precluded convertible husbandry, which involved alternating lands between the two uses. Collective management of the fields inhibited the adoption of new crops since a consensus was necessary among the farmers in order for change to occur. Pasturing the village livestock in a single herd led to overgrazing, the spread of animal diseases, and the inability to control breeding. According to the critics, 'open-field farmers were impervious to new methods' (Ernle 1961: 199).

Enclosure is supposed to have rectified these problems by bringing land under exclusive private control. Communal controls were abolished, so that each owner – and thus each farmer – had exclusive control over his or her property. The scene was set for the enterprising farmers to take the lead in adopting new crops and improving the quality and care of their animals.

The case for the backwardness of the open fields and the modernity of the enclosures has rested mainly on eighteenth-century commentaries. In an extravagant phrase, for instance, Arthur Young (1813b: 35–6) contrasted 'the Goths and Vandals of open fields' with 'the civilisation of enclosures'. There is some truth to this opinion, but inquiries by historians have shown that open fields were not nearly as backward as has been claimed. Havinden (1961) was one of the first to question the conventional indictment of open fields. He showed that such villages in Oxfordshire did indeed adopt new crops – in this case sainfoin. Yelling (1977: 146–232) strengthened the case with additional local comparisons, but remained unconvinced that open fields were really as flexible as enclosures. Allen (1989) has refined the assessment with a series of regional studies. These show that open field villages adopted new crops and increased the share of grass when these innovations were profitable. However, enclosed villages always adopted the new methods more fully than did open field villages.

Enclosure also led to greater output, but the increase was much less than the growth in production that occurred between 1700 and 1850. Chronology suggests this conclusion: much of the enclosure took place in the second half of the eighteenth century, when agricultural output stopped growing. Comparisons of corn yields in open and enclosed villages buttress the case. The data collected by Arthur Young on his tours of the 1760s show that yields of the main crops were 7–12 per cent: higher in enclosed villages (Allen and O'Gráda 1988: 98). Turner (1986: 691) found a larger increment – 11 per cent to 23 per cent – in his sample drawn from the 1801 crop returns. A limitation common to both of these studies is that they did not standardise the comparisons by soil type. Allen (1989: 72) used data drawn mainly from Board of Agriculture county reports prepared between 1794 and 1816 and divided them into districts with relatively uniform environments. On the boulder clays of Cambridgeshire, Bedfordshire and Huntingdonshire, enclosure resulted in yield increases of 10–39 per cent for beans, barley and oats (but only 3 per cent for wheat) because the consolidation of property facilitated the installation of drains in the furrows that had formerly divided the open field strips. In other regions, the yield increases were generally less than 10 per cent. While enclosure did have some impact on yields, the boost was only a small part of the doubling that took place between the middle ages and the nineteenth century.

Both Turner (1986) and Allen (1992) have combined their findings on yields with estimates of the impact of enclosure on cropping to measure the overall effect on output. Turner found that enclosure had little effect on total corn production, although declines were more frequent than advances. Allen found that enclosure increased corn production on the boulder clays where yields went up substantially, lowered output marginally on light soils where turnip cultivation was introduced, and substantially reduced output where there was large-scale conversion of arable to pasture. Allen also included animal products in his comparison. He found that enclosure raised real farm output 12 per cent on the boulder clays in the East Midlands and by 20 per cent on high-grade fattening pastures. Otherwise, eighteenth-century enclosures led to only minor increases or even reductions. As with the results on yields, the important finding is that the output increases that followed enclosure were small, as was the growth in output that occurred in English and Welsh agriculture during the industrial revolution.

Enclosure affected the inputs in English agriculture as well as the output. The acreage of improved land increased substantially between 1700 and 1850. Enclosure was fundamental to this upgrading. In 1700, the waste that was later improved was legally common land. Only when it was enclosed and brought under individual control was it worthwhile for anyone to improve it.

Enclosure had a small impact on capital formation. The stock of fixed capital increased as landlords paid for the hedging, ditching, road building, etc. that accompanied enclosure. The capital supplied by farmers also increased as flocks were expanded and livestock upgraded to take advantage of the improved pastures and greater production of winter forage. However, Table 4.4 suggests that the total effect was not substantial during the eighteenth century – agricultural capital did not rise greatly before 1800.

The most hotly debated issue is the impact of enclosure on employment. In this regard, one must distinguish the charge that enclosure led to the expropriation of peasant lands from the impact of enclosure on labour demand *per se*. It is probable that many fifteenth-century enclosures did involve lords' usurping the land of small farmers and the destruction and depopulation of the villages concerned (Beresford 1954; Allen 1992). Such extreme results did not occur in the eighteenth and nineteenth centuries, since legal titles were protected in both parliamentary and non-parliamentary enclosures. There were still people at risk of losing property, however – principally cottagers who pastured stock on commons without a legal right to do so. They lost that privilege at enclosure. Moreover, even cottagers with legal common rights may have been worse off after enclosure since their land grants may not have generated as much income as their grazing right had previously. The losses were particularly serious for women (Neeson 1989; Humphries 1990).

There are strongly divergent views on the effect of enclosure on the demand for labour. Critics of enclosure have generally charged that people were put out of work, while defenders have claimed that enclosure created new jobs. In the modern literature, Chambers (1953) has championed the latter view and argued that the improved agriculture required more labour to hoe the turnips, thresh the additional corn, trim the hedges and scour the ditches. Recently, this view has been challenged. Snell (1985) has used poor law evidence to argue that enclosure led to increased seasonal unemployment rather than the greater stability in employment expected by Chambers. Allen (1988) used Young's survey data to measure the impact of enclosure on employment. He found that enclosures had little effect on farm employment unless they led to the conversion of arable to pasture, in which case employment declined. In some regions, eighteenth-century enclosures did have this result. However, the total arable acreage increased slightly in this century (Table 4.2), so enclosure did not lead to a general decline in agricultural employment.

This review of the evidence about the impact of enclosure on agricultural outputs and inputs suggests that it had a positive but small effect on productivity. This conjecture is confirmed by measurements of total factor productivity. McCloskey (1972, 1975, 1989) suggested that the impact of enclosure on productivity could be inferred from the movement of rents. Indeed, a rise in rent was the landlord's incentive to enclose, and, in the eighteenth century, the conventional expectation was a doubling from 10s. to 20s. per acre. A stylised example shows how this increase might have arisen and its relationship to total factor productivity. In an eighteenth-century open field village, output, as measured by farm revenue, was about £3.5 per acre. The cost of the labour, capital and materials applied to the land (including the opportunity cost of the labour and capital of the farmer and his family) was about £3 per acre. The difference, or Ricardian surplus, was £5 or 10s. If the market for farm tenancies were competitive, then rents would have been bid to equal this level. Suppose that enclosure involved no change in employment or capital per acre but resulted in an increase in output to £4 per acre. With costs the same, Ricardian surplus and rent would have risen to £1 (= £4 − £3). In this example, the doubling of rent that followed enclosure was a consequence of the accompanying output increase.

While rents doubled, total factor productivity also increased but by a smaller proportion. Total factor productivity rises when output rises with respect to the 'bundle of inputs' used in production. In both the open and the enclosed village in this example, the 'bundle' is the same – namely £3 of labour, capital and materials per acre of land. Output, however, increased from £3.5 to £4, i.e. by 14 per cent. That is the rise in total factor productivity.

The overall impact of the enclosure of open fields on the growth in productivity in English agriculture was less than 14 per cent for four reasons. First, the rent increase following enclosure was probably less than a doubling (Allen 1992; Clark 1998a). Second, the assumption that rental markets were always in competitive equilibrium so rents always equalled Ricardian surplus has been questioned – the rise in surplus may, in fact, have been less than the rise in rent (Allen 1982). Third, only 21 per cent of the farm land of England and Wales was enclosed between 1700 and 1850. Setting aside the first and second points, the enclosure of the open fields raised the total factor productivity of English and Welsh agriculture only 3 per cent ($=14$ per cent $\times$ 0.21). This is an inconsequential amount compared to the 50 per cent increase that took place over the period.

Enclosure did make another contribution to productivity growth in the same period – namely the reclamation of waste. This contribution can be analysed similarly using Gregory King's figures. In the eighteenth century, about 3 million acres of 'forest, parks, and commons' were enclosed and improved as well as 3 million acres of waste. According to King, the rental value of the first type of land was 3.5s. per acre c. 1700 and the latter was worth 1s. per acre. If the annual value of these lands was raised to 9s., the value of enclosed pasture, then the total value of English agricultural land, increased from £8.75 million to £10.025 million – a gain of 23 per cent. Such a rent gain translates into a total factor productivity increase of about 7 per cent. This increase may well be an overstatement of the efficiency gains of the enclosure of waste since it values the improved land at a rent equal to the most productive land in King's account. The overall conclusion must be that the enclosure movement made little contribution to agricultural productivity growth during the industrial revolution.

AGRARIAN CHANGE AND ECONOMIC GROWTH

Even if enclosure was not of great importance in boosting output or efficiency, it is possible that agricultural change *in toto* made an important contribution to economic development. The potential linkages include:

1. increasing output
2. providing a home market for manufactures
3. generating new capital by increasing the savings from the agricultural surplus
4. releasing capital by reducing the agricultural demand for investment
5. releasing labour by reducing the agricultural demand for workers.

Most of these functions were not performed by British agriculture during the industrial revolution.

1. Output grew less rapidly than the population during the industrial revolution. Production and consumption per head declined, and the drop in consumption would have been much greater had imports not expanded to meet demand. Prices rose to allocate the limited supply of food. The result was downward pressure on working-class living standards and a deterioration in stature during the first half of the nineteenth century. If one asks how British agriculture fed the expanding population during the industrial revolution, the answer is – badly.

2. Agriculture did not provide a home market for manufactures. O'Brien (1985: 780) and Crafts (1985a: 133–4) independently estimated that the consumption of manufactures by agriculturalists increased about one third between 1700 and 1800 – a century when industrial production increased more than threefold (Crafts 1985a: 32). After 1800, the importance of the agricultural market became even less important. Exports and the urban economy absorbed the manufacturing output – not agriculture.

3. Industrial and commercial capital formation were not financed by tapping the agricultural surplus. Landlords received the bulk of the surplus – that is, the value of production less the consumption needs of farmers and labourers – in Britain as rent. While some landlords invested in urban and commercial activities, many borrowed instead. Crouzet (1972: 56) endorsed Postan's (1935: 2) 'view that "surprisingly little" of the wealth of rural England "found its way into the new industrial enterprises"'. Crafts (1985a: 122–5) has calculated that agricultural savings financed little non-agricultural investment.

4. Agriculture did not release capital by reducing its demand for investment. Instead, as Table 4.4 indicates, agricultural capital increased. Any other result would be surprising in view of the eighteenth-century emphasis on rising investment as the source of rising agricultural output.

5. One way in which British agriculture may have contributed to economic growth was through the release of labour. Here the conclusion depends on the definition adopted. The most straightforward meaning of 'labour release' is that farm employment declined. Male employment in agriculture was constant in the eighteenth century and rose in the first half of the nineteenth. The employment of women and children declined throughout. If these 'freed' workers were re-employed in industry, then the resulting rise in manufacturing output would have been an indirect contribution of agrarian change to economic development. But this is a big 'if'. Most of the boys and women did not leave their villages. Only if employment were found in rural industry would it have been found at all. Throughout the industrial revolution, the employment prospects of women in the rural textile industries, their biggest employer, were declining in the face of mounting competition from factories. In 1724, Defoe wrote, 'The Farmers' Wives can get no Diary-Maids . . . truly the Wenches Answer, they won't go to Service at 12*d.* or 18*d.* a week, while they can get 7*s.* to 8*s.* a Week at Spinning' (Pinchbeck 1969 [1930]: 140). By

the 1830s, if not by 1800, these jobs had disappeared. Agricultural redundancies then resulted in structural unemployment rather than increased manufacturing output.

The problem of structural unemployment was greatest in southern England. Williamson (1990: 178–218) has shown that southern urban wages were much higher than rural wages, even allowing for the higher living costs and lower quality of life in the cities. There was no comparable disequilibrium in the north. Despite the fact that a large share of children born in rural England moved to cities when they reached adulthood, migration was not enough to equalise wages. This failure to allocate labour efficiently reduced the national income several per centage points, according to Williamson (1990: 211). The fact that enclosures ceased to be depopulating during the industrial revolution may have meant – ironically – that agrarian change was less significant in raising the national income than traditional accounts suggest.

A LONGER-TERM PERSPECTIVE

This is a dreary assessment. Did agrarian change really contribute so little to the industrial revolution? The answer depends critically on the time period. One reason why the industrial revolution could proceed in the face of a largely static agriculture was that agriculture had already revolutionised itself between 1600 and 1750, as Figure 4.1 shows. In that period, yields, output and labour productivity all increased sharply. Crafts (1985c) has urged that declining farm employment is not the appropriate definition of labour release; instead, he proposes that a rise in output per worker that allows a decline of the fraction of the workforce in agriculture is a more revealing concept. In Crafts's terms, labour was released from British agriculture between 1500 and 1750 when the agricultural share of the population dropped from 74 per cent to 45 per cent and agricultural labour productivity rose 54 per cent (Allen 2000). The agricultural revolution did not run concurrently with the industrial revolution but rather preceded it.

5

Industrialisation and technological change

KRISTINE BRULAND

Contents

Introduction   117
Competing views of innovation and industrialisation   120
Sectoral patterns of technological advance: the
    patenting evidence   122
Sectoral patterns of change: technological histories   126
   Agriculture   126
   Food and food processing   129
   Glass manufacture   133
The 'major innovations'   135
   Textiles   135
   Steam power   142
Conclusion: Interpreting the pattern of technological
    change   145

INTRODUCTION

Technological change was a central component in the industrialisation process of the late eighteenth and early nineteenth centuries, and thus in the making of the modern world economy. Nevertheless, more than two centuries after the beginnings of industrialisation, our understanding of the factors that impelled and shaped the development, diffusion and impact of the new technologies of early industrialisation remains far from complete. As a consequence, important questions concerning the place and interpretation of technological change in industrialisation remain unresolved.

The idea that we know relatively little about the sources and outcomes of innovation in the industrial revolution may seem strange, since there is a large historical literature organised explicitly or implicitly around the idea that technological change and industrialisation are intimately linked. Indeed there are many writers for whom new technologies *are* industrialisation, and so the emergence of new techniques is implicitly

or explicitly a fundamental causal event. But the very size of the literature tends to obscure the fact that it actually tells us rather little about
the dynamics of technological change in the industrial revolution, and
particularly its impacts on growth. So although technological change is
usually seen as a central element in the economics of industrialisation
there is frequently no satisfactory account of the relationships between
technological change and industrial growth. To put it differently, there
are few comprehensive treatments of the technologies involved in the
industrialisation process, in the sense of treatments that integrate economic, social and technological dynamics. Although such a task cannot
be achieved within the space available here, nevertheless this chapter
seeks to describe some broad patterns of technological change during
the first industrial revolution, and to place them within an interpretative framework.

The core theme here is the need to understand innovation and technological change in the industrial revolution as an economy-wide process:
that is, as a broad array of changes, across many activities, proceeding at
uneven rates and with different degrees of 'visibility', but none the less
wide in terms of developments and application. Technology – and hence
technological change – in this context will be seen not just in terms of
the technical performance characteristics of products or processes, but
also in the broader sense of methods of organisation, co-ordination and
management.

This chapter aims to do three things. First, it seeks to map some overall dimensions and distributions of technological change in British manufacturing during the period. The reason for this mapping exercise is
that interpretation of the links between innovation and long-term growth
should rest on an informed empirical understanding of the extent and
character of innovation during the period in question. Second, it discusses
questions related to the interpretation of this pattern of technological
change – its sectoral composition, its radical or incremental character,
its causality and so on. Finally, it discusses historiographical debates on
the connections between technological change and economic growth in
the British economy.

The first section addresses interpretative issues following from the
question of whether the industrial revolution should be seen as a narrow
or a broad phenomenon. Traditional histories of the period have focused
on dramatic technological change and productivity growth, in relatively
few industries, particularly textile processes. This literature tends to suggest the importance of radical change in what are here called 'critical
technologies', concentrated in key industrial sectors. A critical technology
can be thought of as one that plays an essential determining role, via direct or indirect effects on output and productivity growth, on the growth
trajectory of any particular period. For many writers the critical technologies of British industrialisation were steam power and mechanised textile

machines (particularly spinning machinery). Recent literature, however, stresses a much wider spectrum of change, and emphasises the importance of incremental innovation across industries. It is important to try to form some broad judgement about the balance and importance of these types of change, since this has implications for how we interpret impulses and incentives to technological change, and causality issues more generally. If, for example, a relatively small array of technologies drove change at that time, then we might want to look for sector-specific causal factors, perhaps related to the dynamics of specific technologies. A different approach would need to consider why it is that a broad-front process of advance was occurring, which – as we shall argue below – must lead us to economy-wide factors, such as general institutional change in legal frameworks, management systems, ownership and control patterns, for example. This broad approach need not assume that all technologies are advancing at the same rates or with the same impacts – it could be consistent with considerable heterogeneity across industries.

Any assessment of competing interpretations must rest on a reasonable understanding of the historical record of technological change. The second section therefore seeks to provide an empirical overview of the sectoral patterns and technical characteristics of technological change during the period, although a full account is of course far beyond the scope of this chapter. This draws on economic histories, histories of technology and business studies; the objective is to give a view of the diversity of technological change during the period. The intention is to look outside the areas of highly visible advance, such as textiles, and draw attention also to the widespread changes in such central areas of economic activity as agriculture, food processing, glass manufacture, machine tools and so on. The aim here is to emphasise the empirical fact that this was an economy with extensive technological change, change that was not confined to leading sectors or highly visible areas of activity. These less visible industries are frequently important when it comes to non-technological forms of innovation: pottery, for example, was a major field of organisational innovation. So we also emphasise the fact that these less glamorous sectors were often the site of major advances in organisational innovations – in vertical integration, in assembly line methods, in work organisation and in distribution, for example.

The conclusion will consider the implications of these contrasting views for general models of economic growth. At the present time, economists and others are increasingly using ideas about technological change during industrialisation as the basis for thinking about growth and change. Most notably we have a widely used Kondratievian–Schumpeterian position, basing models of long-run growth and change on the idea of radical technological discontinuities occurring in critical technologies. These models, and the literature which draws on them, often begin with stylised views of the nature of the industrial revolution, and this is one key area where discussions of the industrial revolution have contemporary resonance. Indeed it is quite common to see contemporary policy documents stressing the importance of innovation in information technology and biotechnology by referring directly to accounts of the role of steam power and machinery in the industrial revolution. If, however, much wider processes of change determine output and productivity growth, then we have before us important issues of principle in understanding productivity growth and indeed overall economic growth during the period.

COMPETING VIEWS OF INNOVATION
AND INDUSTRIALISATION

In 1815 Patrick Colquhoun wrote that 'It is impossible to contemplate the progress of manufactures in Great Britain within the last thirty years without wonder and astonishment. Its rapidity, particularly since the commencement of the French revolutionary war, exceeds all credibility. The improvement of steam engines, but above all the facilities afforded to the great branches of the woollen and cotton manufactories by ingenious machinery, invigorated by capital and skill, are beyond all calculation' (Colquhoun 1815: 68). This view of the relation between technology and manufacturing growth was not uncommon: it focused on a number of highly visible techniques that began to be implemented from the later eighteenth century. Foremost among these were steam engines, cotton spinning machines, and metal working devices and products. These techniques were often associated with specific industries or activities, and it was a short and apparently natural step to link the techniques with the expansion of the industries concerned, and then see these industries as the driving forces of economic growth.

This kind of vision of the technology–industrialisation–growth link began with the first systematic work on the industrial revolution, Arnold Toynbee's *Lectures on the industrial revolution of the Eighteenth Century*. Toynbee (1969 [1884]) focused on five technologies, and argued that it was the intersection of these technologies and the emergence of free-market capitalism as described by Adam Smith that constituted the industrial revolution. The key technologies were the Watt steam engine and the 'four great inventions' which revolutionised the cotton textile industry between 1730 and 1830 – the spinning jenny, the water-frame, Crompton's mule and the automatic mule of Richard Roberts. Toynbee's work had a major impact on subsequent economic history, with its technological emphases being repeated in Paul Mantoux's classic *Industrial Revolution in the Eighteenth Century*, and in a wide range of later works up to and including Landes's *Unbound Prometheus*, which remains the main work on technological development in western Europe. Mantoux focused Part II of his work, 'Inventions and Factories', on exactly the same sequence of textile inventions to which Toynbee drew attention, adding Cort's iron process (Mantoux 1961: II, 193–348). Landes did likewise, adding a brief discussion of power tools and chemicals (Landes 1974: 82–114), although he also noted briefly that 'other branches of industry effected comparable advances' (1974: 41).

The approach based on critical technologies has fed through into contemporary analysis mainly through the ideas of Joseph Schumpeter. In *Business Cycles*, Schumpeter claims that innovations 'concentrate on certain sectors and their surroundings', and that there are discrepancies between the growth of sectors: 'some industries move on, others stay behind' (Schumpeter 1989: 75–6). The central idea is that innovations disrupt equilibria and cannot be smoothly absorbed into the system; however, 'those disturbances must be "big" in the sense that they will disrupt the existing system and enforce a distinct process of adaptation'. This process of adaptation is the so-called Kondratieff wave, a long period of growth and decline as the critical technologies are exploited and then exhausted. What 'big' means in this context turns out to be similar to the technological themes sketched above in the industrialisation literature based on critical technologies:

> Historically, the first Kondratieff covered by our material means the industrial revolution, including the protracted process of its absorption. We date it from the eighties of the eighteenth century to 1842. The second stretches over what has been called the age of steam and steel. It runs its course between 1842 and 1897. And the third, the Kondratieff of electricity, chemistry, and motors, we date from 1898 on. (Schumpeter 1989: 145)

These critical technology notions have been very influential, and it is only in recent years that a counter-emphasis has emerged in which other dimensions of industrialisation have been placed in the forefront of analysis. The reassessment has two elements. First, there has been increasing caution about how widespread technical innovation actually was. McCloskey, for example, emphasised that by 1860 only about 30 per cent of British employment was in 'activities that had been radically transformed in technique since 1780' and that innovations 'came more like a gentle (though unprecedented) rain, gathering here and there in puddles. By 1860 the ground was wet, but by no means soaked, even at the wetter spots. Looms run by hand and factories run by water survived in the cotton textile industry in 1860' (McCloskey 1981: 109). Samuel suggested that hand techniques and innovation were by no means exclusive. He rejected the idea that steam power in particular had economy-wide impacts, arguing that 'the industrial revolution rested on a broad handicraft basis . . . the handicraft sector of the economy was quite as dynamic as high technology industry, and just as much subject to technical development and change' (Samuel 1977: 60). Secondly, there is an emphasis on innovation outside these allegedly core sectors. Von Tunzelmann, for example, argued that 'the usual stress on a handful of dramatic breakthroughs is seriously open to question', and that what mattered was the variety and pervasiveness of innovation (von Tunzelmann 1981: 143). Maxine Berg and Pat Hudson have argued that most accounts of innovation in the industrial revolution in effect focus on process change, on innovation in capital goods (Berg and Hudson 1992). Berg has stressed the importance of a relatively unexamined part of innovation at that time, namely product innovation in consumer goods, especially in products that can be considered luxury goods. This was a key demand-side factor shaping innovation in Britain, and gave rise to major industries. Some of the evidence for this will be outlined below (Berg 2002; see also chapter 13 below).

What are the implications of these different views of industrialisation for understanding the process of change in the British economy from 1760 to 1830? The first view accords with an account in which industrialisation is driven by a small number of rapidly growing industries and by the inter-industry diffusion of a relatively small number of critical technologies that formed the basis of leading sectors. In this account the emphasis is on radical innovation, and an abrupt shift in leading sectors and technological methods (for a recent account, see Freeman and Louca 2001; for an economic history of industrialisation in this framework, see Lloyd-Jones and Lewis 1998). In such views technological change is a determining factor in growth. Within this first approach, technology tends to be seen as a *deus ex machina*; technological change has been treated as something that explains the industrialisation process, but is rarely itself seen as needing explanation. The second view implies a more complex story, in which innovation accelerates on an economy-wide basis, yet is usually incremental and small scale. In this approach, the problem is not so much one of using technology to explain growth, as explaining the wide disposition to innovation across a very broad set of activities: here technology plays no primary causal role, but rather is the phenomenon that needs explanation.

What types of evidence are relevant to deciding between these very different accounts of industrialisation? An obvious starting point is an examination of what we know about the actual processes of innovation and diffusion across the economic activities of Britain at that time. We turn now to this task, looking first at evidence from patenting behaviour, and then at the histories of specific technologies.

SECTORAL PATTERNS OF TECHNOLOGICAL ADVANCE: THE PATENTING EVIDENCE

One of the few available quantitative output indicators for technology is the patent series. A patent is the grant of monopoly rights of use for a new invention – at the time of the industrial revolution for a period of fourteen years – following an application to the Patent Office by an inventor (see also chapter 8 below). Patent applications must disclose details of the invention: these include details of the particular ways in which it is novel, its technical field, and areas of potential application. Patent applications and grants are published, and over time provide an insight into the extent and scope of inventive activity in society. In Britain the patent data map a definite acceleration of technological change from the mid-eighteenth century. Of course patents have obvious limitations as technology indicators: the propensity to patent is shaped by social and economic factors, and varies over time and between industries. Moreover the existence of a patent – which protects a new technical principle – does not imply a commercially viable product or process, since it does not necessarily lead to adoption of the technology. A patent therefore indicates nothing about the economic value of a new technique.

However, the patent series is linked – though in complex ways – to the evolution of industries, and gives us a reasonable guide to the pace and direction of technological advance in industry. Jacob Schmookler, for example, showed that patenting in a number of US industries was closely correlated with industry output (with patents lagging), and that a high proportion of patents within an industry were commercialised; his broad conclusion was that patenting was strongly associated with industrial activity, but more significantly that the lag relationship implied that invention was shaped by economic forces (Schmookler 1962, 1966).[1] Christine MacLeod, in the definitive study of the English patent system, emphasised the point that from its inception in the mid-sixteenth century – as a system of royal grants of monopoly rights in production of some commodities – the patent system was used for widely different purposes by different types of inventors. By the late eighteenth century, however, the system had changed along two dimensions. The first was 'the emergence . . . of two major patenting contexts': one in the mercantile and manufacturing community of London, the other in the manufacturing districts in the north-west of England.[2] The second dimension of change was in the scale of patenting, with a substantial increase occurring after 1750. The Bennet Woodcroft index compiled in the mid-nineteenth century showed a major increase in the gross totals of all patents registered annually after 1750.[3]

---

[1] Nathan Rosenberg, while accepting this relationship, emphasised that it was not an encompassing theory and that invention also rested on independent scientific advance: Rosenberg 1974.

[2] 'One was firmly based in the London mercantile and manufacturing community, chiefly among the higher status crafts; the other in the manufacturing districts of the West Midlands and North-west. What both contexts shared was a highly competitive environment and a degree of capitalization unusual for that period. They also had in common the appearance of engine makers specializing in equipping and servicing workshops and factories. Between them they accounted for over three-quarters of all patents obtained between 1750 and 1800' (MacLeod 1988: 115).

[3] Bennet Woodcroft (ed.), *Chronological Index of Patents of Inventions* (1854), cited in MacLeod 1988: 146.

Table 5.1 Patents for capital goods, 1750–99

Type of invention	1750–9	1760–9	1770–9	1780–9	1790–9	Total
Power sources	10	21	17	47	74	169
Textile machinery	5	6	19	23	53	106
Subtotal	*15*	*27*	*36*	*70*	*127*	*275*
Agricultural equpt	1	3	5	22	27	58
Brewing equpt	0	1	2	4	17	24
Machine tools	1	4	1	2	3	11
Salt making equpt	2	3	2	1	2	10
Sugar making equpt	0	1	7	1	1	10
General chemical equpt	0	3	2	9	9	23
Building tools and machinery	1	2	4	2	5	14
Mining machinery	1	5	3	7	5	21
Metallurgical equpt	6	9	11	18	19	63
Shipbuilding	4	14	7	17	37	79
Canal and road building	2	1	1	2	24	30
Other industrial	1	5	11	13	18	48
Total	34	78	92	168	294	666
% of all patents	37.0	38.0	31.3	35.2	45.2	38.3

Source: Derived from MacLeod 1988: 148.

MacLeod showed that growth was especially rapid in capital goods, which grew sharply in absolute terms but also as a proportion of all patents, making up 45.2 per cent of patents in the last decade of the century. The two fastest-growing categories were power sources and pumps (which of course include steam engines, with James Watt's engine being patented in 1775) and – fastest of all – textile machinery. The time paths of patenting in these categories are shown in Table 5.1. A sustained rise in patenting from 1750 is visible, and the rise is especially strong in the last decade of the eighteenth century: in both power sources and textile machinery about half of all patenting from 1750 occurred in the ten years 1790–9. So these technical categories are strongly present. However, it is important to keep their predominance in perspective. Over the whole period these two groups made up almost exactly 50 per cent of capital goods patents, which means that there was also substantial patenting in other areas. In fact exactly the same time path, with strong growth in the last decade of the eighteenth century, can be seen in agricultural equipment, brewing equipment, shipbuilding, canals, building equipment and metallurgical equipment. As we shall see below, these were large sectors where considerable technological advance was occurring.

Apart from the diversity of patenting, we should note that Table 5.1 refers to capital goods only. These made up just under 40 per cent of all patents during the period 1750–1800. So rapid growth in capital goods should not obscure the fact that innovation was also occurring

Table 5.2 Selected product and ornamenting patents, 1720–1800		
	Birmingham	Total UK
Buckles and fastenings	11	36
Engraving, etching and chasing	1	12
Making and ornamenting frames for pictures and looking-glasses	2	7
Workboxes, music stands, dressing boxes and fire-screens	2	4
Castors, knobs and handles	6	10
Cabinets and other furniture	4	14
Metals and metallic substances		
Plating, tinning, lining and covering	11	35
Ornamenting, inlaying and polishing	3	9
Moulding and ornaments for buildings, coaches, and furniture	5	18
Paper mâché and japanned ware	2	5
Total	47	150

Source: Berg 1998a: 39.

across a wider spectrum of British economic activity (Sullivan 1990: 350). Maxine Berg's work on patents, focusing in particular on the Midlands metal trades, reveals some of the broadness of innovation activity during the early industrial revolution. Her work looks at consumption goods, showing that patents were taken out on a vast number of small, novel processes and products such as buckles and buttons. This suggests small-scale ingenuity, and a process of innovation and technological change involving a much larger number of people and of manufacturing processes and goods than suggested if we just look to the 'heroic' inventions stressed by Toynbee and those who followed his emphases. Table 5.2 shows some of the array of patents related to ornamentation and decoration, both personal and domestic.

These rather humble consumption goods may seem a good deal less exciting than new steam or textile technologies, but that of course does not mean that they have less economic impact. Taken together, there are a large number of them, and they are in areas of high demand and considerable economic significance in terms of the volume of employment and output; many of them rested on new types of production machinery and capital goods. So without far more detailed technological and economic analysis, we could not say that these were in some way less significant fields than those that comprise the textile process, for example.

What can we conclude from this brief look at patenting? The patent series suggests a technological dimension of industrialisation which was certainly apparent to contemporary observers, and which has played a central role in historical writing about the period ever since. However, during the period, the two largest groups of patents, power sources and textile machinery, constituted slightly less than 20 per cent of all patents. Within capital goods, relatively unglamorous activities such as brewing equipment, agricultural implements, machine tools, sugar making equipment and so on exhibit similar rises, although to smaller totals. Finally, there is a large set of consumption goods patents that indicate extensive inventive activity in a wide range of luxury and everyday products. So the patent evidence suggests a very broadly based process of technological change, with major capital goods inventions as important components, but with extensive inventive behaviour occurring across the whole spectrum of economic activity.

SECTORAL PATTERNS OF CHANGE: TECHNOLOGICAL HISTORIES

Beyond the patent record we have a wide variety of technological case studies that, taken together, provide a detailed overview of the range and scope of innovation during British industrialisation. In this section the evidence for a number of important economic sectors is reviewed in terms of the technological advances taking place over the period. We focus in detail on two broad, related types of activity – agriculture and food processing, the latter of which includes the brewing of beer which was a major scale-intensive activity at that time, and then on the glass industry, a prosaic activity perhaps but one with wide uses and impacts on the quality of life.

Agriculture

No account of the technological development of Britain can ignore agriculture, which was the largest economic sector at that time and one of the most significant in terms of technological change. Change within the sector encompassed a complex array of interacting institutional, organisational and technical shifts: 'the century from 1750 to 1850 saw considerable activity and expansion in British agriculture. The new interest in farming under the influence of the great improvers; the opportunity to adopt new ideas resulting from enclosure; the continually increasing population leading to additional demands for food; better means of communication; and the stimulus of the Napoleonic wars, all led to great developments in farming techniques' (Beaumont and Higgs 1958: 1–2).

Technological change in agriculture from 1750 encompassed a wide variety of technical functions within a complex set of agrarian production processes: farm tools, cultivation implements (ploughs, harrows, mowers, wheels for farm vehicles), sowing implements, harvesting equipment (reapers, rakes, hoes, scythes, winnowing and threshing devices, etc.), barn equipment, and drainage equipment. During the period 1750–1850 there was considerable change in the array of techniques, and technological progress occurred across a very broad front (Mathias 1983: 70).

The long and broad character of change had an important effect on the development of specialised equipment supply into the sector. By the 1830s,

> Many small engineering works and foundries had sprung up in the rural districts and market towns of England. Although these catered primarily for the farmer, their effect on farming methods was at first small, consisting mainly of the gradual substitution of cast and wrought iron for wood or stone in the construction of simple farm implements and appliances . . . [however] it was due to their influence that that basic farm implement, the plough, was transformed in the early years of the nineteenth century from a crude construction of wood and blacksmith's ironwork into a stronger, handier and far more efficient implement constructed entirely of cast and wrought iron.
>
> (Rolt 1980: 103–4)

Ploughing was then and now a time and energy consuming element in agriculture. The eighteenth century saw continuous change in plough-ing techniques, beginning around 1750 with the Rotherham plough, a smaller and lighter swing plough derived from a Dutch model. This was primarily a design change rather than a change in materials, but it quickly led to materials substitution, with James Small introducing the 'Scotch swing plough' in 1763, involving the extensive use of wrought iron, and then in 1785 an important innovation, the self-sharpening ploughshare patented by Robert Ransome:

> The under surface of the share was cooled more quickly than the upper surface, thus making one side harder than the other and the share self-sharpening. Shares had previously been filed in the field or taken back to the forger for sharpening. When chilled cast iron shares came into use a permanently sharp edge was ensured. The principle of self-sharpening shares is still the same today. (Beaumont and Higgs 1958: 3)

This innovation, as Rolt remarked, was a case of a 'seemingly small inno-vation [that] had an immense effect on the speed and efficiency of arable cultivation' (Rolt 1980: 104). Ransome also took out a third very important patent in 1808, which involved nothing less than the introduction of stan-dardised parts, a revolutionary step that is often held to have occurred much later (and then primarily in the USA). This was for a plough-frame to which components were bolted – new parts could be easily substituted for damaged or worn-out parts, a development that significantly reduced the cost and time involved in plough repair. These innovations were not necessarily small-scale trial and error processes; they certainly led to the formalisation and codification of the technologies used in agriculture, with publication of plans and books covering these techniques.[4] Both the development of standardised parts and the process of codification of

---

[4] These innovations 'inspired such as John Arbuthnot and James Small to consider principles of plough design and to discuss in books the relative merits of the various ploughs in use. They produced plans, tables, and detailed descriptions from which ploughs could subsequently be built' (Beaumont and Higgs 1958: 2–3).

technology are often regarded as watersheds in the evolution of technology as a whole, but the unglamorous origins of these in agriculture is
often neglected.

This broad innovative effort around a particular farming function was
replicated in other areas. For example, the drilling of seed was a problem
approached in diverse ways. The major invention, Jethro Tull's seed-drill
of the early eighteenth century, was the culmination of decades of attack
on the problem by many inventors; it was invented in 1701, introduced
(via a book) in 1731, and an improved geared version appeared fifty years
later, in 1782. Its importance lay in the fact that it was 'the first important step towards the elimination of manual labour in farm operations
in Britain' (Beaumont and Higgs 1958: 5–9; Rolt 1980: 671; Inkster 1991:
305). It should be emphasised that this was not an isolated innovation – it
led to a trajectory of advance, with at least three further important seed-
drill innovations by 1850, and a range of improved seed-drills being developed in a process of change that continued throughout the nineteenth
century.

The innovative effort broadened to all the functions of farming. Tull
himself developed a horse-hoe in the early eighteenth century that was
progressively developed throughout the century (Derry and Williams
1979: 671). The problem of harvesting was also systematically addressed,
at first through incremental improvements to such longstanding tools
as the scythe (Daunton 1995: 46). This was followed with devices that
attempted to replicate the hand actions of skilled farm workers (Balassa
1988: 151). These devices failed, yet between 1780 and 1850 a wide variety
of reaping machines were invented and marketed in Britain and the USA.
In Britain, the importance of this problem can be indicated by the fact
that the Royal Society of Arts offered a prize for its solution in 1812. The
defining solution to this technical problem came in 1831 in the USA, with
the McCormick reaper of 1831, which rapidly became the standard technique for mechanical harvesting. But the noteworthy point is that this
machine was not an isolated act of invention, but rather the culmination
of a sustained inventive effort on both sides of the Atlantic; indeed it has
been claimed that 'the seven essential elements of McCormick's reaper
. . . had already appeared in English patents in the first quarter of the
[nineteenth] century' (Giedion 1969: 152–3).

These examples can easily be multiplied. The mid-eighteenth to early
nineteenth centuries saw the introduction of horse-rakes for haymaking,
then Salmon's haymaking machine (the principles of which are still in
use in haymaking), the threshing machine of Andrew Meikle, the winnowing machine of James Sharp, root and chaff slicers, and drainage
equipment (such as mechanically made pipes) (Beaumont and Higgs 1958:
9–10; Mokyr 1990: 139; Inkster 1991: 306). This was an arena of technological advance with profound impacts on the extent and nature of labour
inputs, and on output.

To what extent did technological change in agriculture depend on the use of advances from outside agriculture itself? Clearly the substitution of cast and wrought iron for wood, and the ability to design new metal-based technologies, relied to some extent on innovations deriving from the iron and steel industries. But the specific advances in casting that led to the self-sharpening plough were made within activities that were specifically focused on agriculture, and it does not therefore seem reasonable to see agriculture in terms of the spread of techniques from elsewhere. Where techniques diffused, it usually post-dated the acceleration of innovation in agriculture in the period discussed here.

This was particularly the case with steam power. Rolt remarked that 'Long after steam power had been successfully applied to manufacture and transport, the British farmer continued to rely solely upon the horse, while the most notable advance in agricultural mechanisation was the substitution of the threshing machine for the flail', and that as late as the early 1840s, 'aside from a few isolated experiments, there had been as yet no attempt to apply steam power on the farm' (Rolt 1980: 102, 104). Ultimately, steam powered technologies did appear: mobile threshing machines, winnowing machines, and cable-drawn ploughs for example. But 'There was little scope for new sources of power until well into the nineteenth century, when determined efforts were made to introduce steam engines into British farms. These were particularly successful in the large farms of the English lowlands such as Norfolk, where techniques of steam ploughing were perfected' (Buchanan 1992: 85).

It seems reasonable to conclude that agriculture was a self-sufficient arena of broad and significant technological innovation throughout the period considered here, and that any consideration of the technological trajectory of the British economy during the industrialisation period should incorporate this as a central component. Of course agriculture can be seen as producing inputs to other industries, such as textiles. But perhaps its most important contribution is to food production, and it is to this we now turn.

Food and food processing

Closely linked with agricultural change were the activities concerned with the processing, distribution and consumption of food. It is worth emphasising that during the industrial revolution these processes were the largest single complex of economic activity; moreover they remained so throughout the nineteenth century (and in fact the food cluster remains a core activity of advanced industrial economies today).

It is sometimes suggested that the 'food complex' was not an important field of technological change during the industrial revolution. For example Sidney Pollard suggested that:

in the mid-nineteenth century the final stages in food-processing such as baking and meat preparation had not yet gone through an 'industrial revolution' as commonly understood. There had been no revolutions in technology there, manual skill or personal know-how were still predominant, there was no central motive power, no factory and no mass production.   (Pollard 1994: 24)

In *The Lever of Riches*, Joel Mokyr concurred: 'Large sectors of the economy, employing the majority of the labour force and accounting for at least half of gross national product were, for all practical purposes, unaffected by innovation before the middle of the nineteenth century. In . . . food processing . . . techniques changed little or not at all before 1850' (Mokyr 1990: 83).

While Pollard and Mokyr are right to suggest that large parts of this major economic activity remained manual, domesticated and relatively static in their technical character, it is certainly not the case that food processing remained unaffected by technological change. (In fact, Mokyr in particular is a good guide to some of the major changes.) On the contrary, within food processing there were areas of change of deep importance, not only for the development and deployment of new techniques, but also for new forms of production organisation and enterprise structure. Certainly it was many years before these innovations diffused fully into the household sector, but the innovation effort in food processing was both widespread and sustained. In this section five areas of change are overviewed: food preservation, refrigeration, baking, brewing and grain milling.

Food preservation. The canning of food was an important achievement in early industrialisation, the basic technique being the vacuum sealing of cooked food. The technique was invented in France in 1795 by Nicolas Appert, using glass jars for storage. In 1810 Peter Durand, an Englishman, proposed the use of tin cans, a method that proved successful (Derry and Williams 1979: 695; Mokyr 1990: 140; Inkster 1991: 305). The early versions of this technique came rapidly into use – they were adopted by the Royal Navy, and canned soup and meat were being consumed by British sailors by 1814. This technology was incrementally improved throughout the nineteenth century, with changes in sterilisation processes, and the use of autoclaves for cooking (Derry and Williams 1979: 691–6). During the 1830s, preservation techniques for milk emerged, with 'condensed milk' being patented in 1835, although diffusion came much later.

Refrigeration. An important arena of technological change from early industrialisation to the present day has been the evolution of techniques for keeping food fresh. Early approaches all involved the use of ice. At first, both in Europe and the USA, this was based on the harvesting of natural ice, and its storage in insulated ice-houses. The main area of use was the fishing industry. Natural ice was being used by the late eighteenth century, with salmon being packed in ice for transport to London by 1786, and sea fish (from Harwich and Grimsby) by the end of the century. This rapidly ran into a supply constraint: 'Since demand clearly exceeded natural supply [of ice] . . . ice-making machines began to be patented in the 1830s and became numerous in the 1850s, the cooling effect depending either upon the expansion of compressed air or upon the evaporation of very volatile liquids such as liquefied ammonia' (Derry and Williams 1979: 698). The basic scientific and technological principle of refrigeration had been known since around 1755, and practical applications were driven by the needs of ice production. About a century of incremental development was necessary before James Harrison patented the first practical commercial refrigeration device in 1856 (Rolt 1980: 112). These changes had important impacts on the fishing industry – the development of large fishing boats ensued, with both refrigeration and onboard tanks for keeping fish alive. The extension of railways to the fishing ports, combined with the use of ice-based preservation, created new distribution possibilities and a large market, with fish being shipped fresh from the main fishing ports. Refrigeration contributed therefore not only to the growth of a new economic activity, but also to a significant shift in diet for urban populations.

Baking. Bread and biscuits were a long-term dietary staple. From the late eighteenth century a series of inventors had attempted to produce massively larger ovens that would permit the large-scale production of bread. Most of these involved either conveyor belts running through a large oven, or a process in which an oven rotated slowly over a fixed heat source (Giedion 1969: 176–7). As with food preservation by canning, the British navy was a lead customer:

> In the first decade of the nineteenth century, Admiral Sir Isaac Coffin (1759–1839) built for the British Navy an oven 'intended for baking sea-biscuits' . . . which he named the 'perpetual oven.' Coffin thus explains the name given to his oven: 'It is called a perpetual oven because the operation of baking may be continued for any length of time.' It was indirectly heated. An endless belt a yard wide and made of loose wire mesh ran the whole length of the baking chamber. At either end, outside of the oven, the belt ran around large cast-iron rollers, which kept it continually moving.   (Giedion 1969: 176–7)

The production of biscuits for sea use was also associated with another epoch-making organisational innovation, namely the assembly line. The machines used for making biscuits were co-ordinated with each other, and with the accurately timed hand operations that were necessary to make biscuits. The principles of synchronisation are in many ways the key element of modern product assembly. Larger-scale ovens followed these innovations in the mid-nineteenth century, followed by automatic mixing and slicing, and by the use of carbonic acid in bread dough (patented in 1856). What we have here is the major technological upgrading of a traditional product – an important but neglected form of innovation during the industrialisation process and after.

Brewing. During the eighteenth century the brewing of beer shifted from small to large scale, although a diverse array of firm sizes persisted within it: 'brewing became a much more specialist activity as home brewing and inn-keeper brewing became less common. By the mid-1820s larger towns usually had several specialist brewers' (Timmins 1998: 108). This had important implications for scale and for the use of technology; as Daunton points out: 'In the course of the eighteenth century, the scale of brewing increased, and in most towns it was amongst the largest and most prosperous businesses . . . the brewers were amongst the first and largest users of steam power' (Daunton 1995: 324).

These firms not only used advanced technologies, they pioneered perhaps the most important organisational innovation of the modern economy, namely the professionally managed, vertically integrated, corporate enterprise. These were capital-intensive operations, and British brewers solved the problems of access to adequate fixed capital by extending ownership; the effect of this was to move away from the family firm as a mode of organisation, and to take an important step towards corporate capitalism. At the same time, the firms integrated backwards into the production of raw materials, and forwards into distribution and the ownership of networks of pubs (Landes 1969: 72; Daunton 1995: 324–5). This somewhat neglected industry has a genuine claim to being both the technological and organisational precursor of the modern economy.

Grain milling. As urban populations increased during the eighteenth century, the demand for flour grew sharply, and the scale of grain milling grew with it. On the one hand this had an important technological component: 'grain milling . . . turned increasingly to steam power in urban locations' (Timmins 1998: 108). On the other hand, as with brewing, there were integrated technological and organisational shifts. Increasingly, small-scale milling was replaced by:

> large, capital-intensive mills which purchased grain in order to supply long-distance markets; water-powered mills on the Thames were some of the largest industrial concerns of the eighteenth century, and steam-powered mills were erected in London . . . As the scale of firms increased, they integrated backward and forward. Large millers purchased their own supplies and cut out the factors, or they moved forward into the trade in flour and cut out the mealmen. The mealmen, in turn, integrated backwards and acquired mills. The whole pattern of supplying bread-stuffs, the basic necessity of life, had become a very different matter from a farmer pitching his wagon in the market-place: it had extended lines of distribution, involving capital-intensive plant and considerable amounts of working capital, with some of the largest concerns in the economy.
> (Daunton 1995: 324)

The examples offered here could readily be extended – into, say, sugar refining, jam manufacture, chocolate manufacture, coffee refining, tobacco processing and so on and so on. It is important to continue to stress the wider implications of this: it is reasonable to claim that the prosaic industries we have mentioned above were not merely adjuncts to industrialisation but leaders of it, and in fact were key bearers of technological change during the industrial revolution.

Glass manufacture

Glass is an important and differentiated industrial product, widely used across the early industrial economy and central to the development of industrialisation. Glass comprises both domestic products (bottles, glasses, lamps, mirrors, etc.) and important industrial inputs: containers, sheet glass and cast plate glass (of widely differing types, usually used for windows), and a complex specialised product, namely optical glass. As with the food industry, the rate and impact of technological change is subject to differences in interpretation. Derry and Williams suggested that the transformation of glass making into a machine industry was a slow process: 'It was, indeed, far from complete even in 1900 . . . in glassmaking the craftsman and the ancient, and often secret, traditional processes were not quickly swept aside by industrial change' (1979: 583, 592). Yet, reviewing the eighteenth century, Berg was able to conclude that the glass industry 'experienced major technological or organisational changes in the period [1700–1820]' (Berg 1994: 53). These views are not necessarily contradictory – although many hand processes remained, the period none the less also saw sustained innovation.

Glass was one of the few large-scale production activities in early industrialisation, along with textiles and iron manufacture (Mathias 1983: 185). It was a sector of steady innovation. In the seventeenth century an important innovation, the reverbatory furnace, had emerged; its basic principle was the separation of fuel and raw material, and this made possible the substitution of coal for wood and charcoal as a fuel (Landes 1969: 53–4; Mokyr 1990: 106; Timmins 1998: 43). In the late eighteenth century the production of plate glass was revived in Britain (where it had been produced on a small scale in the seventeenth and early eighteenth centuries) with the construction of a very large plant at Ravenhead, near St Helens, by the British Plate Glass Company (Timmins 1998: 109). In the 1830s cylinder processes were introduced for the manufacture of sheet glass, and in the 1840s machinery for grinding and polishing sheet glass was developed and diffused (Singer 1958: 367; Daunton 1995: 229). These innovations were important in the development of companies that have played a major long-term role in British manufacturing: for example, the cylinder process was introduced in the 1840s by the St Helens Crown Glass company, which became Pilkington Brothers, a firm that remains a major producer and innovator in glass (Timmins 1998: 201). Finally, 'from 1859 onwards there was a series of patents in various countries for bottle-making machines, and in 1887 the semi-automatic Ashley machine, used at Castleford in Yorkshire, provided the first commercial success' (Derry and Williams 1979: 698). In blown-glass products, some important innovations related to plant layout and organisation: 'manufacturers evolved a distinctive cone-shaped factory, with the furnace in the middle, together with the pots of molten glass, and plenty of space around it for the glass "blowers" to exercise their skill' (Buchanan 1992: 179). It should be noted that many of these innovations were in fact diffusions from western Europe, principally from Germany and France. The cylinder process came from Lorraine and the German states, although it probably originated in France (Singer 1958: 367; Mokyr 1990: 106).

The most knowledge-intensive component of glass production was however in optical glass:

> The closest link with the scientific advances of the period of the industrial revolution is in the steady progress of optical glass. It was in 1758 that John Dollond, a practical optician, was awarded a patent for the achromatic lenses that he had been constructing, contemporaneously with Moor Hall, for about a quarter of a century; they were made by cementing a convex lens of crown glass to a concave lens of flint glass.   (Derry and Williams 1979: 592)

Many of the key developments in optical glass occurred in western Europe: glass manufacturing processes were developed in Switzerland by Pierre Guinand, in France by Bontemps and Lerebours, and in Germany by Franubhofer. These advances diffused to Britain via a Birmingham manufacturer, Lucas Chance, who purchased and patented the Bontemps technique in 1837. After the 1848 revolution Bontemps himself came to the UK and worked directly with Chance Brothers, who became major producers of optical, telescopic and camera lens glass. These developments became the object of specific research programmes in Britain, not only among manufacturers but among interested scientists such as Herschel and Faraday, who took charge of the Royal Society investigations into optical glass in 1824 (Singer 1958: 359–60; Derry and Williams 1979: 592–3).

The material in the sections above has been intended to demonstrate the extent of innovation in what are often thought to be rather stable, undynamic sectors of the economy. The kinds of experience represented by these activities could easily be expanded: in such activities as pottery and ceramics, machinery and machine tools, instruments and mining, important and persistent patterns of innovation can be found. Pottery, for example, was an important area of organisational innovation, particularly in the Wedgwood enterprise. McKendrick showed some years ago that Wedgwood's product innovations were accompanied by changes in plant layout and labour organisation and management that were in many respects the earliest important form of modern workplace organisation (McKendrick 1961). In machinery and machine tools there were numerous important innovations: the screw cutting lathes of Jesse Ramsden in the 1770s, the boring machines of John Wilkinson in the mid-1770s, specialist machines for making watches, the carriage lathes of

Henry Maudesley in the late eighteenth century, new woodworking lathes and planers (such as that built by Joseph Bramah in 1802), large-scale lathes and metal planing machines invented by Richard Roberts in 1817, Nasmyth's machines for accurate cutting of hexagonal nuts in 1829 and many others that were developed at that time (on these and related machine making technologies see Burstall 1963; Saul 1970; Derry and Williams 1979; Daumas 1980; Mathias 1983; Cantrell 1984; Inkster 1991; Buchanan 1992). Some of these developments, such as Wilkinson's accurate and large-scale boring machines, made possible such innovations as the Boulton and Watt steam engine, since all of the Watt engine cylinders were bored with Wilkinson's machinery. The growth in variety, scale and accuracy of machine tools (by 1830 Maudsley was using a bench micrometer accurate to 0.0001 inch) was of profound importance for production across many sectors).

The pervasiveness and extent of innovation across the industries outlined above give us reasonable grounds for a general conclusion, namely that innovation was not confined to alleged 'leading sectors' of the economy, but rather was present, often in an intense way, across virtually all economic activities. This does not of course mean that we can ignore the sectors such as textiles and steam power that have driven so much of the historiography of industrialisation; on the contrary, they deserve close examination.

THE 'MAJOR INNOVATIONS'

Textiles

Together with steam power, textile machinery has been the emblematic technology of the industrial revolution, to the extent – as we have seen – that many histories of the industrial revolution have seen textiles not only as the primary site of innovation but also as the driving force of economic growth. While we can contest both the singularity of the technological changes, and their impact on growth, it nevertheless remains the case that this was indeed a major sector of change, in which considerable explanatory challenges remain: 'This "story", endlessly narrated, has never been explained by historians, who lack a general theory able to account for the major breakthroughs in technology that occurred in textiles over the eighteenth century' (O'Brien *et al.* 1996: 155). The evolution of textiles equipment in the eighteenth century was in part a process of transition away from domestic manufacture to factory production. The first factory production of textiles began in the early eighteenth century in the production of silk thread and cloth, based on silk throwing machinery patented by Thomas Lombe and based on modifications of Italian technology. Lombe's patent expired in 1732, leading to entry in the industry:

by the 1770s there were about thirty silk mills in the Midlands, mainly supplying handloom weavers in London (Kirby and Rose 1994: 38).

The real expansion occurred however in cotton textiles. The major innovations began with the mechanisation of hand techniques, which then developed into new elements of mechanical technology (see Chapman 1972 for the best overview of the technical developments). The sequence is usually associated with four key technologies: Kay's flying shuttle, Arkwright's water-frame, Crompton's spinning mule and Cartwright's loom, but we could add into this such major developments as Roberts's automatic mule (a machine which introduced the principle of error-actuated servo-control, and which Marx claimed 'opened up a completely new area in the capitalist system'). The first development occurred in cotton spinning, with the spinning jenny design by the Lancashire spinner James Hargreaves coming into use in the 1760s. This was a hand powered device which made it possible for a strong and skilled operator to work with more than one spindle at once; it 'reproduced the actions of the hand spinner' utilising a system of spindles with a movable carriage (Mann 1958: 278). In the early 1770s this was followed by Arkwright's water-frame, which introduced two significant innovations: first a series of rollers which drew and spun the thread, and second, water power to drive the rollers. Shortly afterwards a new technology emerged, Samuel Crompton's spinning mule, so called because it was a hybrid, mixing elements of the Hargreaves and Arkwright approaches. This machine was working by 1779, and over the next fifty years was subjected to a great number of improvements which considerably increased its productive capacity; variants of this machine formed the staple device around which the development of the textile industry occurred. It was the dominant technology for almost a century. The mule permitted large increases in productivity: so much so that the technical development of the cotton sector as a whole is often written in terms of the imbalance between spinning and the other processes of cotton manufacture. It was not superseded until the Roberts automatic mule of 1825, a radical breakthrough that was, in effect, the first truly automatic machine in the world. What we have here is an interrelated series of 'macro-inventions' appearing over a relatively short time period. The technological history of the industry therefore involves questions concerning the impulses to these processes of discovery, combined with the impulses to diffusion, as well as a wide array of smaller-scale inventions and innovations in textiles. O'Brien *et al.* point out that between 1700 and 1850 there were 2,330 textile patents in the UK, and this extensive range of patents is far from encompassing all of the innovative activity of the period in this sector (O'Brien *et al.* 1996: 165–7).

These technological changes were associated with rapid industry growth. Between the late eighteenth century and the middle of the nineteenth century the cotton textile industry in Britain grew spectacularly, in the absolute size of output, in labour productivity, in the scale of enterprises, in capital employed, and in the proportion which it contributed to national income. The gross value of output grew from £0.6 million in 1760 to £30 million in 1815 (Deane and Cole 1967: 185–8). In spinning, the number of operative hours required to process 100 lb. of cotton declined from 2,000 in 1760 (using Crompton's mule) to 135 in 1825 (using Roberts's automatic mule) (Catling 1970: 60). Between 1797 and 1850 the average annual input of raw cotton per factory rose by over 1,000 per cent, which reflects an increase both in physical productivity and in the average size of enterprises (since the number of enterprises less than doubled during the same period) (Chapman 1972: 70).

These dramatic productivity shifts should not be seen simply as the result of technological change. First, it is important to remember that the textiles sector comprised more than cotton: it included flax, silk and woollen manufactures, plus the manufacture of such products as lace and hosiery. Hosiery and lace manufacture remained domestic hand technology tasks, and in spinning the input of human skills remained strong even after mechanisation (Samuel 1977: 19). Moreover it is important to remember the overall complexity of the textile processes: textile manufacture involved many differentiated products, with processes involving raw material preparation (cleaning, combing and so on), spinning (with many different types of output), various types of weaving, bleaching, dyeing and printing, plus the operations involved in working up cloth outputs into products. Within the textile production chain mechanisation was very uneven, and so cannot exclusively account for the productivity growth experienced by the industry.

Within textiles, production was shaped not only by technical change but also by major organisational innovations associated with the factory and changing managerial control. These organisational innovations should be borne in mind when considering the longer-term impacts of the industrial revolution, since the factory permitted not only the application of power and the adoption of new techniques, but also the organisation and intensification of labour. In fact such organisational and managerial elements were central problems in the early factory system (see chapter 2). These points lead to two broad explanatory problems: first, explaining the sequence of textile equipment innovations, and secondly, understanding and explaining the organisational innovations within which the new techniques were put to work.

There is no comprehensive historical explanation of the sequence and array of invention in textiles. O'Brien *et al.* (1996) offer perhaps the clearest steps towards an explanation. They stress contextual features of path dependence (Britain had been a major textile producer and exporter across the whole range of processes and fabrics for a very long period), and of changes in the political economy of the industry (particularly changes in the supply and price of cotton from the Americas, and the emergence of protection against Indian cotton fabrics and hence a process of import substitution). On the inventions themselves they strongly emphasise the importance of an eighteenth-century social milieu committed to technical improvement and invention – a critical mass of human capital based on 'widespread interest in natural philosophy, mechanics, automata, and even in technological fantasies, among the upper and middle ranks of British society, including members of the ruling elite' (O'Brien *et al.* 1996: 175).

The diffusion of the major innovations, however, depended critically on organisational change. The development of the factory involved the concentration and supervision of the process of production under one roof, but before this control could even be attempted a labour force had to be assembled. Once assembled it had to be maintained. There were here, as Pollard remarks, 'two distinct, though clearly overlapping difficulties; the aversion of workers to entering the new large enterprises with their unaccustomed rules and discipline and the shortage of skilled and reliable labour' (Pollard 1965: 160). Where the factory simply concentrated production, without changing the technical means of production and therefore without the opportunity to change the composition and skill requirements of the labour force, there was found to be great difficulty in maintaining a workforce. In weaving and hosiery, where it was possible for the domestic worker to produce outside the discipline of the factory, he often did so: as one hosier, Robert Cookson, reported to the Committee on Woollen Manufacture:

> I found the utmost distaste on the part of the men, to any regular hours or regular habits . . . The men themselves were considerably dissatisfied, because they could not go in and out as they pleased, and go on just as they had been used to do; and were subject, during after-hours, to the ill natured observations of other workmen, to such an extent as completely to disgust them with the whole system, and I was obliged to break it up.
>
> (*Committee on Woollen Manufacture*, evid. of R. Cookson, quoted in Pollard 1965: 162)

The second problem, that of skilled labour, was of a very different character. In the first place, the skilled labourers were not necessarily concerned to avoid the factory, for it formed a major market for their skills; indeed some could only be applied within industrial production. Rather they were concerned to exploit the increased demand for skilled labour that the growth of the factory system engendered. The industrialisation of the late eighteenth and early nineteenth centuries led to an extreme shortage of skilled labour in every important sector of the economy (Pollard 1965: 167–72); the textile sector was dependent on skilled wood and metal workers because most of its machinery was made within individual enterprises, until the arrival of standardised machinery in the second quarter of the nineteenth century:

The early wooden textile machinery was made by the men who used it, or directly to their order by mechanics of many kinds – loom-makers, clock-makers, cabinet-makers, instrument-makers, and men with the mechanical hobby; the 'engineers' of that day being primarily pump-makers. Having learnt to make machines, the makers often set up as spinners, so that from both sides there was intermixture. McConnel and Kennedy of Manchester combined the two businesses in the early years of the firm. Henry Houldsworth, who, after six years at Manchester, went to Glasgow in 1799, still called himself a cotton-spinner and machine-maker in 1824. 'A great many manufacturers make their own machinery?' the Chairman of the parliamentary committee of that year said to one expert witness: 'they do', was the reply. Some of the largest firms long continued to do so – the Strutts at Belper, for example. But by 1820–30 the professional purveyor of machines made with the help of other machines, the true mechanical engineer of the modern world, was just coming into existence – in Lancashire and London where the demand was at its maximum.

(Clapham 1926: 152)

Arkwright and Strutt were 'continually advertising' for woodturners, clockmakers, smiths etc., who were employed in machine making. A stern line was taken on apprentices in wood and metal trades who broke their contracts: Arkwright had one imprisoned, and offered a reward for the capture of another (Fitton and Wadsworth 1958: 105–6).

So there were problems in building a labour force. But there were also problems in maintaining that labour force in the face of a high labour turnover and continuing resistance to work in the factory. The problem of skilled labour was ameliorated in two ways: first, as industrialisation progressed, the education system and the apprenticeship system began to increase the supply of skilled workers (see chapter 12), and second, the growth of a specialised machine building industry based on highly paid skilled labour and producing more or less standardised cotton machinery displaced the problem away from the cotton mills themselves. It is probable that this specialised industry consolidated its labour force by differentiating it sharply in terms of skills, wages and status from that of the factory operative; John Foster, for example, in his study of Oldham, argues that the growth of machine building implied the development of a labour aristocracy (Foster 1974: 228–9).

In the mills the problem of labour turnover remained: 'one of the most enlightened firms, McConnel and Kennedy regularly replaced spinners who had not turned up within two or three hours after starting time on Mondays, on the reasonable presumption that they had left the firm: their average labour turnover was twenty a week, i.e. about 100 per cent a year' (Pollard 1965: 182). The Strutts' records from Belper and Milford show 1600 departures between 1805 and 1812, which with a total labour force of about 1,300 would indicate an annual turnover of 16 per cent (Fitton and Wadsworth 1958: ch. 9). But these records deal with those who gave notice, and not with those who ran away, left without notice or were dismissed. These are precisely the most important groups when considering turnover, so the true figure is probably much higher.

These turnover problems are associated with the control and intensity of work. An important aspect of the mechanisation of the cotton industry, and the continuous process of technological innovations, was its effect on the intensity of work. As Catling (1970: chs 9–11) showed, not only was unremitting attentiveness required, but the intensity of production was such that repair and maintenance tasks on the machines had to be performed while the machine was in motion, at considerable physical risk. Thus on a pair of typical late-period mules of 1,200 spindles each, about five or six threads would be breaking each minute. Clearly the work of repairing broken ends could never be neglected for more than a few minutes and was a most important staple task (Catling 1970: 156). In view of the fact that the machinery was powered from a central power source under the control of the master, we might expect to find evidence of an increase in the speed of operation of machinery; and indeed there is abundant evidence of this. The following is from a spinner's evidence to Factory Commission hearings in 1840:

> Q. Is 10 hours' labour now at cotton spinning in a factory any more intense than 10 hours' labour was within your recollection? – A great deal more so.
> Q. What does it arise from? – It arises from the extra quantity that is produced, and the extra speed; a great deal more yarn is produced than in former day: this is all taken from the spinner.
> Q. A greater quantity of yarn is turned off in a given time than formerly? – Yes.
> Q. That is brought about by the increased speed of the machinery? – Yes.
> Q. That requires increased exertions on the part of all engaged in that machinery, in order to effect that purpose? – Yes, another thing that helped it: the competition of the workmen with one another: those two circumstances combined have rendered that necessary.
> Q. It is your opinion that 10 hours' labour as a cotton spinner now involves a severer duty, and requires as much exertion, as 12 hours did when the speed of machinery was much slower than it is now? – Yes; 10 hours now would be sorer on the operative than 12 would have been in the year 1827, or 1828, or thereabouts.
>
> (Evidence of Henry Dunn, Factories I: 1840–1)

An important point here is that the technical innovations of cotton are associated with a new organisational form, the factory. Productivity grew not simply because of new techniques, but because of the intensification of work permitted by factory organisation. But the problems of intensification of work, labour turnover and labour resistance also played an important role in shaping the trajectory of technological innovation in the cotton industry. The most notable case of this was the Roberts self-acting (i.e. automatic) mule, patented in 1825.

Where workers possessed skills which were indispensable to the production process then they also possessed a certain power to resist managerial control, which in addition gave them an advantage in bargaining over pay rates, work speeds, and so on. In this context, technical innovation was not simply a process of increasing the technical capacity to produce output, but might also have had implications for the particular skill mix of a production process, hence for the kind of labour required, hence for the overall power of the cotton managers in the organisation of production. The development of engineering capabilities and mechanisation generally held out the possibility for managers to 'innovate around' labour problems.

In *The Philosophy of Manufactures* (1835), Andrew Ure gave a concrete example of this. He remarked that in cotton spinning, the mule spinners had 'abused their powers beyond endurance, domineering in the most arrogant manner . . . over their masters. High wages, instead of leading to thankfulness of temper and improvement of mind, have, in too many cases, cherished pride and supplied funds for supporting refractory spirits in strikes'. After a series of such strikes in Lancashire towns 'several of the capitalists . . . had resort to the celebrated machinist Messrs Sharp and Co. of Manchester, requesting them to direct the inventive talents of their partner, Mr. Roberts, to the construction of a self-acting mule, in order to emancipate the trade from galling slavery and impending ruin' (Ure 1967: 366–7). The result was Roberts' self-acting mule, a major breakthrough in factory automation. Its construction was no small undertaking, for Ure estimated its development costs at £12,000 (Ure 1967: 368; Catling 1970: 64). This was, perhaps, however a small price to pay, for as Baines remarked: 'One of the recommendations of this machine to the spinners is, that it renders them independent of the working spinners, whose combinations and stoppages of work have often been extremely annoying to the masters' (Baines 1966: 208).

There were many other examples of innovations aimed at reducing the power of labour – in calico printing machines, self-acting dyeing and rinsing apparatus, sizing machines for warp dressing in power loom weaving, and carding and combing machines (Bruland 1982). So the organisational problems of the cotton sector were also intricately linked to the innovations that are normally held to characterise it.

What can we conclude from the record of innovation in the textile sector? There is no question that this was a major growth industry, with immense productivity change, and a significant site for the development and adoption of new technologies. But it would be wrong to see this sector as being driven in its development by technical innovations, since many changes were the result of a complex interaction between technology, work organisation and managerial practices. It would be mistaken also to see textiles as a *sui generis* driver of growth in the economy as a whole.

It was one sector among many that were innovating at that time, and it was far from being the only sector to generate sustained productivity growth.

Steam power

The 'critical technologies' approach to British industrial growth ascribes the expansion to the effects of the deployment of new techniques as the primary agent of economic advance, and its strongest version is written around the steam engine: 'If we were to try to single out the crucial inventions which made the industrial revolution possible and ensured a continuous process of industrialisation and technical change, and hence sustained economic growth, it seems that the choice would fall on the steam engine on one hand, and on the other Cort's puddling process which made a cheap and acceptable British malleable iron' (Deane 1965: 130). As I have argued above, this type of approach has a long history stretching back at least to the first systematic use of the term 'industrial revolution' in the work of Arnold Toynbee. However the strong emphasis on the primacy of steam power among the technologies of industrialisation goes back much further, into the nineteenth century itself. A classic statement of the alleged benefits of steam was made by Andrew Ure, writing in 1835. It is worth quoting this at some length, since the structure of the argument has been very important over the years, and continues to be reflected in the advocates of 'critical technology'-based growth theories even today:

> There are many engines made by Boulton and Watt, forty years ago, which have continued in constant work all that time with very slight repairs. What a multitude of valuable horses would have been worn out in doing the service of these machines! And what a vast quantity of grain they would have consumed! Had British industry not been aided by Watt's invention it must have done with a retarding pace in consequence of the increasing cost of motive power, and would, long ere now, have experienced in the price of horses, and scarcity of waterfalls, an insurmountable barrier to further advancement, could horses, even at the low prices to which their rival, steam, has kept them, be employed to drive a cotton mill at the present day, they would devour all the profits of the manufacturer.
>
> Steam engines furnish the means not only of their support but also of their multiplication. They create a vast demand for fuel; and while they lend their powerful arms to drain the pits and raise the coals, they call into employment multitudes of miners, engineers, shipbuilders and sailors, and cause the construction of canals and railways; and while they enable these rich fields of industry to be cultivated to the utmost, they leave thousands of fine arable fields free for the production of food to man, which must otherwise have been allotted to the food of horses. Steam engines, moreover, by the cheapness and steadiness of their action, fabricate cheap goods, and procure in their exchange a liberal supply of the necessaries and comforts of life, produced in foreign lands.   (Ure, cited in Morgan 1999: 107)

Ure's arguments have been repeated many times since. On the one hand he is arguing that steam overcame a fundamental energy crisis for the British economy – alternative energy sources would have been so expensive as to slow down or stop industrialisation completely. On the other, there is an argument about backward and forward linkages. Steam produced a backward demand for coal (and, it is sometimes argued, iron and steel), and forward linkages into manufactures (usually argued to be textiles).

How valid are these ideas? A surprising feature of the literature on technology and industrialisation is that there are very few systematic studies of the impact of specific technologies. However, in the work of Nicholas von Tunzelmann (1978) we have a detailed assessment of the extent of use of steam power, and of its economic impact – in effect a quantitative assessment of the validity of ideas such as Ure's about steam. Von Tunzelmann's aim was 'to combine economics, engineering and history to reassess the contribution of the steam engine to British economic growth during the industrial revolution'.

The work draws on an influential approach to the assessment of large technology impacts, which has given rise to much debate, that of Robert Fogel (1964). The 'social savings' method pioneered by Fogel to assess the growth impacts can be described as follows. Any particular process innovation that displaces some prior process, either across sectors of the economy or by the effective creation of a new sector, diffuses essentially because it cuts total costs of production. Whether it diffuses slowly or quickly, via the replacement of worn-out equipment or by causing functional plant to be scrapped, will of course depend on the particular configuration of fixed and variable costs involved. These cost reductions can be represented as the difference between the resource costs involved in the old and new modes of fulfilment of some economic function. Such resource-cost differences, called the 'social savings', can be seen as the 'contribution' of the new process to national income at some specified time. The analysis is carried out via the formation of a 'counter-factual example': we know what the technical facts were at some point, so let us assume that they were otherwise, and attempt to quantify the costs of the counter-factual example. Fogel's counter-factual example assumed that the American railway network, which Schumpeter held to be the crucial sector of nineteenth-century American economic growth, was bombed out of existence in 1890. Fogel then calculated the costs of fulfilling the same transport functions through the canal system, coast-to-coast shipping around Cape Horn, etc. His conclusion is well known: the railways contributed less than 5 per cent to the US national income in 1890, a striking result which 'clashes with the notion that economic growth can be explained by leading sector concepts' (Fogel 1964: 236).

What about steam power in the UK? In fact, two principal techniques are deployed in von Tunzelmann's investigation. On the one hand there is an assessment of the social savings contributed to the economy by steam power. The second technique is a rather more empirical assessment of the backward and forward linkages of the steam engine in the economy.

Von Tunzelmann makes a very careful assessment of the number and utilisation of steam engines in Britain in the early nineteenth century – in effect he carries out an industrial census of steam engines in British industry. In terms of social savings, two cases are worked out: the first examines replacement of the Watt engine alone, while the second looks at all types of steam engines. The first case involves the supposition that all Watt engines are replaced by early atmospheric steam engines of the Newcomen/Savery types. Then the aggregate fixed and variable savings on the Boulton and Watt engine, and its pirate copies, on plausible patterns of use, are assessed at between £226,000 and £233,000 in 1800. A reasonable estimate of national income in that year is £210 million. This implies that

> the social saving estimated for 1800 is very low even by the normal standards of such reckonings. For Boulton and Watt engines alone (including their pirates) the social savings over atmospheric engines can be put at about 0.11 per cent of national income in 1800. If total real output was then growing at its average rate for the take-off years, the level of national income reached on 1 January 1801 would not have been attained much before 1 February 1801 without James Watt.   (von Tunzelmann 1978: 286)

A similar, rather more intricate estimate for the replacement of *all* steam engines by animal and water power places the social savings at approximately 0.2 per cent of 1800 national income: 'If all steam engines, Watt and atmospheric alike, were hypothetically replaced with other means of motive power (a combination of water and wind would be optimal), the setback would have been about two months. These are upward-biased figures' (von Tunzelmann 1978: 287).

The other effects investigated in the text are possible backward linkages (into the development of the iron and coal industries) and forward linkages (especially to cotton, via the effects of steam power on the diffusion of automatic machinery in that sector). In opposition to those historians who allege a 'mutual sustenance of the steam engine . . . and the iron industry in the late eighteenth century', it is pointed out that, at the peak of production and sale of Boulton and Watt engines at this period, 'their consumption of iron would have amounted to under one-quarter of one per cent of annual output' (von Tunzelmann 1978: 286). He moreover points out that 'If all the engines operating in the textile industries had suddenly been swallowed up by the ground in the middle of 1838, and all blast furnace capacity in the country had then been set to work to smelt the iron required to rebuild them, it would have taken under a month to complete the task' (von Tunzelmann 1978: 109).

Backward linkages to coal were rather more substantial, though still arguably very small: possibly as much as 10 per cent of 1800 coal output was consumed in steam engine furnaces, though there are possible upward biases here, and anyway most historians have considered the technical development of coal to have taken place before the industrial revolution.

Nor do the forward linkages to cotton look much more impressive. These linkages came relatively late in the development of the cotton sector, 'when the cost of supplying power fell and this happened to influence the nature, extent, and mode of employment of machines driven by power', whereas – it could certainly be argued – the crucial period of cotton development came much earlier, in the acceleration of output which occurred between 1770 and 1800. The major technical innovations in cotton, until the development of Roberts's self-actor in 1825–30, were not developed for steam power; water power long dominated the power-intensive textile processes – 'rarely have I unearthed cost reductions from steam-powered inventions in textiles on the scale often intuitively supposed' (von Tunzelmann 1978: 294).

The method of social savings used by von Tunzelmann is certainly open to criticism on conceptual and methodological grounds (for an excellent critique of the social savings method, see O'Brien 1977). However the underlying empirical basis of his work, which demonstrates rather limited diffusion of steam relative to other power sources, has not been challenged, and his critique of the alleged backward and forward linkages of steam also remains unchallenged. What we can conclude here – in what is after all one of the very few detailed empirical examinations of a critical technology – is that the claims made for steam as a driving force for growth are seriously overdone. This does not mean that the impact of steam is non-existent – it would not have diffused or survived as a technology if it had no advantages. But those advantages do not necessarily add up to support for the extreme views of those who advocate a steam-driven view of industrialisation.

CONCLUSION: INTERPRETING THE PATTERN OF TECHNOLOGICAL CHANGE

This chapter opened with the suggestion that the technological aspects of early British industrialisation continue to present intellectual challenges; technological dimensions of industrialisation are far from fully researched, and are likely to remain a productive area for students in the future. The 'critical technologies' argument seems to obscure most of these problems, mainly because it rests on an implicit technological determinism in which a small number of innovations – whose provenance and trajectories are more or less unexplained – account for the basic growth dynamic of what was already a large and complex economy. While those who support these arguments often criticise the attempts to quantify the impacts of critical technologies (see for example Freeman and Louca 2001: 31–5), the proponents of the critical technologies arguments in general offer little evidence concerning the economic impacts of steam, railways and so on. Conceptual arguments as to precisely how the radical technological breakthroughs in textile machinery, steam power and the like fed through into economic outcomes are often absent, as is any form of quantitative evidence linking the industry concerned to the wider economy.

The alternative that has been explored here is that innovation was a broad process, pervasively embedded in many industries, even those that were essentially matters of hand technology. Samuel argued, in a chaotic but fascinating paper, that 'in speaking of the primacy of labour power one is referring not to single instances, or to curious survivals, but to a dominant pattern of growth', one that was 'quite as dynamic as high technology industry, and just as much subject to technical development and change' (Samuel 1977: 45, 61). There is in fact a wide array of evidence from business, technological and industrial histories to lead us to the firm conclusion that innovation in the industrial revolution was present across virtually all activities that comprised the British economy at that time. Clearing the ground on this issue is important in itself, but it also generates much wider questions. If we recognise that technological change during early industrialisation was not a matter just of steam, textiles or any other particular heroic breakthrough, but was rather a matter of extensive development across a very wide range of technologies, then we open up a new array of research issues. The wide scope of technological development in Britain after the early eighteenth century suggests a general social propensity to innovate. Exploring this propensity ought to lead us first to an adequate causal account of extensive technological change, secondly to a more satisfactory account of the relations between the different fields of technological and economic change, and finally to a better understanding of the economic causes and impacts of innovation.

6

Money, finance and capital markets

STEPHEN QUINN

Contents

Introduction: the British financial system in 1873   147
Payments to 1800   151
Commercial finance to 1800   157
Nineteenth-century reorganisation   161
Securities   167
Conclusion   173

INTRODUCTION: THE BRITISH FINANCIAL SYSTEM IN 1873

Walter Bagehot, editor of *The Economist*, published *Lombard Street* in 1873. Bagehot rejected the title 'Money Market' because he wanted to convey to readers that he was dealing 'with concrete realities' (Bagehot 1873: 1), and reality in 1873 was that the bricks-and-mortar components of the London money market around Lombard Street were banks: the Bank of England, private banks, joint-stock banks and discount houses. In Bagehot's words, these banks formed 'the greatest combination of economical power and economical delicacy that the world has ever seen' (Bagehot 1873: 2). However, the two centuries of financial development that produced Lombard Street also sheltered once-innovative, now-dated arrangements like England's decentralised regional banking system (Cottrell 1980: 16). In 1873, Britain had 376 private and joint-stock banks, of which ten were Scottish and 296 – 80 per cent – of the remaining 366 banks were English and Welsh banks outside of London (see Table 6.1). Similarly, two-thirds of England's £393 million of commercial bank deposits were outside of London, and most of Britain's 481 Trustee Savings Banks were also outside London (Table 6.1; Horne 1947: 379–85).

Regional banks were mostly local concerns, and London acted as the hub that integrated the regions into a larger financial system. On an

Table 6.1 British banks in 1873					
	Britain	London	London-based Provincial	Provincial England and Wales	Scotland
Commercial banks	376	61	9	296	10
Joint-stock banks	135	17	9	99	10
Private banks	241	44	0	197	0
Bank branches	2,558	90	433	1,188	847
Deposits, in millions	£469	£131	£52	£210	£76

Sources: English commercial banks are from Capie and Weber 1985: 423, 576, and Scottish banks are from Checkland 1975: 497, 743.

average day in 1873, provincial banks had £9 million on deposit with correspondent banks in London and £5 million in cheques and notes being cleared – mostly using the London Clearing House (Capie and Weber 1985: 280, 475). London was also where banks that needed cash sold bills of exchange. While no aggregate figures for the scale of rediscounting are available, the practice was common. For example, the middle-sized Liverpool Commercial Banking Company was rediscounting 15 per cent of its bills in 1873 (Nishimura 1971: 45). London was the place to sell bills of exchange because the money market was so deep (that is, there were many diverse institutions operating within it). In addition to commercial banks, London had discount houses whose sole form of lending was discounting bills of exchange. In 1873, £60 million of the kingdom's £445 million in bills (assuming an average usance of three months) were held by London discount houses (King 1936: 261; Nishimura 1971: 93). The robust competition meant provincial banks, along with commercial and industrial concerns, could rely on being able to sell a 'good' bill in London (Collins 1988: 151–3).

Market depth applied to foreign bills of exchange also, and half of all bills drawn in Britain in 1873 were foreign bills (Nishimura 1975: 93). The international character of London included many foreign banks. While the number of foreign banks in London is not known, between 1870 and 1873 twelve foreign and two colonial banks were formed in London while branches of Credit Lyonnaise and Deutsche Bank were also opened (Cottrell 1991: 45; Newton 1998: 79). By 1877, foreign bank deposits were £107 million or one-fifth the size of all deposits in British commercial banks, and London was even being used to finance trade that never passed through Britain (Capie and Weber 1985: 254; Davis and Gallman 2001: 129–30). The London money market had evolved to redeploy money from regions of net saving to regions of net borrowing – both domestically and internationally.

London performed a similar function for long-term securities by combining domestic and international markets; however, the supply side of London's stock market was dominated by government and railway securities. In 1873, the total value of securities on the London Stock Exchange

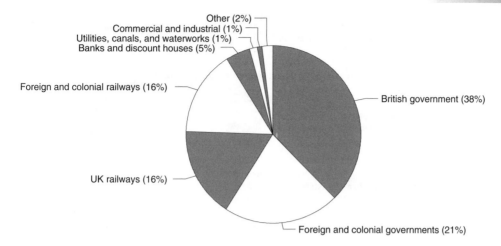

Other (2%)
Commercial and industrial (1%)
Utilities, canals, and waterworks (1%)
Banks and discount houses (5%)

Foreign and colonial railways (16%)

British government (38%)

UK railways (16%)

Foreign and colonial governments (21%)

was £2,270 million (Michie 1999: 88). Figure 6.1 shows that over half of the market's value was government debt and that British government debt was 80 per cent larger than the combined listings of all foreign and colonial governments. Railways comprised an additional third of the market's value and were equally divided between domestic and foreign railways. The initial public offerings of these securities were handled by various institutions: the Bank of England managed issues of British government securities, domestic railways issued their own securities, and major foreign issues were handled by London's merchant banks (Cottrell 1980: 182, Davis and Gallman 2001: 168). In contrast, commercial and industrial securities accounted for less than 1 per cent of the London market. The small amount of industrial capital that was raised by public issue was usually floated through local channels outside of London, and the resulting regional stock exchanges were small. While the London Stock Exchange had around 2,000 members, Britain's ten provincial stock exchanges in 1873 were served by 299 brokers, and half of those brokers were concentrated in Liverpool and Manchester (Cottrell 1980: 152).

London's dominance was self-reinforcing because financial agglomeration in the metropolis attracted non-banking financial intermediaries like insurance companies, which were major holders of securities. The delicacy of the situation was that everyone looked to London for money in an emergency, yet the actual amount of money was limited. Commercial banks averaged 10 per cent reserve-to-deposit ratios and discount houses were even more leveraged (Capie and Weber 1985: 78). The total amount of debt in the British money market was roughly five times the actual value of coins in Britain, and the value of the stock market was larger still (see Figure 6.2). A rush to convert bills, deposits or securities into coins endangered the entire chain of credit, and Bagehot stressed in *Lombard Street* that the Bank of England should act as a lender of last resort to mitigate such panics. Although the Bank of England had only

Figure 6.1 Sectoral shares of London stock market in 1873

Source: Michie 1999: 88.

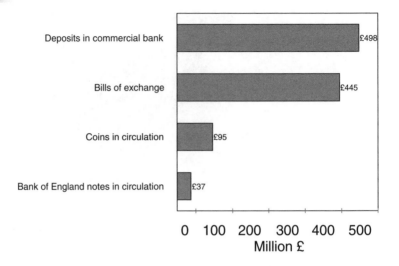

Deposits in commercial bank — £498

Bills of exchange — £445

Coins in circulation — £95

Bank of England notes in circulation — £37

0   100   200   300   400   500
Million £

Figure 6.2 Deposits, bills, coins and banknotes in 1873

Sources: Coins, notes and deposits from Capie and Weber 1985: 325, 432. Bills (assumes average usance of three months) from Nishimura 1971: 93.

£37 million in circulating banknotes, it could issue more notes during panics, and the Bank of England did this by rediscounting bills during panics in 1847, 1857 and 1866. However, Bagehot wanted the Bank of England to make it a committed policy before the next panic, so that faith in the Bank of England would avert panic in the first place.

To explain why the British financial sector of 1873 had this structure, this chapter focuses on the effects of two forces on the development of Britain's financial intermediaries. Shocks, especially political ones, rapidly changed the financial environment through events like wars, regulations and bubbles. The Glorious Revolution of 1688 and the wars with France from 1793 to 1815 were of particular importance. Within each era's political and economic environment, financial intermediaries like bankers and brokers engaged in the incremental mitigation of perennial economic problems through the innovation and diffusion of financial technology. Economists categorise the problems as adverse selection, asymmetric information, credibility, moral hazard, risk, and transaction costs. The common direction of Britain's incremental financial evolution was to improve the ability of people to get money – liquidity taken in a general sense. The layering of shocks with incremental development over the years since 1688 produced the mixture that was British finance and capital markets in 1873.

How the financial system developed is important because money and finance are the mirror image of virtually every economic activity. Arrangements for payment, whether immediate or deferred, must be made, so money and finance lubricate an economy (Cameron 1967: 2). The less friction an economy has with its lubrication, the better the 'real' side of the economy operates, so financial development is repeatedly examined as a leading source of economic growth by researchers in economic development and macroeconomics as well as by economic historians (Cameron

1967; Goldsmith 1969; Levine 1997; Khan 2000; Davis and Gallman 2001; Ferguson 2001). The British experience up to 1873 is of particular interest because of Britain's role in industrialisation, world trade and the development of other nations. However, what stands out is the advance of British finance itself. In 1688, Britain was a financial backwater. In following centuries, British finance surpassed rivals, particularly Holland and France, in its ability to facilitate trade, mobilise savings, withstand crises, and expand the number, type and geographic range of marketable assets (Neal 2000). In 1873, other nations had finally caught up with Britain in some areas such as corporate banking, but Britain was the still the pre-eminent financial nation of the world. To outline that development, this chapter focuses on the innovations and the diffusion of those innovations that together made the financial system work better for all the other aspects of economic development.

PAYMENTS TO 1800

In early modern Europe, the most advanced ways of paying for things were by coins, bills of exchange and bank transfers. A variety of other things were also used, like groceries, tokens, wool, tobacco, nails, etc.; however, coins, bills and bank accounts each offered a way to pay which was superior to others in some respect. Coins were the most secure, but coins were the most expensive to move, protect and assay (i.e. check for purity). Bills of exchange were similar to a modern traveller's cheque and could be mailed, but bills had the risk of not being paid when they came due. Transfer within a bank's ledger provided fast settlement, but the risk of the bank's failure was ever present. These three ways of paying formed the technological frontier of the early modern payments system, and, in Britain before 1688, only London offered all three.

The effectiveness of each way depended on how well it eased transactions by flowing from person to person, but frictions, such as costs and risks, slowed the flow. From 1688 to 1873, Britain decreased both the costs and risks of making payments through innovations like banknotes, clearinghouses and branch banking. To conceptualise the development of the payment system as a technology, one can arrange means of payment along a line based on the trade-off between the risk of the medium becoming illiquid and the transaction costs of use (Berger *et al.* 1996). Figure 6.3 presents this relationship as a trade-off between costs on the vertical axis and risk on the horizontal axis. Viewing the payments system this way allows us to see the development of the payment system as innovation that moves the frontier closer to the origin by reducing cost or risk.

The other aspect of monetary development was moving transactions located outside the frontier up to best practice. As with other technologies,

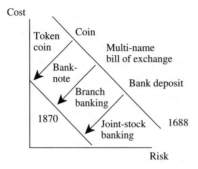

Cost

Token coin   Coin

Multi-name
bill of exchange

Bank-
note

Bank deposit

Branch
banking

1870

Joint-stock
banking   1688

Risk

Figure 6.3 Innovation
of the payment
system, 1688–1870

Source: See text.

diffusion of best practice determines how much an economy benefits from innovation. For example, British coin technology underwent an innovation when the production of coins by mill press replaced production by hammer during the reign of Charles II (1660–85). Milled edges were an improvement because their texture easily revealed if coins were clipped or shaved. Milled edges helped avoid the cost of weighing coin, yet the technology was not fully implemented until the entire stock of British silver coins was reminted in 1696 (Li 1963). Until the Great Recoinage, milled coins were hoarded, and their benefit to commerce was not realised.

The Great Recoinage was also a shock with the unintended effect of putting Britain on the path to the gold standard. Until 1696, England was on a silver standard, meaning that a troy ounce of sterling silver was set by law to be worth 62 pence, and the value of a gold guinea was set by the market (Feavearyear 1963: 346). To reduce the price of gold during the recoinage crisis of 1696, the price of a gold guinea was capped at 22 shillings. At that price, gold bought more silver in Britain than it did on the continent, so arbitrage pulled gold in and pushed silver out (Quinn 1996). The problem was realised early on by Sir Isaac Newton, Master of the Mint from 1699 to 1727. Newton lowered the price of a guinea by 6 pence in 1699 and still concluded in 1702 that 'Gold is therefore at too high a rate in England by about 10 [pence] or 12 [pence] in the Guinea' (Newton 1702: 137). In 1717, the value of a guinea was again reduced by 6 pence, but gold at 21 shillings a guinea was still overvalued.

Under the bimetallic standard of 1717, gold slowly displaced silver over the course of the eighteenth century. Because silver coins were far more useful for small, everyday transactions than gold coins, the disappearance of silver from the British monetary stock was a problem (Sargent and Velde 1999). By 1787, only the smallest and most worn silver coins still circulated, and only minimal amounts of new silver coins were being produced (Redish 2000: 141–2). In 1816, the solution was adopted to abandon bimetallism and introduce token silver coins. Token coins are coins with less metal content than their stamped value, so export is no longer profitable. Token coinage also creates large profits, called seigniorage, for the mint. Unfortunately, counterfeiters could also earn the same high profits, so successful token coins required a hard-to-counterfeit technology. The solution was the use of a steam engine along with steel collars to create perfectly round and polished coins at a level of exactness unattainable by human powered presses. In 1816, parliament adopted the technology, created token silver coinage and formally put Britain on the gold standard (Redish 1990: 802).

Even with milled or pressed edges, coins were heavy. A £100 bag of pre-token silver coin weighed 32 pounds, so although large quantities of coin could be used for payments, they had a high viscosity in terms of lubricating the economy. To avoid coin for local payments, Renaissance moneychangers had earlier developed deposit banking in Italy, so two merchants could go to a banker and transfer funds from one account to another (van der Wee 1997: 175–6). While avoiding the use of coin, deposit banks introduced the risk of runs and bank failures. Bank failures create a shock to the monetary system because suddenly a medium of exchange, bank accounts, becomes illiquid and people scramble for alternatives. Authorities in Europe responded to the shock of bank failures in different ways. Amsterdam, Barcelona, Naples and Venice created municipal banks that were not to engage in lending, so they would always have sufficient coin on hand (Usher 1943; Avallone 1997; Dehing and Hart 1997; Mueller 1997). Other places responded by outlawing deposit banking. In England, a royal monopoly on money changing prevented banking until the mid-seventeenth century (Munro 2000). In Antwerp, banking was outlawed beginning in 1489 (van der Wee 1977). Without deposit banks, people relied solely on personal promises in the form of written notes or entries in merchant ledgers (Kerridge 1988). Unlike bank transfer, payments using these methods were limited to circles of personal familiarity and were not final until the promises were settled.

Transfer (negotiability) improves the use of promises by allowing the reuse of trusted promises over a chain of purchases. A London court recognised the legality of transfer among merchants as early as *Burton v. Davy* in 1436 (Munro 2000). Unfortunately, the opportunity to transfer a promise creates an incentive to misrepresent the creditworthiness of the promise, and this moral hazard problem limits the effectiveness of transfer. In 1507, Antwerp addressed the moral hazard by making every person in the chain of transfer liable for the debt (van der Wee 1977). The most convenient way to record the chain of transfers was to have people sign the back of the promise, so endorsement became the standard way to record this contingent liability.

The innovation of transfer by endorsement diffused across mercantile Europe and jumped from local payments to the medium of exchange used for international payments called the bill of exchange. A bill of exchange orders someone in a distant location to pay a specified sum in the local currency. For example, a merchant might pay sterling in London to buy a bill that orders repayment in Dutch guilders in Amsterdam a month later. Again, Italians first developed bills of exchange, but British merchants began adopting bills of exchange in the 1300s for international remittances, especially in the wool trade (Munro 2000). Bills of exchange allowed merchants to avoid shipping bullion and so became the dominant means of international payment. As commerce developed within nations, bills of exchange were also drawn solely in domestic money and were called inland bills of exchange.

For bills of exchange to work, the person who wrote the bill (the drawer) had to arrange for someone to pay the bill at the other end (the acceptor and payer). The risk in using a bill of exchange was that the acceptor would fail to accept the bill, so innovation focused on ensuring the credibility of acceptance. Italian bankers built the first network for bills of exchange by placing family members in various cities and fairs to assure acceptance. Bankers in seventeenth-century London used agents (Neal and Quinn 2001). Penalties were also developed, and Britain was part of the Law Merchant tradition of ostracising abusers (Rogers 1995). Transfer by endorsement improved the flow of bills, because bills drawn from far away could circulate locally if at least one of the signatures was trusted locally. The more signatures a bill had, the more secure the bill was; however, endorsers of a bill of exchange were liable until the bill was finally paid, so a multi-signature bill of exchange falls between coin and a bank deposit on the frontier of the payment system in Figure 6.3.

While coins and bills of exchange were well established in Britain by the seventeenth century, deposit banking had only begun in London during Cromwell's Protectorate (1649–60). Cromwell relaxed economic regulation in general, and banking by goldsmiths developed from the existing businesses of pawn brokering and retail credit (Quinn 1997). The transforming path of British banking, however, began with the initially small innovation of the banknote. The European payments system based on deposit banks and bills of exchange worked well for those people with means and reputation, but many people were lacking in either means or reputation. A solution was for a banker to issue to the customer a banknote, which is the banker's promise to pay. Bank drafts perform the same function. Of course anyone could write a note, but only where banks were permitted could someone develop the reputation necessary to issue notes that would be widely accepted at face value. An additional innovation was to transfer banknotes by bearer instead of by endorsement. Since the value of the note depended on the reputation of a well-known banker, endorsement added no net value but did create a chain of unsettled payments until the bill was finally paid. In contrast, transfer without liability, 'by bearer', created finality for someone at the time the banknote was used. By reducing cost without increasing risk, the banknote payable to bearer moved the payments system frontier inwards towards the origin (Figure 6.3).

Banknotes altered how banks were financed and how the payments system worked. Banks could buy assets to push notes into circulation, and the notes did not come right back for redemption because people wanted to use the notes as a means of payment. The potential was greater if the public's willingness to hold and reuse banknotes increased as more people used banknotes. Such a network effect on the demand for banknotes rewarded an initially aggressive purchase of financial assets, and the Bank of England did exactly that in 1694. To help finance the Nine Years War (1688–97) against France, the Bank of England scheme had the public subscribe £1.2 million to create a corporate bank that would purchase a £1.2 million annuity from the government. Although investors pledged to the full amount within two weeks, the actual money was collected from investors in stages running for months, so the Bank of England paid the government with banknotes. After that, the Bank of England purchased more government debt from the public with banknotes. By March 1696, the Bank of England had £2 million worth of banknotes in circulation, and about half of those notes offered no interest – their only value was as a means of payment (Horsefield 1983: 264).

Although begun in London, banknote-style banking expanded rapidly in Scotland. In 1695 the Bank of Scotland was founded in Edinburgh by act of the Scottish Parliament. Unlike the Bank of England, the Bank of Scotland was prohibited from lending to the Scottish government. In 1727, the Royal Bank of Scotland became the second Scottish joint-stock bank, and a note duel soon followed as the two banks competed for the banknote market. The competition forced the Bank of Scotland to suspend convertibility for eight months in 1728 until legal pressure forced the bank to resume payment. The Bank of Scotland then adjusted its notes by inserting a clause allowing the bank's directors to suspend payments, but they had to pay interest on notes they suspended. The Royal Bank of Scotland did not incorporate the clause until 1762 but was ready to make the adoption if needed (Checkland 1975: 68). The suspension clause was rarely resorted to, and the option to suspend may have prevented runs in the Scottish system, but the clause was outlawed by Parliament in 1765 (White 1995: 26).

In 1747, a third Scottish joint-stock bank was granted a charter (Checkland 1975: 97). Private banking spread to Glasgow, and another bank war broke out between Glasgow and Edinburgh, but the new Glaswegian banks could not be crushed, and private banking spread to Aberdeen, Ayr, Dumfries, Dundee and Perth (Checkland 1975: 91–138). In 1771, the Bank of Scotland and the Royal Bank of Scotland began par acceptance and regular weekly clearing (settlement of inter-bank liabilities) of the provincial banks which integrated the Scottish note market. Edinburgh acted as the hub for the Scottish system and connected Scotland to London via bills of exchange. In May 1772, Scotland had thirty-one banks, of which twenty-one were in Edinburgh including the three limited-liability joint-stock banks (Checkland 1975: 135).

The stability of the Scottish system was tested when the Ayr Bank went on a three-year bill-discounting/note-issuing spree. The failure of a London–Edinburgh banking house allied with the Ayr Bank in June 1772 touched off a panic that ruined thirteen private Edinburgh banks along with the Ayr Bank (Checkland 1975: 134). The liquidity crisis was controlled when the Bank of Scotland and the Royal Bank of Scotland accepted Ayr banknotes that were secured by the property of Ayr Bank's owners. The par acceptance of provincial notes was restarted in 1774, and the Bank of Scotland began to establish branches around Scotland. In contrast, the Royal Bank of Scotland developed correspondent relationships with provincial banks except for one branch in Glasgow. Private banking again began expanding both in and out of Edinburgh.

By contrast, the development of banknotes in England was dominated by the privileges parliament granted the Bank of England. Parliamentary Acts in 1697, 1707 and 1709 granted the Bank of England a monopoly on corporate banking in England and forbade partnerships of more than six members from issuing banknotes payable on demand (Horsefield 1983: 134, 139). As a result, London bankers largely abandoned note issue in favour of deposit banking (Clapham 1944a: 162). The effect, however, was limited to London because the Bank of England refused to branch, so Bank of England notes were only redeemable in London. When far from London, the notes would circulate at a discount to cover shipping costs, which discouraged their regional circulation until the Bank of England began opening branches in 1826. While free to issue notes, English banks were limited in size, so banking spread slowly beyond London. In 1750, perhaps a dozen country banks operated, but their numbers grew in waves of expansion (1765–6, 1770–1 and 1789–93) to 280 banks in 1793 (Pressnell 1956: 4–11). The expansion of country banknotes outside of London and the Ayr crisis prompted parliamentary restrictions. In 1775, notes less than one pound were prohibited, and the minimum amount was raised to five pounds in 1777, so banknotes became suitable only for larger transactions (Pressnell 1956: 140).

The number of London banks doubled from 1760 to 1800, and many were country bankers moving to the capital (Clapham 1944a: 165). The local dominance of the Bank of England meant that, in London, Bank of England notes supplanted gold for high-valued settlement, and London banks came to use Bank of England notes as reserves instead of specie (gold coin). The Bank of England became the depository for roughly one-third of the kingdom's gold as country banks put extra gold into their London correspondents who, in turn, put the gold into the Bank of England (Clapham 1944a). When gold flowed into Britain, the Bank of England's note issue expanded, such as when capital fled France and the continent after 1789. However, when France stabilised its monetary system in 1795 and invasion scares mounted, gold flowed out of Britain and the Bank of England contracted note issue (Clapham 1944a: 267–72).

The other consequence of the dominance of Bank of England notes in London was that private banks in London moved to offering customers chequing accounts, and, to reduce the cost of processing cheques, thirty-one City banks created a clearinghouse in 1773 (Joslin 1954). The clearinghouse minimised the actual transfer of Bank of England notes between member banks by processing off-setting balances by ledger. Members of the London Bankers Clearing House did not share their books with each other, so the clearinghouse did not perform the same level of monitoring and co-insurance that nineteenth-century clearinghouses did in the United States (Holland 1910; Gorton 1985). The clearinghouse protected its advantage as deposit banking expanded in the nineteenth century by excluding joint-stock banks until 1854 and private country banks until 1858 (Pressnell 1956: 130; Kindleberger 1993: 80).

Along with local payments, early bankers offered remittance services to London. To connect localities to opportunities in London, country banks established correspondent relationships with London banks. The relationships usually followed from the regular flow of bills of exchange between country and City deriving from an economic speciality (Pressnell 1956: 84). In return for a balance in London, the London bank would pay the notes and bills of exchange of the country bank, execute stock or annuity orders, assist in times of tight money, and offer other services as needed (Pressnell 1956: 80, 88). The correspondent system created a hub-and-spoke structure permitting people to move money between places (London, countryside and overseas) and to change the form of their savings from demand (notes and deposits) to securities via the London stock market or international bills of exchange via the London money market.

COMMERCIAL FINANCE TO 1800

Banknotes, demand deposits and bills of exchange were means of paying for things, but they were also means of borrowing. A bill of exchange was a loan with a fixed duration. Banknotes and deposits were loans usually payable on demand. The dual nature of these instruments was how banks simultaneously introduced new media of exchange and mobilised savings for the economy. Banks borrowed by offering deposits and notes that customers preferred over coin. Banks then lent most of that money by discounting bills of exchange (Pressnell 1956: 293). Having deposits and notes as liabilities meant banks needed liquid assets, so banks preferred bills to other types of loans, such as overdrafts. On both the asset and liability sides of their business, banks were focused on liquidity.

Banks were an innovation in lending because most eighteenth-century lending was book credit extended to purchasers. Merchants routinely offered ledger credit to their customers, and such credit was common as early as the late seventeenth century (Earle 1989: 409–14; Muldrew 1993).

The eighteenth-century West Riding textile industry provides an example of the chain of credits that financed most industry and commerce. Textile manufacturers could purchase wool directly from farmers for cash, but they often got wool from staplers (middlemen who held stock of wool in warehouses) on credit (Hudson 1986: 112). Indeed, a typical artisan woollen manufacturer could be extended credit by suppliers for the full range of inputs (wool, labour, fulling, scribbling, carding, tools and rents), which made entry into the industry very easy (Hudson 1986: 190–1). Manufactured cloth was then consigned to a factor (a sales agent) at London's Blackwell Hall market who sold the fabric to drapers, warehousemen and merchants. Buyers for the domestic market demanded credit of six months to twelve months while buyers for the international market wanted longer credit (Hudson 1986: 156). Larger manufacturers might wait that long, but most manufacturers arranged to collect their sales revenue quickly either from their London factors, who found buyers, or from warehousemen who actually took ownership of the fabric (Price 1980: 105). The London middlemen, rather than manufacturers, came to specialise in supplying commercial credit to merchants, and the greatest of these, such as Samuel Fludyer, dominated the mid-century London woollen market (Price 1989; Smail 1999: 55). Big wholesalers in other industries like linen, iron and groceries also were major sources of credit and often had larger capitalisations than their merchant customers (Price 1980: 112–13).

The predominance of commercial credit created a demand for both sides of the emerging banking business. To repay credits, businesses needed demand deposits, banknotes, bills of exchange or other means of payment, so the supply of these means of payment was the principal function of country bankers (Pressnell 1956: 136). The other aspect of credit was that accounts receivable were illiquid, so when the inflow of credits (accounts receivable) proved too slow to cover payments due (accounts payable) a demand for external borrowing was created. The standard way for merchants to borrow externally was for the business to draw a bill of exchange and then sell the bill at a discount for cash. For middle- and working-class households, pawn brokers were a key source of external credit (Lemire 1998: 113).

Quasi-banking emerged incrementally as innovators across Britain began to offer these services. Manufacturers occasionally produced tokens and notes to pay their workers, but far more often they solved the means-of-payment problem by paying workers with groceries (Hudson 1986: 156–8). Industrialists who had regular trade with London supplied bills of exchange and remittance services (Hudson 1981: 380–1). Also, wholesalers issued bills to producers that circulated as a medium of exchange within regions like the West Country (Smail 1999: 55).

On the lending side, most borrowing outside the chain of trade credit was kept within the close circles of information limited by family, religion or business (Hudson 1986: 211). Scrivener attorneys extended that range by using the information generated from their privileged legal positions to act as brokers who connected savers with borrowers. Across Britain, but especially in Lancashire and Yorkshire, local attorneys were relied upon by large landowners, trusteeships, spinsters, widows and other savers to find suitable borrowers (Anderson 1969b; Hudson 1986: 211–17). This function was similar to notaries in France (Hoffman *et al.* 2000). Savers delegated the finding of opportunities to attorneys via brokerage, but savers knew exactly to whom their money was being lent because the loan was still direct. Delegated lending developed on the edges of attorney finance when landed gentry deposited funds with their London scriveners for use at the scrivener's discretion until a suitable mortgage investment appeared (Melton 1986), or when attorneys, acting as estate agents, held and used a landowner's rents for short periods (Hudson 1986: 214). In London, wholesalers borrowed money from investors to help supply commercial credit (Price 1980: 142).

Commercial banking evolved as attorneys, manufacturers, warehousemen, merchants and other people took the next step of combining payment services and delegated lending. A quasi-banker's earliest notes would often be payable with interest after a certain date, but the evolution of full banking brought the use of notes payable on demand, because customers valued the liquidity (Thornton 1802: 170). The advantage of banking was that combining the supply of media of exchange with the supply of external lending was often a superior form of intermediation than supplying each function separately. The supply of liquidity complemented delegated lending because customers wanted notes and deposits for their use as means of payment, so money was lent to a bank at little or no rate of interest and without much regard as to what the bank would do with it. Indeed, the less depositors had to bother knowing about a bank's lending decisions, the greater the value added by the delegated lending function of a bank. It was the banker's job to assess lending opportunities (Newton 2000).

Unfortunately, the asymmetry of information between depositor and banker also created an opportunity for bankers to abuse depositor trust, but many early banks mitigated the problem of moral hazard by openly lending to partners, their family and their related businesses. Open insider lending by banks meant that depositors knew the business and family groups that were behind the bank and could judge the risk accordingly. Many country banks were established to finance the business ventures of the partners, and they were similar in this regard to the early banks of nineteenth-century New England (Pressnell 1956: 292; Lamoreaux 1994). For example, bankruptcies of these industry–bank alliances often did not treat the manufacturers as separate from their banks (Hudson 1981: 384–5). The limitations of business-based or family-based banking were that the failure of the business ruined the bank and that the success of the business venture often transformed the business from a borrower to a source of savings, so the bank had to begin finding outside lending opportunities.

Even when commercial banks moved beyond insider lending, moral hazard was still addressed by the liquid nature of the bank's notes and deposits. Liabilities that can be withdrawn on demand or presented for payment on demand are a constant threat. Because of the psychology of a bank run, even a few prominent withdrawals can cascade into a run, so only a few customers can effectively monitor and threaten a bank (Calomiris and Kahn 1991). The threat of bank runs, especially for partnerships facing unlimited liability, mitigates moral hazard and causes bankers to place a premium on liquid assets, so the ability to convert bills into money separates a double coincidence of wants regarding investment duration. In the case of bills, a borrower agrees to pay the bill on a fixed day in the future, but liquidity means that the bank can hold the debt for less than the full duration. Disconnecting a borrower's and a lender's view of a loan's duration promotes lending by allowing more combinations of people to find beneficial exchange. Transfer of financial assets was difficult throughout early modern Europe, so discounting of bills of exchange was the principal means of liquid commercial credit available in the eighteenth and nineteenth centuries (van der Wee 1977). The dual nature of bills of exchange as loans and as means of payment even mingled within the ledgers of country banks. Bank lending by bill involved discounting a bill of exchange by the discount rate, but standard practice for accepting deposit of a circulating bill of exchange was for a country bank to give full value and immediate access to a demand account customer (Pressnell 1956: 293).

The combination of commercial credit, attorney brokerage, insider lending and external bank loans was sufficient to finance early industrialisation (Pollard and Ziegler 1992: 21). The long-term capital requirements of early mills were not large, so mortgage and retained earnings were often sufficient to finance fixed investment in the eighteenth century (Pollard 1964; Hudson 1986: 262). The contribution of external lending was to free retained earnings from duty as cash reserves. To see how, consider a firm's supply and demand for funds (Neal 1994). The supply schedule was a combination of cash, borrowing and equity. A firm's cash reserve was from the retained earnings of earlier profits, and eighteenth-century firms placed an emphasis on 'accumulating a reliable cushion of liquid assets' (Ellis 1998: 104). External funds might then be available from a banker or through an attorney. Finally, a firm could issue new stock or accept new partners to gain funds, but the opportunity cost of equity was considered greater than borrowing. The composite supply schedule is presented in Figure 6.4.

A firm's demand schedule for funds began with any fiscal shortfall that had to be paid. Such demands carried a high willingness-to-pay because

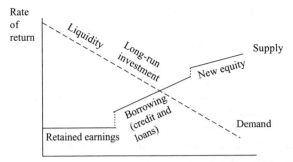

Quantity of financing

Figure 6.4 Supply and demand for industrial finance *c.* 1790

Source: Neal 1994: 176.

the opportunity cost of not meeting these obligations was ruin. After non-deferrable expenses comes the entrepreneur's opportunity for long-run investments in the company. The remainder of the demand curve was short-run opportunities such as extending credit to customers, increasing production or repaying credit not yet due. The composite demand schedule is also presented in Figure 6.4. Because immediate obligations must be addressed first, a firm without access to external borrowing had to hold internal funds as precautionary reserves, so the availability of external debt to cover short-run liquidity needs freed internal capital for investment purposes.

Shifts in the components of supply and demand demonstrate the power of shocks to ruin firms. For example, trade cycles were a common feature of the era. In a trade boom, revenue would easily flow in; internal profits would grow, providing room for expansion of long-run investment and opportunistic short-run lending. A downturn, however, reduced revenues, so firms had less internal profit exactly when the demand from immediate obligations increased, so a liquidity crisis on top of a trade crisis was devastating (Pressnell 1956: 468). The supply schedule would shift up and the right tail of the middle (borrowing) component of the supply curve would truncate as lenders rationed credit. The more the system of external lending eased business access to money during regular periods, the more the same businesses became vulnerable to disruptions of that system, and studies have found that bankruptcy correlated with trade and liquidity crises (Duffy 1985; Hoppit 1987; Neal 1994). The evolution of the British financial system in the eighteenth century increased this channel through which large shocks propagated through the domestic economy.

NINETEENTH-CENTURY REORGANISATION

The Revolutionary and Napoleonic wars with France and the Panic of 1825 that followed triggered a series of shocks, crises and innovations that reorganised the British system of money and banking. The transformation began with the suspension of the convertibility of Bank of England notes into gold. War with France was causing a drain of gold out of the Bank of England that became precipitous in early 1797, so on 26 February the King ordered the Bank of England to suspend convertibility (Clapham 1944a: 272). Suspension drove coinage out of circulation, and the Bank of England responded to the demand for money by expanding the supply of its notes through bill discounting, including the rediscounting of bills from London bankers. Discounting supported the government's war effort because London banks could invest heavily in high-return government debt and easily borrow from the Bank of England at a fixed rate of 5 per cent should the banks require momentary liquidity. Discounting was also very profitable for the Bank of England since notes could be issued without any gold backing; however, the Bank of England did ration its discounting to keep credit levels from growing too much (Duffy 1983).

Banknote issue also expanded outside of London. Parliament responded to the lack of coinage for small payments by lifting restrictions on small-denomination banknotes in March 1797. The expansion of credit and the freedom to issue small-denomination notes promoted the expansion of country banking, but another factor at work was an increased demand for banking by industry. The success of Napoleon's Continental Blockade and the need to arm Wellington's Peninsular Campaign shifted resources within Britain towards heavy industry such as metallurgy (Neal 1990: 205). From 1797 to 1810, the number of country banks in England and Wales almost tripled from 230 to 783, and the growth of private banknotes was especially demanded by industry (Pressnell 1956: 11, 148). The increase in supply of banknotes brought inflation. The price of gold peaked in 1813 at 36 per cent above its pre-suspension level. Figure 6.5 plots the price of gold in London from 1790 to 1830. Rapid deflation followed in 1814 and 1815, yet not until 1819 did the Resumption Act order the Bank of England to restore convertibility. The Bank of England responded by building up its stock of gold, reducing the number of notes in circulation, and keeping the discount rate at 5 per cent in an era of falling rates (Neal 1998: 55). The resulting final spurt of deflation allowed the Bank of England to restore convertibility in 1821.

War finance also disrupted the relationship between country banks and London bankers. The expansion of country banking and industrial growth during the wars increased demand for country bank discounting on London when London was reducing the supply of rediscounting (King 1936: 6). With high wartime rates on government debt, London bankers favoured the more secure government debt over the bills offered by country banks (Neal 1990: 217). Also, the Bank of England would not rediscount bills for country banks. Even the secondary market was problematic because the Bank of England would only discount bills of less than sixty-five days, which excluded two-thirds of the bills sent to London by country banks (Pressnell 1956: 99).

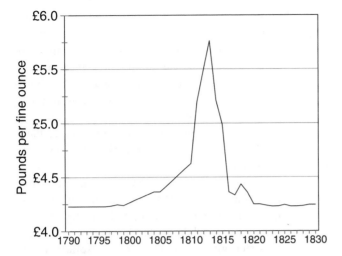

Figure 6.5 Price of gold in London, 1790–1830

Source: Officer 2002.

To improve the liquidity of bills, bill brokers emerged who charged a fee to connect buyers and sellers. The brokers' 'primary function then quickly came to be that of receiving bills from the "industrialist" banker and arranging for the discount either in London or by the "agricultural-ist" country bankers' (King 1936: 6). Bill brokers took no position on the bill itself, and brokers claimed that they screened borrowers on behalf of investors, so country banks using brokers suffered fewer losses (King 1936: 16). With peace and the subsequent fall in rates on government debt, brokers gained further business when private bankers were slow to reduce their discount rates and the Bank of England refused to reduce its discount rate at all (King 1936: 27–8). Bill brokering rapidly increased the liquidity of the secondary market for bills and bolstered the eighteenth-century system of localised banking. In terms of Figure 6.3, bill brokerage improved the ability of bills to move between the countryside and London.

The spread of commercial banking across Britain also brought banking panics. In 1793 the end of a trade boom and speculation in canals had forced many country banks to suspend payments. As mentioned above, in 1797 the Bank of England was granted the suspension of convertibility to forestall a crisis. Even during the Suspension Era, private banks failed in waves of runs between 1810 and 1813 caused by bad harvests and the downturn in foreign trade (Pressnell 1956: 466–70). An even larger panic hit Britain in 1825 when about fifty English banks went bankrupt and more suspended payments.

Scotland, however, seemed 'almost immune to the virus' (Clapham 1944b: 102), so the Scottish system became a template for English banking reforms. In 1826, Parliament allowed banks beyond 65 miles from London to become joint-stock banks of more than six members; 117 were created from 1826 to 1844, and only nineteen failed or closed (Cottrell and Newton 1999: 84). The new joint-stock banks displaced over half the traditional country banks by 1844, but most joint-stock banks remained local in lending and ownership, with one-fifth having been converted from private banks (Cottrell and Newton 1999: 90–2, 103). Often, joint-stock banks continued insider lending and used shares as collateral (Hudson 1986: 224). In 1833, Parliament expanded joint-stock banking to London, but joint-stock banks operating in London were prohibited from issuing notes to avoid direct competition with the Bank of England. By 1844, London had five joint-stock banks that averaged three times the deposits per bank of private London banks, but private banks were still twelve times more numerous (Cottrell and Newton 1999: 103).

What did not happen until the 1860s was extensive bank amalgamation or bank branching. Many banks found that the benefits of diversification were outweighed by the challenges of managing branches (Newton and Cottrell 1998: 121–2). Also, joint-stock bank development was stymied from 1844 to 1857 by legal restrictions such as a minimum capital requirement of £100,000 and a minimum share value denomination of £100, and only six new joint-stock banks were formed from 1844 to 1857 (Collins 1988: 74). A key element of the Scottish model of joint-stock banking, however, was not introduced to England until limited liability for shareholders was finally made legal in 1858 and 1862; then a rapid expansion of joint-stock banking and bank branching followed (Newton and Cottrell 1998: 127). A consequence of the expansion of bank size was the growth of overdraft services at the expense of discounting bills of exchange. Increasing scale of bank operations meant joint-stock banks had less need for the liquidity that bills offered, so they favoured the convenience that overdrafts offered.

Another consequence of the Panic of 1825 was the geographic expansion of the Bank of England. The government pushed the Bank of England to establish branches so local money markets could be stabilised through the direct supply of Bank of England notes and discounting (Kindleberger 1993: 86). The Bank of England did not want to expand, but the government threatened to revoke the Bank of England's monopoly, so, from 1826 to 1829, the Bank of England established eleven branches in Manchester, Gloucester, Swansea, Birmingham, Liverpool, Bristol, Leeds, Exeter, Newcastle, Hull and Norwich (Ziegler 1990; Neal 1998: 72). To discourage local note issue, the Bank of England branches offered favourable terms to banks that did not issue notes (Pressnell 1956: 152). Also, the branches supplied coinage, that was particularly useful to industrialists for paying wages. To secure this advantage, in 1829 Parliament banned notes below £5 in England and Wales. As a consequence, the composition of the English monetary stock became dominated by commercial bank deposits, and commercial banknotes gradually became unimportant (Collins 1983: 390).

Still another consequence of the Panic of 1825 was that London banks discovered that the Bank of England could not be relied on to assist other banks during a crisis. In the eighteenth century, London's banking system had become based on Bank of England notes, but the Bank of England avoided lending to banks, especially the rediscount of bills of exchange that a private bank had already discounted. The Bank of England was a for-profit operation and resisted offering assistance to competitors at the Bank of England's expense (Goodhart 1988). Expectations were altered, however, during the suspension era when the Bank of England liberally rediscounted bills of exchange for banks. With the return of convertibility, the Bank of England returned to its aversion to rediscounting. During the liquidity crisis of 1825, the Bank of England's first instinct was to build reserves and restrict lending (Clapham 1944b: 98). In 1825, London bankers were caught between the demand on them for rediscounts by their country bank correspondents and the Bank of England's refusal to supply London bankers with rediscounts. This painful experience caused London private bankers to develop greater cash reserves and demand interest-paying call deposits (King 1936: 62–3). With banks willing to take a rate of return on call deposits less than what bills of exchange offered, the largest bill brokerages began to supply the service. In doing so, the brokerages became dealers – discount houses – who took demand deposits from banks and invested the money in bills of exchange.

The transformation from bill brokerage to discount house was encouraged in 1830 when the Bank of England began permitting discount houses to rediscount with the Bank (King 1936: 89). This seemingly innocuous policy change by the Bank of England rerouted the flow of emergency funds from the Bank of England through discount houses instead of directly to banks (King 1936: 89). The mediation of discount houses between banks and the Bank of England caused the Bank of England's rediscount policies to focus on systemic needs rather than on whether particular banks deserved assistance (Capie 1999). Bill dealing and rediscounting was further changed by the 1833 repeal of the usury ceiling on bills of exchange of up to three months. For discount houses, the spread between the rates offered on call deposits and the rates available on bills was no longer limited. For the Bank of England, instead of having to restrict the quantity of discounting supplied at 5 per cent, the Bank of England could instead raise rates to reduce the quantity demanded. The flexibility allowed the Bank of England's discount rate to become the primary policy instrument calibrating the Bank of England's relationship with the discount houses.

Discount houses were also critical to the new form of British banking. The combination of the note-issue ban in London and the presence of Bank of England branches outside of London meant that most joint-stock banks chose not to finance by note issue but instead sought deposits. As a result, country banknote issue (private and joint-stock) peaked in 1836 (Newton and Cottrell 1998: 126). Joint-stock banks made deposit-based liabilities profitable by keeping low cash reserves and rediscounting bills to provide liquidity when needed (King 1936: 39–40). London's discount houses became the key intermediaries as joint-stock banks rediscounted bills of exchange on a daily basis, and joint-stock banks increased the volume of the bill market by buying bills when funds were deposited and selling bills when funds were withdrawn. Similarly, joint-stock banks put their cash reserves to profitable use as call loans to discount houses (King 1936: 42).

As with other new financial technologies, the new discount market was pushed to an unsupportable extreme. The ease of rediscounting caused banks to discount more bills and bills of less quality, yet the security of a bank's endorsement lulled discount houses into ignoring the volume and quality of liabilities banks were creating (King 1936: 94). Those pushing the limits of the system included joint-stock banks that discounted the bills of merchant houses specialising in Anglo-American trade. When the scale of the American-based liabilities became clearer in 1836, the Bank of England refused to discount the bills, so a panic began, based on the weakness of the affected merchant houses and their banks. The Bank of England then chose to reverse policy, and the panic subsided, but the Bank of England was locked into a generous rediscount policy for three years. The moral hazard created by the Bank of England's easy liquidity caused banks and discount houses to lack restraint. The increasing supply of Bank of England notes, however, scared continental markets into a run on the currency side of the Bank of England in 1839 out of fear that the Bank of England would not be able to maintain convertibility (King 1936: 97). In response, the Bank of England increased the discount rate to 6 per cent, limited rediscounts and pushed London into a severe liquidity crisis (King 1936: 82).

The failure of the Bank of England in the 1830s to balance its role as defender of the pound and rediscounter of last resort fuelled a reformatory agenda that became law in 1844. Members of the currency school believed that the freedom to issue notes caused swings in the overall price level and created instability. The Bank of England and other members of the banking school felt that so long as notes were issued with reasonable gold backing – thought to be 33 per cent by the Bank of England's Governor – that note issue did not threaten price stability (Kindleberger 1993: 91). The Bank of England's failure during panics in 1836 and 1839 gave the currency school the upper hand in government, and, in 1844, the Bank of England was split into an Issue Department and a Banking Department with the goal of limiting note issue (Kindleberger 1993: 91). The Issue Department was given the monopoly on the issue of Bank of England notes while the Banking Department was given all the remaining business of the Bank of England. The Issue Department was allowed £14 million in fiduciary notes, after which every additional Bank of England note issued had to be fully backed by gold. To limit further the supply of banknotes, existing English banks could not expand their note issue, while existing Scottish and Irish banks could only expand issue with full gold backing like the Bank of England now had to have (Collins 1988: 72). Finally, no new note issuing banks were allowed anywhere in Britain.

While the Bank Act of 1844 created strict currency controls, the discount policy of the Bank of England remained largely unrestricted because rediscounts could be created by deposit liabilities instead of notes. The exception was when withdrawals from the Bank of England demanded more notes than could be supplied, but here an *ad hoc* solution was found. During panics in 1847, 1857 and 1866, the Treasury waived the penalties for violating the constraint, so the Bank of England was free to supply emergency liquidity (Kindleberger 1993: 94). The very suspension of restrictions on Bank of England note issue was enough to end the domestic portion of the panic of 1847 (Dornbusch and Frenkel 1984).

The era of domestic panics ended when the Bank of England committed to emergency rediscounting while minimising moral hazard problems. The solution adopted by the Bank of England was to commit to offering easy access to rediscounting during panics but to charge a high rate of interest to penalise those who most exposed themselves to the threat of a liquidity crisis. The policy was most prominently championed in the 1860s and 1870s by Walter Bagehot, and the adoption of Bagehot's policy by the Bank of England in the 1870s along with the growth of bank branches and the amalgamation of banks created a very crisis-resistant payments system (Ogden 1991). In the following decades, individual banks failed and international exchange-rate crises threatened the pound, but domestic panics on the banking system ceased (Capie 1999: 125–6).

SECURITIES

The evolution of large-scale finance in Britain was also framed by shocks and by liquidity enhancing innovations. More so than with short-run finance, liquidity was crucial for solving the differences in time horizons between suppliers and demanders of capital. For example, the dominant consumer of long-term capital from 1688 to 1873 was the British government itself, and the advent of reliable, liquid government debt allowed the British government to borrow extraordinary amounts in the eighteenth century compared to Holland or France (Neal 1998). Even after the introduction of securities by foreign governments, transportation, financial services and industry, British government debt in 1873 still accounted for 38 per cent of the London Stock Exchange (Figure 6.1).

The revolution in the finance of the British government began with the Glorious Revolution of 1688. The ascension of Holland's William of Orange to the English throne brought a new constitutional compromise. Parliament would support William's Holland in the Nine Years War (1688–97) against France, but William III would recognise parliament's control of the public revenue (North and Weingast 1989). The settlement also created the national debt because funded debt was created under parliament's direct authority to commit specific tax revenues to maintenance of the debt it authorised (Dickson 1967). The involvement of parliament complemented the introduction in England of the Dutch practice of long-term borrowing by annuity, and lower interest rates on government debt resulted (Wells and Wills 2000; Quinn 2001; Stasavage 2002). Annuities backed by the expansion of taxation by parliament created a revolution in military finance essential to Britain's emergence as a Great Power (Brewer 1988; O'Brien 1988).

Annuities, however, were difficult to transfer, so their secondary market was limited by their lack of liquidity, and the Bank of England was an innovation that addressed this problem. By the 1690s, the use of joint-stock organisation by companies was well established (Harris 2000: 39–46). Because stock was much easier to transfer than government debt and government debt formed more than 90 per cent of the Bank of England's revenue-producing assets, Bank of England stock was, in effect, a more liquid form of government debt (Neal 1990: 15). After the success of the Bank of England, annuities were sold to other joint-stock companies: the Million Bank in 1695, the New East India Company in 1698 (£2 million) and the South Sea Company in 1711 (£9 million). Also, the Bank of England expanded its holding of government debt in 1697 and 1709 in exchange for extensions of its charter and parliamentary prohibitions on competing banks noted earlier (Acres 1931: 101). In all these cases, parliament traded support for a company in exchange for corporate borrowing, and the public supported the scheme by either buying stock, swapping government debt for stock or accepting banknotes.

The new stock deepened the secondary market for securities in London. Even companies that did not absorb government debt, like the Royal Africa Company and the Hudson's Bay Company, experienced an increase in trade activity (Carlos *et al.* 1998). Deepening the market meant that buyers and sellers had increasing confidence that a trading partner could be found. The key intermediaries in deepening the market were brokers and jobbers. Brokers specialised in matching buyers with sellers while jobbers actually bought and sold their own positions. Although maligned in their day, jobbers created liquidity for sellers and a constant market for buyers in a manner similar to what warehousemen provided for trade goods (Michie 1999: 23–4). Most long-run investors rarely bought or sold, but the volume of business generated by short-run holders, especially merchants, kept intermediaries in business, so long-run investors enjoyed low-cost liquidity (Michie 1999: 26).

Government borrowing by annuity was introduced in the 1690s, but annuities came to dominate government borrowing during the War of the Spanish Succession (1701–13) (Dickson 1967: 358–60). By the coronation of George I in 1714, interest charges were consuming half of the government's yearly revenue (Roseveare 1991: 53). While Britain won both wars, roughly one-third of the debt, £15 million worth, was irredeemable – meaning that the government could not force repayment of the 99-year annuities (Dickson 1967: 92–3). The solution to the government's debt problem was to extend the mechanism of debt-for-equity swaps to their logical extreme through the conversion of the irredeemables and other annuities into stock. In 1720, the South Sea Company outbid the Bank of England for the right to create stock and swap it for most of the outstanding government debt. At the time, a similar scheme under the direction of the Scotsman John Law seemed to be succeeding in Paris (Neal 1990). By mid-1720, more than 80 per cent of privately held annuities (£26 million) were voluntarily exchanged for South Sea stock (Dickson 1967: 522–3). The windfall for the government was that annuities costing the government between 6 and 9 per cent were transformed into debt owed to the South Sea Company paying 5 per cent and could be redeemed.

Individuals traded their annuities for South Sea Company stock out of an expectation that stock prices would rise. A bubble formed because investors were inexperienced about how to value these new securities, and new types of securities also led to later bubbles in canals, foreign debt, and railroads. The bubble was also inflated by extensive credit creation. The South Sea Company only required subscribers to put down a fraction of the subscription in cash. To circumvent Parliament's prohibition on corporate banking, the South Sea Company used a partnership called the Sword Blade Company to issue banknotes that were used to finance more purchases of the South Sea stock. While Sword Blade notes only functioned as a medium of exchange in Exchange Alley, that circulation was sufficient to support a price increase that reached ten times par in the summer of 1720. Annuity holders responded enthusiastically to the opportunity to swap annuities for stock which lent credibility to the scheme (Neal 1990 109). By the end of August 1720, the South Sea Company's assets were £75 million in subscribed cash, £26 million in swapped annuities, £11 million in loans, and £17.5 million in unissued stock, while liabilities were only £8 million owed to the government in various pledges and £5 million in bonds (Dickson 1967: 125, 134, 160–1; Murphy 1986: 161–2).

The bubble burst because most of the South Sea Company's £75 million in cash was pledged rather than in hand, and, when collecting the cash began to look very unlikely because that amount of money was beyond the ability of the banking system to create, stock prices plummeted (Neal 1990: 109). Liquidation spread, London banks suffered runs, the prices of East India Company stock and Bank of England stock fell, and the Sword Blade Company failed on 24 September 1720 (Dickson 1967: 158; Neal 1990: 106). Investors clamoured for legislative relief, and parliament ruled that the South Sea Company would not collect the remaining cash due; however, the annuity–stock swaps were ruled final, and the £26 million in annuities collected through the stock swaps were restructured into marketable government annuities that provided enough secondary market trading to maintain the broker-jobber infrastructure of the London market (Neal 2000: 128).

Although the South Sea annuities were finally paid off in 1850, parliament continued to issue new annuities (Roseveare 1991: 59). Because each new issue was based on a different revenue fund, these securities collectively became called the Funds, and, from 1749–52, Lord Treasurer Pelham directed the consolidation of the Funds into one perpetual annuity paying 3 per cent interest per year called the Three Per Cent Consol (Dickson 1967: 228–41). The Consol was simple and secure, with a deep secondary market. The liquidity of the Consol promoted investment because it reduced the money that a bank, insurance company or other business had to hold for precautionary purposes.

In the decades following the Bubble, the market for government debt also consolidated around the Bank of England. New annuities were issued through the Bank of England eight times from 1727 to 1751. Instead of purchasing annuities, transferring annuities or collecting interest on annuities at the Treasury in Westminster, investors came to conduct the business much more conveniently at the Bank of England. The Rotunda of the Bank of England, opened in 1765, was popular for trading because transfer of both Consols and Bank of England stock was registered there (Michie 1999: 32). Securities trading also occurred outside of the Bank of England, and in 1773 a syndicate built a stock exchange in Sweetings Alley and charged for people to trade there (Michie 1999: 31). The benefit for traders was a common set of rules and regulations; however, the exchange was not a closed system, and the exchange's Committee for General Purposes lacked the power to exclude defaulters or adjudicate disputes (Michie 1999: 34).

Another consequence of the South Sea Bubble was the passage of the Bubble Act in 1720 that prohibited the formation of publicly traded joint-stock companies except by government charter or act. The act was a piece of special-interest legislation pushed by the South Sea Company to suppress rival schemes during the Bubble (Harris 1994). Although famous, the Bubble Act was easily circumvented and eventually repealed in 1825 (Harris 1994: 623–6; 1997). Circumvention was especially important for the growth of insurance, which benefited from economies of scale. When the incorporation of new life insurance companies was blocked by the Bubble Act, new companies instead organised around private trusts that were effectively the same as joint-stock companies (Supple 1970: 54–61). The exception was marine insurance, because the Bubble Act contained a clause that granted joint-stock charters to the Royal Exchange Assurance and London Assurance and prohibited any other company or partnership from underwriting marine insurance (Supple 1970: 32–3). Because both joint-stock companies expanded slowly and because the exclusivity clause kept out new companies until it was repealed in 1824, Lloyd's private underwriters dominated marine insurance in the eighteenth century (Supple 1970: 53, 186).

Liquid, secure government securities also played an essential role in the development of insurance. Insurance companies needed liquid assets to meet unexpected claim demands, so insurance companies preferred securities to mortgages, and government debt was particularly favoured. For example, from 1734 to 1784, government securities rose from being 22 per cent to 54 per cent of the Royal Exchange Assurance's assets, and in 1840 their share peaked at 70 per cent (Supple 1970: 74, 314). Mutual fire insurance societies also made heavy use of South Sea annuities and Consols (John 1953: 144–5). The reliance on the liquidity of government securities by insurance companies only declined in the middle of the nineteenth century as life insurance companies grew so large that cash requirements could be confidently predicted (Supple 1970: 314).

English savings banks also relied on government debt. Begun in Ruthwell, Scotland, in 1810 as a charity, savings banks allowed the working class to earn interest on small-value deposits (Horne 1947: 43). The concept was wildly popular with members of the upper class who desired to promote thrift among the working poor, so, by the end of 1815, all of Scotland except the far north had access to a savings bank (Horne 1947: 50). The concept soon moved south; however, private banks in England would not pay savings banks for deposits like Scottish banks did. The English solution was for the government to offer savings banks a guaranteed, above-market rate of return for money invested through the Bank of England into a special account of the national debt (Horne 1947: 77–8). The bill became law in 1817, and about 150 new savings banks formed within twelve months after passage. The total amount those savings banks held in their special fund at the Bank of England increased by an average of one million pounds per year over the next thirty years (Horne 1947: 116) and provided a way for working-class Britains to gain access to reasonable rates of return on their savings yet still have the ability to liquidate those savings if needed.

The Napoleonic Wars also brought changes to the stock market. War shocked the market for government securities with increased volume and volatility, while refugees from Paris and Amsterdam brought experienced traders who were new to the London market (Michie 1999: 33–4). The resulting problem of traders defaulting began harming the liquidity of government securities, so the exchange on Sweetings Street organised to limit access to the market. In March 1801, the stock exchange changed itself into a subscription room with rules of behaviour, controlled admission, administration paid by subscriptions, monitoring, and enforcement by the threat of expulsion (Michie 1999: 35). The exchange soon refused admittance to members whose principal business was not brokering or jobbing, to avoid linkages between external business failure and members going bankrupt (Michie 1999: 38–9). Positions between members could be substantial, and the illiquidity of assets in bankruptcy threatened the system. The institutional firewall was made formal in 1812 when the exchange ruled that all members had to be solely stock brokers or jobbers (King 1936: 39).

The tension between brokers and jobbers then kept the exchange from imposing additional limits (Davis and Neal 1998: 41–2). Brokers wanted fixed commissions and transparent bid-ask spreads that jobbers opposed. Jobbers also opposed limits on the number of brokers or limits on trade with non-members desired by brokers. In such a competitive environment, brokers favoured adding new listings, so gaining access to the exchange was not constrained, and the success of British government securities in London attracted a wave of new securities from foreign governments after the Napoleonic Wars. Merchant bankers like the Barings and the Rothschilds arranged for issues by France, Prussia, Spain, Denmark, Russia, Austria and the new nations of Latin America (Neal 1998: 61–4). Despite the offerings of safe securities like French debt, many investors with little information gambled on new nations like Peru and related foreign mineral companies. Despite the deserved collapse of some foreign securities during the panic of 1825, the flotation of foreign securities by merchant banks remained an important aspect of the London market.

New domestic securities, however, were slow to develop. The first joint-stock canal was formed in 1766 (Harris 2000: 97). A boom in joint-stock canals came later and peaked in the early 1790s, but most canal capital was raised locally, often along the path of the canal itself where property owners would be most benefited (Thomas 1973: 6). Most canal shares were never traded, and many canal companies discouraged speculation and jobbing of shares by limiting the amount of shares any one person could hold, so organised trade was limited and centred in London (Thomas 1973: 6–7). Similarly, joint-stock gas works and water works were local affairs, often with limited individual holdings with little secondary trading. The development of provincial auctioneers into stock brokers instead relied on the growth of railway securities in the 1830s which coincided with the growth of joint-stock banks mentioned earlier (Thomas 1973: 10–11). At the peak of the first railways boom in 1836, brokers in Liverpool and Manchester created formal exchanges (Thomas 1973: 18–19).

After the first wave of railways established profitability in the early 1840s, a second wave of railways formation began and the source of capital shifted from insiders who would directly benefit from the new railways to outsiders and the London market (Killick and Thomas 1970: 97–102). The change was essential because railways required such substantial amounts of capital (Reed 1999: 10). Margin buying, investor exuberance, inadequate accounting and a rush to be the first to lay track turned the second railway wave into a bubble. The number of railway companies listed on the Liverpool exchange increased from thirty-eight in 1836 to one hundred in 1844, and to 305 in 1845 (Thomas 1973: 33). Numerous provincial stock exchanges appeared in 1844 and 1845, but only a few exchanges survived the collapse of the bubble in late 1845. Table 6.2 shows the retrenchment of railways after the bubble by listing the number of railway companies listed by exchange at the end of 1845 and 1846.

Table 6.2   Changes in the number of railways listed by stock exchange

	End of 1845	End of 1846	Percentage change
Liverpool	305	233	−24%
Manchester	166	105	−37%
Leeds	77	69	−10%
Bristol	72	29	−60%
Birmingham	88	21	−76%
Sheffield	105	36	−66%
London	204	147	−30%

Source: Thomas 1973: 33.

For the next quarter-century, British investment focused on foreign securities as the London stock market assumed its 1873 balance of domestic and foreign securities. From the mid-1850s to the 1870s, investment in foreign securities increased fivefold and included new securities issues from thirty-four nations, Indian and colonial governments, foreign railways, and private companies operating overseas (Davis and Gallman 2000: 158). By 1873, a quarter-million British savers directly owned paper securities; however, far more savers reached the securities market through deposits and life insurance policies. While commercial banks were by far the largest intermediaries shepherding British savings, insurance companies did account for about one-fifth of all the assets held by UK financial institutions (Davis and Gallman 2000: 88). Savings banks accounted for an additional 10 per cent of all financial assets, and savings banks represented more than 3 million depositors (Horne 1947: 389, 392). In 1873, British savers had a variety of intermediaries with which to access the securities market.

CONCLUSION

From 1688 to 1873, shocks and incremental innovations created a new system of finance for the British economy. Britain began with coins, bills of exchange and local credit networks. London also had deposit banking. The Glorious Revolution was the first great shock and triggered a revolution in government finance marked by the Bank of England, the South Sea Bubble, the Three Percent Consol and restrictions on English banking. As a consequence, banking developed more quickly in Scotland than in England, but the market for securities in London became robust. The Napoleonic Wars were the second great shock and triggered token coins, savings banks, discount houses, the London Stock Exchange, a wave of new foreign securities after 1815, the panic of 1825, Bank of England branches and joint-stock banking in England. As a consequence, commercial banks replaced banknotes with deposits, and London's money market and securities market became the largest in the world.

Lesser shocks also mattered. Railway bubbles created provincial stock exchanges, repeated panics turned the Bank of England into a lender of last resort, and limited liability laws brought branches and bank amalgamation. Still, the adoption of most new financial technology throughout Britain was incremental. Chains of commercial credit led to specialised financiers like staplers and warehousemen. Brokers, like attorneys, developed local networks of external credit. Quasi-bankers integrated lending with the supply of means of payment, and insider lending became delegated lending. Joint-stock banks and railway finance only slowly moved beyond their local beginnings, and, even by 1873, little British industry was financed by the national market.

Another consequence of the evolutionary nature of British financial development was an element of path dependency. The particular sequence of English financial development produced a system resistant to reform based on lessons available from other systems such as Scotland, America or the continent. For example, many authors have commented that England suffered from greater banking regulation relative to Scotland (Cameron 1967: 98–9; Checkland 1975; White 1995). A consequence, however, was that England took a different developmental path focused on the deepening of the secondary market for bills of exchange and especially on the development of discount houses (Cameron 1967: 58–9). The London money market created a resilient source of liquidity that supported bills of exchange as a means of payment, bills of exchange as a means of lending, and a banking system that relied on both functions of the versatile bill of exchange. The Bank of England also used the bill market to conduct her discount policy. As Bagehot concluded in *Lombard Street*, 'A system of credit which has slowly grown up as years went on, which has suited itself to the course of business, which has forced itself on the habits of men, will not be altered because theorists disapprove of it, or because books are written against it' (Bagehot 1873: 160). Instead, rapid change followed macro-shocks that disrupted business habits, and slow change followed micro-improvements to the flow of business.

7

Trade: discovery, mercantilism and technology

C. KNICK HARLEY

Contents

Introduction	175
The commercial revolution	176
The American trade	181
The industrial revolution and trade	186
Repeal of the corn laws	187
Trade and growth	190
The importance of trade and why Britain did not 'depend' on trade	191
Mercantilism, trade and growth	195
Trade and the industrial revolution	198
Conclusion	202

INTRODUCTION

In the mid-eighteenth century Britain was the world's greatest trading nation. Manufacturers exported a wide variety of textiles and hardware. Rich London and Bristol merchants imported tropical goods and more modest provincial merchants dealt in Baltic timber and grain. Two centuries earlier, England had been an economic backwater, exporting unfinished heavy woollen cloth to the Low Countries for further finishing before sale throughout Europe. During the century and a half after 1750, British firms and British investors provided leadership in industrial revolution technology and policy shift that created a fully globalised trading world.

Trade from the mid-sixteenth century to the end of the industrial revolution may be envisaged, somewhat oversimply, in two periods. Until the late eighteenth century, incorporation of the Americas drove change. The British industrial revolution introduced a shorter second period that lasted until about 1850. Late in the eighteenth century, British firms in a few key industries developed technological superiority over producers elsewhere. As British firms adopted superior technology and competition among them drove prices down, they captured world markets. Since the new cotton textiles depended on a tropical raw material, new import trades grew as well. In 1846 repeal of the corn laws symbolised a shift in policy from mercantilism to free trade. Later in the nineteenth century, a new phase of multilateral globalisation occurred, driven primarily by technology that dramatically lowered transportation costs, reinforced by liberal economic policy and population growth.

THE COMMERCIAL REVOLUTION

The broad dimensions of British trade from the Restoration to the American Revolution are illustrated in Table 7.1 and Figure 7.1 (comparisons over time are not entirely appropriate since the 1660s data relate only to London). Broad trends are clear. Initially Britain exported woollen textiles to Europe. In the eighteenth century, distant markets, particularly in the American colonies, became important. Imports initially came mainly from continental Europe; about half were manufactured goods – mainly linen from north-western Europe – with the remainder split between wine and spirits and various raw materials. By the end of the period, imports from Europe still predominated but manufactured goods had less importance and imports were raw materials – raw silk and dye-stuffs from southern Europe for the textile industries and iron and timber from the Baltic. The most dramatic change in imports, like that of exports, was the rise of distant markets. Initial expansion occurred in oriental goods: spices – particularly pepper – and cotton and silk textiles. In the eighteenth century the imports of new tropical and semitropical staples – sugar, tea and tobacco – grew rapidly to make up nearly 30 per cent of all imports in the 1770s (Davis 1954, 1962, 1973, 1979; Minchinton 1969). The bulk of Britain's trade remained focused on nearby areas of Europe. Exports remained primarily woollen cloth but some change was underway by 1660. At the beginning of the seventeenth century British merchants exported heavy unfinished woollen cloth to more advanced textile centres in the Low Countries for finishing and final sale. After 1568, revolt in the Spanish Netherlands and the Thirty Years War severely disrupted this trade. Many skilled Protestant craftsmen and merchants escaped the horrors of war and religious persecution on the continent and brought their skills and capital to England. English firms began to produce lighter, more finished, woollen (and worsted) cloth – the New Draperies – and established a flourishing trade with southern Europe independent of the Low Countries.

Although Britain's European trade developed and remained the source of most trade, the rise of long-distance trade attracted the attention of contemporaries and historians. These trades introduced exciting new

Table 7.1 Official values of British trade, 1663–1774 (£000)

	1663 & 9 (London only)				1699–1701				1772–4			
	World	Europe	East	Americas	World	Europe	East	Americas	World	Europe	East	Americas
Exports	2,039	1,846	30	163	4,433	3,772	122	539	9,853	4,960	717	4176
Manufactures	1,734	1,562	19	153	3,583	2,997	111	475	8,487	3,816	690	3981
Woollens	1,512	1,423	19	70	3,045	2,771	89	185	4,186	2,849	189	1148
Metal	44	15		29	114	31	10	73	1,198	295	148	755
Imports	3,495	2,665	409	421	5,849	3,986	756	1,107	12,735	8,122	1,929	2,684
Manufactures	1,292	1,077	215		1,844	1,292	552		2,157	1,364	792	1
Pepper	80		80		103		103		33		33	
Tea	0				8		8		848		848	
Sugar	292	36		256	630			630	2,360		2,360	
Tobacco	70	1		69	249			249	519	1		518
Re-exports					1,986	1,660	14	312	5,818	4,783	63	972
Manufactures					746	491	3	252	1,562	959	7	596
Sugar					287	287			429	428		1
Tobacco					422	421	1		904	884		19

Sources: Davis 1954, 1962.

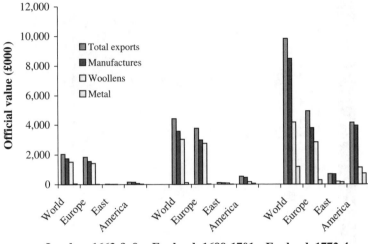

London, 1663 & 9   England, 1699-1701   England, 1772-4

Figure 7.1 British exports, 1660s, 1700s and 1770s

Source: Table 7.1.

goods – printed calicos and silks, porcelain, sugar, tobacco and tea – to everyday use in the eighteenth century and expanded European horizons (see chapter 13). The trade demanded large capital and new forms of organisation. The East India and West India merchants epitomised new wealth, sophistication and political influence that had accumulated in London as a result of a commercial revolution.

The Spanish and Portuguese discovery of sea routes at the end of the fifteenth century created the long-distance trades to the Orient and to America. The voyages of discovery had been motivated by the search for new routes to Asia and brought eastern goods to Europe. Dutch merchants, despite the revolt against Spain, quickly re-established their mercantile presence in the Iberian peninsula and came to dominate trade by the late sixteenth century. The Portuguese initially attempted to restrict the growth of Asian trade to maintain prices and profits, but Dutch and British competition led to dramatic decline in the European prices of Asian goods. In England the price of pepper – the main spice from the East – fell to less than a quarter of its 1570 price by 1660 (Clark 2001b: 60).

The trade tapped into existing networks in Asia but became dominated by the great Dutch and English East India companies whose success rested on institutional and financial innovations. The Dutch East India Company led the way early in the seventeenth century by displacing the Portuguese in the Spice Islands and innovating in business structure. In 1612 the company shifted its organisation from adventures in individual voyages – as had long been common in European long-distance trade – to a company with a permanent capital that was not redistributed to the investors at the end of each voyage. The British company soon adopted similar structure (Neal 1990). The companies' success rested on mobilising the large capital that supported permanent presence in the east. The heavily capitalised companies required not only profitable trading ventures but also a secondary market for company shares. This market developed in the already quite sophisticated seventeenth-century Dutch and English capital markets. The Dutch company's control of Java and the Spice Islands forced the British to relocate to India – a second-best solution – and obtain spices by Asian trade. The companies flourished for two centuries on the basis of their organisational skill and military strength, their trading monopolies and the success, particularly of the English company, in developing European markets for Indian cotton textiles and Chinese tea.

Europe's Asian trade exhibited a peculiarity that is as central to its understanding as the institutional innovations of the East India Companies. While Europeans eagerly imported eastern goods, little corresponding eastward flow of European goods developed. Instead, trade was financed by an eastward flow of gold and silver that many Europeans (and subsequent historians) found disturbing. In fact, trading had become multilateral and the bullion and specie came from America. European demand for eastern goods was certainly high, but Asian demand for bullion and coin was so great that the rise of European trade with the east should be seen primarily as a consequence not of trade routes to the east but of the discovery of America.

European discovery of America had extraordinary repercussions on world trade. The dramatic conquest of Mexico (1519–22) and Peru (1531–5) established Spanish dominance and incorporated the Americas into world trade. The changes that followed were unlike anything that occurred before or since. International trade reflects an equilibrium in which traders in different countries engage in profitable exchange. Although at times political events create large adjustments, trade usually evolves gradually as new technologies reduce production and trading costs and as political changes ease or hamper exchange. America was quite different. Eurasian and American societies had developed in isolation. In the Americas, Europeans found that, sometimes after protracted periods of discovery and development, they could produce four principal commodities at much lower cost than previously prevailed in Eurasia. Chronologically the first was the humble codfish of the northern continental shelf – to which we will return briefly. The most spectacular was precious metal – silver and gold. A century or so after the conquest, the great plantation crops of sugar and tobacco became important.

The *Conquistadores* plundered native treasures, but the great bullion flows from America were mined. American deposits were far richer than any remaining in the Old World. Table 7.2 presents estimates of the annual flow of bullion to Europe; about 2 million rix-dollars of additional silver annually flowed directly to Manila from Mexico around 1700 (Attman 1986; Giraldez and Flynn 1994). The bullion flows were large. In the mid-1780s all British domestic exports were worth about £11.4 million or

Table 7.2 Circulation of precious metals, 1550–1800 (millions of rix-dollars per year)							
	1550	1600	1650	1700	1750	1780	1800
Production							
Spanish America	5	11–14	10–13	12	18–20	22	30
Brazil (gold)	–	–	–	1	9–10	4	3
Shipments to Europe							
To Spain	3	10	8–9	10–12	10–15	15–20	20–5
To Portugal	–	–	–	0.5	8–10	3	2
Europe to the East	(2–3)	4.4	6	8.5	12.2	14.7	18

Source: Attman 1986: 33.

48.5 million rix-dollars; so bullion shipments from America had a value equal to about half of British exports.

Gold and silver were monetary metals and could be easily sold (or equivalently, used to purchase goods) world-wide. The increase in money drove down its real value through price inflation and the purchasing power of silver in Europe declined to approximately a third of its pre-discovery level in the sixteenth and seventeenth centuries. The monetary use of gold and silver was not confined to Europe so, as their value in Europe fell, European traders found that profits could be made using silver and gold to buy goods elsewhere. If we assume roughly that monetary demand was proportionate to population so that additions to the money stock would eventually distribute themselves in proportion to population, we can begin to appreciate the nature of early modern trade between America, Europe and Asia. America, with only about 2 per cent of world population, was clearly going to sell most of the gold and silver it mined to the rest of the world for other goods. The output of the American mines, of course, flowed initially in colonial trade to Spain and Portugal – the Spanish crown collected 20 per cent as tax. However, the population of Spain and Portugal did not exceed that of the Americas in 1600 and so very little of the bullion remained in the Iberian peninsula. Much spread to the rest of Europe as Spanish Habsburg monarchs fought expensive wars against the Protestant Reformation. Most of the rest bought European goods for consumption in the peninsula and in America. But western Europe was only a small part of the monetised economy of the Old World. Economically advanced China and India each had a population twice that of western Europe, and the population of eastern Europe, the Ottoman Empire and the trading states of central Asia approximately equalled that of western Europe. American treasure spread throughout these Old World societies in an exchange of specie from Europe for valuable, easily transportable goods from Asia.

The inherent logic of the distribution of the extraordinary windfall of rich American mines was reinforced by domestic developments in China. Kenneth Pomeranz has recently summed up the situation (2000: 159–61):

From roughly 1400 on, China was essentially remonetizing its economy after a series of failed experiments with paper money and a grossly mismanaged copper coinage . . . [S]ilver was becoming the store of value, the money of account (and often the actual medium) for large transactions, and the medium of state payments for this huge and highly commercialized economy. The enormous demand for silver this created made it far more valuable in China (relative to gold and to most other goods) than anywhere else in the world: and China itself had few silver mines. Consequently, China was already importing huge amounts of silver (mostly from Japan, and to some extent from India and Southeast Asia) in the century *before* Western ships reached Asia. When Westerners did arrive, carrying silver from the richest mines ever discovered . . . they found that sending this silver to China (whether directly or through intermediaries) yielded large and very reliable arbitrage profits – profits so large that there was no good reason for profit-maximizing merchants to send much of anything else . . .

[W]e need to see silver itself as a good: a refined product with a mineral base, which was well suited to an important function and which the West could produce far more cheaply than any place in Asia (excepting, in certain periods, Japan).

. . . What is important here is a more specific point: that the West's huge comparative advantage in the export of silver sucked in trendsetting prestige goods from Asia. This helps to explain why so many other exotic goods flooded into Europe – they paid for silver.

It is only a slight exaggeration to characterise the first trading impact of the European discovery of America as an exchange, in China, of American silver for oriental luxury goods. The exchange was enormous because of both a discontinuous expansion of the supply of silver from America and an expansion of demand for silver in China. The trade was fundamentally multilateral. Spanish America demanded European goods that passed through Spain but to a considerable extent were imported from elsewhere, including Britain. Trade with Spain provided other Europeans with the bullion that they traded to the east. The Chinese obtained silver by selling goods both directly to the European East India Companies and by exchange through South Asia. From the British point of view, this Asian intermediation occurred via the East India Company that sent silver to India. Indians then sent silver to pay for Chinese exports (Chaudhuri 1978, chs. 1 and 8; Flynn 1986; Doherty and Flynn 1989).

THE AMERICAN TRADE

In the eighteenth century, two American crops – sugar produced on the slave plantations of the West Indies and tobacco from Virginia and Maryland – played a greater role in British (and European) trade than did all trade to the east. The Europeans introduced sugar cane from the Mediterranean, but the sugar trade depended unambiguously on American resources. Before Columbus' voyages, sugar was expensive – a spice or medicine of the well-to-do and item of ostentatious consumption by kings and princes (Mintz 1985: 44–90). The Spanish and the Portuguese introduced sugar into the Canaries and Madeira in the fifteenth century and began the practice of importing African slaves to provide labour. While the price fell somewhat, sugar remained extremely expensive. Columbus introduced sugar into the West Indies and the Portuguese began cultivation in northern Brazil about a generation later. Informed investors quickly realised that with a suitable labour force the West Indian islands and north-eastern Brazil could produce large quantities of sugar at a cost far below the pre-Columbian European price. The history of the Caribbean for the next two centuries is largely that of exploiting opportunities for sugar cultivation with capital and labour imports (if one is willing to encompass the slave trade in such an anodyne phrase).

Tobacco, a New World plant, was the Americas' other great export staple. Initially it was a medicine in Europe, widely grown in small quantities in the Caribbean and elsewhere in the mid-sixteenth century. The English settlers began growing tobacco at Jamestown shortly after its founding in 1607 and it proved extremely productive. The Chesapeake colonies became the major tobacco producing areas of the seventeenth-century world and the rapid expansion of tobacco exports caused tobacco prices to fall steeply after the first decade of the seventeenth century. West Indian planters abandoned the crop to concentrate on sugar, and after 1630 the islands quickly transformed from a principally white society with a mixed agriculture to slave-plantation-based sugar cane monoculture. In the Chesapeake, tobacco was grown on farms that ranged from small family plots to considerable plantations. The labour force, expanded by immigration, remained overwhelmingly white until the end of the sixteenth century (85 per cent of the 1700 population was white). Soon thereafter, large slave imports began, and by 1780 black slaves made up nearly 40 per cent of the population (McCusker and Menard 1985: 136).

The stages of the exploitation of both tobacco and sugar were similar. Both started as scarce luxuries that fetched high prices in Europe. Production in America, although it carried with it the vast uncertainty of an unexplored environment, promised high profits to those who would succeed. These uncertain but promising conditions still prevailed around 1625 when new English colonies on Barbados and in Virginia began sugar and tobacco production. A hundredweight of sugar from Brazil cost between £4 and £5 in London early in the seventeenth century. By about 1660, the price had fallen to around £2 per cwt but sugar remained very profitable and cultivation expanded rapidly in Barbados, the Leeward Islands and Jamaica. The price fell below £1 in the 1680s (Sheridan 1974; McCusker and Menard 1985: ch. 7). Tobacco's seventeenth-century history was similar. In the 1620s it sold as high as 20 pence per pound in the Chesapeake, but by the 1680s it had fallen to a penny a pound (McCusker and Menard 1985: ch. 6). In the eighteenth century, price stabilised and the American colonies continued to increase exports of sugar and tobacco. Sugar was the more spectacular, with Britain's imports growing 17.5 times or at a rate of 4 per cent per year in the seventy-five years leading to the American Revolution, while tobacco shipments grew at about 1.6 per cent per year for more than a threefold increase. Important differences existed between the two staples, however. Tobacco's growth depended on finding markets elsewhere in Europe. Sugar from the British colonies, in contrast, went almost exclusively to Britain, drawn to a large extent by the spectacular development of tea drinking that accompanied the fall in the retail price of tea.

Although tobacco was widely grown, by 1740 the Chesapeake shipped as much tobacco as Spanish, Portuguese, Turkish, Russian, Dutch and German sources combined (Price 1964: 500). The British Acts of Navigation stipulated that tobacco had to be shipped to a British port in the first instance, but most was then re-exported – two-thirds by the 1710s and over 85 per cent by the 1770s (Price 1973: 849). About a third of the re-exports went to northern and central Europe via Dutch ports, and 20–30 per cent was bought by the French tobacco monopoly. British consumption increased only slightly faster than population and probably more slowly than national income.

The spectacular growth of sugar, on the other hand, was entirely domestic. Sugar re-exports amounted to 75 or 80 per cent of the amount retained for home consumption at the end of the seventeenth century but sugar from the British West Indies lost its competitive position, particularly to sugar from the French island of Saint-Domingue (modern Haiti). By the middle of the century, the British trade statistics show re-exports equal to about 10 per cent of imports but this sugar sold in Ireland – a market reserved to sugar from British colonies by British legislation. Elsewhere in Europe, French sugar was cheaper. Why then did the trade in sugar from the British West Indies increase so rapidly even though the retail price, which had fallen spectacularly in the seventeenth century, probably increased slightly? Per capita consumption on the eve of the American Revolution was about twenty times the level it had been at the beginning of the century. The explanation rests in another important connection between American and Eastern trade – tea.

The British East India Company started shipping of tea directly from Canton at the end of the eighteenth century. As early as 1724, a London merchant observed: 'The Consumption of Sugar in England, by the great use of Tea and Coffy is very much encreased, of late, especially by the cheapness of Tea which will alwise enlarge the Consumption.' Tea followed the familiar pattern of initial high prices that encouraged the expansion of the trade followed by fall in the price and the growth of consumption. The price fell from about £3.5 a pound at its first introduction in 1652 to about £1 at the end of the century (Sheridan 1974: 28). In the eighteenth century, tax dominated the British retail price and, not surprisingly, stimulated widespread smuggling, which clouds our knowledge of the tea market. In the 1720s and 1730s taxes on tea considerably exceeded price net of taxes that the East India Company received at its sales. None the less, the price of tea after paying taxes fell quite dramatically, to a little below 40 per cent of its 1725 price in the early 1770s (Cole 1958, 1975; Mui and Mui 1975). Contemporaries estimated that consumers sweetened a pound of tea with between 12 and 16 pounds of sugar. The cost of the combination was overwhelmingly tea. At wholesale prices in 1725, one pound of tea cost over 132 shillings while adding 12 pounds of sugar brought the cost just over 150 shillings. The price of sweetened tea fell by about 1.2 per cent per year from 1725 to the early 1770s, implying a very high price elasticity of demand for tea of about 9. This was the period during which the British developed their extraordinary demand for sugar (Myntz 1985: ch. 7 explores the evolution of sugar consumption, which peaked in 1901 at more than 90 pounds of sugar per capita).

The American mainland colonies need integration into this story of staple trades. They were key markets for British exports and, after all, they became a great economic power in a few generations after the American Revolution. By 1770, the non-staple, non-slave colonies north of Maryland contained two-thirds of the white population, if only 45 per cent of the total population, of British America (including the West Indies). These colonies played a key role in the eighteenth-century diversification of Britain's exports by developing multilateral trading opportunities that arose from the staples. Although woollen textile exports grew, by the 1770s other exported manufactured goods exceeded them in value. Some two-thirds of the export of the 'new' industrial goods went to America. Without the northern mainland colonies, the exchange of British manufactured exports for tropical imports could not have developed to the extent that it did. In the early seventeenth century, the West Indian colonies became essentially sugar cane monocultures that depended on imports from the northern American mainland colonies for a large portion of their food and raw materials but purchased only limited amounts of manufactured goods.

New England – although its original financiers had hoped to profit on American resources – was not settled for staple production. The region lacked valuable minerals and was unsuitable for staple agriculture. The Puritan commonwealth, none the less, drew immigrants during the 'great migration' in the troubled 1630s leading up to the outbreak of the English Civil War, and its 13,500 population in 1640 surpassed the 8,100 in the tobacco region of the Upper South. Thereafter New England attracted few immigrants but a high birth rate caused population to grow at an annual rate of 2.7 per cent from 1640 to 1770. New Englanders, although non-economic considerations dominated their motivations, needed exports and they developed them in multilateral opportunities that Atlantic trade presented. Fishermen from Europe's Atlantic littoral fished the Grand Banks cod and sold their catch in Spain and the Mediterranean in the sixteenth century. New Englanders quickly exploited this resource, which provided them with a staple-like export (Grafe 2001). In addition, they sold food (particularly dried fish), timber and, increasingly importantly, shipping and other mercantile services to the British West Indian sugar colonies.

The middle colonies lacked New England's early religious impetus and developed somewhat later; the British captured New York from the Dutch in 1664 and Pennsylvania was established in 1682. They had better agricultural potential but still they too lacked staple exports that could be sold profitably in Europe. Their eighteenth-century expansion also rested on multilateral trade in Britain's Atlantic Empire. Colonists financed imports of manufactured goods from Britain by selling flour, grain and meat to West Indies plantations and with income earned from shipping and commercial activities based in Philadelphia and New York (Shepherd and Walton 1972; McCusker and Menard 1985).

Britain occupied the central position in a multilateral world trading system that developed from the exceptional seventeenth- and eighteenth-century American opportunities in mining and then in sugar and tobacco. By the late seventeenth century, Britain's growing long-distance trade had developed a pattern that persisted for a century and a half. Imports, consisting heavily of tropical primary staple products, were paid for by exports of manufactured goods and the earnings from shipping and other international services. Multilateral trading was central to the pattern. Much of this trade occurred within the British Empire, at least nominally directed by the mercantilist regulations of the British Acts of Navigation, which like other European powers' mercantile regulations controlled long-distance trade with the east and the Americas. The mid-seventeenth-century British Navigation Acts were designed to protect British shippers from Dutch competition – at that time the world's leading commercial and shipping economy. The acts stipulated that goods from Asia, Africa and America could be imported into Britain and her possessions only in British ships. Imports from European ports could only be carried by British ships or ships of the country of the imports' origin. Further certain 'enumerated' colonial staples – particularly sugar, tea and tobacco – had to be shipped to a British port, even if their ultimate market was elsewhere, and colonial imports of European goods had to pass through a British port. The acts certainly created artificial ties between the colonies and Britain, and British shipowners and merchants expanded under the shelter they provided from competition from more efficient Dutch competitors (Harper 1939). A disproportionate share of British exports sold in the mainland colonies in North America. Americans outside the staple producing colonies of the South paid for British goods by selling agricultural goods to the West Indies and to southern Europe. The northern mainland colonies sold more than half their export in the West

Indies – principally, but not exclusively, to British sugar colonies. The pattern did not, however, completely derive from mercantilist regulation. New England and Newfoundland fish, the grain of the middle colonies and the rice of the lower South also found eager buyers in southern Europe. In turn, payment for these exports contributed to England's access to Spanish and Portuguese American silver and gold that were exchanged for textiles and tea in the trade to India and China. Trade with Africa, although relatively small in the context of total trade, played an important multilateral role because the African slave trade provided the labour needed to expand the American plantations. Europeans bought slaves from African slave traders with manufactured goods from Europe and Asia.

THE INDUSTRIAL REVOLUTION AND TRADE

Following the cotton spinning innovations of the late 1760s, technology drove developments in British trade. Improved production methods allowed British firms to capture export markets with cheaper goods while the cotton industry's essential raw material created a huge new import trade with the American South. The great industries of the industrial revolution – cotton, iron, engineering and coal – were deeply involved in trade. And their growth made 1840 Britain an urban industrial society. Great industrial cities – Manchester and its ilk – were much smaller than London to be sure, but of a new character, with factories and proletariat and the absence of a traditional establishment. Manchester's industry was created by the technology of Arkwright, Crompton and Watt and by foreign trade. Nearly two of every three pounds of yarn and yards of cloth were exported and all the raw cotton arrived in Liverpool. This urban industrial society, so dependent on trade, shook the foundations of Britain's aristocratic society. A factory-owning middle class with growing economic power had already forced reform on parliament and now agitated for free trade. Their employees, the new 'proletariat', raised more radical demands in the People's Charter – manhood suffrage, secret ballot, equal electoral districts, abolition of property qualifications for MPs, payment for MPs, and annual parliaments.

Inventions reduced cotton yarn cost in 1820 to less than a fifth of its 1780 level (Harley 1998). Spinners happily sold to foreigners seeking cheap yarn. Similarly, Britain's new coke-based iron technology lowered costs in metal-using industries, stimulating sales at home and abroad. The introduction of railways overseas, beginning in the 1830s and accelerating in the following decades, created large overseas markets for Britain's low-cost iron rails (Fremdling 1977). At mid-century, British firms so dominated the world's modern industry that many contemporaries, and historians after them, talked of a British monopoly. Paul Bairoch (1982: 288–97) has calculated that in the middle third of the nineteenth century Britain produced some two-thirds of the world's output of 'new technology' products. During this period, the exports of textiles and other goods cheapened by Britain's new industrial technology (aggregated at, say, 1800 prices) grew much faster than either 'real' national income or 'real' industrial production aggregated at the same prices.

The growth of exports was not confined to the goods of the famous industries of the industrial revolution. Some have suggested that this should be taken as evidence to support an older view of the industrial revolution, which sees technological change cheapening British industrial goods generally, and to challenge the recent view that sees technological change largely confined to the famous industries (Temin 1997). However, the expansion of trade is consistent with the recent view of localised technological change. British population grew very rapidly, creating an expanding demand for imported food. The famous industries' large exports were driven by falling prices and so they earned much less from overseas than the expansion of the volume of their exports would seem to indicate. Furthermore, cotton required massive imports of raw materials. As a result, exports of other traditionally exporting industries also expanded to help to finance growing import demand (Harley and Crafts 2000).

REPEAL OF THE CORN LAWS

In the middle of the nineteenth century the politics of trade shifted as Britain led the dismantling of the restrictions of eighteenth-century mercantilism. The repeal of the corn laws in 1846 was the great symbol. Britain's political consensus shifted radically from supporting a trade policy of protecting vital interests – particularly the landed interest and those of East and West Indian traders – to a commitment to free trade.

Repeal of the corn laws presents something of a paradox. It radically changed the politics of tariffs, but actually tariffs fell only slightly and the ratio of tariff revenue to the value of imports actually remained higher than in France until the 1870s (Nye 1991; Irwin 1993). None the less, 'free trade' – which meant foreswearing the use of tariffs to protect domestic interests although retaining some for revenue – took on a near constitutional status in Britain that removed the possibility of protective tariffs from usual political discussion. Britain's leaders changed policy in response to various forces: industrialisation and urbanisation altered British society; growing population, both in Britain and elsewhere, changed the economics of the grain market (Fairlie 1965, 1969); the Reform Act of 1832 altered the politics; agitation outside of parliament became more effective; economic crises demanded action from the administration.

Eighteenth-century mercantilism was a complicated amalgam of ideas and policies. The Acts of Navigation, tariffs, bounties and prohibitions became an almost incomprehensible collection of statutes from an age in which 'the British parliament seems rarely to rise to the dignity of a general proposition'. Two separate principles motivated regulation; either it protected domestic interests or it provided revenue for the state; occasionally it did both. The Navigation Acts were valued because they strengthened the shipping and trading that supported maritime interests that underlay the successful 'blue water strategy' in the eighteenth-century wars against France. Duties on spirits, tobacco, tea and sugar complemented similar excise taxes and provided about a quarter of government revenue (Brewer 1988: ch. 4). Early in the eighteenth century, however, protection of special interests became entrenched and most of the regulations, at least measured by simple counting, aided interest groups (Davis 1966). Agriculture – the great interest of the aristocratic classes that ran the state – received aid through export bounties at times of low domestic price and duties that protected from cheap imports. The Customs protected British textile manufacturers from Irish linen and Indian cotton, ironmasters from cheap Swedish iron, and much else. Adam Smith heaped scorn on this policy in *The Wealth of Nations*: 'It cannot be very difficult to determine who have been the contrivers of this whole mercantile system: not the consumers . . . whose interests have been entirely neglected: but the producers, whose interest have been so carefully attended to' (1976 [1776]: 626).

Under ideological attack such as Smith's, administrators in the 1780s began tentatively to simplify and rationalise the customs, without changing the basic philosophy. Revenue needs of the Napoleonic Wars interrupted these stirrings of rational tariff policy. The income tax – 'the oppressive and inquisitorial tax' to contemporaries – was repealed with the peace, but other war taxes remained to pay the debt incurred in financing the war (over half the budget down to the 1850s). Protection of interests as well as revenue continued to shape tariff policy. Parliament reacted to sharp post-war declines in grain prices with new protective corn laws. High wartime duties on timber had both raised revenue and, through strong discrimination in favour of Empire timber, promoted a Canadian timber industry that joined the West Indian sugar planters as an interest to be protected. Policies to protect established interests generally recommended themselves to Britain's aristocratic political elite; they had been badly frightened by revolution in France.

Rationalisation of the tariff structure resumed in the 1820s with the removal of contradictory or inoperative duties, but even this modest programme was far from complete in 1840. On the eve of the move to free trade the tariff remained complex and consciously protective of British interests (Davis 1966; Clapham 1926). The tariff contained prohibitions on imports of live or dead meat, duties on 'slave-grown' sugar two or more times higher than those on sugar from British colonies, drawbacks on timber for use in the mines of Cornwall or in churches, eighty-odd different specifications of skins – from badger to weasel – with associated duties, export duties on coal and wool, and over 2,000 import duties on items ranging from agates to zebra wood. But as sources of revenue many duties were superfluous; seventeen of 721 articles in the tariff schedule produced 94.5 per cent of the tariff revenue (Parliamentary Papers 1840: 102).

Political and economic events brought the tariff to the forefront of parliamentary concern in the early 1840s. Severe economic recession created distress in manufacturing districts and, by curtailing revenue from customs and excises, brought a crisis in government finance. Distress strengthened the already powerful political challenge, mainly outside of parliament, to the corn laws – a particularly iniquitous tax on the poor's food for the benefit of the rich. In 1842 Prime Minister Peel acted decisively to strengthen government finance and unexpectedly reintroduced the income tax, which provided revenue that permitted tariff reform; the corn laws and the timber duties were modified. Return of prosperity allowed Peel to undertake further tariff reform in 1845 – including the removal of the import tax on raw cotton and lowering of the sugar duties.

Distress convinced Peel that protecting the agricultural interests with tariffs on food was both morally wrong and in the long run politically unsustainable; the majority of his Tory party, however, remained committed to protection. In the fall of 1845 bad weather brought on a food crisis by seriously damaging the grain harvest and spreading potato blight throughout northern Europe. This forced Peel's government to act. It became apparent that the potato blight would bring famine to Ireland in the New Year. The government split; Peel and most of his closest associates advocated immediate repeal but failed to convince their fellows. The government resigned, only to resume office when the opposition Whigs failed to form a government. Peel then brought repeal before parliament in face of opposition from most of his party, securing passage with opposition support (Gash 1986: chs. 9, 10, 15, 16).

Repeal had great political impact (Gash, 1986: 714):

> It is easy now to see how contemporary opinion exaggerated the effects, both baneful and beneficial, of the repeal of the corn laws. But the significance of the action taken by Peel in 1846 was symbolic; and as a symbol it was rivalled only by the Reform Act of 1832 as the decisive event in domestic politics in the first half of the nineteenth century. The Reform Act had been a gesture of deference to public opinion and the enhanced stature of new political classes. After 1832 the aristocracy continued to govern the country but it governed on trust. In that situation there were two dangers that might have destroyed the good effects of reform. One was that the aristocracy might be unable to carry out its trust for lack of internal cohesion; the other that it would fail to recognise the terms of its trusteeship. By 1845 the corn laws had been elevated in the public mind into a test of governmental integrity. Peel's response and the sacrifice it entailed did more than anything else to heal the social breach and restore public confidence in the good faith of a system which was still essentially oligarchic.

Almost immediately Benjamin Disraeli, who emerged as the leader of the protectionist majority of the Tory party that split from Peel, recognised that the reimposition of protection would subject the established order – the Tory's overwhelming concern – to savage and perhaps fatal popular attack (Blake 1966: 278–84). On the other side of the House, Whigs, Radicals and Peelites, despite their many differences, all opposed protectionism.

Repeal of the corn laws did not immediately end Britain's tariffs. Import duties on consumption goods continued to provide a large portion of government revenue but the principle of removing protective tariffs had been achieved and only consolidation remained. Gladstone's 1860 budget, and the associated Cobden–Chevalier Free Trade Treaty with France, removed the last vestiges of the protective system. The British Customs had been transformed from its Byzantine eighteenth-century structure to revenue duties on a little more that a dozen imports. Tariffs on sugar (complicated by West Indian interests and Brazilian slavery), tea and coffee, spirits, wine and tobacco remained important in a tax system that included comparable excise taxes on domestic production. These duties, as the French in particular pointed out with respect to wine, continued to distort trade and protect some British interests (Nye 1991), but return to old-style protection was politically precluded in Britain for two generations. Britain's unwavering free trade supported expansion of world trade for more than half a century.

TRADE AND GROWTH

The development of Britain into the first modern industrial economy occurred in tandem with the expansion and increasing sophistication of its foreign trade and growth is, after all, our primary interest in studying British economic history. Many commentators have posited a causal link from trade to growth, even suggesting that growth depended on trade. From the mid-seventeenth century onward, British trade expanded and diversified. Merchant wealth and financial sophistication developed in private merchant firms and in great trading corporations, like the East India Company, engaged in long-distance trade to the Orient and America. The 'Commercial Revolution' developed the legal, financial and commercial institutions that supported the subsequent 'industrial revolution' (see chapters 6 and 8). During the industrial revolution the great progressive industries – textiles, metal working and coal – grew by selling world-wide. The correlation between British exports and incomes suggests dependence. Eighteenth-century Britain surpassed Holland as the mercantile and commercial capital of Europe; the industrial revolution occurred in Britain and not in Holland. Britain's nineteenth-century place as 'workshop of the world' rested on the great export industries.

Statistics appear to confirm the impression of trade's importance (Crouzet 1980). The proportion of national income derived from exports and spent on imports nearly doubled relative to national income during the eighteenth century (despite a sharp setback during the American War of Independence when exports fell by more than a quarter). The ratio of trade to national income continued to grow in the nineteenth century, although somewhat surprisingly it hardly increased during the industrial revolution itself, when British cotton textiles firms quickly found large overseas markets for products of their improved technology, but did so at sharply lower prices. Imports, of course, increased along with exports. Britons in the heyday of Victoria's reign spent at least one out of every four pounds on foreign goods, a higher share than in France or Germany, and much higher than in the United States. Some three-quarters of all imports were foods and raw materials and imports were frequently the major, or even only, source of supply.

Britain was the pivot of international trade and events affecting her trade, such as the commercial revolution in long-distance trade or the move to free trade in the middle decades of the nineteenth century, might be expected to react on the British economy for good or evil with special force. In the decade 1876–85 (the earliest dates with usable statistics) Britain exported about 38 per cent of manufactured goods in world trade; a few decades earlier, the share had no doubt been larger (Hilgerdt 1945: 157–8). This position of dominance was unique, approached but not equalled even by the United States, whose share in world manufactured exports peaked at 27 per cent in 1950. Only after the First World War did the United States exceed Britain in exports of all kinds (with American wheat and British coal included in the accounting) and only after the Second World War in total exports of manufactures (Maizels 1963).

THE IMPORTANCE OF TRADE AND WHY BRITAIN DID NOT 'DEPEND' ON TRADE

Britain and the world, then, appear to have been mutually dependent, yet the size of trade is not necessarily a good guide to its importance. Trade alters economic structure as trading economies allocate resources in response to trading opportunities, and certainly trade promoted British industrialisation. In the eighteenth century Britain purchased tropical goods like sugar and tobacco by producing more manufactured goods and exporting them to customers, particularly in America. In the nineteenth century, industrial exports purchased a wider range of food and raw materials. We need, however, to be careful in talking about the dependence of an economy on trade. A careless reading of the statistics suggests that removing trade might have cut national income by 25 or 30 per cent and British wheat consumption (for example) by 80 per cent – after all, these were the shares of foreign supplies in national income and in wheat consumption. The volume of a trade, however, is a poor guide to how much the economy's prosperity depends on it. The issue is simplest to see in the case of a single commodity. Victorian Britain, denied imports of wheat, would grow more wheat and other home-grown foods with the resources that had previously produced exports to pay for foreign wheat. Foregoing wheat from the fertile plains of Illinois or the Ukraine would have a cost, but the loss to British wellbeing would be much less than the whole value of the wheat imported.

The reasoning here is characteristically economic, focusing as it does on the alternatives to acquiring goods by trade. A stress on exports rather than imports as the things-to-be-desired is non-economic. One hears it said, for example, that Britain had to import corn and timber and wine in order to give foreigners the wherewithal to buy British manufactures. A person or nation fully employed, however, yearns to acquire goods, not to get rid of them. Exports are an unfortunate sacrifice that people or nations must make to acquire imports for consumption. As Adam Smith remarked in his attack on the mercantilist doctrine that an excess of exports over imports should be the goal of policy: 'Consumption is the sole end of and purpose of all production . . . The maxim is so perfectly self-evident, that it would be absurd to attempt to prove it' (Smith 1976 [1776]: 625). Correct determination of the contribution of trade to economic welfare involves estimating the loss involved in reallocating resources devoted to the production of goods for export and instead using them to produce substitutes for domestic imports.

Although the volume of trade is an inappropriate yardstick, the gains from trade properly conceived may still seem large. For example, O'Brien and Engerman (1991) argue that export industries employed an increasing proportion of the labour force in the eighteenth century which the economy would have had trouble employing in the absence of growing trade. If so, reducing trade would have eliminated jobs in export industries and the workers would have produced goods of much lower value than the imports obtained by trade. It is not entirely clear whether O'Brien and Engerman feel that, even in the long run, markets in the early modern British economy lacked the flexibility to reallocate resources to domestic use or whether they feel that their productivity in alternative uses would have been very low.

In a somewhat different vein, Kenneth Pomeranz (2000) has recently argued, comparing China and Europe, that Britain's ability to trade manufactured goods for food and raw materials with America was key to the success of the industrial revolution, because it released Europe from biological limits to growth. The argument seems overblown. The great food imports came late in the nineteenth century, well after the industrial revolution; much of Europe imposed tariffs to frustrate American food imports; and much of Britain's food and raw material imports did not come from American sources. None the less, it is useful to investigate the likely magnitude of income loss that could have occurred if exports had been unavailable as a means of acquiring imports.

Calculating the benefits of trade, or alternatively the cost of abandoning it, is of little significance in itself, for no historical issue turns on the literal abandonment of British foreign trade, but it provides useful background to more modest experiments in counterfactuals and checks exaggerated opinions of Britain's dependence on trade. Foreign trade can be viewed as an industry that produces imports, say wheat, in exchange for sacrifices of exports, say cotton cloth. The 'productivity' of this industry is the rate at which a quarter of wheat exchanges for yards of cloth, i.e. the 'terms of trade'. The price of Britain's exports of cotton cloth, iron, coal, shipping services and so forth divided by the price of imports of wheat, lumber, tobacco, raw cotton and so forth is the terms of trade, and indicates the amount of imports a unit of exports can buy. The gains from trade depend on the extent that trade changed the terms of trade between goods imported and exported and on the importance of the foreign trade 'industry' relative to other, domestic, industries. The ratio of exports (or imports) to national income rose from about 0.08 early in the eighteenth century to about 0.30 by the end of the nineteenth. If trade made imported goods 10 per cent cheaper, and the share of trade were 0.19 of income (its average for the two centuries), national income would rise on this account by no more than (10 per cent) * (0.19), or 1.9 per cent.

The matter of concept settled, the remaining question is the difficult counterfactual one of how much the terms of trade would have moved had Britain lacked trading opportunities. Clearly, without trade the price of now-abundant exportables like cloth would have fallen relative to the price of now-scarce, land-intensive importables like wheat. In other words, the terms of trade would have deteriorated. How much? Since no such event occurred we cannot answer this question precisely, but the actual course of the terms of trade over the nineteenth century, shown in Table 7.3 and Figure 7.2, gives some guidance. The massive fall from 170 in 1820 to 100 in 1860 resulted from Britain's ingenuity in making exported cotton cloth cheaper, which more than overcame the effect of the push of population in Europe against supplies of grain. The (smaller) rise thereafter was a consequence of the full application of steam and steel to the making and, especially, the shipping of food and raw materials to Britain from hitherto remote parts of the globe. Although no exact guess is possible, perhaps the 70 or 30 per cent fall and rise in the terms of trade can provide a guide to the terms of trade implied by self-sufficiency in, say, 1860. Not much

Table 7.3 The terms of trade, 1820–1910	
1820	170
1840	130
1860	100
1880	110
1900	130
1910	130

Source: Imlah 1958.

Figure 7.2 Terms of trade, 1796–1913

Sources: Imlah 1958; Davis 1979; Crafts 1985.

of a rise in the price of German toys relative to British clocks, perhaps 10 per cent, would have been necessary before domestic production would have replaced shipments into or out of Britain. But quite a large rise would have been necessary to stop wheat and raw cotton coming in or textiles going out, so powerful were the forces of specialisation in these goods. With a tariff of 40 per cent, British farmers fed the nation in years of good harvest under the corn laws. A doubling of the price of cotton cloth exports during the cotton famine caused by the American Civil War sharply reduced exports but only by a third, but the experiment is flawed because the prices of Britain's competitors in this market went up as well. As an illustration we may consider that a prohibition of trade might have reduced the price of exportables relative to importables by, say, 50 per cent. The share of imports in income to multiply the 50 per cent would be half the way from zero, under the prohibition, to the 25 per cent that actually occurred in 1860. Self-sufficiency in 1860, then, would have cost Britain only (50 per cent) ∗ (0.125) or about 6 per cent of national income.

Six per cent of national income – or even, if, improbably, the terms of trade effect were twice as great, 12 per cent – looks small beside bold metaphors of Britain's 'dependence' on foreign trade. Indeed, the calculation is worthwhile only to loosen the grip of the metaphor (for other attempts see Kravis 1970, 1973; Crafts 1973). Even on the absurd premise of no foreign trade at all, Britain's loss would have been small relative to nineteenth-century growth of about 2 per cent per year that increased income some sevenfold. True, had Britain suddenly been denied all trade by strike or edict, the immediate effects would have been larger (cf. Crouzet 1958, 1964; Olson 1963). The experiment relevant to all the history of this period except times of war and blockade, however, is not a sudden denial of trade but a failure of it to grow over a long term. It is precisely the steady and rapid growth over two centuries that has led people to attribute to foreign trade a major role in economic growth.

The previous calculations focus on the gains trade provides from reallocating resources in response to comparative advantage. Unfortunately, economists have long recognised that such reallocation, on which their techniques focus, does not explain very much of the economic growth we observe in modern economies. It is possible to imagine forces that would have increased trade's long-run influence. This is particularly tempting in Britain's case since we often loosely, but mistakenly, use the term 'industrialisation' as a synonym for modern economic growth. The empirical impact of possible dynamic influences, however, was probably small. Like many traditional historical narratives, some modern analytical models emphasise learning by doing as an important source of technological change and hence growth (Helpman and Krugman 1985). However, trade implies not only that some industries grow relative to the size they would have been without trade but also that some are smaller. Therefore a net gain in technological progress requires that the gains from learning in the expanding industries exceed the losses from failing to learn in the industries from which resources were drawn. The dynamic British industries would have been large even if they had not captured export markets, and there is no evidence that the expansion from trade contributed learning that would not have occurred in somewhat smaller industries. Expanding trade could also have increased growth, if by chance the people enriched by the extension of foreign trade, such as East and West Indian merchants, cotton manufacturers and coal owners, saved or invested more than the people impoverished by the trade, such as timber owners and silk manufacturers. New industries probably had more scope for learning by doing, and income earners more orientated towards capitalist expansion may have saved and innovated more than those orientated towards aristocratic privilege, but there is no persuasive evidence that these effects were large. Britain was left with, say, its 6 per cent – no trivial sum, to be sure, but measured against the whole rise in output per worker of roughly 80 per cent from 1855 to 1913, only one thirteenth of the story.

MERCANTILISM, TRADE AND GROWTH

Britain's transformation from an economic backwater into Europe's leading economy with sophisticated commercial and financial institutions and a large manufacturing sector occurred during the mercantile era of growing long-distance trade. Two important issues have long attracted historians' attention. First, trade developed in the context of mercantilist imperial regulations, conflict and warfare among European empires. How much of Britain's success depended on policies that supported military and naval success? Second, Britain's – and more widely, Europe's – growing trade was intertwined with imperialism. In the New World, the conquerors displaced indigenous societies and enslaved the population to exploit the mines. When the indigenous societies failed to provide adequate labour, they imported as many as 10 million African slaves for labour. In the east, the Dutch controlled the Spice Islands and the British developed hegemony in India. In the centuries that followed, Europeans became spectacularly richer while the peoples that fell under European control did not. Were European success and non-European stagnation two parts of a single process in which Europeans became rich by exploiting the rest of the world (Williams 1944; Wallerstein 1980)? Temporal relationships have led many to conclude that success in war and imperial exploitation were keys to Europe's economic success, but more careful examination of the historical details and economic connections casts doubt on these positions.

In the eighteenth-century imperial wars, Britain adopted a 'blue-water strategy' that exploited its island position. The navy protected the British Isles from invasion and harassed French trade while the British subsidised continental allies to fight land campaigns against France. The 'blue-water strategy' was expensive, since fleets required greater and more sustained outlays than armies and subsidies required large amounts of cash at short notice. Success rested on Britain's superior ability to tax and to borrow at least as much as on its island position (Baugh 1988, 1998; Brewer 1989; O'Brien 1998, 2000; chapter 8 below). Shipping and commerce were central to the strategy's success. Merchant shipping provided the manpower for wartime fleets. Duties on imports provided significant, but by no means overwhelming, revenue. Probably more important, the commercial establishment in London lent large amounts to the government on short notice – an indispensable British asset in time of war.

Even though British politicians paid close attention to trade and shipping interests, it would probably be incorrect to place excessive emphasis on power politics in the development of British trade, and by possible extension, on growth. Despite naval domination in most of the wars, Britain gained little territory and the loss of the thirteen mainland American colonies, the greatest territorial change in eighteenth-century empires, went decisively against Britain.

The eighteenth-century British Empire was not exceptionally large or prosperous. The Spanish, French and English sugar islands in the West Indies all had about the same population (300,000 to 350,000 around 1750). The British islands were high-cost producers, unable to compete with the rapidly growing output of French Saint-Domingue without protection. During the eighteenth century, French trade to the West Indies grew more rapidly than British, and merchants in the French Atlantic ports dominated the re-export, of sugar and coffee to northern Europe (Crouzet 1996). Even in 1750, Spanish America's population of 10.5 million provided a much larger market than British America's 1.5 million. Portugal's colony in Brazil had a population equal to that of all of British America. The British Empire's size or trading contribution can hardly have made the decisive contribution to Britain's lead in the emergence of modern economic growth.

Somewhat ironically, the northern mainland American colonies – undesirable from a mercantilist view and established well before Britain became an aggressive participant in European imperial conflicts –

provided the main support to the trading pattern that accelerated Britain's industrialisation. By financing their imports by selling food, raw materials and commercial services to the staple exporting colonies they allowed Britain to expand exports of manufactured goods other than the traditional woollen textiles to a much greater extent than would have been possible with only bilateral trade. The French Empire, in contrast, had considerable difficulties supplying food and raw materials to its sugar colonies and failed to develop export trades in manufactured goods comparable to Britain's. However, the independence of the thirteen colonies hardly affected trade. Attempts to limit American trade with the West Indies failed because West Indian interests depended on American imports. British exporters retained their American markets after Independence. Re-emergence of European war in 1793 following the French Revolution only reinforced the American connection for Britain's manufactured exports to the Americas. American neutrality expanded multilateral trade to the Caribbean and South America and Britain's exports surged (Cuenca Esteban 1997).

Europe's imperialistic military success, the horror of the African slave trade, and global inequality of incomes today, have led some scholars to maintain that the tropical trade of the seventeenth and eighteenth centuries rested on Europeans' aggressive exploitation of power and that in the process Europe extracted resources from the rest of the world that made a unique contribution to Europe's growth. The modern debate on this issue still refers to 'Capitalism and Slavery' (see Williams 1944, an Oxford doctoral thesis written by Eric Williams, later the first prime minister of Trinidad and Tobago). Williams argued that the slave trade and the sugar plantations yielded great profits that played a key role in the mobilisation of capital for Britain's industrial revolution. Williams's view is now seen as overblown and the slave trade as not exceptionally profitable, but debate continues (Inikori 1987; Solow 1991a; Morgan 2000). Barbara Solow (1985) presents calculations that show that slave profits equalled a large portion of industrial investment, but this calculation is misleading. It rests primarily on the fact that the investment requirements of the British industrial revolution were very small relative to national income or the incomes of property owners. Solow's slave-related profits grow from under three-tenths of 1 per cent of national income in the late eighteenth century to close to 1.5 per cent by 1770, but total income from wealth was close to half of Britain's national income. Consequently, her calculation would be duplicated for many other potential investors without providing any useful clues. It is hard not to agree with the recent assessment made by David Eltis and Stanley Engerman – two leading scholars of the slave economies of the Caribbean – that 'sugar cultivation and the slave trade were not particularly large, nor did they have strong growth-inducing ties with the rest of the British economy' (2000: 123).

The Navigation Acts forced colonial trade through Britain, potentially enriching Britain at the expense of the colonies. In sugar, the most valuable of the traded staples, however, mercantile restriction hurt British income for the benefit of West Indian plantation owners by reserving the British market to high-cost British colonies. Sugar from the French colonies would have saved British consumers money. Mercantilist restrictions that required colonists to purchase manufactured imports from Britain seem to have had little effect. The American colonies continued to purchase almost exclusively from Britain after Independence just as they had before. The Navigation Acts' requirement that tobacco sold in continental Europe pass through British ports distorted trade in Britain's favour. The distortion has been studied by economic historians interested in the role of economic grievances in the American Revolution in classic studies in the New Economic History that combine clearly specified models with detailed historical data (Thomas 1965; McClelland 1969; Thomas and McCloskey 1981). The cost to the colonies was small and the gain to Britain even smaller. The extra expenses of shipment were not large and were balanced by the considerable credit and marketing services that British, particularly Scottish, merchants provided to the Chesapeake planters. After Independence British merchants continued to handle a substantial portion of American tobacco exports to continental Europe (Davis 1962).

A broader set of connections to European imperialism and European growth has been suggested by a 'global economy' literature that raises a large number of issues beyond the profitability of the slave trade (Wallerstein 1980). These writers see the increase in the economic and political power of merchants engaged in long-distance trade and the rise of port cities and their associated manufacturing hinterland as key features in the social and economic transformation of Europe into a capitalist society. These arguments rest on still poorly articulated and largely untested views of the dynamics of growth that require a very large weight to be placed on small parts of the early modern economy. After all, trade was a relatively small part of even Britain's economic activity and the long-distance trade to Asia and the Americas was a small part of trade. It is hard not to agree with O'Brien's (1982) conclusion 'that the periphery was peripheral' in the development of modern economic growth in north-western Europe.

TRADE AND THE INDUSTRIAL REVOLUTION

Exports are often seen as crucial to Britain's growth during the industrial revolution. They increased much faster in volume than total output and the most dynamic industries exported very large proportions of their output. Some commentators have concluded from this that the demand for

Figure 7.3 Exports as proportion of national income, 1700–1913

Source: Imlah 1958: 94–8.

these exports was a crucial causal factor in growth (Cuenca Esteban 1997). This conclusion is almost certainly inappropriate. Calculation of volume, or 'real' values, by aggregating quantities at the unchanged prices of a base year is an indispensable tool for removing distortions that arise in periods in which the value of money changes such, as during the inflation caused by American treasure in the sixteenth and seventeenth centuries. But when the relative prices of goods change radically, 'real' values have ambiguous meaning. During the industrial revolution exports grew not because foreign demand for British goods at the prevailing price increased, but because technological improvements caused a fall in prices that attracted foreign buyers. As Figure 7.3 shows, because prices fell the value of the larger volume of exports actually grew more slowly than the value of total output over the period 1800 to 1830.

We sometimes see reference to Britain benefiting from a monopoly in industrial revolution industries, but this is unfortunate; there was clearly no monopoly despite Britain's dominance. Firms were small and entered the British industry easily. As a consequence, technological improvements lowered costs, and competition caused prices to fall as well. Lower prices passed the benefits of technology to consumers; the foreign two-thirds of cotton textile customers shared the benefits equally with domestic customers. Competition among firms meant that the British gained little from the rapidly growing exports but the rest of the world gained from cheap textiles. Had the British industry been able to act as a monopolist and sold at a higher price, Britain would have benefited more.

Cotton textiles that British firms exported earned foreign exchange that bought raw materials and foodstuffs. In the twenty-five years after the Napoleonic War, technological progress reduced the capital and labour needed to spin and weave a piece of cotton cloth in Lancashire by nearly half, and competition among firms drove textile prices down in step. In 1840 an exported piece of cloth could purchase only half the foreign goods it had commanded at war's end (Imlah 1958). Because price declines and exports transferred benefits of technological change to foreign consumers, conventional aggregation of national income overstates the benefits to Britain of the cotton industry's growth. Table 7.4 illustrate the magnitudes involved. In 1841 Britain produced 5.2 times the

Table 7.4 Cotton textile production and consumption yielded, 1815–41: effects of terms of trade

	Quantities		Prices	
	1815	1841	1815	1841
Output	100	520	1.0	0.5
Raw cotton	25	161		
Consumption				
Cotton	40	208	1.0	0.5
Imports	35	75.5	1.0	1.0
Aggregate consumption			Index, 1815 = 100	
1815 prices	75	283.5	378	
1841 prices	55	179.5	326	

Source: See text.

cotton textiles it had produced in 1815. About 60 per cent of output was exported in both years. Think of the foreign exchange earned from the export sales first paying for the industry's imported raw cotton, with the remainder purchasing imports for consumption. In 1815, raw cotton imports cost about a quarter of the industry revenue; in 1841 the proportion was somewhat higher at 31 per cent. About 35 per cent (60 per cent minus 25) of the output in 1815 was exported for foreign consumption goods. In 1841 about 29 per cent of a much larger output was exchanged for such consumption goods. This was 4.3 times as many textiles as in 1815 but these exchanged for only 2.15 times as many foreign goods because revenue from a given piece of cloth could now purchase only half as many imports. The cotton textiles produced increased more than fivefold, but the consumption (British-consumed cotton goods and imports) it provided increased less than fourfold. The growth of exports increased the industry's size and social impact but had modest impact on national income.

Repeal of the corn laws has also at times been seen as making a major contribution to British growth. The height of the tariff and its changes are illustrated by the ratio of tariff revenues to the value of imports in Figure 7.4 (the measure misses the effect of outright prohibitions or duties so high as to be prohibitive). In 1841, import duties equalled 35 per cent of the value of imports and by 1881 they had fallen to only 6 per cent. Peel's political change, however, contributed only modestly to this decline. More than three-quarters of the revenue before 1846 came from the duties on sugar, spirits and wine, tea and coffee, and tobacco, which remained after repeal ('that the labouring classes should bear their share of the burden in a form in which it will be palpable and intelligible to them', as Gladstone said in presenting his 1860 budget). These revenue tariffs were able to decline between 1841 and 1881 because government expenditure declined from 9 per cent of income to 6 per cent and imports rose from 12 per cent of income to 30 per cent (in part owing to falling tariffs). Import duties could have fallen to about 9 per cent of imports and still have provided the same share of government revenue. By 1881, new tax sources – primarily income tax and estate duties – provided a little over a fifth of revenue and a shift of tax burden from customs duties to excise taxes further lowered customs duties to 6 per cent of the value of imports (McCloskey 1980: 309–13).

Trade theories help to evaluate the impact of repeal and emphasise that the impact on the distribution of income is greater than on its size.

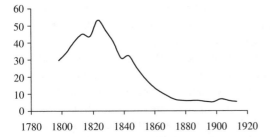

Figure 7.4 Tariff
revenues as
percentage of value of
retained imports

Source: Imlah 1958:
121, 160.

The categories of the simple theory of trade – importables, exportables and non-traded goods – corresponded well in Victorian Britain to agriculture (including some mining), manufacturing, and the residual sector, services. The early 1840s tariff raised the price of land-intensive raw materials and food relative to the price of manufactures and services, as would be expected of a tariff designed by committees of landlords in parliament and imposed on the imports of a nation buying little but raw materials and food from the rest of the world. The first effect of free trade is obvious: removing high tariffs reduced British landlords' income relative to their countrymen. Political argument at the time took it as axiomatic that what landlords lost the workers would gain, because protection of British corn producers was a tax on the mainstay of the workers' diet. In the event the real wages of workers did rise sharply after the 1840s but real rents of landlords did not fall until a generation later. Neither event is strictly relevant, however, for history was not a controlled experiment in which all factors except tariffs were held constant. In fact it is unlikely that a controlled experiment would have produced the symmetry contemporaries expected because landlords and workers were not in fact symmetrically located in the British economy. Removal of tariffs affected both the prices of goods and the incomes of labourers, capitalists and landlords. Landlords were located, of course, in agriculture and their incomes would fall. But workers were not committed to one vulnerable sector and were located everywhere: in the very agriculture made worse off by the fall of protection, in manufacturing made better off, and mostly in the vast sector of goods and (especially) services that did not cross Britain's borders. Most of the distributional consequences of the fall of protection was to shift income from wealthy landlords committed to (importable) agriculture to wealthy capitalists committed to (exportable) manufacturing, and even this was no dramatic amount.

Contemporary critics of the corn laws, and later historians, emphasised that agricultural protection was a tax on food and saw its impact working through the cost of living. The corn laws made grain expensive. The poorest classes spent nearly half their income on grain-based food while the richest spent only a negligible portion. One calculation suggests that the higher prices of corn probably decreased real wages of unskilled workers around 1830 by between 12 and 24 per cent (Williamson 1990b).

This calculation is uncertain (it probably overestimated the decline of grain prices by failing to consider an increase in prices in the Baltic), but the tax on food had large distributional impact.

The tariff also affected the size of national income but even the direction of this effect is in doubt. Free traders past and present have had no doubts whatever. Just as an individual who restricts his dealings with the rest of the world is worse off, so too, they argued, is the nation. British landlords may be made better off by a tariff on corn, but because the nation as a whole must be worse off with less access to corn, the loss to the rest of the nation is necessarily larger. But the argument is flawed. A monopolist can raise the price of what he sells and his income by withholding supply; so can a country. As we have seen, technological leadership gave Britain's cotton textiles, iron and machinery dominant positions during the industrial revolution but competition among small firms ensured that technology lowered prices rather than increased firms' profits. The tariffs of the early nineteenth century provided Britain with some monopoly advantage in these new industries by restricting British willingness to accept foreign goods. Since Britain was the dominant supplier and the main buyer of many foreigners' exports, foreigners faced with the tariff received less cloth and iron for their exports and Britain's terms of trade were better than they would have been. By abandoning protection Britain magnanimously chose not to exploit its unique position of mid-century market power. Paradoxically, protection began to recover its political appeal only at the end of the century, when potential monopoly was gone forever. In the time of greatest enthusiasm for free trade the usual argument is probably the reverse of the truth. The move towards free trade in the 1840s and 1850s probably reduced Britain's national income slightly (McCloskey 1980; Irwin 1988; Crafts and Harley 2003).

CONCLUSION

Britain's early modern economic growth intertwined with an international economy that was undergoing epochal change. Expanding foreign trade accompanied the increasing sophistication of the British economy in the century before the industrial revolution. Furthermore, the rapid growth of the industries that transformed the British economy and its society in the early nineteenth century in response to the new technologies of the industrial revolution owed much to export markets.

International trade unambiguously enhanced Britain's industrialisation. The opportunities that Columbus's discovery of America presented to the Eurasian economy profoundly affected Europe's relationship with the rest of the world. A new multilateral network of trade developed and comparative advantage in this context promoted British industrialisation.

Initially, American treasure sent to the Iberian peninsula purchased British textiles. In the eighteenth century, Britain financed sugar and tobacco imports by selling a multitude of manufactured goods to the North Americans, who supplied food and timber to the West Indies. Finally, when the industrial revolution greatly cheapened British textiles and hardware, firms in these industries found their products in demand world-wide. By exporting manufactured goods, in most cases in multilateral trading networks to buy imported foodstuffs, including tropical sugar and tea, the British economy became much more industrialised than it would otherwise have been.

Trade undoubtedly stimulated Britain's industrialisation, but it is much more difficult to develop causal connections from trade growth to the emergence of sustained modern economic growth. Specialisation and trade, of course, provided gains for the economy, but quantifying these gains shows them to have been quite small compared to the growth that emerged after the industrial revolution. Certainly there may have been gains from developing new industries and from the rise of specialised urban traders and financiers but we do not have any reliable way to measure these effects and they are likely to have been small. Certainly, growth caused some trade and the reverse is less clear. Most obviously, during the industrial revolution innovations cheapened goods, and exports grew in response. Earlier, Britain's exceptional eighteenth-century success in emerging as a powerful state in international politics and a great commercial power was as much an implication of the positive forces that were causing economic growth as a cause of those forces. After all, the opportunities that presented themselves to Europe after Columbus discovered America were not particularly directed towards Britain.

8

Government and the economy, 1688–1850

RON HARRIS

Contents

Introduction   204
Regulation   206
Public versus private ownership   211
Fiscal policy: taxation and expenditure   214
Property rights   225
Conclusion   235

INTRODUCTION

According to a well-worn myth, the British industrial revolution was a revolution that took place in the market, that was financed by private capital, and the agents of which were individual entrepreneurs.[1] The government, which had no industrialisation policy, played no significant role in this revolution. Rather, it gradually adopted a *laissez-faire* policy. Taxation was very low by modern standards and had no substantial redistributive consequences. Government expenditure conformed to early modern patterns and mainly took the form of military and crown expenses. The state owned neither means of production nor infrastructure and even its landownership had been dramatically reduced over the two previous centuries. Though some remnants of Tudor and Stuart regulation existed, particularly in the labour market and in overseas trade, such regulation was not effectively enforced and was in the process of being abolished. The minimal role of the state was unique to Britain. Elsewhere, government played an important role in inhibiting industrialisation (as in France or China), in creating industrialisation engineered from above (as in Germany and Japan) or in encouraging and subsidising private sector industrialisation (as in the USA). The more exceptional that Britain

[1] I am grateful to Martin Daunton, Stanley Engerman, Joshua Getzler and Joel Mokyr for valuable comments on drafts of this chapter.

was in terms of the role of government, the more attractive this minimal role became as a potential explanation of why Britain was the first to industrialise. If the first industrial revolution took place in a 'night watchman' state, should not economists, inspired by this interpretation of the roots of the industrial revolution, recommend free-market industrialisation as the prescription for industrialisation in eastern Europe and the Third World today? This view of the industrial revolution was most popular in the 1950s and 1960s.

This *laissez-faire* view can be contrasted with a state-centred view. The state-centred view has a dual origin: it is rooted in the fiscal–military nature of the state and in the definition of efficient property rights. The first origin attributes much to the financial revolution that began in 1688. This revolution was manifested in the rise of taxation, borrowing and financial institutions (see chapter 6). There was a strong connection between the financial revolution and Britain's rise to world mastery in the eighteenth century. The creation of a large national debt enabled Britain to finance its navy and colonial armies. As a result, Britain could, and France could not, meet the challenge of increasing costs and distances of the new global and technological wars. A financial–military nexus emerged. Merchants, city financiers and parts of the aristocratic landed elite supported this nexus and benefited from it, and the British economy prospered. The Empire and the trade it generated expanded markets, enabled specialisation, and provided surplus capital and raw materials; the rest of the story is well known.

The second origin is institutional. The political and legal institutions of Britain, notably parliament, the common law and the constitution, created the preconditions for the functioning of the market. The state created institutions that defined and protected property and lowered transaction costs. These included tradable government bonds, bills of exchange, insurance schemes, joint-stock companies, patent law and contract law, among others. These institutional innovations facilitated the development of overseas trade, capital markets and technological inventions, and the rest followed.

Britain was not exceptional in that it had a minimal or idle government. On the contrary, Britain's representative and constitutional monarchy and common law judiciary created the most active state apparatus in Europe, one that tirelessly conducted wars and/or created property rights. This context for Britain's industrialisation shows today's policy makers that political reforms, such as the formation of a representative parliament and an independent judiciary, and the adoption of rights-protecting constitutions should be the first step on the road to industrialisation and wealth.

Neither of these two views, in their extreme versions, is adhered to by many historians these days. But they encapsulate the stakes in terms of historical interpretations, economic theory and contemporary politics. They may also provide a dialectic tension, beginning with the extremes and moving to a more complex and refined synthesis. As such, I will use them as a motivating starting point for the present chapter.

Can these two historiographical views be reconciled? One route towards reconciliation emphasises timing. In the first half of the eighteenth century, Britain was a fiscal–military and/or credible property-rights generating state. By the middle of the nineteenth century it had been transformed into a *laissez-faire* state. Another route emphasises the division within British capitalism between overseas commerce and high finance on one hand, and provincial industry on the other. The government played a key role in creating the British Empire and facilitating overseas trade, but not in industrialising Britain itself. A third route argues that it is all relative. Compared to the seventeenth century, government in our period was big, while compared to twentieth-century governments, it was small. A fourth way of bringing together the two historiographical approaches is by saying that it is all a matter of where one aims the spotlight. There are numerous ways of viewing the role of government and each may point in a different direction. I will take this fourth route as my organising framework and examine, one by one, the role of the state in regulation, in ownership of enterprises, in fiscal activity and in defining property rights.

REGULATION

Was the British economy substantially regulated by the state during the industrial revolution? Was it becoming progressively more, or less, regulated? After examining the statute books up to 1700, one might conclude that Britain was heavily regulated. Here one finds laws regulating production (notably in the woollen sector), labour (the Statute of Artificers), movement of people (the poor laws), shipping (the navigation laws), overseas trade (various monopolies), maximum interest rates (the usury laws), note issuing (the Bank of England Charter), and the activity of stock brokers (a 1697 act later extended and prolonged). To this list can be added the Bubble Act of 1720 that regulated the formation of joint-stock companies. This is an impressive list that could suggest that the government was highly interested in the economy, had a clear economic policy and was able to implement it by legal-regulatory means.

Much of this regulation was abolished in the first half of the nineteenth century. The wage-fixing and apprenticeship requirements of the Statute of Artificers were repealed in 1812–13. The new poor law replaced the old poor laws in 1834. The East India Company's Indian monopoly was abolished in 1813. The Bubble Act was repealed in 1825, the corporate and note issuing monopoly of the Bank of England in 1826, the corn laws in 1844, the usury laws in 1854 and the navigation laws between 1850 and 1854. Can we conclude from this second list that eighteenth-century mercantilism and regulation were replaced by nineteenth-century *laissez-faire*?

While the statute book is a readily accessible historical source that allows statutes to be easily listed, counted and quantified, it is not very good for learning more than the basics of regulation. It does not answer two very essential questions: why were specific pieces of regulation passed and what was their impact on the economy? I will not expand here on the first question but I will elaborate on the second, arguing that the effect of the statutory regulation on the economy is far from straightforward. I would like to relate to two aspects in the discussion: the level of enforcement and the level of maintenance.

The level of enforcement of economic regulation was not uniform. Attempts to regulate the labour market, or more specifically the poor, the unemployed and young and temporary workers, were relatively successful. Here the interests of masters, estate owners and local gentry were aligned with those of the regulators. In the case of taxation, which was not only a source of income but also a regulatory measure, things were more complicated, as the interests of the state and of some of its tax payers were often in conflict. However, here the state invested great effort in enforcing its laws. By 1782 there were almost 8,300 full-time tax collection employees, an impressive number by contemporary standards. But when we examine other sorts of regulation, the enforcement picture is much gloomier. The Board of Trade had only 122 employees in 1782 and the number of employees in other departments who dealt with the enforcement of economic regulation was even smaller. Overseas trade monopolies and the navigation laws were evaded by smuggling and the forgery of documentation. Evasion of domestic regulation of the capital and goods markets required even less effort. Here the interests of traders, bankers, manufacturers and brokers often prevailed over those of the state. The lack of police and other enforcement agencies, the meagre number of administrators, the absence of public prosecution, the small budgets of the non-taxing civil departments of the government, and the lack of coordination, provide much of the explanation for the gap between regulation in the statute books and its effect on the economy.

It is argued that as the nineteenth century progressed, civil government expanded. The budget of its civil departments grew. Administrative personnel, particularly regulation inspectors, increased in number (MacDonagh 1958, 1961). The enforcement of regulation became more effective. Some historians debate the reasons for this administrative growth or the capabilities of the administrators, but not the general trend (Bartrip 1982; Harling and Mandler 1993). If enforcement was stronger in the middle of the nineteenth century, one can argue that the economy was more tightly regulated in this period than a century earlier, when regulation in the books was more extensive but regulation in practice weaker. To this one should add the fact that, while many regulations disappeared from the statute books, several important regulatory acts, including the Factory Act of 1833, the Joint-Stock Companies Act of 1844 and the Railway Act of 1844 (to which I will return), were added.

Much research has been done on the enforcement of various pieces of regulation and there is still plenty of room for additional research. The task is complicated because of the lack of primary sources and for various methodological reasons. Here, my aim is not to evaluate the level of enforcement in various sectors and periods, but only to reiterate the importance of the gap between the formal legal rules and the economic practice in any discussion of state intervention by way of regulation.

The weaknesses of Tudor and Stuart regulation were a result not only of inadequate enforcement by the executive branch but also of its drafting and maintenance by parliament. The ceiling on interest in the usury laws was bypassed by adding risk fees, by fictitiously increasing the sum of the original loan, issuing bonds below par, playing with exchange rates on foreign bills or adding profit-sharing elements. When parliament drafted the usury laws, it did not sufficiently account for enforcement problems or for the complexity of the credit market. A much more intensive and sophisticated legislative effort was needed to produce sustainable usury regulation.

Some regulations were not updated to fit the changing reality. For example, the Statute of Artificers applied only to vocations existing when the original 1563 law was passed. Entrants to newer professions were not subject to the seven years of required apprenticeship, to wage control or the like. Furthermore, the level of wages fixed in this statute had to be periodically updated to suit inflation and labour market changes. Parliament did not do this. As a result, the Statute of Apprentices and its offspring became increasingly detached from reality as time went on. This was not a problem of enforcement. Parliament needed to invest time and effort in drafting the regulation in a manner that would be sufficiently detailed and would address the complexities and variety of contexts of real life. It took maintenance work to keep the regulation current. The British parliament often did not do this. The navigation laws were a notable exception that demonstrated the investment required for real economic engineering, and, as such, emphasises the norm of inadequate legislative maintenance.

Crude legislative work, in turn, left much room for the judiciary. Generally speaking, regulation in the form of specific rules limited the role of ex-post judicial interpretation while regulation in the form of general and abstract – and often cryptic – standards called for such interpretation. The Bubble Act is a good example of the role of the judiciary in determining the effects of regulation. The act was drafted and passed in the period of the turmoil of the South Sea Bubble. It was hastily drafted and was intended to serve the immediate interest of the South Sea Company in advancing its scheme for converting the national debt. The act was not abolished in the aftermath of the Bubble and was not maintained thereafter. When it resurfaced in the early nineteenth century, again with interested parties acting as private prosecutors, judges needed to interpret the vague sections of the act before it could be applied. The interpretation of some judges was that any business association that contained elements of limited liability or transferable shares was illegal. Other, more liberal judges read the 1720 act as prohibiting only companies that had fraudulent intentions (Harris 2000: 60–81, 235–45). Thus the effects of the Bubble Act on the economy were determined by judges rather than by legislators. There are other examples of the important role of the judiciary. I shall return later to one of these: the role of the judiciary in interpreting section 6 of the Statute of Monopolies, which was the sole statutory base of English patent law during the industrial revolution.

To complicate things still further, I would like to introduce the regulatory role of the common law, and to move directly to one of its most complex manifestations, the interaction between statutory regulation and common law regulation. It is sometimes argued that there was a tradition of economic liberalism within the common law which dated back to the early seventeenth century and to Edward Coke, a tradition augmented in the eighteenth century by Lord Mansfield (Atiyah 1979: 112–38). This tradition could not be fully manifested in fields well regulated by parliament, but when fields of economic activity were left outside of the realm of parliamentary legislation, or if parliament decided on deregulation, common law judges, so it is argued, could step in and ensure free markets.

I would like to problematise this claim. In several important contexts when parliament abolished outdated regulatory statutes, the courts stepped forward and sustained the regulation, this time basing the prohibition on the common law. An antiquated doctrine, of unclear origins, held that some forms of price manipulation in the market – forestalling, engrossing and regrating – were illegal. This doctrine was primarily directed at the market for essential food supplies, particularly corn. In 1772 parliament was persuaded to abolish the ancient statutes that fixed penalties for these offences. However, common law judges, in a famous 1800 case and on other occasions, maintained the prohibition and sanctions on these market practices. They held that the basis for this prohibition could be found in the ancient common law, and thus was not abolished by the repealing statute.

Similarly, when parliament intervened in 1799 and 1800 and again in 1824 and 1825 to determine the legality of workers' combinations, common law kept resurfacing. The old common law crime of conspiracy was applied in the eighteenth century to workers who combined to raise wages. In 1799 (and in an amended version in 1800) the first nation-wide Combination Acts were enacted to void and criminalise combinations and contracts whose purpose was to raise wages, to decrease working hours, to reduce the quantity of work or to prevent persons from employing workers at will. The acts did not prevent employers from turning to a parallel track and suing on the basis of common law conspiracy.

Employers continued to do so in circumstances in which they considered that the common law would lead to better and swifter results than the statutory offence. The 1824 Combination Act proclaimed that workmen who entered into any combination specified in the act would be exempt from prosecution 'under the common law or the statute law'. By this, it not only repealed the statutory prohibition on workers' combinations but also pretended to abolish the common law offence. A year later the losing side was able to regroup and pass the 1825 Combination Act that repealed the 1824 act and with it the statutory intervention in the common law of conspiracy. What common law judges did thereafter was to interpret the act to determine, sometimes narrowly, the boundaries of its application. Outside of these boundaries, they continued to apply, often harshly, the common law of conspiracy against workers and their unions (Orth 1991). What the story of conspiracy strikingly demonstrates is that, though parliament was the undisputed sovereign, it could not create common law doctrines and it was considered poor form for it to declare common law doctrines void. Furthermore it is evident that the judiciary applied its own policies to the organisation of labour continuously between the eighteenth century and the middle of the nineteenth century and beyond. Its policies were shaped independently of enactment or repeal of legislation and of the ongoing political struggles in parliament. Judges tended to be more conservative than legislators because they adhered to ancient common law doctrines and precedents and were not influenced by the writings of political economists or by the lobbying of emerging social and economic interest groups.

My third and last example is that of the invention of a common law prohibition of the formation of joint-stock companies, after the repeal, in 1825, of the statutory prohibition, the Bubble Act. Interested members of parliament tried to repeal the Bubble Act. The Board of Trade decided to join in and lead the repeal itself. Lord Chancellor Eldon objected to the repeal. After failing to block the bill in Cabinet and in parliament, he declared that he viewed the formation of joint-stock companies to be illegal by common law. After the repeal, Eldon prompted common law judges to act accordingly, and some of the judges followed his lead (Harris 1997). This instance again demonstrates the interaction between statutory regulation and common law regulation. The Lord Chancellor here acted in three interchangeable capacities: as a member of Cabinet, as the head of the House of Lords and as a senior judge. This example is particularly perplexing because, when resorting to common law, Eldon and the courts could not find a single precedent on which to base their prohibitive attitude.

This mode of judicial decision-making, which compensated for the withdrawal of the legislator from the regulation of a specific issue by reviving common law regulation, can be interpreted as a manifestation of an interventionist and paternalist judicial policy. A conservative judiciary attempted to block a more liberal and market-orientated government and parliament. I do not argue that all the common law judges objected to free markets and supported regulation. But I reject the claim of Atiyah and others that they were, on the whole, passionate supporters of economic liberalism. The judgements varied according to economic contexts, legal doctrines, judges and cases. If anything can be said on a more general level, it is that some of the key common law and Chancery judges of the closing decades of the eighteenth century and opening decades of the nineteenth, the heyday of the industrial revolution, including Chief Justice Kenyon, Lord Ellenborough and Lord Chancellor Eldon, were more, and not less, interventionist and restraining than their predecessor Lord Mansfield. A claim, based on parliamentary deregulation alone, that the British state became less interventionist in the nineteenth century, which ignores judicial re-regulation, is misguided.

To conclude, in order to advance the discussion of the regulatory role of the state in the period 1700–1850, we have to move beyond listing or even counting statutes. Different statutes had different scopes. Counting clauses is not sufficient either, because at times single clauses (as with patents and joint-stock companies) had considerably more impact than statutes containing dozens of clauses (like those that aimed at regulating a single sector in a limited region). Public acts and private acts had different impacts, but neither disregarding the private ones nor giving the two equal weight is sufficient. A move from the statute books to the real world is essential.

A good first step is studying the resources invested in enforcing the statutes – budgets and employees – but this is only a first step. Much more can be done to integrate local enforcement and private enforcement. Actual prosecution in court can teach us much. The court played a multiple role: it created common law regulation, interpreted statutory regulation and enforced both. Its role as a regulator is an important but often neglected facet of the regulatory scene. It receives less attention from economic historians than statutory regulation because cliometricians do not possess sufficiently good theories and methodologies to deal with it (Harris 2003). The only generalisation I am willing to espouse at this stage is that, in the books, regulation provides a very limited view of the forms and extent of the state's role in the economy. While awaiting further research on the actual effects of regulation, we shall turn in the next sections to other roles of the state in the economy that should receive at least as much attention as regulation.

PUBLIC VERSUS PRIVATE OWNERSHIP

While industry overall (with the exception of royal dockyards and arsenals) was in private hands during the first industrial revolution, infrastructure and utilities were not in purely private hands. Three of the most interesting examples of the complex mixture of private and public ownership are turnpike roads, water supply projects and railways. The failure of local government to maintain and improve the king's highways led to the development of a new institution, the turnpike trust, which first appeared in full in 1706 (see chapter 11). Turnpike trusts were created by acts of parliament, usually for a renewable period of twenty-one years. The acts named trustees who were empowered to raise money, conduct improvement works, close the road with gates and collect tolls from passengers. A turnpike trust did not have joint stock. Yet the money it used was private loans, not state money. The entrepreneurs involved did not receive dividends. Yet they benefited personally from its earnings by way of interest, salaries, freight hauling, etc. In fact, the state granted some property rights to groups of entrepreneurs over a section of road for a fixed period of time in return for investment in that road, subject to some regulation of the exercise of these property rights (Albert 1972; Pawson 1977; Harris 2000: 86–100). England did not privatise its king's highways. It created a private–public partnership, more or less along the lines of modern BOT (Build, Operate, Transfer) schemes.

Urbanisation took the government by surprise. Governmental reaction to the rapid growth of cities was, as we shall see in the next section, one of inaction. A notable exception was water supply. Here it is often assumed that the response was successful because the central government stepped aside, pushed aside local government, and let privately owned enterprise in. Entrepreneurs who raised capital on the stock market petitioned parliament for incorporation and then invested large sums in developing sources of drinking water, bringing the water to town centres and distributing it through a newly constructed network of mains and pipes. Is this another example of the positive role of the market and of private ownership in the unfolding of the industrial revolution? No. Things in fact were more complicated: the state played various roles in the functioning of these seemingly private companies. Until the passage of the General Incorporation Act of 1844, the state controlled the use of the corporate form. Until that time, parliament incorporated some water supply undertakings and refused to incorporate others. At the time of incorporation, parliament determined two major aspects of the activity of the water supply companies. First, parliament determined the limits on the powers of these companies to infringe on the property rights of city dwellers in order to construct pipes and works. Second, parliament determined the level of competition in the field when deciding whether or not to grant regional monopolies.

In the case of London, the New River Company achieved a dominant position by the early nineteenth century, acquiring or driving out of business most of its eighteenth-century rivals including the London Bridge Water Works and the York Buildings Company. In 1806–7, parliament authorised the incorporation of the West Middlesex Company and the East London Company and the two began competing with the New River, one invading its eastern neighbourhoods and the other its western areas (Rudden 1985; Foreman-Peck and Millward 1994). A decade of competition drove down prices but also the quality of service, and parliament was again called upon to act. The next decades were marked by an attempt to divide London into one-company monopoly districts and at the same time to regulate the quality of water and service. But important issues such as the responsibility of water companies for cholera and typhoid epidemics, for drains and waste water, or their obligation to provide water to every household within their territory remained unsettled. This led to the establishment of numerous Royal Commissions and Select Committees and to the passage of many general and private acts of parliament. Edwin Chadwick became the leading mid-nineteenth-century reformer in this field. He proposed to consolidate the water supply companies and local sewers commissions into a single public body. While this proposed body was being discussed in parliament, he exchanged ideas with John Stuart Mill regarding it. What is interesting about this exchange and about much of the contemporary discourse as a whole is the consensus that existed as to the undesirability of private companies. Unlike Adam Smith who, three-quarters of a century earlier, had viewed water supply as a sector that should be in the hands of private joint-stock companies (as opposed to individual entrepreneurs), Mill believed that it should be in public hands. The discussion dealt only with the nature of the public body: should it be central or local, should it be staffed by elected representatives or by professional experts (Schwartz 1966)? In the end, the lobby for the water companies was able to block Chadwick's centralisation proposal for a while longer. But even so, water supply was not truly private. At the supposed heyday of *laissez-faire* and entrepreneurship, the state was engaged in massive regulation of water supply and seriously considered its nationalisation.

Railways provide another interesting example of the presence of the state as a factor in the development of infrastructure and of the link between regulation and public ownership (see also chapter 11). When the first railway scheme, the Stockton and Darlington, was conceived in the early 1820s, its promoters had to turn as a first step to parliament. An act of parliament was needed both for incorporation of the railway company and for enabling land expropriation. This involved the state in the development of the railway sector, beginning with the very first line. The value of the technology itself was discussed in the House of Commons. An elaborate set of standing orders made parliamentary scrutiny very detailed and expensive. Every bill went through a trial-like process in which its technical, financial and legal aspects were examined and all affected parties heard. By controlling entry, parliament not only shaped individual projects but also the formation of the network and the level of competition (Kostal 1994: 110–43). This was not done intensively or through any coherent policy. Until 1844, state intervention was felt primarily by way of private bills incorporating specific companies. In that year, a major general statute, Gladstone's Railway Act, was passed. This act, comparable in scope to the Interstate Commerce Act (which was the first major federal regulation of big business – railways – in the US and has been widely studied by historians), has not always received the attention it deserves. It regulated various aspects of the services and rates of the railway companies. It strengthened the Board of Trade Railway Department so that it could supervise the implementation of the regulation. It required railway companies to issue financial reports. Most importantly (and unlike the ICC Act), it empowered the state to buy out, twenty-one years after their authorisation, railway companies formed after 1844. In fact, in the heyday of *laissez-faire*, parliament enabled the government to nationalise much of Britain's railway network, an option the state did not exercise when it became relevant in the 1860s. But the existence of the threat influenced business practices, prices and profits in the sector and facilitated the passage of more substantial regulation in 1868 in return for relinquishing the nationalisation option (Parris 1960; McLean and Foster 1992; Foreman-Peck and Millward 1994).

Thus the commonly held view that British economic growth was achieved by private enterprise is only partly correct. Manufacturing was indeed in private hands, but, as shown in this section, infrastructure and utilities were not purely private. The state not only authorised and shaped the undertakings in these fields, but in some cases also retained a degree of control over them or considered nationalising them. As we shall see in the next section, the state also played a significant role in encouraging and subsidising overseas trade, particularly within the expanding Empire.

FISCAL POLICY: TAXATION AND EXPENDITURE

The 1970s and 1980s witnessed renewed interest in examining the role of government in the economy through its fiscal, rather than regulatory, activity. I will sketch this trend, beginning with revenues, in the form of taxation and borrowing, and moving on to expenditure. Taxation was on the rise during the eighteenth century. In the century beginning in 1715, tax revenues rose tenfold in current prices and about fourfold in constant, inflation-adjusted prices.

The increase is lower, but still significant, when adjusted to the increase in population (an increase of 250 per cent) and to the increase in production (its proportion of the GDP rose from about 10 per cent to 18 per cent – though these figures are more tentative, as are GDP growth figures). The rate of rise in taxation in Britain was considerably faster

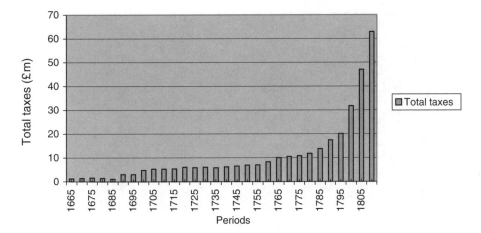

than in France, and probably the fastest in Europe. The real burden of taxation (relative to production and to population) in Britain by the middle of the eighteenth century was about twice as high as in France – its chief rival – and by the close of the century about three times as high (Mathias and O'Brien 1976).

Figure 8.1 Total tax revenue, 1665–1805
Source: O'Brien 1988: tab 4.

The composition of tax revenues was changing. The most remarkable change was the decline of direct taxation on manifestations of wealth and income and the rise of excise, levied on the purchase of consumption goods. The share of excise in total tax revenues rose from 26 per cent at the beginning of the eighteenth century to 50 per cent in the middle of the century, and decreased very moderately thereafter. The share of direct taxes decreased from 36 per cent to 15–20 per cent (to increase sharply for a few years during the Napoleonic Wars with the introduction of Pitt's short-lived income tax). It was argued that the shift from direct to indirect taxation had considerable redistributive effects (O'Brien 1988). While the rich carried much of the burden of direct taxation (on land and houses, servants and carriages), excise was levied mostly on basic consumption (salt, bricks, printed cloth, domestic spirits, etc.) of the middle and even the lower classes. The magnitude of the redistribution and the question of how much tax was paid by each social group, and the more complicated question of whether the social groups that paid more actually carried the burden or shifted it elsewhere via the market, are still being debated.

The state revenue system experienced two institutional transformations late in the seventeenth century, transformations whose effects on eighteenth-century government was immense. While during the Tudor and early Stuart reigns, non-parliamentary revenues (crown income, sales of lands and monopolies, and mint profits) comprised about 75 per cent of total revenues, these dropped to about 3 per cent of the total after the Glorious Revolution. This put parliament in control of the revenue side of British fiscal policy. The system of tax collection changed after

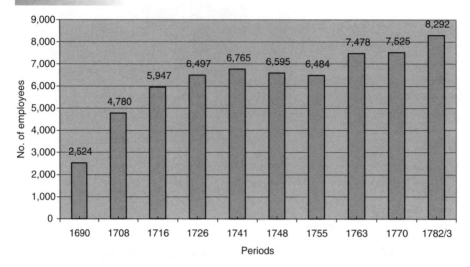

Figure 8.2

Employees in fiscal bureaucracy, 1690–1782/3

Source: Brewer 1988: tab 2.

the Restoration and the Revolution from tax farming[2] to direct collection by government departments. This was reflected in the growth of the tax collection bureaucracy from a few hundred employees during the Interregnum to 2,500 in 1690 and to over 8,000 in 1782/3, making revenue department employees by far the largest group of government employees (Brewer 1988).

The transformation of taxation in terms of overall revenue, composition and the levying and collection institutions, had far-reaching political and economic consequences. Among others, it created the precondition for another major transformation: the creation of the national debt. A variety of institutional novelties coupled with the changing tax system to bring this about. They included the subjection of the crown to parliamentary supervision through the Bill of Rights; the linking of loans to specific taxes that were supposed to provide the assured stream of income out of which interest would be paid – the so-called funded debt; and the incorporation of the Bank of England as a pivot that connected private lenders with the Exchequer. These political-constitutional-institutional changes were completed by the time the Hanoverians arrived in 1714. They enabled the Hanoverians, so it is argued, to make the credible commitment that they would repay what they borrowed. This was a novelty, because the Stuarts had been unable to convey credibility in the previous century, both because of their practice of forcing loans and stopping the payment of debt, and because they did not create institutional safeguards that would prevent them from repeating these practices (North and Weingast 1989; Weingast 1997). I shall examine the actual credibility of the Orange and Hanoverian crown in the next section. Whatever its cause, the result

[2] Under tax farming, private institutions paid the government a lump sum fee for the right to collect tax. This transferred both the cost of collection and the risk of default from the government to the private contractor.

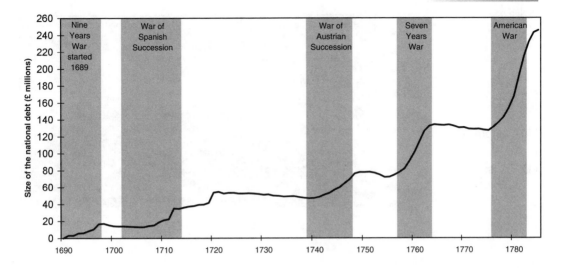

Figure 8.3 Growth of national debt, 1690–1780s

Source: Brewer 1988, Fig. 4.6.

of the change was stupendous. National debt jumped from around £1 million in 1688 to £15m a decade later, to £78m in 1750 and £244m in 1790. The trend was remarkable, and indeed exceptional, by European standards (Dickson 1967).

What did the government do with all the new resources, tax and loan money, at its disposal? It conducted wars. Total expenditure fluctuated considerably between war years and peacetime. The task of the newly created national debt was to flatten this fluctuation and enable massive government military expenditure during war years, to be repaid by tax money in the years of peace that followed.

Eighteenth-century British expenditure was pre-modern in the sense that it was mainly military. But its size constantly grew until it reached a modern scale, enabling Britain to operate more ships and soldiers in more remote parts of the globe than in past centuries and most importantly on a scale with which the French fiscal system could not compete (Kennedy 1987; Brewer 1988; Ferguson 2001; see also table 8.1).

How did these military expenses contribute to Britain's economic growth? Wars disrupt trade and bring destruction and casualties. But a nation that is able to win wars can minimise these and partly offset them by spillover effects, territorial expansion and, in the long run, also by increasing trade. It is argued that the British regime tended to wage more profitable wars than the French regime and to have the means ultimately to win these wars (Hoffman and Rosenthal 1997). Britain was able to fight its long eighteenth-century wars on foreign soils, spend

Table 8.1 Size of navies, 1689–1815 (Ships of the Line)

	1689	1739	1756	1779	1790	1815
Britain	100	124	105	90	195	214
Denmark	29	–	–	–	38	–
France	120	50	70	63	81	80
Russia	–	30	–	40	67	40
Spain	–	34	–	48	72	25
Sweden	40	–	–	–	27	–
United Provinces	66	49	–	20	44	–

Source: Kennedy 1987, Table 5.

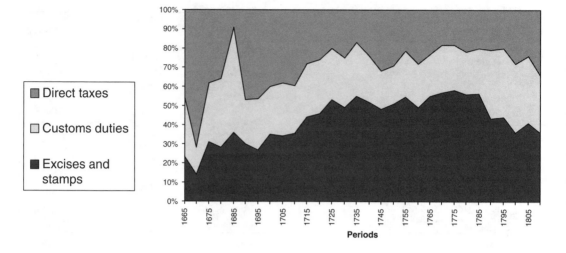

Figure 8.4 Allocation of government expenditure, 1665–1805

Source: O'Brien 1988: tab 1.

more money on them and win more of them. In this way, it improved its relative political and economic position *vis-à-vis* France, Spain and the Netherlands.

Wars have been fought throughout human history, by all regimes and nations. What was unique in eighteenth-century Britain, and thus is relevant to our discussion, was how the wars were financed. A central aspect of the financial revolution was the emergence of a stock market. The state, wishing to borrow money from private individuals, issued bonds. Primary and secondary markets in government bonds soon appeared. These featured specialised brokers and jobbers, trading techniques, meeting places, investment and information networks, regulation, and a stock market press. A market in corporate shares soon followed (Neal 1990; see also chapter 6 above). In a sense, the share market enjoyed positive externalities of the government bond market. Its players were free riders on the bond market institutions. By the canal age, the share market, together with the bond market, was well established, and with the advance of the railway the former surpassed the latter in volume (Michie 1999; Harris 2000: 168–98, 216–23).

Can we conclude that the government played a major role in the formation of a share market that, in turn, financed industrialisation? To answer this question we need to address several elements. I will deal with only one of them, the assertion that the government bond market and the corporate share market competed with one another. One manifestation of this assertion is the application of the 'crowding-out' discussion in fiscal policy to eighteenth-century Britain. In our case, the idea is that the British government attracted investors who would otherwise have invested in the private sector (Mokyr 1987; Williamson 1987). During the most critical phase of industrialisation (1789–1815), the British government raised unprecedented sums of money in order to finance its costly involvement in the Revolutionary and Napoleonic Wars. This, so the argument goes, hampered the rate of investment and growth in the industrial revolution.

Did the government bond market create the share market or compete with it? Probably both. But while the benefits for the share market from the prospering of the stock market are tangible, the disadvantages are not. Contemporaries did not believe in a crowding-out thesis. A few ultra-conservative politicians expressed the concern that the rise of the share market would curtail the government's ability to raise money for fighting the next war (Banner 1998). But the key economic ministers did not hold such views and businessmen did not express reverse concerns. Despite the rise of the share market, with every war the government was able to raise more money, peaking in the years after 1789. This did not prevent the investing public from engaging in speculative investment in the private market in wartime: during the canal mania of the 1790s and the share boom of 1805–7.

This presentation of the problem at hand is somewhat simplistic because the distinction between private and public markets and funds is not always clear (Alborn 1998). The Bank of England and its stock had characteristics of both. The conversion of the national debt into South Sea Company shares in 1720 also blurred this distinction. The ever-important case of the East India Company further complicates any attempt to distinguish clearly between a government bond market and a private share market. The money raised by this company was used both for overseas trade with India and China, and for financing the Company's army and other expenses related to the conquest and governing of India. In fact, turning India into the 'Jewel in the Crown' of the British Empire was a joint private–public venture. Thus even if the two markets competed for investors, the moneys they raised often ended up in the same place. Furthermore, government stock attracted foreign (particularly Dutch) investors and risk-averse investors such as widows, orphans and trustees who would not consider investing in even the most solid shares. This suggests that the markets complemented each other, attracting investors of different types.

So far we have discussed revenues and military expenditure. The British state between the years 1700 and 1850 was indeed a warfare state, not a welfare state. But does this mean that it performed no other functions of the modern state? Some such functions – education, housing, environmental protection and medical services – were provided on a very low level, by modern standards, up to the middle of the nineteenth century. The government devoted no administrative employees or budgets, and almost no parliamentary attention in the form of commissions or legislation, to these spheres of activity.

Results of the passivity of the government were vividly felt, and can be best exemplified by the state of the rapidly growing industrial towns.

These towns were speedily built from the start, with minimal investment in social overheads. The consequences were familiar to contemporaries from Chadwick to Engels and are confirmed by modern research. The underinvestment in infrastructures such as roads, pavements, lighting, drainage, water supply, sewage and public building had immediate effects. The towns were ugly, crowded and polluted, breeding high mortality and morbidity. The economic effects of this underinvestment are debatable. Williamson stresses the possibility that higher investment in towns could have left less available capital for investment in industry. In addition, higher investment in towns might have had to be borne by the poor urban population in the form of higher taxes or lower wages (Williamson 1994). This reminds us that there were no free lunches and that the state as such could not carry the burden of social overheads for the fast-growing towns. But the state could determine the trade-off between producing more commodities and having a healthier environment, or between a higher real wage and a better overall quality of life.

Other state functions to which twentieth-century central governments devote a large share of their budgets were performed in our period with very low central government expenditure. The English criminal system is a good example of a function that was performed cheaply by the central government. The low costs were achieved by a combination of factors, some dating back to the early days of the common law and some to eighteenth-century measures. Henry II and his successors constructed the superior royal courts as low-cost, high-impact courts. No more than ten to twelve judges sat on these courts at any given time throughout their history and only three or four of these were normally involved in criminal litigation. Several devices, including the assize system, the jury, the adversarial procedure and court fees, transferred much of the costs of operating this slim system to the parties and communities involved (Baker 1990). Lesser criminal offences were tried by the quarter sessions, local government courts. Justices of the Peace, whose main duties involved local administration, presided over these courts (Landau 1984). Though the central government partly supervised these local institutions, it did not finance them with Treasury money. Policing and prosecution was also to a large degree the responsibility of local government, at the parish and county level. The victims themselves, the informers, the locally hired watchmen and private prosecution associations complemented the system (Beattie 1986; Hay and Snyder 1989). Only after 1829, and more so after 1856, did professional police forces and state prosecution officers appear. The punishment structure was another means of economising on state costs. The introduction of capital punishment for a large number of offences in the eighteenth century, the 'Bloody Code', to compensate for the low level of prosecution, enabled the maintenance of higher deterrence levels at lower cost. Transporting and whipping, which were less expensive than imprisonment, were the most common punishments.

Interestingly, imprisonment was used primarily for the collection of civil debts and thus paid for primarily by the debtor or the creditor. An important element in reinforcing the system was its marketing; to increase its legitimacy, it was packed with majesty, justice and mercy (Hay and Snyder 1989). All these measures amounted to an unorganised, unprofessional and decentralised, but low-cost, system of keeping public order.

A differently structured system enabled the state to ensure the provision of relief to the poor and the disabled, while rolling its costs on to local communities. The famous acts of 1597 and 1601 codified earlier Tudor laws and practices and defined the old poor law system. This system was in force until the new poor law replaced it in 1834. The old poor law was a framework created by the central government that compelled small local government units, the parishes, to bear the responsibility for relief to the poor. Each parish was responsible only for its own poor. Each parish had to finance the relief from its own sources. In order to do so, it was empowered to collect local taxes. Churchwardens and overseers of the poor in each parish were put in charge of implementing the law. They were granted the authority to fix and collect taxes and to allocate relief. Parish vestry and Justices of the Peace were obliged by law to supervise them. The law did not fix the details of taxation and relief, leaving much discretion to individual parishes. Indeed variations in the types and burden of taxes among parishes were maintained for a long period of time. In most parishes poor rates were collected from all occupiers of real estate. The total collection of this local tax increased sharply from £400,000 in 1696 to almost £4.5 million in 1802/3. To demonstrate the magnitude and growth trend of poor law collection, two relevant figures are worth mentioning: its amount rose from 0.8 per cent to about 2 per cent of national production and from 11 per cent to 21 per cent of central government direct and excise tax revenue (Slack 1990: 9–26).

Initially, the focus of the poor law was on vagabonds, beggars, and maimed and disordered soldiers returning from the wars, whom the central government expected the parishes to discipline and contain. The law's application was gradually extended to orphans, widows and elderly men. In the next stage, it was extended to poor able-bodied men. Until 1782, the law required that the able-bodied be entitled only to indoor relief; that is, relief on the condition that they reside at workhouses.

As we have seen, total expenditure of the old poor law increased tenfold during the eighteenth century. The real expenditure per capita increased only fourfold. This disparity can be explained by the spreading of poor law relief. While in 1696 the law relieved only 3.6 per cent of the population, by 1803, it relieved 14.7 per cent of the considerably larger population (about 9 million compared to about 5 million in 1696). By then more than 90 per cent of the relief was granted outdoors, much of it to the able-bodied. The timing and scope of the large-scale extension of relief to able-bodied men has been debated. Contemporary critics of the old poor law, and generations of historians, pointed to the years 1782–95 as a major turning point. In 1795, the Speenhamland standard of relief that linked the level of payment to the price of bread and the size of the worker's family was introduced, and was soon legally adopted by many parishes, particularly in the south and the east. Generous payments, in the form of outdoor relief, to able-bodied workers became widely available. The level of total parish expenditure went out of control as it was linked to external factors – the birth rate and the price of wheat.

The problem with the rising expenditure was not only how to finance it. Unlike military expenditure, poor relief expenditure, which took the form of transfer payments, had more immediate and consequential effects on the incentives of individuals across the English economy. Contemporaries and historians were highly critical of the old poor law system in its late eighteenth- and early nineteenth-century incarnation. Adam Smith argued that it was detrimental to the labour market because it prevented labour from migrating freely to developing regions, particularly to towns, because workers lost their entitlement for poor relief as soon as they left their parish of origin. Thomas Malthus argued that the relief standards encouraged the rise of the birth rate and was bound to lead to overpopulation and demographic crisis. Nassau Senior and Edwin Chadwick, the dominant members of the poor law Commission, whose report led to the repeal of the old poor law in 1834, concluded that the law encouraged indolence, and worse, rather than checking poverty, led through a snowball effect to 'a universal system of pauperism'. Later historians stressed the damaging effects of the poor law to the rural parish economy as a whole, particularly to the yeomanry and to cottage industry.

In recent decades more attention has been given to the localised nature of the old poor law. The central government created a framework, but administration was on the parish level. The seemingly clear distinction between outdoor relief and indoor relief was blurred by historians. They emphasised the variety of types of workhouses, ranging from sweatshops to night shelters to elderly infirmaries, and of outdoor relief schemes ranging from allowances to the disabled, elderly, orphans and the like, to family allowances, to subsidy of wages, rotation in the employment of the poor among rate payers and employment of the poor by the parish itself, particularly in road maintenance (Daunton 1995: 447–74). Therefore, assigning able-bodied paupers to outdoor relief did not necessarily mean that they could avoid working, and assigning them to workhouses did not necessarily force them to work even if they were able to do so.

While parishes varied considerably in area and population, most of them were small enough (12,000 of the 15,000 parishes in 1831 had fewer than 800 inhabitants) to allow close personal familiarity. Thus, separating the able-bodied from the disabled was not based on clear formal, not to say legal, guidelines. The overseers, the rate payers and the parish community in general were more often than not familiar with the parish poor, their abilities and motivations and their family history. Much discretion was exercised in each case to determine whether the individual pauper was able-bodied or disabled, or partly able, and to tailor the relief scheme to that individual, his or her dependants, and the conditions in the parish.

Economic historians, aware of this communal and regional diversity in the application of the poor law, gradually developed a more positive view of its effects. Blaug was the first to argue that by the late eighteenth century the poor law became an enlightened system for dealing with the significant seasonal fluctuations (say between midwinter and harvest time) in the demand for agricultural labour in arable farming and particularly in the grain producing regions of the south and east (Blaug 1963). Boyer (1990, 1997) suggested viewing the outdoor relief system within the framework of implicit employment contract theory. In areas of lower seasonality, such as the pasture regions of the west, annual employment contracts were preferable. In areas in which seasonality was high, seasonal layoffs complemented by poor relief during the seasons of unemployment was the selected institutional form. The advantage of this contractual form was enhanced by the distributional effect of the poor law. The redistribution was not from rate payers to paupers but rather from rate payers who did not employ wage earners (family farmers, shopkeepers, artisans) to labour hiring farmers (often holders of more lands) who could lay off their workers during the off season without letting them starve or migrate. The farmers in fact enjoyed a subsidy at the expense of the workers, as the sums they saved on wages were higher than the rates they paid to the parish. They could not have benefited from a similar subsidy had they employed their labourers on the basis of annual contracts.

More recently Solar (1995, 1997) suggested analysing poor relief as a form of insurance. In a way, this is an extension of Boyer's analysis from viewing the law as offering unemployment insurance to viewing it as offering all-inclusive social security coverage. Yet, while Boyer analysed the employers' perspective, Solar examined the workers' perspective. The irregularity of employment, the fluctuation of real wages, and the human life-cycle traditionally made land a more stable source of main or supplementary subsistence. The introduction of relief in England by way of the old poor law allowed individuals to switch to wage-earning work. Relief entitlements were sufficiently secure to allow them to take the risks involved in leaving the land or not settling on it when they had acquired the means to do so. As a form of social insurance, the poor law affected more than the 14 per cent or so that received relief in the early nineteenth century. It affected the decisions of all those individuals, numbering anywhere between one-third to four-fifths of English society, who lived near poverty and feared for their subsistence at some point during their life-cycle or at times of external crisis. The poor law was an efficient form of insurance because of its communal nature, which limited problems of moral hazard, and its coverage of the whole population, which eliminated problems of adverse selection. It was generous and successful enough to be termed a miniature welfare state or a predecessor of the modern welfare state.

We now reach a stage in the historiography of the poor law in which many features that were considered to have negative economic impact in the past are now interpreted as positive features. The poor law enabled yeomen to leave their lands, facilitated enclosure and the formation of larger farms, allowed labour mobility, and even eased the pressure to get married and have children in the absence of an old age pension. But if the old poor law was so beneficial, why was it so harshly criticised by contemporaries and eventually replaced in 1834 by a new poor law? The new poor law pretended to replace Elizabethan paternalism with a modern system that gave primacy to the market, but, in fact, insisted on eliminating all that was economically good in the old law by centralising the system, ousting discretion and reinstituting the workhouse requirement in order to stop outdoor relief to the able-bodied. A full discussion of the new poor law is beyond the scope of the current chapter. I will only suggest two explanations for this puzzle. One, that the new law was in many respects a codification of laws and practices developed before 1834 and represented a continuation of the old poor relief system rather than a break with it. Focusing on expenditure figures and not on legal changes, it is evident that change was gradual and fluctuated. Expenditures correlated not to the replacement of the old law by the new one, but rather to the long-term changes in agriculture and industry and the external shocks caused by wars. Expenditures rose between the mid-eighteenth century (decades before the legal amendments of 1782–95) and the end of the Napoleonic War in 1815, and began to decline thereafter, long before the old poor law was abolished (Boyer 1990: 1–43; Lindert 1994: 381–5). Another explanation is that the old law was abolished despite the objections of those who operated it and benefited from it: magistrates, farmers and rural labourers. The opponents of the new poor law were not 'all the ignorant and timid around the country' as Nassau Senior overconfidently stated. The new poor law may have been enacted as a result of the failure of liberal political economists' theories to recognise the advantages of the old law, as a way to weaken the countryside and strengthen the centre, owing to a change in the balance of political power on the parish level between those who benefited from the old law and those who subsidised them, or because of a change in the ethos of the gentry (Mandler 1987, 1990).

The universality and comprehensiveness of its poor law made England exceptional by European standards. In other places one found either national systems that were badly financed and did not provide substantial relief; inadequate systems created by local governments that were substantial only in affluent towns but may have been non-existent in rural areas; or voluntary charitable systems, not regulated by the state, that offered no legal commitment towards the poor. Assigning to English poor law a negative effect on growth when in fact it offered a higher standard of relief and when Britain was growing faster than the rest of Europe is perplexing. In this sense the current stage of the historiography of the poor law seems to be more in line with a comparative perspective.

PROPERTY RIGHTS

Since the 1990s, following in the footsteps of Coase, Demsetz, Alchian and North, economic historians have focused more of their interest on institutions in general and property rights in particular. This trend makes the state an important subject of study. The most important role of the state in facilitating economic growth is believed to be the way it defines and enforces property rights. Property rights regimes are less conducive to growth and wealth creation when the rights are undefined or vague, as this gives rise to common pool problems and to wasteful behaviour.[3] This is also true when assets remain with individuals who do not put them to optimal use, because they cannot be easily transferred to users to whom these assets have higher value (Eggertsson 1990; Barzel 1997). England was able to perform the role of defining, enforcing and conveying property rights better than other European states (and on a par with the Netherlands). This, in North's view, laid the groundwork for Britain's rapid economic growth and political dominance (North 1990: 130, 139–40). I would like to discuss the formation and protection of property rights in Britain by delving into specific manifestations of property rights, in an attempt to bridge the more abstract discussions in economic theory and history and the more concrete discussions of legal historians.

The prime example given by North and Weingast of a growth-conducive change in property rights is that of the Glorious Revolution of 1688 and subsequent political developments that enabled the state to commit credibly that it would not confiscate its subjects' assets. Though they make some reference to the protection of property rights in all types of assets, the core of their argument deals with the rights of government lenders. The constitutional change enabled the state to convey credibly that it would repay its bond-holders. In addition, while the government was allowed to confiscate the assets of its subjects in the form of taxes, it was no longer allowed to do so without the consent of parliament (North and Weingast 1989; Wiengast 1997). This in turn enabled the government

---

[3] When assets are owned in common, there is an incentive for each co-owner to exploit the asset to the full, because any individual restraint will be undermined by the opportunistic behaviour of other co-owners. Thus common land tends to suffer from overgrazing, common fisheries from overfishing.

to avoid confiscating other assets, for example by expropriating land or forcing loans, in order to finance its wars.

The North–Weingast thesis provides important insights for the study of the English state and economy. Yet, some aspects of the thesis are problematic. The Bill of Rights of 1689, unlike the American Bill of Rights of 1789, did not limit the government's ability to confiscate property and did not require compensation for this. While it subjected the government's taxing power to parliamentary approval, the bill did not limit parliament's taxing powers, and did not require any representation or consent of those tax payers who were not represented or were underrepresented in parliament. In fact, as depicted in the section on fiscal policy, throughout the eighteenth century, tax burdens increased and money – and property – of underrepresented subjects financed the imperial-mercantile project of the overrepresented landed, financial and commercial elites.

Expenditure, unlike revenues, was not subject to parliamentary supervision by the constitutional revolution. The eighteenth-century English constitution, unlike the American constitution, did not contain an appropriations clause. In the aftermath of the Glorious Revolution, parliament attempted to achieve control over expenditures. However, it was unable to develop the administrative tools required for supervising a highly complex system of lists and accounts, paymasters and departments, suppliers and wage recipients, arrears and debts that was the British Treasury. As late as 1780, Edmund Burke still argued that the first lord of the treasury could not 'make even a tolerable guess, of the expenses of the government for any one year', and if he could not, parliament certainly could not (Roseveare 1973). A century after 1688, the fiscal system still did not provide parliamentary approved itemised annual budgets (Desan 1998). The issue at hand during much of the eighteenth century was the creation of centralised Treasury control over expenses, not parliamentary control over the Treasury. The accountability of the Treasury to parliament developed incrementally later and reached a landmark only in 1866–8. Even if state creditors were able to achieve some degree of supervision over borrowing and taxation, they did not achieve such supervision over the level of expenditure and its goals. The crown and the Cabinet could involve parliament, the tax payers and the nation as a whole in overseas wars and create budgetary deficits. State creditors could not ensure that the state would not become insolvent.

Undoubtedly, the constitutional revolution and institutional change made it more difficult for the government to default on its debts. But they were designed with the 'Stop of the Exchequer' of 1672 in mind. On that occasion, Charles II borrowed increasingly large sums, not against specific taxes but against the revenues in general, and at some point, for some years, the Exchequer had to stop paying the interest and principle on some of the loans, particularly those held by goldsmith-bankers (Horsefield 1982). The likelihood of a stop of this kind was considerably reduced after 1689, when the linkage between specific loans and specific taxes was institutionalised. The establishment of the Bank of England created a barrier between public debt holders and the Exchequer but did not prevent the creation of credibility problems for the Bank itself during the crises of 1797 and 1825. The South Sea Bubble of 1720 was a harsh reminder to lenders that the government could still find ways to evade repaying debts even after it seemed to be bound to pay them. This time, instead of stopping payment as in 1672, the government, in cooperation with the South Sea Company, lured the public to exchange the high-interest and irredeemable debt for South Sea shares that turned out to be almost worthless (Dickson 1967; Neal 1990). Later governments found other ways not to pay their creditors in full.

Could the British state find better ways to ensure credible commitments that protected its subjects' property rights? The state used constitutional and legal tools in order to impose shackles on its own freedom of choice. A series of laws passed between 1689 and 1702, notably the Bill of Rights and the Act of Settlement, were intended to achieve this effect. The problem with attributing a committing power to these statutes was that they were not entrenched. Unlike the American constitution, and some later constitutions, the statutory elements of the English constitution could be amended by simple majority legislation passed according to the regular legislative procedure. While the American constitution limited the ability of state (and later also the federal) legislatures to expropriate property or breach contracts by regular majority legislation, the English constitution did not restrict parliament from doing so.

The dominant characteristic of the English political and constitutional system, both before and after 1689, was the sovereignty of parliament. This meant that parliament had the right to make or unmake any law whatsoever and that no other person or body had the right to override or set aside the legislation of parliament (Dicey 1915; Goldsworthy 1999). Two conceptions threatened to undermine this dominant principle: that of constitutional conventions and that of natural rights. The first, in one of its interpretations, entailed that parliament could not legislate contrary to some understandings and practices that had commonly been observed for generations. The second held that there existed natural and universal principles and rights that were above parliament-made law. It is important to remember that in eighteenth-century Britain these conceptions were entertained primarily by political philosophers and legal theorists, but were marginal in actual political discourse and constitutional doctrine. In these, the principle of the sovereignty of parliament was the mainstay. But even had they been more widely accepted, neither of these conceptions could have helped a government that wished to constrain itself and convey credible commitments. The government could instantaneously create neither new constitutional conventions nor operational natural rights. Furthermore, conventions or natural rights could formally restrain parliament only in the presence of institution-alised judicial review of legislation. The growing independence of the English judiciary was evident long before 1688. But the judiciary was not granted, by the constitutional revolution or at anytime before or after the revolution, the power to perform judicial review, and it could not legitimately self-proclaim such power.

Therefore, creating credible commitment in England was a compli-cated matter. Constitutional and legal measures as such had limited value in advancing them. However, institutions were more complex than the laws that created them. The Bank of England could theoretically be dis-solved through the same procedure by which it was formed: annulment of its charter or repeal of the act authorising it. In practice, such a move was not simple. Though the stock market, which had been established informally and was not sanctioned by any law, could be banned alto-gether by regulation, it was unlikely that the state would do this. This was partly due to institutional inertia. As the Bank of England developed the bureaucratic capability to handle the national debt, the Exchequer lost this administrative ability. As the public began lending money di-rectly to the state (through the Bank), earlier lenders and brokers, such as the City of London and the goldsmiths, lost their ability to handle the lending. It was partly a matter of vested interests. Once a new set of in-stitutions was in place, a variety of private interests clustered around it. These interest groups were likely to oppose further change (Olson 1982). In our case, such interest groups included Bank officers, Bank sharehold-ers, stock brokers and jobbers, and ultimately the creditors of the state. Such groups lobbied the crown, the ministers and parliament. Their lobby was not necessarily based on representation nor on their electoral power.

The threat of removing a king, voting down a ministry or impeach-ing an office holder existed both before and after 1689. But it was not likely to be exercised for the protection of the property of those lacking political power. The political power structure remained a key factor in the stability of the system of public finance. As long as it held strong, it could convey, more credibly, commitments to preserve the property rights of lenders. In other words, the Whigs were linked to certain fi-nancial interests and, when in power, were able to protect their property rights, while the Tories were linked to other interest groups and tried to protect their property rights (Carruthers 1999). To sum up, constitutional institutions intermingled with informal institutions, institutional inter-ests, individual interests and party politics to provide a growing, though not an absolute, degree of protection to the property of state creditors. Surprisingly, this mid-level of protection was not necessarily injurious to public finance, as evident in the fact that the crash of the South Sea Bubble did not set back the achievements of financial revolution.

Government bonds were one type of new property created and ex-panded during the financial revolution. In the remainder of this section,

I will discuss the construction and protection of three additional types of property: land, slaves and intellectual property in technological innovations.

Property rights in land were the major form of assets of the time. I will touch upon land only briefly because the issue is an extremely complex one that cannot be discussed here satisfactorily, and because it is extensively discussed elsewhere in the literature (Simpson 1986; Cornish and Clark 1989; Baker 1990; Getzler 1996, 2004). Property rights in land in the Britain of 1700–1850 did not develop in a way that the property rights school prescribes as encouraging economic growth. Private property in land was not well defined. Establishing rights in privately held land, in the absence of a formal system of registration of title, was a very cumbersome matter, both in terms of legal procedure and in terms of evidence required. Though there was a marked shift from commonly held lands in the open field system to privately owned land resulting from enclosure, the contribution of this shift to economic efficiency is debatable (Allen 1992; Neeson 1993; G. Clark 1998a; see also chapter 4 above). Land was not fully commodified and was not made freely transferable until the late nineteenth and early twentieth centuries. The main reason for this was conflicting interests of the landed elite. On one hand, this elite wanted to ensure continuity of family estates across generations and to guarantee its exclusivity in wealth and political power. This was achieved through various legal mechanisms such as the strict settlement, which prevented sons from transacting in family lands and dismantling their fathers' estates and forced them to pass the estates on to their own sons (Spring 1993). On the other hand, landowners wanted to be able to transfer their property rights in order to increase consumption and make use of non-landed investment opportunities. The basic tension between the two opposing motivations could be mitigated only very partially by various legal and business constructions such as the trust, the mortgage and the lease. As a result of the restrictions on transactions, lands were often not put to the most valuable use.

Property rights in land were not clearly defined and were not freely transacted, but were they effectively protected? Yes, in the sense that one subject could not deprive another of his lands by use of force, nor could the government routinely confiscate the lands of its subjects. But land *was* expropriated by the state for a variety of purposes. Most commonly land was taken by acts of parliament from its owners and given to promoters of transport and utility projects, such as canals and railways, docks and water supply (Kostal 1994: 144–80). In the USA, where property rights were protected by the constitution, taking of land was restricted and a complicated doctrine of eminent domain had to be developed. In some countries on the continent, where land could be arbitrarily taken by an absolute national or local ruler, things were apparently simpler. In a way, the British level of protection of property rights in land had advantages over both stronger and weaker protection. In Britain, parliament served as a focal point, the meeting place of various interest groups. The promoters of a canal project had to negotiate in parliament with the landowners whose land the canal was to cross, mill owners whose water flow would be disturbed, and turnpike road trustees whose revenues might be reduced. Compensation in the form of money, exchange of lands or shares in the profits could be offered. The case of canals is only one of many examples. Parliamentary encroachment of property rights in lands, after due negotiation, could be found in many hundreds of private and public acts of parliament in the period 1700–1850. To be sure, the bargaining was done within state institutions, not on the open market. Land could be priced and transferred on the basis of the political influence of the contending groups. But nevertheless, land was likely to be transferred to those who would put it to more valuable use and was less likely to be transferred to those who could not increase wealth. The negotiations and the subsequent legislation involved considerable transaction costs, often higher than the contractual transaction costs. But this form of conveying rights in land had its advantages, as the conveying instrument was statutory and not contractual, and its enforcement was accordingly more effective. It is hard to imagine the unfolding of the transport revolution in a regime of strict protection of property rights. The English regime opened the door to expropriation of lands by private acts and enabled four modes of transport (river navigation, turnpike roads, canals and railways) to succeed one another between 1700 and 1850.

Slavery was an integral component of the triangular trade of the British Empire, whose core was in North America and the Caribbean islands. At the turn of the nineteenth century, slave-produced commodities, particularly sugar, were still the basis of the economy of the West Indies. By that time, the share of the Atlantic slave trade handled by British ships was the largest ever, almost 45,000 slaves annually, representing around 60 per cent of the total trade. This is not to say that slave-related trade represented a large share of British overseas trade or that it played an important role in industrialisation, neither of which was the case. But slavery was definitely essential for the business of many British individuals and companies. In 1807, parliament abolished the slave trade in the Empire. By doing this it not only regulated trade and deprived slave traders and their investors of their expectations of high profits. It also affected the property rights of West Indies plantation owners because the slave population there (unlike in the USA) was not self-reproducing. In 1833, parliament partially emancipated slaves in the colonies and in 1838 the process was completed, with full emancipation of all West Indies slaves. This was a blatant encroachment of property rights. Williams (1944) argued that the economic basis of slavery in the West Indies plantations died out gradually after 1776, and that abolition became possible only when slavery became unprofitable. If this was indeed the case, then the property rights encroached were redundant. But most economic historians today dismiss this argument and claim that the slave-based plantation economy was doing well, and even strengthening, up to its abolition (Solow and Engerman 1987; Heuman 1999). It is clear today that parliament did expropriate valuable property rights. Nevertheless, there was nothing in the English constitution to protect slave owners from expropriation.

To be fair, it is important to mention that compensation of £20 million was granted to slave owners in the 1833 Emancipation Act. But this was not required by the English constitution. It was paid as part of a political compromise whose aim was to lessen the opposition of the West India lobby, which was still quite strong in parliament. But unlike the deals regarding expropriation of land for the construction of transportation networks, discussed above, here the deal was not between two economic interest groups. The anti-slavery movement was a popular movement, motivated by religious, moral and national sentiments (Colley 1992: 350–60). The pro-slavery lobby was outnumbered in parliament by the abolitionists and did not have equal bargaining power. It could not buy out the abolitionists even though its aim was pursuing a profitable business. The price paid for securing the legislation did not reflect the economic value of the property rights expropriated.

Comparison with the USA is again illuminating at this point. The import of slaves into the USA could be stopped only after the original settlement entrenched in the Constitution, which prohibited federal intervention in the slave trade, expired in 1808. As late as 1857, the US Supreme Court, resting on the protection of property rights in the Bill of Rights, invalidated an Act of Congress that prohibited slavery in some federal territories. As is well known, it took a Civil War and coercion by the North to amend the Constitution and abolish slavery in the USA.

A new type of property, defined and expanded during the industrial revolution, was intellectual property, in the form of patents. I would like to demonstrate the advantages of mid-level protection of property rights using the case of intellectual property rights and the history of patent law. Long before the industrial revolution, the English crown granted monopolies of various sorts. The later Tudors used grants of monopoly, among other things, to encourage foreign craftsmen and innovators to settle in England and make use of their skills and knowledge in the country. Elizabeth and the early Stuarts extended the use of monopoly to inventions by Englishmen. The crown viewed the grant of monopolies for inventions as part of its discretionary prerogative. The hostility of parliament and of the common law judges to the use of monopolies by the crown, as a means of extracting independent income and increasing political power, led to the enactment of the Statute of Monopolies in 1624. The statute prohibited the grant of monopolies by the crown without parliamentary authorisation. However, as part of a compromise, a number of exceptions were made to this rule. Section 6 of the Statute of Monopolies exempts the grant of monopoly by way of letters patent for 'the true and first inventor' of 'new manufactures' for 'the term of fourteen years or under'. This section created the statutory basis of English patent law for the entire span of the first industrial revolution. It meant that the crown could continue the practice of granting monopolies on inventions at the crown's discretion. Such grants were not subject to any criteria or procedures. These monopolies were enforceable as any other crown patent, charter or franchise. Only in 1852 did a new patent law, establishing a patent office, replace it.

Does this mean that the English state had sufficiently defined intellectual property rights long before the industrial revolution? Or that it did not define them efficiently until after the revolution? Can patent law have explanatory power for the outburst of inventive activity specifically in England? In the second half of the eighteenth century, but not earlier? These questions cannot be answered on the basis of the Statute of Monopolies alone. As with regulation, here too, in order to advance our understanding, we need to encompass private and specific legislation; the practices of the administration with respect to granting and enforcing patents; and the role of common law and the judiciary with respect to interpreting the statute, expanding rules beyond it and handing down remedies for infringement.

Until the early eighteenth century, the crown manipulated the grant of patents for its own ends. Thereafter, the system was one of registration, involving time and money, but without an examination of the content of the patent or its value. After 1711, it became more common to ask inventors to append details of the method of their invention to their petitions. In some instances, the officers insisted on the inclusion of detailed drawings. By 1734, the request for specification became the standard practice, but it was only forty-four years later that this practice was embodied in the laws of England, not via legislation but as a result of Lord Mansfield's 1778 *Liardet* v. *Johnson* decision. The reports on this case are incomplete. They are based less on law reports than on newspapers and pamphlets and a brief mention in Mansfield's notebooks. Nevertheless, it is assumed that in this case Mansfield ruled that specification should be sufficiently full and detailed to enable anyone skilled in the general field to understand and apply the invention without further experiment (Adams and Averley 1986; Adams 1987).

Did the emergence of the new requirement for specification represent progress in the direction of creating more defined and enforceable intellectual property rights? A plausible explanation for the emergence of the practice is that as patents accumulated – many of them centred on a limited number of fields such as carriages, bleaching, oil and spinning – the task of the law officers of the crown became more complicated. They were obliged to grant patents only within the powers conferred to them by the Statute of Monopolies, that is, only to new manufacture. They found it more and more difficult to determine whether a petition submitted to them was indeed for a novel method or machine. By asking for specification, they did not intend to put the petitions under their own careful professional scrutiny. They continued to register them as before. The idea was to transfer the burden from themselves to other interested parties (MacLeod 1988). In some circumstances, this also meant that the state was no longer a party to the ensuing litigation. An important implication of this shift was that the definition of the property rights of inventors was done ex-post and not ex-ante. Neither the crown officers nor the courts provided inventors with detailed rules regarding the submission of specifications. Inventors could go to the trouble of investing in experiments, specification, patenting, production and marketing, only later to face a court suit that would void their patent.

This indeed happened to some of the most notable inventors. Arkwright lost his 1775 carding machine patent in 1785 mainly on the grounds of unsatisfactory specification. In the process, he was involved in three trials over four years, losing not only the patent but also a great deal of time and money. Boulton and Watt were occupied for more than two decades with the validity of their 1769 fire engine patent. They realised at some point that it was not well specified, and their concern grew after Mansfield's 1778 decision in *Liardet* v. *Johnson*. They became involved in the litigation of other inventors, including Arkwright, in an attempt to achieve advantageous court decisions. They considered petitioning for a new patent. They lobbied parliament for an act that would prolong their patent, hoping that this would also protect it from invalidation. Finally, they reached a conscious decision to put up with a bearable level of infringements rather than risk losing a claim in court which would mean invalidation of the patent altogether. Only in 1794 did they dare to go to court, employing the leading lawyer of the time.

The problem of patent law was wider and graver than the question of specification. It resulted from the fact that the statutory basis of intellectual property rights in inventions throughout the industrial revolution was one old clause, Clause 6 of the 1624 Statute of Monopolies. The rest had to be created by judges who could not do much to expound the law when hearing only one case in the period 1750–69 and twenty-one cases between 1770 and 1799 (Dutton 1984: 69–85).

Since judges, unlike legislators, cannot set their own agenda, they depend on the flow of cases into their courtroom. In this case, the flow was less than one case per year, and many of these cases were decided on evidence or on minor points of law. To this, one should add the fact that creating detailed rules in this field of law was exceptionally complicated, because judges could not apply legal doctrines borrowed from other fields of law since they had to deal with technical issues unfamiliar to lawyers, and because the nature of innovations was changing rapidly. A

Table 8.2 The number of patent law cases, 1750–1849

	1 Patents granted	2 Cases	3 Patents disputed	4 2 as % 1	5 3 as % 1
1750–69	297	1	1	0.3	0.3
1770–99	1,418	21	16	1.5	1.1
1800–29	3,510	61	50	1.7	1.4
1830–9	2,453	47	38	1.9	1.5
1840–9	4,581	128	104	2.8	2.3

Source: Dutton 1984: Table 8.2.

manifestation of the unsettled state of patent law can be found as late as 1795 in a note written by Watt himself listing 'Doubts and Queries upon Patents'. The eight queries on Watt's list can be classified into four main issues. What is patentable? What should be included in specifications? What is the relationship between newer and older patents? What kind of use of monopoly power will be considered illegal? Only well into the nineteenth century, with the increase in litigation and the formation of a series of parliamentary committees leading to the 1852 act, did more detailed and settled rules begin to emerge.

But was the unsettled nature of patent law detrimental to the rate of inventions and to economic growth? Khan and Sokoloff (1998) argue that property rights in technological innovations were broader and better defined in the USA than in Britain. In the USA, eight federal patent acts were passed between 1790 and 1842 while in Britain the first act to be passed after 1624 was the 1852 act. As a result, US patent law encouraged a higher level of inventive activity among more varied social groups and in a wider array of industries. This claim is not unquestionable. Measuring inventive activity and its impact on economic growth is a tricky business. Britain seems to have done quite well in terms of inventions and growth in the period discussed here. It is not clear that the USA did better. Many contemporary Europeans envied the British spirit of invention and patent system.

Furthermore, a patent law that would better define and more strictly protect property rights would have social costs. It could provide more incentives to inventors but it would also slow the rate of diffusion and increase the monopoly rent of inventors at the expense of manufacturers and consumers. It would result in the allocation of more resources to research that could potentially lead to patentable inventions at the expense of other inventions. What the English system offered was ex-ante incentives that sometimes only partly materialised ex-post (Mokyr 1990: 247–52). Some patents were invalidated by the courts, others were not strictly enforced. Infringement was quite common. Though inventors did not always extract in full the profits they initially expected to gain from their monopolies, the incentives were sufficient for inventors to remain in business and to do well. The state was there to play around with the patent system when it led to undesirable results or when the inventor's lobby was strong enough. Parliament prolonged the duration of Boulton and Watt's patent from fourteen to thirty-one years. It made special grants to Lombe (when denying the renewal of his silk throwing patent), Crompton (who never took a patent on his mule) and Cartwright (who lost his patent to creditors). It granted small pensions to other inventors. But it granted no money to inventors such as Arkwright and Tennant, who prospered despite losing their patents. Not least in importance were the non-monetary benefits, in the form of prestige, ceremonies and patronage, granted by the state to its privileged inventors. When the state had a strong or symbolic interest in an invention, as was the case with the water chronometer (from which accurate longitude at sea could be calculated for the benefit of the navy and of merchant shipping), a special prize was offered in advance to increase incentives. It seems as though clearly defining property rights in advance was not necessarily the optimal contribution that the state could offer to economic growth. Other sorts of ex-post interventions, in the form of court decisions and private acts of parliament, had considerable impact on technological innovation and diffusion.

CONCLUSION

It used to be possible for scholars to conduct their discussion of the role of government in the British economy between 1700 and 1850 on the basic assumption of the existence of two distinct spheres: the market and the state. The questions they asked concerned how the first expanded at the expense of the second, or how the second interfered with the first. Theoretical and historiographical trends of the last few decades have blurred this clear-cut distinction between the state and the market. The state seems to have surfaced almost everywhere in the economy. It not only regulated markets but also created them. It not only protected property rights but also defined them. It did not either own enterprises or leave them to be owned by private individuals, but was also a partner in joint public–private undertakings, be they new modes of transportation or new imperial conquests. It seems more appropriate to speak now of the state within the economy rather than of the state and the economy.

It was not only the relationship between the state and the economy that was problematised. The state itself is viewed today as a less homogeneous entity. The early focus on central government policy or parliamentary regulation turned out not to be sufficient. We now devote more attention to private acts, to bureaucrats, to the judiciary and to local government. The private bill procedure served as a venue through which conflicting interest groups could clash and negotiate. The state served as a mediator or a meeting place. Private acts reflected agreements between interest groups and forced resolution in disputes. They created and abolished monopolies; created regulations and exempted from regulations; defined property rights and expropriated property. Bureaucrats collected taxes, authorised expenditures, inspected compliance to regulations and registered property rights. The judiciary not only handled litigation but also interpreted parliamentary regulation and declared common law regulation. The judiciary itself was not uniform. It accommodated competing sets of doctrines and norms and competing courts and judges. Local government, from the county level down to the parish level, was involved in the economy in various ways through various bodies and office holders. Its activities were financed at times by the central government, at times by local taxes, at times by consumers and at times by private entrepreneurs. The central direction and supervision of these activities varied in degree. Often central and local functions intermingled.

The ever-important question, what was the contribution of the state to the first industrial revolution, has not been satisfactorily answered in this chapter. Was the British advantage over other European countries in having a representative and constitutional government? Such an advantage enabled the collection of more taxes and the borrowing of more funds. But this money was used for fighting wars and bringing about destruction to the benefit of the few, not for investment in infrastructure and welfare to the benefit of all. Did the English advantage over continental systems lie in the fact that the English had a common law and not a Roman-based legal system? Weber (1954) ascribed explanatory power in Europe's economic rise to the rationality of European law. Posner (1998) argued that the common law's logic drives it towards efficiency, and implied that it was a more efficient form of law than continental codification and legislation. But for Weber, England created a problem; its law was less rational and less systematic than continental legal systems and he found it difficult to explain why it was that the English, of all European legal systems, industrialised first. As we have seen in this chapter, English law did not seem to be particularly instrumental to business needs and did not define, transfer or protect property rights in a very efficient way. We are still left with the puzzle as to whether the peculiarity of the English common law encouraged or hindered economic growth.

The British way seems to have been the middle road: not an entrenched constitution but not royal despotism, not super-rational and organised Roman law but not total identity of law with politics, not completely centralised but not overly decentralised, not a state taken over by big business and robber barons but not a planned-from-above economy. Hindsight shows us that something in this mix did the trick, since Britain experienced unprecedented economic growth, by both comparative and inter-temporal standards, during the 150 years discussed here. But which elements of the mix contributed more to growth, which contributed less and which hindered it? More research by economic, political and legal historians, pragmatically employing the theoretical tools of the various disciplines and better utilising some of the less-explored historical sources, will be needed before a new synthesis can emerge.

9

Household economy

JANE HUMPHRIES

Contents

Introduction   238
Evolutionary and structuralist–functionalist theories of
    the household and the economy   239
The size and composition of the pre-industrial household   241
The size and composition of the household in the
    industrial revolution   244
Self-interested individuals and households of mutual
    advantage   246
Continuity as well as change: live-in service and
    domestic enterprise   250
Wage earning households in the industrial revolution   257
The household economy, the standard of living and
    consumption   263
Conclusions   266

INTRODUCTION

In many times and places, household and economy were overlapping in-stitutions. Indeed, the word economics comes from the Greek *oeconomica*, meaning the science or art of managing a household. The traditional household brimmed with economic activities. Based on kin but extended to include living-in servants, apprentices and lodgers, it was the scene of production as well as consumption and reproduction. Allocation of labour and resources was not egalitarian, but all members participated. In contrast its modern counterpart has suffered a dramatic 'loss of func-tion'. Needs that were formerly met by family members working within the home are now met by outside agencies, and individuals interact with the wider economy and society not through their households but inde-pendently. The household has wasted economically, shrunk in apparent size and become dependent on the earnings of its male head, or very recently its two adult earners (Parsons 1959).

The contrast between pre-industrial and modern families implicates economic change in the household's loss of function. Urban industrial life not only involved significant changes in how goods and services were produced but also reallocated the transformed activities between the household and the market economy. This chapter is about these processes as they occurred for the first time in the context of another pioneer experience, industrialisation in Britain in the eighteenth and nineteenth centuries: 'ours was the society which first ventured into the industrial era, and English men and women were the first who had to try to find a home for themselves in a world where the working family, the producing household, seemed to have no place' (Laslett 1965: 18). Questions are raised about the timing, conceptualisation, explanation and implications of the changes in the household economy, particularly the implications of the changes for well-being and for understanding industrialisation itself. Answers involve establishing what the households of the past looked like, how they behaved and why they behaved as they did.

The recent recognition of the household as a respectable topic of research means that theorising has often run ahead of empirical evidence (Laslett 1972a). Thus the chapter begins with the shock caused when empirical findings on the size and structure of pre-industrial households caught up with established evolutionary and structuralist–functionalist theories of the household. Next it summarises the evidence on households' measurable characteristics during industrialisation and the search for explanation in a theory of mutual advantage. The chapter notes the survival of features of the pre-industrial household such as live-in service and domestic production and describes the heterogeneous historical experiences of wage earning households. Finally the household economy provides a fresh perspective on ongoing mainstream debates about the standard of living and consumption during the industrial revolution.

The chapter disputes grand theories of structural differentiation, which polarise the pre-industrial and post-industrial household. But it also rejects excessive emphasis on continuity, which presents the household as independent of economic change. Instead the households of the industrial revolution emerge as relatively autonomous. They and their members adapted to, resisted and created economic change.

EVOLUTIONARY AND STRUCTURALIST–FUNCTIONALIST THEORIES OF THE HOUSEHOLD AND THE ECONOMY

Evolutionary theories explained the historical development of the household as a process of differentiation (Parsons and Bales 1965). A society undergoing economic change necessarily differentiates its household-based social structure. New institutions like firms, schools, trade unions and the welfare state met functions that previously had been undertaken by the household. Kinship relations also underwent functional specialisation, becoming dominated by a system of small nuclear family units. The modern 'thin' family was adapted to the need for social and geographical mobility. The primary responsibility for household support rested on the male head, the breadwinner, whose 'job' linked the family to the economy. The division of activities between the family and the market allowed values essential to the success of the modern economy to prevail in the marketplace while others more relevant to reproduction and caring could survive in the home. The economic transition was paralleled by a change in values. The increasing dominance of small nuclear affective families was both the result and the reflection of 'the rise of individualism'.

Identifying the industrial revolution as the crucible of change allowed historians to link evolutionary models of the household to economic development and so piggyback on standard periodisation. Traditional interpretations of industrialisation emphasised the importance of mechanisation and economies of scale in promoting the transition to the factory system. Household-based production units could no longer compete and gave way to households as collections of waged workers, the 'family wage economy', a stage in the evolution towards the modern 'male-breadwinner family system' (Clark 1968; Tilly and Scott 1978).

Structuralist–functionalist and evolutionary accounts of the household were essentially teleological, arguing back from a known present to a generally agreed upon but imprecisely described and dated past. The elegance of the model of structural differentiation alongside the attraction of what William Goode has called the 'classical family of Western nostalgia' promoted a superficial comparison of 'pre-industrial' and 'post-industrial' households consistent with the inevitable triumph of individualism. In depicting the changes in the household as successful adaptations to economic growth and development, sociologists, historians and economists were in danger of reading historical change as linear and seeing pre-industrial households as homogeneous, static and traditional.

Support for evolutionary accounts came from the long line of social commentators, beginning with first-hand observers, who perceived industrialisation, particularly factory labour, as undermining family life by providing individual economic independence (Gaskell 1833; Engels 1845). Historians contrasted the free-standing family farms and artisan households of the seventeenth century, which produced for sale and subsistence, with the wage earning households of the nineteenth century. But while rich in detail and varied in chronological and geographical location, such studies could not provide the basis for a quantitative analysis of the dimensions of change. Major suppositions were left unchallenged, including the belief that, before the industrial revolution, producing households were universally and necessarily larger and more complex (Laslett 1972a), and that the advent of industrialisation brought a transition from the extended to the nuclear family (Flandrin 1979).

Polarising the history of the household into pre- and post-industrial was increasingly out of sync with the revisionist view of the industrial revolution as involving continuity as well as change. Moreover, both evolutionary and structuralist–functionalist models of the household fell increasingly foul of growing empirical evidence, which suggested that the relationship between industrialisation and the household was more involved. Surprising evidence demonstrated that the English household was not only small and nuclear long before industrialisation but also remarkably homogeneous across time and space, with perhaps important implications for understanding England's precocious economic development.

THE SIZE AND COMPOSITION OF THE PRE-INDUSTRIAL HOUSEHOLD

Some scholars had long resisted the sentiment that the pre-industrial household was large and complex by pointing to surviving empirical evidence on household size (Laslett 1972a: 1–13; Wall 1972: 191). The breakthrough came with the collection and analysis of surviving English 'listings' by the Cambridge Group for the History of Population and Social Structure (Laslett and Harrison 1963; Laslett 1969, 1972b). These documents enumerated every individual of a particular settlement according to the household in which he or she belonged, and so enabled the systematic quantitative study of household size and composition over time and across communities of different types. The findings were cataclysmic for the presumption that pre-industrial households were large and complex. Households were small. The majority contained fewer than five persons, and membership was customarily confined to parents and their unmarried children. Some households contained servants, but there were remarkably few complex households containing grandparents, parents and grandchildren.

Tables 9.1 and 9.2 present the estimates of household size and key quantifiable characteristics of household structure (percentages of households with kin, lodgers and servants) respectively from the hundred 'pre-industrial' communities originally studied.

The tables also provide comparable figures for England and Wales, and (following Anderson 1971b and 1972) for Preston and Swansea for 1966, to show how 'modern' the pre-industrial family appeared. True the pre-industrial family was larger and much more likely to contain servants, but not much larger, and crucially had only about the same likelihood of including kin. The large and complex households of western nostalgia

Table 9.1   Number of persons per household (percentage in various communities)

	Household size										Mean household size
	1	2	3	4	5	6	7	8	9	10+	
Pre-industrial communities 1564–1821 (N = 100)	6	14	17	16	15	12	8	5	3	5	4.8
England and Wales 1966	15	31	21	18	9	4	1	1	0	0	3.0
Preston 1966	18	32	19	15	8	5	2	1	1	0	2.9
Preston 1851	1	10	16	17	14	12	10	8	5	8	5.4
Rural Lancashire 1851	3	12	13	12	14	12	11	9	6	9	5.5
York 1851	5	15	16	18	14	13	7	5	3	5	4.7
Nottingham 1851											4.47
Ashford 1851											4.85
Pre-industrial communities 1650–1749 (N = 45)											4.696
Pre-industrial communities 1740–1821 (N = 50)											4.776

Sources: Figures for England and Wales 1966, Preston 1966 and rural Lancashire 1851 from Anderson 1972: table 7.1. Figures for York 1851 from Armstrong 1972: table 6.1. Figures for Nottingham and Ashford from Armstrong 1972: 211. Figures for pre-industrial communities from Laslett 1972b: table 4.4.

Table 9.2   Percentage of households with kin, lodgers and servants for various communities

	Percentage of households with:		
	kin	lodgers	servants
Pre-industrial communities 1564–1821	10	<1*	29
England and Wales 1966	10	–	0
Swansea 1966	10–13	<3	<3
Preston 1851	23	23	10
Rural Lancashire 1851	27	10	28
York 1851	22	21	20
Nottingham 1851	17.3	21.8	11.7
Ashford 1851	21	17.5	16.9
Potteries 1861	18	18	9–11

Sources: See Table 9.1. Potteries figures calculated from Dupree 1995: tables 2.2, 2.4 and 2.8b.
* Probably an underestimate, see Anderson 1972: 220.

appeared just that, as far as English history was concerned: figments of a collective imagination that yearned for a more sociable and less isolated family life.

The precocious development of wage labour in the English country-side contributed to the high frequency of small households of two or three people (for the relatively small size of labourers' households in the pre-industrial sample see Laslett 1972b: 154). But generally, pre-industrial households were not collections of proletarians. The empirical evidence for the widespread existence of household production was too ubiquitous to be disputed. Why then were households so small and simple? What forces had produced these modern-looking households in a pre-industrial environment? The answer required locating the producing activities of the household in their demographic, economic and cultural context. Conditioning variables were specified as fertility, mortality, expectation of life, age at marriage, propensity to stay in the parental home after marriage, and relative frequency of widows and eldest sons taking over the headship of the household after the death of the master. Extended families were rare, produced by freak coincidences within the conditioning variables, 'fortuitous outcomes of demographic eventualities and economic conveniences, and of particular strong personal attachments as well' (Laslett 1972a: 73).

Continuity was assured by the priority given to demographics. These ripped and tore families into the simple shapes observed. Low life expectancy for example put an upper limit on the proportion of all families that could include grandparents (Wrigley 1969). But economic and cultural factors also mattered. Late marriage as well as early death constrained the maximum frequency of three-generation households and residential preference determined what proportion of those who were demographically able to live with kin actually chose to do so. Economic conditions, in turn, could bring forward or push back the age at marriage, and cultural norms could require or not the formation of an independent household on marriage. Demographic history was to show the importance of these variables in understanding English population growth (Wrigley and Schofield 1981; Wrigley *et al.* 1997; and chapter 3 above). In the longer term, economic changes could also influence mortality and fertility.

The discovery that the pre-industrial household was small and simple exploded belief in the rise of individualism as a universal explanation of familial change, and prompted speculation about the role of household structure in economic development. 'England had been the first of the world's societies to undergo [an industrial revolution], and it seemed quite possible that her pioneering role might have had something to do with the simple structure and small size of English households before ever industrialisation began' (Laslett 1972a: 49). Perhaps the history of the household provides another brick in institutionally driven accounts of the first industrial revolution.

Subsequent research on pre-industrial household size and composition tended to confirm the initial findings (Schurer 1992; see Wall 1983 for a comparative European perspective). But the vision of stable continuity left by the English empirical tradition was misleading. Very different demographic, social and economic forces can produce similar outcomes. The seemingly constant household could disguise a maelstrom of underlying change. Moreover, further scrutiny of the evidence suggested that far from exhibiting continuities both with the past and the present, the households of the industrial revolution were themselves distinctive.

THE SIZE AND COMPOSITION OF THE HOUSEHOLD
IN THE INDUSTRIAL REVOLUTION

Even within the original evidence, there were suggestions that the contrast was not between pre- and post-industrial households but between the households of the industrial revolution and those that went before and came after. Laslett subdivided his original data into two sub-periods, 1650–1749 (forty-five communities) and 1750–1821 (fifty communities), to suggest that smaller households were more common in 1650–1749, although mean household sizes for the two periods remained close (see Table 9.1). Ironically it looks as though household size swelled just as England began to industrialise.

This intriguing suggestion was endorsed by Michael Anderson's (1971a) pioneering study of household structure in the industrial revolution. Anderson calculated household size and the percentages of all households that contained kin, lodgers and servants, from a 10 per cent sample taken from the enumerators' books of the 1851 Census for Preston. The Lancashire cotton town was viewed as a 'half-way house between a predominantly rural pre-industrial England, and the predominantly urban-industrial/commercial post-capitalist England of the present day' (1972: 215). Anderson's findings are shown in Tables 9.1 and 9.2, which also include summary statistics of household size and structure from a number of other samples to identify the effects of industrialisation and to check whether Preston was indeed representative of an environment in transition. These include: first, a rural sample that Anderson drew with the object of comparing the family structure of migrants to Preston with the family types which were found in the villages from which in-migrants came; second, another sample drawn from the enumerators' books of the 1851 Census, but for York, a very different kind of mid-nineteenth-century town, in which 'true factory or large-scale production was unknown' (Armstrong 1972); third, evidence for Nottingham and Ashford, nineteenth-century towns which were comparable with Preston and York respectively (Armstrong 1972); and finally, a sample from the 1861 Census for the Potteries, another comparable manufacturing community (Dupree 1995).

Mean household sizes in Preston and rural Lancashire were much higher than the 1960s benchmarks and somewhat higher than the pre-industrial mean. This was partly a product of the comparatively high proportions of households that contained kin in comparison with modern and pre-industrial communities. Table 9.3 provides some detail on the kin relationships. Ten per cent of Preston households contained parents and married children, a family composition that was rare in pre-industrial England and uncommon too in rural Lancashire. Households that contained other kin were also more numerous in Preston than in the

Family type	Pre-industrial communities	England and Wales 1966 (approx.)	Preston 1851	Rural Lancashire 1851	Potteries 1861
No related person		17	4	5	5
Married couple only	90	24	10	12	12
Parent(s) and unmarried children only		49	63	56	65
Parent(s) and married child(ren) but no other kin		5	9	6	
Parent(s) and married child(ren) with other kin	10	0	1	0	8
Other combinations of kin		4	13	21	10
All (percentage)	100	99	100	100	100
N =		1,533,954	1,240	855	1,432

Table 9.3 Structure of the families of household heads

Sources: See Tables 9.1 and 9.2. Figures for Potteries calculated from Dupree 1995: table 2.2.

pre-industrial communities, though rural Lancashire had an even higher incidence.

Was Preston's pattern of co-residence the product of its urban-industrial environment? Here the comparison with other nineteenth-century communities is instructive. All the nineteenth-century communities shared Preston's relatively high incidence of extended family living but there were differences in household composition. Oldham, another nineteenth-century textile town, emulated Preston's incidence of parents co-resident with married children (Table 9.3; Foster 1974). But the surprising popularity of this type of household did not extend to Northampton or South Shields, where only 5 and 4 per cent of all households respectively included parents and married offspring (Foster 1974). On the other hand, households that contained other kin were relatively numerous in Northampton (12 per cent) and South Shields (11 per cent).

Preston also had far larger proportions of households containing lodgers in comparison with both pre-industrial and 1960s England. Households with lodgers were much less common in rural Lancashire, though still more frequent than in the pre-industrial or modern communities. About one-fifth of households in all the industrial towns took in lodgers. Preston had the highest proportion at 23 per cent, with the other towns close behind in a cluster.

The proportion of households with servants in Preston was much lower than in the pre-industrial communities, while they had practically disappeared in modern England. Mid-nineteenth-century rural Lancashire closely resembled the pre-industrial communities. The relatively low proportions of households with servants in the other industrial towns suggest that servants were disappearing from urban industrial households, although again Preston stood at the extreme of experience. Moreover, one-fifth of households in the market towns continued to include servants.

Subsequent studies have confirmed a relative rise in extended family living during the mid-Victorian era in Britain and the USA. Ruggles (1987) analysed twenty-seven separate studies of sixty-eight data sets drawn from localities and national samples in England and America between 1599 and 1984. Although the majority of households never contained extended kin, the minority that did approximately doubled between 1750 and the late nineteenth century, to about 20 per cent of all households (Ruggles 1987: 6). While these findings gave no heart to the old myth that there was a transition from the extended family to the nuclear family at the time of the industrial revolution, they also exploded the new myth that American and English family structure was always and everywhere overwhelmingly nuclear. However, the range of experience suggested by the community studies counsels against taking Preston as a benchmark even for mid-nineteenth-century urban industrial Britain, let alone the environment as a whole. Any explanation of household composition must address not only Preston's often extreme characteristics but the variation around it marked out by the other towns.

SELF-INTERESTED INDIVIDUALS AND HOUSEHOLDS OF MUTUAL ADVANTAGE

The structuralist–functionalists and the English empiricists failed to translate their macro-models into an account of the human decisions involved in the formation and dissolution of households and the drawing of their boundaries. The former depicted adaptive behaviour taking place at the level of society as a whole, while the latter focused on the measurable characteristics of households detectable in historical records. More recent approaches such as the New Home Economics (Becker 1965, 1981) and the 'family strategies' perspective envisaged the household as adopting the size, composition and employment structure that was most advantageous collectively (Tilly and Scott 1978; Hareven 1982). How these decisions came about and were acted upon remained mysterious. What was needed to tie the patterns in size and composition to potential social and economic explanatory variables was a credible account of individual behaviour with respect to household membership. Without such a microanalysis of the household, its history had no driving force.

The explanatory vacuum at the micro-level left by the other approaches was filled by Anderson's instrumentalist utilitarian account of family relationships. In Anderson's work the 'economic conveniences' that Laslett had acknowledged could influence size and structure emerged in a fully developed micro-theory of the household based on reciprocal exchange and mutual advantage.

Co-residence was explained by reference to the advantages and disadvantages that individuals experienced as a result of household membership (Anderson 1972: 226). In particular, large numbers of individuals from one group of kin (say married children) would only be found co-residing with another group (say widowed parents) if the present value of average, lifetime economic advantages of doing so outweighed the economic disadvantages. Benefits had to be mutual and calculated on the understanding that co-residence implied some sharing of resources if required.

The theoretical framework facilitated an explanation of the distinguishing features of the households. The propensity of rural households to contain kin was easily explained. North Lancashire, unusually for nineteenth-century rural England, had a high proportion of prosperous family farms on which kin were employed to mutual advantage (see also Williams 1963). But on-going economic co-operation could not explain the high propensity of Preston's wage-dependent households to harbour kin.

To some extent the tendency to include kin simply represented 'piling up' or 'huddling', as individuals sought to spread rents over larger numbers in rapidly growing cities. But there was another advantage to co-residence, for networks of relatives often helped individuals obtain work. Where kinsmen had small businesses they could provide employment, and thereby overcome various information problems in hiring and monitoring. Even where households were fully wage dependent, access to employment could be eased by the information and introductions provided by parents, uncles, cousins, in-laws and siblings.

What about the higher incidence of married couples co-resident with parents, unusual seemingly everywhere but Preston and Oldham? Again the answer lay in mutual advantage. Members of the working class who survived to old age faced deprivation unless they could live with married children, sharing rent and common consumption. Young married couples could benefit from savings on rent, but the downside of sharing with parents loomed large. As relatives aged they were likely to become liabilities. Denied co-residence, old people would be saved by the poor law from absolute destitution (Thomson 1991; Smith 1998; Thane, 2000). These considerations kept the proportions of co-resident parents and married children down in pre-industrial rural areas and most nineteenth-century towns. In Preston and Oldham, poverty was less intense and there was more room to manoeuvre (Foster 1974; Anderson 1972). More importantly, the cotton industry offered employment for married women, thus creating a demand for substitutes to provide childcare and housework. By providing these services, elderly relatives could reciprocate for bed and board. Everybody gained. Later work on the Potteries, where poverty was also less biting and local industry again afforded employment for married women, confirmed these links with family structure and composition echoing those of the textile towns (Dupree 1995; see Table 9.3).

Local opportunities for children's employment also influenced family composition. In Preston children worked in the mills and as child-minders, and did not have to leave home in search of jobs, as did children in pre-industrial England, most rural areas of industrialising England, and even York. Guaranteed employment, orphaned relatives or the underemployed children of kin were attractive additions to Preston households, thus explaining the large numbers of 'parentless children' detected among other kin.

The proportions of households containing servants and lodgers were also plausibly related to mutual advantage. In Preston the relative absence of small businesses, the homogeneity of income levels and the existence of jobs for young people that did not involve co-residence meant that servants were relatively uncommon, while in Preston and York the relatively high costs of housing increased the incidence of lodging.

Thus mutual advantage explained not only the distinctive patterns of co-residence observed in Preston in comparison with pre-industrial households but also the variations across nineteenth-century industrial and non-industrial towns. These were related to local differences in housing, poverty, employment opportunities for women and children, mortality and migration. For example, the dominance of the nuclear family in the Potteries and the low incidence of sharing with people outside the nuclear family, related to the lower migration into the Potteries and the more plentiful supply of housing (Dupree 1995).

Moreover, contrary to the conventional wisdom, as the industrial revolution got underway, households acquired new functions as they shed old ones. The organisation of early industrial labour markets devolved many functions onto workers' own families. Relatives, even when themselves only employees, often had the power to hire directly. Spinners hired their own piecers, potters their mould runners, hewers their drawers (Shaw 1903; Smelser 1959, 1967; Humphries 1981). Family teams of workers extended beyond their well-documented presence in spinning factories (Smelser 1959; Collier 1964) to many other early industrial workplaces. Working with other family members had advantages. Patriarchal authority and familial loyalty were adapted to create effective hierarchy within the labour process, and in dangerous workplaces the presence of trusted and reliable work-mates increased individual security. Thus, in the badly ventilated mines of the industrial revolution, family members were preferred as co-workers in the belief that they were more likely to afford assistance in the event of danger (Humphries 1981). The primitive and contested nature of work evaluation in the early mills and mines, where workers were often on piece-rates, also put a premium on including family members in the work team. Their presence where work was checked and weighed guarded against cheating by managers and foremen and they could be relied upon to struggle for advantages in the allocation of work and access to equipment (Humphries 1981). Help finding work was particularly important to newcomers to towns and cities, and strengthened ties with more distant kin, ironically creating a motive for extending households in ways which were rare among pre-industrial producing households.

Today historians have become accustomed to the invasion of economics, and rational economic man pops up in the strangest places. But in 1971, historians accustomed to think of family relations as normative and affective, balked at his appearance in the households of the industrial revolution. Reference to norms, which freed individuals from interminable computation while ensuring an efficient response, did little to calm their unease. The reduction of emotional attachments to 'particular non-marketable household commodities' seemed 'unsubtle' (Ruggles 1987: 17). The circumstantial nature of the evidence, inferring intention from outcome, was suspect, prompting Anderson himself to look for supportive accounts of motivation (1972: 231), many of which were however consistent with more solidaristic interpretations of family relations (Dupree 1995: 25).

Non-economic explanations of family structure were offered as supplements if not alternatives. The 'personal attachments' that Laslett had grudgingly accorded a role in explaining unusual family forms were generalised in cultural and emotional explanations of the rise in extended family living during industrialisation. Urbanisation, mobility, and widespread economic and social change created unprecedented turmoil and sense of insecurity, causing many to retreat into the home, the family and intense affective relationships (Lasch 1977; Ruggles 1987). Demographic conditions too had changed in ways that were favourable to extended families. Increased longevity and earlier marriage, by increasing the availability of kin, expanded the proportion of the population that could choose to live with relatives (Ruggles 1987: 125).

The economistic approach to the household collided with alternative emotional and cultural interpretations over the extent to which families provided assistance. It was easy to find examples of help but difficult to assess whether they were isolated or representative. Care for the elderly was an important issue. Although the Elizabethan poor law required children to support aged parents, poor law records and lists of poorhouse inhabitants suggest that by the eighteenth century responsibility for the elderly was shouldered by the parish (Thomson 1991; Thane 2000). On the other hand, that families only provided help 'where exchanges were reciprocal and fairly immediate' (Anderson 1971: 8) was disputed. Some historians could find little evidence of a 'calculative orientation' among family members (Roberts 1988: 172; see also Finch 1989). Care or food was often provided even when poverty held back subsidies. Networks of non-pecuniary assistance were particularly important for women (Finch 1989; Ross 1993). By subsidising kin and neighbours who were providing help, the old poor law may have strengthened family and community relations so that they withstood pressure on other occasions. The persistent miserliness of the old poor law in the north and west (King 2000) left the family, for all its drawbacks, as a major provider of assistance in the industrial districts. The hardening of attitudes in the south and east at the end of the eighteenth century, and the transition to the new poor law in the 1830s and 1840s, similarly left the family as an outpost of welfare provision. The massive retrenchment in poor law expenditures after 1834, since needs could scarcely have fallen in line, suggests that families filled some of the gap.

The survival and structure of the family among the wage-dependent working class owed much to the reciprocal services that members were able to provide. Changing economic conditions afforded new opportunities for reciprocal exchange as well as sweeping away old ones, and help was perhaps less conditional than earlier thought, with most kin prepared to offer assistance until their own nuclear family was jeopardised (Humphries 1977; Dupree 1995). But all was not change. Evidence for the retention of traditional features by an important minority of households not only supports the revisionist claim that organisational transition was gradual but also helps to explain why that was so.

CONTINUITY AS WELL AS CHANGE: LIVE-IN SERVICE AND DOMESTIC ENTERPRISE

Pre-industrial households frequently included live-in servants, who, along with apprentices, were a significant component of the labour force, representing around 15–20 per cent of the adult male population (Stone 1966). Service provided a bridge from childhood to adulthood tailored for a society constructed around families rather than individuals (Caunce 1991). With the exception of domestic service, however, living-in has been regarded as 'one of the large reptiles of economic history, extraordinarily successful in its time and driven rapidly to extinction when times changed' (Kussmaul 1981: 134). The relatively low proportions of households that contained servants in Preston was held by Anderson to auger 'the ultimate decline to which this class was destined' (1971a: 81).

The demise of live-in service is dated from the late eighteenth century when economic conditions moved sharply to disfavour it. Yet as late as the mid-nineteenth century, significant proportions of households in some communities continued to include servants, trade assistants and apprentices (see Table 9.2), suggesting that the institution and its fate are ripe for reconsideration.

Live-in farm servants hired annually and paid largely in kind provided solutions to some of the problems associated with agricultural labour. The traditional service contract made it easier to align incentives, and reduce monitoring and muster costs (Woodward 2000). In return, resident service cut the costs of travelling to work and insured the worker against rising rents and food prices. That most live-in farm servants were young and single testifies to the importance attached to an independent household on marriage and to the value in the service contract of the on-the-job training and experience. For most farmers a mix of live-in servants and independent wage labourers best met their needs, the proportions depending upon farm type and price variations (Kussmaul 1981).

Changes in the seasonality of marriage provided indirect evidence of the decline of service. Marriage for farm servants frequently occurred shortly after their last yearly hiring, the annual wages allowing them to form an independent household (Kussmaul 1981). Changes in the proportion of all marriages that took place in October provided a rough guide to the importance of service and were used as an indicator of trends over time. Farm service apparently fell from 1750, with a slight reversal during the Napoleonic Wars but a sharper slide thereafter (for a discussion of the hazards of this method see Snell 1985: 85; Woodward 2000). Service for a full year guaranteed settlement under the old poor law.[1] Thus changes in the proportion of all settlements obtained by yearly hiring, as revealed in settlement examinations, provided another rough indicator of the decline in service (Snell 1985). According to this evidence, the decline in service was not regionally uniform but progressed fastest in the south-east, where it was advanced by 1820. Contemporary social commentary corroborated these trends, claiming that the decline in 'traditional' service with its enforced intimacy between employer and employee contributed to the yawning gulf in class relations (see Snell 1985 for a summary).

The decline of service was related to its costs and benefits. The cause was not industrialisation *per se*, though the transition to capitalism in agriculture played an underlying role. Movements in food prices, reflecting demographic conditions, made the room and board of servants expensive or cheap compared with day wages and so determined long swings in the composition of farm labour (Kussmaul 1981). The inflation of the Napoleonic Wars operated as a sharp disincentive to indoor service. With rising expenditure on poor relief and diminishing anxieties about the availability of harvest labour in overstocked rural labour markets, aversion to forms of hiring that bestowed settlement grew (Snell 1985). New preferences for privacy on the part of both the farmer and the servant (Pinchbeck 1969[1930]), increasing farm size and the disappearance of family farms (Moses 1999) also contributed.

Recent work based on the printed and manuscript census returns and oral histories suggests that farm service did not disappear as rapidly as previously believed but remained important through the nineteenth century, especially in the north of England, Scotland and Wales (Devine 1984;

---

[1] Under the poor law, poor persons seeking assistance in cash or kind had a right to apply to local overseers of the poor only in their parish of settlement. Birth within a parish created an automatic right of settlement, but settlement could also be acquired through apprenticeship and certain extended periods of employment.

Short 1984; Howkins 1994; Caunce 1997b; and see also Kussmaul 1981). Thus by 1871, the final year for which a distinction was made between servants and labourers in the census, in England only 16 per cent of hired workers were servants. But in Scotland most permanent farm workers, and in Wales and Ireland more than half of the total, continued to fall into this category (Howkins 1994: 60). Even in the south-east of England, where decline proceeded fastest, in 1831 between 15 and 38 per cent of the agricultural labour force were 'farm-servants' (Snell 1985: 84).

Service survived even in arable areas and on large-scale capitalist farms. For example in the East Riding as late as the 1920s over half of farm workers were servants (Caunce 1991). Service's resilience stemmed from its adaptability. In the East Riding, with the transition to capitalist farms, new or extended farm houses included accommodation for servants away from that occupied by the farmer and his family, thus preserving the institution of service alongside the preference for privacy (Moses 1999). Elsewhere servants were housed in a bothy or separate structure, or boarded with foremen (Howkins 1994). From about 1780, living-out forms of farm service also developed (Snell 1985). Service survived, but it did so in part by detaching itself from co-residence.

Outside agriculture, live-in service offered analogous advantages and disadvantages to masters and servants. The same economic changes that discouraged farm service also undermined living-in in trade and industry. Yet the proportions of households with servants and trade assistants in fourteen sub-districts from the published Census Report of 1851 suggest that living-in was still widespread (Armstrong 1972: table 6.12; see also the evidence for York and Ashford, market towns and railway termini, in Table 9.2 of this chapter).

Domestic servants fared differently. The generally adverse conditions were, in the case of male domestics, exacerbated by the taxation levied on them at a time when men were needed for the army and navy. But female service was held to have increased, promoted by the absence of competing job opportunities, especially in rural areas. Recent work has cast doubt on this view by questioning the validity of nineteenth-century census enumeration of female domestic servants and the related back projections on which the purported increase was based (Higgs 1983; Schwartz 1999). The proportion of living-in maidservants may even have declined from 1780 to 1851.

Apprentices were also numerically and economically important workers who traditionally lived in. The apprentice was bound by indentures (a training contract, typically five years in length) to a tradesman who was covenanted to teach him his trade. The apprentice contributed to the costs of his training and maintenance by working for the master during the contract, and by paying a premium up-front. The apprentice lived with the master as part of the family. Training extended to learning the way of life associated with the future occupation (see chapter 12).

While the legal history of apprenticeship is well known, trends in its quantitative significance remain vague (see Dunlop 1912). Surviving town employment books suggest that apprentices probably counted for about 5 per cent of the early industrial urban population, but maybe 10 per cent in some parts of London where many boys went to be trained (Earle 1989; Humphries 2002). That the institution declined is agreed, but the timing and explanation remain unclear (see Snell 1985). One tendency is to associate decline with the diminishing control of the guilds a century or so before the industrial revolution. Snell is one of the few historians to attempt to document the decline in terms of the reduced times actually served and the growth of illegal apprenticeships as revealed in settlement examinations. His evidence suggests regional differences in the timing of the decline and a different chronology between guilded towns and more rural contexts. The length of the term served declined from the mid-eighteenth century, especially after 1780 and with 1811–20 seeing most change (Snell 1985; see also Rushton 1991). Lane (1996), however, argues for a much more gradual decline, unaffected by the repeal of the Statute of Artificers in 1814.

Apprenticeship too survived by adapting to the new conditions. 'Clubbing-out' apprenticeships where the apprentice remained at home or boarded, and worked with the master during the day much like a journeyman, became increasingly common after 1780 (Snell 1985). These were similar to the living-out forms of farm service that developed in the same period. Shorter-term apprenticeships also gained in popularity (Snell 1985).

All forms of living-in service were put under pressure by late eighteenth- and early nineteenth-century conditions: high food prices, overstocked labour markets, reluctance to help employees gain settlements, and a desire by employers to create social distance from employees. As a result, households shed workers and contracted. Yet these employment forms did not disappear as speedily or as universally as implied in Kussmaul's vivid metaphor. The conditions that made live-in service unattractive were particularly chronic in the agricultural south-east, significantly the main focus of both Kussmaul and Snell's research. In other regions and sectors conditions favoured living-in. Over time the factors that had undermined service faded: food prices came down from wartime levels, and in 1834 yearly hiring ceased to be a criterion for settlement. The significant minority of households that contained servants (including but not only domestic servants), trade assistants and apprentices in 1851 testifies to co-residence's survival as more that a quaint relic. On the other hand the adaptations that in part preserved service moved it out of the household and reduced the yearly bond to an employment contract.

Living-in was associated with the traditional master–servant relationship, and hence its disappearance with the demise of small-scale production. Suggestions that living-in survived in some sectors and adapted to changing conditions are consistent with the view that small and micro units of production remained important until well on into the nineteenth century (Berg 1994; Howkins 1994).

In agriculture, the processes of enclosure, increasing size of farms and changes in land tenure had long worked together to separate small-scale proprietors from the land and make them wage dependent. Perhaps 60 per cent of families were in receipt of wages by 1700, though some of these may have retained some vestigial rights to land (Tilly 1984; Snell 1985). The extensive development of waged labour in the early modern countryside has long been held to be one of the deep roots of the industrial revolution, and through the constraints on proletarian households' size to have contributed to the small families of the era.

During the eighteenth century, small freeholds were bought up and landlords eliminated secure leases. The former yeoman lands passed into the hands of the gentry and the aristocracy. Small farms were combined and leased to large-scale capitalist farmers (Allen 1992; chapter 4 above). By 1830 another 15 per cent of families had been added to the wage earning class (Tilly 1984). Over the same time horizon, the remnants of diffused property ownership in the form of common rights, which had continued to be exploited by some members of proletarian households, were expunged (Martin 1984; Snell 1985; Malcolmson 1988; but see also Shaw-Taylor 2001). The result was the consolidation of the great estate and the emergence of the three-tiered social structure of rich landlord, substantial tenant farmer and poor landless labourer.

But this process did not proceed at the same pace throughout the British Isles (Devine 1984; Howkins 1994). Outside the arable south-east, large-scale capitalist agriculture and proletarianisation were not universal. For example, the survival of family farms in northern Lancashire has already been linked to the propensity of rural households to include kin and servants.

Outside agriculture, the standard story was of an inexorable shift away from family firms and businesses towards larger-scale production units. But while huge capitalist enterprises dominated the imaginations of contemporaries and some historians, more recent research has demonstrated that these coexisted with a varied industrial organisation (Berg 1994). As late as 1840, over 75 per cent of British manufacturing was in diverse, dispersed and unspectacular industries. Artisan production flourished alongside networks of putting out, and both were often symbiotically interrelated with centralised capitalist enterprises (Hudson 1986; Levine 1987; Rose 1988; Berg 1994; chapter 2 above). Small-scale production was sometimes threatened, the fate of the handloom weavers held up to exemplify the experience of handicraft manufacturers in the age of mechanisation. But remember that the handloom weavers persisted as independent producers well on into the nineteenth century, still numbering some 200,000 in 1840 (Bythell 1969). Elsewhere small-scale manufacturing survived and indeed sometimes flourished, for example in the metal industries of Birmingham and the Black Country, the hosiery trades of the Midlands, and the myriad consumer industries ranging from furniture and shoe manufacturing to the tobacco and food industries (Berg 1994).

Experts on industrial organisation have pointed out that small-scale production units can offset diseconomies of scale by being flexible and responsive, producing high quality, and networking among themselves (Piore and Sable 1984; Best 1990). Producing households that employed resident servants and kin were particularly well placed to develop these competitive advantages. Resident servants were available for work twenty-four hours of the day, facilitating fast responses to orders. Apprentices and kin-workers who had often been trained within the household had reliable skills. Quality was relatively easily monitored.

Recent discussions have highlighted the importance of trust in facilitating economic co-operation, which, while mutually advantageous, is threatened by the ability of individuals to renege on prior agreements about the divisions of rewards and responsibilities. Household-based production units, especially if they employed kin, provided trustful environments. Kinship ties represented networks of relationships within which disputes could be mediated, settlements negotiated and, in the last resort, multi-sided punishments in the form of social and economic shunning threatened, without the costs of calling in exogenous authorities. The on-going kinship relation held both master and man to the implicit employment contract and so ensured co-operation, which, while efficient, could not be maintained by a solely market relationship. This was probably particularly important in the small-scale sector, where liquidity was short and payments often had to be postponed until the contract was fulfilled. The frequency with which journeymen sought out relatives as masters or co-workers suggests the importance of trust in economic exchange, especially in contexts (small-scale sector, early industrialisation) when contracting was not routine. Family businesses, which took in kin as servants, could continue to benefit from co-residence without sacrificing household intimacy. Moreover business networks across firms, important in sustaining and initiating enterprise, were built on kinship as well as community links (Pearson and Richardson 2001).

Thus the persistence of small and micro enterprise provided a niche for household production, co-residence and kin-service. But in turn these features also actively contributed to the resilience of the small-firm sector.

Household production units shaded imperceptibly into self-employed households. Ubiquitous in industrialising Britain, they provided another niche for household-based economic co-operation. In the countryside every village had its blacksmith, carpenter and butcher and such households were multiplied in the towns and cities and augmented by masons, bricklayers, plumbers, glaziers and all the myriad trades represented in the census listing of occupations.

Households of manufacturers involved in putting out occupied a position between the self-employed households of tradesmen and the households of waged workers. Middlemen supplied raw materials, marketed the finished products and sometimes rented out the equipment. But the household organised production.

Households engaged in artisan production, self-employment and making to order shared a constitutional tendency for all family members to become involved. Income depended on output. Ancillary processes in production, such as winding, seaming, stitching, doing the accounts, minding the shop and supervising the apprentices, unless done by other family members, took the primary producer's time or involved payments to outsiders, in both cases reducing family income. Not surprisingly, descriptions of such households from working-class memoirs or contemporary observation document the widespread and advantageous involvement of wives and children (Vincent 1981). Natural categories like age and gender provided a division of labour within the mini-production team. Multifaceted interdependence along with ongoing and intimate contact reduced the incentive and ability to shirk, and so made the monitoring of effort and quality less necessary. Rarely separately remunerated, and disguised behind job descriptions such as 'assisting', these contributions enabled many domestic units to remain competitive.

But there was a darker side to these advantages. Family labour had the potential for exploitation, pressure from falling prices of output leading to household members being worked longer and harder to keep the family enterprise afloat (Medick 1976). Thus as piece-rates and earnings fell in handloom weaving, families responded by employing more of their members, their wives and their children, and increasing output in a bid to maintain incomes (Lyons 1989). In the framework knitting community of Shepshed, by 1851, the inability of families to survive on the low earnings of male heads of households had pulled increasing numbers of other family members into the trade: 80 per cent of households contained at least two people employed in some branch of the trade and 50 per cent contained three or more, an incidence of 'wage-earning co-residence' appreciably higher than among agricultural labourers or tradesmen and craftsmen (Levine 1977: 27; see also Rose 1988). In trades, hard times led to increased numbers of apprentices. Of course 'adding workers' and increasing output only exacerbated the situation of oversupply.

The tendency of household-based production units to respond to pressure on prices by increasing labour input resonates with modern interpretations of the industrial revolution that conceptualise its early phase in terms of increasing labour input rather than increasing labour productivity (Crafts and Harley 1992; Crafts 1994; de Vries 1994; Voth 2000). But this was an 'industrious revolution', driven not by aspiration to higher incomes and new consumer goods but by the desire to maintain standards. In the terminology of de Vries (1993), it involved a coerced rather than a willing transfer of domestic production and leisure time into market work. Its empirical investigation awaits a closer look at family employment levels and living standards.

WAGE EARNING HOUSEHOLDS IN THE INDUSTRIAL REVOLUTION

The 'family wage economy' was susceptible to the same degenerative tendencies as producing households squeezed by declining piece-rates or prices. Faced with falling wages, the responses at the level of the household, adding workers or working longer and harder, if replicated on a wide scale, reduced wages further, leaving households no better and maybe even worse off while putting out more effort (Medick 1976).

Marx and Engels were not alone in recording these tendencies, though they were unusual in understanding them as inevitable aspects of capitalist progress. Modern historians have traced these effects on the household economies of hand workers as they came into competition with mechanised production (Levine 1977; Rose 1988; Lyons 1989). In this view, the households of the early industrial economy, especially those of domestic manufacturers competing with mechanised production, were characterised by a low ratio of non-workers to workers, high participation rates of wives and mothers, and early working for children. To the extent that mechanisation itself freed manufacturing production from the need for physical strength, enabling women and children to be employed, and reducing wage rates, it too was associated with an intensification of work.

An increasingly 'work rich' but 'time and welfare poor' early industrial household, while consistent with anecdotal evidence and studies of specific trades, jarred with the belief that industrialisation marked the transition from a pre-industrial family economy in which everyone was involved in production to a male breadwinner family system in which women and children were dependent on men. How important was the intensive phase of family employment and over what time frame did it give rise to the male breadwinner family? There was no agreement on either question (Creighton 1996). With only patchy empirical evidence on women and children's work and isolated studies of family employment structure, the debate shed more heat than light (Thomas 1988).

Whether early industrialisation really saw an increase in the intensity of family employment was disputed (Richards 1974). The increasing visibility of women's and children's work as it emerged from the privacy of the household may have misled observers. Whether the intensive employment of women and children reached its peak in domestic production or was matched in the early factories was also debated (Pinchbeck and Hewitt 1973). Nor was it clear how intensive family employment squared with accounts of women's work in which the movement of production outside the home, by making it hard to combine productive with domestic activities, undermined women's independence. Not that everyone agreed that the disappearance of producing households had deleterious effects on the status and well-being of women. At least it freed the home from the dirt, noise and stress of the workplace (see Pinchbeck 1969[1930]). In optimistic accounts, the nascent capitalist economy provided opportunities for women and girls and liberated them from patriarchal control.

There was also debate about why these 'work-rich, time and welfare-poor' households gave way to the male breadwinner family system. Some economic historians emphasised supply conditions, particularly the income effects associated with increases in men's earnings which allowed more leisure for women and children (Nardinelli 1990). As budget constraints relaxed, the male breadwinner family system was preferred, giving a Whig twist to the history of the household! Others saw working men as advancing their own position at the expense of working women. Demands for family wages and agitation for protective labour legislation, while perhaps genuine expressions of concern for women and child workers, could alternatively be interpreted as attempts to legitimise men's claims to a pay premium while excluding competing workers from the better-paid jobs. Whatever the mix of motives, the proclamation of womanly standards that extolled motherhood and housework, and derided working wives, undoubtedly reinforced patriarchal social norms. By linking their demands to a hierarchical gender order that was familiar and cherished, working-class men induced sympathy and allied with men from other classes (Benenson 1984; Rose 1992; Seccombe 1993).

These struggles took place in a class context. Elements among the employing classes were sympathetic to the demand for family wages because they realised that the employment of women and children could lead to the physical and mental deterioration of the working class as a whole. Perhaps too the campaigns for family wages and protective labour legislation represented the defence not of patriarchal privilege but of family integrity and working-class living standards. Working-class women as well as men may have seen the advantages in a strategy that freed married women from the drudgery of the double shift and enabled children to go to school, while reducing the supply of labour and raising wages (Humphries 1977).

Doubt was expressed about whether patchy and often inconsistent empirical evidence could ever resolve the disagreements (Thomas 1988). Systematic studies of the employment structure of households were rare, and often time and industry specific (see Collier 1964; Levine 1977; Rose 1988; Lyons 1989). But recently, working-class household budgets, recovered from a variety of original sources, have allowed trends in household employment and incomes to be tracked for a number of broad occupational groups (Horrell and Humphries 1992, 1995a, 1995b). Figure 9.1 summarises the evidence on trends in the composition of family incomes.

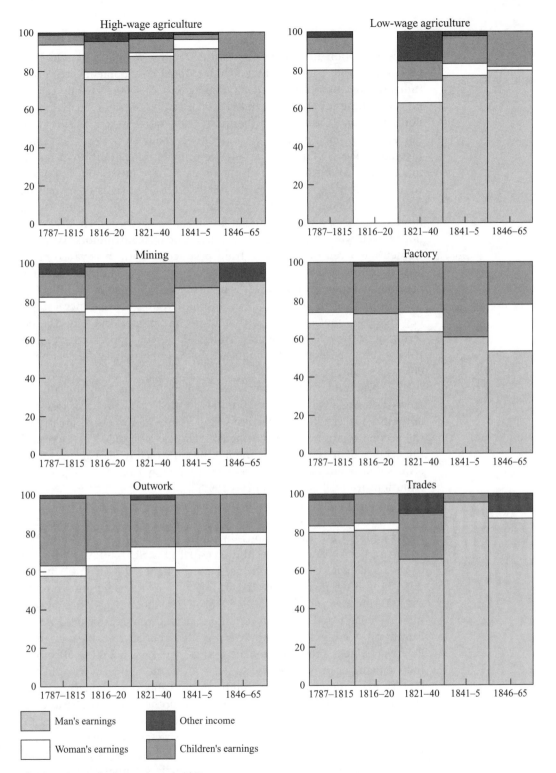

Figure 9.1 Contributions to household income

Source: Horrell and Humphries 1995a.

The transition to a male breadwinner family system seems to have been a precocious but patchy and interrupted development. Before the industrial revolution was underway many families were already reliant on the earnings of husbands and fathers. Families of factory workers and domestic manufacturers had the most democratically sourced incomes. But even here men on average contributed about 60 per cent of family income. In factory families the relative contributions of different family members held constant through the industrial revolution, but in domestic manufacturing families by the 1840s there were signs of increasing dependence. Equally striking was that for all families, including those headed by factory workers and domestic manufacturers, children and not women were the most important secondary contributors. Working women's apparent detachment from productive work in advance of industrialisation is consistent with the evidence that middle-class women became increasingly dissociated from business from 1680 on (Hunt 1996). In the course of the industrial revolution, families became increasingly dependent on men's earnings, though not in any uniform way. The petering out of married women's earnings and their opportunities to contribute through self-provisioning were not as important as the decline in children's contributions.

The structural change associated with industrialisation initially increased the relative weight of families headed by factory workers and domestic workers. But the declining importance of domestic industry by the second quarter of the nineteenth century, alongside the increased importance of artisan and mining families in which men's earnings were always dominant, drove the aggregate trend away from more equal contributions (Horrell and Humphries 1997).

While assigning some role to the driving force of male earnings, the trends in individual occupations leave room for demand-side, institutional and cultural explanations. In southern agriculture, declining job opportunities for women and children (Snell 1985; Sharpe 1999) produced a growing dependence on inadequate and stagnant male earnings. In contrast, in mining, increased male earnings provided a beneficent route to the male breadwinner family, though protective labour legislation by prohibiting women and children from underground work, also played a role. Families headed by factory workers provided another tier of experience. Relatively high and buoyant male earnings were not enough to offset the inducements of own wage effects for women and children. Nor did the Factory Acts immediately cut children's contributions, though perhaps the increased contribution from wives and mothers after 1845 was a response to limits on child employment (see also Rose 1988; Dupree 1995). For these families there was a phase of intensive family employment consistent with a voluntary industrious revolution motivated by economic opportunities. In contrast it was stagnant male earnings that enforced the persistently high contributions from other family members in the households of domestic manufacturers. Tradesmen's families illustrate that occupational identities could be associated with idealised household employment patterns that were relatively independent of earnings. The skilled tradesman aspired to a male breadwinner family structure even if he did not earn a family wage.

It would be wrong to conclude that the contributions of women and children were unimportant. Women's contributions were underestimated because housework and caring were not counted, and self-provisioning and taking in lodgers were hard to value. Self-provisioning activities, such as gleaning, growing potatoes, keeping a cow or pig, or collecting firewood, common strategies to augment family earnings in the eighteenth-century countryside (Humphries 1990; King 1991), were curtailed by urbanisation and the privatisation of rural resources. Some rural households that were fortunate enough to retain access to resources adapted provisioning activities, replacing cows with pigs for example. These remained able to generate resources worth 10 to 20 per cent of men's earnings at the end of the industrial revolution (Horrell and Humphries 1997). As opportunities to forage faded, increased labour migration boosted the demand for lodgings, and provided wives and widows with the chance to augment family incomes by selling their domestic services or a share of their accommodation (Davidoff 1979; see also Table 9.2).

Children were important secondary earners. When trends in child participation rates are related to the growing numbers of children characteristic of the period, they suggest an increase in the absolute input of child labour time. In addition, the relatively high and increasing participation rates in factory districts and the influx of population into such areas implies a massive increase in children working in factories: a near doubling from 1787–1816 to 1817–39 according to Horrell and Humphries's (1995) estimate. Although the boom in child labour was not sustained, the new quantitative evidence (see Tuttle 1999) rehabilitates an older theme in industrial revolution studies: the exploitation of small children (Hammond and Hammond 1932; Thompson 1963). Historians may be well advised to revisit the role that children played in British industrialisation, especially as it looks unusual in comparison with other nineteenth-century industrialisers (Cunningham and Viazzo 1996).

The contributions of women and children were crucial in supporting families through the family life-cycle and associated poverty cycle. The newly married couple, especially if the wife continued working, fared well. But when babies arrived and the mother's efforts were curtailed, the ratio of dependants to wage earners rose and there was pressure on family income. Older children's entry into the labour force, by driving down the ratio of dependants to workers, inaugurated a new, more prosperous phase. Thus men's relative earnings declined in importance in the middle stages of the life-cycle when children's earnings made up about one-third of income with some variation by occupation (see Horrell and Humphries

1995: fig. 2). But these balmy times were soon threatened by the declining productivity of the ageing head of household and the tendency of grown children to seek independence and ultimately themselves embark on a similar familial cycle. Children's confrontation of the dependency hump associated with their own increasing families probably coincided with parents' ageing, inhibiting intergenerational assistance. Stylised accounts of the family life-cycle have been given substance through the vivid descriptions of the pressures on family resources as fathers aged and siblings multiplied (Vincent 1981; Ross 1993).

For one important group of households, women's and children's contributions were not only helpful but vital: those households either temporarily or permanently without a male breadwinner. High mortality left large numbers of widows, while desertion, sickness and unemployment also threw women and children on their own resources. In the turbulent years of the industrial revolution both sources of female headship may have been increasing. But whether increasing or not, households headed by women comprised between 10 and 20 per cent at any point in time (Humphries 1998). Given the overall importance of male earnings, it is not surprising that these households, despite their predictably higher rates of female and child participation (Humphries 1998), often relied on poor relief and other assistance to remain together as families (Snell and Millar 1987; Horrell *et al.* 2001).

Children from such families, as well as orphans and *de facto* orphans, were in the vanguard of the industrial labour force (Rose 1989). The poor law, manufacturers through their recruitment policies, and the institution of pauper apprenticeship collaborated in this draft. By opening its doors to 'parentless children' and actively recruiting workhouse orphans, the extended family of the factory and mining districts also reallocated child labour to where it was needed.

The male breadwinner family system came about in different ways and over varied time scales for families facing heterogeneous local conditions. This conclusion is consistent with research on the industrial revolution, which emphasises regional and industrial diversity (Berg and Hudson 1992), and with feminist research, which emphasises a varied female experience (Honeyman and Goodman 1991). Political and cultural as well as economic factors promoted it. *En route* some families experienced an intensive phase of employment but they did so in different ways and with different welfare implications, some in response to opportunities to earn and buy, others pressurised by falling piece-rates or wages. But over and above the variety and diversity of the industrial revolution, originating before and sprawling beyond its horizons a great transformation did take place. Industrialisation did not introduce the male breadwinner family. But in its tumult, by varied routes with significant interruptions and heterogeneous welfare implications, more households adopted this form.

THE HOUSEHOLD ECONOMY, THE STANDARD OF LIVING AND CONSUMPTION

The history of the household economy provides a fresh perspective on two of the most contested aspects of the industrial revolution: the standard of living debate and the role of consumption. Historians of the standard of living concentrated on men's real wages, assuming that these moved in line with both their own and women's and children's earnings. Unearned contributions to family incomes, such as self-provisioning and poor relief, and changes in numbers of people dependent on male earnings were ignored. The household budgets provide direct evidence on these points, as anticipated in the discussion in the previous section of widespread but unevenly developing dependence on male earnings.

Levels and trends in family incomes varied widely, depending on the occupation of the male head and the region of observation. Aggregating according to the changing importance of the specific occupational groups, and using the best available cost of living index (Feinstein 1998) to deflate nominal incomes, suggests that on average real family incomes fell 14 per cent from 1791/5 to 1816/20. Improvements in the 1830s were eroded by the recession of the 1840s, leaving the average working-class family by 1846/50 with a 24.9 per cent higher real income, hardly a rich reward for the generation that lived through the industrial revolution (Horrell and Humphries, forthcoming). Consistent with the failure of other family members' contributions to track male earnings, household incomes grew less than did male earnings. This relatively pessimistic picture fits with recent definitive work on real wages if account is taken of changes in dependency (Feinstein 1998). Feinstein guessed that the increasing burden of dependants on workers characteristic of the period meant that family living standards were about 10 per cent lower than those implied by real wage trends by mid-century (Feinstein 1998: 650). An adjustment of this order to his estimate of welfare improvement up to the 1840s leaves it reassuringly close to the estimated growth in real family income reported above.

Household-based accounts confirm other well-known aspects of the era, for example the persistent poverty of agricultural families, and the stagnation of family incomes in domestic manufacturing in the 1830s and 1840s. They also highlight the depth and frequency of setbacks in material progress, which have been hidden by trends in relatively static wage rates. The household data also suggest that the distribution of income across families was becoming more unequal (Horrell and Humphries 1992). Increasing dependence on male earnings also hints that the distribution within families was becoming less egalitarian, though whether this was offset by growth in overall income depended on the type and location of the household.

Consumption has provided more than its share of awkward corners in the jigsaw of the industrial revolution (see chapter 13). Social historians of the early modern period, noting the appearance of new market commodities in household inventories and other sources, identified 'a consumer revolution', which it was tempting to link causally through demand to the industrial revolution that followed. But a consumption-led interpretation of the industrial revolution was not easily squared with the findings of economic historians from the national accounts. Crafts (1985), for example, estimated that real per capita consumption grew at 0.47 per cent per annum between 1780 and 1821, hardly consistent with a bout of frenzied spending. It was none the less sufficiently strong to jar with the stationary or even falling real wages of the period. Did a revolution in spending characterise the early modern economy, precipitating the industrial revolution in its wake? And if so, how did it happen in the face of stagnant wages? Various scholars sought reconciliation by hypothesising an increase in labour input. Does the history of the household economy support the idea that an industrious revolution enabled a consumer revolution?

The traditional definition of the household was in terms of consumption: the bed, board and hearth that members shared. But as urban industrial life transformed and reallocated the productive activities of the household it also transfigured the content, scale and allocation of consumption. The pre-industrial agricultural household produced much of what it consumed. The specialised early modern producing household had to resort to the market to sell its output and to buy goods to eat, drink and wear. In the family wage economy, individuals pooled their earnings and bought what they needed from the market (Tilly and Scott 1978). Consumption was 'commodified'.

One of the earliest accounts of the consumer revolution argued that the increased employment of women and children, by boosting working-class family incomes, increased demand for manufactures and encouraged industrial expansion (McKendrick 1974). A more sophisticated version of the same approach linked commodification to an increase in women's and children's market work (de Vries 1993). The relative cost and attractiveness of market commodities lured women, in particular, into wage labour so that they could replace domestic production with purchased substitutes. But an industrious revolution, which involved increasing female participation rates and family incomes, is hard to square with the evidence presented above from household budgets. A recent argument, which partly avoids this conflict, postulates an increase in the length of the working week and year as the way in which working people reconciled stagnant wages with the desire to consume (Voth 2000). While consumer aspirations remained the main driver, about a quarter of the increase in hours was prompted by the increase in dependency.

Table 9.4 Expenditure on necessities as a proportion of men's earnings (%)						
	High-wage agriculture	Low-wage agriculture	Mining	Factory	Outwork	Trades
Expenditure on food and housing as % of men's earnings						
1787–96	98	114	115	121	136	124
1810–17	–	–	98	–	70	78
1824–5	–	–	111	54	–	–
1830–40	156	75	–	72	128	81
1841–54	100	107	85	98	177	82
Adult equivalent expenditure on food as % of men's earnings						
1787–96	27	31	26	54	35	30
1810–17	–	–	31	–	21	29
1824–5	–	–	35	17	–	–
1830–40	31	21	–	23	34	19
1841–54	24	32	26	31	50	24
(Sample)	(45)	(93)	(29)	(37)	(37)	(13)

Notes: Adult equivalence scale uses 1.7 for man and wife and 0.5 for each other household member.

Source: Horrell 1996.

Attempts to test these various hypotheses on household-level consumption founder on the lack of surviving evidence. A rare attempt to investigate whether working-class families shared in the consumer boom, albeit limited by the small sample of sufficiently detailed budgets available and their possible selectivity bias, is instructive (Horrell 1996). There was little sign that a growing part of men's and other family members' earnings was becoming available for discretionary consumption. Table 9.4 indicates that there was some improvement for families headed by men in some occupations, but this was often short lived, while for others, such as outworking and agricultural families, necessities took an increasing proportion of men's earnings. In only a few occupations, and not in all families in these occupations, were men able to earn enough to feed and shelter their families. The minority contributions of women and children by and large went not on discretionary spending but on necessities, with little change over time. There is little support here for the idea that women and children worked to finance expenditure on the new manufactured goods produced by the factories of the industrial revolution (Horrell 1996). Nor is there evidence that working-class budgets responded to urbanisation or the decline of self-provisioning, a blow to accounts of consumption spending that emphasise commodification.

How was consumption allocated within the households of the industrial revolution? Bargaining models suggest that allocations reflect individual contributions filtered through familial and community notions of deserts. An increase in dependence on male breadwinners skews household resources away from women and children, and without strong gains in male earnings family income may not increase enough to offset the reallocation. The breadwinner effect on distribution outweighs the bread-winner effect on total availability, to leave some family members worse off. Although there are few quantitative studies (but see Horrell and Oxley 1999), qualitative evidence documents severe inequality in the allocation of food, particularly meat, in working households in the late Victorian heyday of the male breadwinner family system (Ross 1993). Children who earned may have had access to better diets but dependent children had to rely on their mothers' sacrifices (Pember-Reeves 1913; Oren 1974). Work in the industrial revolution was often hard and dangerous, so dependence had its benefits. But in the transition to the male breadwinner family system, in households where incomes stagnated, dependence had costs borne by women and children around their own kitchen tables.

Reconciliation of the evidence on real wages and family incomes with that on aggregate consumption and the diffusion of consumer goods awaits a careful piecing together of the diverse experiences of different types of family over time and across space. The evidence from probate inventories for the late seventeenth and early eighteenth centuries (but see King 1997), along with the probable timing of commodification, assigns de Vries's voluntary industrious revolution to the early modern period. Later theories must rely on the demand of the middle classes to kick-start the manufacturing economy. Only fortunate working-class families shared in this consumer boom. The harder work and longer hours of many men, women and children during the industrial revolution were motivated by pressure to provide necessities in the face of stagnant wages and increased numbers of dependants.

CONCLUSIONS

Both long-run changes and short-run variations in economic conditions shaped the household economy. Many operated outside the time frame of the industrial revolution. For example, wage dependence, an important underlying cause of the high frequency of small households in the English countryside, long preceded industrialisation, as did those same small households. Similarly the transition to large-scale centralised production was far from complete by the mid-nineteenth century, allowing producing households of various kinds to survive into the post-industrial era.

Economic factors were not alone in shaping households. Mortality grimly limited the household's long-run size and structure and contributed to its short-run variation across the industrial towns of the nineteenth century. Institutions, for example the poor law, by shifting the costs and benefits of including or excluding kin or resident employees, helped redraw household boundaries. Cultural factors also mattered.

Old ideas linking marriage to the formation of an independent household contributed to the persisting rarity with which married children lived with parents. New ideas about affective familial relationships and the desirability of privacy contributed to the declining frequency with which households included servants.

Households' responses to economic changes were not narrowly deterministic. They could resist, speed up and divert economic pressures. Strategies chosen and their success depended on initial conditions and local opportunities. Hence across the towns of the industrial revolution, against varying backgrounds in terms of poverty, employment opportunities for women and children, housing availability and migration, new kinds of mutual advantage emerged to be exploited through co-residence. These pulled and tugged but also teased and tempted households into new shapes, sizes, occupational structures and internal dynamics.

But households did not just offer temporary and contingent refuge. Individuals struggled to keep their families together and would sacrifice their own advantage in the interests of collective survival. Nor did concern for family invariably foster narrow individualistic interest. Perceived economic pressures on family life did occasion class action and organised resistance.

Households and the individuals within them could react to the opportunities of the changing economy and seize the new industrial day. But their ability to do so depended on many factors outside their immediate control. Not surprisingly, the winners and losers in the industrial revolution varied systematically by household type and geographical location.

The household's partial autonomy, its non-economic dimensions, and the long roots and delayed effects of many of its economic determinants explain why historians have been hard pressed to tell a standard story or to fit their subject into the stiff periods of the industrial revolution. The household's history, like an increasing number of topics, appears occupationally and regionally differentiated, and unfolds on a time scale that transcended industrialisation.

10

Living standards and the urban environment

HANS-JOACHIM VOTH

Contents

Introduction 268
Real wages 271
Heights and physical well-being 273
Working hours 276
Consumption and household budgets 280
Urbanisation, mortality and the value of life 283
Composite measures of welfare 288
The standard of living and macroeconomic performance 291
Conclusions 293

INTRODUCTION

Few topics in economic history generate more controversy than the British industrial revolution – and arguably no debate in economic history is more famous than the 'standard-of-living debate'. In the post-war period, the question of whether the early stages of modern capitalism led to an improvement or a decline in workers' living standards became as hotly contested as many of the Cold War's other theatres. Marxist historians argued that, in exchange for ever longer hours of grinding toil in the factories, the working classes had little to show by 1850 in terms of living standards except for a few cotton goods (Hobsbawm 1972). Optimists such as Max Hartwell pointed to gains in real wages and life expectancy, and to the move to the cities as the escape from the 'idiocy of rural life' (Karl Marx).

When O'Brien and Engerman (1981) discussed the issue in the first volume of *The Economic History of Britain*, they emphasised that future research would most likely have to focus on three topics: improvements in the measurement of real wages, of inequality, and of the changes in welfare not measured by income. Twenty years on, it appears that their intuition was remarkably prescient – two of these areas have contributed most to our reassessment of changes in living standards between 1760 and 1850. The issue of inequality, however, is too controversial to permit firm conclusions (Williamson 1985; Feinstein 1988). Consistent wage series by skill category have proven extremely difficult to compile, and there is no conclusive evidence that the share of total income paid to capital rather than labour moved significantly; the issue will therefore not be covered in this chapter.

I will examine the remaining two research themes in greater detail below. The task of giving a coherent overview is complicated by the great number of indicators that can and have been used to shed light on trends in living standards. Nor do the different variables suggest a uniform direction of change. Much of the difficulty in synthesising the state of the debate arises from conflicting trends, with different variables moving in opposite directions. Even where they converge, sizeable subgroups of the population (as distinguished by class, gender, age or location) may have experienced substantially different changes, in terms of either magnitude or direction. The echoes of economic change 250 years ago resemble the dissonant tones of a Hindemith or Schönberg concert, not the harmonies of a classical symphony. To discern patterns at all requires more than just active listening.

As a first introduction to the trends I discuss in greater detail below, consider the overview of a few indicators in Table 10.1. GDP per capita in 1760 was a mere 1,803 dollars, measured in 1992 purchasing power – Britain was marginally richer than India and Bolivia are in 2000, but a little poorer than Armenia and Indonesia. If the Britain of 1760 were an independent country today, it would rank 149th out of 208 countries (World Bank 2001). Some ninety years later, per capita income had grown substantially – today, Britain's GDP per capita in 1850 would give it a rank ahead of China, but behind Lebanon and the Philippines. Wages apparently improved substantially less than production per head, rising by only 4 per cent over the sixty years between 1760 and 1820, and by less than a quarter for the period 1760–1850 as a whole. Yet to compare across time using 1992 dollars is to ignore radical changes in the range of goods and services that money can buy today – from anaesthesia to better lighting, radios, telephones, education and airtravel.[1] Alternative measures may provide a more intuitive guide to living standards in the past.

Heights were very low by modern standards, a measure often used as an indicator of the 'biological' quality of life. More than 80 per cent of males in Britain in 1966 would have been taller than their average ancestor 200 years earlier; and the first century of industrialisation probably brought little or no improvement, depending on the height series we use. Even the highest levels recorded in the most optimistic series only reach

---

[1] There is some evidence that the value of new goods is substantially underestimated in cost-of-living indices (Nordhaus 1997).

the 25th percentile of modern heights (Floud *et al.* 1990: 10). Height differences between the classes were astoundingly large, indicating that children from the lower classes rarely enjoyed adequate nutrition. Recruits to the Sandhurst military academy, normally drawn from the upper strata of society, towered over their peers from London slums. In 1790, for example, the average 14-year-old boy at the Royal Military Academy was a full 14 cm taller than his contemporary from a disadvantaged background (Floud *et al.* 1990: 197).

Workloads were high by any standard, even before the industrial revolution. While developed countries today often have working years of 1,500 to 2,000 hours, England may well have had substantially longer hours as early as 1760. The data are hardly more than tentative, and comparisons of absolute levels are highly problematic. Yet the trend, which may be a little easier to establish, also points upwards. By the middle of the nineteenth century, working hours had reached levels that were probably higher than ever before or since.

A life expectancy in 1760 of 34.2 years appears very short by modern standards. In 1999, even Sub-Saharan Africa recorded average life expectancies of forty-eight years. Inadequate nutrition as well as ineffective medical intervention combined to keep death rates high. Nor was progress rapid over the following ninety years. By 1850, Englishmen – and women – could expect to live five more years at birth. This increase is less than the one seen in the Middle East and North Africa between 1990 and 1999 (an additional nine years) and the same as in Latin America over the same period. Similar conclusions apply to infant mortality. With the exception of Sierra Leone, no country in 1999 had higher death rates than Britain in 1850 or in 1760.

Literacy rates improved during the first century of industrialisation – even if the standard used is relatively low, measuring the percentage of bridegrooms who could sign their names (Schofield 1973). This is still less than in Sub-Saharan Africa today, but higher than in a number of Third World countries. By the middle of the eighteenth century, this rate had grown by 13 per cent, putting Britain ahead of present-day Senegal and Pakistan, and on a par with Morocco.

Most social scientists would agree that civil and political rights are important aspects of the standard of living. Compiling comprehensive indicators is difficult, as it requires judgements about the indicators included as well as their calibration. One familiar scale, applied to Britain by Crafts (1997), measures progress in these two dimensions on a scale from 1 to 7, with 1 the best possible score. Universal suffrage remained a long way off during the industrial revolution. At the same time, there were clear constitutional limits on the king's powers, and the Glorious Revolution had established the sovereignty of parliament. A score of 3 appears appropriate. Civil rights such as the right to a fair trial, an independent judiciary, freedom of speech and the right to form associations are also crucial facets of human progress. Compared to many European countries

Table 10.1 Selected indicators of the standard of living, 1760–1850										
decade	Y	W	H1	H2	WK	E	M	L	R1	R2
1760	1,803	(109)	167.4	171.1	2,576	34.2	174	48.5	3	3
1780	1,787	100	168	164.6	2,952	34.7	173	49.5	3	3
1800	1,936	103	168.9	164.6	3,328	35.9	145	52.5	3	4
1820	2,099	113	170.7	167.2	3,342	39.2	154	54.5	3	4
1830	2,209	120	170.7	165.6	3,356	40.8	149	57.5	3	3
1850	2,846	135	165.3	164.7	3,185	39.5	156	61.5	3	1
% change 1760–1820	16.4	4.1	2.0	−0.9	29.7	14.6	−11.5	6	0.0	33.3
% change 1760–1850	57.8	23.9	−1.3	−1.3	23.6	15.5	−10.3	13	0.0	−66.7

Note: Percentage change relative to starting level for all variables except literacy, where the figure stated is the gain in percentage points.

Sources: Y income per capita in 1992 ppp-adjusted US-$; Crafts 1997: 623.
W   1780 = 100; full-employment real earnings; Feinstein 1998a: 652–3 except for 1760, which is based on Lindert and Williamson 1983a, spliced to the Feinstein series.
H1   Average height of recruits aged 20–3, by decade of birth; Floud *et al*. 1990: 142–7.
H2   Average height of recruits aged 20–3, by decade of birth; Komlos 1993, 1998, pvt. comm.
WK   Number of working hours per year; Voth 2001. Values for 1780 and 1820 based on linear interpolation.
E   Life expectancy at birth; Wrigley *et al*. 1997: 614.
M   Infant mortality rate; Wrigley *et al*. 1997: 224.
L   Literacy rate; Schofield 1973.
R1   Political rights index (range from 1 to 7, with 1 being the best score); Crafts 1997.
R2   Civil rights index (range from 1 to 7, with 1 being the best score); Crafts 1997.

at the time, Britons enjoyed a relatively high degree of civil liberties. At the same time, political repression grew during the Napoleonic Wars and thereafter, with the government using increasingly repressive measures to crack down on Luddites and 'Captain Swing' riots. The tide turned from the 1830s onwards. Greater press freedom and greater opportunities for forming civic organisations and assemblies did much to reverse the earlier decline in civil liberties, and by 1850, most of the important human rights in this regard were respected (Crafts 1997: 624).

In the context of numerous indicators that show gradual change, sometimes of varying tendency, only one variable stands out – demographic growth. Population surged at an unprecedented rate during the classic period of the industrial revolution (Wrigley and Schofield 1981; Wrigley *et al*. 1997; see also chapter 3 above). Few other variables show radical discontinuities (Clark 2001b). The apparent lack of a clear, strong trend in living standards is nothing short of remarkable in this context. Earlier episodes of demographic expansion and contraction had strong effects on economic well-being, as Malthus predicted. It can be argued that the most remarkable feature of the period 1750–1850 was the absence of a sharp collapse in per capita income (Mokyr 1999).

REAL WAGES

The oldest – and in some ways most narrow – of all the indicators of the standard of living has been most important in changing our

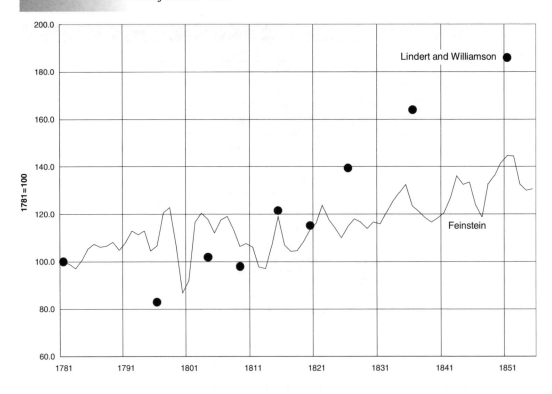

Figure 10.1 Real earnings in Great Britain, 1781–1855

Source: Feinstein 1998a: 643.

understanding of the industrial revolution. The quality of real wage indices has improved markedly since the 1980s. Instead of reworking the same old data, collected by Bowley and Wood at the end of the nineteenth century, recent research has at last expanded the number of professions covered in the nominal wage series (Feinstein 1998a). Even more importantly, a new cost of living index now includes information on a much wider range of household items. This momentous effort in data collection has strongly reinforced pessimistic interpretations of the course of living standards during the industrial revolution.

In the 1980s, optimists could point to the course of real wages as their strongest piece of evidence, declaring confidently that 'the debate should be over' (Lindert and Williamson 1983a). The most sanguine estimates implied that real wages for adult men increased by over 80 per cent between 1820 and 1850. Some revisions by later authors reduced this figure to 62 per cent (Crafts 1985b). Also, other authors found that wages of skilled workers surged between 1770 and 1815 (Botham and Hunt 1987), and that the income of clerks in banks and the East India Company increased drastically (Boot 1991, 1999). One of the first pieces of evidence that contradicted these results was new information from budget surveys. Horrell and Humphries (1992) showed that total family income probably failed to keep up with prices over the period 1791–5 to 1816–20. Declining opportunities for female employment drove a wedge between family budgets and the wage gains of males.

What overturned the optimistic verdicts, however, was a fundamentally new view not of trends in nominal wages, but of prices. While the new Feinstein series differs from the Lindert and Williamson nominal wage index in some respects, it follows a broadly similar trend over time. Prices of consumer goods, however, fell markedly less after the end of the Napoleonic Wars than earlier authors appreciated. The new consumer price index contains information on twelve food items plus beer, as well as data on candles, coal and clothing. It also uses a more accurate rent series. In addition to using improved and new series, Feinstein also changes the base year and expenditure weights in his index series. Every single one of his corrections diminishes the extent of the price decline after the end of the Napoleonic Wars. While most adjustments are relatively small – adding series for potatoes, milk and cheese reduces the total fall in prices by 3.2 per cent – the cumulative effect is substantial. Lindert and Williamson had concluded that the cost of living declined by 51 per cent between 1810/14 and 1849/51; the new figure is 37 per cent (Feinstein 1998a: 640–2). The new index covers most of the commodities bought by working-class households. In particular, the new series on the price of clothing – and evidence on its robustness – as well as the collection of good data on rents strongly suggest that future revisions are likely to be small.

As a result of these revisions, the overall increase in real full-time earnings is reduced to a little over 30 per cent. Also, Feinstein was one of the first to derive confidence intervals for his estimates of real wage increases. Consequently, the often invoked 'uncertainty arising from incomplete historical data' can finally be quantified. He calculates that real full-time money earnings may have increased by as little as 19 per cent or by as much as 55 per cent between 1778/82 and 1848/52. This rules out stagnation, but even the upper bound is markedly below the earlier estimates by more optimistic authors. Further research has tended to reinforce these conclusions by, for example, showing that Feinstein's estimates of real wages may be too optimistic for the period 1790–1820 (Clark 2001a). Taking unemployment and short-time work into account further reduces real wage growth to a less than 30 per cent increase over the period 1780 to 1850 as a whole. Since wages probably fell between the 1760s and 1780s, the overall gain in purchasing power was even more limited. These figures may still convey too optimistic an image of living standards once changes in a wider range of indicators is considered, as the following sections argue.

HEIGHTS AND PHYSICAL WELL-BEING

Over the last few decades, income as a measure of living standards has been much criticised (Tobin and Nordhaus 1973). The main objection is that it represents an input in the production of well-being, not an output. To the extent that wages rise because they compensate for urban disamenities or the riskiness of particular kinds of work, measuring income may seriously overstate gains in the standard of living. Also, while income at low levels of development is essential for purchasing additional food, housing or health care, it is also often associated with the purchase of products that harm physical well-being, such as alcohol and tobacco.

Few research programmes created more enthusiasm at their inception than the use of body measurements to establish trends in living standards. The stature of children and adults has become the focus of numerous studies since the 1980s. Height is a measure of net nutritional status from birth to age 25. In most populations today, growth ceases at age 18 or even earlier. The amount of nutrients consumed, as well as their composition, is crucial for growth. So are the claims on nutrient intake – calories used up to cope with heat, cold or disease, or to withstand the rigours of work. What matters is the net nutritional balance: the amount of calories and protein available for growth. Children deprived of adequate nutrition can experience 'catch-up' growth. If adequate food becomes available at some stage up to age 25, growth resumes. Height gains at such relatively late stages in life can be dramatic: on American plantations, slaves went from being severely stunted in childhood to terminal heights that were an easy match for European populations (Steckel 1986). Also, there is increasing evidence that the nutritional status of mothers affects children for most of their lives.

Height seemed an attractive indicator of physical well-being because it is not an 'input' measure, such as income. Instead, it captures net outcomes (Fogel 1984; Komlos 1989). Despite the collection of enormous amounts of data, however, firm conclusions from this research programme are few and far between. The original intention was to cast light on living standards for periods when data on incomes were scarce or unavailable. Indeed, some scholars tried to derive estimates of per capita income based on the co-movement of heights and income in later periods (Brinkman *et al.* 1988). However, it appears that height and income are not highly correlated, at least during the eighteenth and nineteenth centuries; some of the correlations used to extrapolate income per capita backwards were spurious (Mandemakers and Van Zanden 1993; Crafts 1997). Anthropometric history abounds in examples showing that poorer populations were often taller, and that economic development often proceeded side-by-side with falls in average heights (Steckel 1986; Nicholas and Steckel 1991). The fact that military recruits from rural areas – which often had relatively low per capita incomes – were markedly taller than their urban peers strongly suggests that the disease environment and the relative price of food may have been more important than total income (Steckel 1995). The relationship is further complicated by the fact that inequality has an impact on average stature that is several orders of magnitude larger than that of GDP (Steckel 1983). Most scholars working in the field now accept that stature and per capita income may not be highly correlated over significant periods of time and in cross-sections, and that one cannot serve as a proxy for the other. Also, there appears to be no systematic association between industrialisation and a decline in heights (Steckel and Floud 1997).

Historians of height have tried to side-step the issue, arguing that stature represents a more comprehensive indicator of the 'biological standard of living' (Komlos 1993; Baten and Komlos 1998). Deviations of trends in height from those for income would then have to be indicative of broader changes in physical well-being. This is because the *direct* benefits of greater stature are extremely limited. While greater life expectancy for adults and lower infant mortality rates are beneficial in themselves, greater heights are not. Stature is useful only in so far as it has indicator value for other characteristics that are associated with a higher standard of living. More immediately useful measures of health outcomes include life expectancy and mortality, as well as proxies for human capital such as education and literacy that may facilitate better hygiene, etc.

Unfortunately, while more comprehensive indicators of living standards that incorporate information on infant mortality, life expectancy and literacy appear highly correlated with stature in the twentieth century as well as over the very long run, the same is not true during earlier periods. Periods with increasing life expectancy and falling infant mortality sometimes witnessed declining heights (Crafts 1997). This is all the more surprising since modern cross-sectional data from Norway show that gains in stature are normally associated with reductions in mortality (Waaler 1984) – a pattern also found among Union army recruits during the American Civil War (Costa 1993). It is because of divergent trends in average heights and life expectancy that, during specific historical periods such as in Britain 1760–1850, changes in height can be poor indicators of physical well-being.

Conceptual issues therefore often make it difficult to map from stature to the standard of living in general (Crafts 1987b), especially when trends over time are concerned. Even if these were resolved, heights would have relatively little to say about the evolution of living standards in Britain during the industrial revolution. This is for two reasons. First, the direction of change has proved difficult to establish. Second, the magnitude of observed changes is too small to suggest meaningful differences in living standards. The most commonly used data set contains information on the heights of 108,000 recruits for the British Army and Royal Marines, and of boys entering the Marine Society in London as well as Sandhurst. While Floud *et al.* argue that heights increased over the period, Komlos finds evidence of a decline in the same data (Floud *et al.* 1990; Komlos 1993). The cause of this peculiar divergence of views is that all of the data from military sources are affected by left-hand truncation of the underlying height distribution. Armies imposed minimum heights standards.

Recruits below a certain height were routinely rejected. To adjust to the fluctuating demands of the armed forces, standards varied over time. Also, they were enforced to a varying degree. While it is possible to correct these biases with quantitative techniques, few of the data actually fulfil the requirements for their use (Wachter and Trussell 1982). Data on the stature of transported convicts do not suffer from truncation, and the results obtained from this source appear more stable. They show a decline in average heights (Nicholas and Steckel 1991).

Even if results were unambiguous in their direction, the magnitudes involved are too small to inspire much confidence in any conclusions based on anthropometric data. Floud *et al.* find that average heights increased by 3.3 cm, from 167.4 cm to 170.7 cm, between 1760 and 1830, and that they then fell to 165.3 cm. Even without the reversal since the 1780s, increases of 0.47 cm per decade would hardly be sufficient as a basis for strong claims about changes in living standards – overall, average heights increased by 1.97 per cent between 1760 and 1830, according to Floud *et al.* (or 0.28 per cent per decade). Komlos (1993) found a decline of 1.3 per cent. Nicholas and Steckel (1991) also calculate that convict heights fell between 1780 and 1815 by approximately 1 per cent of the starting level.

These are small differences, compared to changes in heights during other periods. Between 1900 and 1950, average male heights in Britain increased by 8 cm, or 1.6 cm per decade (Steckel 1995). This represents a rate of change that is more than five times higher than the one observed during the most favourable episode of the industrial revolution (using the optimistic results from Floud *et al.*). Moreover, interpretation of trends in heights – even if their direction could be established unambiguously – is complicated by the considerable variability of estimates over short periods. The overall decline between 1760 and 1850 according to Floud *et al.* is 2 cm. However, estimated heights appear to change very markedly within a few years. For example, the Floud data show a decline by 3.1 cm over a five-year period from 1832 to 1837, followed by a 2.2 cm gain in the next five years. Estimated heights change so much from decade to decade that, over the period as a whole, 95 per cent of all observations lie within a 8 cm interval between 164.6 cm and 172.6 cm – four times larger than the overall change between 1760 and 1850. Independent of the statistical significance of these results, it would be hard to argue that a historically meaningful difference exists once sampling biases, problems with truncation because of minimum height standards, and the deficiencies of historical data in general are taken into account.

WORKING HOURS

Ever since the writings of William Blake and Karl Marx, the industrial revolution has been synonymous with long hours of arduous toil, often by children and women, under dangerous and unhealthy conditions. Europe's 'dark satanic mills' producing cotton textiles saw the longest working years recorded in human history – around sixty-five to seventy hours per week, or some 3,500 hours per year. Compared to these figures, the working week in the Third World today is relatively short, averaging forty to fifty hours (Acemoglu *et al.* 2002). Did such long hours exist before the industrial revolution? Or did the great shift of labour out of agriculture and into industry coincide with a move towards much longer working hours? Changes in the hours of work would have strong implications for the standard of living debate – if money incomes rose only because of more work, it becomes much harder to argue that living standards improved (O'Brien and Engerman 1981). A comprehensive view of welfare implications would have to take into account the value of leisure lost (Usher 1980; Crafts 1985a). To do so would be particularly useful since the potential magnitudes of change involved are substantial.

Data on working hours before the industrial revolution are very rare. What few there are can only shed light in an indirect way, and may be of questionable reliability. A considerable degree of variation by region, occupation, gender and age aggravates problems of representativeness for any particular source. Despite the weaknesses of the data, many historians have argued that average working hours for males of prime working age between 1750 and 1850 increased, by between 20 and 35 per cent (Freudenberger and Cummins 1976; Tranter 1981; Crafts 1985a).

Research since the 1990s offers some qualified support for this belief. Hours were probably already long in agriculture, and may not have changed much during the industrial revolution (Clark and van der Werf 1998; Voth 2001). Outside agriculture, there is some evidence that people in 1830 and 1850 worked longer than their great-grandparents did in 1760. Using witnesses' accounts from the courtroom, new estimates of the length of the working year in London and in the industrialising north of England have been compiled (Voth 1998, 2001). The main factor responsible for longer hours, according to these results, was not a longer working day. Instead, work was performed on many more days in the year. What had curtailed total labour input in pre-industrial times was a large number of festivals and holy days, both religious and political in nature. Also, when workers set their own schedules, they were prone to take Monday off – a practice know as 'Saint Monday' (Thompson 1967).

The courtroom evidence strongly suggests that Mondays and holy days were indeed days of leisure during the middle of the eighteenth century, and that they had become days of regular work by the first decades of the nineteenth century. Yet the persistence of practices such as Saint Monday is controversial (Reid 1976, 1996), and a considerable degree of regional variation may make it more difficult to ascertain national trends (Hopkins 1982.) At the moment, it appears that the balance of evidence favours increases in total workloads during the industrial revolution for males

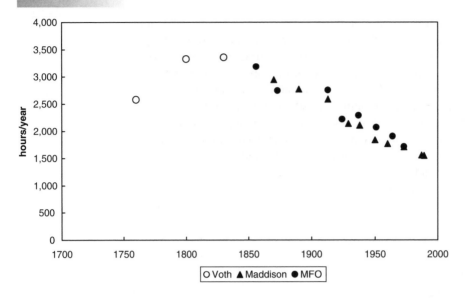

Figure 10.2 Working hours in Britain in the long run

Source: Matthews *et al.* 1982; Maddison 1991; Voth 2001.

of prime working age. The direction of change is much more clearly established than the magnitudes involved. Despite numerous efforts since the 1980s, it appears unlikely that the quality of the data will match that on wages, mortality or literacy in the near future.

Using witnesses' data to construct tentative estimates of annual labour input, we can compare total annual working hours before and after the industrial revolution. They suggest a relatively rapid increase during the second half of the eighteenth century, and then stagnation or a slight decline from a peak around 1830. If the findings are even broadly correct – and can be compared with the data derived from very different sources for later periods – then total hours before the onset of full industrialisation were approximately as 'short' as they were around 1900.

Increases in the length of the working year may have been mitigated by declining work opportunities for women, and less child labour. Earnings data show that females may have participated in paid work to a considerable extent. In the late eighteenth century, 65 per cent of married women had either non-zero earnings or a recorded occupation. Household budgets suggest that the earnings opportunities of women declined as industrialisation spread. Many of the old cottage-shop industries were more compatible with the skills of women and their preferred modes of working than the factory-based system of production (Horrell and Humphries 1995). The story differs somewhat for different occupations, and is complicated by an apparent increase in female contributions to family income in the second quarter of the nineteenth century. None the less by the middle of the eighteenth century, women's participation rates had fallen to 45.3 per cent, and their share of total family earnings was often below its peak (Horrell and Humphries 1995: 98–107; see also chapter 9 above).

Child labour may have begun to decline during this period. It is possible that the reduction began before the Factory Acts (Nardinelli 1980), over the period 1815–35. However, other scholars using the same sources find that child labour was and remained high in many industries, including cotton (Tuttle 1999). Therefore, the idea that child labour was a necessary but transitory phase of industrial development that enabled the formation of a disciplined workforce appears questionable (Galbi 1997). What is also unclear is the extent to which an increase or a decline in the prevalence of child labour occurred between 1750 and 1810. Child labour was common enough in agriculture (Kussmaul 1981; Humphries 2001); it is not obvious that increasing employment outside the primary sector would have necessarily led to greater employment of children and adolescents. The data from various enquiries reported to parliament do not suggest a substantial decline in child labour before the 1830s. At the moment, the potentially more important issue of employment shares during the middle of the eighteenth century remains largely unresolved because of substantial data problems.

Child labour matters because it is one of the key characteristics of the British industrial revolution (Humphries 2001), and because the welfare implications of changes are less ambiguous than, for example, in the case of women. The increasing dependence of women on male earnings is likely to have reinforced patriarchal patterns of behaviour, even if more time spent in the home could also have been used for the production of non-market goods. Less child labour may have led to a reduction in family earnings, but would normally be seen as welfare improving none the less. Early work, especially in mines and factories, often led to injuries and disabilities. Even children who were not maimed or afflicted by debilitating disease as a result of early work – often from the age of 9 or earlier – were left permanently stunted (Humphries 1997). Also, their chances to acquire greater skills, either through schooling or apprenticeships, were often reduced dramatically. The normal premises of utility maximisation do not apply when economic agents cannot chose 'freely' – as is the case with children (Humphries 2000). While the trend may or may not have been downwards, the extent of child labour remained relatively high throughout the industrial revolution. As late as 1851, the census suggests that 36 per cent of children aged 10–14 worked, and the rates based on autobiographies are even higher (Humphries 2001: 17). This implies that child labour in industrialising Britain was broadly as common as in Africa and Asia in 1950, and more frequent than in India and Brazil at that time.

Evidence on working hours among children and women suggests that the increases in male hours may have been balanced to a certain extent by declining work for women and (possibly) children, at least in classic paid employment. Magnitudes are hard to establish at the aggregate level, since most of the evidence is highly concentrated at the regional or sectoral level. To the extent that total hours worked in the British economy grew net of these countervailing forces, estimates of consumption and income growth need to be corrected. Calculating the value of leisure lost is not straightforward. However, if the average wage rate is used as the opportunity cost of leisure (Usher 1980), then most of the relatively modest gains that traditional accounting methods used to show disappear (Voth 2001). Instead of growing by 0.38 per cent per year between 1760 and 1830 (equivalent to a total gain of 30 per cent), consumption may only have increased by 0.04–0.05 per cent per year (a total increase of 3 per cent).

This argument would be further reinforced if work intensity increased. Evidence on this is very patchy indeed. What there is largely compares piece-rates with weekly wages. Dividing the former by the latter yields an index of physical output per week (Clark 1987, 1991a). Much of this research reveals that levels of work effort in Britain during industrialisation were high, that the move to factories increased them, and that they may have risen over time. Clark finds that workers in factories may have worked up to one-third harder (Clark 1994). He also finds that work intensity in English agriculture may have increased by 38–89 per cent (Clark 1987: 427).

If some of the observed rise in output was bought not just by longer hours, but by harder toil, the overall productivity gains would be even less impressive than is currently thought. In welfare terms, however, the implications may well be ambiguous. Clark (1994) argues that factory discipline functioned as an effective pre-commitment device, enabling workers to overcome short-sighted preferences for leisure. The underlying assumption is that, in a competitive labour market, firms that do not offer adequate compensation for extra work intensity would have found themselves without workers eventually. Given that much of the recent evidence, especially in terms of real wage trends, shows that the Lewis model of surplus labour may describe the situation of industrialising Britain more adequately (Feinstein 1998a), this interpretation will remain highly controversial.[2]

CONSUMPTION AND HOUSEHOLD BUDGETS

The old optimistic case quickly ran into one problem: if incomes grew, what were they spent on? Further work on purchases of basic foodstuffs,

---

[2] The Lewis model builds on the concept of a dual economy, composed of a traditional and a modern sector. Because labour is abundant in the traditional sector (agriculture), its reallocation to the modern sector does not cause a fall in agricultural output – the marginal product of labour in the traditional sector is essentially zero. This implies that wages may only rise above subsistence levels once the modern sector becomes sufficiently large to affect agricultural wages.

Table 10.2	Consumption of luxury goods (in pounds of weight) and standard-of-living indicator (in pounds sterling)						
					Standard-of-living indicator, based on:		
	Sugar	Tea	Tobacco	Borda ranking	Sugar	Tea	Tobacco
1794–6	16.03	1.6	1.12	6			
1795–9					15.96	16.09	8.78
1804–6	22.86	1.74	1.14	2			
1805–9					17.03	16.04	9.32
1814–16	17.35	1.57	0.97	7			
1815–19					15.54	15.29	8.58
1824–6	21.64	1.61	0.91	6			
1825–9					16.64	15.49	10.9
1834–6	20.72	1.88	0.98	4			
1835–9					16.51	15.88	14.12
1844–6	22.26	1.85	1.03	3			
1845–9					17.79	16.20	16.84
1854–6	33.11	2.43	1.2	1			

Source: Mokyr 1988.

as well as luxury items such as sugar, coffee, tobacco and tea, has demonstrated that the history of consumption offers little support for the view that living standards improved markedly. These findings are largely corroborated by household budgets.

Joel Mokyr (1988) was among the first to wonder whether luxury consumption supported optimistic interpretations of the industrial revolution. He examined commodities that were not produced domestically, such as tea, coffee, sugar and tobacco. Because they were imported, it is relatively straightforward to establish total volumes consumed. Spending on these goods probably represented only a small share of total expenditure (Figure 10.3). None the less, since they are generally regarded as superior goods, their consumption should have risen by more than 1 per cent for every percentage point gain of income, thus making them a particularly sensitive indicator of trends in incomes.

Instead of rising rapidly, however, rates of increase remained modest for most luxury commodities. Tobacco imports per inhabitant were broadly stagnant, while sugar and tea consumption began to rise after the end of the Napoleonic Wars. Yet not all of the increase can be seen as a sign of increasing riches: prices of some of these goods declined in relative terms, making them easier to purchase. By adjusting for these changes, Mokyr constructs an index of 'latent' purchasing power, revealed by the pattern of imports (Table 10.2, final three columns). Consumption of sugar, adjusted for price changes, only rose by 14 per cent between the 1790s and the second half of the 1840s (Mokyr 1988). The respective figure for tea is 2.3 per cent. In the case of tobacco, this indicator stagnates until the 1820s, but then doubles. We can rank periods by the amount of

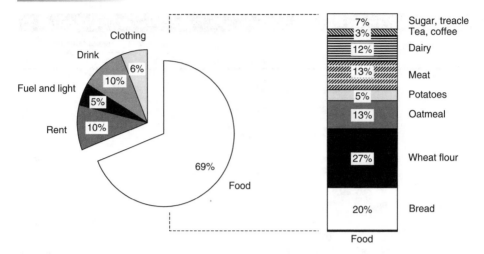

Figure 10.3
Composition of
working-class
expenditures, 1788/92

Source: Feinstein
1998a.

each commodity available per head of the English population and aggregate these rankings into a single score per time period according to the 'Borda rule'.[3] This shows that 1804–6 recorded relatively high levels of luxury consumption. The 1820s, on the other hand, marked a low point. Despite improvement in the 1830s, it was not before the 1850s that consumption of luxury products exceeded levels seen in the 1800s. With the exception of tobacco, there is therefore no sign of people spending much more money on the kind of goods that would have been most likely to attract additional purchases, had living standard indeed improved substantially.

This interpretation is indirectly vindicated by the so-called 'food puzzle' that some researchers have identified in industrialising Britain (Clark *et al.* 1995), based on the premise of rapid income growth. They extend Mokyr's question to food consumption in general. The sum of domestic food production plus imports may well have failed to keep up with population growth during the period (Holderness 1989). Clark, Huberman and Lindert try to resolve the puzzle by assuming changes in the relationship between final food consumption and the value added by agriculture and imports. However, the markedly more pessimistic estimates of income growth seen in Feinstein imply that the food puzzle no longer exists – food consumption barely changed, and may have fallen on a per capita basis, because purchasing power was largely stagnant.

There is one part of household budgets that probably saw rising real expenditure: the purchases of durables and semi-durables. While clothing is not customarily classified as a durable good, it provides a stream

---

[3] The Borda rule facilitates the compilation of composite indices, especially where we aggregate across conceptually very different individual indicators. For each variable, the observations (or time periods) are ranked. In our case, we assign a lower rank to a more favourable outcome. Next, we calculate the sum of these scores for each observation (or time period) across all indicators, and again rank them. The outcome is a Borda ranking.

of services for an extended period. A number of indirect indicators suggest that Englishmen and women were accumulating clothing and other (semi-)durables at a higher rate. First, probate inventories show that, during the second half of the eighteenth century at least, even the poor were dying in possession of a larger number of goods than they had half a century before (King 1997). Second, workers were devoting a greater share of their budgets to the purchase of clothes – possibly rising by as much as one half between 1788/92 and 1858/62, from 6 to 9 per cent of the total (Feinstein 1998a: 635). This was, to a large extent, a response to a shift in relative prices. The nominal price of clothing goods probably declined by one-third between the 1770s and the 1850s, at a time when the prices of almost all other commodities in the Feinstein cost-of-living index were rising (Feinstein 1998a: 640). Household budgets show that, while total household spending grew by 43 per cent between 1789–96 and 1830–9 in nominal terms, total expenditure on non-essential items increased by 137 per cent (Horrell 1996). In the absence of growing riches, such a shift was predominantly driven by the relatively lower price of these goods, especially cotton clothing. In contrast to the assertions of those who detect a 'consumer revolution' unfolding in eighteenth-century England (McKendrick *et al.* 1982), changes in material life did not necessarily require substantial income growth (see chapter 13 below).

URBANISATION, MORTALITY AND THE VALUE OF LIFE

Average life expectancy at birth in England rose between 1760 and 1850. Despite this improvement, the history of mortality does not provide unanimous support for an optimistic interpretation of the industrial revolution. First, the levels reached were unimpressive by the standards of England's own demographic history. Second, the experience of important subgroups and regions shows a decline in life expectancy. Third, compared with other industrialising countries at the same level of income per capita, English life expectancy was disappointingly low.

In the very long run, the age of Elizabeth I stands out for the long lives that Shakespeare and his contemporaries could expect. From a peak of 42.7 years in 1581, life expectancy at birth fell for the following century and a half, reaching a nadir of 25.3 years in 1726 (Wrigley *et al.* 1997: 614). By 1826, it had recovered to almost the same level as the one seen 250 years earlier – 41.3 years, before falling back to 39.5 in 1850. The experience of subgroups was often much less favourable.

Housing conditions in Britain during the industrial revolution were dismal. In the *Inquiry into the Sanitary Conditions of the Labouring Population* in 1842, Edwin Chadwick argued that:

> various forms of epidemic, endemic, and other disease [are] caused . . . chiefly amongst the labouring classes . . . by decomposing animal and vegetable substances, by damp and filth, and close and overcrowded dwellings [that] prevail amongst the population in every part of the kingdom, whether dwelling in separate houses, in rural villages, in small towns, in the larger towns – as they have been found to prevail in the lowest districts of the metropolis.
>
> (Chadwick 1842: 369–70)

In early modern Europe, towns in general could exist only because of a steady influx of migrants from the countryside; death rates almost never fell below birth rates. Crowding, unsanitary conditions, and difficult access to fresh drinking water and fresh food, as well as lack of immunity from infectious disease for many of the new migrants from the more isolated areas, all conspired to drive up mortality rates. These difficulties were compounded when a very large proportion of the population began to move to the cities over a relatively short period. Few places inspired quite the same horror as did Britain's industrial cities – which is why Friedrich Engels's description of conditions as 'social murder' is particularly appropriate. None the less, it is worth noting that, by the 1840s, the great cities of industrialising Britain were no longer in danger of disappearing without in-migration: because of strong demographic growth, birth rates actually exceeded death rates (Williamson 1990a: 222). Dreadful as conditions were – especially in the industrialising cities of the north – the period between 1750 and 1850 also saw major improvements in the urban environment, at least in part. Many of the main streets were paved, and gas lighting, street names and house numbers became more common (Reed 2000). Wooden structures with thatched roofs were replaced by brick buildings with tiled roofs, reducing the risk of fires and infection from rats (Appleby 1980); the gradually growing separation of residential areas from the place of work reinforced these benign tendencies. New suburbs began to grow near the major metropolitan centres, while museums, public libraries and government offices were built (Clark 2000).

The great shift out of agriculture and into industry, now seen as the defining characteristic of the industrial revolution, also implied a reallocation of labourers from rural areas and small towns to the cities (Williamson 1990; Crafts and Harley 1992). New industrial cities changed the urban hierarchy. The proportion of the population living in cities approximately doubled over the period, rising from 26 per cent in 1776 to 56.4 per cent eighty years later (see chapter 3 above). Not only did the move to Britain's cities occur earlier than in most other European countries. For any given level of per capita income, British urbanisation was also markedly higher than on the continent (Crafts 1985a: 62). While, for example, other countries showed an urbanisation rate of 23 per cent at the level of per capita income reached by England in 1800, her figure was 33.9 per cent. Nor did the gap decline over time. Forty years later, when almost every second Englishman and woman lived in an urban area, the

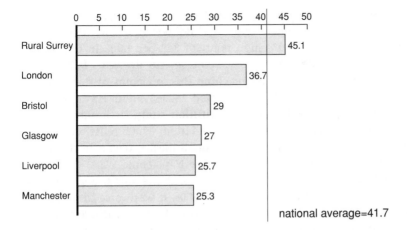

Figure 10.4 Life expectancy at birth (in years) in selected cities and areas, 1841

Source: Szreter and Mooney 1988: 93; Wrigley *et al.* 1997: 614.

European norm suggested that fewer than one in three should have been living in cities.

To put things into perspective, comparisons with the urbanisation experience in the Third World are instructive. Williamson (1990: 220–3) finds that Britain's cities grew more slowly than their counterparts in the less developed countries today. Also, cities and rural areas in poorer parts of the world show very similar mortality and birth rates. In contrast, in Britain the crude rate of natural increase was markedly higher in the countryside than in the cities. In 1842, Chadwick had guessed '[t]hat of the 43,000 cases of widowhood, and 112,000 cases of destitute orphanage relieved from the poor's rates in England and Wales alone', the majority was attributable to unsanitary living conditions, and that at least thirteen years of productive life were lost in each case. The full extent to which life expectancy suffered in the industrial centres of northern England has only been confirmed in recent years. It appears that, in a number of cities at least, Chadwick's number is even an underestimate of the mortality penalty in the cities where conditions were worst.

While life expectancy in the largest city of Europe, London, in 1841 was not far below the national average – though considerably below that of rural areas such as Surrey – the rapidly growing industrial cities of the north experienced very high levels of mortality. Children born in Manchester suffered a penalty of 16.4 years compared to the average for England as a whole. Szreter and Mooney (1998: 105) demonstrate the extent to which the move to the cities extracted a high and growing price in the first half of the nineteenth century. Based on the unusually good data in Glasgow, and the general similarity in the mortality experience of English provincial cities with more than 100,000 inhabitants and Glasgow's, they calculate that average life expectancy possibly fell by six years between the 1820s and 1830s. Improvements beyond that low level were not visible before the 1850s, but it took until the 1870s to reach the same low mortality levels as in the 1820s.

Also, there is growing evidence that the second quarter of the nineteenth century saw a general rise in childhood mortality. Death rates during childhood reached a high point of 348 per 1,000 in the second quarter of the seventeenth century. Some seventy-five years later, it was 25 per cent lower, at 263. After reaching this low point, it started to increase again, reaching 287 in the period 1825–37, and 315 in 1837–54. This trend is apparent in the reconstitution study, undertaken by the Cambridge Group for the History of Population, which relies on parishes that were predominantly in relatively small market towns. In the aggregate, infant mortality increased after the Napoleonic Wars, registering a rise of 10 per cent between the 1810s and the 1820s, and a rise of 11 per cent between the 1810s and the 1850s. It was worse in industrialising areas. Even in relatively small towns with around 15,000 to 20,000 inhabitants, those that had a high share of labour employed in agriculture saw a worsening of infant mortality (Huck 1995). In a sample of nine parishes with substantial employment in mining, the cotton industry and iron manufacturing, infant mortality rose from a low of 151 per 1,000 in 1813–18 to 172 in 1831–6.

What is the value of changes in life expectancy? Usher (1980) suggested an innovative method to adjust real income per capita for changes in mortality. The value of an increase in life expectancy will be equivalent to the extra future consumption that it makes possible – assuming that the gain in life expectancy is not driven by higher income itself. This method has been refined and applied to industrialising England (Williamson 1984). To make such an adjustment, we need assumptions about the extent to which people discount future increases in consumption, and how much they value consumption in their utility function. Depending on the assumptions used, Williamson calculated that the growth of lifetime income over the period 1781–1851 would have to be revised upwards by 0.01–0.16 per cent per year. Even the highest of these figures is relatively low compared to the 'pessimistic' estimates of earnings growth by Feinstein, who calculated that full-time earnings grew by 0.43 per cent per year over the period. The value of changes in life expectancy was small because the gains themselves were relatively small too.

The great move to the cities normally led to wage gains, even after adjusting for the higher cost of housing and much else (Williamson 1990). At the same time, the penalty in terms of higher mortality rates was anything but trivial (Figure 10.4). Was one sufficient to compensate for the other? In a cross-section of English towns, those with higher infant mortality and population density also recorded higher wages. Based on these observations, we can calculate the proportion of the urban wage premium that was simply compensating for urban disamenities. Williamson (1990: 255–6) finds that, relative to rural wages, premiums of 10 to 30 per cent were necessary to compensate workers for moving to the cities of industrialising England. For the south of England, this implies that there were still gains in living standards for those workers making the transition, whereas in the north the gain might be slim indeed, with the disamenity premium accounting for 28 and 83 per cent of the nominal wage gain (Williamson 1990: 186). Once the higher cost of living is taken into account, the increase in living standards seems relatively small. Also, the national figures for wage gains must be adjusted for the fact that some of the apparent real wage gains simply compensated for urban disamenities. In the aggregate, real wage gains need to be reduced by 3 to 8 percentage points (Feinstein 1998a: 650).

An alternative method is to use the observed premiums for risky jobs, and to calculate the proportion of the wage gain that simply compensates for higher mortality risk (Costa and Steckel 1997: 76). In the USA, the risk premium for dangerous jobs in 1969 was about 5 per cent, and surveys show that workers are willing to pay 2 to 4 per cent of annual income for a reduction in job-related mortality risk from 0.1 per cent per year to zero. Costa and Steckel also find that similar or even larger magnitudes prevailed in the nineteenth century. Of course, the use of risk premiums from the twentieth century is not without conceptual difficulties. If we use the figures employed by Costa and Steckel, what does this methodology imply for urban disamenities in industrialising Britain? I use the Princeton life table 'North' to translate life expectancies into mortality rates. The average 25-year-old man in England in 1841 had a 49.4 per cent chance of living to the age of 65. By moving to Bristol (by no means the worst of the industrial cities, see Figure 10.4), his chances would decline to 34.9 per cent. A 15.5 percentage point higher chance of death by age 65 is the 'physical price' of moving – for every seven Englishmen per cohort dying in rural areas, nine would be dead by age 65 in the cities. What is the monetary value of this penalty? If the risk premium is between 2 and 5 per cent, this would imply that he should have demanded a wage premium of 16 to 41 per cent per year to be compensated for the higher risk of early death.[4] Since real wage premiums ranged from 26 per cent in the north to 96 per cent in the south, this would imply that migrants may have shown a net gain in the north, depending on the risk premium used, and that a sizeable advantage was likely in the south. In the north, men in the cities had to last to age 56 to enjoy the same cumulative earnings as their rural peers between age 25 to 65. Fewer than 40 per cent of each cohort of 25-year-olds did, which suggests a certain degree of 'irrational exuberance'. In the south, they only had to live to age 43; approximately 64 per cent managed. In cities with lower life expectancy than Bristol, such as Manchester, even smaller fractions of each cohorts lived to 'break even'. The welfare implications therefore depend on the extent to which we take revealed preferences at face value. If we

---

[4] Because of continuous compounding, the death rates per year would be 1.76 per cent for national average, and 2.6 per cent for Glasgow.

assume that, by moving to the cities, people made an informed choice, we rule out the possibility that their standard of living may have deteriorated as a result. If we allow for some degree of myopia and less than perfect information, and use reasonable figures for the value of years lost, urban disamenities may easily have been large enough to cancel out any increase in living standards for the majority of migrants.

COMPOSITE MEASURES OF WELFARE

As the discussion in this chapter has tried to emphasise, the standard of living is notoriously hard to define. No single variable provides a reliable, comprehensive view. At the same time, policy makers and historians are keen to be able to compare trends over time, nations with each other, or the differential fates of subgroups. In response to these needs, a variety of composite indices that weight a number of indicators have been compiled in recent years. The first attempt of this kind was made in the late 1970s, using a weighted average of infant mortality, life expectancy and adult literacy (Morris 1997). The United Nations Development Programme later developed more advanced versions of this human development index (HDI). In its most commonly used form, it contains normalised indices of national income per capita, life expectancy and educational attainment. The level of each variable is compared to the minimum (the dollar value of a subsistence diet in the case of per capita income, for example) and the maximum values (maximum life expectancy in a human population, e.g. eighty-five years). For a country that has reached complete literacy, the individual component of the index would, for example, record a 1.0 score. A country with a life expectancy of sixty years (assuming a minimum of twenty-five years) would receive a score of

$$\frac{60-25}{85-25} = \frac{35}{60} = 0.583.$$

HDI is simply the weighted average of the three sub-indices.

The choice of indicators included in the index is, however, not compelling. Dasgupta and Weale (1992) offer an alternative index, which also includes information on political and civil rights. Their aim is to compare ordinal measures of well-being, not to provide cardinal measurement. They therefore use the 'Borda rule' to aggregate their sub-indices into their broader measure of well-being (DW-index).

Applying these composite indices to the case of Britain during the industrial revolution is attractive for a number of reasons. First, it permits an explicit approach to the vexed question of weighting the importance of different indicators. Second, the HDI approach allows us to calibrate differences over time, and to compare levels of overall well-being between countries. Third, these indices can serve as a basis for further refinements,

Table 10.3 Alternative indices of living standards in Britain, 1760–1850

	HDI (Crafts)	HDI (new life expectancy)	Pseudo-HDI (Floud heights)	Pseudo-HDI (Komlos heights)	DW (Crafts)	DW (+ working hours)	DW (+ heights*)
1760	0.272	0.254	0.37	0.37	6	6	4
1780	0.277	0.262	0.38	0.35	5	6	6
1800	0.302	0.290	0.41	0.36	4	4	6
1820	0.337	0.307	0.45	0.38	3	3	3
1830	0.361	0.320	0.46	0.40	2	2	2
1850	0.407	0.371	0.44	0.44	1	1	1

Note: *based on Komlos's heights.

Sources: Crafts 1997, own calculations.

taking gender differences or the inequality of income into account (Costa and Steckel 1997; Crafts 1997).

Crafts (1997) was among the first to apply these aggregation methods to the economic history of the industrial revolution. His findings suggest cautious support for the optimistic case: HDI grew in every period he examined, by a total of 49.6 per cent. The DW-index also suggests the same uniform pattern of improvement, and so do the indices taking gender differences and income inequality into account. These conclusions are, however, not compelling. A wider set of indicators can be incorporated into a measure of well-being along the lines of the DW-index. Arguably, work effort necessary to produce income should be included. In a similar spirit, the new wage figures by Feinstein should be incorporated in the index. Also, new data on life expectancy have become available (Wrigley *et al.* 1997). Finally, numerous authors have computed 'Pseudo-HDI' for a number of countries, choosing stature to replace life expectancy (Costa and Steckel 1997; Sandberg and Steckel 1997; Twarog 1997). Since evidence from convict data shows declines in average stature, the Komlos estimate of trends in height time series may be more reliable than the Floud series. Any one of these changes in the series used, or the type of measure included, undermines Crafts's optimistic conclusions somewhat.

Use of the new life expectancy figures reduces estimates of the level of human development uniformly, but by a greater amount in the 1850s than in the 1760s. Gains in the standard of living therefore appear somewhat smaller than initially assumed, but improvement over the period now proceeds more steadily. The same is not true of pseudo-HDI, calculated on the basis of Komlos's height series. Here, there is no improvement until 1800, but a quicker acceleration thereafter.

The DW rankings, once we incorporate additional indicators, also reduce the optimistic implications of Crafts's findings somewhat. Replacing the GDP figures with real wages by itself does not change the rankings. Incorporating additional working hours suggests stagnation for the first twenty years of the industrial revolution. If heights are added to this,

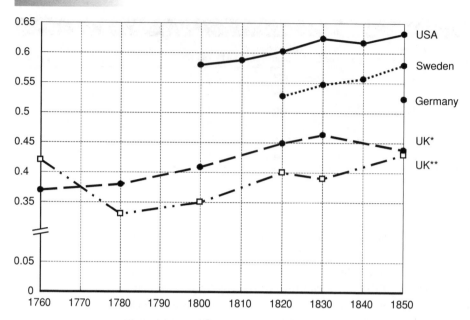

Figure 10.5 Pseudo-HDI for Britain, the USA, Sweden and Germany

Notes: *Incorporating height data from Floud.
**Incorporating height data from Komlos.

Sources: Costa and Steckel 1997; Crafts 1997; Sandberg and Steckel 1997; Twarog 1997; Komlos 1998, own calculations (see text).

the index first falls, and overall conditions do not improve relative to the starting level before the end of the Napoleonic Wars.

How do living standard in Britain compare with those in other industrialising countries? Britain was by far the richest country by the middle of the nineteenth century in terms of per capita income. Yet international comparisons of composite welfare measures give a mixed impression. If the DW-index is used, Britain and Denmark tie for first place in 1860, and Britain is considerably ahead of other European countries and North America on the basis of the human development index. Comparisons using pseudo-HDI, on the other hand, suggest that Britain was doing markedly worse than other countries. There may have been a drastic decline in the second half of the eighteenth century (Komlos 1993, 1998); using the alternative height data, the standard achieved by 1850 was below its peak in 1830 (Figure 10.5).

These results are exclusively driven by the use of heights instead of life expectancy. For those scholars who believe that heights measure physical well-being in a more useful way than life expectancy, Britain's relative performance in terms of physical well-being was extremely disappointing. If life expectancy is used instead, Britain emerges as the world leader by 1860. We have already questioned the extent to which stature is a more important indicator of the 'biological standard of living'. Unless the utility of heights can be established more directly, the weight of the evidence from HDI and the DW-indices suggests that Britain was ahead of its peers by the middle of the eighteenth century. The extent to which the early phases of the industrial revolution saw a decline in overall living standards is still open to debate. The composite indices cannot answer this question conclusively, since results are sensitive to the set of indicators included in the calculations. If additional measures such as working hours are used, the steady march of progress apparent in Crafts's calculations no longer exists. Instead, it appears that no turning point was reached until the 1820s or 1830s.

THE STANDARD OF LIVING AND MACROECONOMIC PERFORMANCE

For a long time, the standard-of-living debate has been strangely divorced from research on macroeconomic performance as a whole. Yet what output the economy generated ended up in the pockets of one group or another; abstracting from terms-of-trade effects and taxes, high rates of output growth would have had to drive up the remuneration of the factors of production (or at least one of them). And if growth was slow, and inequality changed little, then the standard of living for the bulk of the population cannot have increased rapidly. The substantive downward revisions of growth rates introduced by Crafts and Harley have largely withstood a wide range of criticism (Crafts and Harley 1992; Jackson 1992; Berg and Hudson 1994; Cuenca Esteban 1994), even if some of the implications for productivity growth remain puzzling (Temin 1997, 2000). Output per capita growth was modest at best for most of the first hundred years of the industrial revolution, ranging from 0.2 per cent to 0.5 per cent per year from 1760 to 1830, before accelerating to a still modest 1.1 per cent for the period 1830–60 (Harley 1999).

Some critics of the current 'slow growth' orthodoxy combine a belief in rapid technological change and productivity advances with a pessimistic view of changes in living standards (Berg and Hudson 1994). These are contradictory positions. What the last twenty years of vigorous debate have shown is that the 'slow growth' view and the pessimist case for only gradual and tentative increases in living standards reinforce each other.

Productivity growth cannot be higher than the weighted average of rates of increase in the real remuneration of factors of production (McCloskey 1985; Antràs and Voth 2001). A doubling of the real rate of return on capital and of real wages at the level of the economy as a whole implies that productivity doubled, too: each factor of production must be generating output at twice the rate attained before. To use such logic, we need standard assumptions such as that factors of production receive the value of their marginal product. Daunting as these seem, they

Table 10.4 Estimates of productivity growth in England, 1770–1860

Antràs and Voth (2003)	r	w	q	gov	TFP
				change in % p.a.	
1770–1801	−0.4	0.35	0.26	2.60	0.27
1801–1831	0.71	0.25	0.76	1.11	0.54
1831–1860	−0.21	0.68	0.48	0.31	0.33
Harley (1999)	Y	K	L	T	TFP
1760–1800	1	1	0.8	0.2	0.19
1801–1831	1.9	1.7	1.4	0.4	0.50
1831–1860*	2.5	2.0	1.4	0.6	1.0

Notes: r – rental rate of capital, w – real wage, q – rental cost of land, gov – government sector (taxes), Y – output growth, K – capital, L – labour, T – land. Antràs and Voth 2003 use an elasticity of 0.32 for capital, 0.14 for land, 0.08 for government and 0.46 for labour.

Sources: Harley 1999: 183; Antràs and Voth 2003.

are no different from the assumptions necessary to derive productivity estimates from quantity data (Hsieh 1999).

Estimates of slow TFP (total factor productivity) growth, derived from quantity-based productivity measures, broadly provide support for the 'slow growth' view. Table 10.4 compares the productivity growth estimates from both sources. The upper half of the table shows the growth in the real return to each factor. Neither land nor labour nor capital became vastly more valuable during the industrial revolution. Output-based TFP estimates coincide almost exactly with the factor price evidence for the second period, 1801–31. For the first and the third periods, there is a somewhat larger difference; for the first century of the industrial revolution as a whole, both methods strongly suggest that productivity growth was not rapid. To restore credibility to the optimist case, either real wages would need to be revised upwards very substantially or we would need clear evidence that inequality increased markedly. Thus, the quantity-based productivity estimates derived from national accounting exercises, and the standard-of-living evidence on real wages, mutually reinforce each other. The accumulating evidence that output growth was slow implies that productivity increased only marginally. And the failure of real wages, rental rates of capital and land rents to rise markedly supports this view. Alternative estimates using the same approach arrive at even smaller numbers (Clark 2001b). Slow growth and a relatively pessimistic view of the course of living standards during the industrial revolution are simply two sides of the same coin, as dual productivity measurements make clear. The same logic also suggests that, to the extent that real wages actually grew even more slowly than output per capita, inequality may have become worse over time (Feinstein 1998b).

O'Brien and Engerman (1981) pointed out that demographic change may also provide important clues about the course of living standards.

The number of Britons surged from the middle of the eighteenth century onwards, largely as a result of increased fertility (Wrigley 1983; Wrigley *et al.* 1997). If this was a response to better living conditions, it would represent a powerful 'smoking gun' in favour of increasing well-being. However, fertility apparently responded only weakly (and belatedly) to changes in wages (Wrigley and Schofield 1981). According to more recent work, the relationship may be even weaker than originally thought (Lee and Anderson 1999). Also, temporary shocks to the demographic-economic system (such as a sudden drop in mortality because of mild winters, etc.) took a long time to 'die out', reverberating in the system for up to a century. Under conditions such as these, it is hard to infer much about the course of living standards from changes in fertility.

CONCLUSIONS

The standard-of-living debate has remained active for so long because neither side could marshal evidence of a marked and important shift (Feinstein 1998a). Since the 1980s, most new research findings have lent increasing but not unambiguous support to pessimistic views. Crucially, real wages did not increase at anywhere near the rate suggested by earlier estimates. Overall gains between 1760 and 1830 were modest, and included periods of decline. Even by 1850, real wages had only risen by small amounts. What gains there were probably had been bought by longer hours of more intensive work, performed in more dangerous and unhealthy workplaces, by Englishmen and women many of whom lived in the unhygienic, disease-ridden, dark, damp and crowded conditions of British cities during the middle of the nineteenth century. The horrors portrayed by Dickens and his contemporaries were not figments of the imagination; they were real enough. The consequences of these desperate conditions were that infant mortality remained stubbornly high, and even increased in some places; that life expectancy in the industrialising cities of the north was very low, and falling; and that heights probably stagnated or declined as the industrial revolution wore on.

That life was markedly better for the working classes by the 1820s and 1830s than it had been in the 1760s is hard to argue. Wage increases were probably insufficient to compensate for urban disamenities, additional workloads, and the rise in infant and child mortality (Feinstein 1998a). From the 1850s onwards, however, real wages were beginning to pull ahead of prices substantially, and life expectancy was marginally higher than in the 1750s (but not than in the 1570s and 1580s). Working hours may have been somewhat shorter than they had been in the 1830s; child labour was on the wane; and heights began their long-term increase. In the very long run, it is difficult not to be an optimist in the standard-of-living debate: the years 1750–1850 allowed Britain to escape

Malthusian constraints, and to make the transition to modern economic growth.

None of this answers the question as to what would have happened to living standards without an industrial revolution (O'Brien and Engerman 1981). Population growth surged after 1750, and it is hard to imagine that, in the absence of fast structural change, England's economy could have avoided rapidly declining marginal returns to labour (Mokyr 1999: 115). Under plausible assumptions, per capita income might well have fallen by 8 to 18 per cent without an industrial revolution. The principal effect of the mass migration from the countryside to the cities, and from agriculture to industry, was therefore to allow the great demographic expansion to continue unchecked. What actual gains in terms of living standards there were appear small, tenuous, and often interspersed with extended periods of stagnation or decline. Yet compared to what might have happened, living conditions held up remarkably well. As Ashton (1996 [1948]: 129) put it:

> The central problem of the age was how to feed and clothe and employ generations of children that outnumbered by far those of any earlier time. There are to-day, on the plains of India and China men and women, plague-ridden and hungry, living lives little better . . . than those of the cattle that toil with them . . . Such Asiatic standards, and such unmechanized horrors, are the lot of those who increase their numbers without first passing through an industrial revolution.

11 Transport

SIMON VILLE

Contents

Introduction   295
Patterns of transport development   296
  Roads   296
  Inland waterways   299
  Shipping   301
  Railways   305
  Urban transport   307
Competition and industry policy   308
New organisational challenges   314
Assessment of economic impact   319
  Rostow and Szostak as transport advocates   319
  Capital formation   320
  Productivity   322
  Earnings   323
  Social overhead capital   324
  Linkages and spillovers   325
  Market integration   326
  Social savings   328
Conclusion   330

INTRODUCTION

Transport has long been viewed as of central importance to modern British economic history.[1] More than forty years ago, Rostow (1960: 302) viewed the railway as the 'leading sector' of the British economy of the mid-nineteenth century, driving broader economic modernisation through its strong intersectoral linkages. This early interest in the developmental role of transport has given way more recently to a closer

---

[1] This chapter has benefited from feedback provided by Joel Mokyr, Paul Johnson, Martin Daunton, Peter Wardley, Knick Harley and other participants at the 2001 London conference that discussed chapter drafts. Paola Crinnion provided valuable research assistance.

understanding and recognition of its pioneering contribution to be-havioural and structural elements of economic change, particularly in terms of government intervention and corporate innovation.

This chapter will describe the process of transport growth in the eighteenth and nineteenth centuries, and then focus more closely on its political, organisational and developmental impact. Transport systems (including communications) move people, goods and information. This chapter will look at each of these functions in order to reveal the pervasive role of the transport industry in modern British history. The tendencies for transport infrastructure to take the form of a public good, open to all users, and for some transport services to operate in a manner similar to a monopoly explain the interest shown in the industry by governments seeking to assess the private and public costs and benefits involved. The large size and capital-intensive nature of many operating units caused unprecedented organisational challenges for transport companies. The identification of transport as a form of social overhead capital, supporting production across the economy, helps account for its broad-ranging impact on economic development that has been the focus of much of the historiography. In this role transport contributed to the efficient allocation of resources over space, thereby promoting competition between producers, and providing information about alternative consumption possibilities to consumers.

PATTERNS OF TRANSPORT DEVELOPMENT

Roads

Concerted efforts were made to improve the quality of the road system in the eighteenth century. Levels of maintenance had not been commensurate with actual or potential demand from road users. Parishes previously provided road maintenance in their vicinity but the neglect of such duties led to the transfer of responsibility to 'turnpike trusts', beginning in the mid-seventeenth century. Access to these roads was through a turnpike, and users had to pay a toll towards the upkeep of the road. The trusts consisted largely of local entrepreneurs with a strong private interest in road maintenance. The first turnpike trust was established by act of parliament in 1663. After a slow start, the number of turnpikes increased rapidly with the economic expansion of the 1750s and 1760s. Further booms occurred in the early 1790s, 1809–12 and the mid-1820s. In the first of these booms turnpike trusts were established across many areas of Britain; in the second and third phases expansion was particularly linked with the port and dock activities of wartime; and in the final period the industrial expansion of Lancashire and Yorkshire provided a strong incentive. By the mid-1830s around 22,000 miles of roads had been turnpiked or entrusted to Improvement Commissioners, representing about one-fifth of all roads (Barker and Gerhold 1993: 37–8). In a similar fashion, bridge trusts often bore responsibility for the maintenance of bridges and the rapid growth in their construction from the late eighteenth century through to 1830 (Ginarlis and Pollard 1988: 208–12; Harrison 1992: 246, 259–60).

Accompanying these improved institutional arrangements were important developments in road building and haulage technology. John Metcalfe, Thomas Telford and John McAdam have been given much of the credit for the improved quality of roads from the later eighteenth century. Roads were strengthened by packing broken stones into them, and drainage was improved by developing convex surfaces. By 1829 concrete was also being used in roads. Many more tunnels and bridges were constructed in order to avoid steep gradients and long contours, which helped roads to handle heavier traffic and to be passable in inclement conditions. Gerhold (1996) has recently argued that road haulage technology, not road systems, was the key explanation of the growth of road transport services. Improved breeds of sturdier horses ate less and worked harder, and some improvements in wagon design predated the turnpike trusts. Of course, better roads and vehicles went hand in hand: better roads facilitated the shift to lighter more capacious wagons by providing harder, smoother, dryer surfaces with less steep inclines. The consequence of these combined improvements was larger loads, higher speeds, and longer continuous periods of travel, including more overnight movements.

How rapidly did road transport grow? Road transport took many forms, most obviously passenger conveyance and goods shipment including the mail, but a distinction is also drawn between London, provincial, local and private carriers of goods (Barker and Gerhold 1993: 19–33). Several estimates have been made of the growth of the London cargo carriers travelling to the provinces, for whom a variety of evidence survives from directories, advertisements, legal proceedings and business records. Estimates of the growth of capacity (number of weekly services) and output (ton-miles) both show a substantial annual compound growth rate: 0.7 to 1.8 per cent in the former and 1.0 to 2.8 per cent in the latter for 1681–1840 (Table 11.1). For passenger services from London to the provinces, growth rates of weekly services and passenger miles come to 1.9 per cent and 2.8 per cent respectively for 1715–1840 (Table 11.2). It is more difficult to estimate the growth of local and private carriers, for whom little evidence survives. Services were often irregular and undertaken by small carriers, who sometimes combined this with cartage work on farms at harvest and other busy seasons. Distances covered were mostly as little as 25 or 30 miles, and carriers rarely required specialist premises because of the smallness of their operations (normally one or two carts) and their ability to complete most tasks on the same day.

Table 11.1 Growth of the London carrying trade, 1681–1840

	Services per week		Index of ton-miles (1765 = 100)		per week Ton-miles
	Chartres and Turnbull	Gerhold	Chartres and Turnbull	Gerhold	Gerhold
1681	372	346			
1690		348		31	74,700
1705		453			
1715	611		17		
1738		422			
1765	990	493	100	100	243,500
1796–8	1,662	565	169	111	269,800
1808		608		113	274,300
1816–18	3,246	823	344	140	340,700
1826		1,025		152	369,800
1838–40	6,113	1,093	571	149	362,200
Annual compound growth (%)	1.8	0.7	2.8	1.0	1.1

Notes: Figures from Chartres (1977), Chartres and Turnbull (1983), and Gerhold (1988). Chartres and Turnbull's index of services per week, 1715–1840, has been converted to actual services on the basis of Chartres's figure for 1715. Gerhold's figures exclude services covering less than 20 miles to London.

Source: Barker and Gerhold 1993: 22, Table 2.

Table 11.2 Growth in passenger services to selected provincial centres, 1715–1840

Year	Service quotient	Index (1796 = 100)	Passenger miles (000)	Index (1796 = 100)
1715	158	10	67	7
1765	279	18	123	12
1773	376	24	183	18
1796	1,596	100	1,040	100
1816	2,060	129	2,043	197
1840	1,765	111	2,369	228
Annual compound growth (%)		1.9		2.8

Note: Service quotient refers to a quantum of the weekly frequency of coach departures from London to thirty-eight major provincial cities.

Source: Chartres and Turnbull 1983: 69.

Better roads and road transport substantially improved the operation of services: average travel times declined by 20 to 30 per cent over the period 1750–1830 (Jackman 1916: 335–6) and carriers could offer a greater range of service types, from slow coaches to flying wagons (faster but higher price), depending upon whether speed or cost was more important. Regularity was enhanced by less seasonal laying up, as only the most severe winter weather made the new roads impassable. These changes undoubtedly reduced the input costs of transport, and the increased competition associated with the extension of services led to these lower costs being passed on in the form of lower freight rates (Pawson 1977: 297; Barker and Gerhold 1993: 40–3). Contemporaries noted that road transport charges were falling, perhaps by as much as a third (Albert 1983: 55–6). None the less, road carriage remained more expensive than by inland waterway or coastal shipping, particularly for long hauls of bulky materials.

Inland waterways

In the half century or so before 1750, navigational improvements had been made to a number of rivers in response to expanding internal trade. Channels had been cut across winding bends and shallow areas deepened. However, from the second half of the eighteenth century there was heightened interest in the construction of canals, which are defined as deadwater navigations, built as directly as possible, avoiding obstructions such as weirs, and incorporating an adjacent towpath for haulage and locks to adjust to altitude changes. The Sankey Brook Navigation, which was partly opened in 1757, connected the coal mines of St Helens with the river Mersey. The Bridgewater Canal, which was opened in 1761, joined the coal mines of the duke of Bridgewater at Worsley with Manchester. Although the change from river improvement to canal was gradual, these two waterways are often viewed as symbolising the beginning of a period of intensive canal construction that lasted until at least the end of the French Wars in 1815. The demand for transporting bulky raw materials that lay behind their construction reflected the type of service to which canals were best suited. Although the Bridgewater was a short local canal it was soon followed by longer trunk canals connecting different regions, including the Forth and Clyde Canal in 1790, which gave Edinburgh access to the commercial waterway of the Clyde, and the Leeds and Liverpool Canal in 1816, which crossed the Pennines.

In a similar fashion to the turnpike trusts, canal construction required the authority of a private Act of Parliament, and these acts provide a proxy for the intensity of waterway expansion. Table 11.3 shows that in the decade and a half from 1760 canal construction proceeded rapidly. This was then followed by a slowdown for about a decade until expansion rose to a peak in the first half of the 1790s. High levels of construction continued through the first three decades of the nineteenth century, by which time the British canal network was all but completed, with the major exception of the Manchester Ship Canal, which was finished in 1894. The mileage of all inland waterways in England and Wales grew from 1399 in 1760 to 3876 in 1830, a growth rate of 1.4 per cent per annum, with most of this growth attributable to canal construction (Duckham 1983: 109).

Although we lack reliable data on the growth of waterway traffic, expansion was heavily orientated towards freight traffic, especially in bulky goods, such as coal and other minerals, and where only a low rate of

Table 11.3 Growth of inland waterways, 1760–1830			
Years	Mileage	New acts	All acts total
1760	1,399		–
1760–4	–	6	6
1765–9	–	23	29
1770–4	–	23	52
1775–9	–	13	65
1780–4	–	11	76
1785–9	–	11	87
1790–4	–	82	169
1795–9	–	44	213
1800–4	–	47	260
1805–9	–	44	304
1810–14	–	37	341
1815–19	–	30	371
1820–4	–	21	392
1825–9	–	35	427
1830	3,876		–
Annual compound growth (%)	1.4		

Note: In most of these years the vast majority of acts were for extending the powers of existing companies or navigation undertakers.

Source: Duckham 1983: 106.

dispersion in their delivery was required. Many of the earliest canals were promoted and financed by individual entrepreneurs for the benefit of their firms. They were mostly connected with the industrialising regions of Lancashire, the West Midlands and South Wales. The Trent and Mersey ('Grand Trunk') Canal, which formed a link between the west and east coasts of England, was completed in 1777. Its promoter, Josiah Wedgwood, used the canal to ship his pottery to the ports of Hull and Liverpool and receive the raw materials of coal and clay. By the 1790s, canal construction had become more widely spread in terms of geographical location, goods carried and numbers of investors, the latter often as part of joint-stock companies. As such, the canals played their part in weaning investors away from government bonds towards a capital market in industrial finance.

The leading canal engineers, men such as Thomas Telford, John Smeaton, the Whitworths and the Rennies, faced enormous natural obstacles, which required the construction of tunnels, cuttings, embankments, bridges and aqueducts. Such works took many years, as can be seen from the long lag in completing the trunk canals: the Forth and Clyde was completed in 1790, twenty-two years after its act was passed, while the construction of the Leeds and Liverpool took from 1770 to 1816. Waterway transport was largely undertaken in narrow boats pulled by horses from the towpath. There was little use of steam on canals before the middle of the nineteenth century, and even then its use and effectiveness was limited by the narrowness of many canals. Fly boats became common during the early nineteenth century. Like the flying coaches on the roads, they used relays of horses, ran to regular timetables, and often worked all night.

Thus, there were only limited improvements to speed from the canal era. Even the progress of relays of horses was constrained by the time taken to pass through locks. Nor was regularity much improved, since narrow canals could easily flood or freeze over in winter. However, the canal era did create significant additional transport networks, both to make connections between existing river systems and to bring water transport into new areas. Canals reduced transport costs, particularly of bulk cargoes such as minerals on longer distances (see chapter 15 below). Duckham (1983: 131) has estimated a saving of 50 to 70 per cent in the bulk trades, though this figure fluctuated substantially according to the distance carried and the extent to which road transport was still needed at the beginning and/or end of the journey: canals rarely delivered door to door, thus involving expensive transhipment costs compared with journeying entirely by road.

Shipping

The shipping industry faced huge increases in demand in both the coastal and overseas trades in the eighteenth and nineteenth centuries in response to industrialisation, international specialisation of production, and colonialism. Increased household and factory demand for coal 'fuelled' the growth of its interregional trade, particularly that sourced from South Wales and the north-east of England. Rapidly growing volumes of grain, livestock and building materials were all being shipped around the coast of Britain in response to population growth and industrial expansion. In the nineteenth century, European industrialisation and the emergence of the steamship stimulated a major expansion of coal exports. Coastal passenger services covered most British ports by the early nineteenth century, particularly serving business travel and leisure excursions. Their comfort and convenience prevented their immediate extinction by the railway in the mid-nineteenth century. Coasters continued to provide a larger share of domestic transport output (ton-miles) than railways throughout the nineteenth century (Armstrong 1987: 176). Most foreign deployment of the British fleet had been found in Europe at the start of the eighteenth century, particularly in the Mediterranean, the North Sea and the Baltic. Over the next century and a half, growing numbers of vessels entered longer-haul intercontinental foreign trades, particularly as a result of British influence over, and settlement of, distant lands in the Americas, Africa, Australasia and Asia. These trades required large amounts of tonnage because of their long distance; additionally, this involved the carriage of some bulky cargoes such as timber, wool, raw cotton, slaves and migrants. Major technological and organisational advances were essential to enable British shipping to respond to this huge increase in demand.

Steamboat experiments took place on the Clyde in the first decade of the nineteenth century and they were shortly in use as river craft. By the 1820s and 1830s larger engines and more efficient paddles brought steam into coasting. In the 1840s paddles were replaced by more efficient screw propellers and in the following decade the compound engine was patented. Further improvements in engine efficiency with the triple and quadruple expansion engines and the turbine, together with the use of high-pressure boilers, made the steamship efficient on most of the ocean trade-routes (Fletcher 1958: 557; Henning and Trace 1975: 365–8). Steam in shipping brought higher speeds, shorter distances since vessels no longer had to pursue circuitous courses in search of trade winds, and greater regularity through not being reliant upon the vagaries of changing wind directions. Iron and then steel provided greater strength, safety and space in vessel construction. Specific vessel types suited to particular trades were developed, including 'reefers' (refrigerated ships), tankers and ore vessels. Sailing vessels remained an important part of the shipping fleet through the nineteenth century (see Table 11.4), benefiting from some of these innovations, such as iron construction, and improvements in sailing and design efficiency. However, the number of sailing vessels was in absolute decline from the 1860s, and the tonnage of steamships overtook that of sail in the mid-1880s.

Infrastructural developments resulted from the new technologies, including a network of bunkering stations, improved port facilities to accelerate the turnaround of expensive steamers, and the reorganisation of shipyards to adapt to the new construction technologies. Improvements in port facilities, navigational aids (for example the chronometer, the quadrant and lighthouses) and stowage methods additionally enhanced the productivity of a ton of shipping (North 1958; Walton 1967; Ville 1986; Harley 1988; Menard 1996). The laying of the first successful transatlantic cable in 1866 by Brunel's *Great Eastern* steamship, with connections to Japan and Australia by the early 1870s, vastly accelerated international communication, to the great benefit of shipping companies and other international business organisations.

The organisation of ship owning experienced important changes associated with several phases of increased specialisation: the emergence of specialist ship owning firms in the first half of the nineteenth century and the gradual division of the industry into liner companies and tramp owners in the second half. The initial specialisation involved the emergence of a separate occupation of ship owning, decoupled from the mercantile or shipbuilding functions. It was facilitated by the growth of

Table 11.4 Shipping registered in the United Kingdom, 1790–1900

	Sailing ships		Steamships		All ships		Annual compound growth (%) all ships (tons)	Avg ship size (tons)	Carrying capacity (000 tons)	Annual compound growth (%) (carrying capacity)
	Number	000 tons	Number	000 tons	Number	000 tons				
1790					13,557	1,383		102.0	1,383	
1800					15,734	1,699	1.9	108.0	1,699	1.9
1810					20,253	2,211	2.4	109.2	2,211	2.4
1820	21,935	2,436	34	3	21,969	2,439	0.9	111.0	2,448	0.9
1830	18,876	2,168	298	30	19,174	2,202	−0.9	114.8	2,288	−0.6
1840	21,883	2,680	771	88	22,654	2,768	2.1	122.2	3,032	2.6
1850	24,797	3,397	1,187	168	25,984	3,565	2.3	137.2	4,069	2.7
1860	25,663	4,204	2,000	454	27,663	4,659	2.5	168.4	6,020	3.6
1870	23,189	4,578	3,178	1,113	26,367	5,691	1.8	215.8	9,030	3.8
1880	19,938	3,851	5,247	2,724	25,185	6,575	1.3	261.1	14,747	4.6
1890	14,181	2,936	7,410	5,043	21,591	7,979	1.8	369.6	23,108	4.2
1900	10,773	2,096	9,209	7,208	19,982	9,304	1.4	465.6	30,928	2.7
Annual compound growth (%)	−0.9	−0.2	7.2	10.1	0.4	1.7				2.8

Notes:
1. Tonnage figures are net.
2. The Isle of Man and the Channel Islands are included in this table.
3. Carrying capacity reflects the growth rate of steam shipping; thus steamship tonnage is multiplied by 4.

Sources: Mitchell and Deane 1962: 217–19.

marine insurance, which reduced the risks of focusing on a single occupation, while agency and brokerage services provided necessary ancillary support. Lloyds List, from the 1730s, and a growing plethora of publications, provided information to ship owners on shipping movements, navigation and stowage (Craig 1982). Helped by these support services, and drawing upon their evolving expertise, these pioneer owners proved adept at keeping their vessels actively deployed across a wide range of trades (Ville 1993). The later subdivision of ship owners into tramp and liners operators was largely the product of the coming of steam and the ocean cable. The liners provided a fast, regular, timetabled service of mixed consignments on particular routes at fixed freight rates. The slower conveyance of a specific cargo on almost any route at a negotiated rate was undertaken by the older tramp vessels. These differences in shipping operations brought a greater choice of service types for shippers, and more focused expertise.

The ability of the shipping industry to respond to rapid increases in demand was further aided by the growing amount of foreign-owned shipping carrying British trade, a process helped by the repeal of the Navigation Laws in 1848 which had limited the rights of third-party nations to carry British trade (see chapter 7 above). Jackson has estimated that by the middle of the nineteenth century about 40 per cent of tonnage entering and clearing ports in Britain's overseas trade was foreign owned, leading him to conclude: 'the myth of the permanent superiority of the British merchant marine cannot be sustained' (1988: 260).

The UK shipping industry, as measured by vessels registered, grew at an average rate of 1.7 per cent between 1790 and 1900 (Table 11.4). If one takes account of the greater productivity of steamships, growth rates were around 2.8 per cent. How was this rapid technical change and growth financed? For centuries the industry had relied upon a system of tenants-in-common ownership of most vessels, which came to be known as the 64th system, owing to its numerical divisibility. Helped by the statutory requirement of vessel registration from 1788, which revealed details of the ship and its owners, the system endured in the nineteenth century in spite of modern company law and the introduction of limited liability by the mid-nineteenth century. However, an increasing number of steamship enterprises opted for joint-stock company status from mid-century (Palmer 1973: 46).

In the light of these streams of organisational and technical change, it is clear that the speed, regularity and coverage of shipping services all increased substantially during our period. Freight rates were highly susceptible to short-term fluctuations in the eighteenth century as a result of intermittent warfare, which increased the demand for shipping in the form of transport vessels and longer journey times in convoys. The steep rise in freight rates during the French Wars was particularly noticeable. However, there appears to have been a large and sustained fall in freight rates through the nineteenth century under the impact of the increased efficiencies. North's (1958: 549) freight rate index for a variety of North Atlantic cargoes, including timber and grain, shows a fall from an average of 186 in 1816–20 to 77 in 1861–5 (1830 = 100), with the downward trend continuing through the remainder of the century. An alternative index by Harley (1988: fig. 1) shows a similar downward trend in real freight rates from about the middle of the nineteenth century (O'Rourke and Williamson 1999: 36). Finally, an index of coal freight rates shows a strong secular decline throughout the nineteenth century (Hausman 1993: 611).

Railways

Land transport along a pair of raised rails was used by collieries to ship coal between pithead and riverside quay in the eighteenth century. Here gravity transported the cargo the relatively short distance over wooden rails to the quayside and the wagons were returned uphill by the use of horses or stationary engines. However, the 'railway age' begins in the early nineteenth century, and particularly from 1830. The construction of the Liverpool to Manchester railway in that year provided the main features of a modern railway: a reserved track, public traffic facilities, provision for passengers, and mechanical power (Gourvish 1988: 57). The line adopted George Stephenson's new steam locomotive technology embodied in the 'Rocket', which had been tested successfully in locomotive trials at Rainhill in 1829. The line's success initiated a period of intense railway construction in Britain, with peaks of building activity in 1837–40, 1846–50 and 1860–6, during which a series of main trunk lines were completed and then complemented by secondary and branch routes. By 1871 about two-thirds of the network was completed (see Table 11.5). The resulting pattern was a series of main lines radiating from London to connect with the main cities of the British mainland, with the latter acting as satellites for regional and local lines. An amalgamation movement among the railway companies and the establishment of the Railway Clearing House (1842) helped to address problems of service duplication and the lack of connectedness between lines and across schedules.

The Liverpool to Manchester was successful as a passenger carrier as well as for its original use in the cotton trade, an experience repeated by many subsequent lines. Passenger travel did not incur the heavy intercompany transhipment costs

Table 11.5 Construction of the rail network, 1830–1900

	km	Annual compound growth (%)
1830	157	
1840	2,390	28.1
1850	9,797	13.7
1860	14,603	3.7
1871	21,558	3.6
1880	25,060	1.4
1890	27,827	1.0
1900	30,079	0.7
Annual compound growth (%)	7.7	

Source: Mitchell 1975: 316–18.

and delays of early freight movements. Moreover, it soon became clear that the railway could offer long-distance transport to a wider portion of the population than the stage coach because of the lower marginal costs of adding additional carriages, or just open trucks for third-class travel. The railway also became an important mode of information conveyance. Mail was carried from the time of the Liverpool to Manchester and played a central role in the success of the Penny Post from 1840 by absorbing much of the rapid increase in demand as the number of letters delivered by the Post Office grew from 76 million in 1839 to 863 million in 1870 (Daunton 1985: 80, 122–32). In addition, the railway companies played an important role in the evolution of the telegraph network from the 1830s to state ownership in 1870, operating services alongside five specialist telegraph companies (Perry 1997: 416–17).

Construction of the rail network, as with other transport modes, encountered formidable technical problems. The Liverpool to Manchester was built across the inhospitable wetlands of Chat Moss. Major construction works such as the Severn Tunnel (1886) and the Forth Bridge (1890), which survive today, are testimony to the engineering achievements associated with the railway era. Railway companies sought to emphasise the quality and reputation of their services through the erection of architecturally grandiose stations such as those at London St Pancras and Bristol Temple Mead. In contrast to the shipping industry with its centuries-old institutions, railway companies were quick to embrace the new corporate investment opportunities of the Victorian era to pay for these engineering works and extravagant buildings. Indeed, railway stock was the main form of traded instrument on the London Stock Exchange, representing 26 per cent of the nominal value of securities quoted in 1863, and rising further to 49 per cent by 1893 (Michie 1999: 89). Included in these figures are the sale of stock in foreign railway companies, particularly those of the United States, reflecting the sector's role in the growth of British overseas investment. Railways played an initiating and facilitating role in many capital market developments. These particularly included broadening the geographical and occupational base of the investing community through the spread of regional stock exchanges, such as at Liverpool and Manchester (1836) and at Leeds, Glasgow and Edinburgh (1844–5), together with the sale of much lower denominated shares, and the increased use of fixed-interest industrial securities to sustain investment when many companies were yielding very low dividends (Michie 1999: 60–9, 116–17). The railway companies themselves were the largest private business organisations of the mid-Victorian period and the pioneers of many advances in the corporate form, as we shall see below.

Table 11.6 testifies to the very rapid growth of railway traffic, 6.7 per cent per annum for passenger numbers and 7.6 per cent for freight tons. The rapid growth in passenger numbers is noteworthy in spite of the freight motivation for most early railways. Output measured in terms of numbers of passengers and tons of freight doubled in both the 1850s and the 1860s.

Railways in Britain did little to extend the transport network already long established by road, canal and coast. However, their substantial improvements in speed and reductions in cost, particularly for long-distance bulk carriage, were impressive. All writers, contemporary and modern, agree that railway freight rates considerably undercut road and canal, and that rail rates fell further between 1830 and 1870. Second-class rail passenger fares of 2 to 2.5d per mile were well below road rates of similar comfort of 3.5 to 4.5d. Ton-mile canal charges of about 3d were easily beaten by rail rates of 1.67d. By 1870, passenger rail rates had fallen 40 per cent from these figures and freight about 30 per cent (Gourvish 1988: 76–7). The cost of conveying mail by rail fell by two-thirds between 1862 and 1882 (Daunton 1985: 133). While rail transport was much faster than its competitors, the resultant benefits were limited by the relatively short average journey length of about 20–30 miles (Hawke 1970: 64).

Table 11.6 Growth of railway services, 1842–1900 (millions)

	Passengers (numbers)	Freight (tons)
1842	24.7	5–6
1850	72.9	38
1860	153.5	88
1870	322.2	167[a]
1880	596.6	232
1890	796.3	299
1900	1,114.6	420
Annual compound growth (%)	6.7	7.6

Note:
[a] 1871 figure.
Source: Gourvish 1988: 74; Mitchell and Deane 1962: 225–6.

Urban transport

Transport, by its nature, has always been a spatially diverse activity, connecting localities, regions and nations. However, the locus of many transport services lies in a condensed urban environment. The termini of most transport services have been located in the larger towns and cities of Britain, reflecting the agglomeration of population and industry, and therefore transport demand, in these places. Many transport companies have located their head offices in towns and cities, to be close to their major customers. Some towns and cities are themselves intimately connected with the economic activity created by transport, such as Liverpool and Bristol (shipping) or Crewe and Swindon (railways). Urban expansion in the eighteenth and nineteenth centuries additionally created a demand for localised transport *within* individual cities and towns. Such transport was particularly associated with the daily commuting of the workforce and the distribution of consumer goods from local factories, wharfs or warehouses to retailers and in some cases direct delivery to the home.

As Barker has pointed out, urban transport in mid-nineteenth-century Britain predominantly drew upon human and animal power (1988: 134). Costers, porters, hawkers and general dock labour all provided substantial amounts of freight carriage. The number of horses pulling freight vehicles grew rapidly in the nineteenth century and much of this was urban activity (Thompson 1976: 80). Cartage agents like Pickfords found plenty of work transporting goods to and from the new urban rail termini. Passenger transport took many forms, from hackney coaches for the wealthy to cabriolets (cabs) for hire and short-distance stage coaches, the latter being replaced by the more practical omnibus from the 1830s. In spite of some improvements to the efficiency of the omnibus through better design, horse tramways began to spread in the 1870s, the reduced friction of their metal rail yielding a significant saving on horse costs. They were particularly popular in provincial cities such as Glasgow, Edinburgh, Birmingham and Liverpool, whose urban spread was insufficient to justify the heavier investments in underground railways begun in London in 1863 with the building of the Metropolitan Railway. Inanimate forms of urban road transport developed towards the end of the nineteenth century: steam trams from about the 1890s and electric from around 1900.

COMPETITION AND INDUSTRY POLICY

The transport sector has always attracted considerable government attention, and there was no exception to this rule in the period under study in spite of a generally limited role for government in the economy. Thus, for example, road, waterway and railway projects required parliamentary approval. Shipping was subject to a series of statutes, dealing with such issues as ports, registration, safety, manning and trading rights. Doubtless, much of this attention reflected the strategic and defence role of transport, especially shipping. Transport investment reverberated widely through the economy, with the result that governments also sought to influence its domestic impact. Several economic concepts help to clarify these political and legal dimensions, most notably natural monopoly and public goods.

Under natural monopoly it is always cheaper for a single firm to produce the relevant output than two or more firms. This applies to transport because large economies of scale and high minimum levels of operation exist in most transport service industries. Public goods are those which are open to all users, and in which one person's consumption does not prevent another's. To a degree, this is true of transport services; rail, road and waterway may be used by many consumers simultaneously as long as there remains some unused capacity.

The existence of monopoly and public-good features in transport commonly attracts government intervention to address the injustices of anti-competitive behaviour and the market failure represented by the underprovision of services. Monopolists have the power to raise prices and restrict output, both of which are likely to limit the economic benefits of a transport system to a small group of operators. On the other hand, public goods risk being underprovided for the opposite reason: the benefits are too widely dispersed (that is, social utility exceeds private utility), so that the private costs exceed the benefits to the transport company. In practice, as we shall see, transport is not a pure form of natural monopoly or public good, but rather a complex hybrid of both features. Finally, issues of co-ordination and standardisation, critical for a complex network industry, are often not easily handled without some form of intervention.

Therefore, governments must decide how the costs and benefits of improved transport systems are to be distributed among different interest groups. Three direct interests are the providers of infrastructure, transport service operators (carriers) and service users (passengers, merchandise owners). Vertical integration, for example the ownership by oil companies of tanker fleets, helps to reconcile these groups but also extends market power. Indirect benefits from transport investment (known to economists as positive externalities) flow more widely through society, and thus reinforce official interest in the industry.

Road maintenance before the turnpike trusts illustrates an undersupplied public good, since the costs were borne locally and collectively within the parish but the beneficiaries were largely private, including through-travellers from beyond the locality. The introduction of turnpike trusts privatised road use and transferred much of its cost to the user. By mitigating the risks of underinvestment associated with public goods, this change provided a firm basis for higher optimal standards of road maintenance and held out the prospect of the construction of new highways through the support of an income stream from toll charges. The trusts themselves were non-profit bodies in contrast to the for-profit joint-stock companies adopted by canal builders and, later, railway companies. They were initially viewed as supplementing local labour services in road maintenance and thus a more limited role was envisaged than the major new capital expenditures of canal and railway construction.

While providing a solution to underinvestment in roads, the new policy adversely affected local groups who were accustomed to traditional free right of access. They perceived the change, sometimes negatively, as the replacement of a communal institution based on custom and tradition with a cash payment based on a private market transaction (Albert 1983: 36). Popular unrest occurred among colliers and industrial workers in the West Country, Wales and the West Riding of Yorks, sometimes ending in the destruction or avoidance of tollgates and assaults on collectors (Albert 1983: 35; O'Brien 1994: 219). Opposition gradually subsided when the beneficial impact was more clearly understood and concessions were obtained for local users.

A system of tolls existed on many inland waterways before 1750, charged by empowered local trustees or commissioners, sometimes as part of a tradition of river conservancy and often under the influence of town corporations. Such groups did not always serve the best interests of users, continuing levies after improvement costs had been paid and mixing waterway finances with other local services (Duckham 1983: 113–14). In the canal era the joint-stock company was the main instrument of progress, with its more clearly defined rights and responsibilities to serve only an individual waterway, and its ability to raise sufficient funds for the high cost of building new waterways. This lack of a challenge to customary public usage of rivers, and the fact that canals extended transport into new areas, minimised the opposition to their development, although of course there were still some losers from trade diversion.

Distributional questions largely centred on the vertical integration of canal owner and barge operator. As noted above, several of the earliest canals were built by individual entrepreneurs for their own use. Parliament used its control over the passage of the Canal Acts to insist, in most cases, upon a separation of ownership of the canal from the carriage of goods upon it until an act of 1845 reversed this policy. Bridgewater was one of a few permitted exceptions to this policy; others included the Forth and Clyde and the Thames and Severn (Hawke 1970: 232; Duckham 1983: 124). Given the growing investor interest in canal building by the late eighteenth century, the separation of owners from operators did not extinguish the growth of the canal system. Integration of operator and user was not uncommon, for example coal merchants and flour millers who owned their own barges. The largest operators were non-integrated specialists, although they gained alternative market power by operating across several transport modes, the most famous being Pickfords, with a very strong presence on both British roads and waterways (Turnbull 1979).

While the separation of functions enhanced competition, transport infrastructure remained a monopoly that governments sought to control in ways that balanced the private incentive to extend the network with the broader social welfare gain from lower transport costs. The canal's enabling act included a schedule of maximum tolls. In some cases, legal restrictions on canal company dividends were imposed but such a policy was at best intermittent and piecemeal (Duckham 1983: 114). Competition was also aided by the growing variety of investors in canal companies, particularly merchants, bankers and landowners, whose interests might favour lower transport costs or improved land values in the vicinity. Thus, they had an incentive for improved transport services rather than solely seeking to maximise the private returns to the canal company. The average return on capital in canal companies in 1825 has been estimated as 5.75 per cent, suggesting that a competitive equilibrium perhaps existed (Duckham 1983: 123).

Navigational aids for shipping such as buoys and the dredging of deepwater entrance channels were public goods, paid for by a levy on shipping entering and clearing the port. Some infrastructure such as lighthouses was also erected in the interests of passing shipping; this was handled by a national system of shipping dues to avoid non-payment (free-riding) by some ship owners. National ports policy by the sixteenth century had begun to divide all of the coastline into the jurisdiction of a series of legally defined ports, each covering its locality in order to strengthen revenue-raising capabilities (customs duties, shipping and port dues) and to eliminate free-riding by trading at small inlets. By mitigating the risks of an undersupply of public goods, official policy ensured the increased safety and productivity of shipping.

Port infrastructure was becoming far more capital intensive by the early nineteenth century, initially to handle the rising volume of traffic and to safeguard valuable cargoes being warehoused, but by mid-century to serve the needs of large steamships for deep-water berths and rapid turnaround. By 1840, Liverpool boasted nearly 70 acres of dock estate, stretching $2^1/_2$ miles along the Mersey, and receiving 2.5 million tons of shipping (Hyde 1971: 247). These new investments required modern forms of capital raising and organisation, focused on a dock's particular needs rather than taking the general form of a public good. The resulting private dock companies charged dock fees to shipping firms using their facilities. In some ports, such as Hull, this produced monopolists who devoted resources to protecting their dominance at the expense of investing in new facilities (Jackson 1988: 228). Contrariwise, in a large port like London, their very high fixed and low marginal costs created destructive price competition among numerous dock companies. Amalgamations were the initial solution, such as that of the London, St Katherine's and Victoria Dock companies on the Thames in 1864. New investments and price wars continued until a Royal Commission led to the establishment of the Port of London Authority in 1909 to take over the private dock companies and operate again in the public interest (Jackson 1988: 228, 241).

Shipping operated in an increasingly competitive market, which helps explain the ability of the industry to respond effectively to steep increases in demand. The monopoly charters of the overseas trading companies (East India Company, Hudson's Bay Company and others) had been revoked by the early nineteenth century. Under the influence of the changing political economy, British governments believed that national economic and strategic interests were better served by encouraging a general proliferation of ship owners and merchants rather than placing their faith in a few vertically integrated monopolies. The costs of setting up political and economic connections to many parts of the world had now been absorbed by these original companies in return for their monopoly rents. The other remnants of mercantilism, which had included the exclusion of third-country shipping from British trade, were relaxed in the 1820s and finally abolished in 1848 (see chapter 7). Coasting, however, continued to be reserved for British shipping for reasons of defence and because navigating treacherous coastal waters and handling bulk cargoes bred sturdy seaman: a policy known as the 'nursery of seamen'. Low entry and exit costs in shipping and a fragmented ownership structure enhanced competition. Michael Henley and Son, one of the largest ship owning firms operating out of London at the beginning of the nineteenth century, entered the industry through the purchase of cheap second-hand sailing vessels. Their fleet of up to twenty vessels represented only a tiny share of London registered shipping (Ville 1987).

By the middle of the nineteenth century, however, the structure of the industry began to change owing to the new technologies of steam and steel. This generated vessels that were more expensive by dint of their steam power and that could be built much larger, because of the use of steel, to produce scale economies. Thus increased capital indivisibility (larger ships) and intensity (capital substituted for labour) raised entry costs to the industry. The regularity of steam, and improved international communications from the development of the oceanic cable, meant that for the first time regular timetabled shipping services could be offered, but this required a fleet of vessels to operate. As a result of these changed operating conditions, a few large companies emerged as leaders of the British shipping industry. However, speed and regularity are more important sources of competitive advantage for some commodities than others. In the carriage of bulk raw materials such as coal and metallic ores, staples of the demand for shipping, cost is a more important factor. With rapid technical change in shipbuilding and consequentially high rates of obsolescence, some ship owners concentrated on the purchase and operation on demand of second-hand steamers at lower cost. The effect was to divide much of the shipping industry into liner (fast, regular, high-quality) and tramp (slow, irregular, low-cost) shipping services. This segmentation encouraged relatively high degrees of competition, to the extent that groups of liner companies began to form collusive shipping rings from the 1870s in an attempt to exclude the price-cutting tramps from particular trades. It was not until the beginning of the twentieth century, however, that British governments addressed seriously this restraint on competition.

The broad social benefits from railways and the strong monopoly features of the network have been compelling reasons for relatively high levels of government interest. High entry costs were associated with the construction challenges discussed earlier. In addition, acquiring privately owned land could be an obstacle. Therefore, a private act of parliament provided for the legal devices of compulsory land purchase (eminent domain) and the security of limited liability in order to attract a broader range of investors (see chapter 8 above). From the outset, many of the largest investors were business owners who stood to gain directly from improved transport services. This helped to mitigate the risk that the benefits would largely be secured by the railway company rather than service users and the broader community. Competition among railway companies and the initial separation of infrastructure owners from service operators also lessened the threat to competition.

From about the 1840s the competitive structure of the industry began to change. Amalgamations produced larger railway companies with fewer rivals. The acquisition of competing canal companies had a similar effect. Competition from new entrants was lessened by the rising scale economies that were being recognised and acted upon. It soon became apparent that the turnpike model of separate infrastructure owners and freight carriers was unworkable, both technically, because of safety considerations, and economically because of the monopoly power of the former. Governments unwittingly contributed to the trend by deciding in 1840 to prohibit private operators on a line, thus fostering vertical integration in the industry. A 'railway interest' emerged in parliament, initially to support the passage of railway acts against opposition from landlords who feared their land values would be affected and road operators who anticipated a loss of business. Increasingly, though, the interest became vociferous in support of powerful economic rights for the railways (Alderman 1973). Similarly, the growth of managerial capitalism among the railway companies created an executive class that performed to the best interests of the company, rather than the business interests of some of its shareholders (Gourvish 1973). Thus, by 1850 the top fifteen railway companies controlled 61 per cent of total paid-up capital in the industry, rising to 80 per cent two decades later (Gourvish 1988: 83).

Governments took seriously the threat to competition posed by these developments and were pressured by traders organised in chambers of commerce and also well-represented in parliament to oppose the railway interest. However, the idea that politics is dominated by distributional coalitions of producer group interests is not the only explanation of government regulation of the railways. A strong sense of public interest motivated Gladstone at the Board of Trade during the passage of the 1844 Railway Act. Among contemporaries, he showed a close understanding of the operation of natural monopolies and the collusive tendencies of oligopolists. The act was an important piece of legislation that has been neglected by many economic historians in the belief that it became watered down during parliamentary debates. It established a pattern of price and quantity regulation that survived until 1960, and its safety provisions remain today. It has been viewed as shaping the pattern for regulation of natural monopolies in the United States through the 1887 Interstate Commerce Act, which itself was the basis for subsequent legislation (McLean and Foster 1992: 315). The act included an option for nationalisation of the rail system, which was to come into effect after twenty-one years. In practice, these purchase powers were not taken up. However, McLean and Foster (1992: 322) have argued for a behavioural impact: that the *threat* of appropriation influenced investors and managers to keep rates of return below 10 per cent by investing in less productive branch and secondary lines. Thus, the experience of Britain's railways over the next eighty years might be viewed as evidence of the hypothesis that regulated industries produce overcapitalisation (Averch and Johnson 1962).

More effective, though, was the scope for intervention in the amalgamation movement. To commence working together, companies had to seek parliamentary approval. This gave parliament the right to investigate their practices, and the Board of Trade in particular negotiated with the railways the final terms of the amending act. By the 1850s, parliament was looking sceptically at many of the proposed amalgamations. The division of interests between users and railway companies was made clear by mid-century with the debates over discriminatory pricing. Under the terms of the Railway and Canal Traffic Act of 1854, companies were only permitted to price discriminate on the basis of cost, whereas their major motive would have been the degree of competition, charging less where competition from shipping was significant. It is conceivable that some of this anti-monopoly stance was overzealous; several proposed amalgamations of the 1870s that sought to cut costs during a downturn were rejected. Significantly, Irving has attributed the declining performance of railway companies in the late nineteenth century in part to service extensions and improvements required by parliament (Irving 1978). Assessing government policy towards the railway as a whole, Dobbin (1994) has concluded that it had a formative influence on the shift of British industry policy away from the idealised free markets of *laissez-faire* to a form of interventionism designed to mitigate an excessive concentration of economic power.

NEW ORGANISATIONAL CHALLENGES

We have seen in the previous sections that in order to be competitive transport firms often have to operate at a high level of output, employing large amounts of geographically dispersed capital and labour. Firm-level evidence of this is not hard to find. Much of the growth of road transport in the eighteenth and nineteenth centuries was concentrated upon a limited number of operators, agglomerating sizeable road fleets along major trade routes. Gerhold has identified one Frome carrier operating a weekly 'team' to London of five wagons pulled by thirty-nine horses (Barker and Gerhold 1993: 21). Thomas Russell and Company, operating between Exeter and London together with regional services in the early nineteenth century, used about 200 horses and thirty wagons, employed sixty to seventy staff and had premises in each town on the route. These in turn were dwarfed by Pickfords of Manchester with 400 wagons by 1803, and Deacon and Co, serving Yorkshire and Norwich, who were reported to operate with 700 horses, 400 employees and 100 branches by 1838 (Barker and Gerhold 1993: 23).

Since most canal companies were not permitted to act as common carriers before 1845 there were few very large infrastructure enterprises, with typically no more than fifty staff. As with road transport, it was the carrier, lacking a monopoly but with the ability to operate across a wide area, that had the freedom to expand. It was noted earlier that much vertical integration existed between carriers and users of the canal network. However, the largest firms were specialist carriers. Chief among them was again Pickfords, whose services spanned much of England from Liverpool and Bristol in the west to Leicester and London in the east, covered by a fleet which grew from ten canal boats in 1795 to 116 in 1838 (Turnbull 1979: ch. 5).

Shipping generated some very large enterprises, particularly from the mid-nineteenth century with the growth of the major liner companies which exploited huge operational scale economies in the provision of fast timetabled services over major trade-routes. Sometimes, through the aid of government mail subventions, these companies expanded into long-haul trades, including Cunard in the transatlantic trade, Royal Mail in South America, P&O to India and the east, and Elder Dempster to West Africa. By the end of the nineteenth century the 'big 5' of P&O, Royal Mail, Cunard, Ellerman and Furness Withy led the British shipping industry (Boyce 1995). In most cases these firms were not heavily vertically integrated; it was the geographical breadth of their shipping operations, rather than their range of functions, that distinguished them. Some established overseas offices if they traded very regularly with a particular port. In most cases, however, the frequency of their transactions at any port was insufficient to justify setting up a local office, with the additional fixed costs and risks involved. Instead, the agency system was commonly adopted whereby ship owners paid local firms, often specialising in agency and brokerage work, to handle their needs such as the payment of bills, the receipt and delivery of merchandise, and the organisation of victualling and ship repairs.

The railway companies were the true giants among transport enterprise as enormous consumers of fixed capital for construction (bridges, tunnels and stations) and operation (rolling stock). Since the railway system expanded at a time of increasing resort to incorporation among Britain's larger listed firms, this enables size comparisons to be drawn across sectors. By 1850 all of the largest firms listed on the Stock Exchange in Britain were railway companies. Indeed, the top fifteen companies accounted for 62 per cent of total paid-up capital in the UK, thus dwarfing manufacturing industry (Gourvish 1988: 83). The London and North Western Railway (LNWR) had raised more than £29 million by 1851, employed a workforce of 12,000, and operated 800 miles of track (Kirby 1994: 130). This was a giant scale of operations for the time and these figures would have still outstripped most British manufacturers half a century later (Wardley 1999: 102–3). The high degree of co-ordination and interaction required to manage these resources and operate a fast and frequent but safe service favoured the adoption of a single governance structure rather than transacting with other firms. Similarly, these companies had reached output levels where many highly repetitive transactions were most cheaply performed within the company. In other words, railway companies sought to minimise their transactions costs by internalising most activities.

The size and spatial diversity of transport enterprises brought unprecedented organisational challenges yet to be faced in other sectors. These particularly involved the logistical management of large volumes of capital and a sizeable workforce spread over an extensive area, yet requiring very high levels of co-ordination and control for reasons of efficiency and safety. Size and spread of activities worsened problems of workforce control, particularly the risk of unobserved opportunist behaviour from employees. In addition, the fact that transport is a service industry created additional management challenges. Services are non-storable – they are produced at a particular time and place and must be consumed there and then or not at all, leading to the risk of underutilisation. Moreover, demand for transport services varies greatly on a monthly, daily or even hourly basis. Transport firms therefore require managers well skilled in matching a relatively inelastic supply with highly elastic demand. How effectively did they respond to these new challenges?

The challenges were of limited significance for the emerging road and canal network. Most firms were small and localised, helped by the fact that management was generally divided into separate owner and operator firms. However, the leading transport operators, such as Pickfords, had relatively large and spatially dispersed workforces requiring careful monitoring and detailed transport planning. They tackled these challenges in a number of ways. The natural co-ordination yielded by their fast and regular transport services provided them with good up-to-date information about their enterprise. Pickfords spread their management across three regional centres, Manchester, Leicester and London, and linked these with intermediate depots and agencies along the major routes and with their own local manager. Ownership of offices along the route reduced the distance between different outposts of the firm. At the senior strategic level, decision-making was shared across a series of partners and, when the firm came close to collapse in 1817, new partners entered the firm with trust-building kinship ties and connections to strong financial networks (Turnbull 1979: 36–41).

Shipping companies were far more geographically distended, and developed a range of strategies. Internal subcontracting was widely practised. This was also a popular strategy among early factory owners and involved delegating some labour recruitment and management tasks to senior employees. In this case, the appointment of the ship's master was one of the key decisions for a firm; upon him fell the responsibility for hiring his crew, keeping a set of onboard accounts, and conducting business with shipping agents and merchants in foreign ports. Owners relied heavily upon masters' regular correspondence back to the company on trade conditions and the performance of the crew. The threat to withhold monthly payments to seamen's families back in England exerted a powerful form of social control over these distant workforces. The ship owner rewarded his masters with higher pay rates, regular employment and sometimes a share in ownership. The owner also dealt directly with shipping agents through correspondence, and often built up close long-term business bonds through reciprocity (Ville 1981). Ship owners drew upon the services of ship brokers who served as specialist intermediaries in the freight market. Shipping firms also benefited from co-operation with one another (Boyce 1995). The growth of public trading information in the eighteenth century gave the ship owner a further means of assessing the performance of his masters as well as benchmarking the performance of different vessels in his fleet against each other.

The earliest railway enterprises drew upon the experience of canal and shipping companies. The Stockton and Darlington subcontracted major functions such as rolling stock repairs and track maintenance to other companies (Kirby 1993). However, the growth of longer-distance rail lines and company amalgamations from the 1840s required a quite different response: the internalisation of most activities and the modernisation of corporate management. Railway companies were pioneers of modern business organisation, separating ownership from management to create a professional executive class organised into a systematically conceived managerial structure for the company. This idea of 'managerial capitalism' was generally slower to develop in Britain than other comparable nations such as the United States and Germany, but it was notable amongst the railway companies from an early stage. The companies were generally organised into functional departments staffed by professional managers with particular expertise in areas such as engineering, finance, legal matters and traffic operations, enabling them to handle more effectively such issues as safety and maintenance, and matching traffic flows to demand estimates. Mobile and capable professional executives with experience across firms and industries dominated the senior management of Britain's railways by the late nineteenth century; 56 per cent of their chief executive appointments (1890–1909) had worked for at least three other companies (Channon 1988; Hughes 1992).

The separation of ownership from management, a key tenet of the modern business enterprise, solved some problems but created others. A separate managerial class creates a divergence of interests between owner and manager. The risk exists that the manager may use his superior information of some of the day-to-day operations of the firm in an opportunist manner, for example putting private business interests or career promotion ahead of what is best for the company. While this corporate governance problem still exists today, it was particularly serious during this transitionary stage between personal and managerial capitalism because firms had not yet learned ways of exerting closer control over their executives. Moreover, many railway managers had not made the full transition to being professional executives. They maintained personal business interests, often connected to the railway industry where their expertise lay, thereby creating a potential conflict of interest between their professional duties and their private business ventures. An example of this occurred in the 1850s when Daniel Gooch, a manager with the Great Western Railway (GWR), acquired a coal company, Ruabon, along with some fellow employees. The Ruabon became a major coal supplier to the railway under a ten-year contract. A suit against Gooch in the Court of Chancery, alleging undue preference, was unsuccessful, but there remained concern about an employee profiting personally from supply contracts to the company (Channon 1999).

Transport enterprises developed accounting techniques as a management aid. The capital intensity and indivisibility of many major investment items necessitated careful attention to the methods of capital accounting. Financial accounting would aid the assessment and monitoring of geographically distant parts of the enterprise. Arnold (1995) and McLean (1995) have shown how nineteenth-century shipping firms instituted and adopted modern accounting techniques to meet the organisational challenges faced by the industry, but it was the railway companies that made most particular use of accounting techniques. Legislation of the 1840s required railway companies to keep detailed accounts and have them audited half-yearly. Mark Huish of the London and North Western Railway (LNWR) went much further than this by collecting a variety of operating statistics as a tool for managing costs and raising the capacity utilisation of its services. The importance of railway accountants can be illustrated by the fact that the companies employed as many accountants and cashiers as they did engineers, and that the industry was of central importance in the expansion of many successful accountancy firms, including Deloitte's and Waterhouse (Gourvish 1988: 71).

A key part of the new management techniques of the railway companies was their pioneering role in the development of internal labour markets. The companies employed some of the largest and most geographically dispersed workforces of nineteenth-century industry. Internalisation sought to maintain the same employees as long-term members of the company, enabling them to draw on their large workforce to fill positions as they arose. This mitigated many of the costs and uncertainties of labour recruitment, while additionally increasing the company's control over its employees and the work process when compared with either an external labour market or internal subcontracting. Howlett (2000) has shown how the Great Eastern Railway used promotion ladders and seniority wage payments to retain their workforce. Non-wage welfare benefits were used for the same purpose (Kingsford 1970).

ASSESSMENT OF ECONOMIC IMPACT

The question of transport's impact on the economy has produced an extensive historical and conceptual literature, and in the process generated two of the most interesting but controversial historical methodologies, the Rostowian leading sector thesis and the counterfactual social savings calculation. There seems little doubt that the sequential waves of transport innovations in the eighteenth and nineteenth centuries did have an important impact; our challenge is to provide a balanced evaluation of their effects and how these were distributed. In this chapter we have distinguished between direct benefits (or costs) of transport investment to the parties to the contract (owners, operators and users) and the indirect or unintended impact on third parties. The latter are often referred to as externalities or secondary effects. In transport studies, the secondary effects are often more substantial than the direct impact. For example, the negative transport externality of pollution and the positive externality of lower prices can flow widely through the economy.

Rostow and Szostak as transport advocates

Earlier sections of this chapter have highlighted the major developments in each transport mode over our period and summarised the improvements to transport provision that resulted. This involved a mix of reduced freight rates, faster speeds, greater regularity and broader geographic coverage. As previously noted, the effects can be so broad ranging that it is difficult to measure them accurately, particularly for earlier historical periods where our evidence is far from complete. The work of Szostak (1991), however, provides us with at least some conceptual guidelines for evaluating the impact.

Szostak sought to explain why an industrial revolution occurred in England in the late eighteenth century by reference to road and waterway improvements, and used France as a control experiment: a less effective inland transport system here prevented or delayed industrial modernisation. He detailed improvements to the system of inland transport and their effects in a complex flow diagram (Szostak 1991: 29). By widening markets, improving access to raw materials, introducing new distribution methods and reducing inventory stocks, transport improvements fostered the main features of the industrial revolution, namely regional specialisation, increased scale of production and the introduction of new industries. These three features, in turn, created more favourable conditions for an increase in the rate of technological innovation.

A shortcoming of Szostak's analysis is the extent to which it draws upon a view of a British 'industrial revolution' at the end of the eighteenth century that is no longer widely accepted. An alternative longer-term process of industrialisation, which characterises British experience as well as that of other European nations, leaves the Szostak model as telling only the beginning of a much longer story. His model might aptly be applied to the railway age where the new technologies of steam and metal sustained the earlier progress; or to ocean shipping with its influence on the early stages of globalisation. His conceptual framework will help guide our discussion later in this section.

An alternative perspective was provided by Rostow (1960), who argued that modern economic development was driven by a 'leading sector', which experienced very rapid growth as a result of technological innovation. This leading sector ignited a 'take-off' in economic development through the stimulus that it imparted to the macroeconomy, and specifically through its linkages or 'spreading effects' to related industries. Rostow sought to place the railway centrally within his schema of economic development by arguing that it was 'historically the most powerful single initiator of take-offs' (Rostow 1960: 302). His work has been subject to critical analysis; as with Szostak, particular criticism has focused upon his interpretation of the pattern of economic development as a revolutionary change. Again, however, the methodology and nomenclature he developed have survived as valuable tools and will help to guide our analysis in this section.

We begin with an examination of the likely economy-wide impact of transport through its share of national aggregates such as investment, productivity and earnings. Thereafter, we look at more specific aspects of its role: its social overhead capital features; its linkages and spillovers to particular industries and sectors; its impact on market integration; and finally the extent of social savings yielded by transport innovations.

Capital formation

Feinstein has estimated the size and distribution of gross domestic fixed capital formation for the century to 1860, disaggregated by broad sectors: agriculture; industry and trade; transport; and residential and social. Transport's share fluctuates between 15 and 21 per cent before 1840, the peak coming in the 1790s with the boom in canal construction and the increased demand for shipping tonnage during the French Wars. Transport's share then begins to rise in the 1830s with the beginning of railway construction and peaks in the 1840s at 39 per cent with the rapid expansion of the rail network. Feinstein notes that a similar magnitude fall in residential and social (especially housing) occurred in those final two

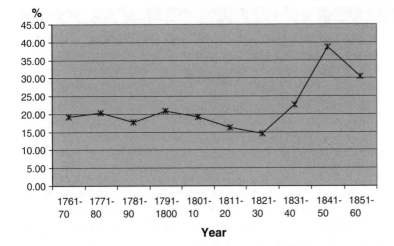

%

Year

decades of our period but is uncertain whether railway investment occurred at the expense of social capital (Feinstein 1981: 133–4; Feinstein and Pollard 1988: 444). His figures are decennial averages. A more disaggregated approach reveals that transport investment was highly cyclical from year to year, as indicated by the canal and road building manias in the mid-1790s and the railway surges in the late 1840s. In the latter case, railway investment may have constituted as much as a half of gross domestic fixed capital formation (Gourvish 1988: 60–1).

The large and highly cyclical nature of transport investment raises questions about its impact upon capital and factor product markets. In particular, is there evidence of crowding out in capital or factor markets, possibly resulting in sub-optimal resource allocation? Since the funds for capital hungry transport projects were often raised during periods of optimism in the hope of future growth in transport demand, did this restrict the opportunities for developing other new industries with important growth potential? Contemporary opinion viewed transport projects as a panacea for economic backwardness, which may have skewed investment. However, it should be remembered that there is a much larger supply of investible funds available during boom periods owing to optimism and higher income levels. Moreover, as we saw earlier, transport played an important role in capital market innovations, which helped to attract additional sources of finance. This growth in capital markets is reflected in a rising investment ratio into double figures during the railway age (Gourvish 1988: 62). Major transport projects requiring parliamentary approval were characterised by a long gestation period from original planning to completion. Thus, projects planned and financed at the top of economic cycles often generated a demand for labour and other production factors during subsequent downturns, providing in some cases a much needed contra-cyclical stimulus to the economy. The second half of the 1840s is a case in point, as we shall see below.

Figure 11.1
Transport's share of gross domestic fixed capital formation in Great Britain, 1761–1860

Source: Feinstein 1981: 133–4.

Table 11.7 Productivity growth in transport by mode (per cent per annum)				
	Roads	Per Canals	Shipping	Railways
Annual compound growth (%)	0.7	0.8	1.4	2.2
	(1690–1840)	(1780–1830)	(1780–1860)	(1830–60)

Sources: Roads, Gerhold 1996: 511; canals, McCloskey 1981: 125; shipping, McCloskey 1981: 125; Harley 1993: 199–200; railways, McCloskey 1981: 125.

Productivity

What evidence do we have for productivity growth in transport that may have mitigated the risks of crowding out by using a fixed amount of resources more efficiently? Many of the sources of productivity growth have been identified in the earlier sections of this chapter. They included better roads, vehicles and horse breeds. On inland waterways this meant better navigation by way of canal and the development of flying services. Shipping benefited from organisational improvements associated with specialist ship owning such as better stowage and navigation, and from rapid technological changes, particularly the shifts to metal and steam. Railways were still in their relative infancy by 1860 but rationalisation through amalgamation and the operation of the clearing house was already impacting upon productivity. As we have also seen on pp. 304–5 above, these improvements were reflected in falling freight rates, and faster and more regular journeys. Calculating productivity change provides us with a single statistic, reported in Table 11.7 which captures most of these varied improvements.

McCloskey evaluated the size and importance of productivity improvements in some of the key 'modernised' sectors of the British economy, 1780–1860. He calculated this by multiplying a sector's annual productivity growth by the weighting of its output in the economy. This led to the result that transport's contribution was the largest among the 'modernised' sectors, that is, 0.23 per cent per annum of the modernised sectors' total growth of 0.52 per cent. McCloskey concluded that 'transportation was therefore among the more notably progressive parts of the economy' (McCloskey 1981: 114; 1994: 252). Table 11.8 reports McCloskey's estimates, and also Harley's (1993) downwards revision of McCloskey's calculations for the modernised sectors. The contribution of shipping is drastically reduced, from 0.14 to 0.03 per cent, by substituting Harley's own productivity growth estimates while retaining the same weightings. Transport's share (0.12) is now slightly behind that of cotton, although the modernised sectors' contribution to national performance is now greater as a result of using Crafts' more recent and more conservative calculations for total productivity growth. Harley's figures are an improvement in that they take some account of productivity in the coastal trade, but his location of productivity improvements in technological changes in the later nineteenth century may understate earlier advances in organisation

Table 11.8 Sectoral contributions to productivity: annual percentage growth, 1780–1860							
		McCloskey estimates		Harley estimates		Ville estimates	
	Share	Productivity	Contribution	Productivity	Contribution	Productivity	Contribution
Cotton	0.070	2.6	0.18	1.9	0.13	1.9	0.13
Worsteds	0.035	1.8	0.06	1.3	0.05	1.3	0.05
Woollens	0.035	0.9	0.03	0.6	0.02	0.6	0.02
Iron	0.020	0.9	0.02	0.9	0.02	0.9	0.02
Canals and railways	0.070	1.3	0.09	1.3	0.09	1.3	0.09
Shipping	0.060	2.3	0.14	0.5	0.03	1.4	0.08
Roads	0.040					0.7	0.03
Sum of modernised sectors	0.330	1.8	0.52	1.2	0.34	1.3	0.42
Agriculture	0.270	0.4	0.12	0.7	0.19	0.7	0.19
All others	0.850	0.6	0.55	0.02	0.02		
Total	1.450		1.19		0.55		0.61

Note: Estimates of roads' share based on evidence in Gerhold 1996: 497–8.

Sources: McCloskey 1981: 114; Harley 1993: 199–200; Table 11.7 above.

and infrastructure. Therefore, we offer a middle point between the work of McCloskey and Harley as a figure for shipping productivity growth. The substantial improvements in road services before the mid-nineteenth century have now been estimated by Gerhold (1996: 511) and can be included. Transport's contribution exceeds cotton's once more. Total productivity growth in agriculture and the 'modernised sectors' aggregates to a figure (0.61 per cent per annum) that is larger than Crafts's (1985: 86; 1987a: 250) aggregate national estimates (0.55 per cent per annum). Harley's lower estimate for transport productivity, when aggregated with the other modernised sectors and agriculture (0.53 per cent per annum), is almost equivalent to the Crafts national figure. This suggests either that all productivity growth in the British economy was confined to the sectors indicated in Table 11.8, or that Crafts's widely recognised downward revisions of national productivity growth for this period are too conservative.

Gemmell and Wardley (1990: 307) have calculated that by 1856 (and through to 1913), 'productivity levels in . . . transport services would appear to have been high relative to manufacturing'. Besides lending some credence to the idea of productivity growth in the sector over the previous century and a half, this additionally suggests that heavy investments in transport were unlikely to have starved more productive sectors of scarce resources.

Earnings

How important were the transport industries as a source of earnings and profits in the British economy? Information on profits is sketchy and there is no compelling evidence for consistently high profits in transport industries. Government intervention, or just the threat of it, may have prevented widespread or persistent monopoly profits, thereby helping to achieve a more efficient allocation of the benefits of new transport systems. It was noted above that the profitability of inland waterways was not exceptional. Davis (1957) doubted whether ship owners achieved outstanding returns in the early eighteenth century, although subsequent periods of war, especially the French Wars, provided exceptional temporary returns to the industry owing to the increased demand for large numbers of transport ships (Ville 1987). The earnings of shipping companies made an important contribution to Britain's trade balance by the boost they provided to invisible earnings. Britain's invisible trade grew more rapidly than its visible trade in the eighteenth century as local ship owners took over much of the international carrying trade from the Dutch (Thomas and McCloskey 1981: 92). Some of the earliest railways, such as the Liverpool to Manchester, achieved good returns, though many later ones, especially regional and branch lines, performed poorly (Donaghy 1965–6). The significance of transport earnings lies perhaps in specific regions and aspects of the economy rather than in national aggregates. Port hinterlands, such as around Liverpool, Glasgow and Bristol, benefited from substantial reinvestment of mercantile profits into evolving trade and industry.

Social overhead capital

While transport featured prominently in a number of economic aggregates, this evidence tells us little about the dynamics of change. Put simply, did transport provide the stimulus to economic expansion or just a reactive force to initiatives elsewhere in the economy? Rostow leaves us in little doubt about the dynamic role of the railway as a leading sector but says nothing of the other transport modes. Figures in the first section of this chapter show that most transport infrastructure and services grew more rapidly than national income throughout the period. This suggests, perhaps, that the transport sector was playing a leading rather than a following role in the accelerated growth of the British economy from the late eighteenth century. However, it does not preclude the possibility that this represented periods of catch-up by transport providers.

A helpful manner of extending this analysis is through transport's role as the major form of social overhead capital (SOC) in the eighteenth and nineteenth centuries. Investment in an economy can usefully be divided into SOC, which supports production across the economy (for example transport, education), or directly productive activities, which involve specific types of production (for example manufacturing). Hirschman (1958), who developed this model, believed expansion in industrial output would stretch the finite resources of SOC and thereby encourage increased investment in transport, communications, education and health. Thus,

SOC is seen as a passive reactor. Alternatively, it has been argued that investment in SOC, by improving the infrastructure for production, can induce directly productive investment in a process referred to as development by excess social overhead capital.

Investing in transport infrastructure ahead of demand is most likely to occur where government plays a proactive role in stimulating economic development. Even in an economy dominated by private investment decisions, transport infrastructures can be built ahead of demand. The belief in transport as a universal panacea for economic backwardness together with the success of early projects often led to investment and construction ahead of demand, as perhaps is illustrated by the 'mania' phases that characterised transport development. The success of the earliest and most viable projects stimulated a 'demonstration effect': industrialists hoped that further investment would yield similar industrial benefits and would avoid 'trade diversion' to neighbouring areas where the transport infrastructure had already been improved, while investors hoped for similar rates of return to earlier projects. In fact, the fears and expectations were often overstated, since the earlier investments were often the most promising. The lack of profitability of many later railway lines and canals became notorious; the demand for them did not yet exist, and in some cases never would.

State provision of subventions to a few steamship companies to carry the mail to areas where there was little commercial trade provides another example of development by excess social overhead capital. From 1839 the Royal Mail Steam Packet Company was paid a subvention by the British government to carry mail to Mexico, Panama, Colombia, Venezuela and the West Indies, while the Pacific Steam Navigation Company began a similar service to the west coast of South America in the following year. In the early 1850s, mail contract payments to the West Indies and Brazil were three times the postage revenue thereby generated (Daunton 1985: 159). Such evidence has caused one writer to note that, 'without British investment in shipping and ancillary services . . . economic growth in Latin America would probably have begun later and at a slower pace' (Greenhill 1979: 265).

Linkages and spillovers

We turn now to look more specifically at transport's links to different sectors and aspects of the British economy. Rostowian backward, forward and lateral 'spreading effects' help us to understand the extent of interconnectedness. These linkages flowed backwards to supply industries, forwards to industries benefiting from improved transport services, and laterally to the local economy. Recent insights into economic development associated with the school of new or 'endogenous' growth theory have emphasised the importance of externalities or beneficial 'spillovers' between sectors. These particularly relate to transfers of 'useful knowledge' that enable industries to modernise and individual firms to enhance their competitiveness (see chapters 1 and 5 above).

Input–output models are used to analyse the multiplier effects of transport investment on supply industries. In his study of German railways, Fremdling (1977) modified Rostow's leading sector concept to a leading sector 'complex' by intertwining the railways with several heavy industries. Mitchell (1964) and Gourvish have each shown the input linkages to several key 'complex' industries including coal, iron and steel, and engineering. The linkages were strongest during the construction booms; thus railways have been estimated to have consumed 39 per cent of pig iron production in 1844–51 and 6–10 per cent of coal output (Gourvish 1980: 24–5). The impact upon iron and steel demand was greater if account is taken of the materials used in engineering products for the industry. Knowledge spillovers from railways particularly relate to their pioneering role in meeting the challenges of large-scale enterprise which was discussed above (pp. 317–18) and the precedents they set for new forms of capital raising in finance markets (see pp. 306–7).

Similar analysis could be used in relation to other transport modes. Ships require large amounts of material in their construction. In the earlier part of the period this necessitated substantial timber imports from the Baltic and North America, but also the use of domestic rolled copper sheet for the sheathing of vessel hulls as a protection against marine life (see chapter 15). The metal steamship drew more heavily upon the domestic coal, iron, steel and engineering industries. Indeed, Palmer (1979: 337–9) has estimated that bunker coal represented 20 per cent of British coal exports by the end of the nineteenth century. Shipbuilding contributed to the clustering of heavy industries in conurbations in Tyneside, Clydeside and Belfast, which yielded local external economies of scale such as a highly skilled workforce (see chapter 14). Canal construction had a limited direct impact on supply industries. However, it provided spillover effects through confronting many civil engineering challenges such as tunnels, bridges and embankments, thereby setting a precedent for railway builders and many areas of construction.

Market integration

Quicker, cheaper, more regular and more comprehensive transport fosters market integration. It provides for the widening of markets, the breakdown of local monopolies and other restrictions on competition, the decline of subsistency, the opening up of new areas to production, and improvements in information flows on which producers and markets rely. It can also concentrate markets by ensuring the necessary food supply and residential expansion associated with urbanisation. Similarly, improved transport impacts upon institutions operating within those markets. Wider markets create the opportunity for larger-scale production and economies of scale. Greater regularity of transport facilitates the reduction of inventories, thus enabling the conversion of circulating into fixed capital to finance such expansion. A more flexible and efficient location of production may result, and provide the opportunity for geographical expansion by individual firms nationally and even internationally. Improved information flows, and increased personal mobility, facilitate the geographical expansion of enterprise.

The impact varied according to transport mode: roads and canals generally stimulated local and regional markets, while railways impacted more on national markets, and shipping on international, reflecting the different types of service and cost functions of these modes. Improved road services in England led to the decline of many local markets and their replacement by fewer, larger regional centres (Pawson 1977: 323). This view has been reinforced for waterways by Turnbull, who argued that the economic impact 'was heavily local and regional'. Most freight movement was over comparatively short distances, and long hauls were restricted by the slow development of trunk routes and the 'extreme parochialism of most canal companies' (1987: 540–1). The major regions of industrial expansion in England by 1800 were inland coalfield areas with a canal network; particular beneficiaries were the urban centres of Manchester, Leeds and Sheffield. Coal prices were reduced through lower transport costs and a redistribution of output in favour of lower-cost producers (Turnbull 1987: 557–8). In Scotland the economic integration of the central lowlands region owed much to transport (see chapter 14).

The integration of national markets through the railway can be seen in the decline of regional price differences between producing and consuming areas that enabled greater regional specialisation of production. These included a concentration of brewing firms at Burton, Alloa and Glasgow, food processing at Reading, and confectionery at Birmingham (Cain 1988: 99). Such firms could be located at their preferred location and use the rail system to distribute to a national market. Chandler (1977) has shown the central role of the railroads in facilitating large national firms in the United States, which were able to draw upon remote sources of raw materials and supply long-distance markets. While transport networks evolved over a longer period of time in Britain, railways with their higher terminal but lower per mile costs helped to create national markets and national firms.

The integration of international markets in the eighteenth century was largely restricted to the North Atlantic. Productivity improvements in the tobacco, rice, oil and bullion trades helped to turn the North Atlantic ocean into 'an English inland sea', according to Menard (1996: 270). Overall, however, Ralph Davis's verdict that the shipping industry contributed 'a very small part indeed' (1962: 391) to the changes associated with the classic industrial revolution period remains the consensus. Lower freights provided consumers with cheaper goods and permitted a greater volume of trade but stimulated no major industrial transformation in Britain, a process we now know to have taken longer and stretched through the first half of the nineteenth century.

Harley has drawn attention to the extension of the European and North American trading economies after 1860 as a result of lower international shipping costs (1994: 324–6). O'Rourke and Williamson (1999: 35) argue more broadly that 'it was falling transport costs that provoked globalization' in the second half of the nineteenth century. Commodity market integration in the form of spatial price convergence and production specialisation is used as evidence of this early period of globalisation. They argue that this was brought about by reduced transport costs, or the reduced transport 'wedge' between export and import prices (O'Rourke and Williamson 1999: 30–1). Primarily, this was the coming to fruition of the major advances in shipping over the last fifty years of the nineteenth century, although improved internal transport helped to mitigate the additional wedge of moving freight to and from port.

As well as providing opportunities for increased export penetration, improved transportation facilitated the growth of multinationals. While British firms did not grow as large and dominant in their home market as American ones, they were particularly noted for their activity in international business in the nineteenth century, which owed much to the falling ratio of transport costs as a share of total production costs. Wilkins (1977: 579) has argued that the growth of European, predominantly British, multinationals in the later nineteenth century can be traced to the speeding up of rail and ship communications, which eased the problems of long-distance management. Improved transportation enabled better international transfer of technologies, more effective monitoring of employees and reduced uncertainty regarding conditions in overseas markets.

Social savings

Of the many possible ways of assessing transport's economic impact, the most novel, stimulating but also controversial has been a counterfactual exercise, the social savings methodology, which asks how the economy would have developed without the railway. The methodology adopted is to estimate the additional costs to the economy of carrying goods by other means in the absence of the railway, using data for a specific year post-dating the actual introduction of the railway. Thus, it is the equivalent of closing down the railway system for a year. The initial advocates of social saving analysed American railroads: Fogel (1964) concluded that the economic impact of the railway was modest, and had been previously overstated relative to its main forerunner, the canal. Within the broader debates of economic development, this conclusion challenged the Rostowian idea of unbalanced development – that innovation in a leading sector could cause the 'take off' of an economy.

Hawke (1970: 241–5) applied the social savings approach to Britain's railways. Using the year 1865, he calculated that the use of railways for passenger traffic yielded a saving equivalent to between 1.5 and 6.0 per cent of national income, depending upon whether a reduction of travelling comfort was deemed acceptable. Hawke looked at freight traffic separately and estimated a saving of about 4 per cent of national income. While his results were not much higher than those of Fogel for the United States, he concluded positively for the important growth-inducing role of the railways. He additionally accepted that the social savings approach provided only a partial examination, mostly of the direct economic impact of the railway, and added to this an assessment of the beneficial external economies of the railways in the form of induced cost-savings and growth-inducing secondary effects to other industries. To capture some of the broader impact Hawke calculates a social rate of return of railways of about 15 to 20 per cent and notes that this might be higher if one takes account of changes elsewhere that were not *dependent* on railways but were *facilitated* by them (Hawke 1970: 405–8).

The methodology has attracted as much attention as its conclusions. Among its shortcomings is the terminal weighting problem; the economy would have developed differently without the railway, perhaps to rely less upon transport services and with a different set of relative freight rates. Thus, the social saving would have been different in reality, probably lower. Imperfect substitutability between the railway and other transport modes is a second problem in collecting data. Hawke has been criticised for the limited evidence he produces of freight rates, which also focuses on coaches and canals for passenger and freight traffic respectively but says nothing about highly competitive coastal shipping.

As a comparison, it is interesting to note that a contemporary of the railway era, Dudley Baxter, undertook a similar exercise in calculating that to have conveyed 1865 railway traffic by canal and road at pre-railway rates would have saved the equivalent of 9 per cent of national income, a not dissimilar result from that of Hawke (Gourvish 1988: 82). An alternative counterfactual model could involve deciding which goods would not have been moved in the absence of the railways and thereby calculating the loss to national income in terms of reduced production and trading. Conceivably, this is a more realistic approach, although assumptions about the competitive structure in transport would still hinder its accuracy. Interest in the social savings concept dwindled from the mid-1970s, after a decade of extensive debate that concluded that the concept provided, at best, only a partial analysis of rail's economic impact.

Foreman-Peck revisited the question in 1991, asking the alternative question: how much higher would national income have been if the performance of the railway system had been better? His reworked social savings calculations for 1865, 1890 and 1910 led him to conclude that 'railways were as important to the late Victorian economy as contemporaries thought, and call into question Fogel's claim that railways were only essential in economies like Mexico or Spain where water was scarce' (Foreman-Peck 1991: 90).

The social saving methodology has never been applied extensively to other transport modes, probably because it was only the railway that was particularly novel, unlike new forms of road and water transport. However, a study of malt movements by canal from Hertfordshire to east London by brewers Truman in the first half of the nineteenth century calculated the 'social saving' as a proportion of the company's expenditure. By this means it was estimated that waterways were a 1 to 3 per cent saving on the roads, while the railway was a saving of only 0.19 to 0.29 per cent on waterways (Jones 1986). Hawke and Higgins (1981: 248–9) calculated a 'conjectural, non-factual' social saving for freight carried on canals over road transport as 1.4 to 6.9 per cent, depending on whether the average journey was closer to 20 or 100 miles. Hawke suspects it was closer to 20, giving a result not very different from Jones.

CONCLUSION

Transport featured heavily in the economic history of Britain in this period. It witnessed the introduction of the railway system and the extension of road, inland waterway, shipping and urban transport structures and services. Technological and organisational changes drove the growth of output and productivity, while financial innovations and legal instruments helped overcome potential impediments. Strategic, monopoly and public good elements of transport attracted an uncommon degree of government attention. Besides questions of defence, particularly associated with shipping, policy makers sought a degree of balance between social and private returns from transport for reasons of both equity (distribution of benefits and costs) and efficiency (optimal levels of investment). Government concern at the market power of some transport firms is not surprising: they were among the largest, most capital hungry, spatially diverse and thus organisationally complex businesses of the time. Responses to these challenges included the development of close working relations with other firms, particularly specialist agencies and intermediaries. For the larger railway companies in particular, new internal information, accounting and labour management strategies were developed under the control of professional executives within new organisational structures. Assessing the overall economic impact of transport services is perhaps the hardest task in light of the pervasive, and difficult to measure, externalities of this major form of social overhead capital. Transport has represented a nationally important form of investment that was increasingly productive over time and frequently drove, as well as responded to, change. It was closely linked to, and facilitated the growth and innovation of, leading industries such as iron and steel, coal, engineering and building materials. The increased speed, coverage, regularity but falling cost of transport services help to support the belief that they facilitated market integration and economic linkages. The impact of transport extended from the local stimulus of road and waterway through the growth of national markets by way of rail, to the early phases of globalisation occasioned by ocean shipping.

12

Education and skill of the British labour force

DAVID MITCH

Contents

Introduction   332
The acquisition of skill and education in 1700   334
   Biological maintenance as human capital   334
   Training and apprenticeship   336
   Education and schooling   340
Trends in human capital accumulation, 1700 to 1860   343
Underinvestment in human capital?   350
The contribution of education and skill formation to
   economic growth, 1700 and 1860   353

INTRODUCTION

Suppose that a deadly plague had swept through Britain in 1860, extermi-
nating its entire population of 23 million people. Suppose then that immediately thereafter a sea-borne group of 23 million unschooled Eskimos
(Inuit) had come upon Britain and settled the initially unpopulated area,
but still possessing all the buildings, machinery and materials of the mid-
Victorian economy at its height. One would expect a massive fall in the
production of the economy to occur, given the unsuitability of Eskimo
skills for the mid-Victorian environment and economy of Britain.[1] This
should be attributed to a mismatch of skills, not to some inherent naïveté
of the Eskimos. Indeed, an analogous transference of the mid-Victorian
British population north of the Arctic Circle would result in a similar initial drop in output relative to Eskimo levels, and survival itself would be

---

[1] William Farr (2001 [1877]: 570), the prominent nineteenth-century statistician, proposed
a similar thought experiment. Farr asked, 'put barbarians in possession of the land, the
mines, the manufactures, the machines, the ships, the triumphant position of these islands
on the sea between two continents, and what would be the result?' I am grateful to Richard
Smith for pointing out this reference.

at stake, given the unsuitability of Victorian English skills for subsisting in an Arctic environment.

Just how large the fall would be is of course subject to considerable speculation. One can get some sense of possible magnitudes by looking at the difference between the actual share of national income going to labour in Britain *c.* 1860 and the share that labour would have received if paid at unskilled wage rates. Labour's share of national income for Britain in 1856 has been estimated at 57.8 per cent (Matthews *et al.* 1982: 164). Gross domestic product for the United Kingdom in 1860 has been put at £683 million (Feinstein 1972: T4). The United Kingdom working population in 1860 was around 12.98 million people (Feinstein 1972). This yields a labour income per working Briton of £30.41. A rough indicator of unskilled earnings would be 10 shillings per week for males and 5 shillings per week for females (based on agricultural earnings in each case). For Britain in 1860, 69.1 per cent of the labour force was male and 30.9 per cent was female (Mitchell 1988). Applying these weights to these wage figures yields a mean wage per unskilled person occupied at fifty-two weeks per year of £22. This implies that, if the non-labour element of national income were to remain unchanged, the reduction of national income per capita would be 15.41 per cent. While this calculation begs many issues, if anything there are reasons for thinking that it understates the loss of output due to lack of suitable skills. To begin with, although farm work has often been taken as setting a floor on adult wages, many common farm tasks did require skill and it is doubtful whether Eskimos could have immediately taken over basic farm labour positions (Mitch 1994). Furthermore, no allowance is made for differences in the age composition of the British and Eskimo populations and for rising productivity (and eventually falling productivity) with age, even in nominally unskilled positions. Consider a rough adjustment for age structure by assuming that the active labour force was between the ages of 10 and 60, with the population aged 10 to 20 at half the productivity of that aged 20 to 60. Based on Mitchell (1988), 29 per cent of the active British labour force in 1861 was aged 10 to 19 and 71 per cent was aged 20 to 59. This lowers the unskilled mean wage per person to £18.76, and raises the reduction in average national income per capita to 21.6 per cent. This latter figure is in line with the estimates proposed by Crafts (1995: 752) in the range of 25 to 32 per cent and William Farr (1877, reprinted 2001) of 25 per cent.

While a decline of national income of at best 35 per cent, using the upper end of Crafts's estimates, resulting from a complete Eskimo repopulation of Britain may seem modest, the attributed share to skill and education is sizeable relative to the corresponding shares that would be attributed to capital and labour. Even the lower estimate above of the skill and education share of 15 per cent is non-trivial relative to the implied combined residual to 'raw' labour and physical capital of 85 per cent.

Skill and education contributed at least one-sixth as much to national income as raw labour and physical capital combined in Britain in 1860. This chapter examines the composition of these skills and how they were acquired, looking first at the conditions around 1700, and then at the developments over the period to 1860. The chapter concludes by evaluating the effect of education and skill formation on overall economic performance.

THE ACQUISITION OF SKILL AND EDUCATION IN 1700

The acquisition of skill and education can be usefully examined with the concept of human capital. According to human capital theory, enhancement of the productive power of the human being entails an investment analogous to that of investment in machinery and similar forms of physical capital. On the cost side of human capital investment, someone may be willing to sacrifice immediate income in order to enhance their future productivity, whether this be by incurring tuition payments and lost earnings to pursue a course of schooling or by sacrificing earnings and paying a premium to undergo an apprenticeship. On the benefit side, just as a machine yields a flow of services over time so does the productive human being. Viewing the productive human as a capital asset yielding a flow of services over time implies some basic influences on its value. As a capital asset, future earnings flows should be discounted to reflect the premium placed on current over future income. The longer the productive human can be expected to yield services because of a lower rate of mortality during the years of active labour force participation, the greater its expected value as a productive asset. From the perspective of a national or other geographical political unit, net emigration of productive labour will reduce the stock of human capital, while net immigration will raise it. British emigration and immigration rates until 1860 were still small enough for these population flows to have little effect on the value of the country's investment in human capital. However, subsequent increases in emigration rates in the last third of the century were sufficiently large to offset the impact of falling mortality on the stock of human capital within Britain (Baines 1994).

Biological maintenance as human capital

For the first few years of life, the family (or substitutes *in loco parentis*) is fundamental in shaping the developing human being: in providing nutrition, in developing language and in instilling formative habits in a variety of dimensions. Population maintenance, not to mention population growth, requires a diversion of resources from other activities and is thus an investment in human capital. Although population maintenance is often taken for granted in the common case of children raised by biological parents, it still presumes sufficiently strong familial attachments over time for the commitment of resources to dependent children to occur. In early modern England, in cases where such attachments were not present, alternative institutional provisions were established.

Apprenticeship was one means used to provide for maintenance of orphans and children in families deemed too poor to support them. In the reign of Henry VIII, provision was made for so-called parish apprentices, ante-dating the 1563 Statute of Artificers which included regulations on vocational apprenticeship (Dunlop 1912). The basic economic and contractual logic of parish apprenticeship appears to be similar to that commonly thought to motivate vocational apprenticeship: the master provided something of value to the apprentice in exchange for the use of the apprentice's labour services. In the case of parish apprenticeship, the master would provide maintenance to the apprentice such as food, lodging and clothing in exchange for the apprentice's labour services. Training in the master's trade was also commonly provided so the apprentice could support him or herself on reaching adulthood. A master should have been willing to do this if the value of the apprentice's labour services at least equalled the cost of maintenance and training services provided by the master. In this regard, the length of service could have been adjusted to bring the expected value of labour services at least into equality with the value of maintenance services. This arrangement would permit the parish to meet its responsibility to provide for the upbringing of impoverished children and youths without burdening it with ongoing payments throughout the period of maturation of a given individual. In so far as there was uncertainty about whether the apprentice would complete the agreed length of service or about the quality of the apprentice's work, the master could be paid an up-front premium in compensation. But this in turn would place the burden on the parish and its rate payers of funding this premium.

In practice it appears that, as a strict economic exchange, parish apprenticeship was frequently not viable: parishes often had difficulty finding masters willing to take on apprentices even with the offer of a one or two pound premium (Dunlop 1912). This suggests that the expected value of labour services provided by the apprentice was less than expected maintenance and training costs. Cross-parish trafficking in parish apprentices developed as overseers in one parish attempted to place their pauper apprentices in another parish in order to shift the burden of dependency to the destination parish. The late eighteenth-century rise in north-west England of textile factories located in rural areas near water sources providing energy, but distant from labour supplies, seemed to open up a new source of demand for parish apprentice labour. Many pauper apprentices were relocated from London and other urban areas to rural textile factories. However, even in these circumstances of labour scarcity, the experience of many factory masters was that parish apprentice labour did not pay: the value of labour services provided was below its maintenance cost (Rose 1989). Parish apprenticeship was generally replaced by other pauper provisions in the early nineteenth century (Pinchbeck and Hewitt 1973: ch. 17).

Training and apprenticeship

After the age of 5 or so, in addition to issues of biological maintenance, an increasing range of conscious choices could be made regarding individual development. Currently, it is expected that the young will spend the period from 5 or so through at least mid-adolescence (age 15 or 16) and possibly into their early twenties in some form of education or training in preparation for future life. With a working life of say forty-five to fifty years, this means that an amount of time equal to 20 per cent or more of total working life is devoted to the acquisition of skill and mental improvement.

In the past, a smaller proportion of (a shorter) working life was typically devoted to acquiring skills, but families were central to this process of education and training. It has been common throughout history for children to inherit the occupations of their parents. In some situations, the inheritance may have been literal, as in the passing on of land or aristocratic title or passing on of a family business. In other situations, the influence may have been more indirect, but significant all the same. And in the course of bequeathing their occupations, parents would also have transmitted skills, knowledge and culture.

Those undertaking apprenticeships in early modern Europe frequently, though by no means universally or even predominantly, entered the same occupations as their parents (Rappaport 1989: 308–10; Epstein 1991: 105).[2] Turning from apprentices to the population at large for the period 1839–43, a sample of marriage registers from some twenty-nine counties of England indicates that 48 per cent of grooms at marriage reported identical occupational titles to those of their fathers. Of course such high rates of inheritance were by no means similar down the occupational hierarchy, as Table 12.1 demonstrates. Furthermore, the relatively large shares of certain occupations in the labour force would imply high rates of intergenerational occupational inheritance simply as a matter of chance over and above any process of skill transmission. That is one factor explaining the high occupational inheritance rate for labourers.

---

[2] Studies of early modern England that emphasise the diverse social and occupational origins of apprentices into particular trades include Ben-Amos 1994; Dunlop 1912; Rushton 1991: 93. Furthermore, Rappaport (1989), cited in the text, emphasises the role of intergenerational occupational inheritance primarily for those entering the Great Companies in London. For apprenticeship more generally, his findings point to more diverse recruitment sources.

Nevertheless, a disproportionate tendency for occupational inheritance is still evident, especially for such occupations as farmers and miners. The greater importance of agriculture in the economy of 1700, with its arguably less diversified occupational structure than the non-agricultural sector, would suggest an occupational inheritance rate at least as high then as a century and a half later.

In so far as the majority of the English labour force in 1700 was involved in agriculture, most children and adolescents prepared for adult work gradually by performing increasingly complex tasks in agriculture as they matured. For the most part the sequence of tasks would have been unstructured but, given that they related to the child's ultimate work setting, would have provided effective training for adult work (Ben-Amos 1994). Even if the child followed in the occupational footsteps of his or her parents, he or she did not necessarily directly receive training or involvement with relevant experiences from them. And both temporary and longer-term separation from one's parents would have been common. Adolescents could be employed in agriculture as day labourers as well as under longer-term seasonal and annual service arrangements. Turnover and migration rates were quite high for farm servants, with many changing employers at least annually (Kussmaul 1981) as well as alternating between casual day employment and longer-term service arrangements (Ben-Amos 1994). Service

Table 12.1   Exact-title occupational inheritance at marriage: percentage of grooms in various occupational categories reporting exactly the same occupational title as their fathers, for grooms from a sample of twenty-nine English counties married during the period 1839–43.

Occupational category	% of grooms listing occ. title of father
Agricultural labourer	16.7
Agricultural skilled	27.8
Construction	46.3
Clerical	16.9
Dealers	29.1
Elite professional	15.5
Farmer	83.6
High commercial	17.4
Skilled metal	39.6
Other skilled	25.5
Skilled textiles	34.6
Hawkers	16.7
Low professional	17.2
Miner	69.1
Mine supervisor	25.0
Manufacturing foreman	12.5
Manufacturing	28.6
Manufacturing labourer	33.5
Manufacturing proprietor	42.9
Military enlisted	0
Military officer	0
Petty trader	25.7
Personal service	11.4
Small farmer	45.3
Semi-skilled metal	33.3
Other semi-skilled	33.3
Semi-skilled textiles	42.7
Titled aristocracy	53.1
Transport	35.4
Transport foreman	37.5
Transport labourer	9.3
Labourer	75.4

Source: Mitch 1993a: 147.

may, in many instances, have simply constituted the highest-paying opportunity available for adolescents and young adults rather than constituting a definite investment in training and acquisition of productivity-enhancing experience. Wages paid to servants increased with age (Kussmaul 1981: 143–5), which can be attributed to growing physical and mental maturation as well as acquisition of agricultural experience. Available evidence does not indicate whether monetary compensation in farm service was lower than in alternative forms of employment and thus whether acquisition of experience in this manner would have required sacrifice of foregone earnings.

Informal arrangements (that is, without an explicitly specified contract regarding length of service and other terms) for receiving instruction or productivity-enhancing experience in particular non-agricultural trades were also common and these could still entail a sacrifice in alternative earnings (Dunlop 1912). While institutional provision for skill acquisition and education is often the focus of discussions of training, simple experience could often be the fundamental basis of skill. Thus, empirically based judgement was the source of skill in iron and steel making and in coal mining (Harris 1976; Berg 1985: 267–8). Despite the presence of informal arrangements for skill acquisition, formal apprenticeship was common in many occupations. Apprenticeship agreements for particular crafts and trades constituted a clearer form of human capital investment than annual or seasonal service in husbandry because the agreements specified that training and experience leading to mastery of the craft in question were to be provided to the apprentice by the master. As with parish apprenticeships, in private apprenticeship agreements the excess of the value of labour services provided by the apprentice over and above the value of maintenance and any remuneration provided by the master would compensate for the cost of training. The investment in skill acquisition implied by working at compensation below that available elsewhere was amplified by agreeing to do so for a number of years in contrast with the annual or seasonal contract that typified service in husbandry.

Since apprenticeship arrangements involved an exchange over time, they were subject to the risk of breach by both parties involved. Apprentices could desert after receiving training but prior to completing a length of service sufficient to compensate for the training; the more general the applicability of the training, the easier it would be to find another employer and the greater the risk of desertion. And the master could fail to provide training sufficient to compensate for the flow of labour services provided by the apprentice. Humphries (2003) has recently argued that English apprenticeship came to be structured in such a way that it was generally self-enforcing with regard to these problems of potential default. Apprentices who deserted would find it difficult to practise the trade in which they had trained, given collective guild solidarity as well as the formal legal protection to masters provided by the Statute of Artificers of 1563. This statute made apprenticeship mandatory for entry into a wide range of occupations and set a seven-year minimum period of apprenticeship for all occupations covered (Dunlop 1912).

Masters who provided inadequate training or reneged on maintenance provisions were subject not only to the sanction of law (though this was frequently difficult to implement) but also to the opprobrium of the local community, of the apprentice's family and of peers in the guild desirous of maintaining its reputation. A further incentive provided to the apprentice to complete his or her contract was that successful completion conferred valuable 'settlement rights' on the individual (which entitled him or her to poor law support from the parish in the event of destitution). The relatively high degree of urbanisation and the large non-agricultural labour force present in England as early as 1700 can in part be attributed, according to Humphries (2003), to the way in which the institution of apprenticeship facilitated rural to urban migration.

However, there are other aspects of apprenticeship that qualify the extent to which it was an efficiency-enhancing institution that facilitated human capital investment. One motive for guilds to establish and enforce formal apprenticeship contracts was to create barriers to entry into the crafts and trades in question and hence to establish and reinforce the monopoly position of those who completed the relevant apprenticeships. Often sizeable up-front premiums were charged by the master to take on an apprentice (Lane 1996: 22–5). The magnitude of these premiums, well over £100 in some crafts, suggests that their function was to serve as a barrier to entry rather than as compensation for a shorter term of apprentice service or as an insurance premium for the risk of apprentice desertion.

Parliament enacted national legislation regulating apprenticeship in clauses in the 1563 Statute of Artificers. That it did so when apprenticeship arrangements could have been left to private contracting or local specification by urban guilds is worthy of note and has been subject to conflicting interpretations. Dunlop (1912: ch. 4) interprets the apprenticeship clauses of the statute as reflecting a desire both to improve and standardise training processes and to minimise possible sources of dispute between apprentices and their masters over contractual arrangements. However, Dunlop (1912: 86) also acknowledges that these clauses did not hinder and probably enhanced the efforts of guilds to establish barriers to entry into various occupations and hence raise the earnings of those employed in them. In any event, the seven-year term which these clauses made standard across the many occupations covered implied allocating a substantial proportion of one's working life to the period of apprenticeship.

Since apprenticeships in early modern England were commonly begun in mid to late adolescence (Dunlop 1912; Rappaport 1989; Ben-Amos 1994) and often did not terminate until youths were in their mid-twenties, the foregone earnings implied by not receiving a direct wage remuneration could be sizeable. The approximate magnitude of the investment involved can be gauged by estimating the opportunity cost (the income foregone) of an apprenticeship at 10 shillings a week, corresponding to an unskilled wage, over fifty-two weeks and for the standard seven years. This of course omits provision for food, lodging and other maintenance expenses which would have been incurred even without serving an apprenticeship and hence is an upper-bound calculation. The foregone earnings involved would come to £26 a year or a cumulative sum over seven years of £182.

A rough estimate for the number of males completing an apprenticeship in 1700 can be put at 11,500.[3] Multiplying this by an investment in apprenticeship of £182 and making what is almost surely an upper-bound allowance of an average service life per apprentice of forty years yields a human capital stock in apprenticeship in 1700 of £84 million.[4] A lower service life per apprentice of twenty-five years to allow for risk of mortality during prime working ages would correspondingly lower the human capital stock in apprenticeship to £52 million.[5] This would appear modest in comparison with Feinstein's (1981) estimate of a physical capital stock for England in 1760 of £810 million and Allen's (1994) estimate of a capital stock in agriculture in 1700 of £183 million.

Education and schooling

Education and the process of incorporation into society in early eighteenth-century England were also conducted through institutions more familiar to twenty-first century readers, namely schools. Despite

---

[3] To obtain this estimate, an estimate of the male population aged 21 in England in 1700 of 41,000 was obtained from the Wrigley–Schofield (1981) estimates of total population in 1701 and their estimate that 16.35 per cent of that population was between the ages of 15 and 24 and assuming that 10 per cent of that group was aged 21 and half of those were male.

To estimate the number of males aged 21 completing an apprenticeship in urban areas, Rappaport's (1989) estimate that two-thirds of all adult males in London in the sixteenth century had completed an apprenticeship was assumed to apply to all 21-year-olds in all urban areas in England in 1700, employing Crafts's (1994) estimate that 17 per cent of the English population in 1700 resided in urban areas, yielding an estimate of 4,670 urban males aged 21 having just completed an apprenticeship. The number of 21-year-olds completing apprenticeships in rural areas is estimated by applying to the estimated rural population an estimate that 20 per cent had completed apprenticeships, based on Ben-Amos's (1994: 79) finding that for migrants into Bristol between 1600 and 1645 from villages, 21 per cent had parents in craft occupations. This yields an estimate of 6,800 21-year-olds in rural areas who had just completed an apprenticeship, giving a total for urban plus rural 21-year-olds completing an apprenticeship of 11,470, which is rounded up to 11,500. This is likely to be a considerable overestimate of the number completing apprenticeships. Humphries's (2003) survey of the extent of apprenticeship suggests that Rappaport's two-thirds figure for sixteenth-century London was considerably higher than in other English urban areas. Moreover, applying Rappaport's sixteenth-century figure to 1700 would overstate the number of completed apprenticeships in so far as Dunlop and others have been correct to argue that apprenticeship had been in decline from the sixteenth century.

[4] Making allowance for the fact that many apprenticeships actually lasted less than seven years would further lower this estimate. No adjustment is made for price changes over time in the cost of apprenticeship. The basic approach of using an estimated service life to convert annual investment flows into a cumulative capital stock is outlined by Feinstein (1978: 35–6; 1981: 130–2).

[5] The downward estimate of an expected service life of twenty-five years was obtained by assuming a 1 per cent risk of mortality per year between the ages of 21 and 61 (based on Baines 1994). This implies that the probability of a 21-year-old surviving for another forty years was two-thirds or an expected service of life of twenty-five years.

the absence of any centrally administered or financed schooling network, one can surmise that by 1700 a substantial minority of English children would have spent at least some time in school. The 1851 Census of Education indicates that, by that date, 60 per cent of boys and 56 per cent of girls aged 5 to 9 were scholars. Relatively sluggish growth of literacy and schools in the century and a half prior to this would suggest that the level of school attendance in the early eighteenth century would have been between perhaps 20 and 40 per cent of this age group. Therefore, attending school in early eighteenth-century England was not an uncommon experience, even for many working-class children (Jones 1938; Hans 1951; Simon 1968; Lawson and Silver 1973; O'Day 1982; Mitch 1993). For this period it is estimated that between 40 and 50 per cent of adults could sign their name (Cressy 1980). Although basic reading and writing skills were often acquired outside of formal schooling during this period, these figures would suggest widespread familiarity with what was done in school. Schools were quite heterogeneous in their financing and in their educational aims (Lawson and Silver 1973; O'Day 1982). The majority of students were probably in private-venture schools, i.e. single-teacher operations (commonly neighbourhood women or dames or elderly men lacking alternative employment) run for profit. The curriculum would have focused on basic literacy and whatever other odd subjects the teacher wanted to throw in. Schools with religious affiliation and support were widespread as well, though religious motives behind the propagation of education did not attain the same level of intensity as in other Protestant regions such as Sweden and Germany (Houston 1988b: 40–8). Philanthropists also supported schools without any formal religious affiliation (Lawson and Silver 1973: 181–2).

A child reaching adolescence around 1700 would have been relatively unlikely to attend school, given the rise in his or her opportunity costs (foregone earnings) with maturation. Traditional grammar schools, together with academies run by and for religious dissenters, did provide some secondary instruction (O'Day 1982: ch. 11). The Universities of Oxford and Cambridge offered higher education, and institutions for more specialised professional training such as the Inns of Court were present in London. Such post-primary education would have been pursued by well under 5 per cent of the relevant age group in early eighteenth-century England. Many children would have made their subsequent way in life through the school of hard knocks: finding employment as adolescents in order to take advantage of their maturing earning power or, in the case of females, helping out at home (Ben-Amos 1994).

Because of its shorter length and the younger age when it would have occurred, with consequent lower opportunity cost, the typical personal investment in formal schooling would have cost considerably less than the typical apprenticeship. For example, three years of schooling between the ages of 8 and 10, perhaps roughly sufficient to acquire basic literacy, can be costed as having direct fees of 6 pence per week and opportunity costs per week usually exceeding no more than 2 shillings. At forty weeks of attendance per year, this implies a total cost per person of £15. Assume that 40 per cent of an estimated 100,000 English 10-year-olds in 1700 had been in school for three years and that the average working life for those reaching the age of 10 was a further thirty-five years.[6] This yields a further cumulative human capital stock in literacy and related primary schooling for males and females of £21 million, about half of the estimated cumulative investment in male apprenticeship of £52 million. This combined human capital stock in both literacy and primary schooling for males and females and in apprenticeship for males in 1700 of £73 million is still well under half of Allen's (1994) estimates of the capital stock in agriculture in 1700 of £183 million.

The benefits from apprenticeship, in terms of a stream of enhanced earnings once qualified, were potentially large. This is suggested by Gregory King's assignment of an annual income per family of £40 for those in artisan and handicraft occupations compared with £15 for labouring people and outservants (Mathias 1979: 186–7). However, the percentage rate of return for schooling may have been higher, relative to its markedly lower opportunity and total costs.

Apprenticeship and formal schooling were by no means incompatible. Indeed in a range of contexts, pursuit of apprenticeship was based on an earlier foundation of formal schooling. This would have occurred in professions such as law and medicine, in which some instruction in basic languages and other disciplines would generally be expected before entering the apprenticeship upon which professional training in the early eighteenth century was generally based. One important activity, for which formal schooling was the foundation for apprenticeship and related on-the-job experience, was that of the merchant. Pollard (1965) has suggested affinities between the education and training of the merchant and that of subsequent industrialists in the early industrial revolution. The merchant commonly mastered both general skills such as basic literacy and more specific skills suitable for commerce such as accounting and mastery of certain modern languages used in trade. Malachy Postlethwayt (1774) proposed in the mid-eighteenth century that a formal commercial academy be set up for this purpose. Although nothing came of this proposal, dissenting academies set up a similar curriculum (O'Day 1982: 208–15, 270).[7] Aspiring merchants commonly started as agents in distant locations as preparation for acquiring more senior status in merchant houses

---

[6] The thirty-five-year expected service life figure for a 10-year-old comes from the admittedly quite crude adjustment of simply adding ten years to the previous rough estimate of a twenty-five-year service life for a 21-year-old.

[7] A lecture given by Leone Levi (1868) in 1868 indicates that at that time, King's College, London was offering classes in physical geography, commerce and commercial law aimed at the aspiring merchant. However, Levi's remarks also suggest that few students were actually taking these classes.

(Ben-Amos 1994: 124–7). Given the creative nature of entrepreneurial activity, it is not clear that training for entrepreneurship can be provided in a systematic way. It was probably at least as critical in guaranteeing a supply of entrepreneurs that relatively few barriers and disincentives were created for those wishing to pursue their entrepreneurial proclivities.

TRENDS IN HUMAN CAPITAL ACCUMULATION, 1700–1860

The century and a half that is surveyed in this volume is commonly seen as a period of profound change and transformation in the English economy. One might expect corresponding evidence of fundamental change in the education of the English labour force. Yet educational histories of this period tend to suggest a pattern more of stagnation than of improvement. However, evidence on schooling and other forms of investment in human capital during this period is fragmentary. This sets the tasks of examining the evidence for educational stagnation and how the relationship between educational trends and economic change can be understood.

Literacy rates as measured by signature rates at marriage provide the most easily quantifiable indicator of trends in education between 1700 and 1860. Signature rates are not without difficulty as measures of reading and writing ability, but nevertheless long-term trends in signature rates are likely to reflect trends in the latter (Schofield 1973; Houston 1988b; Reay 1991). Cressy (1980: 176), having examined a range of sources such as legal documents which indicate signature rates, has suggested that, at the accession of George I in 1714, approximately 45 per cent of men and 25 per cent of women could sign their names (see Figure 12.1). Cressy's assessment is that this reflects continuous improvement since 1500, at which date perhaps at best 10 per cent of men, and an even smaller per centage of women, could sign their names. By this point, as Table 12.2 shows, other countries already had an educational lead over England. North America and Sweden stand out in this regard (Graff 1987: ch. 6). It is also commonly believed that Scotland had higher literacy rates than England, though recent research has qualified this view (Houston 1985). England seems to have been in a similar position to France, and was perhaps behind Germany and Holland, but almost surely ahead of areas in southern and eastern Europe such as Spain, Italy and Russia (Graff 1987: ch. 6). As already suggested, while literacy was not acquired exclusively in schools, these literacy figures probably in some degree reflected the widespread network of primary schools which were present throughout England at this time.

A similar intermediate position in higher levels of educational attainment characterises the international standing of England's universities and scientific establishment in 1700 (Stone 1974; O'Day 1982: 273–5;

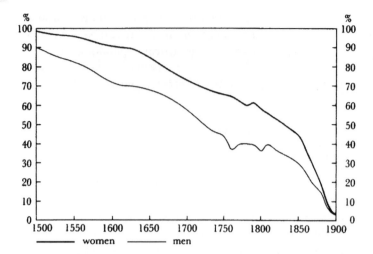

Figure 12.1
Estimated illiteracy of
men and women in
England, 1500–1900

Source: Cressy 1980:
177.

Houston 1988b: ch. 4; Inkster 1991). Scotland and the Netherlands had far more vibrant activity than England in such fields as law and medicine. But despite recurrent disdainful comments about Oxford and Cambridge, these universities did have some scholars making respectable if not exceptionally brilliant intellectual contributions.

Schofield (1973) has made national-level estimates of trends in signature rates for brides and grooms at marriage for England between 1750 and 1840 (see Figure 12.2). Some improvement in ability of brides to sign their name is evident, with the proportion rising from about a third in the 1750s to about half in the 1830s. However, for grooms, any rise was more modest, increasing from perhaps 60 to 70 per cent over this period. Moreover, regional studies focusing on Lancashire, a focal point of the growth of cotton textile manufacture, have found deteriorating signature rates during industrialisation (Sanderson 1972a). This assessment has been subject to some debate. Laqueur (1974) has argued that literacy rates were actually rising modestly in industrialising Lancashire. And Nicholas and Nicholas (1992) have constructed national literacy estimates by occupational grouping, indicating that rates were actually rising during a first phase of industrialisation through the late eighteenth century, followed by a decline which they interpret as reflecting a deskilling phase of industrialisation. More generally, considerable variation in local and regional literacy trends has been noted (Schofield 1973; Stephens 1987). Nevertheless, the preponderance

Table 12.2 Literacy for selected areas in Europe and North America c. 1700		
Region	Male literacy rate	Female literacy rate
England	40%	25%
France	29%	14%
Amsterdam	70%	44%
Moklinta, Sweden (reading ability)	89%	89%
Iceland	Almost 50%	Almost 50%
New England	70%	

Note: Literacy rates for England, France and Amsterdam based on signature rates at marriage.
Sources: Cressy 1980; Graff 1987.

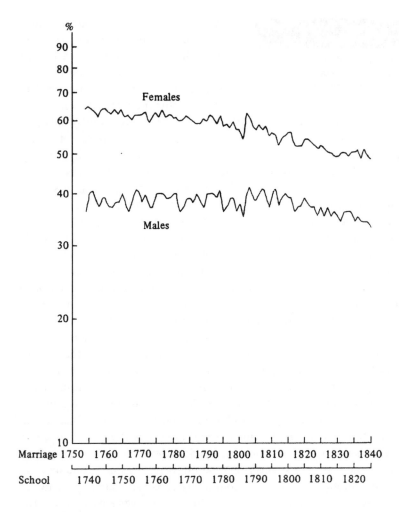

%

of evidence suggests little overall upward trend in literacy rates before the second quarter of the nineteenth century.

Evidence on corresponding schooling trends is much more patchy. In considering likely developments, it is useful to distinguish between the private-venture, for-profit schooling market and schools that were financed at least in part by subsidies. There is no reason to think there were any major changes between 1700 and 1850 in the private-venture schooling market. It is likely to have expanded and contracted with working-class demand. There would seem to have been a ready and elastic supply of those willing to sell instructional services at prevailing market rates (Gardner 1984). There is little reason to think there was an expansion in working-class demand during the industrial revolution period, in so far as neither living standards nor labour market demands for schooled workers were increasing.

Figure 12.2
Estimated annual percentage of males and females unable to sign at marriage, 1754–1840 (from a random sample of 274 English parish registers)

Source: Schofield 1973: 445.

Table 12.3 Proportion of population under 20 in England and Wales who were scholars, 1818–71				
1818	1833	1851	1861	1871
0.128	0.179	0.267	0.346	0.355

Source: Mitch 1982: 10.

Turning to subsidised schools, there does seem to have been an extensive charity school network in the early eighteenth century. However, there is little evidence to suggest clear revival or growth of this network (Simon 1968). Beginning in the early nineteenth century, various religiously affiliated societies do seem to have been active in promoting the growth of schooling provision. The national surveys sponsored by parliament in 1818 and 1833 are themselves evidence of awakened national interest in schooling activity. And in 1833 parliament began to fund the building of schools and subsequently developed apparatus for supporting running costs as well as for the development of curriculum standards and the provision of teacher training and certification. The impact of this was revealed in rising enrolment rates in day schools between 1818 and 1851. Yet private-venture enrolments appear to have kept up with subsidised enrolments throughout this period. The proportion of all scholars who were enrolled in private venture schools was more or less the same, at 60 per cent, in both the 1818 and the 1833 national educational surveys.

Sunday schools experienced the clearest surge of activity in the late eighteenth and early nineteenth centuries. They were virtually non-existent before the late eighteenth century. By the second quarter of the nineteenth century, Sunday school enrolments exceeded those in day schools. While Sunday schools commonly had religious affiliations and sponsorships, they also appear to have offered some secular instruction in basic literacy skills. Historians have differed over the extent to which their expansion was driven by working-class demand for secular education or by the supply of sponsoring religious organisations (Laqueur 1976; Dick 1980). Sunday schools were commonly used as an alternative to day school instruction. Sunday school enrolment rates were positively correlated with child labour force participation and negatively correlated with literacy rates (Laqueur 1976; Mitch 1992; Snell 1999).

The period 1700 through 1860 does not appear to have been one of general expansion or improvement for secondary and university education. Secondary education during the eighteenth century was subject to conflicting forces. Inflation had eroded the value of many grammar school endowments but students seeking commercial and related types of practical education contributed to the growth of dissenting academies (Parker 1969; O'Day 1982). Enrolments at Oxford and Cambridge reached a nadir in the mid-eighteenth century and university enrolments relative to population continued to decline in England through the mid-nineteenth century (Sanderson 1972b: 3; Stone 1974). In any case, no more than a small percentage of the population would have enrolled in secondary or higher education during this period. There does appear to have been an upsurge in more informal intellectual institutions such as literary, philosophical and scientific societies and in free-lance lecture series with quite diverse aims and clientele (Musson and Robinson 1969; O'Day 1982: 210; Inkster 1991) but the magnitude and significance of this activity are difficult to gauge.

Turning to trends in other forms of human capital than schooling, formal apprenticeship is commonly seen as going into decline during the eighteenth century, culminating in repeal of the Statute of Artificers in 1814. Dunlop's (1912) assessment is that compulsory apprenticeship under the terms of the Statute of Artificers was in decline as early as the late seventeenth century. According to her, over the course of the eighteenth century, capitalist master employers who increasingly demanded less skilled labour than that implied by a seven-year apprenticeship term were able to evade the conditions of the Statute. In trades in which guilds were able to maintain their control over entry or in which an extensive apprenticeship period was genuinely required for mastery of the skills involved, apprenticeship, albeit voluntary, persisted into the nineteenth century. Snell (1985), using settlement documents for artisans from southern England, found that the length of apprenticeship terms declined appreciably in the second half of the eighteenth century compared with the first half. He argued that this occurred because apprentices perceived shrinking opportunities for utilising the skills acquired and hence less value in completing their apprenticeships. This decline was in evidence in the apprenticeship documents that Snell examined for women as well. However, Berg (1987: 75) has suggested that the purpose of female apprenticeships was more often to provide support and socialisation while awaiting marriage than mastery of specific crafts. Furthermore, with the decline in the agricultural sector and shift of labour out of agriculture, both the more structured institutions such as service and the more informal exposure to agricultural work that served as training would have been on the decline as well.

Some have argued that the eighteenth-century decline of apprenticeship was followed by further deskilling tendencies in the early nineteenth century, with the rise of outwork or so-called sweated trades and the increasing employment of women in unskilled manufacturing occupations, especially textiles and metal manufactures (Berg 1987). According to this view, the ready supply of low-wage labour, especially female labour, made it profitable to divide up manufacturing processes in clothing, textiles and metal working into specialised steps, each requiring dexterity that it was thought female labour could provide but which did not entail a long period of skill acquisition.

On the other hand more informal sorts of skill acquisition arrangements arose as alternatives to apprenticeship. Boot (1995) has argued that the effective period of training in cotton textile factories could be at least as long as traditional formal apprenticeship, and perhaps as long as ten years, implying comparable magnitudes of human capital investment and well in excess of what characterised typical patterns of formal schooling. It can be argued that such informal arrangements were better suited than traditional apprenticeships to the development and acquisition of the range of new empirically based skills that were important for the newly emerging technologies fuelling industrialisation. Informal training could be adjusted in length to suit newly emerging and expanding skills and occupations. In addition factory masters wanted to instil habits of discipline and routine in their workforce that may have been incompatible with guild and artisan traditions of independence, instead requiring a more coercive approach (Pollard 1959).

Furthermore, Boot (1991) has documented the introduction of age-related clerical salaries in the Bank of Scotland between 1780 and 1830 in contrast to previous apparently level age-earnings gradients for clerical staff in the bank. Boot attributes this change to the effort of the bank to create an internal labour market in response to changing conditions in the clerical labour market. He suggests that this reflected an increasing tendency over time for relevant skills in the bank to rise with age.

Net trends in skill acquisition are difficult to ascertain. Williamson (1985) has argued that there was a rising premium for skill over the first half of the nineteenth century and that this indicates that the demand for skill was rising relative to supply. However, others have questioned his estimates, and available evidence would not seem to support a uniform widening premium for skill over the industrial revolution period (see Mitch 1999: 268–70 for more detail). The redeployment of perhaps a quarter of the male labour force from agriculture into manufacturing (based on Crafts 1994: 45) between 1700 and 1840 and the arguably greater potential of manufacturing than agriculture for investing in skill (as suggested by the much flatter profile of earnings by age for agricultural labourers than for cotton textile workers reported by Burnette (2000)) would seem to imply a net increase in skill acquisition over this period. Baxter's 1867 allocations of the male manual labour force according to skill level indicate that over 60 per cent were in lower or higher skilled occupations (see Table 12.4). This is arguably higher than would have been the case in 1700 as crudely suggested by the 17 per cent of those in the overall categories of general labour, trade, distribution and manufactures, as reported in King's 1688 estimates (Mathias 1979: 189).[8]

---

[8] Lindert and Williamson (1982, 1983b) have proposed adjustments to both King's 1688 figures and Baxter's 1867 figures. Using Lindert and Williamson's readjustment of Baxter's 1867 figures yields 68 per cent of the manual classes in higher and lower skilled occupations (their figure is for all types of labour, not just male labour). Using their readjustment of King's 1688 figures yields 52 per cent of the manual classes in higher and lower skilled occupations. Thus, while Lindert and Williamson's revised estimates still suggest an increase between 1688 and 1867 in the percentage of the manual classes who were skilled, this increase is considerably less than implied by King's 'unadjusted' estimates. Thus there would seem to be a good deal of uncertainty as to the extent of any increase in the percentage of the manual labour force who were skilled during the eighteenth and early nineteenth centuries.

Trends in physical capital accumulation appear to have been much more rapid than those in human capital accumulation. Investment flows in physical capital as a share of national income were substantially larger than investment flows in schooling. West's (1970) estimates of direct educational expenditures of £3 million in 1833 for England is just under 10 per cent of Feinstein's (1978: 76) estimate of annual fixed capital formation for Britain averaged over the period 1831–40 (pro-rated to England's population share). Allowance for opportunity costs could increase schooling investments to as high as a quarter of fixed capital formation. Once allowance is made for workplace training investments as with Boot's estimates, the gap would appear to be considerably smaller. Nevertheless, there is no clear evidence in favour of a marked increase in the rate of human capital investment during the eighteenth and early nineteenth centuries.

Table 12.4 Distribution of men in the manual labour classes across wage categories following Baxter's 1867 classification

Wage category in shillings per week	Premium relative to unskilled wage of 10 shillings per week	Percentage of all adult males in manual labour class
Higher skilled labour and manufactures		
35s.	25s.	1.07%
28–30s.	19s.	20.3%
Lower skilled labour and manufactures		
25s.	15s.	14.8%
21–3s.	12s.	26.1%
Unskilled labour and agriculture		
15–20s.	7.5s.	6.62%
14s.	4s.	29.2%
14.5s.	4.5s.	1.9%

Source: Based on Baxter 1868: appendix IV.

This is suggested by considering the impact of a similar annihilation by plague followed by Eskimo repopulation in 1700 as that considered above for 1860. One can use Gregory King's figures for 1688 to estimate total national income at £44.7 million. Deducting income to nobility and rentiers, to landed agriculture, and to trade and distribution other than seamen, leaves an income of £17.3 million that can be attributed to labour income. Alternative estimates per family for unskilled labour income would be the £15 per family for labouring people and outservants and the £6.5 per family for cottagers and paupers. King estimates a total of 1,360,000 families. Using £15 per family yields an income to unskilled labour of £20.4 million, which is greater than the total labour figure and obviously problematic. Using the alternative lower figure yields an income to unskilled labour of £8.8 million. This leaves a residual for human capital of £17.3 million − £8.8 million = £8.5 million. This in turn produces an estimate of the share of human capital in national income of $8.5/44.7 = 19$ per cent for 1700 compared with the 15.41 per cent estimated above for 1860. However, employing the upper estimates above for 1860 human capital shares in the range of 25 to 35 per cent implies substantially more scope for expansion of the role of human capital during the 150 years in question. This underscores the degree of uncertainty in current knowledge about the quantitative extent of skill formation during this period.

How is one to explain the apparently limited role of human capital in the industrial revolution? One explanation, following Galor and Moav (2000), is that Britain was still at a relatively early stage in the accumulation of physical capital and that returns to physical capital were substantially in excess of those to human capital. Evaluating this possibility requires deciding on the relevant margin for expansion and coming up with economy-wide estimates for the marginal return to each type of capital. On some margins it would appear that returns to human capital were in excess of those on physical capital, thus challenging this explanation. Estimates of both nominal and real interest rates for government bonds and other types of capital investments tend to average in the range of 3 to 7 per cent for the eighteenth and first half of the nineteenth centuries. Estimates of the rate of return to basic literacy for the 1840s are well in excess of 20 per cent (Mitch 1984), and Elbaum (1989) for the early twentieth century estimates a rate of return to apprenticeship of just over 20 per cent. A second explanation is that technical change was not skill using during this phase but was to become so in later periods. This can be explained by the increasing role of science-based technical change later in the nineteenth century and the corresponding increasing importance of formal over informal education. A third explanation is that market failures led to underinvestment in human capital, as suggested by its high relative returns as just noted above.

UNDERINVESTMENT IN HUMAN CAPITAL?

It has been suggested that England was underinvesting in schooling by the mid-nineteenth century, not because of evidence of the high rate of return to schooling but on indications of higher levels of literacy and primary school enrolments in other countries such as the United States and Prussia (see Table 12.5A).

It is difficult to address claims of underinvestment directly, because it is difficult to determine what the optimal level of investment in education is for any economy. Since it is now commonly presumed in modern societies that both the financing and the provision of primary schooling should be subject to government controls, the lag of England behind other countries in establishing such provision has often been seen as reflecting some deficiency (Green 1990).

Closer examination of England's public provision of primary schooling in the eighteenth and early nineteenth centuries mitigates the extent to which there was any underinvestment due to the lack of government in education. There was extensive financing and provision of non-profit schooling from non-governmental sources even prior to the initial government funding of elementary schooling in 1833. The funds came from a diverse mix of organisations and individuals and with diverse aims, including the propagation of religious doctrine, philanthropy and a sense of obligation to the local community. As early as 1818, some 40 per cent of the scholars recorded in a national parochial survey were in schools receiving subsidies. And in a sample of the eight counties of Durham, Gloucester, Hereford, Lancashire, Lincolnshire, Middlesex, Nottingham and Stafford taken from this survey, some 30 per cent of the population resided in parishes clearly identified as having at least one subsidised school and in which comments for the parish indicated that 'the poor are sufficiently provided with education'. An 1833 national parochial survey indicated that only 14 per cent of the population in these eight counties resided in parishes in which no mention was made of subsidised schools (Mitch 1982).

Schools were subsidised in part to redistribute wealth by lowering the fees charged to working-class parents for their children to attend school. Private, unsubsidised fees for working-class schools were typically in the range of 6 to 9 pence a week. Subsidies commonly lowered fees to only 1 or 2 pence a week. With an unskilled labourer or agricultural labourer earning in the range of 10 shillings a week, this subsidy of 4 to 8 pence could amount to 5 to 7 per cent of an adult male head of household's income, thus having a sizeable impact on lowering the direct cost of schooling. Nevertheless, the motive for subsidies was as much to control what was taught and how the schools were run as directly to lower fees. In part this was

Table 12.5A   Male illiteracy in Europe and North America c. 1860

Country	Percentage illiterate
Austro-Hungarian Empire	85
Spain	70
Belgium	40
France	35
England	30
Netherlands	18
United States (white males)	6.6
Prussia	5

Source: Graff 1987; Vincent 2000.

Table 12.5B   Female illiteracy in Europe c. 1860

Country	Percentage illiterate
Spain	90
Belgium	55
France	45
England	37
Netherlands	27
United States (white females)	10.1
Prussia	5

Source: Graff 1987; Vincent 2000.

Table 12.5C   Male school enrolments in several European countries c. 1850: percentage of male children aged 6–14 enrolled in primary schools

Country	Percentage enrolled
Prussia	81
Bavaria	83
France	60
England and Wales	66
Sweden	59

Source: Maynes 1985.

due to religious, doctrinal considerations. Elites wanted to control the religious and moral content of what was taught and instil habits of discipline in working-class children. Over the course of the nineteenth century, efficient instruction in literacy skills did assume increasing priority. Indeed as parliamentary funds were increasingly directed towards education, schools that were found to offer an appropriate curriculum, suitably qualified instructors and adequate facilities were classified as 'efficient', as distinguished from inefficient schools not meeting these standards.

Despite efforts to establish centralised educational standards, primary schools between 1700 and 1860 were established and funded locally, a characteristic that can be explained by the value of on-site supervision in the presence of a geographically dispersed population. This led to considerable regional variation in the provision of schooling, depending on the interests of the local elite in promoting mass education. As parliament became increasingly involved in funding of primary schools in the first half of the nineteenth century this tendency was somewhat reversed. Yet receipt of parliamentary funding was made conditional on matching local funding from sources other than student fees. This tension between the desire to redistribute funds to areas of greatest educational deficiency and the desire to reward local efforts at provision persisted until the landmark Education Act of 1870 filled in the gaps, though earlier provision made partial correctives (see Mitch 1992: 120). John Stuart Mill (1861) noted this tension in the provision of government services between management by those familiar with local conditions and expert, national establishment of standards. While there was much support at the national government level for funding of schools out of local property taxes, this was blocked by Church of England interests which were concerned that such a move would facilitate the spread of secular and non-conformist schools in competition with Anglican-sponsored schools.

Critics of the English educational system have argued that the absence of universal provision for elementary schooling impeded its spread in the eighteenth and nineteenth centuries. Smith (1976 [1776]: 785) claimed that in Scotland provision from the late seventeenth century for every parish to establish and support a school resulted in higher levels of educational attainment in the Scottish population than the English during the eighteenth century. In the mid-nineteenth century, when national comparisons of signature rates at marriage becomes possible, the illiteracy rates for both Scottish brides and grooms were only half of English levels (Cipolla 1969). However, historians have come to challenge the claim of Scottish superiority in primary education (Smout 1969; West 1975). Houston (1985) has concluded that no Scottish superiority over northern England in literacy rates was evident in the early eighteenth century, several decades after the statute establishing Scottish parochial schools was passed. And a number of historians have noted considerable variation across Scotland in levels of school enrolment and rates of literacy, thus challenging the claim of universal access to schooling in all parishes (Smout 1969; West 1975). Furthermore, the 1818 national parochial survey of schools indicates that the majority of Scottish students were enrolled in private not parochial schools. This suggests that parochial provision from local taxes could not keep up with expanding population, especially in industrialising areas of Scotland. Centralised attempts to establish schools had little impact unless followed up with resources to support them, and this entailed local support. The English choice of local and charitable support for education may have been an appropriate way to develop a system of elementary schooling in its initial stages.

Thus the limited extent of subsidised schooling in England prior to 1870 can be attributed to the fact that primary schooling was supported by elite interests and subject to considerable local variation in intensity of support, in contrast with later secondary schooling in England and the United States where democratic redistribution played a stronger role (Lindert 2001; Mariscal and Sokoloff 2000).

THE CONTRIBUTION OF EDUCATION AND SKILL FORMATION TO ECONOMIC GROWTH, 1700–1860

Studies of economic growth during the twentieth century have often found increases in human capital to be a key contributing factor (see Topel 1999 for a survey). However, in so far as the modest literacy increases evident between 1750 and 1840 reflect trends in formal schooling attainment of the English population during this period, this would imply a small contribution to economic growth from this source. One can put the change in adult male literacy rates as going from 62 per cent in 1780 to 70 per cent in 1830 (Schofield 1973). A reasonably generous allowance for the extent to which literacy raised earnings over that of an otherwise illiterate person would be 20 per cent (see Mitch 1993b: 294). Thus, the change in aggregate labour force earnings attributed to rising male literacy can be put at 1.6 per cent (0.2×0.08) and setting labour's share in national income at 0.6 would put the contribution to increased output over the full fifty years at just 0.96 per cent, or 0.02 per cent per year compounded over fifty years. This is a small part of the perhaps 0.2 to 0.5 per cent per annum growth in per capita income during this period (see chapter 1 above). In contrast, for the fifty years between 1871 and 1921, the increase in average years of schooling has been estimated as from 4.2 to 7.4, with a correspondingly larger contribution to economic growth (Matthews *et al.* 1982).

As already noted, the basic factor limiting the contribution of literacy or alternatively primary schooling to growth during this period was the apparently limited increase in the extent of schooling or literacy. The actual levels of investment in schooling were non-trivial relative to national income or physical capital investments. West (1970) has estimated that direct expenditure on primary and related types of schooling in 1833 amounted to about £3 million or about 1 per cent of English national income. This is based on making upward adjustments in reported school enrolments to allow for likely undercounting. Even eliminating West's adjustments as overly generous would still leave an expenditure of £1.5 to £2 million, or at least 0.5 per cent of national income. This amounts to

5 to 10 per cent of annual gross domestic physical capital formation during the 1830s. When allowance is made for opportunity costs of school attendance, which may well have at least equalled direct costs and could have been double those costs, especially for children aged 10 and over, then human capital investment flows in schooling approach 25 per cent of fixed capital formation (Feinstein 1978: 76).

The English industrial revolution offers a number of challenges to conventional views of the role of education in economic growth. First, it offers the example of rapidly growing sectors, often classified as 'leading', in which large segments of their labour forces had little formal education, and in which formal education levels, as measured by literacy, may indeed have actually declined for extended periods of time. Second, the overall improvement in formal educational levels between 1750 and 1860 appears to have been quite modest, despite substantial growth in both total and per capita income. It would thus appear that technological and productivity advances do not always require improvements in educational levels. And it appears that the relationship between education and technology as well as the incorporation of educational requirements into work organisation have changed considerably since 1860.

Nevertheless it is also important to note more indirect contributions made by skill and education during this period. First, as noted above, there were the contributions made by skill acquisition on the job in new industrial activities. Second, some modern studies of the role of education in economic growth suggest that the level of educational attainment may have more impact on growth rates than any changes (increases) in this level (Benhabib and Spiegel 1994; Barro and Sala-I-Martin 1995). In this view, a labour force composed primarily of college graduates is more likely to grow in productivity than a labour force rapidly moving from illiteracy to minimum literacy skills. The importance of initial levels of educational attainment is also implied in the influential view, proposed by Bowman and Anderson (1963), that there is a literacy threshold required for economic development. Whether such a threshold was actually pertinent to England during the industrial revolution is arguable. But, as Table 12.6B shows, English literacy levels were already high enough by 1700 to ensure virtual universal literacy among those engaged in high-level commercial occupations and close to it in other occupations for which literacy was likely to have been of considerable functional value.

And whatever the degree of intellectual stagnation at Oxford and Cambridge or of corruption in English grammar school foundations during the eighteenth century, there is evidence of vibrant intellectual activity elsewhere in English society, whether it be provincial agricultural or literary societies or urban lecture series on scientific and philosophical topics. While one can argue whether England lagged in intellectual leadership behind Scotland or France during the eighteenth century, the home of Newton and Samuel Johnson can hardly be regarded as an intellectual backwater.

Chapters 1 and 5 above argue that Britain's intellectual vibrancy in the late eighteenth century was not confined to literary or scientific spheres but was particularly paramount in the development of economically useful technological innovations. One would expect that such activity would be one of the major losses from an Eskimo repopulation of the British Isles as considered at the beginning of this chapter. While visible institutions for skill transmission and education such as apprenticeship, schools and universities may have played a supporting role, they do not seem to have been critical to developing England's edge in innovative activity at this time; more amorphous factors such as culture appear to have been central. In searching to explain the development of human resources suitable for innovation, one can turn to both supply- and demand-side factors. On the supply side, there was the possibility of recruiting talent suitable for innovative activity from a variety of sources, ranging from immigrants familiar with the science and technology of continental Europe to those trained in dissenting academies or participants in provincial literary and scientific societies. Such pluralistic opportunities for innovative talent have sometimes been offered as an explanation for European technological leadership over Asia and other regions of the world during this period (Mokyr 1990). And arguably this talent was present in England in greater degree than elsewhere at this time. On the demand side, it has been suggested that in Europe generally, and in England in particular, talent faced a higher relative reward in productive rather than in rent-seeking or outright destructive opportunities compared with other regions (Mitch 1999: 273–5).

Table 12.6A Illiteracy by social structure in rural England, 1580–1700

Percentage illiterate	Economic activity or social status
0–10	Clergy and gentry
	Retailers
	Distributors
14–33	Specialist crafts
27–73	Yeomen
37–52	Manufacturers
	Processors
56–68	Village crafts
73–100	Heavy manual trades, husbandmen, labourers

Source: Based on Cressy 1980: 136, Table 6.8.

Table 12.6B Illiteracy by occupation group, 1754–84

Occupation	No.	Percentage illiterate
Gentry and professional	68	0
Officials etc.	20	0
Retail	19	5
Wood	137	16
Estate	29	17
Yeoman and farmers	97	19
Food and drink	57	19
Textile	41	20
Metal	60	22
Leather	78	23
Miscellaneous	81	30
Transport	154	31
Clothing	63	35
Armed forces (non-officer)	180	41
Husbandmen	666	46
Construction and mining	146	51
Labourers and servants	192	59

Source: Schofield 1973: 450.

Thus, assessing the role of skill and education in the British industrial revolution requires distinguishing between levels of skill and education and the changes in those levels. Whatever increases in skill and educational levels occurred appear to be modest, involving a relatively limited share of the labour force. Nevertheless, a substantial share of the output of the English economy in both 1700 and 1860 does appear to have come from the skills and knowledge of its population. And the level of skill and knowledge of its workforce made a substantial contribution to the economic changes which occurred during the intervening century and a half.

13

Consumption in eighteenth- and early nineteenth-century Britain

MAXINE BERG

Contents

Consumption, consumer revolutions and demand	357
Luxury and consumption	362
Addiction, consumerism and foreign trade	364
Consumption, class and gender	369
Gender and household division of consumption	379
Product innovation, fashion and taste	383
Selling, shopping and advertising	384
Consumer politics	385
Conclusion	386

CONSUMPTION, CONSUMER REVOLUTIONS AND DEMAND

There is a paradox at the heart of recent research on the industrial revolution. This is the juxtaposition of theories and evidence of slow economic and industrial growth with alternative theories and evidence of rapidly rising consumer expenditure. Earlier histories linked consumption to elite expenditure on the one hand and rising standards of living on the other. These are no longer considered to be valid. Few now believe that elite expenditure was in itself sufficient to fuel a major increase in consumption, and elite consumer behaviour did not 'trickle down' to sufficiently broad parts of the population. It is also now believed that the living standards of the labouring classes either were static or improved only slowly over the whole of the eighteenth century and much of the first half of the nineteenth century. Yet despite these conventions, theories of a consumer revolution, or at least recognition of evidence of a relatively widespread increase over the period in the possession of consumer goods, have been difficult to dislodge. Indeed they have gathered force since the 1990s, shaping the grand narrative of the period, and replacing the former grand narrative of the industrial revolution. Consumption, is now the major preoccupation of social and cultural historians of the eighteenth and early nineteenth centuries, as it is of the social sciences more generally. Analysis of the broader aspects of consumer practices, and an understanding of the growing diversity of consumption, were left to social and cultural historians. Shifts in consumer behaviour depended on changing tastes, on deploying underemployed resources, especially within the household, and on that vocabulary which economic historians had carefully removed to the cultural sphere, that is, desire, attitude, fashion and emulation (de Vries 1993).

Part of the problem of analysing consumption in the eighteenth and early nineteenth centuries lies in the questions being asked and the period discussed. Much of the discussion of consumption has been directed to the broader concept of demand. Was demand an independent variable in the process of economic growth? What was its place in the explanations of the industrial revolution? Elizabeth Gilboy argued in 1932 that demand should play an equal part in explanations of economic change in the eighteenth century. Her point was revived for the century before this when Joan Thirsk pointed out the significance of consumer industries in the early modern period (Thirsk 1978). McKendrick's large claims for an independent role for consumption in the second half of the eighteenth century, and indeed for a consumer revolution with a direct impact on the industrial revolution, challenged economic historians to clarify theoretical issues, and to reassess evidence on the sources of early economic growth. The result was concentration on a narrowly defined set of issues, and conclusions which denied a significant place to demand (McKendrick 1983). Consumption was framed within estimates of national economic output, and estimates of standard of living. These estimates indicated even slower growth than that of overall output; estimates of growth in personal consumption per head were substantially deflated by issues of 'quality of life' (Crafts 1985, 1997). The case for a consumer revolution was most effectively dismissed by Mokyr, who treated demand as a mere response to supply-led events, arguing that the case had to be made for a pre-existing rise in real incomes. His supply-led model, however, assumed fixed tastes and fully employed resources (Mokyr 1985).

Others denied the impact of foreign demand; there is little evidence of export-led growth, and the bulk of foreign demand was colonial, dependent on the British market's ability to purchase colonial products (Cole 1981; Engerman 1994; Thomas and McCloskey 1994). Domestic demand might arise from population growth, from agricultural improvement or from changes in the distribution of income in favour of those with a larger propensity to consume the products of manufactured industry. Population growth would only shift demand if income rose, and macroeconomic estimates gave little support to this (Crafts 1985). The case made for the expansion of domestic demand in classic accounts by Eversley, Jones and John rested on assumptions about the expansion of the agricultural sector. More recent research has credited little contribution to agriculture in widening the domestic market for industrial goods (O'Brien 1985). There was also little evidence that increased agricultural productivity raised real incomes of the labouring classes (Horrell 1996).

Shifts in the distribution of income provide another set of possibilities for incentives for rising consumption. The impact of movements of agricultural and industrial prices combined with rising rents may have shifted income from the industrial sector to landowners and farmers in the late eighteenth century. There are other arguments that income shifts in the early nineteenth century in favour of the middle classes arose from low-cost labour and industrial and commercial profits. This was reinforced by regressive taxation and investment in the national debt. But this trend towards rising inequality during industrialisation has been disputed (Feinstein 1988; Hudson 1992), and there were no clear effects on consumption, especially of domestically produced manufactures. Consumption patterns have been assumed rather than investigated from conclusions reached on the standard of living (Horrell 1996; Feinstein 1998).

If the economic history of consumption has been too narrowly focused on issues of economic growth, the timing of changes in consumption has been only vaguely specified. Debate draws on evidence of probate inventories from the seventeenth century, prices from the mid to later eighteenth century, and budgets from the late eighteenth and early nineteenth centuries, as if there was a single experience of consumption over the whole period between the 1600s and 1850 (McKendrick 1983; Mokyr 1985; Shammas 1993; Horrell 1996). Some of the dispute over the existence or not of a 'consumer revolution' might be resolved with clearer specification of timing of key consumption trends, but important differences would still remain. In the present context of the questions posed by economic historians and the estimates they provide as evidence, we cannot come to firm conclusions on the extent to which the industrial revolution was demand led. Current estimates of macroeconomic trends in consumption, of economic growth and of standards of living remain at odds with the findings of social and cultural historians. It is likely they will continue to do so if we maintain restrictive assumptions on tastes and household resource allocations. We can only start to move beyond this stalemate by seriously investigating the incentives for changing consumer behaviour.

The more recent economic analysis of consumer behaviour provides some new directions for the history of consumption, directions which lead into close connections with the cultural sphere. Economic analysis of consumer behaviour has been based on a variety of models of price and income elasticity, time use and household decision-making, habits and social norms, and interactive consumer behaviour such as responses to aspirational groups. The central concerns of consumer theory have been with price and quantity, with technologies explaining the success or failure of certain goods. However, the roles of taste and of product characteristics have recently emerged as important determinants of consumer decisions. This develops theories originally put forward in the 1970s arguing that consumers selected among characteristics of goods, and enjoyed accordingly. Preferences were not exogenous, but endogenous; there was an interdependence between products and taste formation (Lancaster 1971; Ironmonger 1972). Economists now investigate the 'active consumer' who takes part in taste formation, responds to new goods, and combines and recombines new and existing goods to create a social identity and a lifestyle (Bianchi 1998).

Few of these theories have thus far been applied to the analysis of consumption in the eighteenth and early nineteenth centuries. Economic historians working on this period have, to a large degree, preferred supply-side explanations, analysing changes in demand only as a function of price and quality change provoked by changing technology. They have assumed consumers to be price takers, and the goods they bought to have no characteristics of their own. The growth of consumption was not considered to provide an important contribution to economic growth, and was therefore sidelined by economic historians. The study of the proliferation of new commodities over the course of the eighteenth and early nineteenth centuries was left largely to social and cultural historians.

Application of an economics of consumer behaviour to other historical periods does open questions that might be raised about consumption in the long eighteenth century. Macroanalysis of consumer demand, diffusion models and time use models have been applied to the study of interwar and post-Second World War consumption of consumer durables and household appliances in the USA and Britain (Bowden and Offer 1994). An economics of product and quality innovation has been applied to consumer and producer durables in the post-Second World War US economy (Gordon 1993; Bresnahan and Gordon 1997). Points arising from these analyses of use to the study of consumption in the early industrial period emphasise the limited extent to which such consumer goods showed up in standard economic indicators such as productivity estimates or proportions of disposable income. The outlay on domestic appliances which claimed only a small fraction of disposable income also profoundly affected household experiences in the twentieth century (Bowden and Offer 1994). Productivity estimates set out in time series based on the national accounts could not recognise a proliferation of product and quality variations in domestic appliances, automobiles, lighting, radios and televisions, computers and photocopiers. The disjuncture between available economic indicators and other narrative evidence of consumer practices and product proliferation has recently led economists to investigate other theories of consumer demand, and to seek out other price deflators to incorporate quality and product differences (Gordon 1990).

Such theories have included the 'time use' analysis of Becker's new household economics. Consumption is treated in terms of time use in the household which produces 'consumption events' by combining inputs of goods, services and time (Becker 1965, 1981). Under this model, time is allocated between market work and household goods and activities. The latter are made by a combination of housework, leisure and market goods. This division of time between the market and household sectors helps to explain the relationship between consumption and labour supply; it also helps to explain the diffusion of different types of consumer goods and activities. Some of these affect the value of discretionary time differently. Using this model, Bowden and Offer distinguish time-saving and time-using domestic appliances: those goods associated with saving housework, such as vacuum cleaners, and those associated with leisure, such as radios and TVs. Time-saving goods are defined as those which release discretionary time; time-using goods are those which are perceived to enhance the quality of time. Not only are consumer durables superior goods for which demand generally increases faster than income, but the different types of consumer durable have very different rates of take-up. The highest rankings in the diffusion of these two classes of durable consumer goods between the 1920s and the 1970s were claimed by time-using goods (Bowden and Offer 1994). This more rapid diffusion process for perceived superior goods can also be tested against processes of consumer demand in the eighteenth and early nineteenth centuries.

A similar use is made of household economics by Jan de Vries in his concept of the 'industrious revolution', which applies the idea of allocations of household resources and time to explain the growing demand for durable consumer goods in seventeenth- and eighteenth-century Europe. This reallocation of household resources, he argues, gave individuals in the household the ability to buy novelties and luxuries. Just as in the case of the consumption of twentieth-century consumer durables, so in the case of early modern consumption, the incentive was provided by the prospect of novelties, luxuries and addictive goods. These were desirable precisely because they were not produced in the household, and the ability to consume entailed a willingness to change tastes (de Vries 1993). De Vries's use of Becker's model of the household allowed him to discuss the allocation of household and individual time between activities for the production of household goods and market activities. Choices over the allocation of labour could generate more cash to buy marketed commodities, but simultaneously take time away from housework, preparing meals and childcare. Such reallocations of time could help to explain increases in durable consumer goods at times when real wages were relatively static. This reallocation of household labour away from self-sufficiency towards market-orientated production and consumption was termed by de Vries 'the industrious revolution', which preceded and accompanied the industrial revolution (de Vries 1993).

These consumer theories have indicated the significance of taste, of choice among different products and qualities, and of responses to perceived non-necessaries, leisure goods and luxuries. This chapter will therefore focus not on the extent to which the consumption of basic foodstuffs and other necessaries rose or fell, but on the role of new goods. It will argue that it was the appearance of these goods, and a consumer culture associated with them, which provided the crucial incentives for changes in consumer behaviour. This did not affect all groups of the population; indeed in specific groups of years over the period, in specific regions, or at various points of the life-cycle, large groups were excluded. But equally, many of these new goods such as sugar, and subsequently tea, rapidly became perceived as necessaries. The chapter will also focus on the consumption of goods rather than the broader consumption of space, services and culture including spas, travel, pleasure gardens, libraries, concerts, clubs and taverns. Many of these provided the social and cultural context for the consumer goods, but they will not be investigated independently.

The 'active' consumer choosing varieties of goods, responding to novelties and fashions, becoming addicted to substances like tea and sugar, changed consumer behaviour over the course of the eighteenth century. The crucial shift in consumer behaviour was generated in the context not of necessaries or common everyday commodities, but of new goods and of luxuries. Goods accorded luxury status by their consumers, from the poor to the rich, and new possibilities of acquiring such goods, provided new incentives to labour, to spend and to take on new cultural modes from dress and domestic rituals to manners.

LUXURY AND CONSUMPTION

The taste for luxury, fashion and addictive substances was addressed during the eighteenth century as the 'luxury debates'. De Vries's questions – does demand have a history, and where did the new consumer aspirations come from – led him to the luxury debates and the importance of the shift identified by eighteenth-century theorists such as Sir James Steuart and Montesquieu from old to new luxuries, from luxuries of the body to luxuries of the home, and to accessible luxuries (de Vries 2002). Over the course of the eighteenth century the luxury debates moved far beyond their traditional concerns with the corruption of wealthy elites. The sumptuary laws which had previously proscribed the wearing of specific types of cloth and of gold and silver lace to all but the elites were repealed or withered away. Bernard Mandeville, the Dutch doctor and political essayist who had made his home in London, provoked a turning point in the discussion of luxury. He accepted traditional associations of luxury with vice, but he also declared luxury to be a public benefit. He furthermore challenged the defining boundaries between luxuries and necessities. Claims to moral virtue in the 'needs' for cleanliness, comforts, decencies and conveniences were no greater than those for luxury housing and furnishings. Men and women, in Mandeville's view, are by their nature self-interested, pleasure-seeking and vain, and they seek luxuries to fulfil these psychological characteristics. By indulging their desire for luxuries, the rich and others who could afford it contributed to the expansion of commerce and the wider employment of the poor (Mandeville 1714).

After Mandeville, luxury was increasingly seen in terms of economic advantage; it turned from a subject of moral discourse into one of political economy. Sir James Steuart argued that the new luxury consisted in 'providing the objects of sensuality, so far as they are superfluous. Sensuality consists in the actual enjoyment of them and excess implies an abuse of enjoyment.' The provision of luxury objects, he argued, encouraged 'emulation, industry and agriculture' (Berry 1994). David Hume and Adam Smith associated luxury almost entirely with commerce, convenience and consumption. Hume argued that luxury was a 'refinement in the gratification of the senses', and the expansion of commerce would make available to all persons not just the necessaries of life, but its 'conveniences' (Hume 1903 [1742]). For Adam Smith, the wealth of a nation lay in its ability to increase the quantity of 'necessaries and conveniences' which its labour could produce or exchange relative to its population. The 'industrious and frugal peasant', who might not enjoy the 'extravagant luxury' of the great, would still be better off than at any previous stage of social development (Smith 1976 [1776]).

Whether an analytical category of political economy, a constantly recurring theme of moral discourse or a literary trope, luxury was at the heart of eighteenth-century debate over consumption, production and trade. It pervaded society, as expressed in Tobias Smollet's comment in *Humphry Clinker* on the London of the 1770s. The trappings of elegant living now pervaded the lives of merchants and tradesmen, and even those lower down the social scale.

> The substantial tradesman, who was wont to pass his evening at the ale house for fourpence half-penny, now spends three shillings at the tavern, while his wife keeps card-tables at home; she must likewise have fine clothes, her chaise or pad, with country lodgings, and go three times a week to public diversions . . . The gayest places of public entertainment are filled with fashionable figures; which, upon inquiry, will be found to be journeymen tailors, serving men, and abigails [ladies' maids], disguised like their betters.
>
> (Smollett 1793)

Luxury was displaced from the mainstream of political economy in the early nineteenth century, as production and labour came to the centre. But it was still a major plank in debates over the distribution of income. Radicals in the 1790s reintroduced the language of sumptuary legislation, and an association of vice with the landed aristocracy. Early socialist theorists distinguished productive and unproductive consumption as well as natural and unnatural wants. Natural wants were those for food, clothing, lodging and objects of convenience (Claeys 1994; Thompson 2001). Unnatural wants were confined to the consumption of luxuries, especially those associated with international commerce. Luxury and consumption was now a factor in the response to the extreme dislocations thrown up by rapid industrialisation.

ADDICTION, CONSUMERISM AND FOREIGN TRADE

A key issue in the luxury debates was the costs and benefits of international trade. Many of the definitions of luxury were connected to foreign imports, from the rest of Europe, but especially from Asia, the Caribbean and North and South America. Most of the historical debate on consumer markets and international trade has focused on the role of exports, and has found this role wanting as a significant source of new demand. But this is to miss the point being made by those engaged in the luxury debates. It was not exports but imports that mattered. European import markets for colonial groceries, especially addictive substances or drugs such as tobacco, sugar, coffee, cocoa and later tea, eclipsed another widely discussed import trade with Asia in luxury manufactured goods – silk, cotton and porcelain. The impact of the trade in colonial groceries was to transform consumer habits and sociability among the middling classes and the labouring poor. The consumption of non-durable goods such as colonial groceries stimulated changes in tastes and new forms of sociability. The East India trade was to escalate the role of fashion marketing, and to have an unprecedented demonstration effect on British consumer goods manufacture. The exotic luxury goods of the Orient fostered a new responsiveness to the sensuality of key goods, especially clothing and ornamental ware.

A global perspective on trade also reveals that much of the growth of domestically manufactured exports depended on world markets opened for the import into Europe of the new groceries. Britain re-exported a significant proportion of these imports. In 1720 the official values of woollen exports and re-exports of plantation groceries and Asian textiles were about equal, and were to continue thus for much of the eighteenth century (Shammas 1990). Over Europe as a whole, the trade going through the Baltic during the seventeenth and eighteenth centuries showed little change in the composition of its northern European commodities, but a mixed category of colonial commodities increased 500 per cent over the period. Pepper, spices and textiles made up three-quarters of total imports before 1740; towards the end of the period tea and coffee were among the prominent imports (Steensgard 1990).

Table 13.1 The composition of British imports, 1699–1800			
Year	Manufactures (%)	Foodstuffs (%)	Raw materials (%)
1699–1701	31.5	33.7	34.8
1752–4	22.2	41.4	36.3
1800	8.4	45.1	46.5

Source: Engerman 1994.

While historians show that exports and imports tended to move in the same direction, they also demonstrate a big shift in the composition of imports. Table 13.1 reveals that foodstuffs, mainly non-essentials like sugar and tea, came to take priority; the share of raw materials increased slightly over most of the eighteenth century, and only increased

Table 13.2 The source of English imports, 1700–98			
Year	Europe	Americas	Rest of the world
1700–1	66.4	19.9	13.7
1750–1	55.3	30.1	14.7
1772–3	45.1	36.4	18.5
1797–8	42.4	32.1	25.5

Source: Engerman 1994.

sharply with the imports of raw cotton at the end of the century (Engerman 1994). Groceries made up less than 10 per cent of the value of imports in the 1550s; by the 1770s they were over one-third of the value, though prices of tobacco, sugar and caffeine drinks were falling sharply (Shammas 1993). The greatest growth of imports between 1700 and the early 1770s was of those sourced in the Americas; after this, it was of those sourced in Asia, as the initiative was taken by imports of tea (Table 13.2). The wider economic impact of these imports remains open to question. O'Brien argues that virtually all of the increment in non-bullion trade between western Europe and the Americas between 1600 and 1800 depended on the exchange of tropical foodstuffs, tobacco and industrial raw materials, most of these cultivated with slave labour. These groceries were luxuries that did little more than complement European food production and did not transform food intake by Europeans. Such imports did not, he argues, contribute a great deal to economic growth; they did not release labour or capital and they did not add value to industry (O'Brien 1991, 1999). But they did have a major economic impact on global economic development. European tastes for exotic groceries fostered the development of colonial monocultures, many cultivated by slave labour.

The history of these colonial groceries is one of the transformation of exotic luxuries into necessities; of how the 'rare, odd and precious could, under particular circumstances, become everyday' (Mintz 1993). These commodities were initially novelties or luxuries, but in the course of the short period 1663–1775 the consumption of one of those commodities, sugar, was to increase twentyfold while population only increased from 4.5 to 7 million. Sugar consumption rose from 4 lb. per person in 1700–9 to 8 lb. in the 1720s. By the 1770s it was 11 lb., and in the 1790s 13 lb. per person (Burnett 1999). Why these substances spread so rapidly through all classes has only recently been addressed. Old explanations of emulation of upper-class habits do not convince. But forms of sociability, adapted to different rituals by class and context, carry far into the role of hospitality, generosity, propriety and sobriety. Tea drinking among the poor became associated with work, rather than a domestic ritual. It involved sociability at work in making it; it was stimulating, hot and sweet, making palatable a meal of cold bread and cheese (Burnett 1999).

The addictive physiological qualities of these foods, combined with hedonistic consumer contexts of rapid gratification, lie behind their rapidly expanding consumer markets. The first mass consumer import was tobacco. Shammas estimates that, by 1670, 25 per cent of the population was using it. London's share of imports was 80–90 per cent. Tobacco usage peaked, however, at the beginning of the eighteenth century at 2 lbs per capita (Table 13.3). A cultural context of men smoking clay pipes in alehouses and coffeehouses was saturated until the rise of cigarette smoking in the twentieth century (Goodman 1993; Walvin 1997; Hilton 2000).

Coffee was also an early import; its consumption in Britain was connected with the spread of coffeehouses as centres of male conviviality and sociability, and with the coincident rise in sugar imports. Originally imported from the Levant, this was an exotic Oriental beverage. The period of most rapid growth of coffeehouses was in the first fifteen years of the eighteenth century, and there were 550 coffeehouses in London by 1740 (W. D. Smith 1995; S. Smith 1996). By 1700, coffee is estimated to have been worth £36,000 a year (as compared with sugar's value of £608,000). By 1750, it was estimated at £75,000, by 1760 at £257,000, and by 1775 at £451,000 (Walvin 1997). But coffee was never, in Britain, to make the transformation from luxury to necessity, as it was in other parts of Europe. Explanations lie in French and English trade and colonial domination, in terms of trade and in culture (Smith 1996; Jones and Spang 1999).

East India Company imports of tea rose from 9 million pounds in the 1720s to 87 million pounds in the 1750s (Walvin 1997). This was the only one of the key colonial groceries to be sourced in the commerce of the East India trade with China, rather than in western colonial plantations. Tea prices declined throughout the eighteenth century, especially after 1784 when tariffs were sharply reduced. Prices fell from 12–36 shillings per pound in 1720 to 2–10 shillings per pound in 1785 (Burnett 1999).

Tea drinking was also started in coffeehouses, and associated with exotic luxuries from the Orient. It was soon to become associated with wealthy households and a ceremonial ritual including the use of porcelain and silver, and mahogany tea tables. It moved from a seventeenth-century association with gentility, refinement and conspicuous consumption to an association among the eighteenth-century middle classes with sobriety, trustworthiness and respectability. It was the centre of polite conversation and behaviour directed by women within private spaces. Its

Table 13.3 Consumption per head of groceries (pounds)							
Coffee		Tobacco		Sugar		Tea (legal and illegal pounds per capita)	
1693–1700	0.04	1698–1702	2.30	1698–9	4.01	1730–9	0.50
1711–19	0.12	1713–17	1.80	1710–19	8.23	1740–9	1.00
1725–9	0.10	1718–22	2.62	1720–9	12.02	1750–9	1.10
1735–9	0.14	1733–7	2.00	1730–9	14.90	1770–9	1.40
		1748–52	1.94	1750–9	16.94	1790–9	2.10
				1770–9	23.02		
				1790–9	24.16		

Source: Coffee, Smith 2001; tobacco, sugar and tea, Shammas 1993.

consumption as a mass commodity used among the labouring classes dates from the 1730s and 1740s. Per capita consumption was 1 lb. a year by the mid-eighteenth century, and an average-sized family consumed 1.5 oz. a week (Burnett 1999).

Tea became entrenched in working-class diets from the latter half of the eighteenth century. Sugar, treacle and tea accounted for over 10 per cent of outlays on food, as compared with 12.3 per cent on meat and 2.5 per cent on beer (Shammas 1984; Burnett 1999). There was a shift from diets dominated by oatmeal, milk and cheese to bread, tea, sugar and butter. Conditions of trade over the course of the eighteenth century fostered further reductions in the price of tea relative to coffee to British consumers, and established it as a mass national drink.

While imports of colonial groceries provided an obvious inducement to changing consumer habits in Britain, an important though more indirect place was occupied by imports of manufactured luxuries. Imports of manufactured goods from Asia declined in relative quantitative significance over the period, but they occupied a vital place in the seventeenth and early eighteenth centuries, and were to have a dramatic impact on British and wider European material culture. They were the seventeenth- and eighteenth-century parallels of twentieth-century time-using consumer durables. As superior goods their diffusion was rapid, and when imports of these goods declined relatively it was only because of import substitution and product innovation in Europe.

The special feature that marks out Asian manufacture was world-class production of fine but affordable consumer wares, marked by diversity, taste and fashion, and produced and traded throughout Asia on a scale not previously encountered in Europe. Some of these goods, especially types of ceramics, silks and calicoes, could be functional and routine parts of everyday life in India and China, but equally, at the higher levels of quality, could be prized as objects of art. Certainly their exotic provenance made them into luxuries in Europe, but, more significantly, their diversity of quality and design, combined with their high-volume production and their long traditions as exportables as well as domestic wares, made them into very special transformative luxuries to Europeans.

The properties of the commodities were crucial. The qualitative features of Indian calicoes and Chinese/Japanese porcelain were vital to their success. Too few economic historians look at what qualitative features underlie the demand in the product markets they study (Chapman 1985; Bianchi 1998; Church 1999; Reynard 2000). These goods were distinctively coloured, patterned and finely textured, and, in the case of porcelain, both heat resistant and translucent. They were also adaptable to the sense of recognition that made them objects of beauty and desire not just in Asia, but in Europe (Goldthwaite 1993; Finlay 1998). The East India companies of Britain and the rest of Europe seized an opportunity to develop luxury and semi-luxury markets for the textiles, seeking out chintz printed on fine cloth to establish a fashion good, then subsequently diversifying to broader qualities (Lemire 1991). They did the same with porcelain, developing middle-class and gentry markets for tea ware, dinner services and armorial ware. Associating these commodities with taste and fashion was crucial to these markets (Weatherill 1988; Visser 1991; Helms 1994; Finlay 1998; Richards 1999). European design was then shifting away from the baroque to the lighter schemes of the rococo, easily accommodating to orientalising influences and soon popularised in European chinoiserie (Scott 1995; Snodin 1995; MacKenzie 1995). Merchants targeted the role of the prosperous middling ranks in early modern northern Europe, where taste was expressed in dress, but also in private domestic practices in dining and drinking rituals.

Imports of two very specific manufactured luxuries from Asia, printed calicoes and porcelain, in the early to mid-eighteenth century made a huge difference to British consumerism and subsequent consumer goods production (see Tables 13.4 and 13.5). Printed calicoes and other cotton textiles, at an early stage, dominated imports from Asia; they made up 67.9 per cent of the value of English East India Company Asian imports in 1668–70, and 80.6 per cent in 1738–40. The English East India Company's imports of chinaware and porcelain accounted at their peak in the early eighteenth century for 13.3 per cent of the total value of its imports; imports of raw silk peaked at the same time at 19.7 per cent. Tea imports from China reached 19.2 per cent of import values in 1722, rising to 31 per cent in 1748 and 39.5 per cent in 1760 (Chaudhuri 1978; Steensgard 1990).

The growth in European demand for Indian textiles was fostered by the East India companies, but subsequently curtailed by European governments. The East India Company forged its success not on mass market textiles, but on more expensive, differentiated fabrics for a discerning class-conscious market. The key to the market was in identifying a wide range of semi-luxury and luxury fabrics, colours and patterns suited to a broad middling class attuned to distinctiveness, fashion and novelty.

These fabrics were clearly seen by their consumers and by contemporary moralists as luxuries partly because they were oriental imports, but more because they were coloured, patterned and fine fabrics. By the later seventeenth century, the Dutch and English companies were each importing over a million pieces of Indian cotton goods. By the eighteenth century, Bengal muslins and Coromandel chintz were the new luxury textiles (Chaudhuri 1982).

Table 13.4 English East India Company imports of chinaware and porcelain

Year	Value (£)	% of Asian imports
1693	6,275	10.4
1697	13,067	8.9
1699	15,282	3.9
1702	18,764	5.0
1704	20,815	13.3
1705	14,338	7.0

Source: Chaudhuri 1978.

Imports of porcelain also played a crucial part. Though it always constituted a relatively small proportion of the East India Company's total trade, it was porcelain to a much greater degree than textiles that defined the 'Orient' to European consumers. There was nothing in Europe to match the translucence, durability and fine distinctive blue and white decoration of Chinese porcelain; it was soon to be imported in bulk, providing

Table 13.5 Estimated East India Company textile imports compared with other commodities (% of invoice value of main imports from Asia)

	1664–70	1696–1705	1731–40
Pepper	20.01	6.14	4.30
Tea	0.02	1.55	9.26
Coffee	0.63	1.24	5.35
Textiles	62.59	64.53	65.35
Silk	0.48	13.56	11.0

Source: Steensgaard 1990.

Europe not just with ornamental novelties but with useful decencies. These manufactured luxuries, unlike most of the colonial groceries, except for tea, were brought to Europe in a context not of colonial domination, but of mercantile enterprise within a strict framework of Asian and European state regulation and Asian intermediaries.

The enormous popularity of these two Asian manufactures established in broad consumer markets in Britain and other parts of Europe and the American colonies provided the key incentive to the development of imitative British goods: a cotton industry producing native printed calicoes, and an earthenware industry producing creamware substitutes for porcelain.

CONSUMPTION, CLASS AND GENDER

If colonial and Asian imports provided the stimulus to changing consumer behaviour in Britain in the later seventeenth and the eighteenth centuries, just how far did this new consumerism reach down the social scale? Did it affect women as much as men, and if so, how different were responses across genders? Was the consumer experience class-confined, the preserve of the wealthy landed elites and the urban mercantile bourgeoisie? Was the expansion of consumption a metropolitan or urban phenomenon confined to particular regions, and bypassed in rural and marginal areas of the country? Were women the sirens of consumption once heralded by Neil McKendrick (McKendrick 1974; Weatherill 1986a, 1986b; Shammas 1990; Overton 2000)? The period of rapid uptake of colonial and Asian commodities in Britain coincided with that of broader consumerism. Extensive studies of inventories demonstrate the widespread expansion of durable consumer goods in the seventeenth century and the first half of the eighteenth (Weatherill 1986a, 1988; Shammas 1990; Overton and Whittle 2000). Yet by the later eighteenth century the possibilities of such widespread consumption appeared to be limited by static and declining living standards.

We turn first to the consumption of the aristocracy, the gentry and the wealthy urban elites of the eighteenth century. Social divisions between the aristocracy and other social classes probably widened over the course of the eighteenth century. Within the ranks of the landed classes, peers maintained their position; if anything knights and gentlemen lost ground. But the ratio of peers' incomes to those of the greater merchants worsened significantly, falling from 7:1 to 3:1. On the other hand, the ratio of their incomes against that of artisans doubled; against that of labourers it increased by 40 per cent. Family incomes per family among the peers increased between the end of the seventeenth century (Gregory King's survey) and the beginning of the nineteenth century (Patrick Colquhoun's survey) from £3,200 to £8,000, a very substantial increase in personal standards of living. This reflected the concentration of the landed elite over the period; the landed aristocracy increased its hold on cultivated land in England and Wales from 15–20 per cent in 1688 to 20–25 per cent in 1790 (Cannon 1984).

There was also a scaling-up of expenditure over the course of the century, as elites sought out symbols of distinction at the same time as access to landed and especially aristocratic status became more difficult. Politeness, civility and taste became social markers more significant than material wealth, and as conventions of lifestyle they demanded socially acceptable consumer expenditure on country houses, furnishings, durables and clothing, servants and leisure (Langford 1989). Civilised conduct, taste, aesthetics and deportment conveyed affluence. Adam Smith set out the close relationship between the consumer goods and those who possessed or wore them: 'The graceful, the easy, and commanding manners of the great, joined to the usual richness and magnificence of their dress, give a grace to the very form which they happen to bestow upon it . . . As soon as they drop it, it loses all the grace, which it had appeared to possess before' (Smith 1978 [1762–3]).

Conveying status and distinction, not just through material wealth but through symbols of taste and refinement, was a longstanding feature of urban societies with substantial mercantile elites and middling classes. The wealthy of Ming China and Renaissance Italy combined rituals of eating and drinking and the private life of domestic interiors with a material culture of porcelain, fine glassware, maiolica, artwork, fabrics and furnishings (Clunas 1991, 1999; Goldthwaite 1993; Welch 1997). The value of many of these goods consisted mainly of the cost of the craft labour that went into their making, and not in value of their materials. This feature was continued in the spending habits of the wealthy in eighteenth-century England as preferences shifted towards lightweight ornamental silver and Sheffield plate, and away from silver whose value was determined only by its sterling worth (Clifford 1999).

Distinction for the wealthy before and just after the sixteenth century relied on 'patina', a sign of the right sort of duration in the social life of things. The cult of the durable consumer good was about family status, and patina was conveyed to objects through surviving family use for several generations (McCracken 1988). By the eighteenth century, distinction was conveyed less by dynasty than by novelty, fashion and taste; and rapid fashion changes in housing styles and interiors demanded the services of architects and upholders, an early form of interior designer (Craske 1999). Thorstein Veblen and Georg Simmel analysed the conspicuous consumption of the rich as the motor driving wider consumer trends. This consumption was associated with Sombart's luxury; it was individual, hedonistic and pleasure seeking, and driven by irrational fantastic desires (Sombart 1913; Miller 1995). But elite consumption was also analysed by Norbert Elias as a 'civilizing process' arising from 'court rationality'. The size, ornamentation and style of houses was coded according to rank; the luxury expenditure to achieve this was 'necessary' as a means to aristocratic social assertion (Mennell 1989). Simmel's 'trickle down' theory and Veblen's theory of emulation were used rather uncritically by historians to convey the wider social impact of the consumerism of the rich. McKendrick used the examples provided by Matthew Boulton and Josiah Wedgwood, who sought out wealthy customers as 'legislators of taste'. Both made commemorative issues of goods for royal birthdays, and sent new patterns to members of the aristocracy. They then produced similar commodities in a variety of cheaper materials accessible to all levels of society. 'The variety of the great will ever be affecting new modes, in order to increase that notice to which it thinks itself exclusively entitled. The lower ranks will imitate them as soon as they have discovered the innovation' (Robinson 1987; McKendrick 1983). Few now hold to a simple emulative model of consumption. Aristocratic consumption, it is now recognised, frequently had dynastic motivations, while that of the gentry conveyed protocol and a sense of belonging as well as the stability of family connections (Douglas and Isherwood 1979; Vickery 1993, 1998; Clifford 1999).

Nevertheless, the expenditure of the aristocracy in the eighteenth century was enormous. Landholding had become significantly more concentrated between the end of the seventeenth century and the early

Table 13.6 Estimated average cost of country houses by estate size, 1770–1800			
Estate size (acres)	Size of house (cu ft)	Cost of new house (£)	Cost of alteration (£)
Greater than 10,000	600,000	22,000	5,500
5,000–10,000	375,000	12,500	3,125
3,000–5,000	200,000	7,000	1,750

Source: Wilson and Mackley 1999.

eighteenth century, reinforced by primogeniture and the development of strict settlement. An increasing political role for those with landed estates further increased valuations, as well as pressures and opportunities for pomp and display (Cannon 1984). The country house became a theatre for the display of wealth, political power, taste and genealogical respectability; it was the largest item of aristocratic expenditure (Wilson and Mackley 1999).

In the first half of the eighteenth century a suitable country seat might be built for £2,000–£3,500, but building costs probably doubled between the 1780s and 1810s. The large majority of country houses in the eighteenth century were built for £3,000–£6,000; in the mid-Victorian period they cost £7,000–£10,000 (see Table 13.6). By comparison, an Arkwright-type mill was insured during the last thirty years of the eighteenth century for £3,000–£5,000 (Wilson and Mackley 1999).

The top 400 landowners had an average income of £10,000. At the top end of the scale, Walpole spent tens of thousands on his house at Houghton in Norfolk, owned two other houses in Richmond Park worth £14,000, and rented a London house at £3,000 per year. His wine bill was £1,000 a year, and his personal expenditure £9,000 in the four years between 1714 and 1718. Great country houses were run by a large and specialised staff of servants: the Duke of Dorset's forty-five servants at Knowle cost £474 per year in wages. Running expenses for the larger establishments could reach the range of £5,000–£6,000. Furnishing an establishment in the new style could cost the £1,000 James Best paid for the refitting of his mansion in Chatham, and the new fashion of the Grand Tour for sons cost £3,000–£5,000 for two years (Burnett 1969).

Incomes for the gentry ranged from £200–£300 up to the wealthiest with incomes close to £5,000, and their lifestyles varied accordingly. In 1790 there were about 800 gentry families with £5,000, and 3,000–4,000 with incomes of £1,000–£3000, with another 15,000 living on a few hundred pounds a year. Their heaviest expenditures were housing conversions, and servants; the prosperous gentry paid wages for between twelve and twenty servants per year (Burnett 1969).

It is to the middling classes and even to the labouring poor that historians have recently turned for explanations of the growth and characteristics of consumption in the eighteenth century. Extensive studies of probate inventories over the period have revealed that each generation from the mid-seventeenth century to the late eighteenth century left behind more and better possessions, but the value of these goods did not increase as a proportion of overall estates (de Vries 1993). The general picture which emerged from these studies was of 25 to 30 per cent of wealth held in consumer goods between the late seventeenth and the eighteenth centuries. The relatively more entrenched social position of the very wealthy was shadowed by the gathering strength of the middling classes. The most common criteria for membership of the middling classes in the mid-eighteenth century were minimum incomes of £40–£50 per year, and liability for payment of the poor rates (a local property tax used to finance the poor law). On the basis of income, these numbers ranged from one to two fifths of the population; poor-rate payers in some large towns might be 30 per cent of the population (Lindert and Williamson 1982; Langford, 1989). The middling groups who possessed a larger and wider array of consumer goods did rise as a proportion of the population over the period, and they had a disproportionate influence on wider consumer habits. There is evidence of a shift in the distribution of income to middling groups between 1750 and 1780, with the proportion of the English population with incomes between £50 and £400 rising from 15 to 25 per cent (Schwartz 1985).

Consumption among these groups of the population has been estimated mainly on the evidence of probate inventories. Studies based on probate inventories cover the period between the mid-seventeenth and mid-eighteenth centuries primarily because of the limitations of the source (Weatherill 1988; Shammas 1990). Probate inventories are lists of moveable possessions that were recorded at death. Such inventories are more widespread and richer in detail for this period than later in the eighteenth century. They provide considerable detail of the possessions and consumer durables of the middling classes; there are relatively few that survive for the poor. Their coverage for women is also limited; they were made only for spinsters and widows. Probate inventories as a source have many other limitations. They provide information only on the accumulation of goods at the point of death, not on the flow of goods, or the timing of their accumulation. They do not distinguish between goods that were inherited and those that were bought. Only consumer durables were recorded, and these rarely included clothing. Many new consumer goods were ephemeral; they were fashion goods, lighter textiles, chapbooks and other paper products, and pottery, and this is a source which only recorded goods still owned by a person at time of death. Only the quantities of the goods and their valuation at death were recorded, and the inventories tell us nothing of their meaning. The valuations assigned to these goods were frequently artificially low, reflecting the conventions of the valuers. Valuations taken at the end of a lifetime also fail to capture the novelty or fashion value of a commodity (Cox 1984; Spufford 1990; Shammas 1993).

Table 13.7 Ownership of goods, 1675–1725							
Social status	Value of total inventory	Value of household goods	Percentage of inventories containing specific commodities				
			Clocks	Pictures	Looking glasses	China	Knives and Forks
Gentry	£320	£55	51	33	62	13	11
High trades	£193	£97	34	35	62	18	7
Intermediate trades	£157	£32	25	29	56	19	11
Low trades	£92	£19	18	15	37	7	3
Widows/spinsters	£82	£18	13	12	36	6	4

Source: Weatherill 1988.

Analysis based on these inventories indicates much greater ownership of eating and drinking utensils, furnishings, books and pictures, looking glasses and clocks and window curtains. Weatherill's data (Table 13.7) indicate that ownership of earthenware and looking glasses roughly doubled between 1670 and 1725, while that of pewter plates, clocks, pictures and window curtains increased by three to five times. The percentages of inventories containing knives and forks, china and utensils for hot drinks rose from virtually none to 10 or 15 per cent (Weatherill 1993). New and decorative goods like pictures and window curtains were much more common in towns, and London dominated for indicators of possession of utensils for hot drinks. Possession of new goods also differed by social status, though often in unexpected ways. Weatherill found that new and expressive goods were more frequently found in the inventories of the middling classes, and especially the urban middling classes, especially tradesmen, than in those of either the gentry or yeoman farmers.

There were also marked regional differences. The much larger data set of 8,000 inventories collected in the study by Overton and Whittle for the two counties of Kent and Cornwall indicates significant additions to the domestic environment in Kent, along with higher levels of consumption. Many new types of furnishings and novelties appeared in the Kent inventories, while the quality of life in Cornwall declined over the period; its consumption was selective, practical and traditional (Overton 2000).

These large-scale studies of probate inventories tell us only about the greater proliferation of consumer goods across middle-rank households into the first part of the eighteenth century. More confined studies based on individual towns, and drawing on the evidence of wills as well as inventories and insurance records, provide a more partial picture into the later eighteenth century. These indicate greater ownership of a wider range of consumer durables, but no sudden or rapid expansion in this. Very high proportions of those leaving wills in eighteenth-century Birmingham and Sheffield made bequests of goods which included clothing, silver, jewellery, linen and china, as well as shop goods and cash (Berg 1993c). Metalworkers insured in Birmingham and Sheffield in a sample drawn from 1776–87 indicated relatively substantial ownership of both trade goods and consumer goods. Over 40 per cent of those insuring goods in Sheffield insured these for values of £100 to £500; in Birmingham nearly 60 per cent of insurers of goods insured at this level (Berg 1993a).

Most houses of the middle rank in the period between the late seventeenth and the early eighteenth century had between three and six rooms, including a general living room or houseplace. This never contained a bed, but did have decorative things such as pictures, looking glasses or a clock, and books. By the early eighteenth century many in this rank had a parlour or best living room with new types of furniture. Weatherill emphasised the special place of cooking in these households, and the social significance of serving meals. Social conventions on the timing of meals, the laying out of the table and the presentation of food were increasingly the subject of conduct manuals and etiquette, but for most people were largely subconscious (Weatherill 1993).

For the middling classes, it is equally important to consider those items which were rarely to be found in inventories, but which expressed imperatives of self-presentation and individuality. Sensitivity to image, and a propensity to buy display goods such as window curtains, mirrors and best clothing, played an important subjective role in consumer expenditure. The clothing that was rarely itemised in inventories was discussed in detail in the texts of wills (Weatherill 1991; Berg 1996). A sample of women who left wills in eighteenth-century Birmingham and Sheffield indicates that 27 per cent of Birmingham female will makers and 25.5 per cent of Sheffield female will makers left bequests of clothing. Their bequests were fully described, and categorised as 'best' or 'everyday' or an item worn on a special occasion (Berg 1996). Relatively high proportions of budgets continued to be spent on clothing, despite declining costs of fabric, because of frequent fashion changes

The real divide among historians arises over the extent to which the labouring classes took part in consumer society in the eighteenth and early nineteenth centuries. Long and heated debates over the standard of living have both opened up the opportunities for and closed off the possibilities of a great deal of labouring-class consumption (see chapter 10 above). Horrell and Humphries's calculations on budgets, followed by Feinstein's recent calculations of the standard of living of the average working-class family, indicate an improvement of less than 15 per cent between the 1780s and the 1850s. Feinstein's calculations for the proportions of budgets are shown in Table 13.8.

Feinstein assumes that the proportions of budgets taken up by tea, coffee, sugar and treacle stayed the same over the period, and used an index for the price of clothing reflecting the rise in the importance of cotton relative to wool and linen (Feinstein 1998). Horrell and Humphries provided the detailed background to these estimates, perceiving retrenchment of demand for products of traditional industries and decreased

Table 13.8 Expenditure in working-class budgets

	% 1788–92	% 1828–32	% 1858–61
Food	69	65	61
Rent	10	11	13
Drink	10	11	12
Clothing	6	8	9

Source: Feinstein 1998.

demand for products of new manufacturing industries, and arguing that, if anything, the low levels of working-class demand put a brake on the demand for manufactured goods. They argued that working-class budgets were relatively stable over the period, and these indicate expenditures on necessaries of about six-sevenths of household income, with little left over for discretionary expenditure (Horrell and Humphries 1992; Horrell 1996).

Such conclusive quantitative judgements have not put to rest flourishing research into the imperatives and stimuli to labouring-class consumption. The budgets used frequently contained hidden moral precepts or agendas, especially over expenditure on tea, sugar and clothing (Styles 1994). There are further disagreements over regional and sectoral divisions of labouring-class living standards. But perhaps the key problem is one of periodisation. The pessimistic positions on budgets and standards of living all refer to the period between the late 1780s and the 1840s, long known to be a time of severe pressure on the labouring poor, from high food prices in the 1790s to trade and industrial crises in the early nineteenth century. Much of the research on expanding consumption refers to the later seventeenth and first two-thirds of the eighteenth century. Allen identifies a divergence in real wages in Europe for 1500–1750 between England and the rest of Europe, with wages in England higher than for her neighbours. The wages of the skilled portions of the labouring classes, furthermore, left the cash to buy the luxuries of the consumer revolution (Allen 2001). Indicators of wages of skilled workers, especially in new industries such as the potteries, did rise over the period between 1770 and 1815 (Botham and Hunt 1987). A great variety of conditions prevailed even among the smallest cottagers of rural Warwickshire. One day labourer who in 1714 left goods, cash and clothing valued at £41 listed as his possessions a cupboard, a table, three chairs, three caldrons and a frying pan, and five pewter dishes, as well as a few beds, and some linens and blankets. Fifteen years later another valued his goods, cash and apparel at only £16, and left similar though fewer items; a higher-status husbandman among them left goods valued at £40, including a clock (Alcock 1993).

One key part of the consumption of the labouring poor was that of colonial groceries and new beverages: tea, sugar, tobacco, gin and rum. The key beverage of choice even among poor households by the end of the eighteenth century was tea sweetened with sugar, both imports from long distances, and this also required fuel for heating water. Tea, sugar and fuel feature as necessities in family budgets, but tea and sugar were also new addictive luxuries which, on existing wages, required substitution away from other food products.

Longstanding disputes over living standards do not dislodge burgeoning evidence of luxury expenditure among those who could not afford
the fashion, respectability or addiction in which they indulged. Even on
Horrell and Humphries's own evidence, during the period of high prices
in 1787–96, 10.6 per cent of working-class expenditure went on non-
essential items, with the largest share spent on clothing. Horrell also
finds an increase in total household spending of 43 per cent over the
period 1800–41, with a rise in spending on non-essential items of 137 per
cent, and on essentials of only 30 per cent (Horrell 1996). Hans Medick
long ago challenged the old market/custom division, as well as the simple correspondence between standards of living and the consumption of
manufactured goods and luxuries. Medick argued that plebeian producers invested a large part of their usually modest monetary income in
consumption, fashion and drinking. Following the cultural anthropology
of Bourdieu, Medick argued that this behaviour provided a form of 'symbolic capital' which interacted with wider plebeian culture (Medick 1982).
Evidence from pauper letters and inventories indicates possession of silver
spoons, watches and rings which were pawned when necessary to raise
cash. Voth has estimated the ownership of watches to be widespread,
approximating to 16–40 per cent in 1750. Even the lower figure would
provide for one third of all males of prime age (Voth 2000). Labourers
in pauper inventories of the late eighteenth century owned a substantial variety of household goods and decorative or semi-luxury items. And
studies of consumption and the family life-cycle show that a family of
four among the rural labouring classes might spend £5 a year on dress,
and more than this at different stages of the family life-cycle (Sokoll 1997;
King 1997; Styles 1994, 2002a).

Clothing was a particularly important marker of style, respectability
and fashion. Correct dress was one of the constantly recurring considerations that underlay the extensive theft of clothing during the period, the
growth of a large and sophisticated trade in second-hand clothing, the
development of fashion styles in adornment and ornamentation, and especially an enormous product diversification in types and costs of fabrics.
Lemire points out the availability even in the late seventeenth century of
flowered, coloured and white cotton calicoes at prices ranging from 9d.
per yard to 1s. 7d. By the 1770s to 1780s over fifty cotton textile fabrics
sold for less that $12\frac{1}{2}$d. per yard, with most of the remaining selling for
13d. to 2s. per yard. Chapmen, pedlars and hawkers over the course of
that century had established oriental cotton textiles as a new decency
among the middling sorts and a new want among the labouring poor.
A cotton gown, by the mid-eighteenth century, formed the basis of a female servant's appearance; this might cost 6–7s., or 8s. ready made, the
equivalent of at least a week's wages for many working people; they also
bought gowns for over twice this amount (Lemire 1991; Styles 2002).

Wages of female servants ranged widely between metropolis and
provinces and between houses of the very rich and more middling class

houses; they might be as much as £15 per annum by the end of the eighteenth century, but with many earning under £4 per annum. Most of these servants lived in; they spent most of what they earned on clothing, and they bought new fashionable clothing, as well as workday wear, even if they had to go into debt to do so. This included lengths of fabric for gowns of printed cotton or linen and even occasional worsted-silk mixes and silks. They bought petticoats, and sometimes stays; they had accessories ranging from neckcloths to hats and shoebuckles. 'They combined the costly and stylish with the cheap and mundane . . . they comprised a financially circumscribed, but huge and free-spending market for new, fashionable clothing' (Styles 2002).

If new clothing was not to be afforded by the labouring poor, then the market in second-hand clothing was highly developed, especially at inland markets, ports and dense population centres. Pawnbrokers conducted a lively trade in pawned clothing, and pedlars and earthenware hawkers accepted worn clothing in exchange for other goods, then selling this clothing on. Clothing was a kind of currency, easily convertible into cash. There were 260 officially designated pawnbrokers listed by the end of the eighteenth century, and Colquhoun estimated that there were in London alone several thousand receivers and hawkers of second-hand goods, including clothing. Clothing was by far the most commonly pawned consumer item in the 1770s, and women were the most active pawners (Lemire 1998). Clothing was one of the most commonly stolen commodities in the eighteenth century, accounting for over 27 per cent of recorded larceny cases, and the greatest percentage of all prosecuted thefts (Beattie 1986; Lemire 1990). Ornamentation and fashionable adornment were so important to style that second-hand clothing was transformed through the addition of scarves, patterned stockings, shoe buckles, waistcoats, a hat, and a variety of ribbons and buttons, and stolen items were quickly reassembled in unrecognisable forms (Lemire 1997). Clothing featured in the wills of those who had very little else to leave, and it was frequently described in detail. Birmingham and Sheffield widows who appeared to have no house and little cash, still bequeathed shifts, gowns, petticoats, caps, bits of lace and handkerchiefs (Berg 1996).

Among the very poor who were pauperised at various points of their lives, inventories reveal a variety of household goods and decorative items that indicate once better times in their life-cycle. The range of goods the working population could expect to own had expanded to such a degree by the late eighteenth century that even the poor might have more in their inventories than their better-off middling ancestors of the early years of the century owned (King 1997). But it was particular types of goods that were considered to be necessary to basic self-respect and decency. Deep shame was expressed in pauper letters that reported the pawning of outdoor clothes and shoes. One woman wrote, 'I was oblig'd to put my only decent Gown in pledge . . . and have not been able to go out of doors or even to a place of worship.' A male pauper wrote, 'My old Great Coat which hides the Rufull tokens of want and Poverty – will take 2/6 to Redeem' (Sokoll 1997). The poor law authorities did respond to the perceived needs of the poor for respectable dress, providing regular sets of new clothing for paupers in a wide range of different types of cloth and different colours, and made in the 'current fashion'; regular replacement once or twice yearly allowed for the accumulation of clothing (King 2002).

Aspirations to fashionable dress, among better-off industrial workers and journeymen, but also among ordinary working people, were especially expressed in leisure clothing which marked a connection between appearance and independence. James Bisset, who was working as a journeyman in a Birmingham toymaker's in the later eighteenth century, lost his position, and found himself in debt for £20, the whole value of which was for the clothing he owned (Berg 1998b). Other journeymen and industrial workers owned wigs and fashionable hats, or plated buttons and buckles (Lemire 1996; Harte 2001).

To conclude on the dynamics of labouring-class consumption, there remains a divide between findings of declining or stable standards of living, and those of rising demand for consumer goods, especially addictive food goods such as sugar and tea and fashion goods such as clothing (see chapter 10). Clothing in particular did account for rising real expenditure. The reasons for this increase in consumption without prior growth in incomes can be sought in changes in prices; prices of cotton textiles fell by approximately one-third from the 1770s to 1850. And lighter textiles, and more frequent fashion changes, pushed for a higher proportionate ownership of clothing. The enhanced hedonic value of clothing provided by perceived improvements in quality and fashion change could increase the utility gained by consumers of these goods, and they might substitute these for other goods, including necessaries and housing standards. Another means of consuming in the absence of changes in income was debt, a constant feature of labouring-class life (Finn 2000).

GENDER AND HOUSEHOLD DIVISION OF CONSUMPTION

Evidence on the variety and value of men's clothing raises questions over the accepted gender analysis of eighteenth- and early nineteenth-century consumption. Sombart and Simmel, both writing at the turn of the twentieth century, associated the incentives to the growth of consumption with sexuality. Sombart, in *Luxury and Capitalism*, wrote that the principal cause of the expansion of trade, industry and finance capital over the whole period between 1300 and 1800 was the demand for luxury goods, especially by the *nouveaux riches*, courts and the aristocracy. An intensification of the demand for luxuries, sexual and political in origin, made fashion a driving force of the social elites. Sombart explained the rise of luxury, ultimately, by the psychological impulse to gratify the senses; this was rooted in turn in sexuality. Mistresses, courtesans and salon culture provided the sirens of consumer society (Sombart 1967 [1913]). Simmel identified a dynamic behind fashion, a dynamic also rooted in psychological impulses, but in this case impulses of imitation and emulation. He identified a fundamental conflict in society between adaptation to our social group and individual elevation from it. It was class based, so that imitation from below of a given pattern was followed by flight towards novelty and distinction from above (Frisby and Featherstone 1997). The key actors here were not courtesans but female domestic servants.

The identity which has come to be assumed between consumption and women arises from gendered presentations of the luxury debates, especially as conveyed in these influential texts by Sombart and Simmel, as well as Thorstein Veblen's *Theory of the Leisure Class*. They were the source of Neil McKendrick's claim for female agency, and especially that of servants in spreading the desires for consumer goods. Women's desires for consumer goods have been assumed to be generic, driven by leisured conspicuous consumption, female vanity and fashion. Not only servants and courtesans but female industrial workers were assumed to be subject to such desires. Young spinners were condemned by moralists for spending the money they earned in domestic manufacture in 'buying fine clothes and other gawdy gew gaws' (Berg 1985). Such assumptions also lie behind theories of household behaviour such as de Vries's 'industrious revolution'. De Vries's theory rests on intra-household decisions over labour, leisure and consumption taken among husbands, wives and children. De Vries, like McKendrick, drew attention to the rising decision-making role of the woman of the household (assumed to be a wife). The wife in the de Vries model takes on a primary role as decision maker in consumption, and occupies a strategic place at the intersection of reproduction, production and consumption. She is an 'active consumer' rather than a passive victim of fashion manipulators. Her willingness to shift her tastes must be combined with power in household decision-making; both convert to her ability to buy novelties and luxuries in the marketplace for herself and the household (de Vries 1993). That power in decision-making depends in turn upon a specifically targeted demand for female labour such as existed in the new consumer industries of the proto-industrial period and the early stages of the industrial revolution (Berg 1993b). There is also, however, no evidence that increased female employment in low-wage labour entailed more access by women to family decision-making. Evidence of women's unequal access to food in the household, frequently through self-denial (see chapter 9), might also be found in other consumer goods, for example clothing versus drink and tobacco.

While de Vries's theory of the 'industrious revolution' places gender at the centre of explanation, it does not address the actual practices of women's and men's consumption. Evidence here is lamentably thin;

supposition drawn mainly from literary analogy provides an edifice of gendered representations, with emphasis on fictions, eroticism and the male gaze (Bermingham and Brewer 1995; de Grazia and Furlough 1996; Kowaleski-Wallace 1997). Women's possession of moveable consumer goods has also been assumed to be an indication of their subordinate status within the family; their baubles a poor compensation for lack of landed property and housing. Evidence on gender differences in possessions and buying practices must be gathered in painstaking research on household inventories, the study of the text of wills, household accounts, family correspondence, diaries and autobiographies.

Lorna Weatherill's classic studies of the middling orders based on probate inventories from 1660–1760 identified few major differences in possessions between men and women; certainly higher proportions of women had new and decorative goods than did the men from similar classes, but these differences were too small to warrant the suggestion of a women's subculture in the ownership of goods. She emphasised that women's possessions indicated that they saw themselves as part of a family and household (Weatherill 1986b; Shammas 1990). Even the limited evidence of meaning and motivation available from inventories can, however, indicate the special part played by the women of the household in cooking and in the arrangement and serving of meals. Inventories provide insight into the use of space as well as the quantities, variety and placement of material possessions. Such evidence reveals the symbolic as well as practical importance of cooking, which was done by the wife or housekeeper rather than servants until the later eighteenth century, occupying a central part of the household, and carried out with simple and functional cooking equipment. A different material culture for the serving and eating of meals included decorated pottery and porcelain, knives and forks, conduct and manners over serving, and rituals of tea drinking, and all set in 'front stage' locations in the household (Weatherill 1993). Evidence of bequests made in wills rather than indices of possessions at death show sharp differences between men's and women's perceptions of what they owned. The women of Sheffield and Birmingham left substantially more bequests containing clothing, jewellery, linen and silver than did men. The really striking differences in the wills, however, was in their presentation of goods and the networks of legacies. Women provided very detailed descriptions of their things: clothes, light furnishings, marked and table linens, tea and china ware were personal and expressive goods, conveying identity, personality and fashion. Their bequests presented a carefully coded inventory of their things embedded in statements about their networks of family and friends. The men left few details of their clothing and furnishings, and generally passed these on to direct family members. The women who left these wills added new commodities to old inherited possessions; they cannot be easily categorised either as fashionable conspicuous consumers or as simple bearers of household or family well-being. For their wills indicate a whole range of clothing, light furnishings and ornaments clearly perceived as personal possessions, and, as such, richly described and sensitively distributed among friends and family (Berg 1993c).

Women's diaries such as that of Elizabeth Shackleton, a woman of the lesser Lancashire gentry, provide insight into the day-to-day expenditure of women and the meanings they attached to the goods they bought. Much of this consumption was the skilled provisioning and servicing of a household, based on the gathering and sharing of information with other women on prices, quality and availability. A woman's purchase of fashionable clothing, furniture and china displayed her social status and gave her personal pleasure, but it also expressed a wide range of other motivations and meanings, from family history to individual memory and sociability (Vickery 1993, 1998).

Our knowledge of the practices of women's consumption from the mundane and daily to the magnificent and episodic is still patchy, with little on life-cycle, class and rural–urban differentiation. The evidence we have does however challenge the gendered stereotype of the rapacious female consumer. A corresponding picture of male consumer behaviour is almost wholly lacking. Men have not featured with any significance in histories of fashionable consumption, perhaps because of those same stereotypes of separate spheres which so underpinned assumptions about the female consumer (Breward 1999).

Men did much more of the shopping for new consumer goods than we imagine. They were frequently delegated in trips to provincial towns and the metropolis, or even abroad to buy for the household. Some took the initiative, as in the case of Ben Franklin who sent a package of English cloths to his wife in 1758, describing them as: '156 yards of cotton, printed curiously from copper plates, a new invention, to make bed and window curtain. Also 7 yards of printed cottons blue ground, to make you a gown' (Lemire 1991). Male dress in the eighteenth and early nineteenth centuries was as laden with fashion as was women's, and male diarists reveal active and enthusiastic shopping activity among men, as well as the full range of motivations and sensibilities over their possessions that women did (Finn 2000). Their clothing provided access to respectability, and was valued accordingly in their insurance policies (Berg 1993c, 1998a). Specific articles of masculine dress such as wigs, and specific attributes of masculine interiors such as dining rooms and their ornamentation with fireplaces, tables and punch bowls, form only the beginnings of research (Nenadic 1994; Harte 2001). Research is still very limited on masculinity and consumption, hampered as it has been by a discourse of separate spheres.

Women's association with the buying of china, satirised in the eighteenth century as a symbol of female superficiality and depraved attraction to things, had some basis in gendered consumption. Certainly women were avid consumers of chinaware; they were of great importance to Wedgwood's success. Their association with chinaware stems from their place in tea drinking. Women occupied a central part in the rituals and symbols of tea drinking. They shopped for chinaware, they ran many of the china shops, and they became noted connoisseurs. But men too played their part. There is widespread evidence in inventories, wills and diaries of men collecting of chinaware. Men's art and print collections and vase mania also attest to this acquisitive consumerism (Weatherill 1986a; Kowaleski-Wallace 1997; Nenadic 1997; Clayton 1998; Richards 1999; Young 1999; Uglow 2002b).

Consumer aspirations across class and gender stimulated the rapid and extensive proliferation of new commodities from the later seventeenth century onwards. The supply-side responses to these aspirations were in turn to generate wider and deeper demand for these goods, bought to satisfy desires for fashion, respectability and sociability, or for convenience and comfort. These new consumer goods were generated through technological change, but above all through product innovation.

PRODUCT INNOVATION, FASHION AND TASTE

As we have seen, qualitative characteristics underlay the rapid growth in demand in Europe for particular imported luxury consumer goods, notably Indian calicoes and Chinese porcelain. Product innovation based in 'imitative principles' followed on from these imports, generating a special range of British consumer goods particularly targeted at middling class consumers.

Mercantilist policies throughout the eighteenth century, prohibiting the importation of Indian calicoes and French silks and imposing heavy duties on French chinaware and Chinese porcelain, certainly stimulated import substitutes. New 'imitative' invention was to produce objects or materials as good as Chinese, Venetian or French imports, but it was also to produce an inventive combination or reinterpretation of traditional principles. In the case of Britain, we can see that the new goods were not just cheaper copies of goods already available to the aristocracy, but were genuine novelties sought out initially by urban middling groups (Weatherill 1988; Berg 2002).

We have seen how consuming these new commodities was connected with specific cultural settings of taste, gentility, politeness and fashion. Many of the new consumer goods, from clothing to furniture, from tea and dinner services and punch bowls to silver plated cutlery and candlesticks, conveyed consumer sensibilities in dining, drinking and visiting rituals. Taste, in a country which was not dominated by the court, was developed as a science and an art. Consumers were educated in or initiated into good taste, or they relied on intermediaries from milliners and mercers to toymen and upholders.

Not just taste but fashion was to drive forward product innovation and consumerism. France is usually credited with a consumer market based in luxury and fashion, and Britain with one based in substantial simple goods and solid comforts. But British product innovation, based in imitative principles, also followed fashion cycles, and in the second half of the eighteenth century was to seize the initiative from France. A fashion market for linen, emphasising variety, novelty and diversity, was developed through a sophisticated and cosmopolitan mercantile network, based in Dublin and Glasgow as well as London. The more rapid innovation in Britain than France in the new calicoes and muslins prompted a transfer in fashion initiative to Britain in the last quarter of the century (Chapman and Chassagne 1981; Collins 1999).

Fashion markets prevailed not just in textiles and clothing, but in furnishings and decorative ware, and Britain was also to take the initiative in these in the last half of the century. New British imitative products – English lead glass crystal, Staffordshire earthenware and especially creamware, Sheffield plate, English light furnishings in mahogany and veneers, and especially tea tables, Axminster and Kidderminster carpets, and a whole range of ornamental metalwares from japanned trays to Birmingham buttons, buckles and brassware, tea and coffee urns – all scooped home and foreign markets because they were fashion leaders.

SELLING, SHOPPING AND ADVERTISING

This proliferation of new goods also speeded up distribution and intensified and transformed retailing over the century. Local fairs and markets were by no means anachronisms, but burgeoned over the period. There were 3,200 fairs in England and Wales in 1756. Though most were specialised, and focused on agricultural goods, it was also common to sell chinaware and glassware at them (Chartres 1985). Similarly, pedlars and hawkers sold the full range of fashion goods. By no means a relic of the past or of a poorly serviced countryside, the pedlars were innovative, aggressive and pushing salesmen and women. They were the commercial salesmen who used large-scale advertising in the towns they visited, and wide use of trade catalogues and extended credit. They were most densely concentrated in Britain in the Midlands and the Home Counties, areas that also had the highest number of shops (Mui and Mui 1989; Fontaine 1996).

Shops were also ubiquitous in eighteenth-century Britain as well as Holland and France. Excise records for 1759 show a ratio of population to shops for England and Wales of 43:1; a later survey in 1785 indicated an average of 55 persons per shop. Such shops ranged from the general chandler to highly specialist shops such as booksellers, mercers, drapers and china sellers which might be found in every small town. They were purveyors of the full range of colonial groceries to all parts of the country. Shops meant fixed premises and fixed prices; they had the advantage of reducing the price of information; as price takers they accepted a fixed percentage above wholesale prices. For the innovative dealer in fashion goods, they also meant an opportunity for new kinds of retailing, indeed for making retailing and shopping themselves a fashion.

Shops became warehouses, galleries, auctions, emporia, bazaars, indeed a new leisure activity. The department store was no nineteenth-century invention; it existed in the Royal Exchange from the seventeenth century, and this centralisation of fashion shops was combined with shop interiors furnished with mirrors and pictures, tables and chairs, and candle lighting (Walsh 1995). Not just shops, but showrooms and galleries, high-profile auctions, and private views of new lines were celebrated tactics pursued by metropolitan and provincial retailers. One of the most successful retailing innovations for new products was warehouse selling, a different kind of fashion retailing. From the 1730s in London it conveyed a large shop, high turnover, bulk selling and low prices. Its principle was deliberate low pricing to promote ready-made clothing, especially cotton petticoats, caps and shirts as well as shoes and hats. The cotton boom of the 1780s and 1790s was the golden age of the drapery warehouses. Warehouse selling complemented the East India Company sales and auctions, and fast-paced selling targeted a price-conscious middling class market. Concentrations of warehouses in spa towns such as Bath played the same role as modern designer discount outlets and seasonal sales, in spreading fashion buying across the middling classes (Robinson 1964; Lemire 1991).

The taste for shopping was spread further through advertising, which, by the end of the eighteenth century, was highly developed in newspapers, periodicals, almanacs, trade cards and trade catalogues. By the 1730s, daily news sheets and advertisers throughout England devoted 50 per cent of their space to advertisements. Highly illustrated trade cards proliferated in Britain from the 1730s to the 1770s, advertising an enormous range of goods, designs and ornamentation. Trade catalogues appeared in numbers from the 1750s, frequently providing plates of groups of commodities, especially brassware, silver plate, ornamental ironwork and metalwork, and glassware and ceramics, demonstrating product complementaries and designs. Series or collections of consumer goods were thus actively constructed by merchants, factors and manufacturers. The catalogues provide evidence of extensive selling by factors and agents, and in international markets (Berg and Clifford 1998).

CONSUMER POLITICS

While this chapter has focused on the consumption of new and non-necessary goods, consumption was, at its most basic level, a deeply political issue expressed in long and intense conflict over the price of bread. Food riots and the 'moral economy' of the crowd throughout the eighteenth century, succeeded by agitation over the corn laws, placed rights to subsistence and markets at the centre of political agendas throughout the eighteenth and nineteenth centuries. Luxuries, even those that had become necessities, were not just moral, but political issues. Anti-slavery agitation was galvanised around sugar consumption and consumer boycotts; consumer boycotts so effectively developed in the American Revolution continued into Chartist political tactics (Breen 1988; E. P. Thompson 1991; Midgley 1992). Consumption formed a key focus for the early co-operative movement, from selling the output of producer co-operatives, to alternative forms of retailing, and to the early formation of the consumer co-operative movement itself (Webb and Webb 1921; Taylor 1983; Thompson 1988).

The state also represented consumption as integral to politics. The luxury debates convey the longstanding ambivalence of states and particular social groups towards the growth of consumption. Sumptuary legislation which attempted reinforcement of social hierarchies through dress codes and other constraints on consumer behaviour was accompanied by concerns over vice and corruption. Legislators feared loss of national independence through excessive reliance on foreign luxuries, and social commentators linked consumer trends with an increasing inequality in the distribution of income. Taxation was a key manipulator. The bulk of eighteenth-century taxation, at levels to support a military and imperial state, was raised through indirect taxation of commodities. Excise duties on beer, malt, hops, soap, salt, candles, leather and glass were complemented by customs duties on tea, sugar, spirits and tobacco. This taxation was socially regressive; the middling and labouring classes bore the brunt of the tax burden. Excise duties rose from 26.1 per cent of total taxes in 1696–1700 to 50.6 per cent of taxes in 1751–5. The poor were taxed on items that had become semi-necessities: tobacco, sugar and tea. Taxed items recorded by Eden in the household budgets of the poor – coal, tea, sugar, candles, salt, soap and starch – represented 20 per cent of a labouring-class family's expenditure. Efforts to raise additional tax revenue did not exclude the rich, and politicians expressed some pride in singling out for assessed taxes items of 'unnecessary' expenditure: male servants, hair powder, carriages and pleasure horses, but also houses, windows and newspapers (O'Brien 1988).

CONCLUSION

An economic history of consumption in the transition from the early modern period into the industrial revolution remains open-ended, and in many ways barely begun. The questions asked by economic historians are frequently set within macroeconomic frameworks sharply constrained by restrictive assumptions which diverge considerably from the issues of consumer behaviour of interest to social and cultural historians. Economic historians have, to a large extent, assumed the subject covered under the mantle of incomes, wages and standards of living. Evidence gathered has frequently been at a far remove from the lives of consumers at the time: price series of one type of cotton textile based on export valuations, not what people paid at shops and fairs and to pedlars for pieces of cloth and ready-made and second hand clothing; food price series based on institutions such as hospitals or colleges, and budgets based on poor law surveys and policy proposals. What types of goods there were, their qualities and fashion, what prices were paid, and how they were distributed need to be integrated into an economic history of consumption. The fragmentation, diversity and unevenness of consumer practices make it very difficult to connect consumer behaviour to long-term trends.

14

Scotland

T. M. DEVINE

Contents

Introduction	388
Before industrialisation: Scotland c. 1700	389
After the Union, c. 1707–60	396
Transformation, c. 1760–1860	399
Explanations	401
Industrialisation and Scottish society	413

INTRODUCTION

Sustained investigation of the economy and society of early modern Scotland has occurred only since the mid-1970s. Earlier generations were content to focus almost exclusively on the developments of church and state in the period before the Union of 1707. Out of this neglect came the widespread acceptance of an influential stereotype. It became a commonplace in the textbook literature until the 1960s that the Scottish experience was exceptional in relation both to England and to other 'advanced' European economies. Scotland in c. 1700 was said to be different, not only in its poverty, the archaism of the social structures and the timeless rigidity of the economic system, but also in its insecurity and instability, a direct result of weak central authority and the threat of baronial insurrection. In an article published in 1967 Hugh Trevor-Roper expressed the orthodoxy in succinct terms: 'at the end of the seventeenth century, Scotland was a by-word for irredeemable poverty, social backwardness [and] political faction' (Trevor-Roper 1967: 1,636).

Since then, however, a more complex and subtle evaluation of the national economic condition has emerged, as a growing army of Scottish historical scholars has asked fresh questions and plundered the archives in the search for answers. The corpus of published work has therefore grown significantly, though it has to be acknowledged that the recent historiography still lacks the sheer richness and density of the work on English economic and social history described at length throughout this volume. Key areas, such as demographic history, are constrained by the inadequacy of records. Not one Scottish parish register is suitable for family reconstitution, while even extraction of baptism and burial totals poses serious problems. At the same time, rigorous statistical studies, of the kind which have forced reassessment of the nature and chronology of English industrialisation, are notable by their absence. Indeed the new economic history in general has had little impact on the study of Scottish history. All that said, however, understanding of pre-Union Scotland has been much advanced by recent work. The stereotypes of the past are no longer tenable.

BEFORE INDUSTRIALISATION: SCOTLAND *C*. 1700

In 1700 Scotland had an estimated population of little more than a million, or about one-fifth that of England. The distribution of these inhabitants reflected the natural endowment and topography of the country. Much of Scotland is dominated by mountain and moorland. Even today, after nearly 300 years of improvement and drainage, around two-thirds of the country is still only suitable for rough grazing. In the later seventeenth century, therefore, the main concentrations of population were in the more fertile areas of the lowlands of Aberdeen and Angus, the coastlands of the Forth and Tay, the Solway plain, the Merse of Berwickshire and the lower Clyde valley. Nevertheless, compared to the nineteenth century, when massive migration decisively altered the national demographic profile in favour of the Central Lowlands and the cities of Glasgow, Edinburgh and Dundee, Scottish population was much more widely dispersed in the early modern period. Perhaps as many as half the people lived north of the River Tay.

There were many Scotlands. The country, though small in size and population, was a veritable mosaic of regional societies. The familiar distinction between the Highlands and the Lowlands concealed more subtle differences between the Hebrides on the one hand and the southern and eastern Highlands on the other. Galloway in the south-west retained strong particularist traditions while the Northern Isles had both a Norse legal system and traces of the Norse language well into the seventeenth century. Nevertheless, amid all this territorial complexity, some national generalisations are still possible. Overwhelmingly Scotland was a rural-based society with only around 12 per cent of the population living in towns of over 2,000 inhabitants. The raw produce of the land – skins, grain, wool and coal – were vital trading commodities, though linen and woollen manufactures were also increasingly important. Even in this early

1. KINROSS
2. CLACKMANNAN
3. DUMBARTON
4. TO KINROSS
5. WEST LOTHIAN
6. MIDLOTHIAN
7. EAST LOTHIAN
8. RENEREW

Figure 14.1 Scotland

Source: Devine 1999.

period, however, the significance of urban development should not be underestimated.

Between 1500 and 1600 the proportion of the nation's population living in the larger towns of 10,000 citizens and above nearly doubled, and it did so again by 1700. Edinburgh, the capital and biggest town, had a population of around 30,000 by the early eighteenth century. Aberdeen and Dundee had about 10,000 inhabitants each, while Glasgow had emerged as the second burgh (city or town) in the land by the later seventeenth century, with a population reckoned at 15,000 and growing. Relative to Edinburgh and Glasgow, however, Aberdeen and Dundee were experiencing stagnation in the second half of the seventeenth century. Edinburgh's predominance in Scottish urban life was longstanding, but Glasgow's new pre-eminence reflected the growing importance of developing links to Ireland and the Atlantic economy, which were to prove so crucial to Scottish progress after *c.* 1740 (Lynch 1989: 85–117; Devine 2000: 151–64). The vast majority of other Scottish burghs were little more than villages in this period. Few, apart from Inverness, Stirling, Dumfries and Renfrew, had more than 1,000 inhabitants each. Nevertheless, in some areas, most notably the coastlands of the River Forth, the sheer number and growth of small burghs created a regional urban network to rival any in western Europe in density (Lynch 1992: 24–41). Most urban areas, however, shared a similar insecurity over time because of the high level of their dependence upon the export of a limited range of primary products. This rendered Scottish towns in the early modern period especially vulnerable to sudden fluctuations in the patterns of both supply and demand.

Against this background, much of the thrust of modern historiography has been to challenge the notion of the Scottish economy as peripheral, static and backward. Contrary to a great deal of received wisdom, Louis Cullen argued that Scotland's apparently 'remote' location off the far north-west coast of Europe was a positive advantage, affording easy access to Ireland, a land frontier with England and the possibilities for lucrative commercial connections to the east (Cullen 1989: 226–8). By the seventeenth century, Scots merchants, pedlars and mercenary soldiers were to the fore in port towns across Scandinavia and the north German, Polish and Russian hinterlands. Between 1600 and 1650 anywhere between an estimated 55,000 and 70,000 Scots had migrated across the North Sea (Smout *et al.* 1994: 77–90). These movements helped to consolidate commercial links with Europe's 'inland sea', the heart of economic development in the north of the continent, and so provide an impetus to urban development along Scotland's east coast. Equally, as the centre of economic gravity shifted south to the Amsterdam–London axis and thence towards the Atlantic world, Scotland was also strategically well placed. New prospects opened up for the west coast towns in supplying 'Scotland's first colony' in Ulster and, even before the Union of 1707, exploiting the new commercial opportunities in both America and the Caribbean:

> Scotland's good fortune was that its most advantageous port locations on the Clyde and on the Firth of Forth were both drawing on the same rich hinterland. Hence the growth of the Atlantic trades reinforced the existing wealth of the Lowlands rather than shifted its centre of gravity. The Lowlands, together with Edinburgh and Glasgow, constituted an effective and integrated economy in which talent and capital could be put to the best use and young men able to venture in the western world.   (Cullen 1989: 228)

In comparison, Ireland's Atlantic commercial expansion was constrained, not only by its colonial status but also because the hinterland of the country's western ports was relatively poorly developed.

Scotland's internal economy and society have also been the subject of more optimistic reappraisals which have collectively challenged the notion of national stasis and inertia. The older view of a land still riven by feud and strife has been conclusively refuted. Centralised justice took on a new meaning with the reconstituted High Court of Justiciary in 1672 and the creation of the circuit courts from 1708. The revolution of 1688-9 in Scotland was a remarkably bloodless affair while the infamous Massacre of Glencoe of 1692 is remembered in song and story partly because, by the new standards of the time, the incident was an entirely exceptional atrocity. Glencoe also illustrated the determination of the state to use its muscle against recalcitrant Highland clans. Not surprisingly, therefore, the militarism of clan society was also in decline. The last clan conflict took place in 1688, and thereafter collective violence was confined to cattle raiding and protection rackets in some of the frontier lands of the Highlands (Macinnes 1996: 147-8).

At a more subtle level commercial forces were already opening up tensions within clanship. Markets were developing to the south for Highland goods: above all for cattle which, alone of most Scottish products, did very well in the years after the Union of 1707, but also for timber, fish and slate. The returns from these trades helped to sustain absenteeism and consumerism among the clan elites. Household accounts show a growing appetite for elegant furniture, fashionable clothing, pictures, books and musical instruments. The clan bards were alarmed at the trends and lamented the habits of chiefs who spent longer periods in Edinburgh or even in London and neglected their traditional patriarchal duties. There were already signs that profit was starting to take precedence over the ancient social responsibilities of the landowners. The clans expected the ruling families to act as their protectors and guarantee secure possession of land in return for allegiance, military service, tribute and rental. But the evidence suggests that this social contract was already under acute pressure in some parts of Gaeldom even before the aftermath of the last Jacobite rebellion in 1745 which hastened the final demise of clan society.

Throughout Scotland similar processes were at work to a greater or lesser extent. Landowners had come to regard their estates more as assets from which revenue and profit could be extracted and less as sources of military power and authority. The indicators of this historic transition in the priorities of the Scottish governing classes were very numerous. It can be seen for instance in their domestic architecture. The last fortified house in Scotland, Leslie Castle, was built in 1660. The emphasis was now more on comfort and aesthetic appeal rather than on defence. The tower house was giving way to the country house. There also was a much greater involvement in the wider economy, with the aim of extracting better returns from the landed estate. North-eastern landowners were heavily engaged in the seaborne grain trade to Edinburgh and the Scandinavian countries. The great Border landlords were energetically expanding the numbers of sheep and cattle on their properties. Between 1500 and the early eighteenth century, around 170 new burghs of barony (authorised by the crown but created by lay and ecclesiastical landowners) were founded by landowners, with the majority established in the decades immediately before the Union. Not all – or even the majority – were a success, but the commitment of the elite to small town and village development is undeniable. There were also instances of large-scale investment in harbour and port development, such as that of the Duke of Hamilton at Bo'Ness, Sir Robert Cunninghame at Saltcoats and the Erskines of Mar at Alloa. Not surprisingly, the new economic priorities of the elite filtered through into the public policies of parliament and privy council which they dominated. The records of these two bodies are full of references to attempts made to improve the national economy. These included acts for the encouragement of colonial trade and domestic manufacturing; the foundation of the Bank of Scotland in 1695; the removal of the traditional monopoly rights of the royal burghs in 1672; and a series of statutes to facilitate agricultural improvement. Many of these initiatives were merely fine aspirations rather than real achievements. In a sense, however, this mattered little. What was more important was the confirmation that the Scottish governing classes were now on the side of material progress and lending their considerable political authority to the cause of national economic reform.

Change and material progress can also be identified in the spheres of agriculture, international trade and domestic industry. The first of these was most crucial because of its dominant position in the economy as a whole. Judged over the century from the 1650s to the early 1740s, Scottish farms were remarkably successful in feeding the population in most years and, in some periods, producing export surpluses. Between 1660 and 1700 there were significant shortages only in 1674 and 1693–7. This last crisis has gone down in history as the 'Lean Years' when a series of consecutive harvest failures brought about famine conditions in some areas and effectively reduced the nation's population by death and emigration by an estimated 15 per cent. For some writers, however, this disaster was an aberration, a break in the trend of increasingly stable food supplies, caused by freak weather conditions which also hit Scandinavia and France equally badly. For the following half-century there were difficult times, but not subsistence crises, only in 1709, 1724–5 and 1740–1. This record can be contrasted with the second half of the sixteenth century, when Scotland suffered food shortages in some areas for around a third of the years between 1560 and 1600 (Devine 1994: 2–32).

Why this improvement occurred cannot yet be precisely determined. Some scholars argue that the decisive factor was more benign climatic conditions; others stress the demographic factor as pressure on food supply was reduced by the mortality crises of the 1640s and 1690s and the impact of large-scale emigration. In addition, however, there is also evidence of greater efficiency in the agricultural sector, with a movement to enlarged single tenancies, longer written leases, an expansion of rural market centres, modest increases in grain yields in favoured areas and commutation of rentals in kind to money values.

Parallel changes occurred in international trade. A shift was already apparent away from Scotland's historic commercial connections with Europe and towards England, Ireland and the Atlantic economy. In 1700 an estimated half of Scottish trade by value was already carried on with England in such key commodities as cattle, coal, salt, linen and grain (Smout 1963: 194–236). Scotland's western ports in particular were now closely involved in commerce with the Scottish emigrant community in the north of Ireland. Recent research has also identified industrial expansion in coal, lead mining, and glass and paper manufacture (Whatley 2000: 26). As many as 106 large manufactories, mainly in the towns, were either proposed or established between 1587 and 1707, with almost 75 per cent of these recorded after 1660. But the real industrial triumph was in linen, a sector destined to become Scotland's main manufacturing industry for most of the eighteenth century. In 1599–1600, 18,000 ells of linen were sent to London (an ell of linen equals 37 inches or 94 centimetres). By 1700 the figure was around 650,000 ells, with total exports across the Border running at between 1.2 and 1.8 million yards. The old sixteenth-century raw material staples of skins and fish exports were now being replaced c. 1700 by linen, coal and live cattle.

What broader picture does all this reveal? First, the older orthodoxy of a static economic system no longer fits the facts. Second, the scale of development needs to be kept in perspective. In the critically important agricultural sector, subsistence activity was still dominant in many areas. The estate records of the time are full of references to the large numbers of small tenants, holding less than 20–30 acres, who rarely produced a surplus beyond that which was necessary for family consumption and landlord rents. One estimate suggests that in the first few decades of the eighteenth century only a quarter of Scottish farmers were mainly producing for market (Dodgshon 1981: 243; Devine 1994: 15–16). The changes identified in the rural economy were real enough but they amounted to modest developments *within* the agrarian system rather than basic alterations to the system as a whole. Thirdly, the foundations of some of the changes were hardly secure. The better times of the period 1660–90 were followed by a series of disasters in the following decade which had longer-term effects well into the first quarter of the eighteenth century: the savage demographic and financial consequences of the 'Lean Years'; war with France in 1689–97 and 1701–13; rampant economic nationalism across western Europe which inexorably squeezed Scottish markets, not least in England, where linen duties were raised significantly in 1698, thus contributing to a halving of Scottish exports to the south between 1698–1700 and 1704–6; and last, but by no means least, the serious financial losses associated with the failed expeditions to Darien on the isthmus of Panama.

Finally, there is the issue of the comparison with England. The two countries certainly had some features in common and in that sense the 'exceptionalism' of Scotland has been exaggerated. These included *inter alia* the existence of an agrarian social structure mainly based on landlords leasing farms to tenants, a geographically mobile population and a governing class in each country increasingly committed to national economic advance. However, at the turn of the eighteenth century, the contrasts were perhaps much more apparent. Scotland was undeniably much poorer, a pattern confirmed not simply by the nation's vulnerability to famine but by wage data. The most recent investigations suggest that by the 1730s an English mason or carpenter had, on average, almost a 50 per cent (money wage) margin over his Scottish counterpart (Gibson and Smout 1995: 275–6). Little wonder that Dr Johnson was later to remark that the finest road a Scotsman ever saw led to England! Even in the later period, 1765–95, carpenters in Aberdeen and Edinburgh never reached more than 40–45 per cent of wages of London carpenters and nearly two-thirds of wages in Exeter or Manchester. Mortality figures point to a similar conclusion. Calculations of life expectancy at birth in 1755 give figures of 31 or 32 for Scotland against 36–7 for England (Hunt 1986: 937; Whyte 1995: 117).

Again, while Scotland may not have been significantly out of line with other north-western European countries such as the Scandinavian states, the nation was manifestly less developed than most of England. The industrial sector was both relatively small and suffering the joint impact of war and rising tariffs in the early eighteenth century while, at the same period, industry and commerce accounted for about a third of English national income (Cole 1981: 41). There was also a marked difference in the performance of agriculture, despite the advances described above in Scottish farming in the later seventeenth century. On Scottish east coast estates (the area most favourable to arable farming) *c.* 1700–20, the seed-yield figures for oats were around three to four. On a sample of English estates the yields for the same crop were averaging 6.5 to 8.5, or double the Scottish equivalent (Holderness 1989: 143–5; Devine 1994: 55–6). Indeed current interpretations of the pattern of English wheat yields from probate inventories indicate major gains in the seventeenth and early eighteenth centuries which exceeded those of the period after *c.* 1760 (Daunton 1995: 30; see also chapter 4 above). In the Scottish case these time frames would have to be reversed. Social indicators tell the same story. Access to some land, however minute, was still one of the defining characteristics of Scottish rural society until the second half of the eighteenth century. Small tenants, often renting land in multiple tenure, cottars allocated a patch of land in return for seasonal work on larger farms, and tradesmen with tiny smallholdings, made up the vast majority of the country population. It was a social order that had more in common with patterns in parts of continental Europe than the regions of commercial farming south of the Border.

AFTER THE UNION, *C.* 1707–60

The Parliamentary Union of 1707 was a historic watershed in Scottish political and constitutional history but its short-term economic consequences down to the 1750s are much more debatable.

Several clauses of the Act of Union were devoted to economic matters, but Articles IV and V were the two of most importance. Article IV provided for Scottish entry without payment of custom duty to the English domestic and colonial markets, while Article V stated that all Scottish-owned vessels would now rank as ships of Great Britain, so affording the Scots the privileges of inclusion within the Navigation Acts. The Union created the biggest free-trade zone in Europe at the time and gave Scottish merchants the liberty to trade legally in such profitable American commodities as tobacco, sugar, indigo and rum (a privilege not granted the Irish) and, at the same time, afforded them the protection of the Royal Navy. It all seemed a very good bargain. On the other hand, there was considerable risk as well as much opportunity for Scotland in the new relationship. The bad times of the 1690s had seriously weakened the national economy. The 'Lean Years' had hit agriculture so hard that, as already noted, in some areas of the Lowlands farmers were still paying off rent arrears more than two decades later. In economic terms Scotland was not in good shape and was potentially exposed to more advanced and competitive English industry within the new common market. It was essentially because they recognised this danger that the last Scottish parliament bargained hard to ensure in the Treaty of Union that Scottish-made paper, malt and salt would continue to have a degree of protection after the Union by being relieved of the need to pay the higher English duties for varying periods of time. The problem was that Scotland and England were at different stages of economic development. Scotland's manufacturing base was both slender and vulnerable, while English industry, especially in textiles, was already the most advanced in Europe. The new political integration might well have doomed Scotland to the status of an English economic satellite: a supplier of foods, raw materials and cheap labour for the more sophisticated southern economy but with little possibility of achieving manufacturing growth and diversification in its own right. This was roughly what happened to Ireland in the eighteenth and early nineteenth centuries. Union could well have been the political prelude to 'the development of underdevelopment' rather than the catalyst for a new age of progress and prosperity. Why this was not the outcome is one of the key questions of eighteenth-century Scottish economic history (Devine 1995a: 42–3).

The first few years after 1707 showed that some of these concerns were well founded. English competition soon crushed the finer end of the woollen trade, which was already in difficulties before the union. The levying of duties on linen in 1711 and 1715 imposed an additional handicap on Scotland's most important manufacture. Other industries, such as brewing and paper making, were also badly hit, though it is very difficult to know how far this was due to the harsh winds of free trade after the Union or to a more fundamental economic malaise that was dragging on from earlier crisis years. Certainly there was a widespread political consensus that the Union itself was to blame, and some of the angry resentment that was generated spilled over into support for the Jacobite rising of 1715. The Scots were also taxed more highly, with some of the new impositions being in breach of the Treaty of Union itself. In addition to linen, taxes rose on salt in 1711 and, most notoriously of all, on malt in 1725. These were basic articles of life, and it is not surprising that the increases on them produced a furious political response, including serious urban rioting in Glasgow in 1725. Yet, in the long run, taxation hardly drained Scotland dry. Modern estimates suggest only about 15–20 per cent of tax revenue actually left the country in the five decades after 1707 (Devine 1995: 43). Taxes went up, but apparently most of the additional revenue was still spent on civil and military expenditure in Scotland itself.

It is also difficult to gauge the real effect of what could have been one particularly damaging post-Union development. Increasingly, the Scottish aristocracy and a few of the greater lairds (landowners) sought political opportunity, social position and family influence in London by setting up residence in the capital during the winter months. This absenteeism was not entirely new; it had already started before the Union and became greater after it. From one perspective the temporary migration of the Scots nobility could be regarded as a flight of capital, as aristocratic rentals were increasingly exported to the south to sustain opulent lifestyles in polite English society. Indeed, absenteeism almost certainly forced rents up because, as the duke of Montrose complained in 1708, 'London journeys don't verie well agree with Scots estates' (Campbell 1977: 206). On the other hand, there was also a positive side: the need for more revenue generated in the longer term a search for improved agricultural practices, since a prime determinant of agrarian improvement was the pressure on the Scottish landed class to extract more revenue from their estates in order to support a higher standard of life.

Moreover, after these early difficult years some Scots merchants were beginning to exploit the new free-trade opportunities. Grain and meal exports more than doubled between the periods 1707–12 and 1717–22 and, as commercialisation intensified, protests against meal exports became more violent in some parts of the Lowlands (Whatley 2000: 53–4). In large part this may have been due to the extension of export bounties on grain after the Union. The so-called Levellers Revolt in Galloway in 1724 started when small tenants in the south-west protested bitterly against the large-scale cattle enclosures which were being built to secure more benefit from English demands for stock. These popular disturbances were one important sign that the post-Union market was beginning to have an impact in some regions. Indeed, by the 1720s and 1730s the effect may have been more general. Recent research on the Lowland rural economy in these decades suggests that many of the estates studied were gearing their output of grain and cattle much more to the market. This is indicated by an accelerated movement towards larger single tenancies and the sustained conversion of payment of rentals in kind to money values (Devine 1994: 20–32). In the long run also, one of the key advantages of the Union was that Scots merchants were able to trade legally with the English tobacco colonies of Virginia, Maryland and North Carolina. Even if the golden age of the Clyde tobacco trade lay some years in the future, there was already some evidence of dynamic enterprise by Glasgow merchants in the 1710s and 1720s. By the early 1720s the Scots had captured around 15 per cent of the legal trade in American tobacco to Britain, while smuggling on a large scale had become a national growth industry.

Thus both the prophets of doom and the optimists were proven wrong as the Union relationship entered it third decade. The nation's economy was not in ruins; indeed, there had been some modest recovery from the miseries of the 1690s in such sectors as agriculture and overseas trade. On the other hand, the economic miracle enthusiastically predicted by some pro-Union propagandists had manifestly not taken place. In structural terms the economy in 1750 differed little from that of 1700: economic expansion tended to develop slowly and in accordance with established patterns.

TRANSFORMATION, C. 1760–1860

The principal thrust of the analysis to this point has been to stress the significant material advances in Scotland between the mid-seventeenth and eighteenth centuries which took place within an existing economic and social framework. Despite urban and industrial growth, Scotland remained an overwhelmingly rural-based society, with only one Scot in eight living in towns defined as communities of 4,000 or more inhabitants in *c.* 1750. This traditional pattern, of basic continuity marked by change at the margins, ended abruptly from the 1760s. From then Scotland began to experience a social and economic transformation unparalleled in the Europe of the time in its speed, scale and intensity. The currently favoured view of English modernisation in the eighteenth century as a process characterised by cumulative, protracted and evolutionary development does not fit the experience north of the Border (Crafts 1985; Mokyr 1993).

There the onset of radical and revolutionary change was distinguished by several key features. First, the rate of expansion of the industrial sector was very significant. Between the 1770s and 1790s cotton had overtaken linen as Scotland's premier manufacture. By 1788 Scotland had nineteen of Britain's 143 water powered mills, in 1810 110 and by 1839 192, by which date the capital value of the industry was around £4.5 million. At the same time, however, linen maintained a sustained expansion, especially in Angus, Fife and Perth. Linen output tripled in volume between 1773–7 and 1813–17, to reach an annual average of 26.6 million yards. Exports of linen cloth in the later period stood at 44 million yards in 1831 but had risen to 79 million in 1845. Woollen hosiery production concentrated in the Borders (where it was insignificant in the 1790s) and parts of the Central Lowlands. By the 1840s it comprised a quarter of the UK's output in this sector and had effectively overtaken the west of England in the fine woollen trade. The associated success in textile finishing was symbolised by the construction of the St Rollox works in Glasgow in 1799 for manufacturing bleaching powder. By the 1830s it had become the largest heavy chemical plant in Europe.

Brewing, distilling, paper making and coal mining also all recorded substantial increases in output, but before 1830 textiles were dominant. One knowledgeable contemporary, Sir John Sinclair, estimated that, in the early nineteenth century, cotton, wool, linen and silk accounted for nearly 90 per cent of all Scottish manufacturing employment. By contrast, iron making experienced relatively slow growth, with no new works being built after an initial phase of expansion (from the opening of the famous

Carron Iron Works in 1759 to 1801) until the 1830s. In that decade, however, metal manufacture started to come into its own as the central dynamic in the industrial system, ironically when cotton was experiencing increasingly acute difficulties in external markets. Scottish output of pig iron, which stood at some 37,500 tons in 1830, had shot up to 700,000 tons by 1849, with the Scottish share of British output rising from 5 to 25 per cent. A new industrial complex now emerged with deep linkages between iron making, coal mining, engineering, railway construction and shipbuilding, all of which fashioned the characteristic Scottish manufacturing structure from this period until well into the twentieth century. Capital raised by Scottish railway companies was a mere £150,000 in 1830 but by 1870 had risen to a massive £47 million. Clyde shipbuilding experienced its major phase of global dominance after *c.* 1870 but the remarkably strong connections between the west of Scotland metal industries and ship construction were already in place in mid-century, with the Clyde yards accounting for two-thirds of all British iron tonnage launched between 1851 and 1870 (Whatley 1997: 18–37).

As a direct consequence of the burgeoning manufacturing economy, radical changes took place in Scotland's traditional employment structure. Indeed, it is possible to argue on the basis of this evidence that Scotland had quickly become more industrialised than the rest of Britain. In 1851 43.2 per cent of the employed workforce in Scotland were occupied in industry, compared to a British figure of 40.9 per cent (Lee 1979). A decade earlier, at the 1841 census, a small majority of the Scottish people, 52 per cent, lived in urban-industrial parishes and no Lowland county had a majority of householders engaged in farming. All this was unambiguous evidence of the speed of structural transformation over the previous few decades.

The national pattern of population distribution was recast in dramatic fashion and the rate of internal mobility was extraordinary. In the 1860s many areas of Scotland were losing people, especially in the Highlands, the eastern counties from Moray to Berwick and parts of the far southwest. Only the textile towns of the Borders and the industrial counties of the Central Lowlands were experiencing significant levels of inward migration. It was these areas, too, which drew the Irish, Scotland's largest immigrant group of modern times. By the 1850s there were around a quarter of a million Irish-born, or 7 per cent of the total national population, more than twice the proportion for England (Devine 1990).

As a direct corollary of the last point, the speed and extent of urban expansion should be noted. In a league of European 'urbanised societies' (as measured by the proportion of total population inhabiting towns of 10,000 or more) Scotland was tenth in 1700, seventh in the 1750s, fourth in 1800 and second only to England and Wales in 1850. In the first three decades of the nineteenth century, the rate of growth of Glasgow was reckoned the fastest of any town of its size in western Europe (de Vries 1984: 39–48). The colossus of Scottish urban growth (the number of its inhabitants had reached half a million by 1871), Glasgow was soon to be dubbed 'Second City of the Empire'.

Finally, the voracious demands for foods and raw materials of the urban and industrial areas helped to revolutionise agriculture and rural society throughout Scotland. No part of the country was insulated from the new power of market forces, whether it be the Hebrides, Orkney and Shetland to the north or the Border counties in the deep south. The buoyant markets for kelp, fish, whisky, cattle and sheep commercialised Highland society, dissolved the traditional communal townships, encouraged the division of land into individual crofts and subordinated ancient landownership responsibilities to the new imperatives of profit. Similarly, customary relationships and connections between clan elites and followers swiftly disintegrated as the entire fabric of society was recast in response to the new rigour of landlord demands, ideological fashion and, above all, the overwhelming market pressures emanating from the south. In less than two generations Scottish Gaeldom was transformed from tribalism to capitalism. The most telling sign of the new order was the notorious Clearances, when entire communities were removed from the land to make room for more profitable activity and particularly for the creation of the new economy of sheep-farming.

The scale of the revolution was no less remarkable in the rural Lowlands. There too the explosion in grain and meat prices after *c.* 1780 as a result of urbanisation has been identified as the fundamental dynamic in rapid commercialisation. It was in the two or three decades after *c.* 1760 that a recognisably modern landscape of enclosed fields, trim farms and separated holdings started to take shape in the Scottish countryside. The single farm under one master became the norm as holdings were consolidated between 1760 and 1815. By 1830, most of those who worked in Lowland agriculture were landless male and female servants whose lives were often as much subject to the pressures of labour discipline and enhanced productivity as those who toiled in the workshops and factories of the larger towns. Most remarkably, the cottar class, which in the old world had comprised between a quarter and a third of the inhabitants of many rural parishes, had virtually disappeared, and their smallholdings had been consolidated into larger tenant farms. Significantly, the populations of all Lowland rural counties approached their peak levels at the Census of 1851. By 1861 no Lowland region had a majority of workers employed in agriculture. Scotland was now a different kind of society from that of the early nineteenth century.

EXPLANATIONS

Space does not permit a detailed assessment of the complex range of influences which shaped Scottish economic development from the second half of the eighteenth century. Here the aim is more modest: to move back from the detail in order to bring into sharper relief the key elements in the overall process and, at the same time, to emphasise those particular factors which appear to have been especially relevant to the Scottish experience.

By the later eighteenth century internal market conditions were more favourable to expanding industrial production. Population rose by about 20 per cent between *c.* 1755 and 1801, real wages increased from the 1760s to the early 1790s (in the Central Lowlands at least), a higher population of the Scottish people worked within a market environment than in earlier decades, and there was notable evidence of the increasing size and purchasing power of the urban trading and professional classes. However, while these domestic influences clearly enhanced demand for manufactures, they were much less decisive than external markets. From the 1740s to the 1780s, the new free-trade area created by the Union was crucial, as can be seen from the two examples of the country's principal eighteenth-century industry, linen, and its most successful branch in overseas trade, tobacco.

Linen experienced dynamic growth between 1740 and 1780, with output of cloth stamped by the Board of Trustees for sale rising fourfold over that period. In addition, linen was to play a key role in the early stages of Scottish industrialisation as the most important source of capital, labour and business skills for the cotton manufacture, the 'leading sector' of the industrial revolution. Linen's success seemed to rest to a large extent on the common market created by the Union. In the 1760s, for instance, as much as two-thirds of stamped linen output was sold in the English home market or the American and Caribbean colonies. In the absence of the Union, this core manufacture would very likely have been confronted with an English tariff wall in competition with aggressive Dutch and German rivals. The Scots instead received protection within the Union and were also aided from 1742 by a series of bounties (financial incentives offered by the government) to encourage exports. These, rather than initiatives to improve efficiency, seem to have been the decisive influences on growth. Linen, therefore, was one case where the record shows the impact of Union to be clearly favourable in the long term (Durie 1979).

To some extent it was a similar story with tobacco. The 'golden age' of the Glasgow tobacco trade dates from the 1740s. In 1741, 8 million pounds in weight of colonial tobacco were landed from Virginia, Maryland and North Carolina at the Clyde ports, a figure which had climbed to 13 million pounds in 1745 and, after a further dramatic spurt, to 21 million pounds in 1752. Astonishingly, by 1758, Scottish tobacco imports were greater than those of London and all the English outports combined. In 1771 the highest ever volume of tobacco was landed, a staggering 47 million pounds (almost 21,000 tons). Glasgow had become the tobacco metropolis of western Europe, and in the west of Scotland the profits of the trade fed into a very wide range of industries, funded banks and financed agricultural improvement through merchant investment. It is now acknowledged that the transatlantic trades played a key economic role in the diversification within the Glasgow area, the region that was to become the engine of Scottish industrialisation (Devine 1995b; Whatley 1997: 22–3).

The legitimacy afforded by the Union was crucial to this dazzling story of commercial success. As already noted, Scots traders had been active in the tobacco colonies before 1707, though on a relatively small scale, and much commerce was clandestine in nature. Certainly no London government would have allowed the enormous illegal growth in Scottish tobacco imports outside the Union. Indeed, it was English protests against the boom in Scottish smuggling *within* the Union that led to the wholesale reorganisation of the customs service in 1723 and the formation of a more professional customs bureaucracy (Price 1984). This reflected the great political sensitivity of the issue, since it was widely recognised that much of the Scottish success was at the expense of English merchants. Smuggling before 1707 clearly had its limitations; the Union was therefore a necessary basis for the phenomenal Glaswegian performance in the American trades. Yet those successes were not inevitable. In the final analysis they were won by the Scottish merchant houses adopting more efficient business methods than many of their rivals. The big Glasgow firms were able to drive down their costs by a number of innovations in purchasing, marketing and shipping which made them formidable competitors in American and European markets. So the union did not inevitably *cause* growth in the Atlantic trades; it simply provided a necessary context in which growth might or might not take place. Nevertheless, one reason for fast Scottish growth after *c.* 1760 was that the focus of external trade had decisively moved from Europe to England, North America and the Caribbean, the most rapidly developing marketplace in the world.

International markets remained crucial throughout the period of this chapter, even if, after 1783, the protection of the Navigation Acts was less significant and Scottish industry was able to penetrate non-imperial markets in the USA, South America and continental Europe on a significant scale. From *c.* 1830 pig iron production was sustained mainly by external demand. In 1847, for instance, no less than two-thirds of Scottish-made pig iron was exported. It was a similar story with jute manufacture which, from the 1840s, became the cornerstone of Dundee's economy.

In exploiting the global marketplace, the Scots had several advantages. The Central Lowlands were almost fashioned by nature for industrialisation. By 1800 the region contained by far the largest proportion of urban dwellers of any region, with fully 60 per cent of the total town and city population of Scotland living in Glasgow and Edinburgh alone. Moreover, several areas (and in particular Ayrshire, Lanarkshire and Fife) were rich in coal and ironstone, the most important minerals for early industrialisation, and had the additional bonus of close location to ports, sources of labour in the towns and water transport. The two estuaries of the Forth and the Clyde penetrated deep into the narrow waist of the Lowlands, a natural advantage which was then maximised by the building of three great canals, Monkland (1790), Forth and Clyde (1790) and Union (1822), all of them important for the carriage of coal and other goods low in value but heavy in bulk. With the construction of more roads and the continued expansion of the coastal trade, followed by the railways, the Central Lowlands acquired a first-class transportation network capable of large-scale exploitation of the very favourable geological advantages of the region. Some question the strategic importance of coal and iron in the first phase of industrialisation since they really came into their own as crucial assets only after 1830. However, steam power, and hence the extensive use of coal as a fuel, was already widely employed in both cotton and linen spinning in Scotland by the early nineteenth century. While water power did continue to be used extensively in all sectors of the economy, steam gave a new and decisive competitive advantage to the export-orientated textile industries, not only by allowing unbroken production in all weathers but also through relocation of the mills from the countryside to the cities with their abundant supplies of low-wage labour. The Belfast cotton industry did not possess such easy access to rich sources of coal in the neighbourhood of the city, and so failed to compete with Glasgow and Paisley in the age of steam and fell behind from the 1820s.

The response of Scottish agriculture to industrial growth was equally critical. At the heart of agrarian improvement was the ability of farmers to produce more from a given area of land and also extend cultivation to underutilised areas. Thus more people could move into sectors where food was bought rather than grown, but without prices for essentials going through the ceiling. Certainly oat prices did move upwards. In south-east Scotland they were on average 56 per cent higher in 1765–70 than for the years 1725–50, and prices for 1805–10 showed a 300 per cent increase over pre-1750 values. These price movements were sufficient to generate confidence for rural investment but they did not undermine the purchasing power of labour as money wages in a varied range of occupations were rising even faster between the 1760s and early 1790s, the classic period of agrarian improvement in Scotland. Essentially changes in farm organisation, cultivation methods, land enclosure and new rotations which had evolved over generations in most parts of England were squeezed into a few decades in Lowland Scotland. One telling illustration of the revolution was the trend of oat yields. By the 1790s, even in counties such as Angus and Lanark, which were by no means in the van of agricultural progress, average seed-yields were 1:12 and 1:11 respectively. These were around three times the average of the early eighteenth century and on a par with several regions south of the Border. As William Fullarton reported in some astonishment in the course of his survey of

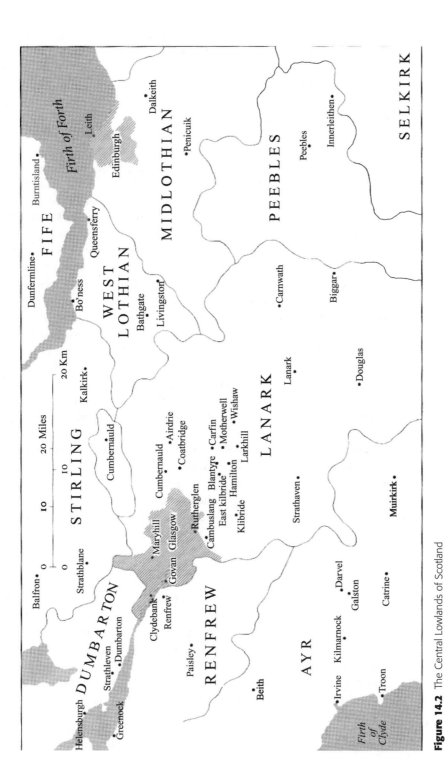

Figure 14.2 The Central Lowlands of Scotland

Source: Devine 1999.

Ayrshire in 1793, 'the third of the farms in crop supplied double or triple the yield formerly taken from the whole' (Fullarton 1793: 21). It was the more intensive application of traditional methods, such as fallowing and the lavish application of lime, combined with the rapid diffusion of sown grasses and turnip husbandry which enabled a heavier carry of stock and hence more manure for the land.

Why market opportunities were grasped so eagerly and effectively is less obvious. In England the current historical opinion is that the great proprietors did not play a central role in the promotion of agricultural change after *c.* 1750 (Beckett 1989: 570–1). The main influences apparently were the lesser gentry, enlightened tenants and land agents. In Scotland the opposite seems to have been the case. In the Highlands, as in the Lowlands, the landed class was at the heart of the process, not necessarily through routine personal involvement but at a more strategic level through the support they gave to their professional factors and agents who actually enforced improvement. Scottish agriculture was less advanced than English and so required a more interventionist approach. The basic advantage of the proprietors was that most land was worked through tenancies governed by leases. They therefore possessed full legal rights of eviction at the end of a lease. This allowed them not only to influence the size and composition of tenantry on their estates but also to build into these contracts mandatory improving clauses enforceable at law. Sheriff Court records demonstrate that landowners had little compunction in using legal muscle to ensure compliance with cropping regulations set out in leases.

Legal developments had added to the power of Scottish landowners to promote improvement. First, as long ago as 1695, the 'Act anent lands lying run-rig' and a second statute in the same year relating to the division of commonties (uninhabited lands with rights of use belonging to adjacent estates) helped to facilitate the process. By the first, individual landlords could take the initiative to exchange and consolidate land held by different proprietors. The second act allowed one landowner to promote a division of commonty rather than wait for a majority to be in agreement. The legislation put in place cheap and effective processes and was clearly designed to assist those lairds in the van of agrarian reform. The rights of Scottish landowners were buttressed further by the development of entail. Through the introduction of laws of entail in 1685 which safeguarded 'entailed' land from forced sales through debts, the succession to an entailed estate was confined to a definite series of heirs. Any proprietor who succeeded could not break this line and he was not permitted to contract debts that would put the property at risk. By 1825 an estimated half of the landed estates of the country were subject to strict entail (Campbell 1988: 93). Entail's great attraction and obvious popularity was that it gave protection and security to the landed family over several generations. But the restrictions made it difficult to raise loans for investment which would then be passed on to succeeding proprietors. An act of 1770 gave some flexibility by allowing an improving landlord of an entailed estate to invest in his property and become a creditor to his heirs up to the value of four years' rental.

But other influences were also significant. The costs of Scottish landownership were rising steeply in the eighteenth century. This was the era of competitive display, when social standing was increasingly defined by material status. More elaborate country houses, interior decoration and the adornment of estate policies became not only fashionable but essential in order to maintain and demonstrate social position. It is noteworthy how many of the great houses of Scotland were either built or significantly renovated during this period. Inverary, Culzean, Hopeton House and Mellerstain were only the most famous examples. This was the era when the remarkable Adam family of architects did their best work, much of which involved the comprehensive remodelling of castellated houses and fortified dwellings of an earlier and more turbulent age. In the later eighteenth century the number of aristocratic and laird houses built from scratch also multiplied. Nearly twice as many were constructed in the 1790s (more than sixty) as between 1700 and 1720. Most of Robert Adam's commissions were for the laird class, even though his best-known work was for the nobility. Also driving up costs was the revolution in interior design and furnishings. At the time of the Union, the domestic furnishings of a typical laird's house were simple in the extreme. Less than fifty years later, the aristocracy was aspiring to standards of unprecedented splendour, with gilded ornamentation, framed paintings, lavish fabrics and elaborate ceiling mouldings. Mahogany furnishings, based on the designs of Chippendale, Sheraton and Hepplewhite, enjoyed remarkable popularity. Nor should it be forgotten that the assimilation of the Scottish nobility into the wealthier English aristocracy subjected them to special additional pressures of expenditure which increased the need to extract more income from their lands.

For all these reasons larger rent rolls became essential to service the new levels of conspicuous consumption and elite material competition of the landed classes. The 'Revolution of Manners' went hand in hand with the popularity of Improvement. But the influences at work were not simply material in origin. They also came from the world of ideas. The Scottish philosophical revolution of the eighteenth century fed through into agrarian reform. The rationalism of the Enlightenment helped to change man's relationship to his environment. No longer was nature accepted as given and preordained; instead, it could be altered for the better, or 'improved' by systematic and planned intervention. In a sense, therefore, Enlightenment thought gave a new intellectual legitimacy to the traditional interventionist role of the landed classes in Scotland by clarifying and systematising the objectives of agrarian reform. Not surprisingly in a society where it dominated the economy, the theorists were fascinated by agriculture. Writers as varied as Lord Kames, James Anderson, Sir John Sinclair and the numerous contributors to the *Statistical Account* and *General Views of Agriculture* of the 1790s formulated ideas about the meaning of Improvement which offered a fundamental critique of the old order and a coherent approach to the development of the new. The crucial links between the intellectuals and the practice of agriculture were the factors and agents who managed the actual routine of farming on the great estates. These were educated men who had often attended a Scottish university, and when they set out their schemes of improvement they were in many instances simply putting into effect the new intellectual orthodoxy that was widely disseminated in the books, pamphlets and journals of the middle decades of the eighteenth century. There was remarkable unanimity about what was bad and had to be changed. Lands 'in a state of nature' were no longer acceptable and had to be enclosed and brought into regular cultivation. Farms held by more than one tenant had to be divided and reorganised. The 'unimproved' regime was vigorously condemned as wasteful and ruinous. What was new was good; the old was bad. This gave the improvers an extraordinary moral and intellectual confidence as they vigorously went about the crusade of thoroughgoing agrarian reformation.

The new imperial context was a basic influence on the momentum of agrarian change. By the later eighteenth century, many Scots were growing rich from the profits of colonial commerce to North America and the Caribbean, from service in the army, and from trade and office holding in India and the East Indies. It was common for some who succeeded to acquire a small landed estate and 'improve' their property from their personal fortunes. By the last quarter of the eighteenth century, for instance, the counties around Glasgow were ringed by the estates of the city's tobacco and sugar lords. At least sixty merchant families were involved in these land purchases between 1760 and 1815 (Devine 1976: 7). It is striking also that many of the architect Robert Adam's clients were not members of the 'old' landed class but men who had made their money in law and commerce. The impact of empire on the land market and improvement comes through in the literature of the time. John Galt's *The Last of the Lairds* concerns the appropriately named Mr Rupees, a 'Nawbob' who 'came hame from Indy and bought the Arunthrough property frae the Glaikies, who, like sae mony ithers o' the right stock o' legitimate gentry, hae been smothered out o' sight by the weed and nettle overgrowths o' mechandise ane cotton-weavry'. Galt depicts Mr Rupees as a man committed to conspicuous consumption on a lavish scale and the generation of more and more profit from his lands.

Though profit-hungry proprietors might own the land, they did not actually work it, and the tenant farmers who did were censured vigorously by improving writers as conservative and hidebound. How then were the new ideas to be transformed into reality against this background of unyielding orthodoxy and traditionalism? Modern research has provided some answers (Devine 1994: 66–70). For a start, not all tenants were as backward as the critics suggested. Even before 1750, the steady emergence of single tenancies and the decay of rentals paid mainly in kind meant more and more had direct experience of serving the market. These enterprising farmers, like their landlords, gained from rising prices after the 1770s. The 'latent' farming bourgeoisie described earlier in this chapter developed further in the new economic context. Nor should it be forgotten that many Scottish tenants were fully literate and that much of the new agricultural knowledge was spread by books, pamphlets and journals. Typical of the standards prevailing in many parts of the Lowlands was the pattern in St Ninian's parish, Stirlingshire, in 1790s: 'Some of our farmers have been favoured with a liberal education. A few of them have been instructed in the rudiments of the Latin tongue. Almost all of them have been taught writing and arithmetic, as well as to read the English language with understanding and ease' (Withrington 1988: 172). As has been argued, 'an educated peasantry more readily turns its back on immemorial tradition because it finds on the printed page an alternative form of authority to custom' (Cullen and Smout 1977: 15). Moreover, improving landlords used a range of incentives to encourage progressive practices. Some covered the costs of enclosure, liming and new farm houses set against obtaining returns through raising rents in the long run. The risk was worth taking because of the huge increases in rents after 1780. Contemporaries estimated that the general level was fairly stable to about 1750, started to move up from the 1760s, doubled between 1783 and 1793, and did so again from 1794 to 1815. Abatements of rent were also allowed in order to permit the result of the new practices to filter through and gain acceptance. As the Earl of Morton advised, rental should be kept at modest levels in the initial phase 'and not so high as to exceed the skill and industry of the tenants . . . as no General can expect good success with a bad disciplined Army' (Devine 1994: 74). In order to attract able tenants, landowners also invested in new farm houses. Some steadings, as in Fife in the early nineteenth century for instance, remained in a 'barbarous' condition, but many others now had substantial, two-storey, slate-covered farm houses, stables, cattle houses, barns, milksheds and strawyards.

Coercion was also used widely and systematically. The approach was based on the improving lease, which set out the detailed instructions for the new cropping prescriptions and to which the tenant had to adhere. Landowners could ensure compliance in a variety of ways: by fining, marginal increases in rent or eviction. Both estate and Sheriff Court records show that breaches of the lease were regarded as a serious offence and could be punished by the loss of the tenancy. These new leases were no longer conventional, generalised documents but contained several pages of written obligations and mandatory instructions concerning fallowing, liming and cropping routines. Nor were they simply paper contracts. On the great estates, bureaucracies of principal factor (estate manager) and sub-factors allowed for careful and regular monitoring. The Earl of Panmure was advised to appoint an inspectorate of three salaried officers to supervise the progress of improvements on his Angus estate. If necessary, they should be supplied with assistants to 'take Inspection and make report annually as said is: That those who do well may meet with the Applause justly due them: That the Backward may be spurred on and that the Obstinately Negligent and Deceitful may be Undone and turned off as an Example *In Terrorem* of others' (Devine 1994: 72). Here indeed was a telling illustration of the threatened use of seigneurial authority in the cause of improvement.

In agriculture the adoption of 'English methods' was important, but they were also crucial in manufacturing. The early phase of Scottish industrialisation was based overwhelmingly on borrowed technology and expertise. Ideas and skills were freely imported from Holland, France and Ireland, but England was far and away the major source. 'Technology transfer' on a remarkable scale took place from south to north, reflecting Scotland's relative backwardness and also the strategy of English business-men who were on the lookout for cheaper labour and low-rented factory sites. The spinning revolution in cotton was entirely based on the seminal inventions of the Englishmen Kay, Hargreaves, Arkwright and Crompton. Men with experience of English mill practice often became the managers of the early factories. The best known of them was Archibald Buchanan who, after serving an apprenticeship at Cromford in Derbyshire, became the technical genius behind the rise of the great Scottish cotton empire of James Finlay and Co. Sulphuric acid manufacture was pioneered at Prestonpans in 1749 by Roebuck and Garbett after their earlier venture in Birmingham. The blast furnace and the coke process of smelting were both introduced from England, as was the coal-fired reverberating fur-nace, which was central to technical progress in the brewing, chemical, pottery and glass industries. Perhaps the most famous example of the penetration of English know-how came with the foundation in 1759 of Carron Company, Scotland's largest manufacturing plant of the day, based on the coke-smelting techniques pioneered at Coalbrookdale. The speed of Scotland's economic transformation also created technical bottlenecks and recurrent shortages of skilled labour which were often relieved by a steady trickle from England of experienced smelters, moulders, spinners and malleable iron workers.

The above is far from being a definitive list but it is enough to demon-strate that Scottish economic progress would surely have been impeded without English technical expertise and skills and, to a lesser extent, those of other countries. But these new processes were assimilated swiftly, confirming that Scotland had the appropriate social, cultural and eco-nomic environment to achieve fast industrialisation. Like a latter-day

Japan, having borrowed ideas from others on a grand scale, the country soon moved rapidly to the cutting edge of the new technology. A whole stream of key inventions started to emanate from Scotland, including James Watt's refinement of the separate condenser for the steam engine (perhaps the fundamental technological breakthrough of the age), Neil Snodgrass's scutching machine, enabling wool to be processed effectively before being spun, Archibald Buchanan's construction of the first truly integrated cotton mill in Britain in 1807, where all the key processes were carried out by power within a single complex, Henry Bell's *Comet* of 1812, which pioneered steam propulsion for ships, J. B. Neilson's invention in 1829 of the 'hot-blast process', which helped to transform iron manufacture by radically reducing the costs of production, and a long series of pathbreaking discoveries in marine engine design.

It is dangerous, however, to focus too much on technology when considering those distinctive advantages which gave the Scots a competitive edge during the industrial revolution. Most tasks, in both agriculture and industry, continued to be done by hand; even in cotton, the most advanced manufacturing sector of all, two of the three core processes, weaving and finishing, remained mainly labour intensive until the 1820s. The cost of labour was therefore critical as was the way in which working people reacted to the strange new manufacturing processes and environments. Undeniably, wages in certain trades were rising in the later eighteenth century. Nevertheless, most Scottish wages remained below those of England, and it was partly because of this attraction that English tycoons like Richard Arkwright were investing in Scottish factories in the 1780s. Arkwright boasted that the lower costs of production in Scotland would enable him to take a razor to the throat of Lancashire. Almost a century later, in the 1860s, when the first rigorous wage censuses became available, Scotland was still unequivocally a low-wage economy in most occupations compared to England. The key test of national differences in this respect was the balance of migration. When good figures were first produced in the 1840s, around 67,000 Scots and English had migrated across the Border. But over three-quarters of this number were Scots, who were plainly much keener to move to the greater opportunities in the south than the English were to move north.

A second advantage for Scottish entrepreneurs was the mobility of labour. Historically the Scots were a migratory people. But in the eighteenth century internal migration became more common precisely at the time when industry needed to attract more workers. Seasonal movement for harvest work from the southern and central Highlands for work in the Lowland harvests was more significant after *c.* 1750. In the same region the first clearances for sheep, the transfer of people from inland straths to the coastlands as the new crofting system was established, and the social strains coming from rampant commercialisation, all led to more internal migration as well as promoting a large-scale exodus of people across the

Atlantic after *c.* 1760. In the Lowlands, agricultural improvement was radically altering the traditional social order and in the process drastically cutting back the large numbers who had always had a legal or customary right to land. The tenant class contracted further and cottar families with smallholdings possessing skills in spinning and weaving were steadily replaced by landless servants and labourers. Those who have little other than their labour power to sell are always more likely to be more mobile than a landholding peasantry who, in the last resort, can rely on their smallholdings as a source of subsistence. Lowland Scotland certainly had larger numbers of people detached from land holding by *c.* 1800 than ever before and the resulting rates of short-distance migration were often remarkable. One case study shows that two-thirds of the families listed for the village of Kippen in Stirlingshire in 1789 were no longer resident there in 1793. In the household of the Earl of Leven and Melville in Fife, 97 per cent of women servants and 90 per cent of men remained for only four years or less in the earl's employment (Houston 1988a: 21). Certainly by comparison with many rural parishes in parts of France and Germany, where most lived and died in the parish of their birth, Scottish internal mobility was a decided bonus for manufacturers keen to hire more labour.

Nevertheless, acute difficulties remained. Skill shortages abounded in coal and ironstone mining, pottery and glass making, bleaching and nail making, and, as already noted, could often only be made good by relying on English workers to hand on their expertise to the natives (Whatley 1997: 21). More seriously, there was the major problem of recruiting labour to the new textile factories and large workshops. The mills crystallised the conflict between the culture of work in the old order and the new. Full-time work, though not unknown, was unusual outside the towns, and the majority of people had little interest in labouring for much longer than their basic needs required. But factory employment was radically different. Costly machinery had to be employed on a continuous basis and that meant long hours, a disciplined workforce and more rigorous supervision of labour. By the early nineteenth century, in the cotton mills night working was not unknown when trade was brisk. Workers normally laboured for six days a week, with Sundays off and usually only a few further days annually. It was hardly an environment likely to attract large numbers of male workers at a time, in the 1780s and 1790s, when work in agriculture and handloom weaving was paying better than ever before.

But this potential recruitment crisis in the early years of industrialisation was avoided. Scottish industry quickly developed a considerable dependence on women and children as sources of low-cost labour. By the 1820s they formed over 60 per cent of the total workforce in manufacturing industry and, in the cotton and flax mills, the proportion of women employed was significantly higher in Scotland than in the industrial areas of Lancashire (Bolin-Hart 1989). Women were also vital as bearers in the collieries, in the preparation of flax and the manufacture of woollen stockings, and in the bleachfields. Again, unlike the pattern in Yorkshire and Lancashire, the immigrant Irish started to stream into the mills as early as the 1790s as both skilled and unskilled labour. It was significant that when the powerful Glasgow Cotton Spinners Association emerged in the early nineteenth century the leadership was dominated by second-generation Irishmen whose families had earlier achieved a position in the industry in the late eighteenth century. In the early 1800s it was reckoned that around half the mill workforce in the city were either Irish-born or of Irish descent. By that time, national population growth in Scotland was starting to accelerate and in the cities the swelling number of migrants was relieving any scarcities that had previously existed in the industrial labour market. But for a period in the 1780s and 1790s, only the recruitment to the mills of Irish immigrants, Scottish women and pauper children prevented a slowing down in the momentum of industrialisation.

INDUSTRIALISATION AND SCOTTISH SOCIETY

Over a mere few decades Scotland had become an industrial society and a force to be reckoned with in the world economy. How far the economic miracle brought significant long-term benefits to the majority of the Scottish people before 1860 is more debatable. The answer to this key question on the relationship between economic change and material welfare is problematic in a Scottish context because the standard-of-living controversy has never attracted the same sustained level of scholarly discussion as in England. As a result, no Scottish cost-of-living index exists for any extended period before 1860. Nevertheless, there are some pointers. A rise in national income and employment opportunities in a still labour-intensive economy allowed Scottish population to increase on a sustained basis from 1,265,000 in the 1750s to nearly 2.9 million by 1851. One estimate suggests that the urban mercantile and professional classes were increasingly significant, comprising about 15 per cent of town populations *c.* 1750 and nearly 25 per cent by the 1830s (Nenadic 1988: 114–15). Material improvement also seems to have been widespread in the Lowlands and southern and eastern Highlands between *c.* 1760 and *c.* 1793. For instance, male agricultural workers in the central belt experienced a real wages increase of 40 to 50 per cent over this period (Morgan 1971: 181–201). This was in contrast to some English regions, especially those distant from the core areas of manufacturing. In Scotland, this initial cycle of improvement was conditioned by intensive agrarian change and industrial/urban growth, a relatively slow rate of national population increase (about half that of England at 0.6 per annum, *c.* 1750–1801), a significant increase in military employment during the war years and a dramatic rise in the involvement of women and children in agriculture and textile work. In addition, the Scots seem to have had a dietary advantage over other UK regions. The traditional diet of oatmeal and milk may have been narrow and monotonous, but it was also very nutritious and helps to explain why Scotsmen were apparently the tallest males in Britain before *c.* 1850 (Floud *et al.* 1990: 73).

Over the next phase, *c.* 1793 to *c.* 1812, the scattered data produce conflicting and ambiguous results, although the most recent assessment suggests that 'Broadly speaking the period of the French and Napoleonic Wars appears to have been one of stagnation [in real wages]' (Whatley 1997: 83). Thereafter, however, the picture darkens somewhat. A survey of average real wages for Glasgow workers in nineteen occupational groups indicates a continuous decline between *c.* 1816 and 1839 and one careful calculation suggests that in 1834 about half of Scotland's handloom weavers, at that date the country's largest group of industrial workers, fell below the primary poverty line as defined by late nineteenth-century social analysts (Treble 1988). Over these decades, too, the index of mortality in the towns, which had fallen between 1790 and 1815, increased dramatically from *c.* 1816–17. Both contemporary comment and the available statistical evidence suggest that mortality from typhus in Dundee, Edinburgh and Glasgow between *c.* 1820 and *c.* 1850 was, in Edwin Chadwick's words, 'greater . . . than in the most crowded towns in England' (Flinn 1965: 99). The harsher times were also punctuated by a series of bitter industrial disputes between capital and labour and acrimonious popular disturbance which did not fade until the 1850s when an uneasy calm started to prevail in the manufacturing districts. Moreover, the impact of economic advance was notably uneven across the country. Nowhere in mainland Britain were the social costs of agrarian capitalism more apparent than in the crofting districts of the Highland, where the people eked out a meagre existence on the margin of subsistence. When the potatoes failed in 1846 whole areas were threatened with starvation, a threat allayed only by massive charitable intervention from the Lowland cities which prevented a human tragedy of Irish proportions (Devine 1988).

The reality was that the economic miracle was a mixed blessing. The sheer speed of Scottish urbanisation for a time quickly overwhelmed existing systems of water supply, sanitation and waste disposal. The new dominance of unfettered market relationships meant the speedy breakdown in some of the paternalistic practices of the eighteenth century. By *c.* 1825 controls over bread prices and legal regulation over work practices and tradesmen's wages had both disappeared. At the same time, the Scottish poor law, which had been remarkably flexible before 1800, had become much more rigorous by *c.* 1840, not least in its formal opposition to the right of the able-bodied unemployed to relief. For many the new urban world was therefore less secure and more vulnerable

Table 14.1   Occupational structure in Scottish cities, 1841

Percentage of Workforce in:	Glasgow	Edinburgh	Dundee	Aberdeen
Printing and publishing	1.12	3.88	0.56	0.91
Engineering, tool making and metals	7.7	6.07	5.59	6.32
Shipbuilding	0.35	0.17	1.14	1.24
Coachbuilding	0.40	0.92	0.21	0.34
Building	5.84	5.73	6.05	5.99
Furniture making and woodworking	1.06	2.73	0.77	0.87
Chemicals	1.22	0.24	0.19	0.37
Food, drink and tobacco	5.24	8.31	5.27	4.66
Textiles and clothing	37.56	13.04	50.54	34.68
Other manufacturing	2.90	3.02	1.29	3.18
General labouring	8.40	3.69	3.84	6.87

Note that occupational classifications in the 1841 Census are questionable and imprecise. The figures here provide an impression of overall structures rather than an exact measurement of them.

Source: Census of 1841 (Parliamentary Papers, 1844, XXVII) and Rodger 1985.

Table 14.2   Occupational structure in Scottish cities, 1841, by sector (percentage of total workforce)

	Professional		Domestic		Commercial		Industrial		Agriculture and fishing	
	M	F	M	F	M	F	M	F	M	F
Glasgow (and suburbs)	4.53	0.57	2.03	31.60	15.09	2.87	73.92	64.59	4.43	0.37
Edinburgh (and suburbs)	13.34	1.93	6.53	70.36	14.10	2.71	62.26	23.61	2.77	1.39
Dundee	4.98	0.88	1.95	27.30	13.70	2.79	76.57	68.65	2.80	0.38
Aberdeen	6.46	2.24	4.05	40.37	14.57	2.44	68.71	53.98	6.21	0.97

Source: As for Table 14.1.

to the cycle of international supply and demand. What compounded the problem in Scotland was the smaller middle class and the weakness of the service sector (outside Edinburgh and its environs) compared with England. As Tables 14.1 and 14.2 reveal, Dundee and Glasgow, the very centres of the new urban industrialism, were alike by the 1840s in their heavy dependency on textile employment, the relative weakness of the professional sector (compared to Aberdeen and Edinburgh) and the large numbers (especially in Dundee) of low-paid female workers. These urban occupational structures were not conducive to long-term stable levels of employment, especially in the difficult trading conditions for textile producers during several years in the 1820s, 1830s and early 1840s.

The broader demographic context should also be borne in mind. The tight labour market of the last quarter of the eighteenth century was moulded in large part by the slow population increase of the period. By the early nineteenth century this pattern had changed to one of more rapid growth: 1.6 per annum between 1811 and 1821 (more than double the rate between the 1750s and 1801) and 2.1 per annum between 1801 and 1851. It was a new demographic scenario of a sustained increase in numbers which may well have swamped rural labour markets, especially after the great demobilisation of soldiers and sailors at the end of the Napoleonic Wars. Though farmers had a need for more hands, the demand for labour was not increasing at anything like the pace of population growth, especially as agricultural income and hence employment opportunities contracted with the slump in grain prices after 1816. One might realistically have anticipated an expansion in structural unemployment in rural districts. This was the experience in the western Highlands – but not in the Lowlands – partly because of the expulsive force of the Scottish structure of engagement for farm service. In the later eighteenth century, it became a major principle of Scottish improving policy that only the population essential for proper cultivation should be retained permanently on the land. Accommodation in and around the farm was strictly limited thereafter to the specific labour needs of the farmer. Cottages surplus to these requirements were pulled down and the building of new accommodation strictly controlled. This inevitably became a mechanism for channelling excess labour off the land, especially when it is remembered that the able-bodied unemployed had no legal right to be relieved under the Scottish poor law, even if occasional assistance was sometimes provided at times of acute difficulty. The combination of this system, a natural and accelerating rise in population and only slowly growing or stagnant employment opportunities in agriculture after 1812–13 helped to impel an increasing movement of people from country to town (Devine 1978: 331–46). In the period c. 1816/17 to the 1840s, parts of Scotland had a growing problem of structural unemployment. But it did not concentrate in the Lowland rural areas and was instead mainly confined to the large towns, the western Highlands and the smaller industrial centres (especially of handloom weavers) in the countryside. This was where the growing pains of the new industrial society were most apparent.

15

The extractive industries

ROGER BURT

Contents

Introduction   417
Location and structure   419
Distinguishing characteristics   423
Markets and prices   427
Institutional development   432
Technological change   436
Conclusion   448

INTRODUCTION

The story of the industrial revolution is usually told in terms of cotton and the textile industry. But men and women did not live by cloth alone. The houses and factories that they lived and worked in were built with brick and roofed with slate; they were heated, powered and lit by coal and its products; their sanitation and water supply were serviced with lead and copper pipes and cisterns; their tools and machinery were of iron and steel; and their household utensils and facilities were of pottery and ceramics. Whereas in the early 1860s the average annual per capita consumption of raw cotton in mainland Britain was around 30 lb., every man, woman and child in mainland Britain could consume something like 10 oz. of tin, 2 lb. of copper, 6 lb. of lead, over 220 lb. of iron and steel, more than 3 tons of coal, and a similar quantity of clays, sand, stone and gravel. The extractive industries were widely dispersed across the country and dominated a number of regional economies, not just in the north of England. The material culture of everyday life was firmly rooted in the products of the nether world and became ever more dependent on it. No matter how the textile sector grew and expanded, it was the domestic extractive industries, and those that processed their products, that dominated the industrial landscape. Overall, Britain's mineralogical factor endowment created the defining context for the whole process of its industrialisation. By facilitating and encouraging the substitution of mineral for organic resources it guided technology in new directions that were particularly rich in innovative possibilities. In metallurgy this led to the final fulfilment of the promise of the Iron Age, initiated millennia before, by making ferrous metals sufficiently cheap and available to become the common material of construction. In the exploitation of heat energy, one of the basic building blocks of all economic activity, the large-scale working of Britain's extensive coal deposits and the invention of machinery to realise their energy, set in train a process that led to a continuous increase in the productivity of capital and labour. As Wrigley has explained, this made it possible 'to construct an industrial society with a capacity to produce material goods of use to man on a scale that dwarfed such production in any earlier period' (Wrigley 1988: 73).

At the base of the 'mineral economy' lay the extractive industries – those that mined and quarried the raw material from its native rock. For all their strategic significance, however, their story remains a shadowy one. Unlike most other topics discussed in these volumes, there is a very limited literature from which to draw an overview of the long-term development of the extractive industries, and there are few debates and reinterpretations to review. The coal industry and its labour force used to attract considerable attention but relatively little has emerged since the 1980s. The non-ferrous mining industries have continued to support widespread research and publication, but most of this work has been antiquarian and provides little academic analysis of the industries' overall economic and social development. Much the same can be said of the whole construction and industrial materials sector, but with an even lower level of academic interest. In the iron industry, smelting has seen exhaustive analysis, but mining has been almost entirely ignored (Willies 1997). Even where studies have been conducted, they are usually more concerned with the markets for final products rather than the economics of the extractive process itself. Thus the detailed volumes on the coal industry pay little attention to the income derived by mines from the frequent joint production of iron ore and clay. Similarly, separate volumes on the history of copper mining and tin mining largely ignore the fact that these products were largely derived from the same workings by the same miners using the same capital equipment (see Burt and Timbrell 1991; Brown 1998). Overall, there has been far greater interest in the role of British capital, entrepreneurs and labour in developing overseas mining in the late nineteenth and early twentieth centuries than has ever been shown in the earlier history of the domestic industry. In many respects it remains the least well-known, and least understood, aspect of modern British industrial history.

LOCATION AND STRUCTURE

Mainland Britain was, and still is, richly endowed with a wide range of minerals, dispersed widely across the country. The principal commercial products may be broadly grouped into four categories: fossil fuels, ferrous ores, non-ferrous ores and what, in the nineteenth century, were known as 'earthy minerals', such as stone, clay and salt. This large and miscellaneous latter group is now known as 'construction and industrial minerals' and that term will be employed here. The only fossil fuel of significant commercial value to be worked during this period was coal, though some small quantities of heavy oil and lignite also found limited local use. Coal was produced in many parts of the country but most came from the north-east, the West Midlands, Lowland Scotland and Yorkshire, in that order, with rapidly emerging mines in Lancashire and South Wales. Iron ore mineralisation was even more geographically dispersed, but again output was dominated by the production of a few leading areas. Unlike coal, however, these changed dramatically during the period, largely because of local problems with the exhaustion of deposits and an evolving interdependent relationship with the coal industry as smelting and refining methods changed. Thus in the early eighteenth century, long-established mining centres in the Forest of Dean and the Weald of Sussex and Kent probably still contributed over a third of total output, with the remainder being drawn from the West Midlands and southern Yorkshire. A hundred years later, however, the Forest of Dean and the Weald had ceased to be of significance (Hart 1971; Cleere and Crossley 1985), Staffordshire and Shropshire had increased their share of a much expanded total to well over a third, and South Wales had emerged as probably the largest single producer. Evolution continued during the nineteenth century as South Wales and the Midlands began to be overhauled, first by mines in Lowland Scotland, and later the north-east and the Furness district of Lancashire/Cumberland (John 1950; Marshall 1958; Harris 1970; Hyde 1977: 12, 123, 181; Warren 1990).

Non-ferrous metal mineralisation was far more confined than iron, and the economics of mining less affected by the local availability of coal supplies. The ores were generally more valuable and able to sustain high reduction costs; the technical problems involved in reducing them were not so great; and cheaply available alternative fuels, such as peat, could often be used (Gill 2001). Thus tin was found and mined only in the south-western counties of Cornwall and Devon (Barton 1967); copper also in the south-west (Barton 1961) as well as north-western Wales (Rowlands 1981), Staffordshire (Robey and Porter 1972) and the southern Lake District (Holland 1986); and lead mainly in the Pennines, north and central Wales, the south-west, and southern Scotland. Silver and zinc were derived from the same mines as lead (Raistrick and Jennings 1965; Lewis 1967; Rowe 1993). Manganese was mined in Devon and central Wales and gold was worked in small quantities in Carmarthen and Merioneth (Rees 1969; Burt and Wilkie 1984; Hall 1988).

Construction and industrial minerals were widely distributed across the country and their production was usually linked to local demand in building, manufacturing and agriculture. Thus limestone was quarried almost everywhere it was found for building stone, furnace fluxes and fertiliser, and low-quality clays were extracted for brick and tile manufacture. Nevertheless, there were some products that were particularly associated with certain localities, and which were distributed to national and international markets. Thus salt was produced in large quantities in Cheshire, with over a third of its total output being exported in 1858. Similarly, china clay production was mainly, but not exclusively, associated with Devon and Cornwall, slate with north-west Wales, gypsum with Derbyshire, fuller's earth with Kent and Gloucestershire, and barytes and fluorspar with the Pennine lead mining districts. The production of these and other materials was a large and highly diversified industry that grew rapidly during the period and has continued to do so ever since. As early as the 1880s, slate was estimated to be the third most valuable mineral in production in England and Wales, behind only coal and iron, and today the construction and industrial minerals comprise by far the largest part of the surviving British extractive sector.

The different industries within the extractive sector varied considerably in their size and value of output. It is not possible to deconstruct the changing relative importance of all parts of the sector – the output of construction and industrial minerals is particularly obscure – but a fairly clear general picture can be compiled for coal and the principal metals. Throughout the period, the coal industry was undoubtedly the largest and most important part of the sector (Pollard 1980). This is usually explained in terms of the transition of Britain from a wood-based to a mineral-based energy economy (Wrigley 1988). It is argued that a widening range of industrial and domestic consumers of timber caused an increasing 'fuel crisis' in Britain from the early sixteenth century and that coal production expanded as a direct response to it (Thomas 1986). Thus Nef estimated a fourteenfold increase in coal output between 1550 and the 1680s (Nef 1932) and by the 1720s it probably already stood around 3.5 million tons annually. This compares with a probable production of around 100,000 tons of non-ferrous ore concentrates at that date and 75,000 tons of iron ore. The value of output is impossible to calculate with any accuracy but again it is likely that the coal industry was a clear leader, followed by non-ferrous metals, because of the relatively high value of their ores. It should be remembered that at this stage the output of iron was still constrained by a dependence on charcoal fuel, notwithstanding the successes of Abraham Darby with coke

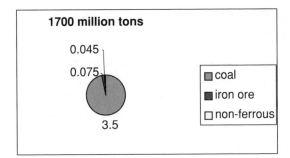

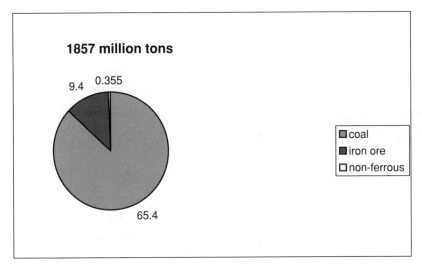

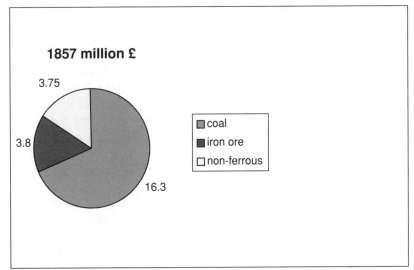

Figure 15.1 Volume and value of mine output, 1720s and 1857

Source: Mineral Statistics 1858.

Table 15.1 Estimated value of some construction and industrial materials produced in England, Wales and parts of Scotland in 1858

Mineral	Value £	Mineral	Value £
Clay (pottery)	285,846	Fuller's earth	13,500
Clay (brick)*	1,000,000	Sands	10,250
Building stone**	4,622,924	Raddle	10,000
Salt	750,000	Fluor spar	4,625
Coprolites	65,500	Rotten stone	750
Gypsum	17,750		
Barytes	15,500	Total	6,796,645

Notes: *Clay estimated at one-third of the cost of the production of bricks and tiles.
**Building stone includes slate and all limestone output.

Source: Mineral Statistics 1858, part II

Table 15.2 Men and women employed in coal and metal mining in 1854

	Coal	Iron	Copper	Tin	Lead
Males					
England	147,070	9,414	17,234	12,879	14,499
Wales	37,314	10,278	97	None	5,982
Scotland	32,969	7,294	15	None	897
Females					
All Areas	2,642	20	3,846	188	371
Total	219,995	27,006	21,192	13,037	21,749
Total number of men and women employed					302,979

Source: Mineral Statistics 1856.

smelting around 1710, and that the domestic demand for bar iron was still largely supplied from abroad (Hyde 1977). Domestic iron production finally took off from the 1760s (Riden 1977), and by the 1850s the position had changed considerably. The regular collection of national production data from the beginning of that decade provides a much clearer picture. The domination of coal had been extended to around 87 per cent by volume of output, with most of the remainder now being made up by iron ore. Coal's lead was somewhat less by value of product, accounting for around two-thirds of total output, while iron and non-ferrous ores divided the other third almost equally. These relative shares reflect the much higher values of metallic ores, particularly those of non-ferrous mines, which were for concentrates and not 'run of mine' production, as was usually the case with coal and iron. Taking the period 1700–1850 as a whole, the volume of coal output probably increased twenty-three times and that of iron by over 140 times, while non-ferrous ore production expanded by only six or seven times (see Figure 15.1).

No regular statistics of output for construction and industrial minerals were collected before the end of the nineteenth century, but a survey of 3,000 quarries in 1858 produced some indicative figures of its size and importance at that time (see Table 15.1). Those conducting the survey thought that these figures considerably understated the real value of output from this sector, however, and it might be better estimated at being around £10 million annually. This would have been roughly equal to one-third of that of metalliferous minerals and coal production.

By 1857 the total annual value of the output of the extractive sector, including construction and industrial minerals, was probably around £40 million a year. This was equivalent to more than 6 per cent of GNP and compares with 18 per cent of GNP derived from agriculture, forestry and fishing, the other main natural resources sector. Total employment in mining and quarrying at that time was probably well over 400,000, which compares with roughly 1.8 million in agriculture, forestry and fishing. There is no detailed breakdown of employment in mining and quarrying for that year, but the distribution in 1854 is shown in Table 15.2. It is notable that female employment is undoubtedly much below the levels seen before their exclusion from underground mining in the early 1840s.

DISTINGUISHING CHARACTERISTICS

Before looking at the causes and character of the expansion of the extractive sector, there are several qualifying issues that need to be considered – issues that set this sector clearly apart from agriculture, manufacturing and other forms of productive activity. First, and obviously, minerals can be mined or quarried only where they are found. Certainly the main centres of mineral production changed over time, with exhaustion, new discovery, and infrastructural changes that eased access problems and reduced costs, but at any one time the industry had to make the most of what was available, where it was available. The product of the mines could be, and was, often transported to other more suitable sites for reduction or manufacture, but the mines and quarries themselves were fixed in their location. By good chance, however, these sites were not often seriously inconvenient in Britain. In that sense it enjoyed an important advantage over many of its future industrial rivals. Minerals were widely dispersed across the country: the two most in need of locational partnering, coal and iron, were commonly found in close proximity; most mining districts were reasonably well served by cheap water transport facilities (rivers and coastal shipping and later canals); and few were remote from emergent urban manufacturing centres. Nowhere in Britain were there important constraints imposed upon industrial expansion and economic development by severe shortages, or excessively high prices, of mineral raw materials.

   Every aspect of the extractive process – technically, organisationally and financially – was heavily influenced by the geological conditions under which minerals were found. Coal mining, for example, was concerned with the removal of a relatively plentiful and cheap soft material from largely horizontally structured sedimentary rocks, frequently containing highly explosive methane gas. It required large numbers of men with limited skills, effectively 'quarrying' the coal by manually 'picking' from the face, and posed an ever present danger of explosion – disastrous both for the consequent loss of life and the physical damage it would inflict on the mine. The need to control ventilation in mines and to move large quantities of material from working areas to the shaft bottom, created opportunities for the employment underground of large numbers of unskilled women and children. By contrast, metal mines, particularly non-ferrous mines, usually worked relatively small, vertical veins of valuable ore in hard rock with little or no risk of gas explosions. They employed comparatively small numbers of skilled men to drill, blast and follow the lode. The work presented innumerable personal hazards, but rarely resulted in mass disaster or serious disruption to mining operations.

Table 15.3 Causes of death among 10,000 males over 15 years old, 1860–2				
Cause of death	All English occupations	Cornish metal miners	Durham coal miners	S. Wales coal miners
Lung disease	2,866	5,596	1,958	3,037
Accident	532	782	1,312	2,158

Source: Kinnaird Commission 1864 (ii).

Ventilation problems were much less prevalent than in coal mines and the volumes of material to be drawn to the surface were much smaller. This minimised the need for the employment of women and children underground and they were used instead in various unskilled and semi-skilled surface 'dressing' operations, where the ore drawn from the mine was crushed and concentrated before being sent for smelting. For much of the period, labour contracts in non-ferrous mines tied families together – men underground and wives and children at surface – in rewarding both the volume and the quality of the final dressed product delivered. By the second quarter of the nineteenth century, however, mechanisation was breaking down that relationship and dressing activity was passing to male labour.

The unpleasant conditions of underground labour also meant that miners, whatever their activity, suffered particularly deleterious effects on their health and/or encountered exceptionally high risks of injury and fatality (Burt and Kippen 2000). In coal mining these problems came mainly from the effects of dust, gas and explosions, while in metal mining they resulted from dust, blasting accidents and falling. In both cases, differing geological conditions were largely responsible for differences in their incidence between area (see Table 15.3).

The incidence of these hazards generally increased over the period as mines became deeper and underground employment became more continuous. Effective regulation of the industry was unknown before the 1840s and was then concerned mainly with removing women and children from underground employment. Attempts to reduce accidents by technological improvements undoubtedly had some impact – e.g. the introduction of the safety fuse for blasting from the 1830s – but in other cases may simply have served to encourage more dangerous practices. The safety lamp, for example, introduced around 1815 to prevent gas explosions in coal mines, never proved entirely reliable, encouraged the working of less well ventilated galleries, and resulted in more lives being lost in the eighteen years following its introduction than in the similar period preceding it (Pohs 1995). To compensate for these dangers, miners received a wage premium compared to other comparable labouring groups but careful measurement of the differences is hampered by the complex systems of employment used in mines (see below, pp. 434–6).

The differing geological conditions under which minerals were found also helped to shape the organisational structures of the industry. Coal seams, usually predictable and often easily worked, were frequently exploited by their owners on their own account during the eighteenth century, while metalliferous deposits, more difficult to prove and very variable in their quality and ease of working, were commonly leased to independent companies of adventurers, as owners sought to spread the risk of their exploitation. This method of working also became common for coal mining in the early nineteenth century as costs and essential investment increased. The high financial risks associated with non-ferrous mining made it a pioneer of extended partnership and, later, of joint-stock forms of organisation, while its occasional bonanzas, and more frequent failures, made those enterprises a notoriously speculative investment on the emergent London Stock Exchange (Burt 1972).

Mining and quarrying are inevitably exhaustive activities. They require constant new inputs of skill, capital and entrepreneurial expertise simply to sustain output but will inevitably finally encounter diminishing returns and rising marginal costs. The question is not *if* but *when* that point will be reached. Well-planned forward investment in prospecting and development will push the event into the future, or signal its approach, but cannot finally avoid it. The problem is compounded by the fact that the point of 'exhaustion' is decided not by the physical removal of the last piece of ore/coal/stone – that never happens – but by the economic viability of the operation. It is estimated, for example, that no more than 20 per cent of the coal *in situ* in most British mines was worth removing and that the remainder was left in the ground. Any sustained increase in prices might have raised that percentage; any reduction, without a comparable reduction in working costs, would have decreased it. Similarly, any long-term increase in market prices might create opportunities for reopening abandoned workings if marginal cost could be held constant at earlier levels. Investment decisions had to be made in the context of complex geological and market predictions that, during this period, were particularly difficult to estimate. Geological science was still in its infancy (Porter 1977) and the systematic geological mapping of Britain not begun until the 1840s (Torrens 2002). The Kent coalfield was discovered by broad observation of the geological structures of South Wales, Somerset, northern France and Belgium, but the more detailed processes of mineralisation were so little understood that industry practitioners continued to take the view that 'only by cutting the ground will the ore be found' (Hunt 1887: 189). All of these problems were further compounded by considerable variations in the quality and 'workability' of mineral 'in sight'. Similarly, the productivity of capital and labour varied widely between and within mines, even given the same quality of inputs. At any point, in any mine, marginal workings could be identified, and these could be taken in and out of production as price levels changed. It was a question not necessarily of opening and shutting particular mines, but of varying production between different parts of a mine (Burt 1984).

A combination of the last two factors makes it particularly difficult to calculate overall levels of capital investment in mining. Purchases of machinery and investments in buildings and surface ancillaries can be identified as in any other branch of industry, but probably the largest investments were in the creation of 'underground structures' – shafts, adits, approach roads, etc. As extraction took place and deposits were worked out, there was a continuing need for additional investment in development work simply to maintain production. If that investment failed to reveal economically viable mining opportunities it was entirely lost and non-recoverable. Equally, working expenditures on current extraction could reveal new deposits and facilitate future working, so effectively contributing to the capital stock of the mine (Claughton 1994). Estimates of total capital formation and capital/output ratios are thus highly speculative. Schmitz reviewed these problems for the non-ferrous mining sector, and made some tentative estimates of fixed capital formation in mines in Devon and Cornwall between 1820 and 1860 (Schmitz 1978), but more detailed national estimates have so far been confined only to the coal industry. Limited source material was again a problem but Feinstein, Pollard and Flinn have been able to suggest some general conclusions. Flinn's overall estimates of capital formation in coal mining between the mid-eighteenth and the mid-nineteenth centuries suggest that annual totals increased rapidly throughout the period, from around £100,000 annually in the late 1760s to £2 million annually in the 1840s. He concluded that the marginal productivity of that capital was improving and that in real terms the capital cost of mining was falling. More precise estimates were intractable, but Flinn found broad agreement with Feinstein in accepting a capital cost of around 4 shillings per ton of coal produced in the 1820s, assuming a total fixed capital at that time of £6 million and an output of approximately 30 million tons. This was slightly up on his own estimate of a capital cost of 2 shillings 6d. a ton in the mid-eighteenth century (Flinn 1984). Notwithstanding the large absolute investment in the coal mines, Feinstein has concluded that gross domestic capital formation in that industry in the eighteenth and early nineteenth centuries was small in relative terms and never accounted for more than 1 or 2 per cent of the national total – a view also supported by Mitchell (1984) in his calculations for the early nineteenth century (Feinstein 1978; Feinstein and Pollard 1988).

Finally, the extractive industries established an early, and particularly bleak, reputation for environmental pollution. Their extraction, processing and consumption became, and have remained, the primary cause of ecological damage in industrial economies everywhere. Although these concerns have now become central to development planning in the industry, they attracted little national attention before the mid-nineteenth century and the industry was subject to no general controls. It was not entirely without regulation however. From the medieval period, customary law in the mining districts had prohibited the pollution of watercourses (Gough 1931; Beare 1994) and people adversely affected were often able to obtain restraining injunctions and/or compensation. From the late seventeenth century, landowners and farmers in Derbyshire successfully prosecuted miners for 'bellanding' – making pasture or rivers poisonous to animals or people by discharging contaminated water – and from the last quarter of the eighteenth century lead smelters across the country invested large sums in long flue systems to protect themselves from similar actions resulting from the fall out of poisonous fumes (Day and Tylecote 1991; Slack 2001). 'Copper smoke' caused similar problems by the precipitation of copper and arsenic particles but had the added hazard of producing a highly toxic 'rain' of sulphurous and sulphuric acid. This was particularly serious in and around Swansea, where copper smelting was concentrated. Here, however, the strategic significance of the industry for the local economy, and the political strength of the smelters, defeated legal attempts to constrain the industry, and effective regulation was delayed until after the mid-nineteenth century (Newell 1997; R. Rees 2000). Similarly, the ravages of hydrochloric acid rain, resulting from the use of salt, pyrites, coal, chalk and limestone in the manufacture of alkalis in south-east Lancashire and Tyneside, were partly compensated by direct legal action but were not subjected to general regulation until 1863 (Dingle 1982). Whatever the level of these relatively localised problems, however, they were as nothing compared to the air pollution resulting from the smelting of iron. In 1845, for example, just one large iron company with works in Brecon and Monmouth was consuming more than a quarter of a million tons of coal a year in its furnaces and the steam engines used to blast them. Iron and smoke were inevitably in joint supply (Clapp 1994). The consequences of this for the urban environment – in the form of smog and acid rain – have been much discussed but its effects on the rural economy remain underresearched. Together with rapidly spreading waste tips from mining, quarrying and smelting, it reduced the productive capacity of agriculture by thousands of acres per year, offsetting gains made in that sector by land reclamation and improvement, and diminishing overall levels of output and productivity.

MARKETS AND PRICES

As has been seen, the production of all minerals increased considerably during this period. That expansion was led by a widening and deepening of demand: widening by finding new markets for minerals already in commercial production and new uses for previously discarded by-products; and deepening by increasing the consumption of existing users. To some degree, the extractive industries provided their own markets by 'feeding' on each other. More ferrous and non-ferrous ores needed more coal to smelt and refine them; more furnaces needed more refractory bricks and fluxes to line and operate them; more mines and miners needed more engines and hand tools to operate them. But more important was the expansion of the wider manufacturing economy and its related urban and transport structures. Thus an increasing range of heat-using technologies – for furnaces, kilns, boilers, ovens and stills – and the substitution of steam technology for traditional water and muscle power, raised the demand for coal (Mugridge 2001). The adoption of 'copper bottoming' of ships in the tropical trades, to protect against worm and fouling, almost invented a demand for rolled copper sheet, while the development of canning greatly increased the consumption of both iron and tin in the production of tinplate (Minchinton 1957). Above all, however, the expansion and urbanisation of the population increased the demand for stone, bricks and mortar for building, lead for roofing and piping, glass for windows, copper and pewter for utensils, pottery for serving and storing food (Rowe 1983). In 1836 the discovery of the method of 'galvanising' sheet iron with zinc created an entirely new product and demand as it became the definitive construction material of European expansion and empire during the later nineteenth century (Cocks and Walters 1968).

Throughout the period, the consumption of the domestic economy was significantly supplemented by overseas demand. Britain had a long history of exporting minerals in semi-manufactured form – e.g. as tin ingots or pig lead – and many of these trades also blossomed. Exports of nearly all minerals increased and for some, overseas markets became the principal source of demand. The growth was seen most spectacularly for copper. This industry had been in its infancy in Britain at the beginning of the eighteenth century but evolved a smelting sector that became a world technological leader by the late eighteenth century, and started to attract complex ores for smelting from mines across the world. The copper smelted from these imported ores was not differentiated from that derived from domestic ores in total export figures but supported an overall level of overseas trade which, by the mid-nineteenth century, was considerably greater than the entire domestic output. The other main non-ferrous metals, tin and lead, were more soundly established than copper at the beginning of the eighteenth century and never developed the same large-scale trade in processing imported ores. The absolute size of their export markets increased over the period but they diminished their share of total output from a massive half to three-quarters of total production in the early eighteenth century to a still respectable third in the mid-nineteenth century. In tonnage terms, all three metals were dwarfed by coal exports, which grew rapidly in their share of domestic output during the early nineteenth century and stood at over 10 per cent of the total by the early 1860s. Iron performed somewhat like copper

Table 15.4	Mineral exports as a percentage of domestic annual production		
	Exports (tons)	Domestic production (tons)	Exports as % domestic Production
Copper			
1700–9 Av.	Minimal		0
1855–9 Av.	22,220	18,660	119
Tin			
1700–9 Av.	1,100	1,410	78
1855–9 Av.	2,100	6,560	32
Lead			
1700–9 Av.	11,840	25,000 (est.)	47
1855–9 Av.	20,120	67,500	30
Coal			
1700–9 Av.	57,700	3,000,000 (est.)	2
1855–9 Av.	5,980,000	66,700,000	9
Iron			
1715–20 Av.	2,305	23,000 (est.)	10
1855–9 Av.	350,000	3,520,000	10

Source: Mitchell and Deane 1962.

in the early eighteenth century, with low levels of output and minimal exports. However, both grew rapidly during the remainder of the period and by the 1850s the relative importance of foreign markets was on a par with the coal industry (see Table 15.4).

Several industrial and construction materials – such as clays and stone – were traded abroad in increasing quantities, and relatively 'new' products such as arsenic began to find major overseas markets from the mid-nineteenth century (Burt 1988). Detailed trade statistics for these products do not appear to have been kept.

So great was the dependence of non-ferrous metal producers on overseas markets that any constriction or interruption to trade could have a profound influence on market prices. Thus war with major trading partners, embargoes, variations in tariffs (some were subject to export as well as import duties), and even prolonged periods of bad weather could cause serious overstocking of the domestic market and cutbacks in activity (Burt 1984). This vulnerability drove the industry constantly to explore new markets and attempt to find ways of redirecting trade throughout the eighteenth and early nineteenth centuries. Different products looked in different directions. Thus, in 1790, while coal, lead and to a lesser extent copper found most customers in Europe, tin looked strongly to the Far East and Africa and almost half of all trade in iron was with the United States and the British West Indies (see Table 15.5). It was only during and after the Napoleonic Wars that these patterns began to change, with a general redirection of trade away from Europe, the emergence

Table 15.5 The geographical distribution of mineral exports, 1790 (%)

	Europe	Far East/Africa	US/Brit. W. Indies
Copper	61	23	14
Tin	54	44	–
Lead	80	11	7
Coal	98	–	1
Wrought iron	27	18	49

Source: Schumpeter 1960.

of alternative domestic sources of supply there and increasing levels of activity elsewhere. Thus by the 1850s over 20 per cent of the overseas coal trade was to Africa, the Americas, Asia and Australasia (Church *et al.* 1986), and rapidly growing lead exports were being driven by new markets in Asia, the Americas and Russia, relegating Europe to second place.

Imports of foreign unprocessed minerals had no significant effect on the British market for most of this period. Coal and stone were never imported in any quantity and initial early eighteenth-century dependency on copper and 'battery' imports dwindled to insignificant levels after the 1720s and remained there until the rapid rise of copper ore imports from the late 1830s. Even then, it was not until the 1860s that imported copper began to have any serious effect on domestic market prices and the profitability of the copper producers. Small quantities of metallic tin were imported from Malaysia throughout the period but most of it was re-exported until the early 1840s. Thereafter imports increased steadily, but it was not until the last quarter of the nineteenth century that they also began seriously to depress domestic ore prices and production. Similarly, imports of lead ore and metal remained small and insignificant in terms of the domestic market until the mid-nineteenth century, when they began to move sharply upwards. Iron was somewhat different. In the early eighteenth century over a third of the British market may have been supplied with foreign iron, and imports increased through to the 1760s and remained fairly steady thereafter. However, much of this was specialist high-quality wrought iron and it accounted for a rapidly shrinking share of the total market as domestic iron production and consumption exploded into life from the mid-eighteenth century. By the end of the Napoleonic Wars, imports of foreign iron were quantitatively insignificant, and continued only for the small-scale manufacture of very highly specialised products.

The great expansion of markets at home and abroad, and the vanquishing of foreign competition, was all achieved without a significant sustained reduction in real market prices. Flinn has shown how coal prices at the pit head increased slightly in real terms over this period while those of most non-ferrous metals maintained a rough long-term parity with changes in producer goods price indices. Only iron experienced a significant secular decline, and that from the early nineteenth century (see Table 15.6).

Certainly there were shorter-term fluctuations, but they appear to have followed no particular pattern, reflecting a wide range of influences in the market. Surprisingly, the price movements of coal and metals in the

Table 15.6 Index of coal and metal prices, 1700–1830			
(Av. 1770–9 = 100 Flinn's base for his coal index)			
Coal	1700 = 95	1830 = 128	(Flinn, pp. 303–4)
Lead, pig	1709 = 70	1830 = 100	(Burt, pp. 303–5)
Tin, white	1700 = 107	1830 = 124	(Schmitz, pp. 293–5)
Copper, bar	1771 = 100	1830 = 117	(Schmitz, pp. 26, 269)
Iron, pig	1710 = 80	1830 = 85	(Hyde, pp. 44, 163)
Schumpter–Gilboy Consumer Goods Index (Mitchell and Dean 1962) 1700 = 100, 1823 = 128			
Source: Hyde 1977; Schmitz 1979; Burt 1984; Flinn 1984.			

early eighteenth century do not appear to support the contention of a developing fuel crisis during that period. New technologies that facilitated the substitution of coal for charcoal in the reduction of metallic ores might have been expected, other things being equal, to have produced a surge in coal prices and a corresponding reduction in metal prices. No such movements are observable (Schmitz 1979; Flinn 1984). Throughout the period, all sectors of the industry appear to have seen near perfect competition between producers, with only coal seeing periodic attempts at price rigging. Mine owners generally acted as price-takers rather than price-fixers. In 1798, for example, there were seventy-six active copper mines in Cornwall alone, with no single producer accounting for more than 12 per cent of total production and the majority less than 3 or 4 per cent. The 'ticketing' system of ore sales, which remained the common form for copper and much lead throughout the period, placed market influence firmly in the hands of the smelters rather than the mine owners. Similar conditions were encountered in the tin market, and, wherever they could, ore purchasers conspired to minimise, rather than maximise, ore prices in order to increase their own profits and maximise the size of the market (Barton 1967; Burt 1984). It is possible that combinations of smelters may have affected the metal markets for short periods during the eighteenth century, but the increasing importance of imported metals in the early nineteenth century would have undermined such activities. Overall, it seems likely that prices were directly determined by marginal costs at the level of production necessary to meet market demand.

The sustained level of prices should not be taken to infer that there were few technological improvements in the extractive sector. As will be seen, there were several highly strategic innovations that affected all parts of the sector during the period. The effects of those changes, however, were absorbed by the increasing difficulties of extracting deeper, more complex and lower-quality minerals. Coal and metal mining in Britain had already been conducted for more than a millennium by the early eighteenth century and the most easily accessible deposits had long since been worked out. A high proportion of output was already coming from mines deep enough to cause difficult technical problems, and even with improved methods the obstacles to the major expansion of production would be acute (Flinn 1984). In particular, deeper mining meant rising drainage, ventilation and drawing costs that would constantly challenge the best technology of the day.

INSTITUTIONAL DEVELOPMENT

Like the manufacturing sector, the extractive industries saw major changes in organisation and technology during this period – changes that also helped to stabilise costs in the pursuit of ever more complex and difficult mineral deposits. At the beginning of the eighteenth century, large swathes of the extractive sector were still in an essentially 'proto-industrial' stage of development, dependent on the enterprise of small groups of self-employed workers, operating mine and quarry leases with little more than simple implements and hand powered machinery, alongside parallel activities in agriculture. Certainly there were some large-scale operations in all sectors of the industry but these were still usually undertaken primarily by the mineral owners, acting either alone or in concert with a few local merchants and tradesmen. During the next hundred years, however, most of that industry was transformed into a modern corporate structure, drawing capital from regional and national markets to facilitate heavy fixed investment, employing a full-time labour force, and dependent on specialised systems of professional management (Burt 1998a).

As in other branches of modern capitalism, the foundations of these new structures were established by institutional changes. Of these, the most important were those relating to property rights. Mining, and to a lesser extent quarrying, normally require high long-term fixed investment to open and develop workings, and security and transferability of ownership define the parameters under which the industry operates. Studies of the origins and evolution of mining law in the frontier areas of the United States and Australia during the second half of the nineteenth century have clearly demonstrated its pivotal role in the development of the industry (Libecap 1986), but in Britain the subject has received comparatively little attention. This is possibly because mining law here evolved gradually from the early medieval period and there were no major departures or innovations during the eighteenth and nineteenth centuries to attract attention. Certainly mining saw nothing to compare with the contemporary struggles over surface rights instigated in the agricultural sector by the process of parliamentary enclosure.

In Britain, unlike continental Europe, common law had long held that minerals were the private property of the owners of the surface. As has been seen, they occasionally worked them on their own account or, with rising costs and increasing risks, leased them to separate companies of miners. The mineral owners sometimes took a share in these companies but always derived an income from rents and royalties on their lessee's output. The level of the latter as a percentage of output generally declined over the period but continued to generate high total revenues for some throughout. In 1860, for example, the Duchy of Cornwall derived an annual £24,885 from mining and quarrying, or slightly more than a third of the total estate receipts. Twenty years earlier, with a smaller total income, mining and quarrying had contributed well over half of the Duchy's income (Burt 1987).

Over time, clear arrangements had evolved for the alienation and disposition of mineral property, by both the owners and the lessees. There was, however, one important exception to these arrangements which, at the end of the seventeenth century, threatened security of tenure in the important non-ferrous sector of the industry. This was the crown's claim to all mines yielding the precious metals gold and silver. Throughout the seventeenth century, these claims had been vested in the Company of Mines Royal which periodically tried to exercise them. While gold was rarely encountered in Britain, silver was commonly found in association with lead and, to a lesser extent, copper. Any private company producing those minerals stood in constant fear of being dispossessed. The limitation, if not removal, of that threat, as much as any positive change in the law, was an important precondition for establishing the necessary confidence for large-scale private sector investment in the industry. It finally came in the 1690s, not through legislation, but by judicial decision, and the 'Terror of the Mines Royal' was removed (Lewis 1967). The issues surrounding the claims of royal prerogative can be seen in the context of the recent discussion of the institutional and political changes set in train by the 'Glorious Revolution' of 1688. The close and careful definition of royal prerogative rights to minerals – which were now far more restricted than in any other part of Europe – was one element of those institutional changes that ushered in the financial developments that laid the foundations for the wider industrial revolution (North and Weingast 1989; Ekelund and Tollison 1997; Wells and Wills 2000).

Secure property rights could lay the foundations for large-scale enterprise but new corporate arrangements were necessary to bring them to fruition. The financing of heavy investment in often highly speculative mining operations presented particular problems. Large numbers of investors needed to be brought together and arrangements made for them to spread or limit their risks. Joint-stock organisation would have been particularly attractive but, with the exception of the London Lead Company and a few other smaller operations with their own parliamentary charters, it was generally unavailable after the Bubble Act of 1720 (see chapter 8 above). Special arrangements were made within common law for mining ventures to have a large number of partners, but they frequently proved inadequate. The most successful method of circumventing the restrictions was found within regional codes of mining law. In the Stannaries of Devon and Cornwall, for example, 'cost book companies' were evolved from the early eighteenth century, which brought together hundreds of large and small investors, and even offered means of limiting individual liability. Also used outside of the south-west, they brought extended investment opportunities to mining more than a hundred years before such facilities were commonly available in other parts of British industry. The difficulty of financing expensive and risky mining operations led mining companies to be in the vanguard of the adoption of joint-stock limited liability forms of company organisation from the 1850s (Burt 1998b).

New methods of company formation brought together the finance necessary to establish large, highly capitalised operations, but it needed the evolution of new management systems to operate them. With labour often accounting for up to two-thirds of total operating costs, the control and motivation of the workforce presented a particular challenge. Like the early manufacturers, mining and quarrying enterprises in the early eighteenth century had to grapple with the problem of disciplining a still essentially proto-industrial labour force for the first time (Jenkin 1927) – and they had the additional problem of ensuring regular and diligent labour in the dark and labyrinthine conditions of underground workings. Most sectors of the industry – certainly coal, iron, non-ferrous metals and slate mining – tackled these problems through variations of a system of partnership working, where groups of miners took responsibility for working particular 'pitches' and pay was related to output. Regular opportunities were given to partnerships to change pitches to accommodate variations in their productivity and working conditions (Samuel 1977; Benson 1980; Colls 1987). In some systems, the miners became effectively sub-contractors, supplying all of their own materials and taking a share in the risks of the enterprise. If the conditions and productivity of their working areas improved, they received higher than expected earnings; if these deteriorated, they carried part of the extra cost of working them for the duration of their contract. The Cornish 'tribute' system was the most sophisticated of these arrangements. It tied earnings either to the quality of the ore produced, or to the volume of ground extracted. Under the patronage of John Taylor and Sons, an influential national and international consulting partnership, it became the industry standard for non-ferrous mining. Through the Taylors' connections with the metropolitan intellectual community, this system also came to the attention of contemporary commentators such as Charles Babbage, who advertised it widely as a model for labour arrangements everywhere (Price 1891; Burt 1977).

Complex systems of performance-related pay make it extremely difficult to calculate general earnings levels. Pay varied between the different

kinds of underground work and the partnerships undertaking them, between mines and regions, and over time. Earnings were subject to numerous deductions and payments in kind and were influenced by wide-
ranging levels of trade union activity, from increasing strength in some
coalfields to near invisibility in the metalliferous mining districts. In the
most general and tentative of terms, however, it would appear that the
average earnings level for miners of all types was around 12d. (1 shilling)
per day at the beginning of the eighteenth century and then increased
gradually over the century. The strongest growth was probably seen in
the most rapidly expanding coal districts and the slowest in the declining metal mining fields, such as the Somerset Mendips. By 1790 earnings
stood around 16d. a day for metal miners and 20d. to 30d. for coal miners. During the ensuing inflationary war years they moved forward more
sharply, to around 24d. a day for metal miners and up to 50d. a day for
coal miners by 1816. They fell back slightly during the post-war deflation,
but by the late 1820s had recovered a roughly similar position. By the
1850s most metal miners were earning around 30d. a day and coal miners probably had fallen back to about 40d. Overall, miners in all sections
of the industry appear to have done reasonably well during the industrial
revolution, with many seeing a significant real increase in their standard
of living. They all achieved considerably higher earnings than agricultural workers everywhere and did at least as well as semi-skilled labour
in neighbouring manufacturing. Those who increasingly chose to capi-
talise on their skills in overseas mining districts did significantly better
again (see Burt 1984, Flinn 1984, Church 1986, Burt and Kippen 2000).

It was not only the labour force that required innovative management.
Careful account was also needed for the tens of thousands of pounds
spent each year on fuel, candles, timber, iron and steel, rope, leather, oil,
hemp, picks, shovels, drills, gunpowder, stationery and a host of other bits
and pieces. Here the professionalisation of management went hand-in-
hand with the evolution of accountancy and improved book keeping techniques (Boyns and Richards 1995). Unlike manufacturing industry, where
management was commonly undertaken by owners and partners during this period, mining companies evolved a dependency on specialised
professional managers from early in the eighteenth century. There were
several reasons for this. First, mining companies pioneered large-scale industrial organisation and were among the first to confront the problems
of managing a large, full-time, mixed-gender labour force and controlling
a large financial turnover. Second, as has been seen, mining operations
were obliged to develop extended partnerships and independent companies from an early date, and even developed mechanisms for effectively
limiting investor liability. There was rarely the sense of private ownership
and commitment that was encountered in manufacturing and there was
a greater preparedness to accept employee management. Third, workplace
management was a particularly unpleasant task and one that needed to

be undertaken by people familiar with the job. Fourth, and again unlike manufacturing industry, there was an available supply of good-quality talent. Britain had no formal mining schools before the 1850s but it had developed a highly efficient informal system of on-the-job 'apprenticeship' management training from an early date. Under-managers, drawn mainly from the ranks of working miners, could progress by stages to overall 'captain' status, and captains themselves often established clear career structures as they moved from smaller to larger workings. At every stage the criterion for progression was proven technical and commercial success. Clearly, in practice, their competence and honesty were variable, but the best were equal to the occasional few trained in the mining academies of continental Europe. By the mid-nineteenth century they already filled most managerial positions in mining districts throughout North and South America, and they maintained their domination of the international industry until they were finally displaced by the graduates of a rising number of schools of mining after 1890 (Harvey and Press 1989).

TECHNOLOGICAL CHANGE

Institutional development paved the way for technical changes in the means and methods of mining – and was in its turn influenced by those changes. The first of the great new technical innovations was the comparatively simple process of applying gunpowder to the breaking of rock. In place of the laborious process of chipping and wedging the work face, short holes were drilled, powder and fuse inserted, the hole blocked up and the charge fired, 'shooting out' shattered rock or mineral. The process was first developed in central Europe around the mid-seventeenth century and it was gradually introduced into England in the decades around the beginning of the eighteenth century. It was not until the second quarter of that century, however, that it became common. When it did, it revolutionised miner productivity on a scale never previously seen. The new technique benefited all parts of the extractive sector, but its use was far more constrained in coal mining, where the possibility of igniting natural explosive gas gave it potentially disastrous consequences. Some sections of the construction and earthy minerals industries, where producers required large and carefully cut products, also made only limited use of the technique.

The improvement in productivity brought about by the introduction of gunpowder was considerable, but it was not sustained after the first half of the eighteenth century. In all sectors of the industry, output per underground worker remained little changed between the 1740s and the introduction of the coal cutter, machine drilling and dynamite explosives in the late nineteenth century. The mechanisation of surface dressing operation had some marginal effect in facilitating the extraction of more

	Manchester cotton firms, 1841			Cornish metal mines, 1837		
Size of firm	Number of firms	Number of employees	Share of total %	Number of mines	Number of employees	Share of total %
Small 1–150	54	3,989	12.5	115	5,626	20.8
Medium 151–500	62	17,806	55.8	35	9,677	35.8
Large 501–1,000	8	5,408	17.0	5	3,317	12.3
Very Large 1001 & over	4	4,700	14.7	5	8,408	31.1
Total	128	31,903	100	160	27,028	100

Table 15.7 Employment structure of Manchester cotton firms, 1841, and Cornish metal mines, 1837

Source: Lemon 1838; Lloyd-Jones and Le Roux 1980.

mixed material but this was generally confined to the non-ferrous sector. Everywhere major increases in output were produced mainly by a direct multiplication of the numbers employed. There were two ways of achieving this but both could incur expensive penalties. Either 'adventurers' (mining investors) could seek the lateral extension of working into new, previously undeveloped areas, or they could follow the deposits to greater depths. The former might be possible using existing extractive practices but commonly involved much higher transport costs as mining diverged from the established centres of consumption. The latter opened new and often rich deposits but required high and continuing expenditures on complex pumping, drawing and ventilation processes. Also, as underground workings radiated out from deep shafts, an increasing percentage of the work time and energy of miners was 'lost' in getting to and from their workplaces.

While the problems of deep mining had been largely resolved for metal mining by the mid-nineteenth century, and workings were going down well over 1,000 feet, for coal the pursuit of seams at depth created increasing dangers from gas and ground instability. This did not prohibit deep development in coal mines – some pits in Yorkshire, for example, matched the deepest Cornish mines with depths of well over 1,000 feet by the 1830s – but it was less common. Thus, in very general terms, the coal and iron mining industries, which were able to exploit widely distributed mineral reserves, tended to opt for lateral development, while the more geographically restricted non-ferrous industry tried to expand production by exploiting lodes at ever greater depths. In the early 1850s, for example, there were over 2,000 collieries operating in England and Wales while the number of tin and copper mines amounted to no more than a few hundred. Similarly, the production of some non-ferrous mining districts tended to be dominated by the output of a small number of particularly large producers, employing large numbers of men, women and children. In 1853, for example, more than 50 per cent of Cornwall's copper output came from just 10 per cent of its active mines (*Mineral Statistics* 1853). The data in Table 15.7 show that, as early as 1837, the proportion of

Cornish miners working in establishments with more than 500 workers exceeded 43 per cent, whereas in the Manchester cotton mills at this time only 32 per cent of workers were employed in enterprises of this size (Lemon 1838; Lloyd-Jones and Le Roux 1980, 1982). At this date the Consolidated and United Mines operation in Cornwall, employing 1,730 men, 869 women and 597 children, was possibly the largest single private industrial employer in the country.

Care must be taken not to draw these lines too strongly however. From the first years of the nineteenth century, several collieries working deep seams in the north-east employed over 500 workers each, with at least one exceeding 700, and in 1820 the average for each colliery in that area was 342 workers (Flinn 1984). Similarly, not all non-ferrous mines worked deep deposits. The lead mines of the Pennines and central Wales, for example, commonly exploited shallow deposits with a fairly small labour force. In the quarrying sector, the depth of workings was less relevant but the need for heavy investment in a transport infrastructure could also encourage large-scale working. Thus Richard Pennant employed 400 workmen in his slate quarry at Penrhyn in North Wales in the 1790s, and by the mid-nineteenth century that number had risen to nearly 2,000 (Samuel 1977).

The introduction of gunpowder blasting in the early eighteenth century not only eased the problems of ore extraction, but also greatly facilitated the sinking of shafts and the driving of underground tunnels. Here it played a crucial role in helping to overcome the 'drainage crisis' that was beginning to constrain the expansion of many mining districts from the early seventeenth century. As mines had sunk ever deeper to sustain and increase output they had also progressed further below the water table, and flooding or 'unwatering' problems had grown steadily. Bailing and pumping equipment, of ancient and medieval design and still largely hand powered, frequently proved inadequate to the task. One solution was to drive long drainage levels (adits) under the deepest mine workings from neighbouring low-lying land. Some such projects had been tried before the advent of powder blasting, but progress had proved too slow and expensive. With powder, speed was greatly increased and drainage systems, sometimes tens of miles in length, began to be pieced together in many mining districts during the later eighteenth and early nineteenth centuries. They made a major and lasting contribution to minimising mine operating costs and can be regarded as a significant investment in the capital infrastructure of many mining districts. However, they presented only a partial solution to the drainage problem. It continued to take years to bring the adits to completion and profitable mines might need to be suspended for the whole of that time. Alternatively, where primitive pumping systems could cope with the inflow of water, the mines frequently had sunk below the adit level before it arrived, so greatly reducing its final benefit. Clearly, there was a pressing need for better and cheaper methods of pumping.

Pumping technology was revolutionised from the early eighteenth century, not by any strategic improvements in the pumps themselves, but in the machines that drove them. On the one hand, traditional power sources, muscle and water, were greatly improved, and on the other, an entirely new power source was rapidly introduced. It was the mining industries that called forth and nurtured the steam revolution that was later to sweep across the rest of the industrial system. From Thomas Newcomen, the Devonian metal merchant, who was inspired by the pumping problems of south Devon tin mines in the earliest years of the eighteenth century, through James Watt and his attempts to improve the efficiency and fuel consumption of atmospheric engines distant from cheap fuel supplies, to the great Cornish steam engineers of the early nineteenth century, it was the requirement of mines for a cheap and reliable source of pumping power that drove one of the main lines of development of steam technology (Barton 1969). Equally, steam power had become the dominant source of motive power in mining districts across the country long before it began to make any significant impact in many manufacturing districts (Kanefsky 1979).

However, the general adoption of steam power within the extractive sector did not follow an easy and regular path. In Cornish tin, copper and lead mines the early up-take of Newcomen atmospheric engines was constrained by their high fuel consumption and the elevated level of local coal prices, which resulted not just from long-distance transportation costs, but also from a tax on coal brought by coastal shipping. The suspension of those duties in 1739, together with efficiency improving inventions in engine design and operation, provided the foundations for a more rapid up-take, and by 1775 there may have been well over seventy engines in the county. Fuel consumption on remote metal mining sites everywhere continued to be a major issue, however, and the arrival of the far more efficient Watt engine was greeted with enthusiasm. Over eighty Watt and similar 'pirate' engines were erected in Cornwall during the last quarter of the eighteenth century, roughly matching all of the atmospheric engines accumulated in the previous sixty years (Barton 1969). Many of the older atmospheric engines were displaced and found new homes in the rapidly expanding coal industry, where plentiful supplies of waste coal gave fuel costs a lower priority than reliability and simplicity of operation. The continuing Cornish demand for ever greater power and minimum fuel costs continued to force technology forward and spawned a rapidly expanding local steam engineering industry in the early nineteenth century. That industry became a world leader in the design and production of high-efficiency pumping engines. By the middle of the nineteenth century its engines had spread beyond the non-ferrous mining districts to the coal mines, where they replaced older atmospheric and Watt engines as some mines sank below their pumping capacity (Church 1986). Nevertheless many of those older engines continued to find use in parts of the coalfields until well into the twentieth century.

Drainage was not the only use for steam power. In all areas, particularly the coal districts, winding engines and their associated headgear became a characteristic feature of the landscape, as steam was applied to the movement of both men and materials in rapidly deepening shafts. Frequently, in the eighteenth and early nineteenth centuries, the same engines were arranged to work both pumps and winders, but by the mid-nineteenth century an increasingly powerful range of expensive and specialised machinery was becoming the norm. From the early nineteenth century, steam power was also applied to surface crushing and separating operations at metal mines, as well as to a widening range of fans and other ventilation devices in coal mines (Hill 2000). Altogether, the use of steam power in mining and quarrying was very extensive by the 1850s and was probably equal to that in the rest of the industrial sector combined. Unfortunately, there are no reliable counts of engines in use at this time, or estimates of their total horsepower, but Kanefsky has conjectured the position in 1870. He estimated that at that time there was 500,000 to 550,000 hp (horsepower) in coal mines, 50,000 hp in non-ferrous mines, 10,000 hp in iron mines and 10,000 hp in quarries (Kanefsky 1979). These figures undoubtedly represented a considerable increase on the level at the mid-century but probably reflect reasonably accurately the balance of distribution of steam usage between the different parts of the extractive sector.

Although the increasing use of steam power usually takes centre stage in histories of the extractive sector, the wider and more intensive use of improved water power – itself an important natural resource – made an equal, and sometimes much greater, contribution to the expansion of output for most of the eighteenth and early nineteenth centuries. In the high and wet non-ferrous mining districts of the Pennines, Wales and the south-west, for example, waterwheels and water pressure engines continued to provide a major source of power (Gill 2001). They not only proved cheaper and easier to install, maintain and operate than steam engines but also, with a power output sometimes in excess of 100 hp, were more than equal to the pumping requirements of relatively shallow workings. Almost everywhere they were used for powering crushing, washing and separating machinery and started the substitution of mechanical for human power in all of the most arduous surface processes. Without those changes, the potential to expand mined output would have been strangled by the inability to process and concentrate run-of-mine material before despatch to customers and/or smelters. Even in the south-west, the home of steam powered pumping machinery, waterwheels continued in

use at many mines, large and small, for a range of underground and surface purposes, particularly where small-scale power units were required
(Barton 1968). Thus Devon Great Consols, the world's largest copper mine
at the mid-century, employed eight steam engines and thirty-three waterwheels in the 1860s, most of them on the dressing floors. Kanefsky
estimates that, as late as 1870, waterwheels generated around 25,000 hp
in non-ferrous metal mines, which was roughly equal to half of that generated by steam (Kanefsky 1979). It is likely that twenty years earlier the
share of water power was considerably greater and that for most of the
eighteenth century it was the most important mechanical power source
utilised by the industry.

Everywhere muscle power – human and animal – also continued to
make a major contribution alongside water and steam. It was used in
operating a wide range of localised underground pumping, haulage and
ventilation equipment and was mainly responsible for the surface separation of mixed materials. Over time there was a clear tendency to substitute animal for human labour, but with the low cost of unskilled workers
it made little progress except for the more arduous tasks such as winding, where horse powered whims could be easily introduced. In coal mining, even the difficult task of hauling coal to the shaft bottom remained
largely the preserve of women until their exclusion from underground
labour by the 1842 Mines Act. Thereafter the use of ponies spread rapidly
and remained an important feature of the industry until well into the
twentieth century (Church 1986). At metal mines, underground horse
haulage was occasionally employed from the eighteenth century but it
generally remained uncommon. Equally their surface operations were
mainly dependent on hand operated wheelbarrows, though rail systems
were introduced at some of the larger workings from the early nineteenth century. Precise, quantifiable assessment of the comparative role
of muscle power has never been attempted but it is likely that it remained
comparable with mechanical sources of power in many mines and most
quarries until well into the nineteenth century.

While improvements in rock breaking and the application of mechanical power kept down costs in the primary processes of mining and quarrying, innovations in smelting and refining greatly increased the efficiency
of converting metallic ores into final marketable products. To the extent
that it is the overall marginal cost of that final product which determines market prices and consumer demand, improvements in ore reduction were as much part of the extractive process as the primary processes
themselves. The technical and economic integration of mining and smelting also meant that improvements in ore reduction techniques could
unlock the exploitation of lower-quality and more complex ores. During
the eighteenth and early nineteenth centuries, the improvements in the
smelting and refining of ores were myriad and to discuss them in any detail would need a metal-by-metal examination that is beyond the scope of

this chapter. However, one particular innovation stands out. It improved the efficiency of lead and tin smelting, virtually created the domestic copper industry, and finally realised the potential of cheap wrought iron. It was the reverberatory, or cupola, furnace which made its first appearance in the last decades of the seventeenth century. By utilising reflected heat, this furnace separated fuel and ore/metals, and provided the key to the substitution of coal/coke for increasingly expensive charcoal. More than any other single innovation, it provided the solution to the increasingly pressing 'fuel crisis' of the late seventeenth and early eighteenth centuries and released British metallurgy from the constraints of medieval technology. The 'reverberatory revolution' started with lead in the late seventeenth century, rapidly diffused to tin and copper two decades later, and was completed for iron after 1780.

The first large-scale introduction of the reverberatory furnace is usually associated with the London (Quaker) Lead Company's operations in north-east Wales, and Derbyshire in the early eighteenth century (Bevan-Evans 1963). Neighbouring coal deposits provided cheap fuel in these districts and the success of the new furnace had made it common in all of their works by the late 1720s. The earlier 'ore hearth' furnace was not entirely vanquished however. In some other lead districts, such as the Yorkshire Dales and the more remote northern Pennines, it continued in use for another 150 years. This was because transport difficulties kept coal costs high, while the blast-hearth, up-dated by various design and construction improvements, could make use of cheap local peat fuel and continued to deliver good results. Both furnaces presented serious environmental hazards by venting large quantities of poisonous 'fume' into the atmosphere, which settled on surrounding agricultural land, depressing vegetation and poisoning farm animals. Together with the discharge of contaminated mine water into river systems, again threatening human and animal life as well as fish stocks, this prompted some of the earliest public concerns about, and control of, ecological pollution. Thus to protect themselves against legal action by local farmers, and to recover valuable material, it became common for mines to construct complex systems of settling-pits and for smelters to built long horizontal flue systems from their larger works. Many of these still survive today as symbols of those concerns (Gill, 2001).

Although reverberatory furnaces affected only part of the lead industry, they transformed the organisation of tin smelting. Until the early eighteenth century, tin ore had been smelted in simple blast-hearths similar in design to those used for lead. These were small-scale installations, sited close to the mines and 'streaming' operations, and they relied on charcoal as their fuel. As early as 1706, however, they began to be replaced by coal fired reverberatories, which presaged a fundamental change in the size and structure of the industry. The limited fuel requirements of these meant that they continued to be sited within the south-west, rather than moving closer to the coalfields, but they produced a 'balling together' of smelting around a smaller number of centres of production. This in turn concentrated market power into the hands of the smelters and produced important changes in the structure of the tin trade (Day and Tylecote 1991). Furnaces continued to evolve during the eighteenth and nineteenth centuries, and English designs emerged as an industry standard, installed in tin producing districts across the world.

The reverberatory furnace transformed lead and tin but it effectively invented the modern British copper industry. Notwithstanding Tudor and Stuart efforts to import central European technology to establish this strategic industry in England, it had languished throughout the seventeenth century as high fuel cost in primitive traditional open furnaces made the English product uncompetitive with foreign imports. In the 1690s, however, John Coster, previously employed at a lead cupola in Bristol, successfully adapted that furnace, and the use of coal fuel, for the production of second-quality copper. A new smelting and refining industry then developed rapidly in the Redbrook district, just to the north of Bristol. In its early years it relied largely on previously discarded ores, brought in by sea from Devon and Cornwall. Gradual improvements in technique, particularly the substitution of coke for coal fuel, gradually improved the quality of the product and the range of its potential uses, but most was consumed by the local brass industry, which also saw a period of rapid expansion (Day 1973; Day and Tylecote 1991). By the early 1720s, Bristol was the undisputed centre of the country's rapidly expanding copper industry – but things were about to change.

The Costers, a prominent smelting partnership that had integrated backwards into copper mining, began to look for alternative reduction sites. They had experimented with a limited primary smelting operation at Hayle on the north coast of the Cornwall but looked to establish a new, more convenient secondary capacity nearer to coal supplies, just across the Bristol Channel, in Swansea. Their early success there attracted other entrants to the industry, particularly during the 1730s and 1740s, and by the mid-century Swansea was already beginning to rival Bristol's ascendancy. A few years later, a third centre of activity also began to emerge along the coast of Lancahire and north-east Wales. These sites were also conveniently located to exploit nearby coal deposits and were used to smelt the rising tide of copper ores produced in Anglesey from the early 1770s. However, with the decline of the Anglesey mines from the 1790s, most of this capacity was relocated to South Wales. Throughout these years most of the copper continued to be consumed in brass manufacture, much of that industry being based locally and around Bristol (Cocks and Walters 1968). From the 1770s large quantities of copper plate began to be used for the protective sheathing of the hulls of sea-going merchant and naval vessels, particularly those engaged in tropical waters (Harris 1964).

In general terms, the story of British copper smelting from the mid-eighteenth century was increasingly that of Swansea. Unlimited supplies of cheap coal, good sources of clay for making furnace refractory linings, deep-water access for shipping, low labour costs, and above all dynamic business partnerships and continuous cost reducing and quality improving innovation, underpinned its success. During the next half-century, it built on that success to turn its national reputation into world renown. The cupola-based 'Welsh Process' of ore reduction turned Britain from the backward cousin of central European technology in the early modern period to an undisputed world leader in copper technology and a logical focus for the rapidly expanding production of copper mines across the world. So efficient were its techniques, and so competitive its costs, that, from the 1830s, new mines in distant Chile found it more profitable to ship their ores on a six- to nine-month round trip via Cape Horn to Swansea, rather than to attempt to smelt them at home – a decision which was later to be repeated by mines in Arizona, Colorado, Australia, New Zealand and many other countries (Fell 1979). It was not until the last decades of the nineteenth century that Swansea finally lost this advantage in copper smelting and began its long decline to twentieth-century extinction (Hughes 2000; Rees 2000).

The modernisation of the iron industry owed much to copper and brass. Abraham Darby, the Shropshire ironmaster who first successfully substituted fossil fuel for charcoal in smelting iron during the second decade of the eighteenth century, had enjoyed a previous career in brass manufacture in the Bristol region. However, it was not the reverberatory furnace that initially provided the way forward. The much higher temperatures needed to reduce iron ores required blast furnace technology. At the beginning of the eighteenth century, that process was high cost in England because of the increasing shortage of traditional charcoal fuel, and the industry's output was low and stagnating. Darby was the first to find a technical solution to that problem, substituting coke for charcoal in those furnaces, but his early methods proved a commercial failure. His fuel costs were not markedly lower than those of charcoal smelters; the furnaces were more expensive to build; they required a more powerful blast; and they produced a lower-quality product. Charcoal producers may have encountered steadily rising costs, but for the moment they enjoyed a domestic market that was heavily protected by tariffs and the high transport costs encountered by foreign suppliers, and most unsurprisingly rejected the new technique.

The balance finally began to shift in favour of coke smelting from the 1750s, however, and a rapid conversion to the now well-known technique underpinned a major expansion of production. This reversal of fortunes has been explained partly in terms of continuing changes in smelting and partly by associated developments in the refining sector of the industry. In smelting, the cost of coke fuel continued to fall while that for charcoal progressed sharply upwards, finally tilting the cost advantage in favour of the coke product. Simultaneously, changes in refining technology began gradually to remove the cost advantage long enjoyed by charcoal smelted pig in that process. This was important, even critical, because, unlike Darby who consumed his blast furnace output directly in producing thin walled castings, the great majority of iron users wanted not crude and brittle pig iron bar, but relatively soft and malleable wrought or bar iron, i.e. pig iron that had been heated to remove sulphur and much of its carbon content. The problem had been that the refiners' forges used charcoal as fuel and that the lower-quality coke-produced pig needed more heat and more fuel to process it. Any savings in smelting costs that could have been achieved by the switch to coke fuel were more than lost by the higher charges at the refining stage. The challenge was also to substitute coke for charcoal without contaminating and reducing the quality of the final refined product and to reduce the cost differentials for the differently produced pig iron. The first major advance in this direction was made by the Wood brothers, with their 'potting and stamping process', introduced in the 1760s and widely adopted thereafter. But it was Henry Cort's exploitation of the reverberatory furnace in his 'puddling process', first patented in 1783/4, that was to have the greatest effect on the industry's longer-term growth. Following further critical improvement by Richard Crawshay in the 1790s, puddling in cupola furnaces quickly became the industry standard, sharply reducing costs in real terms and helping to triple the output of bar iron between 1794 and 1815. It continued as the main method of refining throughout the nineteenth century and was a principal support of Britain's progress to becoming one of the largest and most efficient iron producers in the world (Hyde 1977; Harris 1988). The reverberatory furnace had arrived late in the iron industry but its impact was at least equal to its earlier achievements in the non-ferrous sector.

Before leaving the issue of smelting and refining, it should be noted that improvements in technology not only facilitated an expansion in the total volume of output from the mining sector but also greatly influenced the range of ores that could be profitably worked, and the broad geographical distribution of mining activity. In this context, it is important to remember that minerals do not occur as single homogeneous products but come in many and varied forms – there are, in other words, many different types of coal, stone and sand and many different ores of iron, lead, copper and tin. They occur sometimes together and sometimes far apart. They are suitable for different purposes and present different challenges in their market preparation. Given a certain level of technology, some are workable and some are not. Technical change can open up new opportunities and potential. This can be seen time and again in all parts of the extractive sector but it can be particularly well illustrated by one key improvement in iron smelting in the 1820s. The British

Isles had been extensively mineralised with a wide range of iron ores, but one group offered particular economic advantages for their exploitation. These were the 'Clay Band' argillaceous ores and the 'Black Band' carbonaceous ores that were often found alternated with coal beds in many of the country's coalfields. This arrangement meant that in many instances the same mines could furnish the smelters with both the ore and the fuel to run their furnaces. Under the constant pressure to minimise costs, the industry had tended to become heavily dependent on these deposits, and down to the second quarter of the nineteenth century most iron was produced from Clay Band argillaceous carbonate ores. The potential of the Black Band ironstone deposits in the Scottish Lowlands also had been noticed by David Mushet at the beginning of the nineteenth century but the difficulties of smelting these had meant that they remained largely ignored.

This changed after 1828, following the invention of the comparatively simple 'hot blast' process by James Neilson. His initial motivation was simply further to reduce furnace operating costs by heating the air flow into blast furnaces, but the technique had two far more important strategic consequences. First, it permitted the use of raw coal rather than coke in the furnaces, and second, it raised furnace temperatures and facilitated the reduction of Black Band ores. Birch concluded that this was 'the most important single invention in the industry in the age of iron' (Birch 1967). It unleashed the economic potential of Welsh anthracite deposits, which had never been suitable for coking, and it opened the door to the exploitation of the vast Scottish Black Band reserves. The iron industry in both countries was given an immediate boost. In Scotland the technique had been adopted in all ironworks within eight years and output began to rocket from 24,500 tons in 1823 to over 300,000 tons in 1843. The number of furnaces increased five times to well over a hundred, and Scotland's share of total UK output went up from 5 per cent to 25 per cent. In South Wales, anthracite fuelled blast furnaces were yielding upwards of 60,000 tons of pig iron annually by the early 1840s (Meade 1882). In the longer term, the introduction of hot blast also helped to open up the working of a wide range of other iron ores in Britain, most notably the large haematite reserves of the north of England. Increasingly complex mixes of ores were used to produce different types and different qualities of metal. In the iron industry, as in other metals, the link between technological change and the supply of raw materials is fundamental. In short, it gave economic viability to the working of minerals that had previously been ignored and, in so doing, reorganised the locational forces that determined the distribution of the main centres of production (Atkinson and Baber 1987).

While institutional and technological changes played a crucial role in increasing efficiency within the extractive sector, external improvements in transportation could make an even greater contribution to minimising final product delivery costs (Fairbairn 1992). Heavy, bulky, low-value goods depended entirely on effective low-cost transportation systems if they were to be moved any distance for profitable manufacture and distribution. Primitive road conditions in the eighteenth century, and the frequent need to convey minerals by pack horse or small cart, meant that land carriage charges could double the total cost of minerals every 10 miles – but equally it was known that the same quantity of material could be conveyed twenty times as far by water for the same unit cost (Flinn 1984). Accordingly, efforts were made everywhere to exploit the facility of water transport – by coastal shipping, rivers and canals – and/or to improve the efficiency of linking land carriage by investment in roads, tramways and railways. The east coast coal trade from Newcastle to London was well established centuries before the industrial revolution, and coasting routes generally continued to carry a very large percentage of all of domestic coal output throughout the period. The development of the south-western copper industry was entirely dependent on the capacity to carry ore and coal coastally – the ore to the coalfields of Redwood and Swansea for smelting, and the coal as return cargo to fuel the mines and the domestic demands of mining communities. Equally the lead districts of central Wales developed an early dependency on carrying ore coastally to smelting works in Neath, and that trade was a powerful motivating force for the construction of the Neath canal in the first years of the eighteenth century. Similarly, the need to reduce the cost of carrying stone, coal and clay from mines near St Helens to smelters and salt boilers on the Lancashire coast was a driving force behind the construction of the Sankey canal in the mid-1750s. Indeed, there was not a river improvement or canal promotion anywhere in England during the eighteenth and early nineteenth centuries that did not refer to the savings that would be offered to the movement of minerals of one description or another. And the savings could be very considerable. Against land carriage costs of around one shilling per ton mile in the eighteenth century, canal and river carriers could reduce rates to 2d. per ton mile and coastal shippers by as much again (Burt 1984).

Not every mine was conveniently placed for water transport however. Many were located in some of the most remote parts of the British Isles – such as the lead districts of the northern Pennines and central Wales – and most needed at least some overland connection. Traditionally this had been provided by pack horses, but from the early eighteenth century there were attempts to reduce costs by constructing 'wagonways'. These were putative tramways, with the road surface being 'hardened' by the installation of wooden rails with flanges to hold and guide the wagon wheels. They became particularly common in the coal districts, where their intensive use and heavy wear led to up-grading with cast iron and then wrought iron rails in the later eighteenth century. Iron fabrication created the potential for saving on construction and maintenance costs, by transferring the flange from the rail to the truck wheel, and also established the conditions for the substitution of steam for horses as the principal source of power. At first provided by stationary engines, and from 1815 by locomotives, these became the nursery of the future railway revolution. By the beginning of the second quarter of the nineteenth century, nearly all of the coal consumed in England was shipped via complex and integrated systems of tramways, canals, rivers and coastal routes, with comparatively little touching the regular road system. Other branches of mining, producing higher-value products, could sustain the higher costs of land transportation over short distances, but even these had invested in local tramway systems by the early nineteenth century. Thus the lead mining interests of the Derbyshire Peak District constructed a 33 mile tramway to connect the Cromford and High Peak canals, while the tin, copper and china clay producers of Cornwall invested in separate 'railway' systems in the twenty years after 1806 (Rowe 1993). As late as 1819, a large granite quarrying venture on Dartmoor in Devon constructed a traditional 8 mile wagonway, and a short linking canal, to convey building stone to the nearest navigable water on the River Teign, and a small quay to aid coastal transhipment to London. In every sector of the industry, improved transportation was essential to minimise internal production costs – mines to smelters to manufacturers – as well as the delivery price in final markets. It was as much a factor in maintaining price levels in a sector facing ever decreasing returns as any of its other internal improvements in methods and machinery.

CONCLUSION

The story of the extractive industries outlined here has an uneasy relationship with the broader picture of British economic growth outlined in other parts of this volume. On the one hand the performance of most parts of the industry reinforces the current view of steady 'evolutionary' growth, rather than any 'revolutionary' surge in output. During the eighteenth and early nineteenth centuries, the output of lead and tin ores increased by an average of less the 1 per cent per annum, with no clear points of discontinuity from a slowly rising trend (Mitchell and Deane 1962). Copper was a little more volatile. After an initial rapid rate of expansion when sustained domestic production was established in Britain for the first time, copper ore output levelled off during the second quarter of the eighteenth century but then grew at an average annual rate of around 2.75 per cent down to the mid-nineteenth century. Coal production probably never sustained an increase of much over the 2 per cent annual average for the period 1700–1860, and only iron ore production seems to have enjoyed rapid rates of short-term growth, amounting to an average of 4.5 per cent per annum in 1796–1860. Similarly, productivity growth probably remained low throughout. After an initial surge following the introduction of gunpowder blasting in the early eighteenth century, miner productivity remained roughly constant in most parts of the industry until the late nineteenth century. The productivity of capital, that might have been expected to have benefited from investment in a new range of steam and improved water power technology, was constantly held back by the need to work minerals of diminishing quality under increasingly difficult conditions.

On the other hand, unlike many sectors of the economy, growth in the extractive industry appears to have been mainly demand led. Ore and metal prices saw no major reduction over the period as most parts of the industry struggled to meet increasing consumption by a widening range of users in both the producer and consumer goods sectors. There were some technological innovations – such as the copper bottoming of ships and railways construction – that produced sudden and unexpected surges of demand, but most of the up-take of the increasing output of metals and minerals was not from the new large-scale, urban-based manufacturing and construction industries; rather it was from expanding activity by myriad small and traditional workshops and craftsmen – e.g. nail makers, edge-tool makers, blacksmiths, plumbers and whitesmiths – found in provincial towns and villages across the country. Wrigley (1988) may be right in observing the emergence of a new mineral-based *energy* economy during the period, but a mineral-based *materials* economy had long been firmly established in England. If there was an important substitution effect during the period, it was not minerals for organics but minerals for minerals. Lower-cost materials were substituted for higher-cost ones – e.g. iron pipes for copper and lead, pottery and tin plate for pewter, bricks for masonry – and reduced overall production costs encouraged increasing demand for final products.

With its firmly established mineral-based economy and material culture, Britain's capacity to feed its industry and rapidly expanding towns with fuel and raw materials was just as important for the process of economic development as its ability to feed its expanding population with basic foodstuffs. An early and continuing dependence on imports could easily have stifled the process of change through shortages, raised prices and diminished incentives in a wide range of key growth sectors. The comparative experience of many other European nations, whose industrialisation was slowed and hampered by poor mineralisation and/or its inconvenient location, illustrates the strongly negative effect of such deficiencies. From the medieval period to the twentieth century, healthy surpluses of metals and minerals played a strategic part in balancing both national and private accounts. Thus they provided the second-biggest export earner after textiles – so helping to generate the overseas earnings required to purchase imports of other essential raw materials such as cotton – and were one of the principal supports of estate incomes, joining with agricultural profits and rents in providing a crucial source of capital for industrial investment, urban expansion, transport development and government finance. Most significantly, however, it was the overall balance of resources that created the context within which the epoch-making innovations of the British industrial revolution were conceived. Similarly, the need to move increasing quantities of heavy, bulky low-value minerals provided the pioneering incentive for the improvement of Britain's rivers and the construction of its canal, tramway and railway systems. Without the exploitation of their extensive mineral resources, many regions that pioneered the industrial revolution – such as the West Midlands, South Wales and Cornwall – would have remained sparsely populated areas of second-rate agriculture, and the demographic, social, cultural and political profile of Britain would have been cast in a very different mould.

16

The industrial revolution in global perspective

STANLEY L. ENGERMAN AND
PATRICK K. O'BRIEN

Contents

Introduction: the rise of Britain and its economy,
    1660–1815   451
Britain and European powers in the world economy,
    1492–1713   453
European economic development, 1500–1800   455
Exogenous and endogenous forces behind the rise of the
    British economy, 1713–1815   458
Britain's international relations   460
Convergence and relative decline   462

INTRODUCTION: THE RISE OF BRITAIN AND ITS ECONOMY, 1660–1815

Between 1660 and 1815 Great Britain rose to become the world's leading commercial and military power, surpassing its European rivals, and all other national economies around the world.[1] Although dating the industrial revolution now seems a pointless exercise, it makes sense to begin an account of Britain's long transition to geo-political and economic primacy at the Restoration (1660) and to recognise that its maritime hegemony and economic superiority was widely feared at the Congress of Vienna (1815).

Britain simultaneously achieved both power and plenty, with its relatively rapid rate of growth of per capita income and of international trade, as well as its precocious structural change from agriculture to

---

[1] We may at this juncture in the process of devolution wish to make more of the relative backwardness of the other kingdoms (Wales, Scotland and above all Ireland). There are data (wage levels, even per capita incomes), and there is a substantial literature on industrialisation in the Celtic periphery, which provide perspective on the English experience and help to deal with the process of integration (see Cullen and Smout 1977, and chapter 14 above).

manufacturing. Although there had been some shift to industry prior to 1660, subsequent changes made Britain the world's richest economy by the start of the nineteenth century. Its dominant navy and powerful army and its fiscal ability to fund armed conflict meant that the British usually emerged victorious from wars with other European powers, a geo-political hegemony that was to persist down to the First World War.

In centralising and strengthening the power of the state, Britain followed the basic outlines of mercantilism, a policy which was also pursued by most other European nations. This meant extensive regulations externally, over foreign trade, shipping and colonial economic activity. British mercantilism existed, however, within a domestic framework of *laissez-faire* and private enterprise that differed from other nations, and also with a strategy for colonisation less dependent on direct governmental investment and administration in settling and building up satellite economies overseas.

During the early modern period European nations were not the only areas to experience economic growth and geo-political expansion. The empires, countries and regions of Africa and Asia were also part of an embryo world economy, and autonomous developments on other continents interacted with those happening in Europe, particularly western Europe. Although the focus in discussing eighteenth- and nineteenth-century economic changes has traditionally been on just one small segment of the world's second-smallest continent, it is important to understand the importance that other parts of an interdependent world played in influencing the pace and pattern of change in the British and other European economies (P. K. O'Brien 1997).

Nevertheless, the timing and the nature of Britain's industrial revolution remain, as other chapters in this volume demonstrate, major topics for debate. Did the industrial revolution occur as a sharp jump during a short period of years of the eighteenth and the first quarter of the nineteenth century, or is it best seen as a gradual process of slowly accelerating growth over the course of a much longer span of time, going back to the middle ages or forward to a more fully industrialised economy later in the nineteenth century? Were the major improvements concentrated in only a few industries, such as cotton textiles and iron, or was economic development the result of a broadly diffused process influencing many sectors of the economy? (See chapters 2 and 5.) Were the structural foundations of the industrial revolution to be found in nationally distinctive economic, political, legal, social or cultural changes? And what was the relative importance of internal compared to external factors in accounting for British development? (See chapter 7.) Continuing debates among scholars demonstrate the controversial nature of the causes and consequences of the changes that we believe represent the industrial revolution. Nevertheless, it is clear that whatever might be argued about the timing and the process of change, the economy of Britain after the

Table 16.1	World population, 1500–1900 (millions)						
	Asia	Europe (w/USSR)	Africa	South and Central America	North America	Oceania	Total
1500	245	84	87	39	3	3	461
1600	338	111	113	10	3	3	578
1700	433	125	107	10	2	3	680
1800	631	195	102	19	5	2	954
1900	903	422	138	75	90	6	1,634

Source: Biraben 1979.

Congress of Vienna looked quite different compared to its level at the time of the Treaty of Utrecht (1713), and was by then regarded as economically and politically superior, not only by the British but also by other nations of the world. These changes, whatever their pace and extent, continue to be represented as the outcome of the British industrial revolution.

BRITAIN AND EUROPEAN POWERS IN THE WORLD ECONOMY, 1492–1713

Estimates of population for earlier times provide contexts for international comparison. Before 1800, Europe accounted for less than 20 per cent of the world's population (see Table 16.1). That ratio had increased somewhat since 1500, owing, in some measure, to a dramatic (nearly three-quarters) decline in Native American populations after they came into sustained contact with European settlers. The European population in 1600 was about the same as that of Africa, each being about one-third of the population of Asia. Both China and India had larger populations than Europe at that time. Asia accounted for almost three-fifths of the world's population. It was, however, Europe that was expanding, via settlement and trade, into other continents. Although this commerce generated reverse flows of ideas, artefacts, raw materials, consumption goods and botanical transfers from Asia, Africa and America to Europe, no sustained movement of ships and peoples from other continents to Europe or to the Americas occurred, except for the involuntary movement of slaves – a movement that took place on European and American vessels.

Within Europe, the British represented less than one-tenth of the overall population (see Table 16.2). In 1600, the total population of Britain and Ireland was equal to about one-third that of France, was below that of German-speaking states, and was roughly equal to that of Spain. Europe and its American offshoots were not among the world's major urbanised areas until about 1850. Europe had just seven of the world's twenty-five largest cities in 1600, and only six in 1700. China, India and Japan were

Table 16.2	Population of selected western European nations, 1500–1870 (000s)						
	France	Netherlands	Germany	Spain	Portugal	Great Britain	Ireland
1500	15,000	950	12,000	6,800	1,000	3,142	800
1700	21,471	1,900	15,000	8,770	2,000	6,640	1,925
1820	31,246	2,355	24,905	12,203	3,297	14,142	7,084
1870	38,440	3,615	39,231	16,201	4,353	25,974	5,419

Source: Maddison 2001 183, 232, 247.

more heavily represented among the nations with large cities (Chandler and Fox 1974). Britain's economy did benefit from its island location, which lowered the costs of providing defence from attacks across its borders but also raised the costs of continental action, which operated to restrain military involvement in European power politics. Spin-offs from public investment in the Royal Navy for overseas commerce and a plethora of good natural harbours added to the advantages of a location that was conducive to intra-European and Atlantic trade.

Among the major civilisations of the ancient world, only two had emerged in Europe. Both Greece and Rome had developed external empires around large urban societies on the southern extremities of the Mediterranean Sea. Eventually both declined in wealth and power. No successor empires to Rome developed in that part of the continent for several centuries. Rich nations existed throughout the non-European world before the industrial revolution, combining wealth with learning and innovation, and with organisational and technological developments. Asia, China and India had populous and developed regions, as did Japan, Indonesia and the Ottoman Empire.[2] In the Americas, Mexico (Aztecs) and Peru (Incas) contained politically powerful and sophisticated economic societies. Within Africa, several polities with urban areas flourished. Some of these regions may have had per capita incomes and enjoyed standard of living equal to or above those in Europe before 1500 (Maddison 2001). The Chinese empires were technologically innovative, but, as with other parts of Asia and Africa, contained masses of poor people and great concentrations of wealth. For more than a century after the Black Death (1347–50), when about one-third of its population died, western Europe seemed potentially a less promising region for early industrialisation and technological progress than China, which was also affected by the plague. The widespread declines in population due to the Black Death generated quite different economic and political outcomes in different parts of Europe (Herlihy 1997).

[2] For an interesting discussion of economic change in the early modern and modern eras, with an argument as to the conditions making for ultimate European success, see Jones (1987). For recent discussion of comparative economic development in Europe and elsewhere, particularly Asia, see Landes (1998), Frank (1998), and Pomeranz (2000). For a survey of the debate, see Goldstone (2002).

Thus, at the start of the fifteenth century, other parts of the world besides Europe had levels of wealth and knowledge that seemed to promise long-run expansion. That situation changed once Europeans (led by the Portuguese) began to expand geographically, down the west coast of Africa, across the Atlantic, and into the Indian and Pacific Oceans. Transcontinental commerce increased during the sixteenth century, under western Europe's political, military and economic dominance. This occurred in the Americas, where the Spanish,

Table 16.3   GDP per capita in various regions of the world, 1500, 1820 and 1913 (1990 international dollars)

	1500	1820	1913
Western Europe	774	1,232	3,473
Western offshoots	400	1,201	5,257
Eastern Europe and USSR	483	667	1,501
Latin America	416	665	1,511
Asia (exc. Japan)	572	575	640
Japan	500	669	1,387
Africa	400	418	585
World	565	667	1,510

Source: Maddison 2001: 28, 126.

Portuguese, Dutch, French and British invested in colonies and maritime bases and attracted inflows of settlers from Europe.[3] Only a few European settlers went to South-East Asia and the Ottoman Empire, and within these areas long-distance trade represented only a minor share of total production. Commerce multiplied, not only in those regions where European contact and violence had led to profound changes in the economies and cultures of indigenous populations, but also in places like India where (as Marx complained) the British, the merchants and the colonial rulers did little to transform the culture and social arrangements, or to change traditional techniques and modes of production. Nevertheless, at first relatively and later absolutely, the non-European world began to lose ground economically, politically and militarily to Europe (see Table 16.3).[4]

EUROPEAN ECONOMIC DEVELOPMENT, 1500–1800

Even prior to the British industrial revolution, there were significant shifts in economic and political power within Europe. It took nearly three centuries after Columbus's voyages before British success was secured. In the time of Columbus and for some two centuries thereafter, the rich countries of early modern Europe were in the southern part of the continent, along the Mediterranean. From the middle ages onward, the city-states of the Italian peninsula expanded, on the basis of trade, finance and industrial production, and they achieved artistic, literary, scientific and architectural grandeur, even during political and social turmoil. With the discovery and colonisation of the Americas, and the development of

[3] For estimates and examinations of the flows of people from Europe and Africa across the Atlantic, broken down by European nations, see Eltis (2000).

[4] Income estimates dealing with these patterns of change are presented most recently in Maddison (2001). For earlier estimates, see Bairoch (1981).

Table 16.4 Relative per capita incomes, the Netherlands and Britain, 1500–1913

	A	B
1500	~	99.0
1650	~	
1700	145.0	150.2
1750	120.0	~
1800	82.9	~
1820	74.2	85.9
1850	75.6	~
1913	~	78.6

Source: Column A, de Vries and van der Woude 1997: 707 (midpoint of two estimates for the Netherlands). Column B, Maddison 2001: 90.

sea routes around the Cape of Good Hope and across the Indian Ocean to South and East Asia, the locus of Europe's economic and political power shifted to Spain and Portugal. Spain, for a time, was not only politically dominant on the European continent, but also the most successful power in the Americas. Spain (along with Portugal) had a lead of about one century over other European nations in the settling and exploitation of the Americas, and was able to colonise and trade with areas that were previously wealthy. Before the arrival of Cortes in Mexico and Pizarro in Peru, both had sophisticated societies with great wealth and complex political organisations. Mexico and Peru together contained about three-fifths of the total Native American population of the Americas (Denevan 1976). Their size, commercial sophistication and considerable mineral wealth (particularly silver and gold) provided Spain and Portugal with immense and immediate riches and two centuries of economic growth, even if they did not provide the basis for long-term sustained economic development (K. O'Brien 1997). Over the centuries, the costs of European and Atlantic warfare weakened Spanish power. The Spanish Habsburgs attempted to dominate the European continent as well as the Americas. Spanish decline was due in part to their engagement in more wars in the sixteenth, seventeenth and eighteenth centuries than other European nations, but perhaps more important was the frequency with which they lost.

In the early years of the seventeenth century, when the British overseas expansion both across the Atlantic and around the Cape of Good Hope really began, Britain confronted yet another rival for the dominance of global commerce – the Netherlands. The Dutch possessed well-developed commercial and shipping networks, political stability, and surplus capital to invest at home and abroad (Israel 1995). They controlled much of Europe's transatlantic shipping until challenged after 1651 by the British Navigation Acts. The Dutch attempts to create large colonies on mainland North America and in Brazil failed, owing to military weakness attributable to a relatively small domestic population (about one-third the size of British population in 1750). Nevertheless, it seems certain that the per capita income of the Netherlands continued to exceed British levels until the end of the eighteenth century (see Table 16.4). The Dutch decline was due to various political and military events, particularly the occupation by the French from 1795 to 1815. During this period of decline there was also some loss of interest in science and mechanical arts, an interest regained only in the second quarter of the nineteenth century.

Nevertheless, the successful Dutch fiscal and financial measures were emulated by Britain. Unlike other European nations, the Dutch invested more heavily in South-East Asia and investments in their East Indian colonies continued to yield benefits to the metropolis for a prolonged period.

Yet it was France that emerged as the greatest threat to British hegemony in world commerce in the seventeenth and eighteenth centuries (Crouzet 1990). France was nearly three times larger than Britain in terms of area and population. French mercantilism competed with British, economically and geo-politically. While the outcome of this rivalry, as seen after the Seven Years War (1756–63), seemed easy in retrospect to predict, during the eighteenth century the writings of British and French economic pamphleteers and statesmen had expressed considerable uncertainty as to the eventual resolution. Indeed the outcome of the competition seemed in doubt right up to the start of the French Revolution (1789) and the Haitian Revolution (1791). These conflicts, and the ensuing Napoleonic Wars, led to a thirty-year hiatus in French economic growth. The slave rebellion in Haiti meant the loss of the richest region in the Americas, and Haiti's subsequent economic collapse meant that a major trading partner had shrunk to insignificance (Engerman 2000).

Estimates of French economic output and foreign trade suggest that they may well have grown at rates comparable to those of Britain from 1700 to 1790, and then again from 1820 to 1900 (See O'Brien and Keyder 1978; Crouzet 1990). The British, unlike the French, experienced very rapid growth and trade expansion between 1780 and 1820, even during the American Revolution and the Napoleonic Wars. Despite their relatively favourable eighteenth-century economic performance, by the end of the century the French had fallen behind the British, economically and militarily. Although the loss of Canada to the British after the Seven Years War indicated the differences in military prowess, its loss was of limited significance economically. Voltaire dismissed it as a conflict 'about a few acres of snow', and the discussion at the post-war settlement centred on whether the British should take Canada or the small Caribbean island of Guadeloupe. It was the outcome of the Revolutionary and Napoleonic Wars (1793–1815) that provided a clear demonstration to contemporaries of Britain's preponderant naval, military and economic power.

The other nations of western Europe, such as Belgium, Switzerland and the German states, generally had some increase in economic growth in the eighteenth century, but their increases and structural changes were not as dramatic as those of Britain, despite similarities in politics and culture. None had early colonial empires, but this could be as much an effect as a cause of their slower economic growth. The German states were not unified until the middle of the nineteenth century, which limited their economic and political development. Within the British Isles, Ireland experienced relatively rapid growth of population and income, with a basically unchanged economic structure, until the onset of the collapse in the Irish Famine of the late 1840s. This led to a decline in population, because of both increased mortality and extensive migration, although per capita incomes for those surviving and remaining did increase (O'Gráda 1993).

EXOGENOUS AND ENDOGENOUS FORCES BEHIND THE RISE OF THE BRITISH ECONOMY, 1713–1815

The rapid demographic and economic growth of the Spanish, Portuguese, British and French Americas was due both to the migration of Europeans, as free and as indentured labourers, and the transportation of black African slaves. The slave trade accounted for over three-quarters of the movement of men, women and children to the New World in the years before 1800, and this established important political and trading relations between several European nations and various states within Africa. Europeans generally traded with Africans on the Atlantic coast, because the disease environment and the military power of African states located in the interior limited the possibility of inland capture and control by Europeans. The slave trade grew rapidly until about 1808, when constraints on that infamous commerce were introduced, by both Britain and the United States, and it was subsequently ended by other states in the nineteenth century. While the transatlantic slave trade continued into the 1860s, the major post-1820 recipients of slaves were Brazil and the Spanish Caribbean colonies, particularly Cuba. The ending of the slave trade and then emancipation in the 1880s had a significant impact on the economy and society of many New World colonies. The effects were less on Africa, where an internal slave trade persisted and where a trade in palm oil and other commodities replaced the Atlantic Ocean trade in slaves.

The American colonies turned out to be highly productive, in terms both of agricultural staples, at first mainly sugar and tobacco and later grains, cotton and coffee, and of minerals (particularly precious metals). All European nations with colonial empires followed their own variant of mercantilism, and imposed controls on trade and production designed to benefit the home country. Political if not economic conditions changed, however, when many colonies achieved political independence from Europe. The American Revolution created the first newly independent nation in the New World, and the Haitian Revolution the second. In the first quarter of the nineteenth century most, but not all, of the Spanish colonies of Latin America won their independence, while Brazil freed itself from Portugal in 1822.

The British colonies on the mainland of North America, settled one century after those of Spain, had not been European settlements of first choice because their climates and resource bases looked less desirable than those colonies in the Caribbean and Latin America. The initial

British New World settlements were in the West Indies, but this shifted after the start of the eighteenth century. Over time, as crops and settlement patterns evolved, temperate North America became the richest area not only in the Americas but in the world (McCusker and Menard 1985). With new agricultural and industrial technology, the success of the United States reflected its favourable demography and endowment.

The traditional attention paid to a first British industrial revolution has underplayed some important aspects of developments in other areas of the world and their relations with Britain. Foreign connections gave rise to a number of different roles in economic development. They were markets for exports and sources of imports of raw materials for use in production as well as for consumption, sources of capital and labour and of ideas and beliefs, and were of considerable importance in providing more land ('ghost acreage') to offset the Malthusian problem of high population density (Jones 1987). There will be, however, no need to argue whether the basic cause of British economic growth is to be found in external, rather than internal, factors. The magnitude of foreign relations may not have been very large, but clearly some factors from outside the British Isles influenced the rate and pattern of growth and, conversely, British growth affected all nations and regions.[5]

In the early stages of its economic development Britain, as did the Netherlands and other European nations, received factors of production, goods and ideas from elsewhere on the European mainland as well as from other parts of the world. Small inflows of labour, primarily of skilled workers from elsewhere in Europe, certainly played a part in the emergence of several English industries, particularly textiles. In the middle ages funds had been supplied by Italian bankers to the monarchs. In the seventeenth and eighteenth centuries Dutch capital flowed into the realm. Ideas and consumer novelties, including tropical groceries, were brought back to Britain by travellers from other countries as well as by Englishmen and Scots. New luxuries as well as more standard consumer goods were imported, meeting basic needs and inspiring greater industriousness among workers (chapter 13 above). The shares of foreign trade to domestic production and of factor movements to total factor inputs remained relatively low, compared with many of the later developers, and with the higher magnitudes Britain displayed in the nineteenth century. Clearly Britain, an economy already rich in some important natural

---

[5] There have been scholarly debates both on the magnitude of the contribution of overall foreign trade to British economic growth, and on the developmental importance of specific trades, such as the slave trade and the export of cotton textiles. The attention to foreign trade is based upon the argument of limited prospects for the British economy without external developments, a counter to the argument that it was the efficiency of the internal economy that permitted Britain to succeed in international markets, but as yet there appears to be no clean-cut resolution of this issue. The seminal work on the impact of the slave trade on the British industrial revolution is *Capitalism and Slavery* by Eric Williams (1944), See also O'Brien and Engerman (1991) and Inikori (2002).

endowments, especially coal, mineral ores and fertile soils, was also an economy and society benefiting from external influences.

In its economic development, Britain drew upon scientific and technical knowledge from other nations. While developments in science, both as a method of inquiry and as a cosmology, were important, the particular uses to which Britain was able to put this knowledge were a key factor in its economic growth. The role played by technology, and by empirical applications by engineers and artisans, led to more successful commercial improvements and a broader diffusion among economic sectors than did the greater attention given to advances in scientific knowledge elsewhere (Jacob 1997).

BRITAIN'S INTERNATIONAL RELATIONS

During its long transition to a successful industrial economy, connections between Britain and the world, politically and economically, were numerous and significant. Britain became a source of labour to various parts of the world, as part of the process of settling new areas on different continents. Major outflows of migrants from the seventeenth to the nineteenth century went to the West Indies, to the North American mainland colonies that became the United States and Canada, and to Australia, New Zealand and South Africa. This outflow consisted of free migrant labour (some of whom were subsidised), as well as indentured servants. There were also shipments of convict labour, first to the United States and then, after American independence, to Australia. In the eighteenth and nineteenth centuries, Britain received some immigrants, mainly skilled and professional labour, but the outflow from the British Isles (especially the Celtic fringes) was significant. Britain received capital from the Dutch in the eighteenth century, and these funds may have played some indirect role in the early financing of the industrial revolution. By the nineteenth century, however, Britain had become the major source of capital internationally, providing loans and credits to private individuals, corporations, states and nations throughout the world, including its colonial empire.

By 1860 the United Kingdom accounted for about 30 per cent of Europe's exports, because of both its economic size (representing about 20 per cent of Europe's 1870 income) and its policy of relatively low tariffs. The basic pattern of exporting manufactures, particularly textiles, and importing agricultural commodities persisted throughout the classic era of free trade, 1846–1914. The United Kingdom's share of world industrial production rose from an estimated 4.3 per cent in 1800 to 19.9 per cent in 1860, when its share of exports in its national income rose to a peak of about 20 per cent (chapter 6 above).

Britain was at war, at sea and on land, for many years between 1660 and 1815, mainly with other European nations (see Table 16.5). These wars, although critical in seizing power from the Dutch and the French, did, however, involve considerable drains of labour, capital, and natural resources from the private economy. Under certain conditions (including the long-term presence of under- or unemployed factors of production, and given favourable outcomes flowing from peace settlements), wars could be considered (as they were at the time) to be profitable undertakings.

Table 16.5 Number of years per nation at war, 1450–1900				
	Great Britain	France	Netherlands*	Spain
1600–50	17.5	24.0	36.0	48.0
1650–1700	26.0	22.5	26.5	34.0
1700–50	29.0	25.0	18.0	29.5
1750–1800	26.5	25.5	11.5	19.0
1800–50	26.0	18.0	14.5	30.0

Note: *For the period 1560–1600, the Netherlands were at war for 48.5 years.
Source: Wright 1965: 653.

In addition, it has been argued that mobilisation for and fighting of wars promoted British state-building, by centralising power in the monarchy and parliament, which led to the development of an effective governmental tax and expenditure system (Winch and O'Brien 2002).

Wars are generally not like zero-sum games. Wars, even those that are won, involve costs to all participants in terms of resource use foregone and the destruction of capital (physical and human). For example, the expansion of the British merchant marine (the world's largest by the late eighteenth century) was costly to build up, but it has been frequently argued that, in the absence of investment in the navy, Britain could have remained a second-rate political and economic power. Before the Seven Years War Britain engaged in war mainly with European powers, although these wars quite often spread to include battles outside Europe over colonial possessions. In the nineteenth century, Britain became involved in numerous colonial wars in remoter parts of its empire, as well as with the nations of Asia and Africa. This required the continued presence of maritime bases and military capacity in these areas, at some cost to British tax payers, which reduced the net benefits from imperialism.

By the start of the nineteenth century Britain was unique in the size of its world-wide empire (Canny 1998; Marshall 1998). Even after the loss of the United States in 1783, a loss whose costs were mitigated by the continuing high level of trade and commercial relations between the two independent countries, the British maintained the world's largest empire, with a population many times that of the metropole. Colonies served as sources of agricultural commodities, based on the pool of cheap manpower, but expenditures on imperial defence and the protection of trade limited the overall profitability of the Empire. Although debate on the profits of imperialism goes back to the classic works of Smith, Hobson, Lenin and others,[6] it was only after the end of World War II that

---

[6] For more recent discussions see Davis and Huttenback (1986), Ferguson (2001), and O'Brien and Leando Prados de la Escosura (1998). And for the contemporary views of the economists, see Wood (1983).

the Empire was drastically reduced. This was primarily due not to any major change in, or concern with, economic profitability to the British, but rather to a shift in moral sentiments and political beliefs and realities influencing the willingness to bear the direct and indirect costs of ruling foreign territories.

CONVERGENCE AND RELATIVE DECLINE

The nineteenth century was clearly when Britain became the world's major power, economically and politically. Britain's economy was growing rapidly, its Empire was expanding, British naval power was the key to a world-wide 'Pax Britannica', and the British economy was regarded as the one that rivals believed needed to be overtaken. Although the Dutch possibly had a higher per capita income at the start of the nineteenth century, and the United States probably surpassed Britain by its end, Britain was recognised as the world's economic leader throughout the long nineteenth century (1815–1914).[7] Although there was a decline in per capita income relative to the United States towards the end of the century, it was the impact of World War I on British capital investments overseas, on manpower and on budgetary conditions that meant that the relative decline was not to be reversed. Nevertheless, throughout the twentieth century, the British economy still experienced absolute growth in per capita income, and an improving standard of living for most of its population.

During the first half of the nineteenth century, Britain was at its zenith as a world economic power. The United States and the western European nations had per capita incomes of roughly three-quarters of the British level (see Table 16.6). There was a great concern on the part of other nations to catch up with Britain, for both economic and political reasons, and convergence (of income levels, trade volumes, levels of industrialisation and technology) was seen as an important policy goal by many European nations. The measures to be pursued were often based on the implementation of what were felt to have been British techniques, although some sought to adopt different methods. Several of the follower nations imposed high tariffs on manufactured imports, unlike the increasingly free-trade British. Important in Britain and elsewhere in Europe were policies introduced for increased education and public health. The growth of heavy industries was seen as central to convergence. In addition to economic goals, nations undertook military build-ups, as the growth of armies and navies were seen as a necessary aspect of the catching-up process. Although there were wars among other continental

---

[7] Leandro Prados de la Escosura's recent estimates (2000) suggest a United States lead earlier in the nineteenth century.

Table 16.6 GDP per capita, selected countries, 1820–1913 (1990 international dollars; Great Britain equals 100)						
	France	Germany	Netherlands	United States	Switzerland	Belgium
1820	58.0	49.9	85.9	59.3	60.3	62.2
1870	53.8	52.2	79.0	70.1	63.1	77.3
1913	67.7	70.8	78.6	102.9	82.8	81.9

Source: Maddison 2001: 185, 247.

European and Asian powers, between the end of the Napoleonic Wars and the First World War no wars occurred between Britain and any other western European nation apart from during the Crimean War.

Prior to the American Revolution, the per capita income of the thirteen continental colonies was probably close to or perhaps slightly below that of the British metropolis. With American independence, however, there was a period of about two decades over which the United States per capita income declined, at a time when British growth rates remained high. The United States followed the basic British policies of mercantilism. Even with high tariffs on manufactures, the American economy remained heavily concentrated upon the production and export of agricultural commodities with the continued import of manufactured goods, mainly from Britain. After the War of 1812, the United States, while still predominantly an agricultural economy, began to grow rapidly, with westward expansion of both the northern agricultural and the southern cotton economies, as well as developments within manufacturing. Raw cotton exports went mainly to England, and cotton accounted for about half of all US exports in the first half of the nineteenth century. As the size of the manufacturing sector increased, and agricultural productivity continued to improve, the American economy began to grow more rapidly than did the British. Even with the slowdown associated with the American Civil War, it seems certain that sometime between 1880 and 1900 the United States surpassed the British in per capita income and became the world's leader. By this time, the exports of manufactures exceeded those of agricultural commodities, and the United States became the world's leading industrial power. The American lead, starting at the end of the nineteenth century, persisted throughout the twentieth century, a period when Britain's relative position continued its decline, although the absolute level of income continued to rise.

On the European continent several nations sought to offset British commercial and political hegemony and to surpass the British economically. Her most serious competitors were the two largest nations of western Europe: France and Germany. Rivalry with France went back to before 1688 and, although the French did well after 1820, they were unable to grow sufficiently rapidly to close the gap with Britain until quite recently. Alone in western Europe, France had little out-migration, to the United

States and elsewhere, and (unlike Britain) its external capital flows went mainly to nations of continental Europe.

Germany, after unification, undertook both geo-political and economic actions necessary to become a great power. It is often believed to have been the most successful of the national economies on the mainland, although its achievements were probably more impressive in the military than the economic sphere. Germany's policies of high tariffs and of technical education helped to spur the growth of heavy industries, and its expenditures on armaments and warships provided credible military threats to Britain by the end of the century. In Prussia and other parts of eastern Europe, the abolition of serfdom in the first half of the nineteenth century provided for a greater degree of labour mobility internally, as well as leading to extensive external emigration, mainly to the United States. Serf emancipation probably helped to increase the growth rate of several economies, at least in the long run, although they have continued to lag well behind Britain. The nations of western Europe and the British dominions overseas were gaining on the British, economically. Britain no longer seemed unique in the world. Nevertheless, Britain maintained economic and political leadership within Europe, and its position as a major world power continued into the twentieth century.

Bibliography

Place of publication is London unless otherwise stated. All references to the *Economic History Review* are to the Second Series, unless otherwise stated.

Acemoglu, D., Johnson, S. and Robinson, J. 2002. Reversals of fortune. *Quarterly Journal of Economics* 117: 1231–94.

Acres, W. M. 1931. *The Bank of England from Within*, I. Oxford.

Adams, J. 1987. Intellectual property cases in Lord Mansfield's Court Notebooks. *The Journal of Legal History* 8: 18–24.

Adams, J. N. and Averley, G. 1986. The patent specification – the role of Liardet v Johnson. *The Journal of Legal History* 7: 156–77.

Albert, W. 1972. *The Turnpike Road System in England, 1663–1840*. Cambridge.

  1983. The turnpike trusts. In Aldcroft and Freeman 1983.

Alborn, T. L. 1998. *Conceiving Companies: Joint-Stock Politics in Victorian England*.

Alchian, A. A. and Demsetz, H. 1972. Production, information costs, and economic organisation. *American Economic Review* 62: 777–95.

Alcock, N. W. 1993. *People at Home: Living in a Warwickshire Village 1500–1800*. Chichester.

Aldcroft, D. H. and Freeman, M. J., eds. 1983. *Transport in the Industrial Revolution*. Manchester.

Alderman, G. 1973. *The Railway Interest*. Leicester.

Alexander, D. and Ommer, R., eds. 1979. *Volumes not Values*. St. John's, Newfoundland.

Allen, G. C. 1929. *The Industrial Development of Birmingham and the Black Country 1860–1927*.

Allen, R. C. 1982. The efficiency and distributional consequences of eighteenth century enclosures. *Economic Journal* 92: 937–53.

  1983. Collective invention. *Journal of Economic Behaviour and Organisation* 4: 1–24.

  1988. The growth of labour productivity in early modern English agriculture. *Explorations in Economic History* 25: 117–46.

  1989. Enclosure, farming methods, and the growth of productivity in the South Midlands. In Grantham and Leonard 1989.

  1992. *Enclosure and the Yeoman*. Oxford.

  1994. Agriculture during the Industrial Revolution. In Floud and McCloskey 1994.

  1999. Tracking the agricultural revolution. *Economic History Review* 52: 209–35.

  2000. Economic structure and agricultural productivity in Europe, 1300–1800. *European Review of Economic History* 3: 1–25.

  2001. The great divergence in European wages and prices from the middle ages to the first world war. *Explorations in Economic History* 38: 1–37.

Allen, R. C. and O'Gráda, Cormac 1988. On the road again with Arthur Young: English, Irish, and French agriculture during the Industrial Revolution. *Journal of Economic History* 48: 93–116.

Anderson, B. L. 1969a. Provincial aspects of the financial revolution of the eighteenth century. *Business History* 11: 11–22.

Anderson, B. L. 1969b. The attorney and the early capital market in Lancashire. In Harris 1969.

Anderson, M. 1971a. *Family Structure in Nineteenth Century Lancashire*. Cambridge.

1971b. Family, household and the industrial revolution. In M. Anderson, ed., *Sociology of the Family*. Harmondsworth.

1972. Household structure and the industrial revolution; mid-nineteenth century Preston in comparative perspective. In Laslett and Wall 1972.

1980. *Approaches to the History of the Western Family 1500–1914*.

1990. The social implications of demographic change. In F. M. L. Thompson, ed., *The Cambridge Social History of Britain 1750-1950*, 3 vols. Cambridge.

1996. *British Population History: from the Black Death to the Present Day*. Cambridge.

Antràs, Pol and Voth, Joachim 2003. Effort or efficiency? Factor prices and productivity growth during the English Industrial Revolution. *Explorations in Economic History* 40: 52–77.

Appleby, A. 1980. The disappearance of plague: a continuing puzzle. *Economic History Review* 332: 161–73.

Arbuthnot, John 1773. *An Inquiry into the Connection between the Present Price of Provisions and the Size of Farms*.

Armstrong, J. 1987. The role of coastal shipping in UK transport: an estimate of comparative traffic movements in 1910. *Journal of Transport History* 8: 164–72.

Armstrong, W. A. 1972. A note on the household structure of mid-nineteenth-century York in comparative perspective. In Laslett and Wall 1972.

Arnold, A. 1995. Accounting information and historical research in the shipping industry. *International Journal of Maritime History* 7: 105–15.

Ashton, T. S. 1939. *An Eighteenth Century Industrialist, Peter Stubs of Warrington, 1756-1806*, Manchester.

1954. The bill of exchange and private banks in Lancashire 1790–1830. In T. S. Ashton and R. S. Sayers, eds., *Papers in English Monetary History*. Oxford.

1996 [1948]. *The Industrial Revolution 1760–1830*. Oxford.

Atiyah, P. S. 1979. *The Rise and Fall of Freedom of Contract*. Oxford.

Atkinson, M. and Baber, C. 1987. *The Growth and Decline of the South Wales Iron Industry 1760–1880*. Cardiff.

Attman, A. 1986. *American Bullion in the European World Trade: 1600–1800*. Göteborg.

August, A. 1994. How separate a sphere? Poor women and paid work in late Victorian London. *Journal of Family History* 19: 285–309.

Avallone, P. 1997. Public banks, trade and industry in southern Italy, seventeenth to eighteenth century. In Teichova *et al.* 1997.

Averch, H. and Johnson, D. L. 1962. Behaviour of the firm under regulatory constraints. *American Economic Review* 52: 1052–69.

Babbage, C. 1963 [1835]. *On the Economy of Machinery and Manufactures*. New York.

Bagehot, W. 1873. *Lombard Street, a Description of the Money Market*.

Baines, D. 1994. Population, migration and regional development, 1870–1939. In Floud and McCloskey 1994.

Baines, E. 1966 [1835]. *History of the Cotton Manufacture in Great Britain*.

Bairoch, P. 1965. Niveau de développement économique de 1810 à 1910. *Annales: Economies, Sociétés, Civilisations* 20: 1091–1117.

1981. The main trends in economic disparities since the Industrial Revolution. In P. Bairoch and M. Levy-Leboyer, eds., *Disparities in Economic Development since the Industrial Revolution*. New York.

1982. International industrialization levels from 1750 to 1980. *Journal of European Economic History* 11: 269–333.

1988. *Cities and Economic Development: From the Dawn of History to the Present*.

Baker, J. H. 1990. *An Introduction to English Legal History*, 3rd edn.

Banner, S. 1998. *Anglo-American Securities Regulation: Cultural and Political Roots, 1690–1860*. Cambridge.

Barker, H. 1997. Women, work and the industrial revolution: female involvement in the English printing trades, 1700–1840. In H. Barker and E. Chalus, eds., *Gender in Eighteenth Century England*.

Barker, T. C. 1960. *Pilkington Brothers and the Glass Industry*.

1988. Urban transport. In Freeman and Aldcroft 1988.

Barker, T. C. and Gerhold, D. 1993. *The Rise and Rise of Road Transport, 1700–1990*.

Barro, R. and Sala-I-Martin, X. 1995. *Economic Growth*. New York.

Barton, D. B. 1961. *A History of Copper Mining in Cornwall and Devon*. Truro.

1967. *A History of Tin Mining and Smelting in Cornwall*. Truro.

1968. *Essays in Cornish Mining History*, I. Truro.

1969. *The Cornish Beam Engine*. Truro.

Bartrip, P. W. J. 1982. British government inspection, 1832–1875: some observations. *The Historical Journal* 25: 605–26.

Barzel, Y. 1997. *Economic Analysis of Property Rights*, 2nd edn. Cambridge.

Basalla, G. 1988. *The Evolution of Technology*. Cambridge.

Batchelor, T. 1808. *General View of the Agriculture of the County of Bedford*.

Baten, J. and Komlos, J. 1998. Height and the standard of living: review article. *Journal of Economic History* 583: 866–70.

Baugh, D. A. 1988. Great Britain's 'blue-water' policy, 1689–1815. *International History Review* 10: 33–58.

1998. Withdrawing from Europe: Anglo-French maritime geopolitics, 1750–1800. *International History Review* 20: 33–56.

Baxter, R. D. 1868. *National Income*.

Beare, T. 1994. *The Bailiff of Blackmoor 1586*. Redruth.

Beattie, J. M. 1986. *Crime and the Courts in England 1660–1800*. Oxford.

Beaumont, O. and Higgs, J. W. Y. 1958. Agriculture: farm implements. In Singer *et al.* 1958.

Becker, G. 1965. A theory of the allocation of time. *Economic Journal* 75: 493–517.

1981. *A Treatise on the Family*. Cambridge, MA.

Becker, G. S. and Murphy, K. M. 1992. The division of labour, co-ordination costs and knowledge. *Quarterly Journal of Economics* 107: 1137–60.

Beckett, J. V. 1989. Landownership and estate management. In Mingay 1989.

Behagg, C. 1998. Mass production without the factory: craft producers, guns and small firm innovation, 1790–1815. *Business History* 40: 1–15.

Ben-Amos, I. K. 1994. *Adolescence and Youth in Early Modern England*. New Haven.

Benenson, H. 1984. The family wage and working women's consciousness in Britain, 1880–1914. *Politics and Society* 19: 71–108.

Benhabib, J. and Spiegel, M. 1994. The role of human capital in economic development: evidence from aggregate cross-country data. *Journal of Monetary Economics* 34: 143–74.

Benson, J. 1980. *British Coal Miners in the Nineteenth Century: A Social History*.

Beresford, M. 1954. *The Lost Villages of England*.

Berg, M. 1985. *The Age of Manufactures: Industry, Innovation and Work in Britain 1700–1820*.

1987. Women's work, mechanisation and the early phases of industrialisation in England. In P. Joyce, ed., *The Historical Meanings of Work*. Cambridge.

1991. Commerce and creativity in eighteenth century Birmingham. In M. Berg, ed., *Markets and Manufactures in Early Industrial Europe*.

1993a. Small producer capitalism in eighteenth century England. *Business History* 35: 17–39.

1993b. Women's consumption and the industrial classes of eighteenth-century England. *Journal of Social History* 30: 415–434.

1993c. Women's property and the industrial revolution. *Journal of Interdisciplinary History* 24: 233–50.

1996. Women's consumption and the industrial classes of eighteenth-century England. *Journal of Social History* 30: 415–34.

1998a. Inventors of the world of goods. In Bruland and O'Brien 1998.

1998b. Product innovation in core consumer industries. In Berg and Bruland 1998.

2002. From imitation to invention: creating commodities in eighteenth-century Britain. *Economic History Review* 55: 1–30.

Berg, M. and Bruland, K. 1998. *Technological Revolutions in Europe: Historical Perspectives.* Cheltenham.

Berg, M. and Clifford, H. 1998. Commerce and the commodity: graphic display and selling new consumer goods in eighteenth-century England. In D. Ormrod and M. North, eds., *Art Markets in Europe 1400–1800.* Aldershot.

Berg, M. and Clifford, H., eds. 1999. *Consumers and Luxury.* Manchester.

Berg, M. and Eger, E., eds. 2002. *Luxury in the Eighteenth Century.*

Berg, M. and Hudson, P. 1992. Rehabilitating the industrial revolution. *Economic History Review* 45, 24–50.

1994. Growth and change: a comment on the Crafts–Harley view of the Industrial Revolution. *Economic History Review* 471: 147–9.

Berg, M., Hudson, P. and Sonenscher, M., eds. 1983. *Manufacture in Town and Country before the Factory.* Cambridge.

Berger, A. N., Hancock, D. and Marquardt, J. C. 1996. A framework for analyzing efficiency, risks, costs, and innovations in payments systems. *Journal of Money, Credit, and Banking* 28: 696–732.

Bermingham, A. and Brewer, J., eds. 1995. *The Consumption of Culture 1600–1800.*

Berry, C. 1994. *The Idea of Luxury.* Cambridge.

Best, M. 1990. *The New Competition.* Cambridge, MA.

Bevan-Evans, M. 1963. *Gadlys and Flintshire Lead Mining in the Eighteenth Century.* Hawarden.

Bianchi, M. 1998. Taste for novelty and novel tastes: the role of human agency in consumption. In Bianchi, M., ed., *The Active Consumer: Novelty and Surprise in Consumer Choice.*

Biernacki, R. 1995. *The Fabrication of Labour: Germany and Britain, 1640–1914.* Berkeley.

Biraben, J.-N. 1979. Essai sur l'évolution du nombre des hommes. *Population* 34, 1: 13–25.

Birch, A. 1967. *Economic History of the British Iron and Steel Industry 1788–1879.*

Blake, R. 1966. *Disraeli.*

Blaug, M. 1963. The myth of the Old Poor Law and the making of the New. *Journal of Economic History* 23: 151–84.

Bolin-Hart, P. 1989. *Work, State and Family: Child Labour and the Organisation of Production in the British Cotton Industry, 1780–1840.* Lund.

Bonfield, L., Smith, R. M. and Wrightson, K., eds. 1986. *The World We Have Gained: Histories of Population and Social Structure.* Oxford.

Boot, H. M. 1991. Salaries and career earnings in the Bank of Scotland, 1730–1880. *Economic History Review* 44: 629–53.

1995. How skilled were Lancashire cotton factory workers in 1833? *Economic History Review* 48: 283–303.

1999. Real incomes of the British middle class, 1760–1850: the experience of clerks in the East India Company. *Economic History Review* 52: 638–68.

Botham, F. W. and Hunt, E. H. 1987. Wages in Britain during the Industrial Revolution. *Economic History Review* 403: 380–99.

Bourgeois-Pichat, J. 1951. La mesure de la mortalité infantile. *Population* 6: 233–48, 459–80.

Bowden, S. and Offer, A. 1994. Household appliances and the use of time: the United States and Britain since the 1920s. *Economic History Review* 47: 725–48.

Bowman, M. J. and Anderson, C. A. 1963. Concerning the role of education in development. In Geertz 1963b.

Boyce, G. 1995. *Information, Mediation and Institutional Development: The Rise of Large-Scale Enterprise in British Shipping 1870–1919*. Manchester.

Boyer, G. R. 1990. *An Economic History of the English Poor Law 1750–1850*. Cambridge.

1997. Poor relief, informal assistance, and short time during the Lancashire cotton famine. *Explorations in Economic History* 34: 56–76.

Boyns, T. and Richards, J. 1995. Accounting systems and decision making in the mid-Victorian period: the case of the Consett Iron Company. *Business History* 37: 28–51.

Breen, T. 1988. Baubles of Britain: the American and consumer revolutions of the eighteenth century. *Past and Present* 119: 73–104.

Bresnahan, T. and Gordon, R., eds. 1997. *The Economics of New Goods*. Chicago.

Breward, C. 1999. *The Hidden Consumer: Masculinities, Fashion and City Life 1860–1914*. Manchester.

Brewer, J. 1988. *The Sinews of Power: War, Money and the English State, 1688–1783*. Cambridge, MA.

Brewer, J. and Porter, R., eds. 1993. *Consumption and the World of Goods*.

Briggs, A. 1963. *Victorian Cities*.

Brinkman, H. J., Drukker, J. W. and Slot, B. 1988. Height and income: a new method for the estimation of historical national income series. *Explorations in Economic History* 253: 227–64.

Brown, I. J. 1998. Ironstone working in the Coalbrookdale coalfield. *Mining History* 13: 79–88.

Brown, J. and Rose, M. B., eds. 1993. *Entrepreneurship, Networks and Modern Business*. Manchester.

Bruland, K. 1982. Industrial conflict as a source of technical innovation: three cases. *Economy and Society* 11: 91–121.

Bruland, K. and O'Brien, P., eds. 1998. *From Family Firms to Corporate Capitalism: Essays in Business and Industrial History in Honour of Peter Mathias*. Oxford.

Brunt, Liam 1997. Nature or nurture? Explaining English wheat yields in the agricultural revolution. University of Oxford, Discussion Papers in Economic and Social History 19.

1999. Estimating English wheat yields in the Industrial Revolution. University of Oxford, Discussion Papers in Economic and Social History 29.

2000. 'Where there's muck, there's brass': the market for manure in the Industrial Revolution. University of Oxford, Discussion Papers in Economic and Social History 35.

Buchanan, R. A. 1992. *The Power of the Machine*.

Burman, S., ed. 1979. *Fit Work for Women*.

Burnett, J. 1969. *A History of the Cost of Living*. Harmondsworth.

1999. *Liquid Pleasures: A Social History of Drinks in Modern Britain*.

Burnette, J. 2000. The wage profiles of agricultural laborers in early nineteenth-century England. Unpublished manuscript.

Burstall, A. F. 1963. *A History of Mechanical Engineering*.

Burt, R. 1972. The London Mining Exchange 1850–1900. *Business History* 14: 124–43.

1977. *John Taylor: Mining Entrepreneur and Engineer 1779–1863*. Buxton.

1984. *The British Lead Mining Industry*. Redruth.

1988. Arsenic and the South Western Mining Industry since the Mid-Nineteenth Century. *Journal of the Trevithick Society* 15: 5–26.

1998a. Proto-industrialisation and 'stages of growth' in the metal mining industries. *Journal of European Economic History* 27: 85–104.

1998b. Segmented capital markets and patterns of investment in late-Victorian Britain: evidence from the non-ferrous mining industry. *Economic History Review* 51: 709–33.

Burt, R., ed. 1969. *Cornish Mining: Essays on the Organisation of Cornish Mines and the Cornish Mining Economy*. Newton Abbot.

Burt, R. and Atkinson, M. 1987. Mining. In C. Gill, ed., *The Duchy of Cornwall*. Newton Abbot.

Burt, R. and Kippen, S. 2000. Rational choice and a lifetime in metal mining: employment decisions by nineteenth century Cornish miners. *International Review of Social History* 45: 1–31.

Burt, R. and Timbrell, M. 1991. Multiple products and the economics of the mining industries: the case of arsenic production in south west England, 1850–1914. *Journal of European Economic History* 20: 379–406.

Burt, R. and Wilkie, I. 1984. Manganese mining in the south west of England. *Journal of the Trevithick Society* 11: 18–40.

Bythell, D. 1969. *The Handloom Weavers: A Study of the English Cotton Industry during the Industrial Revolution*. Cambridge.

Cain, P. J. 1988. Railways 1870–1914: the maturity of the private system. In Freeman and Aldcroft 1988.

Caird, James 1852. *English Agriculture in 1850–1*, 2nd edn, ed. G. E. Mingay.

Calomiris, C. and Kahn, C. 1991. The role of demandable debt in restructuring optimal banking arrangements. *American Economic Review* 81: 497–513.

Cameron, R., ed. 1967. *Banking in the Early Stages of Industrialization: A Study of Comparative Economic History*. Oxford.

Cameron, Rondo 1990. La Révolution industrielle manquée. *Social Science History* 14: 559–65.

1994. Industrial Revolution: fact or fiction? *Contention* 4: 163–88.

Campbell, Bruce M. S. 1983. Arable productivity in medieval England: some evidence from Norfolk. *Journal of Economic History* 43: 379–404.

2000. *English Seigniorial Agriculture 1250–1450*. Cambridge.

Campbell, B. M. S., ed. 1991. *Before the Black Death: Studies in the 'Crisis' of the Early Fourteenth Century*. Manchester.

Campbell, B. M. and Overton, M., eds. 1991. *Land, Labour, and Livestock: Historical Studies in European Agricultural Productivity*. Manchester.

Campbell, R. H. 1977. The Scottish Improvers and the course of agrarian change in the eighteenth century. In Cullen and Smout 1977.

1988. The landed classes. In Devine and Mitchison 1988.

Cannon, J. F. 1984. *Aristocratic Century: The Peerage in Eighteenth-Century England*. Cambridge.

Canny, N., ed. 1994. *Europeans on the Move: Studies in European Migration, 1500–1800*. Oxford.

1998. *The Origins of Empire: British Overseas Enterprise to the Close of the Seventeenth Century*. Oxford.

Cantrell, J. A. 1984. *James Nasmyth and the Bridgewater Foundry: A Study of Entrepreneurship in the Early Engineering Industry*. Manchester.

Capie, F. 1999. Banking in Europe in the nineteenth century: the role of the central bank. In Sylla *et al.* 1999.

Capie, F. and Weber, A. 1985. *A Monetary History of the United Kingdom, 1870–1982*, I, *Data, Sources, Methods*.

Cardwell, Donald S. L. 1972. *Turning Points in Western Technology*. New York.

1994. *The Fontana History of Technology*.

Carlos, A., Key, J. and Dupree, J. 1998. Learning and the creation of stock-market institutions: evidence from the Royal African and Hudson's Bay Companies, 1670–1700. *Journal of Economic History* 58: 318–44.

Carpenter, R. 1994. Peasants and stockingers: socio-economic change in Guthlaxton Hundred, Leicestershire, 1700–1851. Unpublished PhD thesis, University of Leicester.

Carruthers, B. G. 1999. *City of Capital: Politics and Markets in the English Financial Revolution*. Princeton, NJ.

Casson, M. 1991. *The Economics of Business Culture: Game Theory, Transactions Costs and Economic Performance*. Oxford.

1993. Entrepreneurship and business culture. In Brown and Rose 1993.

1997. Institutional economics and business history: a way forward? *Business History* 39: 129–50.

Casson, M. and Rose, M. B. 1997. Institutions and the evolution of modern business. *Business History* 39: 1–8.

Catling, H. 1970. *The Spinning Mule.* Manchester.

Caunce, S. 1991.Twentieth century farm servants: the horse lads of the East Riding of Yorkshire. *Agricultural History Review* 39: 143–66.

1997a. Community structure as a source of innovation in the West Yorkshire textile industry, c1700–1850. *Business History* 39: 26–43.

1997b. Farm servants and the development of capitalism in English agriculture. *Agricultural History Review* 45: 49–60.

Cerman, M. and Ogilvie, S., eds. 1996. *European Proto-Industrialization.* Cambridge.

Chadwick, E. 1842. *Report . . . from the Poor Law Commissioners on an Inquiry into the Sanitary Conditions of the Labouring Population of Great Britain.*

Chambers, J. D. 1953. Enclosure and the labour supply in the industrial revolution. *Economic History Review* 5: 319–43.

1963. The rural domestic industries during the period of transition to the factory system, with special reference to the Midland counties of England. *Proceedings of the Second International Economic History Society Congress*, vol. 2. Aix-en-Provence.

1972. *Population, Economy and Society in Pre-industrial England.* Oxford.

Chandler, A. D. 1977. *The Visible Hand.* Cambridge, MA.

1990. *Scale and Scope: The Dynamics of Industrial Capitalism.* Cambridge, MA.

Chandler, T. and Fox, G. 1974. *300 Years of Urban Growth.* New York.

Channon, G. 1988. Railway pooling in Britain before 1900: the Anglo-Scottish traffic. *Business History Review* 62: 74–92.

1999. The business morals of British railway companies in the mid-nineteenth century. *Business and Economic History* 28: 69–79.

Chapman, S. D. 1967. *The Early Factory Masters.* Newton Abbot.

1972. *The Cotton Industry in the Industrial Revolution.*

1979a. Financial constraints on the growth of firms in the cotton industry 1790–1850. *Economic History Review* 32: 50–69.

1979b. British marketing enterprise: the changing roles of merchants, manufacturers and financiers, 1700–1860. *Business History Review* 53: 205–34.

1985. Quality vs. quantity in the Industrial Revolution: the case of textile printing. *Northern History* 21: 175–92.

1987. *The Cotton Industry in the Industrial Revolution*, 2nd edn. Basingstoke.

1992. *Merchant Enterprise in Britain from the Industrial Revolution to World War 1.* Cambridge.

Chapman, S. D. and Chassagne, S. 1981. *European Textile Printers in the Eighteenth Century: A Study of Peel and Oberkampf.*

Chartres, J. 1977. Road-carrying in England in the seventeenth century: myth and reality. *Economic History Review* 30: 73–94.

1985. The marketing of agricultural produce. In J. Thirsk, ed, *The Agrarian History of England and Wales*, V, *1640–1750*, II, *Agrarian Change.* Cambridge.

Chartres, J. and Hey, D., eds. 1990. *English Rural Society 1500–1800.* Cambridge.

Chartres, J. and Turnbull, G. L. 1983. Road transport. In Aldcroft and Freeman 1983.

Chaudhuri, K. N. 1978. *The Trading World of Asia and the English East India Company 1660–1760.* Cambridge.

1982. European trade with India. In T. Raychaudhuri and I. Habib, eds., *The Cambridge Economic History of India*, I. Cambridge.

Checkland, S. G. 1975. *Scottish Banking: A History, 1695–1973.* Glasgow.

Chorley, P. 1981. The agricultural revolution in northern Europe, 1750–1880: nitrogen, legumes, and crop productivity. *Economic History Review* 34: 71–93.

Church, R. 1970. Labour supply and innovation, 1800–1860: the boot and shoe industry. *Business History* 12: 25–45.

1993. The family firm in industrial capitalism: international perspectives on hypotheses and history. *Business History* 35: 17–43.

Church, R. 1999. New perspectives on the history of products, firms, marketing and consumers in Britain and the United States since the mid-nineteenth century. *Economic History Review* 42: 405–35.

Church, R. A. with Hall, A. and Kanefsky, J. 1986. *The History of the British Coal Industry, III, 1830–1913: Victorian Pre-eminence*. Oxford.

Cipolla, Carlo. 1965. *The Economic History of World Population*. Harmondsworth.

1969. *Literacy and Development in the West*. Harmondsworth.

Claeys, G. 1994. The origins of the rights of labor: republicanism, commerce and the construction of modern social theory in Britain 1796–1805. *Journal of Modern History* 66: 249–90.

Clapham, J. 1926. *An Economic History of Britain: the early railway age, 1820–1850*. Cambridge.

1944a. *The Bank of England: A History. Volume 1 1694–1796*. Cambridge.

1944b. *The Bank of England: A History. Volume 2 1797–1914*. Cambridge.

Clapp, B. W. 1994. *An Environmental History of Britain Since the Industrial Revolution*.

Clark, A. 1968. *Working Life of Women in the Seventeenth Century*.

Clark, G. 1987. Productivity growth without technical change in European agriculture before 1850. *Journal of Economic History* 472: 419–32.

1991a. Labour productivity in English agriculture, 1300–1860. In M. Overton, ed. *Agricultural Productivity in the European Past*. Manchester: 211–35.

1991b. Yields per acre in English agriculture, 1250–1860: evidence from labour inputs. *Economic History Review* 44: 445–60.

1993. Agriculture and the Industrial Revolution, 1700–1850. In Mokyr 1993.

1994. Factory discipline. *Journal of Economic History* 54: 128–63.

1998a. Commons sense: common property rights, efficiency, and institutional change. *Journal of Economic History* 58: 73–102.

1998b. Renting the revolution. *Journal of Economic History* 58: 206–10.

2001a. Farm wages and living standards in the Industrial Revolution: England, 1670–1850. *Economic History Review* 54: 477–505.

2001b. The secret history of the Industrial Revolution. UC *Davis Economic History Working Paper*. Davis, CA.

Clark, G. and van der Werf, Y. 1998. Work in progress? The Industrial Revolution. *Journal of Economic History* 583: 830–43.

Clark, G., Huberman, M. and Lindert, P. H. 1995. A British food puzzle, 1770–1850. *Economic History Review* 48: 215–37.

Clark, Jonathan C. D. 1986. *Revolution and Rebellion*. Cambridge.

Clark, P., ed. 2000. *The Cambridge Urban History of Britain*. Cambridge.

Claughton, P. F. 1994. Carmarthen United: an example of undercapitalisation in a mid-nineteenth century lead venture. *British Mining* 50: 149–57.

Clayton, T. 1998. *The English Print*. New Haven.

Cleere, H. and Crossley, D. 1985. *The Iron Industry of the Weald*. Leicester.

Clifford, H. 1999. A commerce with things: the value of precious metalwork in early modern England. In Berg and Clifford 1999.

Clow, Archibald and Clow, Nan L. 1952. *The Chemical Revolution: A Contribution to Social Technology*.

Clunas, C. 1991. *Superfluous Things: Material Culture and Social Status in Early Modern China*.

1999. Modernity global and local: consumption and the rise of the West. *American Historical Review* 104: 1497–1511.

Coale, A. J. and Demeny, P. 1966. *Regional Model Life Tables and Stable Populations*. Princeton.

Coase, R. 1937. The nature of the firm. *Economica* 4: 386–405.

Cocks, E. J. and Walters, B. 1968. *A History of the Zinc Smelting Industry in Britain.*

Cole, W. A. 1958. Trends in eighteenth-century smuggling. *Economic History Review* 10: 395–410.

   1975. The arithmetic of eighteenth-century smuggling: a rejoinder. *Economic History Review* 28: 44–9.

   1981. Factors in demand 1700–80. In Floud and McCloskey 1981.

Coleman, D. C. 1958. *The British Paper Industry, 1495–1860.* Oxford.

   1983. Proto-industrialization: a concept too many. *Economic History Review* 36: 435–48.

Colley, L. 1992. *Britons: Forging the Nation 1707–1837.* New Haven.

Collier, F. 1964. *The Family Economy of the Working Classes in the Cotton Industry 1784–1883.* Manchester.

Collins, B. 1999. Matters material and luxurious: eighteenth and early nineteenth-century Irish linen consumption. In Hill and Lenn 1999.

Collins, M. 1983. Long term growth of the English banking sector and money stock, 1844–1880. *Economic History Review* 36: 374–94.

   1988. *Money and Banking in the UK: A History.*

Collins, M. and Hudson, P. 1979. Provincial bank lending: Yorkshire and Merseyside, 1826–60. *Bulletin of Economic Research* 31: 69–79.

Colls, R. 1987. *The Pitmen of the Northern Coalfield: Work, Culture and Protest, 1790–1850.* Manchester.

Colquhoun, P. 1815. *A Treatise on the Wealth, Power and Resources of the British Empire.*

Cookson, G. 1997. Family firms and business networks: textile engineering in Yorkshire, 1780–1830. *Business History* 39: 1–20.

Cornish, W. R. and Clark, G. N. 1989. *Law and Society in England: 1750–1950.*

Costa, D. L. 1993. Height, weight, wartime stress, and older age mortality: evidence from the Union Army Records. *Explorations in Economic History* 304: 424–49.

Costa, D. and Steckel, R. 1997. Long-term trends in U.S. health, welfare, and economic growth. In R. Floud, ed., *Health and Welfare during Industrialization.* Chicago.

Cottrell, P. L. 1980. *Industrial Finance 1830–1914.*

   1991. The coalescence of a cluster of corporate international banks, 1855–75. In G. Jones, ed., *Banks and Money: International and Comparative Finance in History.*

Cottrell, P. L. and Newton, L. 1999. Banking liberalization in England and Wales 1826–1844. In Sylla *et al.* 1999: 75–117.

Cox, N. and Cox, J. 1984. Probate inventories: the legal background. *Local Historian* 16: 133–45, 217–27.

Crafts, N. F. R. 1973. Trade as a handmaiden of growth: an alternative view. *Economic Journal* 83: 875–84.

   1976. English economic growth in the eighteenth century: a re-examination of Deane and Cole's estimates. *Economic History Review* 29: 226–35.

   1977. Industrial Revolution in Britain and France: some thoughts on the question 'why was England first?'. *Economic History Review* 30: 429–41.

   1985a. *British Economic Growth during the Industrial Revolution.* Oxford.

   1985b. English workers' real wages during the Industrial Revolution: some remaining problems. *Journal of Economic History* 451: 139–44.

   1985c. Income elasticities of demand and the release of labor by agriculture during the British Industrial Revolution: a further appraisal. In Mokyr 1985.

   1987a. British economic growth, 1700–1850: some difficulties of interpretation. *Explorations in Economic History* 24: 245–68.

   1987b. Cliometrics, 1971–1986: a survey. *Journal of Applied Econometrics* 23: 171–92.

   1994. The industrial revolution. In Floud and McCloskey 1994.

   1995. Exogenous or endogenous growth? The Industrial Revolution reconsidered. *Journal of Economic History* 55: 745–72.

   1997. Some dimensions of the 'quality of life' during the British Industrial Revolution. *Economic History Review* 50: 617–39.

Crafts, N. F. R. and Harley, C. K. 1992. Output growth and the British Industrial Revolution: a restatement of the Crafts–Harley view. *Economic History Review* 45: 703–30.

2003. Precocious British industrialization: a general equilibrium perspective. In Prados de la Escosura 2003.

Craig, R. 1982. Printed guides for master mariners as a source of productivity change in ocean shipping, 1750–1914. *Journal of Transport History* 3rd ser. 3: 23–35.

Craske, M. 1999. Plan and control: design and the competitive spirit in early and mid-eighteenth-century England. *Journal of Design History* 12: 187–216.

Creighton, C. 1996. The rise of the male breadwinner family: a reappraisal. *Sociological Review* 44: 204–24.

Cressy, D. 1980. *Literacy and the Social Order: Reading and Writing in Tudor and Stuart England*. Cambridge.

Crouzet, F. 1958. *L'Economie britannique et le blocus continental, 1806–13*. Paris.

1964. Wars, blockade and economic change in Europe, 1792–1815. *Journal of Economic History* 24: 567–88.

1972. Editor's Introduction. *Capital Formation in the Industrial Revolution*.

1980. Toward an export economy: British exports during the industrial revolution. *Explorations in Economic History* 17: 48–93.

1985. *The First Industrialists: The Problem of Origins*. Cambridge.

1990. *Britain Ascendant: Comparative Studies in Franco-British Economic History*. Cambridge.

1996. *Britain, France and International Commerce*. Aldershot.

Crump, W. B., ed. 1931. *The Leeds Woollen Industry, 1780–1820*. Leeds.

Cuenca Esteban, J. 1994. British textile prices, 1770–1831: are British growth rates worth revising again? *Economic History Review* 47: 66–105.

1997. The rising share of British industrial exports in industrial output, 1700–1851. *Journal of Economic History* 57: 879–906.

Cullen, Louis M. 1989. Scotland and Ireland, 1600–1800: their role in the evolution of British society. In Houston and Whyte 1989.

Cullen, L. M. and Smout, T. C., eds. 1977. *Comparative Aspects of Scottish and Irish Economic and Social History 1600–1900*. Edinburgh.

Cunningham, H. and Viazzo, P. P. 1996. *Child Labour in Historical Perspective, 1880–1985*. Florence.

Daniels, G. W. 1920. *The Early English Cotton Industry*. Manchester.

Dasgupta, P. and Weale, M. 1992. On measuring the quality of life. *World Development* 20: 119–31.

Daumas, M., ed. 1980. *A History of Technology and Invention: Progress through the Ages, the Expansion of Mechanisation*.

Daunton, M. J. 1985. *Royal Mail: The Post Office since 1840*.

1995. *Progress and Poverty: An Economic and Social History of Britain 1700–1850*. Oxford.

Daunton, M. and Hilton, M., eds. 2001. *The Politics of Consumption*. Oxford.

Davenport-Hines, R. P. T. and Liebenau, J., eds. 1987. *Business in the Age of Reason*.

David, P. and Thomas, M., eds. 2003. *The Economic Future in Historical Perspective*. Oxford.

Davidoff, L. 1979. The separation of home and work. In Burman 1979.

Davidoff, L. and Hall, C. 1987. *Family Fortunes: Men and Women of the English Middle Class, 1780–1850*.

Davis, L. and Gallman, R. 2001. *Evolving Financial Markets and International Capital Flows: Britain, the Americas, and Australia, 1865–1914*. Cambridge.

Davis, L. E. and Huttenback, R. A. 1986. *Mammon and the Pursuit of Empire: The Political Economy of British Imperialism, 1860–1912*. Cambridge.

Davis, L. and Neal, L. 1998. Micro rules and macro outcomes: the impact of micro structure on the efficiency of security exchanges, London, New York, and Paris, 1800–1914. *American Economic Review* 88: 40–5.

Davis, R. 1954. English foreign trade, 1660–1700. *Economic History Review* 7: 150–66.

1957. Earnings of capital in the English shipping industry, 1670–1730. *Journal of Economic History* 17: 409–25.

1962. English foreign trade, 1700–1774. *Economic History Review* 15: 285–303.

1966. The rise of protection in England, 1689–1786. *Economic History Review* 19: 306–17.

1973. *The Rise of the Atlantic Economies*. Ithaca, NY.

1979. *The Industrial Revolution and British Overseas Trade*. Leicester.

Day, J. 1973. *Bristol Brass: A History of the Industry*. Newton Abbot.

Day, J. and Tylecote, R. F. 1991. *The Industrial Revolution in Metals*.

de Grazia, V. and Furlough, E., eds. 1996. *The Sex of Things: Gender and Consumption in Historical Perspective*. Berkeley and Los Angeles.

de Vries, J. 1984. *European Urbanization 1500–1800*. Cambridge, MA.

1993. Between purchasing power and the world of goods: understanding the household economy in early modern Europe. In Brewer and Porter 1993.

1994. The industrial revolution and the industrious revolution. *Journal of Economic History* 54: 249–70.

2002. Luxury in the Dutch republic in theory and practice. In Berg and Eger 2002.

de Vries, J. and van der Woude, A. 1997. *The First Modern Economy: Success, Failure and Perseverance of the Dutch Economy, 1500–1815*. Cambridge.

Deane, P. 1965. *The First Industrial Revolution*. Cambridge.

Deane, P. and Cole, W. A. 1967. *British Economic Growth 1688–1959*. Cambridge.

Defoe, Daniel 1727. *The Complete English Tradesman in Familiar Letters*.

Dehing, P. and Hart, M. 1997. Linking the fortunes: currency and banking, 1550–1800. In Hart *et al.* 1997.

Deiaco, E. *et al.*, eds. 1990. *Technology and Investment*.

Denevan, W. 1976. Epilogue. In W. Denevan, ed., *The Native Population of the Americas in 1492*. Madison.

Derry, T. K. and Williams, T. I. 1979. *A Short History of Technology*. Oxford.

Desan, C. A. 1998. Remaking constitutional tradition at the margin of the Empire: the creation of legislative adjudication in colonial New York. *Law and History Review* 16: 257–319.

Desjardins, B. 1995. Bias in age at marriage in family reconstitutions: evidence from French Canadian data. *Population Studies* 49: 165–9.

Devine, T. M. 1976. The colonial trades and industrial development in Scotland, 1700–1815. *Economic History Review* 29: 1–13.

1978. Social stability and agrarian change in the eastern Lowlands of Scotland, 1810–40. *Social History* 3: 331–46.

1984. *Farm Servants and Labour in Lowland Scotland 1770–1914*. Edinburgh.

1988. *The Great Highland Famine: Hunger, Emigration and the Scottish Highlands in the Nineteenth Century*. Edinburgh.

1994. *The Transformation of Rural Scotland: Social Change and the Agrarian Economy, 1660–1815*. Edinburgh.

1995a. *Exploring the Scottish Past: Themes in the History of Scottish Society*. East Linton.

1995b. The golden age of tobacco. In Devine and Jackson 1995.

1999. *The Scottish Nation, 1700–2000*.

2000. Scotland. In Clark 2000.

Devine, T. M. and Jackson, G., eds. 1995. *Glasgow*, I, *Beginnings to 1830*. Manchester.

Devine, T. M. and Mitchison, R., eds. 1988. *People and Society in Scotland*, I, *1760–1830*. Edinburgh.

Deyon, P. 1996. Proto-industrialization in France. In Cerman and Ogilvie 1996.

Dicey, A. V. 1915. *Introduction to the Study of the Law of the Constitution*, 8th edn.

Dick, M. 1980. The myth of the working-class Sunday school. *History of Education* 9: 27–41.

Dickson, P. G. M. 1967. *The Financial Revolution in England: A Study in the Development of Public Credit, 1688–1756*.

Dingle, A. E. 1982. 'The monster nuisance of all': landowners, alkali manufacturers and air pollution, 1828–64. *Economic History Review* 35: 529–48.

Dobbin, F. 1994. *Forging Industrial Policy: The United States, Britain, and France in the Railway Age*. Cambridge.

Dodgshon, R. A. 1981. *Land and Society in Early Scotland*. Oxford.

Doherty, K. W. and Flynn, D. O. 1989. A microeconomic quantity theory of money and the price revolution. In E. van Cauwenberge, ed., *Precious Metals, Coinage and the Changes of Monetary Structures in Latin America Europe and Asia (Late Middle Ages–Early Modern Times)*. Leuven.

Donaghy, T. J. 1965–6. The Liverpool and Manchester Railway as an investment. *Journal of Transport History* 7: 225–33.

Dornbusch, R. and Frenkel, J. 1984. The gold standard and the Bank of England in the crisis of 1847. In M. Bordo and A. Schwartz, eds., *A Retrospective on the Classical Gold Standard 1821–1931*. Chicago.

Douglas, M. and Isherwood, B. 1979. *The World of Goods*.

Drobak, J. N. and Nye, J. V. C., eds. 1997. *The Frontiers of the New Institutional Economics*. San Diego.

Duckham, B. F. 1983. Canals and river navigations. In Aldcroft and Freeman 1983.

Duffy, I. P. H. 1983. The discount policy of the Bank of England during the suspension of cash payment, 1797–1821. *Economic History Review* 35: 67–82.

1985. *Bankruptcy and Insolvency in London during the Industrial Revolution*. New York.

Dunlop, J. and Denman, R. D. 1912. *English Apprenticeship and Child Labour: A History*.

Dupree, M. 1995. *Family Structure in the Staffordshire Potteries, 1840–1880*. Oxford.

Durie, A. M. 1979. *The Scottish Linen Industry in the Eighteenth Century*. Edinburgh.

Dutton, H. I. 1984. *The Patent System and Inventive Activity during the Industrial Revolution, 1750–1852*. Manchester.

Eamon, William 1994. *Science and the Secrets of Nature*. Princeton.

Earle, P. 1989. *The Making of the English Middle Class*.

Edin, K. A. 1915. Studier i Svensk fruktsamhetsstatistik. *Ekonomisk Tidskrift* 9: 251–304.

Eggertsson, T. 1990. *Economic Behavior and Institutions*. Cambridge.

Ekelund, R. B. Jr and Tollison, R. D. 1997. *Politicized Economies: Monarchy, Monopoly and Mercantalism*. College Station, TX.

Elbaum, B. 1989. Why apprenticeship persisted in Britain but not in the United States. *Journal of Economic History* 49: 337–49.

Eley, G. 1984. The social history of industrialization: proto-industry and the origins of capitalism. *Economy and Society* 13: 519–39.

Ellis, J. 1998. Risk, capital, and credit on Tyneside, circa 1690–1780. In Bruland and O'Brien 1998.

Eltis, D. 2000. *The Rise of African Slavery in the Americas*. Cambridge.

Engels, F. 1958 [1845]. *The Condition of the Working Class in England*. Oxford.

Engerman, S. L. 1994. Mercantilism and overseas trade, 1700–1800. In Floud and McCloskey 1994.

2000. France, Britain and the economic growth of colonial North America. In J. J. McCusker and K. Morgan, eds., *The Early Modern Atlantic Economy*. Cambridge.

Epstein, S. A. 1991. *Wage Labor and Guilds in Medieval Europe*. Chapel Hill, NC.

Ernle, Lord 1961. *English Farming: Past and Present*.

Fairbairn, R. A. 1992. The cost of producing lead from Sharpley Lead Mine in Northumberland during the eighteenth century. *British Mining* 45: 28–31.

Fairlie, S. 1965. The nineteenth century Corn Law reconsidered. *Economic History Review* 18: 562–75.

1969. The Corn Laws and British wheat production, 1829–1876. *Economic History Review* 22: 88–116.

Farnie, D. A. 1979. *The English Cotton Industry and the World Market*. Oxford.

Farr, William 2001 [1877]. William Farr on the economic value of population. *Population and Development Review* 27: 565–71, reprinted from the Registrar General's 39th Annual Report.

Feavearyear, A. 1963. *The Pound Sterling.* Oxford.

Feinstein, C. H. 1972. *National Income, Expenditure and Output of The United Kingdom, 1955–1965.* Cambridge.

  1978. Capital formation in Great Britain. In P. Mathias and M. M. Postan, eds., *The Cambridge Economic History of Europe*, VII, *The Industrial Economies: Capital Labour, and Enterprise*, Part I, *Britain, France, Germany, and Scandinavia.* Cambridge.

  1981. Capital accumulation and the industrial revolution. In Floud and McCloskey 1981.

  1988b. The rise and fall of the Williamson Curve: review article. *Journal of Economic History* 483: 699–729.

  1998. Pessimism perpetuated. Real wages and the standard of living in Britain during and after the Industrial Revolution. *Journal of Economic History* 58: 625–58.

  1998b. Wage-earnings in Great Britain during the Industrial Revolution. In S. G. B. Henry, ed., *Applied Economics and Public Policy.* Cambridge.

Feinstein, C. H. and Pollard, S., eds. 1988. *Studies in Capital Formation in the United Kingdom 1750–1920.* Oxford.

Fell, J. E. 1979. *Ores to Metal: The Rocky Mountain Smelting Industry.* Lincoln, NB.

Ferguson, N. 2001. *The Cash Nexus: Money and Power in the Modern World, 1700–2000.*

Finch, J. 1989. *Family Obligations and Social Change.* Cambridge and Oxford.

Finlay, R. 1998. The pilgrim art: the culture of porcelain in world history. *Journal of World History* 9: 141–88.

Finn, M. 1996. Women, consumption and couverture in England, c. 1760–1860. *Historical Journal* 39: 703–22.

  2000. Men's things: masculine possession in the consumer revolution. *Social History* 25: 133–55.

Fisher, F. J., ed. 1961. *Essays in the Economic and Social History of Tudor and Stuart England.* Cambridge.

Fitton, R. S. and Wadsworth, A. P. 1958. *The Struts and the Arkwrights, 1758–1830: A Study of the Early Factory System.* Manchester.

Flandrin, J.-L. 1979. *Families in Former Times: Kinship, Household and Sexuality.* Cambridge.

Fletcher, M. E. 1958. The Suez Canal and world shipping, 1869–1914. *Journal of Economic History* 18: 556–73.

Fleury, M. and Henry, L. 1956. *Des Registres paroissiaux à l'histoire de la population: manuel de dépouillement et d'exploitation de l'état civil ancien.* Paris.

Flinn, M. W. 1970. *British Population Growth 1700–1850.*

Flinn, M. W., ed. 1965. *Report on the Sanitary Condition of the Labouring Population of Great Britain* by Edwin Chadwick. Edinburgh.

  1977. *Scottish Population History from the 17th century to the 1930s.* Cambridge.

Flinn, M. W. with Stoker, D. 1984. *The History of the British Coal Industry*, II, *1700–1830: The Industrial Revolution.* Oxford.

Floud, R. and McCloskey, D., eds. 1981. *The Economic History of Britain since 1700*, I, *1700–1860.* Cambridge.

  1994. *The Economic History of Britain since 1700*, I, *1700–1860*, 2nd edn. Cambridge.

Floud, R., Wachter, K. and Gregory, A. 1990. *Height, Health and History: Nutritional Status in the United Kingdom, 1750–1890.* Cambridge.

Fogel, R. W. 1964. *Railroads and American Economic Growth.* Baltimore.

  1984. Nutrition and the decline in mortality since 1700: some preliminary findings. NBER Working Paper 1402.

Fong, H. D. 1930. *The Triumph of the Factory System in England.* Tientsin.

Fontaine, L. 1996. *History of Pedlars in Europe.* Cambridge.

  2001. Antonio and Shylock: credit and trust in France, c. 1680–c. 1780. *Economic History Review* 59: 39–57.

Foreman-Peck, J. 1991. Railways and late Victorian economic growth. In J. Foreman-Peck, ed., *New Perspectives on the Late Victorian Economy: Essays in Quantitative Economic History, 1860–1914.* Cambridge.

Foreman-Peck, J. and Millward, R. 1994. *Public and Private Ownership of British Industry 1820–1990*. Oxford.

Fortrey, Samuel 1663. *England's Interest and Improvement*. Cambridge.

Foster, J. 1974. *Class Struggle and the Industrial Revolution*.

Frank, A. G. 1998. *ReOrient: The Silver Age in Asia and the World Economy*. Berkeley.

Freeman, C. and Louca, F. 2001. *As Time Goes By: From the Industrial Revolutions to the Information Revolution*. Oxford.

Freeman, M. J. and Aldcroft, D. H., eds. 1988. *Transport in Victorian Britain*. Manchester.

Fremdling, R. 1977. Railroads and German economic growth: a leading sector analysis with comparison to the U.S. and Great Britain. *Journal of Economic History* 37: 583–604.

Freudenberger, H. and Cummins, G. 1976. Health, work, and leisure before the Industrial Revolution. *Explorations in Economic History* 131: 1–12.

Frisby, D. and Featherstone, M., eds. 1997. *Simmel on Culture*.

Frost, P. 1981. Yeomen and metalsmiths: livestock in the dual economy of south Staffordshire 1560–1720. *Agricultural History Review* 29: 29–41.

Fukuyama, F. 1995. *Trust: The Social Virtues and the Creation of Prosperity*. Harmondsworth.

Fullarton, W. 1793. *General View of the Agriculture of the County of Ayr, Edinburgh*. Edinburgh.

Galbi, D. 1997. Child labor and the division of labor in the early English cotton mills. *Journal of Population Economics* 104: 357–75.

Galloway, P. R. 1988. Basic patterns in annual variations in fertility, nuptiality, mortality, and prices in pre-industrial Europe. *Population Studies* 42: 275–302.

Galor, O. and Moav, O. 2000. Das Human Kapital. CEPR Discussion Paper 2701.

  2002. Natural selection and the origins of economic growth. *Quarterly Journal of Economics* 117: 1133–91.

Galor, O. and Weil, D. 2000. Population, technology, and growth. *American Economic Review* 90: 806–28.

Gardner, P. 1984. *The Lost Elementary Schools of Victorian England*.

Garfield, S. 2001. *Mauve: How One Man Invented a Color that Changed the World*. New York.

Garret, E., Reid, A., Schurer, K. and Szreter, S. 2001. *Changing Family Size in England and Wales: Place, Class and Demography, 1891–1911*. Cambridge.

Gash, N. 1986. *Sir Robert Peel: The Life of Sir Robert Peel after 1830*, 2nd edn. New York.

Gaskell, P. 1833. *The Manufacturing Population of England*.

Gattrell, V. A. C. 1977. Labour, power and size of firms in Lancashire cotton in the second quarter of the nineteenth century. *Economic History Review* 30: 95–139.

  1982. Incorporation and the pursuit of Liberal hegemony in Manchester, 1790–1839. In D. Fraser, ed., *Municipal Reform and the Industrial City*. Leicester.

Gautier, E. and Henry, L. 1958. *La Population de Crulai: paroisse normande*. Paris.

Geertz, C. 1963a. *Agricultural Involution: The Process of Ecological Change in Indonesia*. Berkeley and Los Angeles.

  1963b. *Old Societies and New States: The Quest for Modernity in Africa and Asia*. Glencoe, IL.

Gemmell, N. and Wardley, P. 1990. The contribution of services to British economic growth, 1856–1913. *Explorations in Economic History* 27: 299–321.

Geraghty, T. 2002. Technology, organisation, and complementarity: the factory system in the British industrial revolution. Unpublished DPhil dissertation, NorthWestern University.

Gerhold, D. 1988. *The Growth of the London Carrying Trade, 1681–1838*.

  1996. Productivity change in road transport before and after turnpiking, 1690–1840. *Economic History Review* 49: 491–515.

Getzler, J. 1996. Theories of property and economic development. *Journal of Interdisciplinary History* 26: 639–69.

2004. *History of Water Rights*. Oxford.

Gibson, A. J. S. and Smout, T. C. 1995. *Prices, Food and Wages in Scotland, 1550–1780*. Cambridge.

Giedion, S. 1969. *Mechanization Takes Command*. New York.

Gilboy, E. 1967 [1932]. Demand as a factor in the industrial revolution. In R. M. Hartwell, ed., *The Causes of the Industrial Revolution in England*.

Gill, M. 2001. *Swaledale: Its Mines and Smelt Mills*. Ashbourne.

Ginarlis, J. and Pollard, S. 1988. Roads and waterways, 1750–1850. In Feinstein and Pollard 1988.

Giráldez, A. and Flynn, D. O. 1994. China and the Manila galleons. In A. J. H. Latham and H. Kawakatsu, eds., *Japanese Industrialization and the Asian Economy*.

Goldsmith, R. 1969. *Financial Structure and Development*. New Haven.

Goldstone, J. A. 1986. The demographic revolution in England: a re-examination. *Population Studies* 40: 5–33.

2002. Efflorescences and economic growth in world history: rethinking the rise of the West and the British Industrial Revolution. *Journal of World History* 13: 323–89.

2003. Europe's peculiar path: would the world be modern if William III's invasion of England in 1688 had failed? In N. Lebow, G. Parker and P. Tetlock, eds., *Counterfactual History*. New York.

Goldsworthy, J. D. 1999. *The Sovereignty of Parliament: History and Philosophy*. Oxford.

Goldthwaite, R. A. 1993. *Wealth and the Demand for Art in Italy 1400–1600*. Baltimore.

Golinski, Jan 1992. *Science as Public Culture: Chemistry and Enlightenment in Britain, 1760–1820*. Cambridge.

Goodhart, C. 1988. *The Evolution of Central Banks*. Cambridge, MA.

Goodman, J. 1993. *Tobacco in History: The Cultures of Dependence*.

Gordon, R. J. 1993. *The Measurement of Durable Goods Prices*. Chicago.

Gorton, G. 1985. Clearinghouses and the origin of central banking in the United States. *Journal of Economic History* 45: 277–84.

Goubert, P. 1960. *Beauvais et le Beauvaisis de 1600 à 1730*, 2 vols. Paris.

Gough, J. 1931. *Mendip Mining Laws and Forest Bounds*. Frome: Somerset Records Society 45.

Gourvish, T. R. 1973. A British business elite: the chief executive managers of the railway industry, 1850–1923. *Business History Review* 47: 289–316.

1980. *Railways and the British Economy, 1830–1914*.

1988. Railways 1830–70: the formative years. In Freeman and Aldcroft 1988.

Grabher G., ed. 1993. *The Embedded Firm: On the Socio-Economics of Industrial Networks*.

Grafe, R. 2001. Atlantic trade and regional specialisation in northern Spain, 1550–1650: an integrated trade theory–institutional organisation approach. Working Paper, Dept. de Historia Económica y Instituciones, U. Carlos III de Madrid.

Graff, H. 1987. *Legacies of Literacy: Continuities and Contradictions in Western Culture and Society*. Bloomington, IN.

Granovetter, M. 1985. Economic action and social structure: the problem of embeddedness. *American Journal of Sociology* 91: 481–510.

Grantham, G. and Leonard, S., eds. 1991. *Agrarian Organization in the Century of Industrialization: Europe, Russia, and North America. Research in Economic History*, Supplement 5.

Green, A. 1990. *Education and State Formation: The Rise of Education Systems in England, France and the U.S.A.* New York.

Greenhill, R. G. 1979. Latin America's export trades and British shipping, 1850–1914. In Alexander and Ommer 1979.

Griffith, G. T. 1926. *Population Problems of the Age of Malthus*. Cambridge.

Habakkuk, H. J. 1953. English population in the eighteenth century. *Economic History Review* 6: 117–53.

Haber, L. F. 1958. *The Chemical Industry during the Nineteenth Century*. Oxford.

Hajnal, J. 1965. European marriage patterns in perspective. In D. V. Glass and D. E. C. Eversley, eds., *Population in History: Essays in Historical Demography*.

1983. Two kinds of pre-industrial household formation. In Wall *et al*. 1983.

Hall, A. Rupert. 1974. What did the Industrial Revolution in Britain owe to science? In McKendrick 1974b.

Hall, G. W. 1988. *The Gold Mines of Merioneth*. Kington.

Hamilton, H. 1926. *The English Brass and Copper Industries to 1800*.

Hammond, J. L. and Hammond, B. 1924. *The Village Labourer, 1760–1832*.

1932. *The Town Labourer 1760–1832*.

Hanley, Susan. 1997. *Everyday Things in Pre-modern Japan*. Berkeley.

Hans, N. 1951. *New Trends in Education in the Eighteenth Century*.

Hareven, T. 1982. *Family Time and Industrial Time: The Relationship between the Family and Work in a New England Community*. Cambridge.

Harley, C. K. 1988. Ocean freight rates and productivity, 1740–1913: the primacy of mechanical invention reaffirmed. *Journal of Economic History* 48: 851–75.

1993. Reassessing the industrial revolution: a macro view. In Mokyr 1993.

1994. Foreign trade: comparative advantage and performance. In Floud and McCloskey 1994.

1998. Cotton textile prices and the Industrial Revolution, *Economic History Review* 51: 49–83.

1999. Reassessing the Industrial Revolution: a macro view. In Mokyr 1999.

Harley, C. K. and Crafts, N. F. R. 2000. Simulating two views of the British industrial revolution. *Journal of Economic History* 60: 819–41.

Harling, P. and Mandler, P. 1993. From fiscal–military state to laissez-faire state, 1760–1850. *The Journal of British Studies* 32: 44–70.

Harper, L. A. 1939. *The English Navigation Acts*. New York.

Harris, A. 1970. *Cumberland Iron: The Story of Hodbarrow Mine 1855–1968*. Truro.

Harris, J. R. 1964. *The Copper King: A Biography of Thomas Williams of Llanidan*. Liverpool.

1976. Skills, coal and British industry in the eighteenth century. *History* 61: 167–82.

1988. *The British Iron Industry 1700–1850*.

Harris, J. R., ed. 1969. *Liverpool and Merseyside: Essays in the Economic and Social History of the Port and Its Hinterland*. New York.

Harris, R. 1994. The Bubble Act: its passage and its effects on business organization. *Journal of Economic History* 54: 610–27.

1997. Political economy, interest groups, legal institutions and the repeal of the Bubble Act in 1825. *Economic History Review* 50: 675–96.

2000. *Industrializing English Law: Entrepreneurship and Business Organization, 1720–1844*. Cambridge.

2003. The encounters of economic history and legal history. *Law and History Review* 21: 297–346.

Harrison, D. F. 1992. Bridges and economic development, 1300–1800. *Economic History Review* 45: 755–93.

Hart, C. 1971. *The Industrial History of Dean*. Newton Abbot.

Hart, M., Jonker, J. and van Zanden, J. L. 1997. *A Financial History of the Netherlands*. Cambridge.

Harte, N. 2001. Why did eighteenth-century men wear wigs? Unpublished paper to Seminar in Eighteenth-Century Studies, University of Warwick.

Harvey, C. E. and Press, J. 1989. Overseas investment and the professional advance of British metal mining engineers, 1851–1914. *Economic History Review* 42: 64–86.

Hatcher, J. 1986. Mortality in the fifteenth century: some new evidence. *Economic History Review* 39: 19–38.

Hausman, W. J. 1993. Freight rates and shipping costs in the English coastal coal trade: a reply. *Economic History Review* 46: 610–12.

Havinden, M. A. 1961. Agricultural progress in open field Oxfordshire. *Agricultural History Review* 9: 73–83.

Hawke, G. 1970. *Railways and Economic Growth in England and Wales, 1840–70.* Oxford.

Hawke, G. and Higgins, J. P. P. 1981. Transport and social overhead capital. In Floud and McCloskey 1981.

Hay, D. and Snyder, F. 1989. *Policing and Prosecution in Britain 1750–1850.* Oxford.

Headrick, Daniel 2000. *When Information Came of Age: Technologies of Knowledge in the Age of Reason and Revolution, 1700–1850.* New York.

Heaton, H. 1965 [1920]. *The Yorkshire Woollen and Worsted Industries: From Earliest Times up to the Industrial Revolution.* Oxford.

Heilbron, J. L. 1990. Introductory Essay. In T. Frängsmyr, J. L. Heilbron and R. E. Rider, eds., *The Quantifying Spirit in the 18th Century.* Berkeley.

Helms, M. W. 1994. Essay on objects: interpretations of distance made tangible. In Schwartz, S. B., ed. 1994. *Implicit Understandings: Observing, Reporting and Reflecting on the Encounters between Europeans and Other Peoples in the Early Modern Era.* Cambridge.

Helpman, Elhanan, ed. 1998. *General Purpose Technologies.* Cambridge, MA.

Helpman, E. and Krugman, P. D. 1985. *Market Structure and Foreign Trade.* Cambridge.

Henning, G. and Trace, K. 1975. Britain and the motorship: a case of the delayed adoption of new technology. *Journal of Economic History* 35: 353–85.

Hennock, P. 1973. *Fit and Proper Persons: Ideal and Reality in Nineteenth Century Urban Government.*

Henry, L. 1956. *Anciennes familles genevoises: étude démographique: XVIe–XXe siècles.* Paris.

Henry, L. and Blanchet, D. 1983. La population de l'Angleterre de 1541 à 1871. *Population* 38: 781–826.

Herlihy, D. 1997. *The Black Death and the Transformation of the West.* Cambridge, MA.

Heuman, G. 1999. Slavery, the slave trade and abolition. In R. W. Winks, *The Oxford History of the British Empire*, V, *Historiography.* Oxford.

Hey, D. G. 1969. A dual economy in south Yorkshire. *Agricultural History Review* 17: 108–19.

1972. *The Rural Metalworkers of the Sheffield Region.* Leicester.

Higgs, E. 1983. Domestic servants and households in Victorian England. *Social History* 8: 201–10.

Hilgerdt, F. 1945. *Industrialisation and Foreign Trade.* Geneva.

Hill, A. 2000. *The History and Development of Colliery Ventilation.* Matlock.

Hill, J. and Lenn, C., eds. 1999. *Luxury and Austerity.* Dublin.

Hills, Richard L. 2002. *Life and Inventions of Richard Roberts, 1789–1864.* Ashbourne.

Hilton, M. 2000. *Smoking in British Popular Culture 1800–2000.* Manchester.

Hirschman, A. 1958. *The Strategy of Economic Development.* New Haven.

Hirst, P. and Zeitlin, J. 1991. Flexible specialisation vs post Fordism: theory, evidence and policy implications. *Economy and Society* 20: 1–56.

Hitchcock, T., King, P. and Sharpe, P., eds. 1997. *Chronicling Poverty: The Voices and Strategies of the English Poor, 1640–1840.* Basingstoke.

Hobsbawm, E. 1972. The British standard of living, 1790–1850. In S. Lieberman, ed., *Europe and the Industrial Revolution.* Cambridge, MA.

Hodgson, G. M. 1993. *Economics and Evolution: Bringing Life Back to Economics.* Ann Arbor.

Hoffman, P., Postel-Vinay, G. and Rosenthal, J. 2000. *Priceless Markets: The Political Economy of Credit in Paris, 1660–1870.* Chicago.

Hoffman, P. T. and Rosenthal, J. 1997. The political economy of warfare and taxation in early modern Europe: historical lessons for economic development. In Drobak and Nye 1997.

Hoffmann, Walther G. 1965. *British Industry, 1700–1950*. Oxford.

Holderness, B. A. 1976. Credit in English rural society before the nineteenth century, with special reference to the period 1650–1720. *Agricultural History Review* 24: 91–109.

1988. Agriculture, 1770–1860. In Feinstein and Pollard 1988.

1989. Prices, productivity, and output. In Mingay 1989.

Holland, E. 1986. *Coniston Copper: A History*. Milnthorpe.

Holland, R. M. 1910. The London Bankers Clearing House. In H. Withers and R. H. Palgrave, eds., *The English Banking System*, volume XVIII of the *National Monetary Commission*. Washington.

Honeyman, K. 1982. *Origins of Enterprise: Business Leadership in the Industrial Revolution*. Manchester.

Honeyman, K. and Goodman, J. 1991. Women's work, gender conflict, and labour markets in Europe, 1500–1900. *Economic History Review* 44: 608–28.

Hopkins, E. 1982. Working hours and conditions during the Industrial Revolution: a re-appraisal. *Economic History Review* 35: 52–66.

Hoppitt, J. 1986. The use and abuse of credit in eighteenth century England. In McKendrick and Outhwaite 1986.

1987. *Risk and Failure in English Business 1700–1800*. Cambridge.

Horne, H. O. 1947. *A History of Savings Banks*. Oxford.

Horrell, S. 1996. Home demand and British industrialization. *Journal of Economic History* 56: 561–604.

Horrell, S. and Humphries, J. 1992. Old questions, new data and alternative perspectives: the standard of living of families in the industrial revolution. *Journal of Economic History* 52: 849–80.

1995a. Women's labour force participation and the transition to the male-breadwinner family, 1790–1865. *Economic History Review* 48: 89–117.

1995b. The exploitation of little children: children's work and the family economy in the British industrial revolution. *Explorations in Economic History* 32: 485–516.

1997. The origins and expansion of the male breadwinner family. The case of nineteenth century Britain. *International Review of Social History* 42: 25–64.

forthcoming. *Household Budgets and the Standard of Living in the Industrial Revolution*. Cambridge.

Horrell, S., Humphries, J. and Voth, H.-J. 2001. Destined for deprivation: human capital formation and inter-generational poverty in nineteenth-century England. *Explorations in Economic History* 38: 339–65.

Horrell, S. and Oxley, D. 1999. Crust or crumb? Intrahousehold resource allocation and male breadwinning in late Victorian Britain. *Economic History Review* 52: 494–522.

Horsefield, J. K. 1982. The stop of the Exchequer revisited. *Economic History Review* 35: 511–28.

1983. *British Monetary Experiments, 1650–1710*.

Houston, R. A. 1985. *Scottish Literacy and the Scottish Identity: Illiteracy and Society in Scotland and Northern England, 1600–1800*. Cambridge.

1988a. The demographic regime. In Devine and Mitchison 1988.

1988b. *Literacy in Early Modern Europe: Culture and Education, 1500–1800*.

1996. The population history of Britain and Ireland, 1500–1750. In Anderson 1996.

Houston, R. and Snell, K. D. M. 1984. Proto-industrialization, cottage industry, social change and industrial revolution. *Historical Journal* 27: 473–92.

Houston, R. A. and Whyte, I. D., eds. 1989. *Scottish Society 1500–1800*. Cambridge.

Howe, A. 1984. *The Cotton Masters, 1830–1860*. Oxford.

Howkins, A. 1994. Peasants, servants and labourers: the marginal workforce in British agriculture c. 1870–1914. *Agricultural History Review* 42: 49–62.

Howlett, P. 2000. Evidence of the existence of an internal labour market in the Great Eastern Railway Company, 1875–1905. *Business History* 42: 21–40.

Hsieh, C.-T. 1999. Productivity growth and factor prices in East Asia. *American Economic Review* 892: 133–8.

Huberman, M. 1996. *Escape from the Market: Negotiating Work in Lancashire*. Cambridge.

Huck, P. 1995. Infant mortality and living standards of English workers during the Industrial Revolution. *Journal of Economic History* 553: 528–50.

Hudson, P. 1981. The role of banks in the finance of the west Yorkshire wool textile industry, c. 1780–1850. *Business History Review* 55: 379–402.

1983. From manor to mill: the West Riding in transition. In Berg *et al.* 1983.

1986. *The Genesis of Industrial Capital: A Study of the West Riding Wool Textile Industry, c. 1750–1850*. Cambridge.

1991. Landholding and the organisation of textile manufacture in Yorkshire rural townships, *c.* 1660–1810. In Berg 1991.

1992. *The Industrial Revolution*.

1996. Proto-industrialization in England. In Cerman and Ogilvie 1996.

1999. Industrialization in Britain: the challenge of micro-history. *Family and Community History* 2: 5–16.

2001. *Living Economic and Social History*. Glasgow.

Hudson, P., ed. 1989. *Regions and Industries: A Perspective on the Industrial Revolution in Britain*. Cambridge.

Hudson, P. and King, S. 1996. A sense of place: industrialising townships in eighteenth century Yorkshire. In Leboutte 1996.

2000. Two textile townships c. 1680–1820: a comparative demographic analysis. *Economic History Review* 53: 706–41.

Hueckel, G. 1981. Agriculture during industrialisation. In Floud and McCloskey 1981.

Hughes, G. 1992. The board of directors of the London & North Eastern Railway. *Journal of Transport History* 3rd ser. 13: 163–79.

Hughes, S. 2000. *Copperopolis: Landscapes of the Early Industrial Period in Swansea*. Aberystwyth.

Hume, D. 1903 [1741, 1742]. *Essays Moral, Political and Literary*.

Humphries, J. 1977. Class struggle and the persistence of the working-class family. *Cambridge Journal of Economics* 1: 241–58.

1981. Protective legislation, the capitalist state and working-class men: the case of the 1842 Mines Regulation Act. *Feminist Review* 7: 1–35.

1990. Enclosures, common right, and women: the proletarianization of families in the late eighteenth and early nineteenth centuries. *Journal of Economic History* 50: 17–42.

1997. Short stature among coal-mining children: a comment. *Economic History Review* 503: 531–7.

1998. Female-headed households in early industrial Britain: the vanguard of the proletariat? *Labour History Review* 63: 31–65.

2000. Cliometrics, child labor and the industrial revolution. *Critical Review* 133–4: 269–83.

2001. At what cost was pre-eminence purchased? Child labour and the first industrial revolution. Unpublished manuscript, All Souls College, Oxford.

2003. English apprenticeship: a neglected factor in the first industrial revolution. In David and Thomas 2003.

Hunt, E. H. 1986. Industrialisation and regional inequality: wages in Britain, 1760–1914. *Journal of Economic History* 46: 936–66.

Hunt, M. 1996. *The Middling Sort: Commerce, Gender and the Family in England, 1680–1780*. Berkeley.

Hunt, R. 1887. *British Mining*.

Hyde, C. K. 1977. *Technological Change and the British Iron Industry 1700–1870*. Princeton, NJ.

Hyde, F. E. 1971. *Liverpool and the Mersey*. Newton Abbott.

Hyrenius, H. 1942. *Estlandssvenskarna: demografiska studier*. Lund.

Imlah, J. A. H. 1958. *Economic Elements of Pax Britannica: Studies in British Foreign Trade in the Nineteenth Century*. Cambridge, MA.

Inikori, J. E. 1987. Slavery and the development of industrial capitalism in England. In Solow and Engerman 1987.

    2002. *Africans and the Industrial Revolution in England: A Study in International Trade and Economic Development*. Cambridge.

Inkster, Ian 1991. *Science and Technology in History: An Approach to Industrial Development*. New Brunswick.

Ironmonger, D. 1972. *New Commodities and Consumer Behaviour*. Cambridge.

Irving, R. J. 1978. The profitability and performance of British railways 1870–1914. *Economic History Review* 31: 46–66.

Irwin, D. A. 1988. Welfare effects of British free trade: debate and evidence from the 1840s. *Journal of Political Economy* 91: 1142–64.

Israel, J. I. 1995. *The Dutch Republic: Its Rise, Greatness, and Fall, 1477–1806*. Oxford.

Jackman, W. T. 1916. *The Development of Transportation in Modern England*. Cambridge.

Jackson, G. 1988. The shipping industry. In Freeman and Aldcroft 1988.

Jackson, R. V. 1985. Growth and deceleration in English agriculture, 1660–1790. *Economic History Review* 36: 333–51.

    1992. Rates of industrial growth during the Industrial Revolution. *Economic History Review* 451: 1–23.

Jacob, M. C. 1997. *Scientific Culture and the Making of the Industrial West*. New York.

    1998. The cultural foundations of early industrialization. In Berg and Bruland 1998.

Jenkin, A. K. Hamilton. 1927. *The Cornish Miner*.

John, A. H. 1950. *The Industrial Development of South Wales 1750–1850*. Cardiff.

    1953. Insurance investment and the London money market of the eighteenth century. *Economica* 20: 137–58.

    1989. *Statistical Appendix*. In Mingay 1989.

Johnson, P. 1993. Small debts and economic distress in England and Wales, 1857–1913. *Economic History Review* 46: 65–87.

Jones, C. and Spang, R. 1999. Sans-culottes, sans café, sans tabac: shifting realms of necessity and luxury in eighteenth-century France. In Berg and Clifford 1999.

Jones, E. L. 1968. Agricultural origins of industry. *Past and Present* 40: 58–71.

    1981. Agriculture. In Floud and McCloskey 1981.

    1986. A transport private saving calculation for the brewers Truman Hanbury and Buxton, 1815–63. *Journal of Transport History* 3rd ser. 7: 1–17.

    1987. *The European Miracle: Environments, Economies and Geopolitics in the History of Europe and Asia*, 2nd edn. Cambridge.

    1988. *Growth Recurring: Economic Change in World History*. Oxford.

Jones, M. G. 1938. *The Charity School Movement: A Study of Eighteenth-Century Puritanism in Action*. Oxford.

Jones, S. R. H. 1994. The origins of the factory system in Great Britain. In Kirby and Rose 1994.

Joslin, D. M. 1954. London private bankers, 1720–85. *Economic History Review* 7: 167–86.

Joyce, P. 1980. *Work, Society and Politics: The Culture of the Factory in Later Victorian England*. Brighton.

Kanefsky, J. W. 1979. Motive power in British industry and the accuracy of the 1870 factory return. *Economic History Review* 32: 360–75.

Kennedy, P. 1987. *The Rise and Fall of The Great Powers: Economic Change and Military Conflict from 1500 to 2000*. New York.

Kerridge, E. 1988. *Trade and Banking in Early Modern England*. Manchester.

Keyser, Barbara Whitney. 1990. Between science and craft: the case of Berthollet and dyeing. *Annals of Science* 47: 213–60.

Khan, B. Z. and Sokoloff, K. L. 1998. Patent institutions, industrial organization and early technological change: Britain and the United States, 1790–1850. In Berg and Bruland 1998.

Khan, A. 2000. The finance and growth nexus. *Philadelphia Federal Reserve Business Review* January/February 2000: 3–14.

Killick, J. R. and Thomas, W. A. 1970. The provincial stock exchanges, 1830–1870. *Economic History Review* 23: 96–109.

Kindleberger, C. P. 1993. *A Financial History of Western Europe, Second Edition*. Oxford.

King, Gregory 1696. Natural and political observations and conclusions upon the state and condition of England. In George Chalmers, *An Estimate of the Comparative Strength of Great Britain* (1802).

King, P. 1991. Customary rights and women's earnings: the importance of gleaning to the rural labouring poor, 1750–1850. *Economic History Review* 44: 461–76.

1997. Pauper inventories and the material lives of the poor in the eighteenth and early nineteenth centuries. In Hitchcock *et al.* 1997.

King, S. A. 1993. The nature and causes of demographic change in an industrialising township c. 1681–1820. Unpublished PhD thesis, University of Liverpool.

2000. *Poverty and Welfare in England 1700–1850: A Regional Perspective*. Manchester.

2002. Reclothing the English poor, 1750–1840. *Textile History* 33: 37–47.

King, W. T. C. 1936. *The History of the London Discount Market*.

Kingsford, P. W. 1970. *Victorian Railwaymen: The Emergence and Growth of Railway Labour, 1830–70*.

Kinnaird Commission 1864. *Report of the Commissioners Appointed to Enquire into the Condition of All Mines in Great Britain to Which the Provisions of the Act 23 & 24 Vict. c 151 do not Apply, British Parliamentary Papers 1864 XXIV (i) (ii)*.

Kirby, M. 1993. *The Origins of Railway Enterprise: The Stockton and Darlington Railway, 1821–1863*. Cambridge.

1994. Big business before 1900. In Kirby and Rose 1994.

Kirby, M. and Rose, M. B., eds. 1994. *Business Enterprise in Modern Britain: From the Eighteenth to the Twentieth Centuries*.

Komlos, J. 1989. *Nutrition and Economic Development in the Eighteenth-Century Habsburg Monarchy: An Anthropometric History*. Princeton.

1993. The secular trend in the biological standard of living in the United Kingdom, 1730–1860. *Economic History Review* 461: 115–44.

1998. Shrinking in a growing economy? The mystery of physical stature during the Industrial Revolution. *Journal of Economic History* 583: 779–802.

Kosminski, E. A. 1956. *Studies in the Agrarian History of England in the Thirteenth Century*, trans. Ruth Kisch, ed. R. H. Hilton. Oxford.

Kostal, R. W. 1994. *Law and English Railway Capitalism, 1825–1875*. Oxford.

Kowaleski-Wallace, E. 1997. *Consuming Subjects*. New York.

Koyré, Alexandre 1968 [1953]. An experiment in measurement. In Koyré, *Metaphysics and Measurement: Essays in Scientific Revolution*. Cambridge, MA.

Krause, J. T. 1958. Changes in English fertility and mortality, 1780–1850. *Economic History Review* 11: 52–70.

Kravis, I. B. 1970. Trade as a handmaiden of growth: similarities between the nineteenth and twentieth centuries. *Economic Journal* 80: 850–72.

1973. A reply to Mr Crafts note. *Economic Journal* 83: 885–9.

Kriedte, P., Medick, H. and Schlumbohm, J. 1981. *Industrialization before Industrialization: Rural Industry in the Genesis of Capitalism*. Cambridge.

Kussmaul, A. 1981. *Servants in Husbandry in Early Modern England*. Cambridge.

Lamoreaux, N. 1994. *Insider Lending: Banks, Personal Connections, and Economic Development in Industrial New England*. Cambridge.

Lancaster, K. 1971. *Consumer Demand: A New Approach.* New York.

Landau, N. 1984. *The Justices of the Peace, 1679–1760.* Berkeley.

Landers, J. 1993. *Death and the Metropolis: Studies in the Demographic History of London 1670–1830.* Cambridge.

Landes, D. S. 1969, 1974. *The Unbound Prometheus: Technological Change and Industrial Development in Western Europe from 1750 to the Present.* Cambridge.

   1986. What do bosses really do? *Journal of Economic History* 46: 585–623.

   1998. *The Wealth and Poverty of Nations: Why Some Are So Rich and Some So Poor.* New York.

Lane, J. 1996. *Apprenticeship in England, 1600–1914.*

Langford, P. 1989. *A Polite and Commercial People: England 1727–1783.* Oxford.

Langlois, R. N. 1999. The coevolution of technology and organisation in the transition to the factory system. In Paul L. Robertson, ed., *Authority and Control in Modern Industry.*

Langton, J. 1984. The industrial revolution and the regional geography of England. *Transactions of the Institute of the Royal Historical Society* 29: 90–105.

Langton, J. and Morris, R. 1986. *Atlas of Industrialising Britain, 1780–1914.*

Laqueur, T. 1974. Debate: literacy and social mobility in the Industrial Revolution in England. *Past and Present* 64: 96–107.

Lasch, C. 1977. *Haven in a Heartless World: The Family Besieged.* New York.

Laslett, P. 1965. *The World We Have Lost.* New York.

   1969. Size and structure of the household in England over three centuries. *Population Studies* 23: 199–223.

   1972a. Introduction: the history of the family. In Laslett and Wall 1972.

   1972b. Mean household size in England since the sixteenth century. In Laslett and Wall 1972.

   1977. Characteristics of the western family considered over time. *Journal of Family History* 2: 89–115.

Laslett, P. and Harrison, J. 1963. Clayworth and Cogenhoe. In H. E. Bell and R. L. Ollard, eds., *Historical Essays presented to David Ogg.*

Laslett, P. and Wall, R., eds. 1972. *Household and Family in Past Time.* Cambridge.

Lawson, J. and Silver, H. 1973. *A Social History of Education in England.*

Laxton, P. and Williams, N. 1989. Urbanisation and infant mortality in England: a long term perspective and review. In M. C. Nelson and J. Rogers, eds., *Urbanisation and the Epidemiological Transition.* Reports from the Family History Group, Department of History, Uppsala University, 9. Uppsala.

Lazear, E. P. 1986. Salaries and piece rates. *Journal of Business* 59: 405–31.

Lazonick, W. 1991. *Business Organisation and the Myth of the Market Economy.* Cambridge.

Leboutte R., ed. 1996. *Proto-Industrialization: Recent Research and New Perspectives.* Geneva.

Lee, C. H. 1979. *British Regional Employment Statistics, 1841–1971.* Cambridge.

Lee, R. D. 1974. Estimating series of vital rates and age structures from baptisms and burials: a new technique with applications to pre-industrial England. *Population Studies* 28: 495–512.

   1985. Population homeostasis and English demographic history. *Journal of Interdisciplinary History* 15: 635–60.

Lee, R. and Anderson, M. 1999. Malthus in state space: macroeconomic-demographic relations in English history, 1540–1870. Unpublished manuscript, Berkeley, CA.

Lemire, B. 1990. The theft of clothes and popular consumerism in early modern England. *Journal of Social History* 24: 255–76.

   1991. *Fashion's Favourite: The Cotton Trade and the Consumer in Britain, 1660–1800.* Oxford.

   1997. *Dress, Culture and Commerce: The English Clothing Trade before the Factory 1660–1800.*

1998. Petty pawns and informal lending: gender and the transformation of small-scale credit in England circa 1600–1800. In Bruland and O'Brien 1998.

Lemon, C. 1838. The statistics of the copper mines of Cornwall. *Journal of the Statistical Society of London* 1: 65–84. Reprinted in Burt 1969.

Leneman, L. and Mitchison, R. 1987. Scottish illegitimacy ratios in the early modern period. *Economic History Review* 40: 41–63.

Levi, L. 1868. *The Education of the Merchant.*

Levine, D. 1977. *Family Formation in an Age of Nascent Capitalism.* New York.

1987. *Reproducing Families: The Political Economy of English Population History.* Cambridge.

Levine, R. 1997. Financial development and economic growth: views and agenda. *Journal of Economic Literature* 35: 701–9.

Lewis, W. J. 1967. *Lead Mining in Wales.* Cardiff.

Li, M.-H. 1963. *The Great Recoinage of 1696 to 1699.*

Libecap, G. D. 1986. Property rights in economic history: implications for research. *Explorations in Economic History* 23: 227–52.

Lindert, P. 1984. Unequal living standards. In Floud and McCloskey 1994.

2001. Democracy, decentralization, and mass schooling before 1914. Working Paper Series 104. Agricultural History Center, University of California, Davis.

Lindert, P. H. and Williamson, J. G. 1982. Revising England's social tables 1688–1812. *Explorations in Economic History* 19: 385–402.

1983a. English workers' living standards during the Industrial Revolution: a new look. *Economic History Review* 361: 1–25.

1983b. Reinterpreting Britain's social tables, 1688–1913. *Explorations in Economic History* 20: 94–109.

Lloyd-Jones, R. and Le Roux, A. A. 1980. The size of firms in the cotton industry, Manchester 1815–1841. *Economic History Review* 33: 72–82.

1982. Marshall and the birth and death of firms: the growth and size distribution of firms in the early nineteenth-century cotton industry. *Business History* 14: 141–55.

Lloyd-Jones, R. and Lewis, M. J. 1998. *British Industrial Capitalism since the Industrial Revolution.*

Loudon, I. 1992. *Death in Childbirth: An International Study of Maternal Care and Maternal Mortality 1800–1950.* Oxford.

Lucas, Robert E. 2002. *Lectures on Economic Growth.* Cambridge, MA.

Lynch, Michael 1989. Continuity and change in urban society, 1500–1700. In Houston and Whyte 1989.

1992. Urbanisation and urban networks in seventeenth century scotland. *Scottish Economic and Social History* 12: 24–41.

Lyons, J. 1989. Family response to economic decline: handloom weavers in early nineteenth century Lancashire. *Research in Economic History* 12: 45–91.

McClelland, P. D. 1969. The cost to America of British imperial policy. *American Economic Review: Papers and Proceedings* 59: 370–81.

McCloskey, D. N. 1972. The enclosure of open fields: preface to a study of its impact on the efficiency of English agriculture in the eighteenth century. *Journal of Economic History* 32: 15–35.

1975. The economics of enclosure: a market analysis. In Parker and Jones 1975.

1980. Magnanimous Albion: free trade and British national income, 1841/1881. *Explorations in Economic History* 17: 303–20.

1981. The industrial revolution 1780–1860: a survey. In Floud and McCloskey 1981.

1985. The Industrial Revolution 1780–1860: a survey. In Mokyr 1985.

1989. The open fields of England: rent, risk, and the rate of interest, 1300–1815. In D. Galenson, ed., *Markets in History: Economic Studies of the Past.* Cambridge.

1994. 1780–1860: a survey. In Floud and McCloskey 1994.

McCracken, G. 1988. *Culture and Consumption.* Bloomington, IN.

McCusker, J. J. and Menard, R. R. 1985. *The Economy of British North America, 1607–1789.* Chapel Hill.

MacDonagh, O. 1958. Delegated legislation and administrative discretions in the 1850's: a particular study. *Victorian Studies* 1: 29–44.

  1961. *A Pattern of Government Growth, 1800–60: The Passenger Acts and Their Enforcement.*

McEvedy, C. and Jones, R. 1978. *Atlas of World Population History.*

Macinnes, A. I. 1996. *Clanship, Commerce and the House of Stuart, 1603–1788.* East Linton.

Mackelworth, R. 1999. Trades, crafts and credit in a Victorian village: a trading family in Milford, Surrey, 1851–1881. *Family and Community History* 2: 33–43.

McKendrick, N. 1961. Josiah Wedgwood and factory discipline. *Historical Journal* 4: 30–55.

  1973. The role of science in the Industrial Revolution. In M. Teich and R. Young, eds., *Changing Perspectives in the History of Science.*

  1974a. Home demand and economic growth: a new view of the role of women and children in the industrial revolution. In McKendrick 1974b.

McKendrick, N., ed. 1974b. *Historical Perspectives: Essays in English Thought and Society.*

  1982. Josiah Wedgwood and the commercialisation of the Potteries. In McKendrick *et al.* 1982.

McKendrick, N., Brewer, J. and Plumb, J. 1982. *The Birth of Consumer Society: The Commercialization of Eighteenth-Century England.*

McKendrick, N. and Outhwaite, R. B., eds. 1986. *Business Life and Public Policy.* Cambridge.

MacKenzie, J. M. 1995. *Orientalism, History, Theory and the Arts.* Manchester.

McLean, I. and Foster, C. 1992. The political economy of regulation: interests, ideology, voters, and the UK Regulation of Railways Act 1844. *Public Administration* 70: 313–31.

McLean, T. 1995. Contract accounting and costing in the Sunderland shipbuilding industry, 1818–1917. *Accounting Business and Financial History* 5: 109–45.

MacLeod, C. 1988. *Inventing the Industrial Revolution: The English Patent System, 1660–1800.* Cambridge.

Maddison, A. 1982. *Phases of Capitalist Development.* Oxford.

  1991. *Dynamic Forces in Capitalist Development.* Oxford.

  2001. *The World Economy: A Millennial Perspective.* Paris.

Maizels, A. 1963. *Industrial Growth and World Trade.* Cambridge.

Malcolmson, R. W. 1988. Ways of getting a living in eighteenth century England. In R. E. Pahl, ed., *On Work.* Oxford.

Malthus, T. R. 1986a. *An Essay on the Principle of Population as It Affects the Future Improvement of Society with Remarks on the Speculations of Mr Godwin, M. Condorcet and Other Writers* [1798], in *The Works of Thomas Robert Malthus,* I, ed. E. A. Wrigley and D. Souden.

  1986b. *An Essay on the Principle of Population; or a View of Its Past and Present Effects on Human Happiness,* 6th edn [1826], in *The Works of Thomas Robert Malthus,* II and III, ed. E. A. Wrigley and D. Souden.

Mandemakers, C. A. and Van Zanden, J. L. 1993. The height of conscripts and national income: apparent relations and misconceptions. *Explorations in Economic History* 301: 81–97.

Mandeville, B. 1714. *The Fable of the Bees.*

Mandler, P. 1987. The making of the New Poor Law redivivus. *Past and Present* 117: 131–57.

  1990. Tories and paupers: Christian political economy and the making of the New Poor Law. *Historical Journal* 33: 81–103.

Mann, J. de L. 1958. The textile industry: machinery for cotton, flax, wool, 1760–1850. In Singer *et al.* 1958.

1971. *The Cloth Industry of the West of England from 1640 to 1880.* Oxford.

Mantoux, P. 1905. *La Révolution industrielle au XVIIIe siècle.* Paris.

1961 [1928]. *The Industrial Revolution in the Eighteenth Century: An Outline of the Beginnings of the Modern Factory System in England.*

Marglin, S. A. 1974. What do bosses do? The origins and functions of hierarchy in capitalist production. *Review of Radical Political Economy* 6: 60–112.

Mariscal, E. and Sokoloff, K. 2000. Schooling, suffrage, and the persistence of inequality in the Americas, 1800–1945. In S. Haber, ed., *Political Institutions and Economic Growth in Latin America.* Stanford.

Marriner, S. 1986. English bankruptcy records and statistics before 1850. *Economic History Review* 33: 351–66.

Marshall, A. 1890. *Principles of Economics*, 8th edition 1949.

1921. *Industry and Trade: A Study of Industrial Technique and Business Organisation*, 2nd edn.

Marshall, J. D. 1989. Stages of industrialisation in Cumbria. In Hudson 1989.

Marshall, K. 1958. *Furness and the Industrial Revolution.* Barrow-in-Furness.

Marshall, P. J., ed. 1998. *The Eighteenth Century.* Oxford.

Marshall, W. 1788. *The Rural Economy of Yorkshire.*

Martin, J. M. 1984. Village traders and the emergence of a proletariat in south Warwickshire. *Agricultural History Review* 32: 179–88.

Massey, D. 1995. Places and their pasts. *History Workshop Journal* 39: 182–92.

Mathias, Peter 1953. An industrial revolution in brewing, 1700–1830. *Explorations in Entrepreneurial History* 5; repr. in Mathias 1979a.

1979a. *The Transformation of England: Essays in the Economic and Social History of England in the Eighteenth Century.*

1979b. The social structure in the eighteenth century: a calculation by Joseph Massie. In Mathias 1979a.

1983. *The First Industrial Nation.*

Mathias, P. and O'Brien, P. 1976. Taxation in Britain and France, 1715–1810. A comparison of the social and economic incidence of taxes collected for the central governments. *The Journal of European Economic History* 5: 601–40.

Matthews, R. C. O., Feinstein, C. H. and Odling-Smee, J. C. 1982. *British Economic Growth 1856–1973.* Oxford.

Maynes, M. J. 1985. *Schooling in Western Europe: A Social History.* Albany, NY.

Meade, R. 1882. *The Coal and Iron Industries in the United Kingdom.*

Medick, H. 1976. The proto-industrial family economy: the structural function of household and family during the transition from peasant society to industrial capitalism. *Social History* 3: 291–316.

1982. Plebeian culture in the transition to capitalism. In R. Samuel and G. Stedman Jones, eds., *Culture, Ideology and Politics.*

Melton, F. 1986. *Sir Robert Clayton and the Origins of English Deposit Banking.* Cambridge.

Menard, R. 1996. Transport costs and long-range trade, 1300–1800: was there a European transport revolution in the early modern era? In D. A. Irwin, ed., *Trade in the Pre-Modern Era, 1400–1700.* Cheltenham.

Mendels, F. 1972. Protoindustrialization: the first phase of the industrialization process. *Journal of Economic History* 32: 241–61.

1975. Agriculture and peasant industry in eighteenth century Flanders. In Parker and Jones 1975.

Mennell, S. 1989. *Norbert Elias: Civilization and the Human Self-Image.* Oxford.

Michie, R. C. 1999. *The London Stock Exchange: A History.* Oxford.

Midgley, C. 1992. *Women against Slavery: The British Campaigns 1780–1870.*

Mill, John Stuart 1861 [reprinted, 1958]. Of Local Representative Bodies in *Considerations on Representative Government.*

Miller, D. 1995. *Acknowledging Consumption: A Review of New Studies.*

Minchinton, W. E. 1957. *The British Tin Plate Industry: A History.* Oxford.

Minchinton, W. E., ed. 1969. *The Growth of English Overseas Trade in the Seventeenth and Eighteenth Centuries.*

The Mineral Statistics of the United Kingdom of Great Britain and Ireland 1853, 1856, 1858.

Mingay, G. E., ed. 1989. *The Agrarian History of England and Wales,* VI, *1750–1850.* Cambridge.

Mintz, S. W. 1985. *Sweetness and Power.* New York.

1993. The changing roles of food in the study of consumption. In Brewer and Porter 1993.

Mitch, D. 1982. The spread of literacy in nineteenth-century England. Unpublished PhD dissertation, University of Chicago.

1984. Underinvestment in literacy? The potential contribution of government involvement in elementary education to economic growth in nineteenth-century England. *Journal of Economic History* 44: 557–66.

1992. *The Rise of Popular Literacy in Victorian England.* Philadelphia.

1993a. 'Inequalities which every one may remove': occupational recruitment, endogamy, and the homogeneity of social origins in Victorian England. In A. Miles and D. Vincent, eds., *Building European Society: Occupational Change and Social Mobility in Europe, 1840–1940.* Manchester.

1993b. The role of human capital in the first Industrial Revolution. In Mokyr 1993.

1994. Learning by doing among Victorian farmworkers: a case study in the biological and cognitive foundations of skill acquisition. London School of Economics and Political Science Working Papers in Economic History 16/94.

1999. The role of education and skill in the British Industrial Revolution. In Mokyr 1999.

Mitchell, B. R. 1964. The coming of the railway and United Kingdom economic growth. *Journal of Economic History* 24: 315–36.

1975. *European Historical Statistics, 1750–1970.*

1981. *European Historical Statistics 1750–1975,* 2nd rev. edn.

1984. *Economic Development of the British Coal Industry 1800–1914.* Cambridge.

1988. *British Historical Statistics.* Cambridge.

Mitchell, B. R. and Deane, P. 1962. *Abstract of British Historical Statistics.* Cambridge.

Mokyr, J. 1983. Three centuries of population change. *Economic Development and Cultural Change* 32: 183–92.

1987. Has the Industrial Revolution been crowded out? Some reflections on Crafts and Williamson. *Explorations in Economic History* 24: 293–319.

1988. Is there still life in the pessimist case? Consumption during the Industrial Revolution, 1790–1850. *Journal of Economic History* 481: 69–92.

1990. *The Lever of Riches: Technological Creativity and Economic Progress.* New York.

1994. Technological change, 1700–1830. In Floud and McCloskey 1994.

2000. The Industrial Revolution and the Netherlands: why did it not happen? *De Economist* (Amsterdam) 148: 503–20.

2002. *The Gifts of Athena: Historical Origins of the Knowledge Economy.* Princeton.

Forthcoming. *The Enlightened Economy: An Economic History of Britain, 1700–1850.* Harmondsworth: in preparation.

Mokyr, J., ed. 1985. *The Economics of the Industrial Revolution.* Totowa, NJ.

1993. *The British Industrial Revolution: An Economic Perspective.* Boulder, CO.

1999. *The British Industrial Revolution: An Economic Perspective,* 2nd edn. Boulder, CO.

Morgan, K. 1999. *The Birth of Industrial Britain: Economic Change 1750–1850.*

2000. *Slavery, Atlantic Trade and the British Economy, 1660–1800.* Cambridge.

Morgan, V. 1971. Agricultural wage rates in late eighteenth century Scotland. *Economic History Review* 24: 181–201.

Morris, M. 1997. *Measuring the Condition of the World's Poor: The Physical Quality of Life Index.* New York.

Morris, R. J. 1990. *Class, Sect and Party: The Making of the British Middle Class, Leeds, 1820–50*.

Moses, G. 1999. Proletarian labourers: East Riding farm servants c. 1850–1875. *Agricultural History Review* 47: 78–94.

Mueller, R. 1997. *The Venetian Money Market: Banks, Panics, and the Public Debt 1200–1500*. Baltimore.

Mugridge, A. J. 2001. *The Broseley Heavy Clay Industry, with Particular Reference to the District's Brickyards and Roofing Tile Manufactories*. Telford.

Mui, H. and Mui, L. H. 1975. Trends in eighteenth-century smuggling reconsidered. *Economic History Review* 28: 28–43.

 1989. *Shops and Shopkeeping in Eighteenth-Century England*.

Muldrew, C. 1993. Credit and the courts: debt litigation in a seventeenth-century urban community. *Economic History Review* 46: 23–38.

 1998. *The Economy of Obligation: The Culture of Credit and Social Relations in Early Modern England*.

Munro, J. 2000. English backwardness and financial innovations in commerce with the Low Countries, 14th to 16th centuries. In P. Stabel, B. Blondée and A. Greve, eds., *International Trade in the Low Countries (14th – 16th Centuries): Merchants, Organisation, Infrastructure*. Leuven-Apeldoorn.

Murphy, A. 1986. *Richard Cantillon: Entrepreneur and Economist*. Oxford.

Musson, A. E. and Robinson, E. 1969. *Science and Technology in the Industrial Revolution*. Manchester.

Nardinelli, C. 1980. Child Labor and the Factory Acts. *Journal of Economic History* 404: 739–55.

 1990. *Child Labor and the Industrial Revolution*. Bloomington, IN.

Neal, L. 1990. *The Rise of Financial Capitalism: International Capital Markets in the Age of Reason*. Cambridge.

 1994. The finance of business during the Industrial Revolution. In Floud and McCloskey 1994.

 1998. The financial crisis of 1825 and the restructuring of the British financial system. *Federal Reserve Bank of St. Louis Review* 80: 53–76.

 2000. How it all began: the monetary and financial architecture of Europe during the first global capital markets, 1648–1815. *Financial History Review* 7: 117–40.

Neal, L. and Quinn, S. 2001. Networks of information, markets, and institutions in the rise of London as a financial centre, 1660–1720. *Financial History Review* 8: 7–26.

Neeson, J. M. 1989. Parliamentary enclosure and the disappearance of the English peasantry, revisited. In G. Grantham and C. Leonard, eds., *Agrarian Organization in the Century of Industrialization*. New York.

 1993. *Commoners: Common Right, Enclosure and Social Change in England, 1700–1820*. Cambridge.

Nef, J. U. 1932. *The Rise of the British Coal Industry*, 2 vols.

Nelson, R. 1995. Recent evolutionary theorising about economic change. *Journal of Economic Literature* 33: 48–91.

Nenadic, Stana, 1988. The rise of the urban middle classes. In Devine and Mitchison 1988.

 1994. Middle rank consumers and domestic culture in Edinburgh and Glasgow, 1720–1840. *Past and Present* 145: 122–56.

 1997. Print collecting and popular culture in eighteenth-century Scotland. *History* 82: 203–22.

Newell, E. 1997. Atmospheric pollution and the British copper industry, 1690–1920. *Technology and Culture* 38: 655–89.

Newton, I. 1702. Report of the Officers of the Mint about the Preservation of the Coyne. Reprinted in W. A. Shaw, *Select Tracts and Documents Illustrative of English Monetary History 1626–1730*.

Newton, L. 1996. Regional bank–industry relationships during the mid nineteenth century: links between bankers and manufacturers in Sheffield, c. 1850–1855. *Business History* 38: 64–83.

1998. English banking concentration and internationalisation: contemporary debate, 1880–1920. In S. Kinsey and L. Newton, eds., *International Banking in the Age of Transition*. Brookfield, VT.

2000. Trust and virtue in English banking: the assessment of borrowers by bank managements at the turn of the nineteenth century. *Financial History Review* 7: 177–99.

Newton, L. and Cottrell, P. L. 1998. Joint-stock banking in the English provinces 1826–1857: to branch or not to branch? *Business and Economic History* 27: 115–28.

Nicholas, S. J. and Nicholas, J. 1992. Male literacy, 'deskilling', and the Industrial Revolution. *Journal of Interdisciplinary History* 23: 1–18.

Nicholas, S. and Steckel, R. H. 1991. Heights and living standards of English workers during the early years of industrialization, 1770–1815. *Journal of Economic History* 514: 937–57.

Nishimura, S. 1971. *The Decline of Inland Bills of Exchange in the London Money Market 1855–1913*. Cambridge.

Nooteboom, B. 2000. *Learning and Innovation in Organisations and Economics*. Oxford.

Nordhaus, William 1997. Do real-output and real-wage measures capture reality? The history of lighting suggests not. In Bresnahan and Gordon 1997.

North, D. C. 1958. Ocean freight rates and economic development, 1750–1913. *Journal of Economic History* 18: 537–55.

1981. *Structure and Change in Economic History*. New York.

1990. *Institutions, Institutional Change, and Economic Performance*. Cambridge.

North, D. and Weingast, B. 1989. Constitutions and commitment: the evolution of institutions governing public choice in seventeenth-century England. *Journal of Economic History* 49: 803–32.

Nuvolari, A. 2001. Collective invention during the British industrial revolution: the case of the Cornish pumping engine. Research Paper, Eindhoven Centre for Innovation Studies.

Nye, J. V. 1991. The myth of free-trade Britain and fortress France: tariffs and trade in the nineteenth century. *Journal of Economic History* 51: 23–46.

O'Brien, K. 1997. *Narrative of Enlightenment: Cosmopolitan History from Voltaire to Gibbon*. Cambridge.

O'Brien, P. K. 1977. *The New Economic History of the Railways*.

1982. European economic development: the contribution of the periphery. *Economic History Review* 100: 773–800.

1985. Agriculture and the home market. *English Historical Review* 41: 1–33.

1988. The political economy of British taxation, 1660–1815. *Economic History Review* 41: 1–32.

1991. The foundations of European industrialization: from the perspective of the world. *Journal of Historical Sociology* 4: 1–40.

1994. Central government and the economy, 1688–1815. In Floud and McCloskey 1994.

1997. Intercontinental trade and the development of the Third World since the Industrial Revolution. *Journal of World History* 8: 75–133.

1998. Inseparable connections: trade, economy, fiscal state, and the expansion of empire, 1688–1815. In P. J. Marshall, ed., *The Oxford History of the British Empire, II: The Eighteenth Century*. Oxford.

1999. Imperialism and the rise and decline of the British economy, 1688–1989. *New Left Review* 238: 48–80.

2000. Mercantilism and imperialism in the rise and decline of the Dutch and British economies. *De Economist* 148: 469–501.

O'Brien, P. K. and Engerman, S. 1981. Changes in income and its distribution during the industrial revolution. In Floud and McCloskey 1981.

1991. Exports and the growth of the British economy from the Glorious Revolution to the Peace of Amiens. In Solow 1991b.

O'Brien, P. K., Griffiths, T. and Hunt, P. 1996. Technological change during the first industrial revolution: the paradigm case of textiles, 1688–1851. In R. Fox, ed., *Technological Change: Methods and Themes in the History of Technology*. Amsterdam.

O'Brien, P. K. and Keyder, C. 1978. *Economic Growth in Britain and France, 1780–1914: Two Paths to the Twentieth Century*.

O'Brien, P. K. and Prados de la Escosura, L., eds. 1998. The costs and benefits of European imperialism from the conquest of Ceuta, 1415 to the Treaty of Lusaka, 1974. *Revista de Historia Económica* 16: 29–89.

O'Day, R. 1982. *Education and Society, 1500–1800*.

Oeppen, J. 1993a. Back projection and inverse projection: members of a wider class of constrained projection models. *Population Studies* 47: 245–67.

1993b. Generalised inverse projection. In D. S. Reher and R. S. Schofield, eds., *Old and New Methods in Historical Demography*. Liège.

2000. Reconstructing England's demographic history: a comparison of the results from generalised inverse projection and family reconstitution. Paper presented to Workshop on Inverse Projection Techniques. Sabaudia, Italy, 25–27 May 2000.

Officer, L. H. 2002. What was the gold price then? *Economic History Services*, EH.Net. URL: http://www.eh.net/hmit/goldprice/

Ogden, T. 1991. An analysis of the Bank of England's discount and advance behavior 1870–1914. In Foreman-Peck 1991.

Ogilvie, S. 1993. Proto-industrialisation in Europe. *Continuity and Change* 8: 159–79.

O'Gráda, C. 1993. *Ireland before and after the Famine: Explorations in Economic History, 1800–1925*, 2nd edn. Manchester.

Ohlin, G. 1955. The positive and the preventive check: a study of the rate of growth of pre-industrial populations. Unpublished PhD thesis, University of Harvard.

Olson, M. 1963. *The Economics of Wartime Shortage: A History of British Food Supplies in the Napoleonic Wars and in World Wars I and II*. Durham, NC.

1982. *The Rise and Decline of Nations: Economic Growth, Stagflation and Social Rigidities*. New Haven.

Oren, L. 1974. The welfare of women in labouring families: England, 1860–1950. In M. Hartman and L. Banner, eds., *Clio's Consciousness Raised*. New York.

O'Rourke, K. and Williamson, J. G. 1999. *Globalization and History: The Evolution of a Nineteenth-Century Atlantic Economy*. Cambridge, Mass.

Orth, J. V. 1991. *Combination and Conspiracy: A Legal History of Trade Unionism, 1721–1906*. Oxford.

Overton, Mark 1991. The determinants of crop yields. In Campbell and Overton 1991.

1996a. *Agricultural Revolution in England: The Transformation of the Agrarian Economy 1500–1800*. Cambridge.

1996b. Re-establishing the Agricultural Revolution. *Agricultural History Review* 44: 1–20.

2000. Geographies of consumption in early modern England. Paper to the Conference on Georgian Geographies, Paul Mellon Centre.

Palmer, S. 1973. Investors in London shipping, 1820–50. *Maritime History* 2: 42–68.

Pannabecker, John R. 1998. Representing mechanical arts in Diderot's *Encyclopédie*. *Technology and Culture* 39: 33–73.

Parker, I. 1969 [1914]. *Dissenting Academies in England*. Cambridge.

Parker, W. N. and Jones, E. L., eds. 1975. *European Peasants and Their Markets*. Princeton.

Parris, H. 1960. Railway policy in Peel's administration, 1841–1846. *Bulletin of the Institute of Historical Research* 33: 180–94.

Parsons, T. 1959. The social structure of the family. In R. Anshen, ed., *The Family: Its Functions and Destiny*. Chicago.

Parsons, T. and Bales, R. F. 1965. *Family, Socialisation and the Interactive Process*. Glencoe, IL.

Pawson, E. 1977. *Transport and Economy: The Turnpike Roads of Eighteenth Century Britain*.

Pearson, R. 1991. Collective diversification: Manchester cotton merchants and the insurance business in the early nineteenth century. *Business History Review* 65: 379–414.

　　1993. Taking risks and containing competition: diversification and oligopoly in the fire insurance markets of the north of England in the early nineteenth century. *Economic History Review* 46: 39–64.

Pearson, R. and Richardson, D. 2001. Business networking in the industrial revolution. *Economic History Review* 54: 657–79.

Pember-Reeves, M. 1913. *Round about a Pound a Week*.

Penrose, E. T. 1959. *The Theory of the Growth of the Firm*. Oxford.

Perry, C. R. 1997. The rise and fall of government telegraphy in Britain. *Business and Economic History* 26: 416–25.

Pinchbeck, I. 1969 [1930]. *Women Workers and the Industrial Revolution 1750–1850*. New York.

Pinchbeck, I. and Hewitt, M. 1973. *Children in English Society*.

Piore, M. and Sabel, C. 1984. *The Second Industrial Divide*. New York.

Plot, R. 1677. *The Natural History of Oxfordshire*. Oxford.

Pohs, H. A. 1995. *The Miner's Flame Light*. Denver.

Pollard, S. 1964. Fixed capital in the Industrial Revolution in Britain. *Journal of Economic History* 24: 299–314.

　　1965. *The Genesis of Modern Management: A Study of the Industrial Revolution in Great Britain*.

　　1980. A new estimate of British coal production, 1750–1850. *Economic History Review* 33: 212–35.

　　1981. *Peaceful Conquest: The Industrialization of Europe 1760–1970*. Oxford.

Pollard, S. and Ziegler, D. 1992. Banking and industrialization: Rondo Cameron twenty years on. In Y. Cassis, ed., *Finance and Financiers in European History 1880–1980*. Cambridge.

Pomeranz, K. 2000. *The Great Divergence: China, Europe, and the Making of the Modern World Economy*. Princeton.

Porter, R. 1977. *The Making of Geology: Earth Science in Britain 1660–1815*. Cambridge.

Posner, R. A. 1998. *Economic Analysis of Law*. New York.

Postan, M. M. 1935. Recent trends in the accumulation of capital. *Economic History Review* 6: 1–12.

Postlethwayt, M. 1774 [1751], 4th edn; repr. 1971. The British Mercantile College, humbly submitted to public consideration in his *The Universal Dictionary of Trade and Commerce*. New York.

Prados de la Escosura, L. 2000. International comparisons of real product, 1820–1990: an alternative data set. *Explorations in Economic History* 37: 1–41.

Prados de la Escosura, L., ed., 2003. *British Exceptionalism: A Unique Path to the Industrial Revolution*. Cambridge.

Pressnell, L. 1956. *Country Banking in the Industrial Revolution*. Oxford.

Preston, S. H., Keyfitz, N. and Schoen, R. 1972. *Causes of Death: Life Tables for National Populations*. New York.

Price, Derek J. de Solla 1984. Notes towards a philosophy of the science/technology interaction. In R. Laudan, ed., *The Nature of Knowledge: Are Models of Scientific Change Relevant?* Dordrecht.

Price, J. M. 1964. Economic growth of the Chesapeake and the European market, 1697–1775. *Journal of Economic History* 24: 496–511.

1973. *France and the Chesapeake*. Ann Arbor.

1980. *Capital and Credit in British Overseas Trade: The View from the Chesapeake, 1770–1776*. Cambridge, MA.

1984. Glasgow, the tobacco trade and the Scottish Customs, 1707–1730. *Scottish Historical Review* 63: 1–36.

1989. What did merchants do? Reflections on British overseas trade, 1660–1790. *Journal of Economic History* 44: 267–83.

Price, L. L. F. R. 1891. *West Barbary; or Notes on the System of Work and Wages in the Cornish Mines*. Reprinted in Burt 1977.

Prior, A. and Kirby, M. W. 1993. The Society of Friends and the family firm, 1700–1830. *Business History* 35: 66–85.

Quinn, S. 1996. Gold, silver, and the Glorious Revolution: arbitrage between bills of exchange and bullion. *Economic History Review* 44: 473–90.

1997. Goldsmith-banking: mutual acceptance and inter-banker clearing in Restoration London. *Explorations in Economic History* 34: 411–32.

2001. The Glorious Revolution's effect on English private finance: a microhistory, 1680–1705. *Journal of Economic History* 61: 593–615.

Raistrick, A. and Jennings, B. 1965. *A History of Lead Mining in the Pennines*.

Randall, A. J. 1989. Work, culture and resistance to machinery in the West of England woollen industry. In Hudson 1989.

Rappaport, Steve 1989. *Worlds within Worlds: Structures of Life in Sixteenth-Century London*. Cambridge.

Razzell, P. 1993. The growth of population in eighteenth-century England: a critical reappraisal. *Journal of Economic History* 53: 743–71.

1994. *Essays in English Population History*.

Reay, B. 1991. The context and meaning of popular literacy: some evidence from nineteenth-century rural England. *Past and Present* 131: 89–121.

Redish, A. 1990. The evolution of the gold standard in England. *Journal of Economic History* 50: 789–805.

2000. *Bimetallism: An Economic and Historical Analysis*. Cambridge.

Reed. M. C. 1999. Railway investment. In R. W. Ambler, ed., *The History and Practice of Britain's Railways: A New Research Agenda*. Aldershot.

2000. The transformation of urban space, 1700–1840. In P. Clark, ed., *The Cambridge Urban History of Britain*, II. Cambridge.

Rees, D. M. 1969. *Mines, Mills and Furnaces*.

Rees, R. 2000. *King Copper: South Wales and the Copper Trade 1584–1895*. Cardiff.

Reid, D. 1976. The decline of St. Monday, 1776–1876. *Past and Present* 71: 76–100.

1996. Weddings, weekdays, work and leisure in urban England 1791–1911. *Past and Present* 153: 76–101.

Reynard, P. C. 2000. Manufacturing quality in the pre-industrial age: finding value in diversity. *Economic History Review* 53: 493–516.

Ricardo, D. 1951 [1817]. *On the Principles of Political Economy and Taxation*. In *The Works and Correspondence of David Ricardo*, I, ed. P. Sraffa with the collaboration of M. H. Dobb. Cambridge.

Richards, E. 1974. Women in the British economy since about 1700: an interpretation. *History* 59: 337–57.

Richards, S. 1999. *Eighteenth-Century Ceramics: Products for a Civilized Society*. Manchester.

Riden, P. 1977. The output of the British iron industry before 1870. *Economic History Review* 30: 442–59.

Roberts, E. 1988. *Women's Work 1840–1880*. Basingstoke.

Robey, J. A. and Porter, L., eds. 1972. *The Copper and Lead Mines of Ecton Hill, Staffordshire*. Leek.

Robinson, E. 1964. Eighteenth-century commerce and fashion: Matthew Boulton's marketing techniques. *Economic History Review* 16: 39–60.

1987. Matthew Boulton and Josiah Wedgwood: apostles of fashion. In Davenport-Hines and Liebenau 1987.

Rodger, R. 1985. Employment, wages and poverty in Scottish cities, 1841–1914, appendix 1. In G. Gordon, ed., *Perspectives of the Scottish City*. Aberdeen.

Rogers, J. 1988. *Family Reconstitution: New Information or Misinformation?* Reports from the Family History Group, Department of History, 7. Uppsala.

1995. *The Early History of the Law of Bills and Notes*. Cambridge.

Rogers, J. E. T. 1866–1902. *A History of Agriculture and Prices in England*. Oxford.

Roll, E. 1930. *An Early Experiment in Industrial Organisation: Being a History of the Firm of Boulton and Watt, 1775–1804*. New York.

Rollison, D. 1992. *The Local Origins of Modern Society: Gloucestershire 1500–1800*.

Rolt, L. T. C. 1980. *Victorian Engineering*. Harmondsworth.

Rose, M. E. 1989. Social policy and business: parish apprentices and the early factory system, 1750–1834. *Business History* 21: 5–32.

2000. *Firms, Networks and Business Values: The British and American Cotton Industries since 1750*. Cambridge.

Rose, S. O. 1988. Proto-industry, women's work and the household economy in the transition to industrial capitalism. *Journal of Family History* 13: 181–93.

1992. *Limited Livelihoods: Gender and Class in Nineteenth-Century England*.

Rosenberg, N. 1974. Science, invention and economic growth. *Economic Journal* 84: 90–108.

Rosenberg, N. and Vincenti, W. 1978. *The Britannia Bridge*. Cambridge, Mass.

Roseveare, H. 1973. *The Treasury, 1660–1870: The Foundations of Control*.

1991. *The Financial Revolution 1660–1760*.

Ross, E. 1993. *Love and Toil: Motherhood in Outcast London 1870–1918*. Oxford.

Rostow, W. W. 1960. *The Stages of Economic Growth*. Cambridge.

Rowe, D. J. 1983. *Lead Manufacturing in Britain: A History*.

Rowe, J. 1993. *Cornwall in the Age of the Industrial Revolution*. St Austell.

Rowland, J. 1981. *Copper Mountain*. Llangefni.

Rowlands, M. B. 1975. *Masters and Men in the West Midland Metalware Trades before the Industrial Revolution*. Manchester.

1989. Continuity and change in an industrialising society: the case study of the West Midlands. In Hudson 1989.

Rudden, B. 1985. *The New River: A Legal History*. Oxford.

Ruggles, S. 1987. *Prolonged Connections: The Rise of the Extended Family in Nineteenth-Century England and America*. Madison.

1992. Migration, marriage, and mortality: correcting sources of bias in English family reconstitution. *Population Studies* 46: 507–22.

Rushton, P. 1991. The matter in variance: adolescents and domestic conflict in the pre-industrial economy of northeast England, 1600–1850. *Journal of Social History* 25: 89–107.

Sabel, C. and Zeitlin, J. 1985. Historical alternatives to mass production. *Past and Present* 108: 133–76.

Salzman, L. F., ed. 1938. *The Victoria County History of the County of Cambridgeshire and the Isle of Ely*.

Samuel, R. 1977. Workshop of the world: steam power and hand technology in mid Victorian Britain. *History Workshop* 3: 6–72.

Sandberg, L. and Steckel, R. 1997. Was industrialization hazardous to your health? Not in Sweden. In Steckel and Floud 1997.

Sanderson, M. 1972a. Literacy and social mobility in the Industrial Revolution in England. *Past and Present* 56: 75–104.

1972b. *The Universities and British Industry, 1850–1972*.

Sargent, T. and Velde, F. 1999. The big problem of small change. *Journal of Money, Credit, and Banking* 31: 137–61.

Saul, S. B. 1970. *Technological Change: The United States and Britain in the 19th Century.*

Savage, M. 1987. *The Dynamics of Working Class Politics.* Cambridge.

Saviotti, P. 1996. *Technical Evolution, Variety and the Economy.* Cheltenham.

Schmiechen, J. A. 1984. *Sweated Industries and Sweated Labour: The London Clothing Trades.* Urbana, IL.

Schmitz, C. J. 1978. Capital formation and technological change in south-west England metal mining in the nineteenth century. In W. E. Minchinton, ed., *Capital Formation in South West England.* Exeter.

1979. *World Non-Ferrous Metal Production and Prices, 1700–1976.*

Schmookler, J. 1962. Economic sources of inventive activity. *Journal of Economic History* 22: 1–20.

1966. *Invention and Economic Growth.* Cambridge, MA.

Schofield, R. 1973. Dimensions of illiteracy, 1750–1850. *Explorations in Economic History* 10: 437–54.

1985. English marriage patterns revisited. *Journal of Family History* 10: 2–20.

1986. Did the mothers really die? Three centuries of maternal mortality. In Bonfield *et al.* 1986.

1989. Family structure, demographic behaviour, and economic growth. In J. Walter and R. Schofield, eds., *Famine, Disease and the Social Order in Early Modern Society.* Cambridge.

1994. British population change, 1700–1871. In Floud and McCloskey 1994.

Schumpeter, E. 1960. *English Overseas Trade Statistics 1697–1808.*

Schumpeter, J. 1989. *Business Cycles: A Theoretical, Historical and Statistical Analysis of the Capitalist Process.* Philadelphia.

Schurer, K. 1992. Variations in household structure in the late seventeenth century: towards a regional analysis. In K. Schurer and T. Arkell, *Surveying the People.* Oxford.

Schwartz, L. D. 1985. The standard of living in the long run: London 1700–1860. *Economic History Review* 38: 24–41.

1992. *London in the Age of Industrialization: Entrepreneurs, Labour Force and Living Conditions, 1700–1850.* Cambridge.

1999. English servants and their employers during the eighteenth and nineteenth centuries. *Economic History Review* 52: 236–56.

Schwartz, P. 1966. John Stuart Mill and laissez faire: London water. *Economica* 33: 71–83.

Scott, K. 1995. *The Rococo Interior.* New Haven.

Seccombe, W. 1992. *A Millennium of Family Change: Feudalism to Capitalism in North West Europe.*

1993. *Weathering the Storm: Working-Class Families from the Industrial Revolution to the Fertility Decline.*

Seed. J. 1982. Unitarianism, political economy and the antinomies of liberal culture in Manchester. *Social History* 7: 1–25.

1986. Theologies of power: unitarianism and the social relations of religious discourse. In R. J. Morris, ed., *Class, Power and Social Structure in British Nineteenth Century Towns.*

Shammas, C. 1984. Eighteenth-century English diet and economic change. *Explorations in Entrepreneurial History* 21: 254–69.

1990. *The Pre-industrial Consumer in England and America.* Oxford.

1993. Changes in English and Anglo-American consumption from 1550–1800. In Brewer and Porter 1993.

Shapin, Steven 1996. *The Scientific Revolution.* Chicago.

Sharpe, P. 1994. The women's harvest: straw plaiting and the representation of labouring women's employment *c* 1793–1885. *Rural History* 5: 129–42.

1999. The female labour market in English agriculture during the industrial revolution: expansion or contraction. *Agricultural History Review* 47: 161–81.

2002. *Population and Society in an East Devon Parish: Reproducing Colyton, 1540–1840.* Exeter.

Shaw, C. 1903. *When I Was a Child.*

Shaw-Taylor, L. 2001. Parliamentary enclosure and the emergence of an English agricultural proletariat. *Journal of Economic History* 61: 640–62.

Shepherd, J. F. and Walton, G. M. 1972. *Shipping, Maritime Trade, and the Economic Development of Colonial North America.* Cambridge.

Sheridan, R. B. 1974. *Sugar and Slavery: An Economic History of the British West Indies, 1623–1775.* Baltimore.

Short, B. 1984. The decline of living-in servants in the transition to capitalist farming, a critique of the evidence. *Sussex Archaeological Collection* 122: 147–64.

Sigsworth, E. 1959. *Black Dyke Mills: a history.* Liverpool.

Simon, J. 1968. Was there a charity school movement? in Brian Simon (ed.), *Education in Leicestershire, 1540–1940.* Leicester.

Simpson, A. W. B. 1986. *A History of the Land Law,* 2nd edn. Oxford.

Singer, C., Holmyard, E. J. and Hall, A. R., eds. 1958. *A History of Technology,* IV. Oxford.

Slack, P. 1990. *The English Poor Law, 1531–1782.* Cambridge.

Slack, P. and Ward, R., eds. 2002. *The Peopling of Britain: The Shaping of a Human Landscape.* Oxford.

Slack, R. 2001. Farmers versus miners: a case of pollution. *Mining History* 14: 29–32.

Smail, J. 1994. *The Origins of Middle Class Culture: Halifax, West Yorkshire.* New York.

1999. *Merchants, Markets and Manufacture: The English Wool Textile Industry in the Eighteenth Century.*

2001. Credit, risk and honour in eighteenth century commerce. Unpublished seminar paper.

Smelser, N. J. 1959. *Social Change in the Industrial Revolution: An Application of Theory to the Lancashire Cotton Industry 1770–1840.*

1967. Sociological history: the industrial revolution and the British working class family. *Journal of Social History* 1: 17–35.

Smiles, Samuel 1891. *Lives of the Engineers.*

Smith, A. 1961 [1776]. *An Inquiry into The Nature and Causes of the Wealth of Nations,* ed. E. Cannan, 5th edn, 2 vols.

1976 [1776]. *An Inquiry into the Nature and Causes of the Wealth of Nations.* Oxford.

1978 [1762–3, 1766]. *Lectures on Jurisprudence.* Oxford.

1991 [1776]. *An Inquiry into the Nature and Causes of the Wealth of Nations.*

Smith, R. M. 1981. Fertility, economy and household formation in England over three centuries. *Population and Development Review* 7: 595–622.

1991. Demographic developments in rural England, 1300–48. In Campbell 1991.

1998. Aging and well being in early modern England: pension trends and gender preferences under the English poor law, 1650–1800. In P. Johnson and P. Thane, eds., *Old Age from Antiquity to Post-Modernity.*

2002. Plagues and peoples: the long demographic cycle, 1250–1670. In Slack and Ward 2002.

Smith, S. 1996. Accounting for taste: British coffee consumption in historical perspective. *Journal of Interdisciplinary History* 27: 183–214.

2001. The early diffusion of coffee drinking in England. *Cahier des Annales Islamologiques* 20: 245–68.

Smith, W. D. 1995. From coffee house to parlour: the consumption of coffee, tea and sugar in Northwestern Europe in the seventeenth and eighteenth centuries. In J. Goodman, P. Lovejoy and A. Sherratt, eds., *Consuming Habits: Drugs in History and Anthropology.*

Smollett, T. 1793. *Humphry Clinker.*

Smout, T. C. 1963. *Scottish Trade on the Eve of the Union, 1660–1707.* Edinburgh.

1969. *A History of the Scottish People 1560–1830.* New York.

Smout, T. C., Landsman, N. C. and Devine, T. M. 1994. Scottish emigration in the seventeenth and eighteenth centuries. In Canny 1994.

Snell, K. D. M. 1985. *Annals of the Labouring Poor: Social Change and Agrarian England, 1660–1900*. Cambridge.

　1999. The Sunday-school movement in England and Wales. *Past and Present* 164: 122–68.

Snell, K. D. M. and Millar, J. 1987. Lone parent families and the welfare state: past and present. *Continuity and Change* 2: 387–422.

Snodin, M. 1995. English rococo and its continental origins. In *Rococo Art and Design in Hogarth's England*.

Sokoll, T. 1997. Pauper letters. In Hitchcock *et al.* 1997.

Solar, P. 1983. Agricultural productivity and economic development in Ireland and Scotland in the early nineteenth century. In T. M. Devine and D. Dickson, eds., *Ireland and Scotland: 1600–1850*. Edinburgh.

　1995. Poor relief and English economic development before the industrial revolution. *Economic History Review* 48: 1–22.

　1997. Poor relief and English economic development: a renewed plea for comparative history. *Economic History Review* 50: 369–74.

Solow, B. L. 1985. Caribbean slavery and British growth: the Eric Williams hypothesis. *Journal of Development Economics* 17: 99–115.

　1991a. Slavery and colonization. In Solow 1991b.

Solow, B. L., ed. 1991b. *Slavery and the Rise of the Atlantic System*. Cambridge.

Solow, B. L. and Engerman, S. L. 1987. *British Capitalism and Caribbean Slavery: The Legacy of Eric Williams*. Cambridge.

Sombart, W. 1967 [1913]. *Luxury and Capitalism*. Ann Arbor.

Southall, H. R. 1988. The origins of the depressed areas: unemployment, growth and regional economic structure in Britain before 1914. *Economic History Review* 41: 236–58.

Spring, E. 1993. *Law, Land and Family: Aristocratic Inheritance in England, 1300 to 1800*. Chapel Hill, NC.

Spufford, M. 1990. The limitations of the probate inventory. In Chartres and Hey 1990.

Stasavage, D. 2002. Credible commitment in early modern Europe: North and Weingast revisited. *Journal of Law and Economics* 18: 155–86.

Steckel, R. 1983. Height and per capita income. *Historical Methods* 161: 1–7.

　1986. A peculiar population: the nutrition, health, and mortality of American slaves from childhood to maturity. *Journal of Economic History* 463: 721–41.

　1995. Stature and the standard of living. *Journal of Economic Literature* 334: 1903–40.

Steckel, R. and Floud, R., eds. 1997. *Health and Welfare during Industrialization*. Chicago.

Steensgaard, N. 1990. The growth and composition of the long-distance trade of England and the Dutch Republic before 1750. In J. D. Tracy, ed., *The Rise of Merchant Empires*. Cambridge.

Stephens, W. B. 1987. *Education, Literacy, and Society 1830–70*. Manchester.

Stevens, Edward W., Jr. 1995. *The Grammar of the Machine: Technical Literacy and Early Industrial Expansion in the United States*. New Haven.

Stevenson, D., ed. 1986. *From Lairds to Louns*. Aberdeen.

Stone, L. 1966. Social mobility in England, 1500–1700. *Past and Present* 33: 16–55.

　1974. Size and composition of Oxford's student body. In Lawrence Stone, ed., *The University in Society*, I. Princeton.

Storper, M. 1993. Regional worlds of production: learning and innovation in the technology districts of France, Italy and the USA. *Regional Studies* 27: 433–55.

Styles, J. 1994. Clothing the North: the supply of non-elite clothing in the eighteenth-century north of England. *Textile History* 25: 139–66.

　2000. Product innovation in early modern London. *Past and Present* 168: 125–69.

2002. Involuntary consumers? Servants and their clothes in eighteenth-century England. *Textile History* 33: 9–22.

Sullivan, R. 1990. The revolution of ideas: widespread patenting and invention during the industrial revolution. *Journal of Economic History* 50: 340–62.

Sundbärg, G. 1907. *Bevölkerungsstatistik Schwedens*. Stockholm.

Supple, B. 1970. *The Royal Exchange Assurance: A History of British Insurance, 1720–1970*. Cambridge.

Swain, J. T. 1986. *Industry before the Industrial Revolution*. Manchester.

Sylla, R., Tilly, R. and Tortella, G., eds. 1999. *The State, the Financial System, and Economic Modernization*. Cambridge.

Szostak, R. 1989. The organisation of work: the emergence of the factory revisited. *Journal of Economic Behaviour and Organization* 11: 343–58.

1991. *The Role of Transportation in the Industrial Revolution: A Comparison of England and France*. Montreal.

Szreter, S. 1996. *Fertility, Class and Gender in Britain, 1860–1940*. Cambridge.

Szreter, S. and Mooney, G. 1998. Urbanization, mortality and the standard of living debate: new estimate of expectation of life at birth in nineteenth-century British cities. *Economic History Review* 51: 84–112.

Tann, J. 1977. Boulton and Watt's organisation of steam engine production before the opening of the Soho Foundry. *Transactions of the Newcomen Society* 49: 41–56.

Taylor, B. 1983. *Eve and the New Jerusalem*. London.

Teichova, A., Kurgan-Van Hentenryk, G. and Zeigler, D., eds. 1997. *Banking, Trade and Industry: Europe, America, and Asia from the Thirteenth to the Twentieth Century*. Cambridge.

Teitelbaum, M. S. 1984. *The British Fertility Decline: Demographic Transition in the Crucible of the Industrial Revolution*. Princeton.

Temin, P. 1997. Two views of the British Industrial Revolution. *Journal of Economic History* 57: 63–82.

2000. A response to Harley and Crafts. *Journal of Economic History* 603: 842–6.

Terrise, M. 1975. Aux origines de la méthode de reconstitution de familles. Les Suédois d'Estonie de Hannes Hyrenius. *Population*, numéro spécial 30: 142–56.

Thane, P. 2000. *Old Age in English History*.

Thirsk, J. 1961. Industries in the countryside. In Fisher 1961.

1978. *Economic Policy and Projects*. Oxford.

Thomas, B. 1985. Escaping from constraints: the industrial revolution in a Malthusian context. *Journal of Interdisciplinary History* 15: 729–53.

1986. Was there an energy crisis in Britain in the 17th century? *Explorations in Economic History* 23: 124–52.

Thomas, J. 1988. Women and capitalism: oppression or emancipation? A review article. *Comparative Studies in Society and History* 30: 534–49.

Thomas, R. P. 1965. A quantitative approach to the study of the effects of British imperial policy upon colonial welfare: some preliminary findings. *Journal of Economic History* 25: 615–38.

Thomas, R. P. and McCloskey, D. N. 1981. Overseas trade and empire, 1700–1860. In Floud and McCloskey 1981.

Thomas, W. A. 1973. *The Provincial Stock Exchange*.

Thompson, E. P. 1963. *The Making of the English Working Class*.

1967. Time, work-discipline, and industrial capitalism. *Past and Present* 38: 56–97.

1991. *Customs in Common*.

Thompson, F. M. L. 1983. Horses and hay in Britain, 1830–1918. In F. M. L. Thompson, ed., *Horses in European Economic History: A Preliminary Canter*. Reading.

Thompson, M. 1976. Nineteenth-century horse sense. *Economic History Review* 29: 60–81.

Thompson, N. 1988. *The Market and Its Critics: Socialist Political Economy in the Nineteenth Century*.

2001. Social opulence, private asceticism: ideas of consumption in early socialist thought. In Daunton and Hilton 2001.

Thomson, D. 1991. The welfare of the elderly in the past: a family or community responsibility? In M. Pelling and R. M. Smith, eds., *Life, Death and the Elderly: Historical Perspectives.*

Thornton, H. 1802. *An Enquiry into the Nature and Effects of the Paper Credit of Great Britain.* Reprinted 1939. New York.

Tilly, C. 1984. Demographic origins of the European proletariat. In D. Levine, ed., *Proletarianization and Family History.*

Tilly, L. A. and Scott, J. W. 1978. *Women, Work and Family.* New York.

Timmins, G. 1993. *The Last Shift.* Manchester.

1998. *Made in Lancashire.* Manchester.

Titow, J. Z. 1972. *Winchester Yields: A Study in Medieval Agricultural Productivity.* Cambridge.

Tobin, J. and Nordhaus, W. 1973. Is growth obsolete? In M. Moss, ed., *The Measurement of Economic and Social Performance.* Chicago.

Topel, R. 1999. Labor markets and economic growth. In O. Ashenfelter and D. Card, eds., *Handbook of Labor Economics*, IIIC. Amsterdam.

Torrens, H. 2002. *The Practice of British Geology, 1750–1850.*

Toynbee, A. 1969 [1884]. *Lectures on the Industrial Revolution in England.* Newton Abbot.

Trainor, R. H. 1993. *Black Country Elites: The Exercise of Authority in an Industrialized Area, 1830–1900.* Oxford.

1996. The elite. In W. H. Frazer and I. Maver, eds., *Glasgow*, II, *1830–1912.* Manchester.

Tranter, N. 1981. The labour supply 1780–1860. In Floud and McCloskey 1981.

Treble, J. A. 1988. The standard of living of the working classes. In Devine and Mitchison 1988.

Trevor-Roper, H. R. 1967. The Scottish Enlightenment. *Studies on Voltaire and the Eighteenth Century* 48.

Turnbull, G. L. 1979. *Traffic and Transport: An Economic History of Pickfords.*

1987. Canals, coal, and regional growth during the Industrial Revolution. *Economic History Review* 40: 537–60.

Turner, M. 1980. *English Parliamentary Enclosure.* Folkestone.

1986. English open fields and enclosures: retardation or productivity improvements. *Journal of Economic History* 46: 669–92.

Turner, M. E., Beckett, J. V. and Afton, B. 1997. *Agricultural Rent in England, 1690–1914.* Cambridge.

2001. *Farm Production in England, 1700–1914.* Oxford.

Turner, M. and Mills, D., eds. 1986. *Land and Property: The English Land Tax, 1692–1832.* Gloucester.

Tuttle, C. 1999. *Hard at Work in Factories and Mines: The Economics of Child Labor during the British Industrial Revolution.* Boulder, CO.

Twarog, S. 1997. Heights and living standards in Germany, 1850–1939. In Steckel and Floud 1997.

Tyson, R. E. 1986. Famine in Aberdeenshire, 1695–1755: anatomy of a crisis. In Stevenson 1986.

Uglow, J. 2002a. *The Lunar Men.*

2002b. Vase mania. In Berg and Eger 2002.

Ure, A. 1967 [1835] . *The Philosophy of Manufactures.*

Usher, A. P. 1943. *The Early History of Deposit Banking in Mediterranean Europe.* Cambridge.

Usher, D. 1980. *The Measurement of Economic Growth.* Oxford.

Van Ark, B., Kuipers, S. K. and Kuper, G., eds. 2000. *Productivity, Technology and Economic Growth.* The Hague.

van der Wee, H. 1977. Monetary credit and banking systems. In E. E. Rich and C. H. Wilson, *The Cambridge Economic History of Europe*, V. Cambridge.

1997. The influence of banking on the rise of capitalism in North-West Europe, fourteenth to nineteenth century. In Teichova *et al.* 1997.

Vickers, M. 1987. Value and simplicity: eighteenth-century taste and the study of Greek vases. *Past and Present* 116: 98–137.

Vickery, A. 1993. Women and the world of goods: a Lancashire consumer and her possessions, 1751–81. In Brewer and Porter 1993.

1998. *Gentleman's Daughter*. New Haven.

Ville, S. 1981. James Kirton, shipping agent. *Mariner's Mirror* 67: 149–62.

1986. Total factor productivity in the English shipping industry: the north-east coal trade, 1700–1850. *Economic History Review*, 39: 355–70.

1987. *English Shipowning during the Industrial Revolution: Michael Henley and Son, London Shipowners, 1770–1830.* Manchester.

1993. The growth of specialization in English shipowning, 1750–1850. *Economic History Review* 46: 702–22.

Vincent, D. 1981. *Bread, Knowledge and Freedom: A Study of Nineteenth-Century Working Class Autobiography.*

2000. *The Rise of Mass Literacy: Reading and Writing in Modern Europe.* Malden, MA.

Vincenti, W. 1990. *What Engineers Know and How They Know It.* Baltimore.

Visser, M. 1991. *The Rituals of Dinner: The Origins, Evolution, Eccentricities and Meaning of Table Manners.* New York.

von Tunzelmann, G. N. 1978. *Steam Power and British Industrialisation to 1860.* Oxford.

1981. Technical progress during the industrial revolution. In Floud and McCloskey 1981.

1995. Time saving technical change: the cotton industry in the English industrial revolution. *Explorations in Economic History* 32: 1–27.

Voth, H.-J. 1998. Time and work in eighteenth-century London. *Journal of Economic History* 58: 29–58.

2000. *Time and Work in England 1750–1830.* Oxford.

2001. The longest years – new estimates of labor input in England, 1760–1830. *Journal of Economic History* 61: 1065–82.

Vries, Peer, 2001a. Governing growth: a comparative analysis of the role of the state in the rise of the West. Unpublished manuscript, University of Leiden.

2001b. The role of culture and institutions in economic history: can economics be of any help? Unpublished manuscript, University of Leiden.

Waaler, H. T. 1984. Height, weights and mortality: the Norwegian experience. *Acta Medica Scandinavica* 79: 1–56.

Wachter, K. and Trussell, J. 1982. Estimating historical heights. *Journal of the American Statistical Association* 77: 279–303.

Wadsworth, A. P. and Mann, J. de L. 1931. *The Cotton Trade and Industrial Lancashire, 1600–1780.* Manchester.

Wall, R. 1972. Mean household size in England from printed sources. In Laslett and Wall 1972.

1983. The household, demographic and economic change in England, 1650–1970. In Wall, Robin and Laslett 1983.

Wall, R., Robin, J. and Laslett, P., eds. 1983. *Family Forms in Historic Europe.* Cambridge.

Wallerstein, Immanuel. 1989. *The Modern World System,* III, *the Second Era of Great Expansion of the Capitalist World Economy, 1730–1840s.* San Diego, CA.

Walsh, C. 1995. Shop design and the display of goods in eighteenth-century London. *Journal of Design History* 8: 157–76.

Walton, G. M. 1967. Sources of productivity change in American colonial shipping, 1675–1775. *Economic History Review* 20: 67–78.

Walton, J. K. 1989. Proto-industrialisation and the first industrial revolution: the case of Lancashire. In Hudson 1989.

Walvin, J. 1997. *Fruits of Empire: Exotic Produce and British Taste 1660–1800.* Basingstoke.

Wardley, P. 1999. The emergence of big business: the largest corporate employers of labour in the United Kingdom, Germany and the United States c. 1907. *Business History* 41: 88–116.

Warren, K. 1990. *Consett Iron 1840 to 1980*. Oxford.

Weatherill, L. 1986a. Consumer behaviour and social status in England, 1660–1750. *Continuity and Change* 2: 191–216.

　1986b. A possession of one's own: women and consumer behaviour in England, 1669–1740. *Journal of British Studies* 25: 131–56.

　1988. *Consumer Behaviour and Material Culture, 1660–1760*.

　1991. Consumer behaviour, textiles and dress in the late seventeenth and early eighteenth centuries. *Textile History* 22: 297–311.

　1993. The meaning of consumer behaviour in late seventeenth and early eighteenth-century England. In Brewer and Porter 1993.

Webb, B. and Webb, S. 1921. *The Consumers' Co-operative Movement*.

Weber, M. 1954. *Max Weber on Law, Economy and Society*. Cambridge, MA.

Weingast, B. R. 1997. The political foundations of limited government: parliament and sovereign debt in 17th- and 18th-century England. In Drobak and Nye 1997.

Weir, D. 1984. Rather never than late. *Journal of Family History* 9: 341–55.

Welch, E. 1997. *Art in Renaissance Italy*. Oxford.

Wells, J. and Wills, D. 2000. Revolution, restoration and debt repudiation: the Jacobite threat to England's institutions and economic growth. *Journal of Economic History* 60: 418–41.

West, E. G. 1970. Resource allocation and growth in early nineteenth-century British education. *Economic History Review* 23: 69–95.

　1975. *Education and the Industrial Revolution*.

Westall, O. 1997. Invisible, visible and 'direct' hands: an institutional interpretation of organisational structure and change in British general insurance. *Business History* 39: 44–66.

Whatley, C. A. 1997. *The Industrial Revolution in Scotland*. Cambridge.

　2000. *Scottish Society, 1707–1830*. Manchester.

White, L. 1995. *Free Banking in Britain*, 2nd edn.

Whyte, I. D. 1989. Proto-industrialization in Scotland. In Hudson 1989.

　1995. *Scotland before the Industrial Revolution: An Economic and Social History, c. 1050–c. 1750*.

Wilkins, M. 1977. Modern European economic history and the multinationals. *Journal of European Economic History* 6: 575–95.

Williams, E. 1944. *Capitalism and Slavery*. Chapel Hill, NC.

Williams, W. M. 1963. *A West Country Village: Family, Kinship and Land*.

Williamson, J. G. 1984. British mortality and the value of life. *Population Studies* 38: 157–72.

　1985. *Did British Capitalism Breed Inequality?*

　1986. The impact of the Irish on British labor markets during the Industrial Revolution. *Journal of Economic History* 46: 693–720.

　1987. Has crowding out really been given a fair test? A comment. *Journal of Economic History* 47: 214–16.

　1990a. *Coping with City Growth during the British Industrial Revolution*. Cambridge.

　1990b. The impact of the Corn Laws just prior to repeal. *Explorations in Economic History* 27: 123–56.

　1994. Coping with city growth. In Floud and McCloskey 1994.

Williamson, O. 1980. The organisation of work. *Journal of Economic Behaviour and Organisation* 1: 5–38.

　1985. *The Economic Institutions of Capitalism: Firms, Markets, Relational Contracting*. New York.

　1989. Transaction cost economics. In R. Schmalensee and R. D. Willinhg, eds., *Handbook of Industrial Organisation*, I. Amsterdam.

Willies, L. 1997. Ironstone mining in Derbyshire. *Mining History* 13: 1–11.

Wilson, J. F. 1995. *British Business History, 1720–1994.* Manchester.

Wilson, R. G. 1973. The supremacy of the Yorkshire cloth industry in the eighteenth century. In N. B. Harte and K. G. Ponting, eds., *Textile History and Economic History: Essays in Honour of Miss Julia de Lacy Mann.* Manchester.

Wilson, R. G. and Mackley, A. L. 1999. Building the English country house 1660–1880. *Economic History Review* 52: 436–68.

Winch, D. and O'Brien, P. K., eds. 2002. *The Political Economy of British Historical Experience 1688–1914.* Oxford.

Withrington, D. J. 1988. Schooling, literacy and society, In Devine and Mitchison 1988.

Wood, A. 1999. *The Politics of Social Conflict: The Peak Country, 1520–1770.* Cambridge.

Wood, J. C. 1983. *British Economists and the Empire.*

Woods, R. 1985. The effects of population redistribution on the level of mortality in nineteenth-century England and Wales. *Journal of Economic History* 45: 645–51.

2000. *The Demography of Victorian England and Wales.* Cambridge.

Woodward, D. 2000. Early modern servants in husbandry revisited. *Agricultural History Review* 48: 141–50.

Wordie, J. R. 1974. Social change on the Leveson-Gower estates, 1714–1832. *Economic History Review* 27: 593–609.

1983. The chronology of English enclosure, 1500–1914. *Economic History Review* 36: 483–505.

World Bank 2001. *World Development Indicators 2001.* Oxford.

Wright, Q. 1965. *A Study of War*, 2nd edn. Chicago.

Wrightson, K. and Levine, D. 1979. *Poverty and Piety in an English Village: Terling 1525–1700.* Oxford.

Wrigley, E. A. 1969. *Population and History.*

1981. Marriage, fertility and population growth in eighteenth-century England. In R. B. Outhwaite, ed., *Marriage and Society: Studies in the Social History of Marriage.*

1983. The growth of population in eighteenth-century England: a conundrum resolved. *Past and Present* 98: 121–50.

1985. Urban growth and agricultural change: England and the Continent in the early modern period. *Journal of Interdisciplinary History* 15: 683–728.

1986. Men on the land and men in the countryside: employment in agriculture in early-nineteenth-century England. In Bonfield *et al.* 1986.

1987a. *People, Cities and Wealth: The Transformation of Traditional Society.* Oxford

1987b. The classical economists and the industrial revolution. In Wrigley 1987a.

1987c. Urban growth and agricultural change: England and the continent in the early modern period. In Wrigley 1987a.

1988. *Continuity, Chance and Change: The Character of the Industrial Revolution in England.* Cambridge.

1994. The effect of migration on the estimation of marriage age in family reconstitution studies. *Population Studies* 48: 81–97.

1997. How reliable is our knowledge of the demographic characteristics of the English population in the early modern period? *Historical Journal* 40: 571–95.

1998. Explaining the rise in marital fertility in England in the 'long' eighteenth century. *Economic History Review* 51: 435–64.

2000. The divergence of England: the growth of the English economy in the seventeenth and eighteenth centuries. *Transactions of the Royal Historical Society* 6th ser. 10: 117–41.

2002. Country and town: the primary, secondary, and tertiary peopling of England in the early modern period. In Slack and Ward 2002.

Wrigley, E. A., Davies, R. S., Oeppen, J. E. and Schofield, R. S. 1997. *English Population History from Family Reconstitution, 1580–1837.* Cambridge.

Wrigley, E. A. and Schofield, R. S. 1981, 1989. *The Population History of England 1541-1871: A Reconstruction*. Cambridge, MA.

Yelling, J. A. 1977. *Common Field and Enclosure in England, 1450-1850*. Hamden, CT.

Young, A. 1774. *Political Arithmetic*.

1799. Waste lands. *Annals of Agriculture* 33: 12-59.

1813a. *General View of the Agriculture of Lincolnshire*.

1813b. *General View of the Agriculture of Oxfordshire*.

Young, H. 1999. *English Porcelain*. London

Zeitlin, J. 1996. Between flexibility and mass production: strategic ambiguity and selective adaptation in the British engineering industry, 1830-1914. In C. F. Sabel and J. Zeitlin, eds., *World of Possibilities: Flexibility and Mass Production in Western Industrialisation*. Cambridge.

Zell, M. 1994. *Industry in the Countryside: Wealden Society in the Sixteenth Century*. Cambridge.

Ziegler, D. 1990. *Central Bank, Peripheral Industry: The Bank of England in the Provinces, 1826-1913*. Leicester.

Index

Aberdeen, 155, 389, 391
Aberdeenshire, 79
accounting techniques, 318, 435
Acemoglu, D. S., 277
acid rain, 427
Acres, W. M., 168
Act of Settlement, 227
Adam, Robert, 395, 408
Adams, J. N., 232
addictive foodstuffs, 366
administrative growth, 207
advertising, 385
Africa, 270, 279, 454, 458
Afton, B., 102, 103, 108
agricultural revolution
  capital, 106–7, 112, 115
  draining, 106, 109, 111, 128
  and economic growth, 114–16,
    359
  employment, 101, 104–6, 110, 115–16,
    131
    impact of enclosures, 112–13
    labourers' income, 359
  enclosures, 99–100, 110–14
  European comparisons, 97–8
  factors, 96–7, 107–14
  farm sizes, 100, 110
  farming methods, 108–10
  great estates, 98–101, 254, 393, 398,
    406–7
  haymaking, 128
  improvements, 15, 100
  and industrial revolution, 116
  land reclamation, 114
  land tenure, 100
  land use, 103–4
  leases, 406, 409
  livestock, 109–10
  marling, 106, 109
  outputs, 101–3
  ploughing, 127–8, 129
  population, 90–1, 104–6
  productivity growth, 92, 96, 107–14
  reapers, 128

  rents, 108, 110, 113–14, 407, 409
  Scotland, 401, 404–10, 413–16
  seed drills, 109, 128
  technological innovations, 126–9
  tenant farmers, 408
  threshing, 128, 129
  timing, 97
  winnowing, 128, 129
agriculture
  agricultural involution, 87
  child labour, 279
  farm servants, 250–2, 337–8
  medieval England, 99
  migration of workers to factories,
    348
  open field system, 99, 111
  poverty, 263
  prices, 98, 102
  protectionism, 188
  rents, 108, 110, 113–14, 407, 409
  revolution, see agricultural
    revolution
  Scotland, 393–4, 396
  skill acquisition, 337
  social structure, 100
  women and children in, 260
  working time, 277
Albert, W., 212, 299, 309
Alborn, T. L., 219
Alchian, A. A., 42, 225
Alcock, N. W., 376
Alderman, G., 313
alkali, 426–7
Allen, G. C., 39
Allen, R. C., 46, 47, 96, 100, 102, 103,
    105, 108, 111, 112, 113, 114, 229,
    254, 342, 376
Alloa, 327, 393
American trade, 166, 179, 181–6, 192,
    197
Amsterdam, 153
anaesthesia, 13
Anderson, B. L., 159
Anderson, James (1739–1808), 408

Anderson, Michael, 53, 95, 241, 244–6, 247, 249, 250, 293
Anglesey, 443
Angus, 389, 399, 404
aniline mauve, 25
annus mirabilis, 15
Antràs, P., 1, 7, 8, 9, 291
Antwerp, 153, 154
Appert, Nicolas (1749–1841), 130
Appleby, A., 284
apprenticeship
  benefits, 342
  breach, 338–9
  evolution, 252–3
  females, 347
  generally, 17, 139
  industrial revolution period, 347
  living-in apprentices, 250, 252–3
  merchants, 342
  numbers in 1700, 340
  orphans, 335–6
  pre-industrial revolution, 336–40
  premiums, 339
  regulation, 32, 206
  settlement rights, 251, 339
  Statute of Artificers, 208, 253, 335, 338, 339, 347
  succession, 336–7
Arbuthnot, John, 110, 127
architecture, Scotland, 393, 407
Argand oil lamp, 13
aristocracy, 370, 397, 407
Aristotle, 21
Arkwright, Richard (1732–92), 24, 136, 139, 186, 410, 411
  parents, 233, 235
Armitage family, 51
Armstrong, J., 301
Armstrong, W. A., 252
army recruits, 275–6
Arnold, A., 318
arsenals, 211
Ashford, 244, 252
Ashley machine, 133
Ashton, T. S., 40, 41, 50, 54, 294
Asia, 2–3, 279, 453
asymmetric information, 159
Atiyah, P. S., 209, 211
Atkinson, M., 446
Attman, A., 179, 180
attorneys, 53, 159
August, A., 37
Australia, 432, 444
Austria, 172
Austro-Hungarian Empire, 351
Avallone, P., 153, 154

Averch, H., 314
Averley, G., 232
Axminster carpets, 384
Ayr, bank, 155, 156
Ayrshire, 403, 406

Babbage, Charles (1791–1871), 24, 45, 434
Baber, C., 446
Bacon, Francis (1561–1626), 21, 24
Bagehot, Walter (1826–77), 147, 149, 167, 174
Baines, D., 334
Baines, E., 141
Bairoch, Paul, 96, 186
Baker, J. H., 220, 229
bakers, 92
Bakewell, Robert, 109
baking, 131
Bales, R., 239
Bank of England
  banknotes, 149–50, 156–7, 162
  and country banks, 162–7
  effect, 227
  government securities, 149, 155, 168
  Rotunda, 170
  status, 228
Bank of Scotland, 155, 156, 348
banknotes, 149–50, 154–6, 162, 206
bankruptcy, 54
banks
  bank runs, 160
  branches, 164
  clearinghouses, 157
  commercial finance, 157, 158
  country banks, 162
  deposit banking, 151, 153–4
  England, 156–7
  failures, 153
  foreign banks in London, 148
  Italian bankers, 459
  joint-stock banks, 53, 155–6, 163–4
  London and regions, 147–8
  merchant bankers, 172
  panics (nineteenth century), 161–7
  private banks, 53
  regulation, 174
  reorganisation (nineteenth century), 161–7
  savings banks, 171
  Scotland, 147, 155–6, 163, 164, 174
Banner, S., 219
Barbados, 182
Barcelona, 153
Barings, 172
Barker, H., 49

Barker, T. C., 6, 297, 298, 299, 307, 314
barley, 108, 111
baroque, 368
Barro, R., 354
Barton, D. B., 419, 431, 439, 441
Bartrip, P. W. J., 207
barytes, 420
Barzel, Y., 225
Basalla, G., 128
Batchelor, T., 107
Baten, J., 275
Bath, 385
Baugh, D., 196
Baxter, Dudley, 329, 348
beans, 108, 110, 111
Beare, T., 427
Beattie, J. M., 220, 378
Beaumont, O., 126, 127, 128
Becker, G. S., 45, 246, 361
Beckett, J. V., 102, 103, 108, 406
Bedfordshire, 30, 111
beggars, 221
Behagg, C., 34, 38
Belfast, 326, 404
Belgium, 97, 351, 457
Bell, Henry (1767–1830), 411
Belper, 139
Ben-Amos, I. K., 337, 339, 341, 343
Benenson, H., 258
Benhabib, J., 354
Benson, J., 434
Beresford, M., 112
Berg, M., 5, 6, 10, 30, 32, 33, 34, 39, 44,
    48, 49, 122–4, 125, 133, 254,
    255, 262, 291, 338, 347, 374–5,
    378, 379, 380, 382, 383, 385
Berger, A. N., 151
Bermingham, A., 381
Berry, C., 363
Berthollet, Claude Louis de
    (1749–1822), 19, 25
Berwickshire, 389
Best, James, 372
Best, M., 255
Bevan-Evans, M., 442
Bianchi, M., 360, 368
Biernacki, R., 43
Bill of Rights, 226, 227
bills of exchange, 54, 148, 151, 153,
    154, 160, 205
binary codes, 11, 24
Biraben, Jean-Noël, 453
Birch, A., 446
Birmingham
  banks, 164
  business elites, 51

button and pin industries, 39, 384
confectionery, 327
growth, 90
gun manufacture, 38
hardware trades, 33
Lunar Society, 50
metal trades, 39, 255
middle-class possessions, 374, 375
trams, 308
women's possessions, 381
working-class clothing, 378
Bisset, James, 379
Black, Joseph (1728–99), 22, 23
Black Country, 35, 51, 255
Black Death, 58, 59, 454
Blackburn, 51
blacksmiths, 92, 255
Blake, R., 190
Blake, William (1757–1827), 276
Blanc, Honoré, 17
blast furnace, 15, 46–7, 144, 444
Blaug, M., 223
bleaching, chlorine bleaching, 19, 25
'blue-water strategy', 196
Bolin-Hart, P., 412
Bolton, 45, 51
Bo'ness, 393
Bontemps, 134
booksellers, 384
Boot, H. M., 272, 347, 348
Booth, Thomas, John and Richard,
    109
Borda rule, 282, 288
Borders, 393, 399, 400
Botham, F. W., 272, 376
bothies, 252
Boulton and Watt, 43, 135, 142, 144–5,
    233, 235
Boulton family, 51
Boulton, Matthew (1728–1809), 371
Bourdieu, P., 377
Bowden, S., 360, 361
Bowman, M. J., 354
Boyce, G., 315, 317
boycotts, 386
Boyer, G. R., 223, 224
Boyns, T., 435
Bramah, Joseph (1748–1814), 135
Brazil, 182, 196, 279, 458
breast wheel, 12
Brecon, 427
Breen, T., 386
Bresnahan, T., 360
Breward, C., 382
Brewer, J., 168, 188, 196, 216, 217,
    381

brewing
  enterprises, 132
  exports, 6
  industrial revolution, 6
  regional centres, 327
  Scotland, 397, 399
  technology, 131
  trade agreements, 52
  Truman, 330
bricklayers, 92, 255
bridge trusts, 297
Bridgewater Canal, 299, 310
Briggs, Asa, 50, 51
Brinkman, H. J., 274
Bristol
  banks, 164
  copper industry, 443
  eighteenth century, 90
  life expectancy, 287
  merchants, 175
  port hinterlands, 324
  shipping, 307
  Temple Mead station, 306
Britain
  causes of economic growth, 458–60
  economic rise, 451–3
  Empire, 461–2
  European competitors, 463–4
  hegemony, 451–2
  international relations, 460–2
  land surface, 57
  and world economy, 453–5
  zenith and decline, 462–4
Brown, I. J., 418
Bruland, Kristine, 141
Brunel, Isambard Kingdom (1806–59),
      16, 302
Brunt, Liam, 103, 108, 109
Bubble Act, 170, 206, 208–9, 210
Buchanan, Archibald, 410, 411
Buchanan, R. A., 129, 134, 135
Buckinghamshire, 30
burghs of barony, 393
Burke, Edmund (1729–97), 226
Burnett, J., 366, 367, 372
Burnette, J., 348
Burstall, A. F., 135
Burt, Roger, 418, 420, 424, 425, 429,
      431, 433, 434, 435, 447
Burton, 327
business managers, 317–18, 435–6
business networks, 49–53
business women, 49
butchers, 92, 255
buttons, 6, 39, 384
Bythell, D., 254

cabs, 308
Cain, P. J., 327
Caird, James, 103
calico
  Calico Acts, 32
  imitative novelty, 384
  imports, 178, 367, 368
  printed calicoes, 368, 369
  printing machines, 141
call centres, 41
Calomiris, C., 160
Cambridge University, 344, 346–7, 354
Cambridgeshire, 111
Cameron, Rondo, 3, 150, 174
Campbell, Bruce, 58, 108
Campbell, R. H., 398, 406
Canada, 188, 457
canals
  Bridgewater, 299, 310
  capital, 172, 310
  carriage of malt, 330
  carriage of minerals, 447
  companies, 315, 327
  construction, 299, 300, 326
  Cromford, 448
  expropriation of land, 230
  Forth and Clyde, 299, 300, 310, 404
  High Peak, 448
  Leeds and Liverpool, 299, 300
  Manchester Ship Canal, 299
  Monkland, 404
  Neath, 447
  Sankey, 447
  Scotland, 404
  Thames and Severn, 310
  tolls, 310
  traffic, 299
  Trent and Mersey, 300
  Union Canal, 404
Canaries, 182
candles, 6, 12
canning, 11, 130
Cannon, J. F., 370, 372
Canny, N., 461
Canterbury, monks, 79
Cantrell, J. A., 135
Capie, F., 148, 149, 165, 167
capital
  agricultural revolution, 106–7, 112,
      115
  canals, 172, 310
  factory system, 38, 53–5, 149
  foreign capital, 460
  markets (pre-nineteenth century),
      157–61
  mines and quarries, 426, 433–4

capital (*cont.*)
  Netherlands, 459
  reorganization (nineteenth century),
    161–7
  shipping, 304
  transport, 312, 320–1
capital punishment, 220
Capper, B. P., 103
'Captain Swing', 271
carding, 16, 141, 233
Cardwell, Donald, 15, 23
Caribbeans, 181–2, 196, 230, 458
Carlos, A., 168
Carmarthen, 420
Carnot, Sadi (1837–94), 26
Carpenter, R., 30
carpenters, 92, 255
carpet weavers, Kidderminster, 43
Carron Iron Works, 37, 400, 410
Carruthers, B. G., 228
Cartwright, Edmund (1743–1823), 235
Casson, M., 37, 48, 49
Castleford, 133
Catling, H., 137, 140, 141
cattle
  breeds, 109
  numbers, 109
  Scotland, 392, 394, 401
Caunce, S. A., 51, 250, 252
censuses, 62
ceramics, 367
Cerman, M., 30, 34
Chadwick, Edwin, 213, 220, 222, 283–4,
    285, 414
Chambers, I. D., 30, 31, 101, 113
Chance, Lucas, 134
Chandler, A. D., 37, 49, 327
Chandler, T., 454
chandlers, 384
Channon, G., 317, 318
Chapman, S. D., 32, 38, 40, 49, 136,
    137, 368, 384
chapmen, 377
Charities Commission, 10
Charles II (1630–85), 226
Chartists, 186, 386
Chartres, J. A., 101, 102, 298, 384
Chassagne, S., 384
Chat Moss, 306
Chatham, 372
Chaudhuri, K. N., 181, 368, 369
Checkland, S. G., 148, 155–6, 174
chemical industries, 6, 24–6
chemistry, 21
cheques, 157
Cheshire, 420

Chevreul, Michel Eugène (1786–1889),
    25
children
  employment, 247–8, 257–8, 261–2,
    264, 278–80
    agriculture, 260
    rural industries, 35
    Scotland, 412–13
  heights, 274
  mortality rates, 80–1, 82, 86, 286
Chile, 444
China
  Canton, 183
  government interference, 204
  growth, 3
  population, 453
  porcelain, 368, 369
  silver and gold, 180–1
  standards of living, 294, 454
  trade, 180
chinoiserie, 368
chintz, 368, 369
Chippendale, Thomas (1718–79), 407
chlorine bleaching, 19, 25
cholera, 213
Chorley, P., 108
chronometer, 235, 302
Church, R. A., 6, 49, 368, 430, 435, 440,
    441
cigarettes, 366
Cipolla, C., 11, 352
cities, *see* towns and cities;
    urbanisation
civil rights, 270–1
Claeys, G., 364
clans, 392–3, 401
Clapham, Sir John, 4, 37, 41, 139, 156,
    162, 163, 165, 188
Clapp, B. W., 427
Clark, A., 240
Clark, Gregory, 1, 3, 10–11, 40, 102,
    108, 114, 178, 229, 271, 273, 277,
    280, 282, 284, 292
Clark, Jonathan, 3
class, and consumption, 369–79
Claughton, P. F., 426–7
clay, 420, 429
clay pipes, 366
Clayton, T., 383
clearinghouses, 157
Cleere, H., 419
Clegg, Samuel (1781–1861), 26
Cleveland, 46
Clifford, H., 371, 385
clothing, 362, 375, 377–9
clover, 108

Clow, A. and N. L., 6, 25, 26
Clunas, C., 371
Clyde, 302, 389, 404
Clydeside shipbuilding, 326, 400
coal
  exports, 428
  and industrial revolution, 14
  industrial use, 15, 19
  output, 448
  prices, 430
  Scotland, 394, 399, 403
coal mining
  adventurers, 425
  characteristics, 423
  importance, 420–2
  location of coalfields, 33, 419
Coalbrookdale, 410
Coale, A. J., 85
Coase, R., 41, 225
coasting, 311, 447
Cobden, Richard (1804–65), 190
Cocks, E. J., 428, 443
cocoa, 364
codfish, 179, 185
coffee, 190, 281–2, 364, 366, 384
coffeehouses, 366
Coffin, Sir Isaac, 131
coins, 151, 152–3
Coke, Edward (1552–1634), 209
coke smelting, 420, 443, 444
Cole, W. A., 1, 4–5, 8, 14, 101, 102, 103,
    104, 137, 184, 358, 395
Coleman, D. C., 6, 33
Colley, L., 231
Collier, F., 248, 258
Colling, Robert and Charles, 109
Collins, B., 384
Collins, M., 53, 148, 164, 167
Colls, R., 434
colonies
  British Empire, 461–2
  colonial wars, 461
  foodstuffs, 365–7, 376
  and industrial revolution, 14, 458–9
Colquhoun, Patrick, 120, 370, 378
Columbus, Christopher, 181–2, 455
Comber, W. T., 103
Combination Acts, 209
combing, 141
commercial finance, *see* capital
commercial revolution, 190
common law, 209–10
Company of Mines Royal, 433
competition, transport, 308–14
compulsory purchase, 229–30, 312
confectionery, 327

Congress of Vienna, 451, 453
conspiracy, 209–10
constitution
  conventions, 227–8
  England, 227–8
  United States, 227, 231
consumer revolution, 283, 357–62
consumption
  addictive foodstuffs, 366
  advertising, 385
  aristocracy, 370
  boycotts, 386
  and class, 369–79
  debate, 263–6, 357–62
  elites, 370–2
  fashion, 383–4
  and foreign luxury trade, 364–9
  and gender, 379–83
  gentry, 372
  and household budgets, 280–3
  luxury goods, 362–4
  marketing, 384–5
  middling classes, 372–5
  novelties, 362, 383–4
  politics, 385–6
  Scotland, 392
  taxation, 386
  working classes, 369–79
contract enforcement, 18
contract law, 205
convicts, 276
cooking, 381
Cookson, G., 46
Cookson, Robert, 138
co-operative movement, 386
copper
  bottoming, 428
  imports, 430
  markets, 428, 429
  mine locations, 419, 431
  mining technology, 441, 443
  output, 448
  pollution, 426–7
  producers, 437
  smelting, 442
corn
  merchants, 107
  prices, 98
  yields, 108–9, 111–12
corn laws
  origins, 98, 188
  repeal, 176, 187–90, 200–2, 206
Cornish, W. R., 229
Cornwall
  china clay, 420
  copper mines, 431, 437

Cornwall (*cont.*)
  middle-class possessions, 374
  mines, 188, 437
  mining capital, 426–7, 434
  mining revenues, 433
  mining work organisation, 434
  pumping engines, 47
  steam engineering, 439
  tin mining, 419
  transport of minerals, 448
corporate governance, 317–18
Cort, Henry (1740–1800), 15, 23, 121,
    142, 445
Cortès, Hernàn, 456
Costa, D. L., 275, 287, 289
Coster, John, 443
costers, 307
cottars, 396, 401
cotton
  consumption figures, 200
  critical technologies, 120, 136
    spinning machines, 120–1
  duties, 189
  factories
    employees, 37
    married women, 247
    owners, 41
    training, 347–8
  famine, 194
  flying shuttle, 136
  growth, 136–7
  imports, 176, 364
  industrial revolution, 5, 12
  Lancashire industry, 44–5
  production figures, 200
  rural industries, 30
  Scotland, 399
  steam power, 145
  warehouse selling, 385
Cottrell, P. L., 147, 148, 149, 163–5
counterfeiting, 152
country houses, 372, 393, 407
Cox, N. and J., 373
Crafts, N. F. R., 1, 4, 5, 6, 7–8, 95, 102,
    103, 115, 116, 187, 194, 202, 256,
    264, 270, 271, 272, 274, 275,
    277, 284, 289–91, 322–3, 333,
    348, 358, 399
craftsmen
  eighteenth century, 91–2
  family succession, 336–7
  independence, 348
  occupations, 92
  rural crafts, 255
  survival, 254
Craig, R., 304

Craske, M., 371
Crawshay, Richard, 445
creamware, 384
credit
  commercial credit (pre-nineteenth
    century), 157
  industrial revolution, 53–5
  reorganisation (nineteenth century),
    161–7
  securities, 167–73
  trust, 54–5, 159
Cressy, D., 341, 343, 344, 355
Crewe, 307
Crimean War, 463
criminal system, 220–1
Cromford Canal, 448
Crompton, Samuel (1753–1827), 15, 24,
    120, 136, 137, 186, 410
  patents, 235
Cromwell, Oliver (1599–1658), 154
Crossley, D., 419
Crouzet, F., 37, 38, 41, 54, 115, 191,
    194, 196, 418, 457
Crowley, Abraham, 43
Crump, W. B., 41
crystal, 384
Cuba, 458
Cuenca Esteban, J., 4, 12, 197, 199,
    291
Cullen, Louis, 391, 392, 409
Culzean Castle, 407
Cummins, G., 277
Cunard, 315
Cunningham, H., 261
Cunninghame, Sir Robert, 393
Cyfarthfa ironworks, 37

Dale textile family, 40
Dalton, John (1766–1844), 24
Daniels, G. W., 32
Darby, Abraham (*c.* 1678–1717), 420,
    444–5
Darien disaster, 395
Dartmoor, 448
Darwen, 51
Darwin, Erasmus (1731–1802), 22
Dasgupta, P., 288
Daumas, M., 135
Daunton, M., 128, 132, 133, 222, 306,
    307, 325, 396
Davidoff, L., 49, 261
Davis, L., 148, 149, 151, 172, 173
Davis, R., 176, 177, 188, 198, 324, 327
Davy, Humphry (1778–1829), 19, 22
Day, J., 427, 443
de Grazia, V., 381

de Vries, Jan, 6, 76, 90, 93, 256, 264, 266, 358, 361, 362, 373, 380, 456
Deane, P., 1, 4–5, 8, 14, 101, 102, 103, 104, 137, 142, 303, 307, 448
Defoe, Daniel (1660–1731), 107, 115
Dehing, P., 153
Deloitte's, 318
Demeny, P., 85
Demsetz, H., 42, 225
Denevan, W., 456
Denmark, 94, 172, 290
department stores, 385
Derbyshire, 31, 420, 426, 442, 448
Derry, T. K., 128, 130, 131, 133–4, 135
Desan, C. A., 226
Devine, T. M., 251, 254, 391, 394, 395, 396, 397, 398, 400, 403, 408, 409, 410, 414, 416
Devon, mining, 419, 420, 426–7, 434, 441
Deyon, P., 34
diaries, 382
Dicey, A. V., 227
Dick, M., 346
Dickens, Charles (1812–70), 293
Dickson, P. G. M., 168–70, 227
Diderot, Denis (1713–64), 20
diets, 367, 414
Dingle, A. E., 427
discount houses, 148, 165–6
disease, 3
display goods, 375
Disraeli, Benjamin (1804–81), 190
distilling, 399
Dobbin, F., 314
docks, 311
dockyards, 211
Dodgshon, R. A., 395
Doherty, K. W., 181
Donaghy, T. J., 324
Dornbusch, R., 167
Dorset, Duke of, 372
Douglas, M., 371
Dowlais ironworks, 37
draining
  farming, 106, 109, 111, 128
  mines, 438–9
drapers, 384
Drinkwater family, 40
Duckham, B. F., 299–301, 310
Duffy, I. P. H., 161, 162
Dumfries, 155, 391
Dundee, 155, 391, 403, 414, 415
Dunlop, J., 253, 335, 338, 339, 347

Dupree, J., 168, 242, 244, 248, 249, 250, 260
Durand, Peter, 130
Durham, schools, 351
Durie, A. M., 402
Dutton, H. I., 233, 234
dyes, 25, 141, 176

Eamon, William, 20
Earle, P., 157, 253
earthenware, 384
East Anglia, 30, 33
East India Company
  annuities, 168
  luxury textiles, 368
  markets, 178–9
  monopoly, 206, 311
  oriental textiles, 368–9
  private and public finance, 219
  silver trade, 181
  tea trade, 183–4, 366
  wages, 272
East London Company, 213
economic growth
  and agricultural revolution, 114–16
  British phenomenon, 93, 451–3
  East and West, 2–3, 15
  and education, 353–6
  European phenomenon, 93, 455–8
  exogenous and endogenous forces, 458–60
  foreign connections, 459–60
  and foreign trade, 186–7, 190–1, 200–2
  and GNP, 4, 13
  industrial revolution, 1–13
  and inequality, 359
  intellectual origins, 17–27
  and mercantilism, 195–8
  pre-Union Scotland, 394
  rates, 291–2
  reasons, 6–10, 458–60
  and technological innovation, 120–2
  zenith and decline, 462–4
Edinburgh, 155–6, 306, 308, 391, 414
education
  1851 Census, 341
  contribution to economic growth, 353–6
  expenditure, 18, 349–50
  labour force, 334–53
  measurement, 3
  schools, 340–3, 345–6, 350–3
  Scottish tenant farmers, 409

education (*cont.*)
  underinvestment, 350–3
  universities, 341, 343–4
Eggertsson, T., 225
Ekelund, R. B., 433
Elbaum, B., 350
Elder Dempster, 315
Eldon, Lord, 210, 211
electrical technology, 16, 18
Eley, G., 34
Elias, Norbert, 371
elites
  consumption, 370–2
  interest in improvement, 17
Ellenborough, Lord, 211
Ellis, J., 160
Ellman, 109
Eltis, David, 197
embezzlement, 41
emigration, 453, 460
empire, *see* colonies
employment, *see* labour
enclosures, 99–100, 110–14, 229
  Scotland, 401, 406, 409
encyclopaedias, 20
Engels, Friedrich (1820–95), 220, 240,
    257, 284
Engerman, Stanley, 192, 197, 231, 268,
    277, 292, 294, 358, 365, 457
engineering works, 37, 43
engineers, 17
engrossing, 209
Enlightenment, 15, 19–24, 407
entail, 406–7
environmental pollution, 3, 426–7
Epstein, S. A., 336
Ernle, Lord, 97, 111
Erskines of Mar, 393
Essex, 30
Europe
  British trade with, 176
  economic development, 455–8
  economies, 463–4
  income per capita, 462–3
  industrial growth, 93
  population, 57–9, 453–4
  and world economy, 453–5
excise duties, 215, 386, 395, 397
Exeter, 164

factories
  architecture, 43–4
  business environment, 48–9
  business networks, 49–53
  capital, 38, 53–5, 149
  collective innovation, 45–7

costs, 372
debate, 40–2
discipline, 348
evolution and adaptation, 47–55
Factory Acts, 207
family firms, 48–9
forms of enterprise, 42–5
occupational cultures, 52
organisation, 44
predominance of small factories,
    37–40
regional specialisation, 51–3, 327
rise, 28–9, 36–47
subcontracting, 38–9
sweated trades, 347
technology, 39
textiles, 137–41
workforce, 45–7, 91–2
fair trials, 270
Fairbairn, R. A., 447
Fairlie, S., 187
fairs, 384
family firms, 48–9
family reconstruction, 63
famines, 189, 394, 395, 396, 414
Faraday, Michael (1791–1867), 22, 134
farm houses, 409
Farnie, D. A., 33, 49, 50
Farr, William, 79, 86, 332, 333
fashion, 383–4
Feavearyear, A., 152
Feinstein, C. H., 1, 98, 107, 263, 269,
    272, 273, 280, 282, 283, 287,
    289, 292, 293, 320–1, 333, 340,
    354, 359, 375, 376, 426, 427
Fell, J. E., 444
Ferguson, N., 151, 217
fertility, 69–70, 71, 79, 293
Fife, 399, 403, 409, 412
financial system
  financing (pre-nineteenth century),
      157–61
  1825 panic, 161–7, 172
  payments (pre-nineteenth century),
      151
  reorganisation (nineteenth century),
      161–7
  securities, 167–73
  1873 situation, 151
Finch, J., 249
Finlay, R., 368
Finn, M., 379, 382
fiscal policy, *see* taxation
fish, 392, 401
Fitton, R. S., 139
Flanders, 97

Flandrin, Jean-Louis, 241
Fletcher, M. E., 302
Fleury, M., 63
Flinn, M., 58, 60, 414, 426, 427, 430, 431, 435, 438, 447
Floud, Roderick, 270, 275, 276, 289, 414
Fludyer, Samuel, 158
fluorspar, 420
flying shuttles, 136
Flynn, D. O., 179, 181
Fogel, Robert, 143, 274, 328, 330
Fong, H. D., 37
Fontaine, L., 54, 384
food
    baking, 131
    canning, 11, 130, 428
    'food puzzle,' 282
    grain milling, 132
    processing, 327
    refrigeration, 130–1
    riots, 386
    technology, 129–33
foreign trade
    America, *see* American trade
    British advantage, 6
    commercial revolution, 176–81, 190
    demand, 358
    dependence on, 191–5
    and economic growth, 190–1
    European trade, 176
    exports, early modern period, 176
    importance, 191–5
    and industrial revolution, 186–7, 198–202
    long-distance trade, 176–81, 455
    luxury goods, 364–9
    protectionism, 187–90, 192, 195–8, 311, 383, 395, 452, 457
    Scotland, 394, 403
    trading nation, 175–6
Foreman-Peck, J., 213, 214, 329–30
Forest of Dean, 419
forestalling, 209
forgery, 207
Forster family, 40
Forth, 389, 391, 404
Forth and Clyde Canal, 299, 300, 310, 404
Forth Bridge, 306
Fortrey, Samuel, 101
fossil fuels, 18, 419
fossils, 11
Foster, C., 214, 313
Foster, John, 139, 245, 247
Fourcroy, Antoine (1755–1809), 26
Fowler, Robert, 109

Fox, G., 454
France
    agricultural productivity, 97
    Beauvaisis, 79
    Caribbean trade, 196
    Cobden–Chevalier Free Trade Treaty, 190
    coffee consumption, 366
    economy, 463
    eighteenth-century wars against, 188
    engineers, 17
    food preservation, 130
    French Revolution, 16, 156, 457
    glass manufacture, 134
    government interference, 204
    hegemony, 457
    illegitimacy 18C, 70
    imperial trade, 197
    issue of securities, 172
    and John Law, 169
    land surface, 57
    literacy, 343
    Lorraine, 134
    luxury goods, 384
    maternal mortality rates, 83
    mercantilism, 457
    Nine Years War (1688–97), 155, 167
    nineteenth-century GDP, 93
    notaries, 159
    population research, 63
    prenuptial conceptions, 71
    Revolutionary Wars, *see* Napoleonic Wars
    rural population, 412
    taxation, 215
    tobacco monopoly, 183
    transport, 319
    urbanisation, 88–9, 90
    wars with Scotland, 395
Franklin, Ben, 382
Franubhofer, 134
fraud, 49
free-market capitalism, 120
free trade, 187–90, 402; *see also* mercantilism
freedom of association, 270
freedom of speech, 270
Freeman, C., 122, 146
Fremdling, R., 186, 326
Frenkel, J., 167
Freudenberger, H., 277
Frome, 314
Frost, P., 31
Fukuyama, F., 50
Fullarton, William, 404
fuller's earth, 420

Furlough, E., 381
Furness, 419
Furness Withy, 315
fustian, 32–3, 54

Galbi, D., 279
Galileo (1564–1642), 24
Gallman, R., 148, 149, 151, 173
Galloway, 389, 398
Galloway, P. R., 78
Galor, O., 18, 349
Galt, John (1779–1839), 408
Gardner, P., 345
Garfield, S., 25
Garrett, E., 36
gas light, 12, 26, 284
gas works, 172
Gash, N., 189
Gaskell, P., 240
Gattrell, V. A. C., 37, 38, 43, 50
Gautier, E., 63
Gay-Lussac, Joseph (1778–1850), 25, 26
Geertz, C., 87
Gemmell, N., 323
gender, and consumption, 379–83
gentry, 372
geology, 425
Geraghty, T., 40, 42
Gerhold, D., 297, 298, 299, 314, 323
Germany
    agricultural productivity, 97
    Bavaria, 351
    demography, 58
    economy, 457, 464
    education, 341
    glass manufacture, 134
    industrialisation, 204
    land surface, 57
    literacy, 343
    railways, 326
    rural population, 412
    wars, 16
    wool weavers, 43
Getzler, J., 229
ghost acreage, 14, 18, 459
Gibson, A. J. S., 395
Giedion, S., 128, 131
gig mills, 39
Gilboy, Elizabeth, 358
Gill, M., 419, 440, 442
gin, 376
Ginarlis, J., 297
Giráldez, A., 179
Gladstone, William (1809–98), 190, 200, 313

Glasgow
    banks, 155
    brewing, 327
    cotton industry
        growth, 90, 400
    life expectancy, 285
    merchants, 398
    port hinterlands, 324
    pre-eminence, 391
    riots, 397
    St Rollox works, 399
    stock exchange, 306
    textile dependency, 415
    tobacco, 402–3
    tobacco lords, 408
    trams, 308
    typhus, 414
    wages, 414
Glasgow Cotton Spinners Association, 413
Glasgow Philosophical Society, 26
glass, 6, 43, 133–4, 394
glaziers, 255
Glencoe massacre, 392
Glorious Revolution, 150, 167, 225, 270, 433
Gloucester, 164, 351
Gloucestershire, 420
GNP, and growth rate, 4, 13
gold
    Americas, 179–80, 456
    foreign trade, 179
    mine locations, 420, 433
    prices, 163
Goldsmith, R., 150
goldsmiths, 228
Goldstone, J. A., 3, 11, 14
Goldsworthy, J. D., 227
Goldthwaite, R. A., 368, 371
Golinski, Jan, 21
Gooch, Daniel, 318
Goode, William, 240
Goodhart, C., 165
Goodman, J., 262, 366
Gordon, R., 360
Gorton, G., 157
Gott, Benjamin, 22, 41
Gott family, 40
Goubert, Pierre, 79
Gough, J., 427
Gourvish, T. R., 305, 307, 313, 315, 318, 321, 326, 329
government
    administrative growth, 207
    expenditure, 217–18, 226
    fiscal policy, *see* taxation
    and industrial revolution, 204–6

government (*cont.*)
  national debt, 216, 217
    default, 226–7
  passivity, 219
  regulation, 206–11
  and role of judiciary, 208–11
  securities, 167–71, 205, 225
  and share market, 218–19
Grabher, G., 53
Grafe, R., 185
Graff, H., 343, 344, 351
grain, 394
grain milling, 132
grammar schools, 341, 346, 354
Grand Tour, 372
grandparents, 243
granite, 448
Granovetter, M., 53
Great Consols, 441
Great Eastern Railway, 318
Great Western Railway, 318
Greek Empire, 454
Green, A., 350
Greenhill, R. G., 325
Greg family, 40, 41, 42, 50
Gregory, A., 270, 275, 414
Griffith, G. T., 60, 62
Grimsby, 130
gross domestic product, 226, 333
growth, *see* economic growth
Guadeloupe, 457
guilds, 18, 253, 339, 347, 348
Guinand, Pierre, 134
gun manufacture, 38
gunpowder, 436, 438
gypsum, 420

Habakkuk, H. J., 62
Haber, L. S., 6
haberdashery, 12
Habsburgs, 456
hackney coaches, 308
haematite, 446
Haiti, 183, 196, 457, 458
Hajnal, J., 95
Hall, C., 49
Hall, G. W., 420
Hall, Rupert, 21
Hamilton, Duke of, 393
Hamilton, H., 39
Hammond, J. L. and B., 99, 261
Hanley, Susan, 3
Hans, N., 341
harbours and ports, 311, 393
hardware industry, 6
Hareven, T., 246
Hargreaves, James (*c.* 1720–78), 136, 410

Harley, C. K., 1, 4, 5, 6, 7–8, 186–8, 202, 256, 284, 291, 302, 305, 322–3, 328
Harling, P., 207
Harper, L. A., 185
Harris, A., 419, 443, 445
Harris, J. R., 338
Harris, R., 168, 170, 172, 209, 210, 211, 212, 218
Harrison, D. F., 297
Harrison, J., 241
Harrison, James, 131
Harrison, John (1693–1776), 15, 17, 21
Hart, C., 419
Hart, M., 153
Harte, N., 379, 382
Hartwell, Max, 268
harvesting
  failures, 2, 79, 394, 395, 396
  and marriages, 77–9
  technology, 128
Harvey, C. E., 436
Harwich, 130
Hatcher, J., 79
haulage, 297
Hausman, W. J., 305
Havinden, M. A., 111
Hawke, G., 307, 310, 329–30
hawkers, 307, 377, 384
Hay, D., 220, 221
Hayle, 443
haymaking, 128
Headrick, Daniel, 20, 21
Heath's process, 16
Heaton, H., 30, 34, 40, 49
Hebrides, 389
heights, 269–70, 273–6
Heilbron, J. L., 21
Helms, M. W., 368
Helpman, Elhanan, 6, 195
Henning, G., 302
Hennock, P., 50
Henry II (1133–89), 220
Henry, L., 63
Henry, William (1774–1836), 24
Hepplewhite, George (d. 1786), 407
Hereford, schools, 351
Hereford cattle, 109
Herlihy, D., 454
Herschel, J. F. W., 134
Hertfordshire, 30
Heuman, G., 231
hewers, 248
Hewitt, M., 257, 336
Hey, D. G., 31, 32
Higgins, J. P. P., 330
Higgs, E., 252

Higgs, J. W. Y., 126, 127, 128
High Peak Canal, 448
Highlands
    clearances, 98, 401, 411–12
    living standards, 414
    unemployment, 416
Hilgerdt, F., 191
Hill, A., 440
Hills, Richard, 24
Hilton, M., 366
Hirschman, A., 324
Hirst, P., 53
Hobsbawm, Eric, 268
Hobson, John Atkinson (1858–1940),
        461
Hodgson, G. M., 48
hoeing, 128
Hoffman, P., 159, 217
Hoffmann, Walther, 4
Holderness, B. A., 101, 102, 107, 109,
        282, 396
Holland, E., 157, 419
holy days, 277
Honeyman, K., 38, 45, 262
Hopeton House, 407
Hopkins, E., 277
Hoppit, J., 38, 53, 54, 161
Horne, H. O., 147, 171, 173
Horrell, S., 258, 260, 261, 262, 263,
        265, 266, 272, 278, 283, 359,
        375–6, 377
Horsefield, J. K., 155, 156, 226
horse-hoes, 128
hosiery, 30, 255, 399
hot air balloons, 11
Houghton, 372
Houlsworth, Henry, 139
household industries
    decline, 240, 254–7
    environment, 30–4
    occupational cultures, 34–6
    rural industries, 29–30
households
    budgets, 280–3
    consumption, 263–6
    continuity and change, 250–7
    evolution, 238–9
    industrialised wage earners,
        257–62
    live-in apprentices, 250, 252–3
    live-in servants, 245, 248, 250–2
    lodgers, 245, 248
    motivations, 246–50
        industrial revolution, 244–6
        pre-industrial households, 241–3
    standards of living, 263–6

theories, 239–41
wage levels, 263
housing
    country houses, 372, 393, 407
    farm houses, 409
    industrial revolution, 11, 283–4
    middle classes, 375
    Scotland, 393, 407
    tower houses, 393
Houston, R. A., 33, 58, 79, 341, 343–4,
        352, 412
Howe, A., 51
Howkins, A., 252, 254
Howlett, P., 318
Hsieh, C.-T., 292
Huberman, M., 43, 102, 282
Huck, P., 286
Hudson, P., 5, 10, 30, 31, 33, 34, 35, 36,
        38, 40, 49, 50, 51, 52, 53–4, 55,
        158–9, 160, 254, 262, 291, 359
Hudson's Bay Company, 168, 311
Hueckel, G., 98
Hughes, G., 317
Hughes, S., 444
Huish, Mark, 318
Hull, 164, 311
human capital
    concept, 334
    and economic growth, 353–6
    industrial revolution, 343–53
    pre-industrial revolution, 334–43
    underinvestment, 350–3
Hume, David (1711–76), 363
Humphries, J., 113, 248, 250, 253, 258,
        260, 261, 262, 263, 272, 278,
        279, 338, 339, 375–6, 377
Hunt, E. H., 272, 376, 395
Hunt, M., 54, 55, 260
Hunt, R., 425
Huntingdonshire, 30, 111
Huygens, Christiaan (1629–93), 21
Hyde, C. K., 419, 422, 445
Hyrenius, H., 63

Iceland, literacy, 344
illegitimacy, 59, 70–1, 75–6
imitative innovations, 383
Imlah, J. A. H., 193, 199
immigration, 413, 460
imports
    composition, 365
    cotton, 176, 364
    from Europe, 176–8
    linen, 176
    luxury goods, 364–9
    minerals, 430

imports (*cont.*)
  porcelain, 369
  sources, 365
imprisonment, 220
incentives, 27
India
  British hegemony, 195
  calicoes, 368
  child labour, 279
  cotton, 179
  population, 453
  standards of living, 294
  trade, 179, 180
individualism, rise in, 243
industrial enlightenment, 19–24
industrial revolution
  and agricultural revolution, 116
  British phenomenon, 451–3
  and consumption, 357–62
  data, 4, 12
  European event, 14–15, 25
  foreign connections, 459–60
  and foreign trade, 186–7, 190–1,
    198–202
  and government policy, 204–6
  growth rate, 1–13
  and household development, 240–1
  and industrialisation, 2–3
  origins
    British prominence, 16–17
    demography, 18, 19
    exogenous and endogenous forces,
      458–60
    fortunate circumstances, 11–12
    institutional changes, 18
    intellectual origins, 17–27
    technical literacy, 16
    technological progress, 11–13,
      15–16
  paradox, 3
  quantification, 4–13
  regulatory framework, 206–11
  Scotland, 410–13
  and transport, 319–20
  wage earning households, 257–62
information, measuring, 3
inheritance
  occupational inheritance, 336–7
  partible inheritance, 30
  unigeniture, 30
Inikori, J. E., 197, 459
Inkster, Ian, 128, 130, 135, 343–4, 347
inland waterways, 299–301
  canals, *see* canals
  growth rates, 300
  tolls, 309–10

innovation, and consumption, 383–4
institutional changes, and growth, 18
insurance, 52, 171, 173, 205
  marine insurance, 170–1, 304
intellectual activity, 344, 354
intellectual property, 231–5
interest rates, usury laws, 206, 208
international relations, 460–2
Inverary Castle, 407
Inverness, 391
Ireland
  emigration to Scotland, 413
  farm servants, 252
  growth, 457
  linen, 188
  potato famine, 189
  sugar trade, 183
  trade expansion, 392
  underdevelopment, 397
iron industry
  blast furnaces, 15, 46–7, 144, 444
  galvanising sheet iron, 428
  hot blast process, 16, 26, 121, 411,
    446
  imports, 176
  and industrial revolution, 5, 18
  protectionism, 188
  Scotland, 399–400
  technology, 23, 444
  wrought iron, 442
iron ore
  imports, 430
  location of mines, 419
  markets, 428
  pollution, 427
  prices, 430
  value, 420–2
Ironmonger, D., 360
ironstone, 403
Irving, R. J., 314
Irwin, D. A., 187, 202, 368
Isherwood, B., 371
Israel, J. I., 456–7
Italy, 57, 88, 343, 455, 459

Jackson, G., 304, 311
Jackson, R. V., 102, 103, 291
Jacob, Margaret, 22, 460
Jamaica, 182
James Finlay and Co., 410
Japan, 3, 204, 368, 453
Java, 179
Jefferson, Thomas (1743–1826), 2
Jenkin, A. K., 434
Jennings, B., 420
John, A. H., 37, 171, 419

John Taylor and Sons, 434
Johnson, D. L., 314
Johnson, Paul, 54
Johnson, S., 277
Johnson, Samuel (1709–84), 355, 395
joint-stock companies
    1844 Act, 207
    business networks, 51
    common law prohibition, 210
    institutional innovation, 205
    mining, 425, 434
    shipping finance, 304
    statutory prohibition, 170–1, 206
    transport, 309
Jones, C., 366
Jones, E. L., 2, 14, 30, 39, 41, 49, 88,
    330
Jones, M. G., 341
Jones, R., 58, 59
Jones, S. R. H., 40, 459
Joslin, D. M., 157
Joyce, P., 51
judiciary, 208–11, 270
jute, 403

Kames, Henry Home, Lord (1696–1792),
    408
Kanefsky, J. W., 439, 440, 441
Kay, John (1704–c. 1780), 136, 410
Kelp, 401
Kennedy, P., 217, 218
Kent, 33, 374, 419, 420, 425
Kenyon, Chief Justice, 211
Kerridge, E., 153–4
Kershaw family, 51
Key, J., 168
Keyder, C., 96, 457
Keyfitz, N., 86
Keyser, Barbara Whitney, 25
Khan, A., 151
Khan, B. Z., 150, 234
Khan, C., 160
Kidderminster, 43, 384
Killick, J. R., 172
Kindleberger, C. P., 164, 166–7
King, Gregory, 91, 103, 109, 114, 342,
    349, 370, 377, 378, 379
King, P., 261, 266, 283
King, S. A., 32, 34, 35, 54, 249
King, W. T. C., 148, 162, 163, 165–6
Kingsford, P. W., 319
kinship, 95, 255, 256
Kippen, 412
Kippen, S., 424, 435
Kirby, M. W., 50, 136, 315, 317
knitting, 30, 31, 32, 256

Knowle, 372
knowledge, useful knowledge, 18–24
Komlos, J., 274, 275, 276, 289, 290
Kosminski, E., 100
Kostal, R. W., 214, 229
Kowaleski-Wallace, E., 381, 383
Koyré, Alexandre, 21
Krause, J. T., 62
Kravis, I. B., 194
Kriedte, P., 30
Kondratieff wave, 121
Krugman, P. D., 195
Krupp, 16
Kussmaul, A., 95, 105, 250, 251, 252,
    253, 279, 337
Kuznets, Simon, 19

labour
    agricultural revolution, 101, 104–6,
        110, 112–13, 115–16, 131
    children, 247–8, 257–8, 261–2,
        278–80
    early organisation, 248
    emigration, 453, 460
    and enclosures, 112–13
    factories, 45–7, 52, 91–2
    family labour, 255, 256
    internal migration, Scotland, 411–12
    laws, 206, 207
    male breadwinners, 258–62, 265–6
    mines and quarries, 422–3, 434, 438
    mobility, 411–12
    national income, 333
    railway companies, 318–19
    Scotland, 400, 411–13
    skilled labour, 138–41, 412
    skills, *see* skills
    slaves, 182, 195, 230–1, 274, 386, 457
    turnover, 139–40
    women, *see* women
    working hours, 270, 276–80, 412
    working population, 333
lace making, 30, 35
laissez-faire, 204–5, 314
Lake District, 419
Lamoreaux, N., 159
Lanarkshire, 403, 404
Lancashire
    alkali, 426–7
    coal mining, 419
    copper industry, 443
    cotton industry, 44–5
    factory workers, 92
    family farms, 254
    household structures, 245, 247
    literacy, 344

Lancashire (*cont.*)
  nonconformist business networks,
    50
  proto-industrialisation to
    industrialisation, 33
  riots, 39
  rural textile industries, 30, 31, 32
    cotton, 33
    fustian, 32, 54
    printed cotton, 33
  schools, 351
  smelters, 447
Lancaster, K., 360
land
  expropriation, 229–30, 312
  market, 11
  property rights, 229
  tax, 11, 32
  tenure, 100
  use, 103–4
Landers, J., 82
Landes, David, 21, 40, 120–1, 132,
    133
Landsman, N. C., 391
Lane, J., 253, 339
Langford, P., 370, 373
Langlois, R. N., 40
Langton, J., 36, 51
Laqueur, T., 344, 346
Lasch, C., 249
Laslett, Peter, 95, 239, 241–3, 244,
    246–7, 249
lathes, 134
Latin America, 172, 270
Lavoisier, Antoine (1743–94), 25, 26
law enforcement, 207, 211
Law, John (1671–1729), 169
Lawson, J., 341
Laxton, P., 82
Lazear, E. P., 42
Lazonick, W., 43, 49
Le Roux, A. A., 37, 438
lead mining
  Derbyshire, 31
  labour force, 438
  locations, 419
  markets, 428, 429
  output, 448
  Scotland, 394, 419
  smelting, 442
  Wales, 419, 438, 447
  Yorkshire, 442
'Lean Years', 79, 394, 395, 396
leases, 406, 409
Leblanc, Nicholas (1724–1806), 25
Leboutte, R., 34

Lee family, 51
Lee, R. D., 63, 293
Leeds, 41, 90, 164, 306
Leeds and Liverpool Canal, 299, 300
Leeward Islands, 182
legal framework, 18, 206–11
Leicester sheep, 109
Leicestershire, 30, 109
leisure, 280
Lemire, B., 158, 368, 377, 378–9,
    382
Lemon, C., 438
Leneman, Leah, 59
Lenin (1870–1924), 461
Leonardo da Vinci, 17
Lerebours, 134
Leslie Castle, 393
Leven, Earl of, 412
Levi, Leone, 342
Levine, D., 34, 35, 254, 256, 257, 258
Levine, R., 151
Lewis, M. J., 122
Lewis, W. J., 420, 433
Li, M.-H., 152
Libecap, G. D., 432
Liebig, Justus von (1803–73), 24
life expectancy, 270, 283–8
lighthouses, 302, 311
lighting, 13
  gas light, 12, 26, 284
lime, 406, 409
limestone, 420
Lincolnshire, 102, 104, 351
Lindert, P. H., 102, 104, 224, 272, 273,
    282, 353, 373
linen
  duties, 395, 397
  export, 6
  imports, 176
  rural industries, 30
  Scotland, 394, 399, 402
literacy
  growth, 353
  industrial revolution period, 343,
    344–5
  men, 351
  occupational levels, 355
  pre-industrial revolution, 341, 354
  rates, 270
  women, 351
Liverpool
  banks, 164
  business networks, 51
  docks, 311
  growth, 90
  port hinterlands, 324

Liverpool (*cont.*)
  shipping, 307
  stock exchange, 149, 172, 173, 306
  trade, 186
  trams, 308
Liverpool Commercial Banking
    Company, 148
livestock, 109–10
living standards
  civil rights, 270–1
  composite indicators, 288–91
  consumption, 263–6, 280–3
  debate, 268–71
  demographic growth, 271
  elites, 370–2
  and heights, 269–70, 273–6
  households, 263–6
  indicators, 269
  labouring classes, 357, 375–9
  life expectancy, 270
  literacy, 270
  and macroeconomic performance,
    291–3
  middling classes, 372–5
  Scotland, 413–16
  wage levels, 263, 269, 271–3
  working time, 270, 276–80, 412
Lloyd-Jones, R., 37, 122, 438
Lloyd's, 171, 304
local taxation, 32
lodgers, 245, 248
Lombe, Thomas, 135, 235
London
  apprentices, 253
  banks, 156–7, 164
  Blackwell Hall, 158
  docks, 311
  financial centre, 151
  growth, 90
  life expectancy, 285
  Lombard Street, 147
  maternal mortality, 83
  merchants, 175
  morality (eighteenth century), 82
  road transport, 297, 298
  St Pancras Station, 306
  silk handloom weavers, 136
  stock market, 148–9
  subway, 308
  water supply, 212–13
London and North Western Railway,
    315, 318
London Bridge Water Works, 212
London Lead Company, 433, 442
London Stock Exchange, 148, 149, 170,
    171–2

Longhorn cattle, 109
longitude, 235
looms
  Cartwright loom, 136
  handlooms, 44, 254
  horizontal looms, 15
  Jacquard looms, 24
  power looms, 141
Louca, F., 122, 146
Loudon, I., 83
Low Countries, 16, 88, 98
Lucas, Robert, 18
Luddites, 271
Lunar Society, 50
luxury goods
  colonial foodstuffs, 365–7
  consumption, 281–2, 362–4
  foreign trade, 364–9
  oriental manufactured goods, 367
Lynch, Michael, 391
Lyons, J., 256, 257, 258

McAdam, John (1756–1836), 297
McClelland, P. D., 198
Macclesfield, 40
McCloskey, D. N., 7, 12, 108, 113, 121,
    198, 200, 202, 291, 322–3, 358
McConnel and Kennedy, 139
McCormick reaper, 128
McCracken, G., 371
McCusker, J. J., 182, 185, 459
MacDonagh, O., 207
McEvedy, C., 58, 59
machine tools, 5, 134–5
Macinnes, A. L., 392
Mackelworth, R., 55
McKendrick, Neil, 6, 22, 52, 134, 264,
    283, 358, 359, 370, 371, 380
MacKenzie, J. M., 368
Mackley, A. L., 372
McLean, I., 214, 313
McLean, T., 318
MacLeod, Christine, 46, 123, 124, 233
macroeconomics, and standards of
    living, 291–3
Maddison, A., 93, 454, 455, 456, 463
Madeira, 182
mahogany, 384, 407
mail, 306
Maizels, A., 191
Malaysia, 430
Malcolmson, R. W., 254
malt, 330, 397
Malthus, Thomas (1766–1834), 78, 93,
    95, 222, 271, 459
managers, 317–18, 435–6

Manchester
  banks, 164
  business families, 51
  canal networks
  growth, 90, 186
  life expectancy, 285
  McConnel and Kennedy, 138–9
  stock exchange, 149, 172, 306
Manchester Literary and Philosophical
  Society, 24, 50
Manchester Royal Exchange, 50
Manchester Ship Canal, 299
Mandemakers, C. A., 274
Mandeville, Bernard (1670–1733), 362–3
Mandler, P., 207, 224
manganese, 420
Mann, J. de L., 30, 32, 33, 39, 136
Mansfield, Lord (1705–93), 209, 232,
  233
Mantoux, Paul, 40, 97, 120–1
Marglin, S. A., 40
Mariscal, E., 353
marketing, 384–5
markets and fairs, 384
marling, 106, 109
marriage
  age, 73–5, 243
  and economic circumstances,
    76–9
  seasonality, 251
Marriner, S., 54
Marshall, Alfred, 43, 44, 47
Marshall, J. D., 30
Marshall, K., 419
Marshall, P. J., 461
Marshall, W., 108
Marston, 106
Martin, J. M., 254
Marx, Karl (1818–83), 101, 136, 257,
  268, 276, 455
masons, 92, 255
Massey, D., 36
Massie, J., 91, 104
Mathias, Peter, 6, 40, 91, 126, 133, 135,
  215, 342, 348
Matthews, R. C. O., 333, 353
Maudslay, Henry (1771–1831), 16, 135
mauve, 25
Maynes, M. J., 351
Meade, R., 446
meals, 375, 381
Medick, Hans, 30, 256, 257, 377
Meikle, Andrew (1719–1811), 128
Mellerstain, 407
Melton, F., 159
Melville, Earl of, 412

Menard, R. R., 182, 185, 302, 327, 459
Mendels, F., 30, 35
Mendips, 435
Mennell, S., 371
mercantilism, 187, 192, 195–8, 311,
  383, 395, 452, 457
mercers, 384
merchants
  Anglo-American trade, 166
  apprenticeship, 342
  corn merchants, 107
  credit (pre-nineteenth century), 158
  foreign trade, *see* foreign trade
  merchant-manufacturers, 39–40
  putting-out system, 29, 31, 37, 40
Merioneth, 420
metal trades, 255
metals, *see* mines and quarries; specific
  metals
metalwares, 30, 32, 125, 384
metal working, 120–1
Metcalf, John (1717–1810), 297
Mexico, 179, 454, 456
Michael Henley and Son, 312
Michie, R. C., 149, 168, 170, 171–2, 218,
  306
middle classes, 372–5, 413
Middle East, 270
Middlesex, 351
Midlands
  agriculture, 30
  coal mining, 419
  hosiery, 255
  iron ore mining, 419
  knitting, 31, 32
  lace making, 35
  metalwares, 31, 125
  proto-industrialisation to
    industrialisation, 33
  rural metal working, 31
  silk mills, 136
Miles, A., 53
Milford, 139
Mill, John Stuart (1806–73), 213, 352
Millar, J., 262
Miller, D., 371
millinery, 12
milling technology, 132
Million Bank, 168
Mills, D., 32
Millward, R., 213, 214
Minchinton, W. E., 176, 428
mines and quarries
  Black Band ores, 446
  capital investment, 426, 433–4
  categories of minerals, 419, 445–6

mines and quarries (*cont.*)
  characteristics, 423–7
  Clay Band ores, 446
  coal, *see* coal
  cost book system, 47, 434
  danger, 248, 424
  drainage crisis, 438–9
  environmental pollution, 426–7
  exhaustion, 425
  fuel consumption, 439
  growth, 449
  gunpowder, 436, 438
  horses and ponies, 441
  iron ore, *see* iron ore
  labour, 422–3, 434, 438
  locations, 419–23
  male labour, 260
  managers, 435–6
  markets, 427–30
  mineral economy, 417–18, 449–50
  Mines Act 1842, 441
  non-ferrous metals, 419
  organisation, 432–6
  prices, 430–2
  productivity, 448–9
  property rights, 432–3
  pumping systems, 438–40
  reverberatory revolution, 442–3
  smelting, 441–5
  steam power, 428, 439–40
  structure of industry, 419–23,
    424–5
  structure of production, 437–8
  technological improvements, 431–2,
    436–48
  transport, 446–8
  value, 422
  wages, 434–5
  water power, 440–1
  winding engines, 440
Mintz, S. W., 182, 184, 365
Mitch, David, 333, 341, 346, 348, 350,
  351, 352, 353, 355
Mitchell, B. R., 303, 305, 307, 326, 333,
  427, 448
Mitchison, Rosalind, 59
Moav, O., 18, 349
Mokyr, Joel, 14, 16, 19, 37, 41–2, 45,
  128, 130, 133, 134, 218, 234, 271,
  281, 282, 294, 355, 358, 359, 399
Monkland Canal, 404
Monmouth, 427
monopolies
  overseas trade, 206, 311
  royal grants, 231
  state monopolies, 18

Statute of Monopolies, 209, 231–2,
  233
  transport, 308–9, 310
Montesquieu (1689–1755), 362
Montrose, Duke of, 398
Mooney, G., 83, 285
moral hazard, 159–60, 166, 167
Morgan, K., 142, 197
Morgan, V., 413
Morocco, 270
Morris, M., 288
Morris, R. J., 36, 50, 51
mortality
  adults, 80, 85
  children mortality rates, 80–1, 82, 86
  cities, 82–3
  falling mortality, 62
  life expectancy, 283–8, 395
  long 18C, 79–86
  maternal mortality rates, 83–4
  Scotland, 395, 414
  seasonality, 82
  sex differentials, 83–6
  and urbanisation, 283–8
Morton, Earl of, 409
Moses, G., 251, 252
Mueller, R., 153
Mugridge, A. J., 428
Mui, H. and L. H., 184, 384
Muldrew, C., 54, 55, 157
Munro, J., 153, 154
Murdock, William (1754–1839), 17, 26
Murphy, A., 169
Murphy, K. M., 45
Mushet, David (1772–1847), 16, 446
Mushet, Robert (1811–91), 16
muslins, 369, 384
Musson, A. E., 21, 347

Naples, 153
Napoleon I (1769–1821), 2, 162
Napoleonic Wars
  corn prices, 109
  economic impact, 2, 161, 457
  farm prices, 98
  and financial markets, 150, 171
  financing, 218
  and foreign trade, 197
  inflation, 251
  outcome, 457
  repression, 271
  shipping demand, 304, 320, 324
  taxation, 188
Nardinelli, C., 258, 279
Nasmyth, James (1808–90), 16, 135
national debt, 216, 217, 226–7

natural rights, 227–8
navies, sizes, 218
Navigation Acts, 185, 187–8, 198, 206, 208, 304
Neal, L., 151, 153, 154, 160, 161, 162, 164, 167, 168, 169–70, 172, 178, 218, 227
Neath, 447
Neath Canal, 447
Neeson, J. M., 113, 229
Nef, J. U., 420
Neilson, James Beaumont (1792–1865), 16, 26, 411, 446
Nelson, R., 48
Nenadic, Stana, 382, 383, 413
Netherlands
    Amsterdam, 153
    capital, 459
    East India Company, 178–9
    economic growth, 87
    GDP (nineteenth century), 93
    literacy, 343
    mills, 17
    revolt of Spanish Netherlands, 176, 178
    stagnation (eighteenth century), 93
    trade, 178, 185, 456
    universities, 344
    urbanisation, 88
    Zaan area, 17
networks, business networks, 49–53
New Draperies, 176
New River Company, 212
New Zealand, 444
Newcastle, 90, 164
Newcomen, Thomas (1663–1729), 19, 439
Newell, E., 426–7
Newfoundland, 186
Newton, Isaac (1642–1727), 152, 355
Newton, L., 53, 148, 159, 163–5
Nicholas, S., 274, 276, 344
Nicholas, J., 344
Nine Years War (1688–97), 155, 167
Nishimura, S., 148
nonconformist business families, 50
non-ferrous metals
    characteristics, 423–4
    markets, 429–30
    mining, 419
    property rights, 433
    structure of production, 437–8
    value, 420
Nooteboom, B., 45
Nordhaus, William, 13, 273
Norfolk, 102, 108, 129

Norfolk rotation, 110
North, Douglass, 18, 42, 168, 216, 225–6, 302, 305, 433
Northampton, 245
Northern Isles, 389
Norway, 275
Norwich, 90, 164
notaries, 159
Nottingham, 32, 244, 351
Nottinghamshire, 31
novelties, 383–4
nuptiality, 73–9
nutrition, 274
Nuvolari, A., 47
Nye, J. V., 187, 190

oats, 108, 109, 111, 404
O'Brien, K., 456
O'Brien, P. K., 96, 115, 145, 168, 192, 196, 198, 215, 268, 277, 292, 294, 309, 359, 365, 386, 452, 457, 461
occupations
    inheritance, 336–7
    and literacy, 355
    Scottish cities, 415
O'Day, R., 341, 342, 344–5, 346, 347
Oeppen, J., 63, 69
Offer, A., 360, 361
Ogden, T., 167
Ogilvie, S., 30, 34
O'Gráda, Cormac, 96, 111, 458
Ohlin, G., 60, 62
oil, 327
Oldham, 45, 139, 245, 247
Oldknow family, 41
Olson, Mancur, 18, 194, 228
omnibuses, 308
open field system, 99, 111
Oren, L., 266
oriental goods, 176, 181, 364–9
O'Rourke, K., 305, 328
orphans, apprenticeship, 335–6
Orth, J. V., 210
Ottoman Empire, 454, 455
ovens, 131
overseas trade, *see* foreign trade
Overton, M., 92, 97, 102, 103, 108, 370, 374
Oxford University, 344, 346–7, 354
Oxfordshire, 111
Oxley, D., 266

P. & O., 315
Pacific Steam Navigation Company, 325
pack horses, 447
Pakistan, 270

Palmer, S., 326
Panmure, Earl of, 410
paper industry, 6
    Scotland, 394, 397, 399
    trade agreements, 52
Papin, Denis (1647–1712), 21
parishes
    apprenticeship, 335–6
    parish registers, 59, 62, 389
    poor relief, 221, 251
Parker, I., 346
parliamentary sovereignty, 227–8, 270
Parris, H., 214
Parsons, T., 238, 239
Partridge, William, 25
patents
    Bennet Woodcroft index, 123
    capital goods, 124
    case numbers, 234
    law, 205, 232
    ornamental products, 125
    practice, 232–5
    technology indicators, 122–6
paving, 284
pawnbrokers, 378
Pawson, E., 212, 299, 327
payment systems
    banknotes, 149–50, 154–6, 162, 206
    bills of exchange, 54, 148, 151, 153,
        154, 160, 205
    cheques, 157
    coins, 151, 152–3
    deposit banking, 151, 153–4
    factory workers, 158
    groceries, 158
    pre-nineteenth century, 151
    tokens, 158
    transfers, 153–4
Peace of Paris, 2
Peak District, 448
Pearson, R., 51, 255
peas, 108, 110
pedlars, 377, 384
Peel family, 41
Peel, Robert (1788–1850), 189, 200
Pelham, Henry (c. 1695–1754), 170
Pember-Reeves, M., 266
Pennant, Richard, 438
Pennines, 30, 419, 420, 438, 440, 442,
        447
penny post, 306
Penrhyn, 438
Penrose, E. T., 48
pepper, 176, 178, 364
Perkin, William Henry (1838–1907),
        25

Perry, C. R., 306
Perth, 155, 399
Peru, 179, 454, 456
Philip family, 50
Pickfords, 308, 310, 314, 315, 316
pig lead, 428
pigs, 109
Pilkington Brothers, 133
pin industry, 39, 52
Pinchbeck, I., 49, 115, 132, 251, 257,
        258, 336
pinmakers, 92
Piore, M., 45, 255
Platts of Oldham, 37
Plot, R., 108
ploughs, 127–8, 129
Plumb, J. H., 283
plumbers, 255
Plymouth, 90
Pohs, H. A., 424
Pollard, Sidney, 5, 32, 33, 36, 39, 52,
        129, 138, 139, 160, 297, 321,
        342–3, 348, 420, 426, 427
Pomeranz, Kenneth, 3, 14, 180–1, 192
Poncelet, Jean Victor (1788–1867), 12
poor rates 373
poor relief
    effect, 95
    Elizabethan poor law, 249
    and enclosures, 113
    evolution, 221–5
    harshness, 32
    old people, 247, 249
    poor law 1834, 206, 221, 224–5, 250
    Scotland, 404–14, 416
    settlement rights, 251, 339
    Speenhamland system, 98, 206,
        222–4, 249, 251, 339
population
    agricultural labour force, 90–1
    Asia, 453
    birth intervals, 71, 84
    censuses, 62
    changes, 18, 19
    craftsmen, 91–2
    data, difficulties, 60–3, 69
    early modern period, 57
    eighteenth century, 35–6, 65–9
    estimates, 61
    Europe, 453–4
    factory workers, 91–2
    falling mortality, 62
    family reconstruction, 63
    fertility, 18, 62, 69–79, 293
    fertility data, 70
    general data, 64

population (*cont.*)
  generalised inverse projection (GIP), 63
  growth, 2, 7, 11, 58–60
    causes, 60–9
    economic indicator, 271
    intrinsic growth rate, 59–60
    Scotland, 59, 413, 415–16
  illegitimacy, 59, 70–1, 75–6
  lopsided growth, 87–92
  Malthusian thinking, 18
  marriage age, 73–5, 243
  mobility, Scotland, 400–1
  mortality, 79–86
  mortality data, 80, 81, 82, 83, 85, 86
  non-marriage, 76
  nuptiality, 73–9
  parish registers, 59, 62, 389
  prenuptial conceptions, 70–1
  research techniques, 63
  retail trade, 91–2
  Scotland, 389, 391, 413
  seventeenth century, 58
  stable populations, 60
  stillbirths, 71–3
  studies, Scotland, 389
  urbanisation of England, 87–92
  world, 453
porcelain, 178, 364, 366, 368, 369, 382–3, 384
Porter, L., 419
Porter, R., 425
porters, 307
Portugal, 178, 180, 182, 456
Posner, R. A., 236
postal services, 306
Postan, M. M., 115
Postel-Vinay, G., 159
Postlethwayt, Malachy, 342
potato famines, 414
Potter family, 50
Potteries, 244, 247, 248
pottery
  architecture of factories, 43
  exports, 6
  industrial revolution, 6
  potters, 248
  Staffordshire, 52
  technological progress, 134
precious metals
  Americas, 179–80
  foreign trade, 180
  gold, 179, 420, 433, 456
  productivity, 327
  silver, 179, 419, 433, 456

prenuptial conceptions, 70–1
Press, J., 436
Pressnell, L. S., 32, 156, 157–61, 162–3, 164
Preston, 241, 244–5, 247
Preston, S. H., 86
Prestonpans, 410
Price, Derek, 26, 40, 158, 159
Price, J. M., 183, 403
Price, L. L. F. R., 434
prices
  coal, 430
  corn, 98
  farm prices, 98, 102
  gold, 163
  iron ore, 430
  market manipulation, 209
  minerals, 430–2
  oats, 404
Priestley, Joseph (1733–1804), 22
printing press, 15
Prior, A., 50
private ownership, versus public ownership, 211–14
probate inventories, 373–4
productivity
  agricultural revolution, 92, 96, 107–14
  mines and quarries, 448–9
  rates, 323
  technical progress, 6
  total factor productivity, 7–10, 292
  transport, 322–3
property rights, 27, 225–35
  intellectual property, 231–5
  land, 229
  minerals, 432–3
  slaves, 230–1
property taxes, 11, 32
protectionism, 187, 192, 195–8, 383, 395, 452, 462–3
proto-industrialisation, 29–36
  demography, 35–6
  environment, 30–4
  occupational cultures, 34–6
Prussia, 172, 351
public ownership, 211–14, 306
public utilities, 212, 219–20
publicans, 92
puddling process, 142, 445
pumping technology, 47, 438–40
putting-out system, 29, 31, 37, 40

quadrants, 302
Quakers, 49, 442
quality of life, 2, 358

quarries, *see* mines and quarries
Quesnay, François (1794–74), 100
Quinn, Stephen, 152, 153, 154, 168

railway, 305–7
  amalgamation of companies, 314
  centrality, 295
  companies, 306, 313, 315–16, 317–19,
    400
  Liverpool to Manchester, 305, 306
  private ownership, 212, 213–14
  Railway Act 1844, 207, 214, 313–14
  Railway Acts, 313
  railway age, 305
  Railway Clearing House, 305
  railway interest, 313–14
  'Rocket', 305
  securities, 148–9, 172–3, 306
  social savings, 328–30
  stations, 306
  traffic, 306–7
Rainhill, 305
Raistrick, A., 420
Ramsden, Jesse, 17, 134
Randall, A. J., 32
Rankine, William (1820–72), 26
Ransome, Robert, 127
Rappaport, Steve, 336, 339
Ravenhead, 133
Reading, 327
reapers, 128
Reay, B., 343
recessions, 189, 263
Redbrook, 443
Redish, A., 152, 153
Redwood, 447
Reed, M. C., 172
reefers, 302
Rees, D. M., 420
Rees, R., 427, 444
Reform Act 1832, 187, 189
Reformation, 15
refrigeration, 130–1
regional specialisation
  factories, 51–3, 327
  rural industries, 31–3
registration of births, deaths and
    marriages, 59, 62, 77
regrating, 209
regulatory framework, 18, 206–11
Reid, D., 277
religion, and business networks, 49, 50
Renaissance, 15
Renfrew, 391
Rennie, John (1761–1821), 12, 16, 23,
    300

rents, 108, 110, 113–14, 407, 409
rent-seeking behaviour, 18
retailing, 91–2, 384–5
reverberatory furnace, 442–3
Reynard, P. C., 368
Ricardo, D., 2, 87
rice, 327
Richards, E., 257
Richards, J., 435
Richards, S., 368, 383
Richardson, D., 51, 255
Richmond Park, 372
Riden, P., 422
riots, 39, 271, 309, 386, 397, 398
roads, 296–9
  haulage, 297
  maintenance, 309
  technology, 297
  turnpike roads, 212, 230, 296, 309
Roberts, E., 249
Roberts, Richard (1789–1864), 16, 24,
    38, 120, 135, 136, 137, 140, 141,
    145
Robey, J. A., 419
Robinson, E., 21, 347, 371
Robinson, J., 277
Rochdale, 44
rococo, 368
Roebuck and Garbett, 410
Roebuck, Dr John (1718–94), 22
Rogers, J., 63
Rogers, J. E. T., 108
Rogers, James, 154
Roll, E., 43
Rollison, D., 34
Rolt, L. T. C., 127, 128, 129, 131
Roman Empire, 454
roofs, 284
Rose, M. B., 32, 33, 37, 38, 40, 45, 49,
    51, 52, 54, 136
Rose, M. E., 262
Rose, S. O., 254, 256, 257, 258, 260
Rosenberg, Nathan, 24, 123
Rosenthal, J., 159, 217
Roseveare, H., 169, 170, 226
Ross, E., 249, 262
Rostow, W. W., 295, 319–20, 324, 325,
    326, 329
Rotherham plough, 127
Rothschilds, 172
Rowe, D. J., 428
Rowe, J., 420, 448
Rowland, J., 419
Rowlands, M. B., 30, 32, 34
Royal Africa Company, 168
Royal Bank of Scotland, 155, 156

Royal Exchange, 385
Royal Institution, 22
Royal Mail Steam Packet Company,
    315, 325
Royal Navy, 130, 131, 454
Royal Society, 21
Royal Society of Arts, 128
Rudden, B., 213
Ruggles, S., 246, 249
rum, 376
Rumford, Count (1753–1814), 22
rural industries
    environment, 30–4
    household industries, 29–30
    occupational cultures, 34–6
    specialisation, 31–3
    town apprentices, 335
Rushton, P., 253
Russia, 172, 343, 464
Ruthwell, 171

Sabel, C., 32, 33, 34, 39, 45, 255
safety lamps, 424
Saint Monday, 277
Saint-Domingue, 183, 196
Sala-I-Martin, X., 354
Salford, 51
salmon, 130
salt, 394, 397, 420
Salt family, 40
Saltcoats, 393
Samuel, R., 34, 37, 121, 137, 146, 434,
    438
Sandberg, L., 289
Sanderson, M., 344, 346
Sandhurst, 270, 275
Sankey Brook Navigation, 299
Sankey Canal, 447
Sargent, T., 152
Saul, S. B., 135
Savage, M., 36
savings banks, 171
Saviotti, P., 45
Scheele, Carl Wilhelm (1742–86), 19
Schlumbohm, J., 30
Schmiechen, J. A., 37
Schmitz, C. J., 426–7, 431
Schmookler, Jacob, 123
Schoen, R., 86
Schofield, R. S., 60, 61, 76, 77, 78–9, 83,
    243, 270, 271, 293, 343, 344,
    353, 355
schools, 340–3, 345–6, 350–3
Schumpeter, Joseph, 121, 143
Schurer, K., 243
Schwartz, L. D., 37, 252

Schwartz, P., 213, 368
scientific culture, 22, 460
Scotch swing plough, 127
Scotland
    1690s harvest failures, 79, 394, 395,
        396
    Act of Union, 396–7, 402
    agriculture, 99, 393–4, 396, 404–10
    aristocracy, 397, 407
    backwardness, 391–6
    banknotes, 155–6
    banks, 147, 155–6, 163, 164, 174
    brewing, 397, 399
    canals, 404
    cattle, 392, 394, 401
    Central Lowlands, 403–4, 419
    clans, 392–3, 401
    coal, 394, 399, 403
    consumption, 392
    cotton, 399
    domestic architecture, 393
    economic transformation, 399–413
        reasons, 401
    Enlightenment, 407
    farm servants, 252
    foreign trade, 394, 403
    foundries, 37
    free trade with England, 402
    glass, 394
    Highland clearances, 98, 401, 411–12
    Highlands and Lowlands, 389
    historiography, 388–9
    illegitimacy, 59
    industrialisation, 410–13
        social impact, 413–16
    Irish immigrants, 413
    iron industry, 399–400
    iron ore mining, 419, 446
    labour, 400, 411–13
    labour migration, 411–12
    lead mining, 394, 419
    linen, 394, 399, 402
    living standards, 413–16
    mortality, 395, 414
    occupations, 415
    population, 58, 93, 389, 391
    population growth, 59, 413, 415–16
    post-Union period, 396–9
    pre-Union disasters, 395
    pre-Union period, 389–96
    registration of births, deaths and
        marriages, 59
    savings banks, 171
    schools, 352
    stereotypes, 388–9
    tenant farmers, 408

Scotland (*cont.*)
  transport, 327
  unemployment, 416
  universities, 344
  urbanisation, 400–1, 416
  wages, 411, 414
Scott, J. W., 240, 246, 264
Scott, K., 368
scriveners, 159
scutching, 411
scythes, 128
Seccombe, W., 35, 258
securities
  canals, 172
  evolution, 167–73
  foreign securities, 172, 173
  gas and water works, 172
  government securities, 167–71, 205, 225
  London, 148–9, 227–8
  railways, 148–9, 172–3, 306
Seed, J., 50
seed drills, 109, 128
self-actor, 13, 16, 24, 38, 120, 136, 137, 140, 145
Senegal, 270
servants
  farm servants, 250–2, 337–8
  living in, 245, 248, 250–2
  women, 252, 377
service industries, 5
Seven Years War, 457, 461
Severn Tunnel, 306
Shackleton, Elizabeth, 382
Shammas, C., 359, 364, 365, 366, 367, 370, 373, 381
Shapin, Steven, 21
Sharp, James, 128
Sharpe, P., 30, 33, 34, 35, 260
Shaw, C., 248
Shaw-Taylor, L., 254
shear frames, 39
sheep, 109, 401
Sheffield
  growth, 90
  metal trades, 39
  middle-class possessions, 374, 375
  plate, 371, 384
  public grinding wheels, 33
  women's possessions, 381
  working-class clothing, 378
Shepshed, 256
Sheraton, Thomas (1751–1806), 407
Sheridan, R. B., 182, 183

shipbuilding, 326, 400
shipping
  accounting techniques, 318
  coasting, 311, 447
  earnings, 324
  finance, 304
  firms, 302–4, 315, 316–17
  generally, 301–5
  and industrial revolution, 327–8
  insurance, 304
  laws, 206
  liners and tramps, 312
  merchant shipping, 461
  registration, 304
  services, 304–5
  size of European navies, 218
  steamships, 302
  technologies, 15, 302
shoemakers, 92
shoemaking, 6
shopkeepers, 92
shops, 384–5
Short, B., 33, 252
Shorthorn cattle, 109
Shropshire, 419
Sigsworth, E., 30, 38
silk
  Essex, 30
  imports, 176, 178, 364, 367
  Macclesfield, 40
  technology, 135
  weaving, 39
silver
  Americas, 179–80, 456
  foreign trade, 179
  mine locations, 419, 433
Silver, H., 341
Simmel, Georg, 371, 379–80
Simon, J., 341, 346
Simpson, A. W. B., 229
Sinclair, Sir John, 408
Singer, C., 126, 133, 134
skills
  acquisition in 1700, 334–43
  apprentices, *see* apprenticeship
  categories, 348
  contribution to economic growth, 353–6
  farming, 337
  industrial revolution, 343–53
  shortages, 412
  underinvestment, 350–3
Slack, P., 221
Slack, R., 427
slate, 392, 420

slave labour, 182, 195, 230–1, 274, 386, 457
slave trade, 186, 197, 230–1, 458
Smail, J., 31, 49, 55, 158
Small, James, 127
smallpox, 11, 13
Smeaton, John (1724–94), 12, 15, 17, 21, 23–4, 300
Smelser, N. J., 248
smelting
  coke smelting, 420, 443, 444
  potting and stamping process, 445
  puddling process, 142, 445
  reverberatory furnace, 442–3
  technology, 441–5
Smiles, Samuel (1812–1904), 16, 17
Smith, Adam (1723–90)
  class, 370
  division of labour, 45
  empire, 461
  free-marker capitalism, 120, 188, 192
  luxury goods, 363
  pessimism, 93
  pinmakers, 92
  poor relief, 222
  public water supply, 213
  Scottish schools, 352
Smith, R. M., 32, 58, 95, 247
Smith, S., 366
Smith, W. D., 366
smog, 427
Smollett, Tobias (1721–71), 363
Smout, T. C., 352, 391, 394, 395, 409
smuggling, 207, 398, 403
Snell, K. D. M., 30, 33, 113, 251, 252, 253, 254, 260, 262, 346, 347
Snodgrass, Neil, 411
Snodin, M., 368
Snyder, F., 220, 221
soap, 6, 25
social overhead capital, 324
Society of Arts, 22
Sokoll, T., 377, 379
Sokoloff, K. L., 234, 353
Solar, Peter, 32, 98, 223
Solow, Barbara, 197, 231
Solway plain, 389
Sombart, W., 371, 379–80
Somerset, 435
South Sea Bubble, 168, 169–71, 208, 219, 227
South Shields, 245
Southall, H. R., 36
Southdown sheep, 109

Spain
  American bullion, 180, 456
  American trade, 181, 456
  Barcelona, 153
  Habsburgs, 456
  issue of securities, 172
  land surface, 57
  Latin American dominance, 179, 196
  literacy, 343
  sugar trade, 182
Spang, R., 366
Speenhamland system, 98, 206, 222–4, 249, 251, 339
Spice Islands, 178, 179, 195
spices, 176, 364
Spiegel, M., 354
spinners, 248
spinning factories, architecture, 43
spinning jenny, 39, 41, 120, 136
spinning machines, critical technology, 120–1
spinning mule
  critical technology, 120, 136, 137
  organised labour, 43, 141
  patent, 235
  self-acting spinning mule, 16, 24, 38, 120, 136, 137, 140, 141, 145
spinning wheel, 15
spirits, duties, 188, 190
Spring, E., 229
Spufford, M., 373
St Helens, 133, 299, 447
St Ninian's, 409
St Rollox works, 399
Stafford, 351
Staffordshire, 31, 52, 384, 419
stage coaches, 308
standards of living, *see* living standards
Stasavage, D., 168
Statute of Artificers, 208, 253, 335, 338, 339, 347
Statute of Monopolies, 209, 231–2, 233
statutory interpretation, 208–11
steam power
  Boulton and Watt steam engine, 135, 142, 144–5
  critical technology, 120–1, 129, 142–5
  impact, 121
  industrial revolution, 12, 13, 16
  milling, 132
  mines and quarries, 428, 439–40
  Scotland, 404
  and thermodynamics, 26–7
steamships, 302

Steckel, R. H., 274–6, 287, 289
steel industry
   crucibles, 16
   Heath's process, 16
   and second industrial revolution, 18
Steensgaard, N., 364, 368
Stephens, W. B., 344
Stephenson, George (1781–1848), 16,
   305
Steuart, Sir James, 362, 363
Stevens, Edward, 16
stillbirths, 71–3
Stirling, 391
stock brokers, 206
stock exchanges, 149, 173, 306
stock market, 171–3, 218–19, 228
Stockport, 51
Stockton and Darlington Railway, 317
Stone, Lawrence, 250, 343–4, 346
stone, markets, 429
Storper, M., 53
straw plaiting, 35
strikes, mule spinners, 141
Strutts family, 139
Stubs, Peter, 41
Sturm und Drang, 15
Styal factory, 42
Styles, J., 376, 377, 378
succession, 30, 336–7
Suffolk, 102
suffrage, 270
sugar
   consumption, 281–2, 364, 365
   duties, 188, 189, 190
   exploitation, 182–3
   importance, 181–2
   imports, 176, 178
   labouring classes, 376
   Navigation Acts, 185, 198
   plantations, 179
   and slave labour, 386
   sugar lords, 408
sumptuary laws, 362, 386
Sunday schools, 346
Sundbärg, G., 62
Supple, B., 170–1
Swain, J. T., 31, 44
Swansea
   banks, 164
   coalfields, 447
   copper industry, 426, 427, 443, 444
   household structures, 241
Sweden, 62, 83, 188, 341, 343
Swindon, 307
swine, 109
Switzerland, 134, 457

Sword Blade Company, 169
Szostak, R., 41, 319–20
Szreter, S., 35, 83, 285

tailoring, 12
tailors, 92
Tann, J., 43
taste, 383–4
taxation
   arbitrary taxation, 18
   commodities, 386
   direct collection, 216
   direct taxation, 215
   enforcement, 207
   excise duties, 215
   level, 204
   local taxation, 32
   parliamentary consent, 225
   policy, 214–25
   rise, 214–15
   Scotland, 397
   servants, 252
   tax farming, 216
   total revenues
Tay, 389
tea
   consumption, 281–2, 364, 366–7
   duties, 188, 190
   East India Company, 179
   imports, 176, 178, 364
   labouring classes, 366, 376
   Navigation Acts, 185
   tea tables, 384
   trade, 183–4
   urns, 384
technical literacy, 16
technological progress, 117–20
   1760–1815 period, 11–13
   agriculture, 126–9
   case studies, 126–35
   critical technologies, 118–19, 120–1,
      135
   debate, 120–2
   efficiency growth, 6
   evidence of patents, 122–6
   food processing, 129–33
   foreign contributions, 460
   general purpose technology, 6
   glass manufacture, 133–4
   and industrialisation, 10, 117–22
   intellectual foundations, 14
   mining, 431–2, 436–48
   models, 119–20
   origin of East and West divergence,
      15
   post-1820, 15–16

technological progress (*cont.*)
  pottery, 134
  and rise of factory system, 39, 40–2
  Scotland, 410–11
  steam, *see* steam power
  textiles, 135–42
Teitelbaum, M. S., 59
telegraph, 16, 306
Telford, Thomas (1757–1834), 297, 300
Temin, P., 6, 10, 187, 291
tenant farmers, 408
Tennant, Charles (1766–1838), 235
Terrisse, M., 63
textiles
  circulation of labour, 46
  factory owners, 40
    family networks, 51
  factory system, 137–41
  organisational innovations, 137–41
  rural industries, 30, 335
  Scotland, 399
  skilled labour, 138–41
  technological innovations, 135–42
  see also calico; cotton; linen; silk;
    wool
Thames and Severn Canal, 310
Thane, P., 247, 249
thermodynamics, 26–7
Third World countries, 60
Thirsk, Joan, 30, 358
Thomas, B., 88, 358, 420
Thomas, J., 257, 258
Thomas, R. P., 198, 324
Thomas, W. A., 172–3
Thomas Russel and Company, 314
Thompson, E. P., 39, 261, 277
Thompson, M., 308
Thompson, N., 364, 386
Thomson, D., 247, 249
Thornton, H., 159
Three Per Cent Consol, 170
threshing, 128, 129
Tilly, C., 254
Tilly, L. A., 240, 246, 264
timber, 176, 188, 326, 392, 420
Timbrell, M., 418
Timmins, G., 30, 32, 38, 44, 131–2, 133
tin
  imports, 430
  ingots, 428
  locations, 419
  markets, 428, 429
  output, 448
  prices, 431
  smelting, 442
Titow, J. Z., 108

tobacco
  American production, 179, 182–3
  Clyde trade, 398
  consumption, 281–2, 364
  duties, 188, 190
  Glasgow, 402–3
  importance, 181
  imports, 176, 178, 366
  labouring classes, 376
  Navigation Acts, 185, 198
  pricing agreements, 52
  productivity, 327
  slave labour, 182
tobacco lords, 408
Tobin, J., 273
tokens, 158
Tollison, R. D., 433
tolls, 309–10
Topel, R., 353
Tories, 228
Torrens, H., 425
total factor productivity, 7–10
  estimates, 292
  industrial revolution, 7
tower houses, 393
towns and cities
  mortality rates, 82–3
  public utilities, 212, 219–20
  transport, 307–8
  see also urbanisation
Toynbee, Arnold, 97, 120–1, 125,
    142
Trace, K., 302
trade, *see* foreign trade
trade cycles, 161
trade unions, 209–10
training, *see* skills
Trainor, R. H., 50, 51
tramways, 308, 448
transport
  British advantages, 17
  capital, 320–1
  competition, 308–14
  earnings, 323–4
  economic impact, 319–30
    models, 319–20
  and factory system, 41
  finance, 312
  inland waterways, 299–301
  linkages and spillovers, 325–6
  market integration, 326–8
  minerals, 446–8
  monopolies, 310
  organisational structures, 314–19
  passenger services, 298
  policy, 308–14

transport (*cont.*)
  productivity growth, 322–3
  railways, *see* railways
  roads, 296–9
  shipping, 301–5
  social overhead capital, 324–5
  social savings, 328–30
  tramways, 308, 448
  urban transport, 307–8
Tranter, N., 277
Treble, J. A., 414
Trent and Mersey Canal, 300
Trevithick, Richard (1771–1833), 16, 17, 23
Trevor-Roper, Hugh, 388
Truman, 330
Trussell, J., 276
trust
  credit, 54–5, 159
  kinship production, 255
Tull, Jethro (1674–1741), 128
Turnbull, G., 298, 310, 316, 327
Turner, M., 32, 100, 102, 103, 108, 111, 112
turnips, 406
turnpike roads, 212, 230, 296, 309
Tuttle, C., 261, 279
Twarog, S., 289
Tylecote, R. F., 427, 443
Tyneside, 326, 426–7
typhus, 213, 414
Tyson, R. E., 79

Uglow, Jenny, 50, 383
Ulster, 391
unemployment, Scotland, 416
Union Canal, 404
Unitarians, business networks, 50
United States of America
  Arizona, 444
  Bill of Rights, 226, 231
  Chesapeake, 182, 183
  Civil War, 194, 275, 463
  Colorado, 444
  constitution, 227, 231
  consumption, 360
  economy, 463
  household structures, 246
  income per capita, 462–3
  independence wars, 2, 191
  intellectual property rights, 234
  Jamestown, 182
  land rights, 229
  literacy, 344, 351
  Maryland, 184
  mining law, 432

natural monopolies, 313
New England, 159, 184–5, 186, 344
New York, 185
Pennsylvania, 185
Philadelphia, 185
private sector subsidies, 204
railways, 327, 328
Revolution, 458
slaves, 182, 195, 231
trade with Britain, *see* American trade
Virginia, 182
universities, 341, 343–4
urbanisation
  England, 88
  and life expectancy, 283–8
  public utilities, 212, 219–20
  Scotland, 400–1, 416
  through apprenticeship, 339
  transport, 307–8
Ure, Andrew, 20, 141, 142
Usher, A. P., 153, 277, 280, 286
usury laws, 206, 208
utilities, 212, 219–20
Utrecht Treaty, 453

vaccination, 13
vagabonds, 221
Vale of Trent, 31
van der Wee, H., 153, 160
van der Werf, Y., 277
van der Woude, A., 93
Van Zanden, J. L., 274
Vaucanson, Jacques de (1709–82), 17
Veblen, Thorstein, 371, 380
Velde, F., 152
veneers, 384
Venice, 153
Viazzo, P. P., 261
vice, 362, 363
Vickery, A., 371, 382
Ville, Simon, 302, 312, 317, 324
Vincent, D., 256, 262, 351
Vincenti, W., 23, 24
Visser, M., 368
Voltaire (1694–1778), 457
von Tunzelmann, Nicholas, 13, 40, 121, 143–5
Voth, Hans-Joachim, 1, 6, 7, 8, 9, 11, 76, 256, 262, 264, 277, 280, 291, 377
Vries, Peer, 3

Waaler, H. T., 399
Wachter, K., 270, 275, 276, 414
Wadsworth, A. P., 30, 32, 39, 139

wages
  amounts, 333
  England, 376
  female servants, 377
  growth, 1
  levels, 263, 269, 271–3
  male breadwinners, 258–62, 265–6
  and marriage decisions, 76–9
  miners, 434–5
  responses to falling wages, 257
  Scotland, 411, 414
wagonways, 447, 448
Wales
  anthracite mines, 446
  coal mining, 419
  copper mining, 419, 443
  farm servants, 252
  iron ore mining, 419
  lead mining, 419, 438, 447
  manganese mines, 420
  population, 57
  registration of births, deaths and
    marriages, 59
  reverberatory furnace, 442
  riots, 309
  slate quarries, 420
  transport of minerals, 447
  waterwheels in mines, 440
Wall, R., 241, 243
Wallerstein, Immanuel, 3, 196,
  198
Walpole, Robert (1676–1745),
  372
Walsh, C., 385
Walters, B., 428, 443
Walton, G. M., 185, 302
Walton, J. K., 30, 32
Walvin, J., 366
Wardley, P., 315, 323
warehouse selling, 385
Warrington, file makers, 41
wars
  1812–14, 2
  British wars, 460–1
  colonial wars, 461
  Crimean War, 463
  eighteenth-century wars against
    France, 2, 188
  financing, 217–18
  France and Scotland, 395
  Germany, 16
  Low Countries, 16
  Napoleon, *see* Napoleonic Wars
  Nine Years War, 154–6, 167
  permanent warfare, 2
  Seven Years War, 457, 461

US Civil War, 194, 275, 463
US independence wars, 2, 191
War of Spanish Succession, 168
Warwickshire, cottagers, 376
water chronometer, 235, 302
water-frames, 120, 136
water power, 12, 13, 440–1
water supply, 212–13
water works, 172
Waterhouse, 318
waterways, 299–301
Watt, James (1736–1819), 15, 17, 19, 21,
  22, 25, 120, 124, 186, 234, 411,
  439
Weald of Kent, 33, 419
Weald of Sussex, 419
Weale, M., 288
Weatherill, Lorna, 368, 370, 373,
  374–5, 381, 383
weaving
  factories, 38
  handloom weavers, 136, 254, 414,
    415, 416
  silk weavers, 39
  West Yorkshire, 42
  wool weavers, 43
Webb, B. and S., 386
Weber, A., 148, 149
Weber, M., 236
Wedgwood, Josiah (1730–95), 12, 22,
  52, 134, 300, 371, 383
Weil, D., 18
Weingast, B., 168, 216, 225–6, 433
Weir, D., 76
Welch, E., 371
Wellington, Duke of (1769–1852),
  162
Wells, J., 168, 433
West, E. G., 349, 352, 353
West Country, 32, 33, 158, 309
West Indies, 181–2, 196, 230, 458
West Middlesex Company, 213
Westall, O., 41
Whatley, Christopher, 394, 398, 400,
  403, 412, 414
Whigs, 228
whisky, 401
Whittle, 370, 374
Whitworth, Sir Joseph (1803–87), 16,
  300
Whyte, I. D., 30, 155, 174, 395
Wigan, 44
Wilkie, I., 420
Wilkins, M., 328
Wilkinson, John (1728–1808), 17, 134,
  135

William III (1650–1702), 2, 167
Williams, Eric (1911–81), 196, 197, 230, 459
Williams, N., 82
Williams, T. I., 128, 130, 131, 133–4, 135
Williams, W. M., 247
Williamson, J. G., 104, 116, 201, 218, 220, 269, 272, 273, 284, 285, 286–7, 305, 328, 348, 373
Williamson, O., 41
Willies, L., 418
Wills, D., 168, 433
Wilson, R. G., 32, 33, 372
Winch, D., 461
winding engines, 440
wine and spirits, 176, 188, 190
Winlaton works, 43
winnowing, 128, 129
Withrington, D. J., 409
Wöhler, Friedrich (1800–82), 24
women
    agricultural labour, 260
    apprentices, 347
    business women, 49
    and consumption, 379–83
    cotton industry, 247
    diaries, 382
    and enclosures, 113
    factory work, Scotland, 412–13
    farming work, 110
    literacy, 351
    and male breadwinners, 258–62
    maternal mortality rates, 83–4
    middle-class women, 260
    mining work, 441
    rural industries, 34–5
    servants, 252, 377
    unskilled work, 347
    wage earners, 257–8, 264, 278
Wood, A., 31
Wood brothers, 445
Woods, R., 36, 83
Woodward, D., 250, 251
wool
    exports, 176
    industrial revolution, 5
    rural industries, 30, 31, 32, 33
    weavers, 43
    Yorkshire, credit system, 54
Woolf, Arthur (1766–1837), 16
Wordie, J. R., 99, 100

working classes
    budgets, 376
    consumption, 369–79
    living standards, 357, 375–9
working time, 270, 276–80, 412
Worsley, 299
worsted, 31, 33, 34, 176
Wright, Quincy, 461
Wrightson, K., 34
Wrigley, E. A., 11, 14, 15, 18, 35, 60, 61, 69, 70, 71, 73, 74, 76, 77, 78–83, 87, 88–9, 90–2, 93–4, 96, 106, 243, 271, 283, 289, 293, 418, 420, 449

Yelling, J. A., 111
York, 90, 244, 248, 252
York Buildings Company, 212
Yorkshire
    coal mining, 419, 437
    cutlery, 32
    factory workers, 92
    farm servants, 252
    iron ore mining, 419
    lead mining, 442
    machine wrecking, 39
    mortgages, 53
    nailmaking, 32
    proto-industrialisation to industrialisation, 33
    riots, 309
    rural artisans, 31
    rural textile industries, 30
        co-operative mills, 33
        credit system, 158
        household sizes, 34
        wool, 33
        worsted, 31, 33, 34
    textile factories
        circulation of labour, 46
        family networks, 51
        small weaving concerns, 42
        subcontracting, 38
        wool payments, 54
Young, Arthur (1741–1820), 100, 101, 104, 105, 111, 113
Young, H., 383

Zeitlin, J., 32, 33, 34, 39, 45, 53
Zell, M., 30, 33, 34
Ziegler, D., 160, 164
zinc, 419